Contents

مندرجات

Editorial consultant ادارتی مشیر

Dr Muntazir Qaimi
Senior Linguist, Centre of Indian Languages (CIL),
School of Language, Literature and Culture Studies (SLL&CS),
Jawaharlal Nehru University, Delhi

Translation co-ordination ترجمہ تطبیق

Ajit Shirodkar

Translators مترجمین

Salim Khan
Ishrath Malik

Editors مدیران

Gerry Breslin
Lucy Cooper
Kerry Ferguson
Anne Robertson
Paige Weber

Editor-in-chief مدیر اعلیٰ

Dr Elaine Higgleton

Abbreviations مخففات

abbr	abbreviation
adj	adjective
adv	adverb
conj	conjunction
det	determiner
excl	exclamation
n	noun
npl	plural noun
num	numeral
prep	preposition
pron	pronoun
US	American English
v	verb
vi	intransitive verb
vt	transitive verb

Using this Dictionary

Entry words

Entry words are printed in blue bold type.

abbreviation

Inflected forms

The inflected forms of verbs, nouns, adjectives, abbreviations, and numerals are printed in black bold type in brackets.

abduct (abducts, abducting, abducted)

Parts of speech

Parts of speech are abbreviated and printed in italics. When a word can be used as more than one part of speech, the change of part of speech is shown after an empty arrow.

about *adv* **About** means near to something.
تقریباً، لگ بھگ ▷ *prep* **About** means to do with.

Definitions

Definitions give the meaning of the word. In the definition, the entry word is printed in black bold.

abroad *adv* If you go **abroad**, you go to a foreign country.

Usage and regional labels

Usage and regional labels are printed in italics in brackets after the definition.

consequently *adv* **Consequently** means as a result. (*formal*)

Translations

Translations come after the definition and give the equivalent of the entry word in Urdu.

abolition *n* The **abolition** of something is its formal ending. خاتمہ

Examples

Example sentences are printed in italics and show how the word is used.

consist of *v* Something that **consists of** particular things or people is formed from them.
مشتمل ہونا *The cabin consisted of two small rooms.*

ڈکشنری سے استفادے کی ہدایات

اندراج الفاظ

اندراج الفاظ نیلے جلی حروف میں ہیں۔

abbreviation

تصریفی شکل

افعال، اسماء، صفات، مخففات اور ہندسوں کی تصریفی شکلیں قوسین میں سیاہ جلی حروف میں ہیں۔

abduct (**abducts, abducting, abducted**)

اجزائے کلام

اجزائے کلام مخفف اور ترچھے حروف میں ہیں۔ جب ایک لفظ ایک سے زیادہ جزوے کلام کے طور پر استعمال ہوتا ہے تو جزو کلام میں تبدیلی تیر کے نشان کے ساتھ بتلائی گئی ہے۔

about *adv* **About** means near to something.
تقریباً، لگ بھگ ▷ *prep* **About** means to do with.

توضیحات

توضیحات الفاظ کے معنی بیان کرتی ہیں۔ توضیح میں اندراج لفظ سیاہ جلی حروف میں ہیں۔

abroad *adv* If you go **abroad**, you go to a foreign country.

طریقہ ء استعمال اور علاقائی الفاظ

طریقہ ء استعمال اور علاقائی الفاظ توضیح کے بعد قوسین میں ترچھے حروف میں ہیں۔

consequently *adv* **Consequently** means as a result. (*formal*)

تراجم

تراجم توضیح کے بعد دئے گئے ہیں جو اندراج لفظ کے مساوی اردو معنی ہیں

abolition *n* The **abolition** of something is its formal ending. خاتمہ

مثالیں

مثالی جملے ترچھے حروف میں ہیں اور وہ یہ بھی بتاتے ہیں کہ لفظ کیسے استعمال ہوا ہے۔

consist of *v* Something that **consists of** particular things or people is formed from them.
مشتمل ہونا *The cabin consisted of two small rooms.*

a

a *det* You use **a** or **an** before a noun when people may not know which person or thing you are talking about. کوئی، کوئی ایک *A waiter came in with a glass of water.*

abandon (**abandons, abandoning, abandoned**) *vt* If you **abandon** a thing, place, or person, you leave them permanently or for a long time. چھوڑنا

abbreviation (**abbreviations**) *n* An **abbreviation** is a short form of a word or phrase. مخفف

abdomen (**abdomens**) *n* Your **abdomen** is the part of your body below your chest where your stomach is. (*formal*) پیٹ

abduct (**abducts, abducting, abducted**) *vt* If someone **is abducted**, he or she is taken away illegally. اغوا کرنا

ability (**abilities**) *n* Your **ability** is the quality or skill that you have which makes it possible for you to do something. قابلیت

able (**abler, ablest**) *adj* An **able** person is clever or good at doing something. لائق

abnormal *adj* Someone or something that is **abnormal** is unusual in a way that is worrying. (*formal*) خلاف معمول

abolish (**abolishes, abolishing, abolished**) *vt* If someone in authority **abolishes** a practice or organization, they put an end to it. منسوخ کرنا

abolition *n* The **abolition** of something is its formal ending. منسوخ

about *adv* **About** means near to something. تقریباً، لگ بھگ ▷ *prep* **About** means to do with. بارے میں *This book is about history.*

above *prep* If something is **above** another thing, it is over it or higher than it. اوپر *Lift the ball above your head.*

abroad *adv* If you go **abroad**, you go to a foreign country. بیرون ملک

abrupt *adj* An **abrupt** action is very sudden and often unpleasant. دفعتہ، اچانک

abruptly *adv* If you do something **abruptly**, you do it in an abrupt manner. یکایک

abscess (**abscesses**) *n* An **abscess** is a painful swelling containing pus. پھنسی

absence (**absences**) *n* The **absence** of someone or something is the fact that they are not there. غیر موجودگی

absent *adj* If someone or something is **absent** from a place or situation, they are not there. غیر حاضر

absent-minded *adj* An **absent-minded** person is very forgetful or does not pay attention to what they are doing. غائب دماغ

absolutely *adv* **Absolutely** means totally and completely. بالکل

abstract *adj* An **abstract** idea or way of thinking is based on general ideas rather than on real things and events. خیالی

absurd *adj* If you say that something is **absurd**, you think that it is ridiculous or that it does not make sense. فضول

Abu Dhabi *n* **Abu Dhabi** is an emirate in South-East Arabia, on the southern coast of the Persian Gulf. ابو ظہبی

academic *adj* **Academic** means relating to life or work in schools, colleges, and universities. تعلیمی

academic year (**academic years**) *n* The **academic year** is the period of the year during which students attend school or university. تعلیمی سال

academy (**academies**) *n* A school or college specializing in a particular subject is sometimes called an **academy**. اکادمی

accelerate (**accelerates, accelerating, accelerated**) *v* If the rate of something **accelerates**, or if something **accelerates** it, it gets faster. رفتار بڑھنا

acceleration *n* The **acceleration** of a process is the fact that it is getting faster. سرعت

accelerator (**accelerators**) *n* In a vehicle, the **accelerator** is the pedal you press to go faster. ایکسلیریٹر

accept (**accepts, accepting, accepted**) *v* If you **accept** something that you have been offered, you say yes to it or agree to take it. قبول کرنا

acceptable *adj* If a situation or action is **acceptable**, people approve of it. قابل قبول

access (**accesses, accessing, accessed**) *n* If you have **access** to a building or other place, you are able to go into it. رسائی ▷ *vt* If you **access** something, especially information held on a computer, you succeed in finding or obtaining it. رسائی حاصل کرنا

accessible *adj* If a place is **accessible**, you are able to reach it or get into it. قابل رسائی

accessory (**accessories**) *n* **Accessories** are extra parts added to something to make it more useful or decorative. لازمہ

accident (**accidents**) *n* An **accident** is something nasty that happens, and that hurts someone. حادثہ ▷ *n* If something happens by **accident**, you do not expect it to happen. غلطی سے

accidental *adj* An **accidental** event happens by chance or as the result of an accident. حادثاتی

accidentally *adv* If something happens **accidentally**, it happens by chance or as the result of an accident, and is not deliberately intended. حادثاتی طور پر

accident and emergency *n* The **accident and emergency** is the room or department in a hospital where people who have severe injuries or sudden illness are taken for emergency treatment. حادثہ اور ایمرجنسی

accident insurance *n* **Accident insurance** is insurance providing compensation for accidental injury or death. حادثہ بیمہ

accommodate (**accommodates, accommodating, accommodated**) *vt* If a building or space can **accommodate** someone or something, it has enough room for them. سمانا

accommodation *n* **Accommodation** is used to refer to rooms or buildings where people live, stay, or work. رہائش

accompany (**accompanies, accompanying, accompanied**) *vt* If you **accompany** someone, you go somewhere with them. (*formal*) ساتھ دینا

accomplice (**accomplices**) *n* An **accomplice** is a person who helps to commit a crime. شریک جرم

accordingly *adv* You use **accordingly** to say that one thing happens as a result of another thing. نتیجہ میں

according to (**x**) *prep* You say **according to** somebody to show that you are only repeating what you have read or heard, and that it may not be true. بحوالہ، بقول *They drove away in a white van, according to the news.* ▷ *prep* If somebody does something **according to** a set of rules, they follow those rules. بہ مطابق، کے مطابق *They played the game according to the British rules.*

accordion (**accordions**) *n* An **accordion** is a musical instrument in the shape of a box which you hold in your hands. You play it by pressing keys and buttons on the side, while moving the two ends in and out. اکورڈین

account (**accounts**) *n* An **account** is a written or spoken report of something that has happened. سرگزشت ▷ *n* If you have an **account** with a bank, you leave money with the bank and take it out when you need it. کھاتہ

accountable *adj* If you are **accountable** for something that you do, you are responsible for it. ذمہ دار

accountancy *n* **Accountancy** is the work of keeping financial accounts. حساب کتاب

accountant (**accountants**) *n* An **accountant** is a person whose job is to keep financial accounts. محاسب۔ منیم

account for *v* If you can **account for** something, you can explain it or give the necessary information about it. وضاحت کرنا *How do you account for the missing money?*

account number (**account numbers**) *n* Your **account number** is the unique number of your account with something such as a bank. کھاتہ نمبر

accuracy *n* The **accuracy** of information or measurements is their quality of being true or correct. درستگی

accurate *adj* Something that is **accurate** is correct to a detailed level. درست

accurately *adv* **Accurately** means in an accurate manner. درست طور پر

accusation (**accusations**) *n* If you make an **accusation** against someone, you express the belief that they have done something wrong. الزام تراشی

accuse (**accuses, accusing, accused**) *vt* If you **accuse** someone of something, you say that you believe they did something wrong or dishonest. الزام دینا

accused (**accused**) *n* **The accused** refers to the person or people charged with a crime. ملزم

ace (**aces**) *n* An **ace** is a playing card with a single symbol on it. اکا

ache (**aches, aching, ached**) *n* An **ache** is a steady, fairly strong pain in a part of your body. درد ▷ *vi* If you **ache** or a part of your body **aches**, you feel a steady, fairly strong pain. درد ہونا

achieve (**achieves, achieving, achieved**) *vt* If you **achieve** a particular aim or effect, you succeed in doing it or causing it to happen, usually after a lot of effort. حاصل کرنا

achievement (**achievements**) *n* An **achievement** is something which someone has succeeded in doing, especially after a lot of effort. کامیابی

acid (**acids**) *n* An **acid** is a chemical, usually a liquid, that can burn your skin and cause damage to other substances. تیزاب

acid rain *n* **Acid rain** is rain that damages plants, rivers, and buildings because it contains acid released into the atmosphere from factories and other industrial processes. تیزابی بارش

acknowledgement *n* An **acknowledgement** of something is a statement or action that recognizes that it is true. اعتراف

acne *n* **Acne** is a skin disease which causes spots on the face and neck. مہاسہ

acorn (**acorns**) *n* An **acorn** is a pale oval nut that is the fruit of an oak tree. شاہ بلوط کا پھل

acoustic *adj* An **acoustic** musical instrument is one which is not electric. غیر برقی

acre (**acres**) *n* An **acre** is a unit of area equal to 4840 square yards or approximately 4047 square metres. ایکڑ
acrobat (**acrobats**) *n* An **acrobat** is an entertainer who performs difficult physical acts such as jumping and balancing, especially in a circus. نٹ
acronym (**acronyms**) *n* An **acronym** is a word made of the initial letters of the words in a phrase, especially when this is the name of an organization such as NATO. سرنامیہ
across *prep* If someone goes **across** a place, they go from one side of it to the other. آرپار *She walked across the road.*
act (**acts, acting, acted**) *n* An **act** is an action or thing that someone does. عمل ⊳ *vi* When you **act**, you do something. کارروائی کرنا ⊳ *vi* If you **act** in a play or film, you pretend to be one of the people in it. کردار ادا کرنا
acting *adj* You use **acting** before the title of a job to indicate that someone is doing that job temporarily. قائم مقام ⊳ *n* **Acting** is the activity or profession of performing in plays or films. اداکاری
action *n* **Action** is doing something for a particular purpose. کارروائی
active *adj* An **active** person is energetic and always busy. فعال
activity *n* **Activity** is a situation in which a lot of things are happening. سرگرمی
actor (**actors**) *n* An **actor** is someone whose job is acting in plays or films. اداکار
actress (**actresses**) *n* An **actress** is a woman whose job is acting in plays or films. اداکارہ
actual *adj* **Actual** is used to emphasize that you are referring to something real or genuine. حقیقی
actually *adv* You use **actually** to indicate that a situation exists or that it is true. فی الواقع
acupuncture *n* **Acupuncture** is the treatment of a person's illness or pain by sticking small needles into their body. جسم میں سوئی چبھونے کے ذریعے مرض کے علاج کا طریقہ۔
AD *abbr* You use **AD** in dates to indicate a number of years or centuries since the year in which Jesus Christ is believed to have been born. بعد مسیح
ad (**ads**) *abbr* An **ad** is an announcement in a newspaper, on television, or on a poster about something such as a product, event, or job. (*informal*) اشتہار
adapt (**adapts, adapting, adapted**) *vi* If you **adapt** to a new situation, you change your ideas or behaviour in order to deal with it. عادی ہونا
adaptor (**adaptors**) *n* An **adaptor** is a special device for connecting electrical equipment to a power supply, or for connecting different pieces of electrical or electronic equipment together. اڈاپٹر
add (**adds, adding, added**) *vt* If you **add** one thing to another, you put it with the other thing. شامل کرنا، ملانا ⊳ *vt* If you **add** numbers together, you find out how many they make together. جوڑنا
addict (**addicts**) *n* An **addict** is someone who cannot stop taking harmful drugs. عادی
addicted *adj* Someone who is **addicted** to a harmful drug cannot stop taking it. نشہ باز
additional *adj* **Additional** things are extra things apart from the ones already present. اضافی
additive (**additives**) *n* An **additive** is a substance which is added to food by the manufacturer for a particular purpose, such as colouring it. مضاف
address (**addresses**) *n* If you give an **address** to a group of people, you give a speech to them. خطاب ⊳ *n* Your **address** is the number of the house, the name of the street, and the town where you live or work. پتہ
address book (**address books**) *n* An **address book** is a book in which you write

people's names and addresses. نام وپتہ کی کتاب

add up *v* If you **add up** numbers or amounts, or if you **add** them **up**, you calculate their total. جمع کرنا *Add up the total of those six games.*

adjacent *adj* If two things are **adjacent**, they are next to each other. متصل

adjective (**adjectives**) *n* An **adjective** is a word such as 'big' or 'beautiful' that describes a person or thing. Adjectives usually come before nouns or after verbs like 'be' or 'feel'. اسم صفت

adjust (**adjusts, adjusting, adjusted**) *v* When you **adjust** to a new situation, you get used to it by changing your behaviour or your ideas. ہم آہنگ بنانا

adjustable *adj* If something is **adjustable**, it can be changed to different positions or sizes. مطابق پذیر

adjustment (**adjustments**) *n* An **adjustment** is a change that is made to something such as a machine or a way of doing something. ہم آہنگی

administration *n* **Administration** is the range of activities connected with organizing and supervising the way that an organization functions. انتظامیہ

administrative *adj* **Administrative** work involves organizing and supervising an organization. انتظامی

admiration *n* **Admiration** is a feeling of great liking and respect. تعریف

admire (**admires, admiring, admired**) *vt* If you **admire** someone or something, you like and respect them. تعریف کرنا

admission (**admissions**) *n* If you gain **admission** to a place or organization, you are allowed to enter it or join it. داخلہ

admit (**admits, admitting, admitted**) *vt* If someone **is admitted** to a place or organization, they are allowed to enter it or join it. داخل کرنا ▷ *v* If you **admit** that something bad or embarrassing is true, you agree, often reluctantly, that it is true. اعتراف کرنا

admittance *n* **Admittance** is the act of entering a place or institution or the right to enter it. داخلہ

adolescence *n* **Adolescence** is the period of your life in which you develop from being a child into being an adult. نوجوانی

adolescent (**adolescents**) *n* An **adolescent** is a young person who is no longer a child but who has not yet become an adult. نوجوان

adopt (**adopts, adopting, adopted**) *vt* If you **adopt** someone else's child, you take it into your own family and make it legally your own. متبنّیٰ

adopted *adj* An **adopted** child is one which has been adopted. لے پالک

adoption (**adoptions**) *n* **Adoption** is the act of adopting a child. تبنیت

adore (**adores, adoring, adored**) *vt* If you **adore** someone, you love and admire them. پرستش کرنا

Adriatic *adj* **Adriatic** means of or relating to the Adriatic Sea, or to the inhabitants of its coast or islands. بحر ایڈریاٹک سے متعلق

Adriatic Sea *n* The **Adriatic Sea** is an arm of the Mediterranean between Italy and the Balkan Peninsula. بحر ایڈریاٹک

adult (**adults**) *n* An **adult** is a mature, fully developed person. An adult has reached the age when they are legally responsible for their actions. بالغ

adult education *n* **Adult education** is education for adults in a variety of subjects, most of which are practical, not academic. Classes are often held in the evenings. تعلیم بالغاں

advance (**advances, advancing, advanced**) *n* An **advance** is money which is lent or paid to someone before they would normally receive it. پیشگی
▷ *vi* To **advance** means to move forward, often in order to attack someone. آگے بڑھنا

advanced *adj* An **advanced** system, method, or design is modern and has been developed from an earlier version of the same thing. جدید

advantage (**advantages**) *n* An **advantage** is something that puts you in a better position than other people. فائدہ

advent *n* The **advent** of something is the fact of it starting or coming into existence. (*formal*) آمد

adventure (**adventures**) *n* An **adventure** is a series of events that you become involved in that are unusual, exciting, and perhaps dangerous. مہم جوئی

adventurous *adj* An **adventurous** person is willing to take risks and eager to have new experiences. مہم جو

adverb (**adverbs**) *n* In grammar, an **adverb** is a word such as 'slowly' or 'very' which adds information about time, place, or manner. متعلق فعل

adversary (**adversaries**) *n* Your **adversary** is someone you are competing with or fighting against. مقابل

advert (**adverts**) *n* An **advert** is an announcement in a newspaper, on television, or on a poster about something such as a product, event, or job. اشتہار

advertise (**advertises, advertising, advertised**) *v* If you **advertise, or advertise** something such as a product, event, or job, you tell people about it in newspapers, on television, or on posters. اشتہار دینا

advertisement (**advertisements**) *n* An **advertisement** is an announcement in a newspaper, on television, or on a poster that tells people about a product, event, or job vacancy. (*written*) اشتہار

advertising *n* **Advertising** is the business activity of encouraging people to buy products, go to events, or apply for jobs. تشہیر

advice *n* If you give someone **advice**, you tell them what you think they should do. مشورہ (ترجیح)

advisable *adj* If you tell someone that it is **advisable** to do something, you are suggesting that they should do it. (*formal*) قابل مشورہ

advise (**advises, advising, advised**) *vt* If you **advise** someone to do something, you tell them what you think they should do. مشورہ دینا

aerial (**aerials**) *n* An **aerial** is a piece of metal equipment that receives television or radio signals. ایریل

aerobics *npl* **Aerobics** is a form of exercise which increases the amount of oxygen in your blood and strengthens your heart and lungs. ہواپاشی

aerosol (**aerosols**) *n* An **aerosol** is a small container in which a liquid such as paint is kept under pressure. When you press a button, the liquid is forced out as a fine spray or foam. ایروسول

affair (**affairs**) *n* You refer to an event as an **affair** when you are talking about it in a general way. واقعہ

affect (**affects, affecting, affected**) *vt* When something **affects** someone or something, it influences them or causes them to change. اثر انداز ہونا

affectionate *adj* If you are **affectionate**, you show your fondness for another person in your behaviour. پیارا

afford (**affords, affording, afforded**) *vt* If you cannot **afford** something, you do not have enough money to pay for it. استطاعت رکھنا

affordable *adj* If something is **affordable**, people have enough money to buy it. قابل استطاعت

Afghan (**Afghans**) *adj* **Afghan** means belonging or relating to Afghanistan, or to its people or language. افغانستانی ▷ *n* An **Afghan** is a person from Afghanistan. افغان

Afghanistan *n* **Afghanistan** is a republic in central Asia. افغانستان

afraid *adj* If you are **afraid** of someone or **afraid** to do something, you are frightened because you think that something horrible is going to happen. ڈرا ہوا

Africa *n* **Africa** is the second largest of the continents. It is located to the south of Europe. افریقہ

African (**Africans**) *adj* **African** means belonging or relating to the continent of Africa. افریقی ▷ *n* An **African** is someone who comes from Africa. افریقی

Afrikaans *n* **Afrikaans** is one of the official languages of South Africa. افریقانس

Afrikaner (**Afrikaners**) *n* An **Afrikaner** is one of the white people in South Africa whose ancestors were Dutch. افریقانز

after *conj* If something happens **after** another thing, it happens later than it. بعد میں *He arrived after I had left.* ▷ *prep* If something happens **after** another thing, It happens later than it. بعد *I watched television after dinner.* ▷ *prep* If you go **after** a person or thing, you follow them or chase them. پیچھے *They ran after her.*

afternoon (**afternoons**) *n* The **afternoon** is the part of each day which begins at 12 o'clock lunchtime and ends at about six o'clock. سہ پہر

afters *npl* **Afters** is a dessert or sweet. (*informal*) میٹھا

aftershave *n* **Aftershave** is a liquid with a pleasant smell that men sometimes put on their faces after shaving. آفٹر شیو

afterwards *adv* If something is done or happens **afterwards**, it is done or happens later than a particular event or time that has already been described. بعد ازاں

again *adv* If something happens **again**, it happens another time. دوبارہ

against *prep* If something is **against** another thing, it is touching it. کے سہارے *He leaned against the wall.* ▷ *prep* If you play **against** someone in a game, you try to beat them. خلاف *The two teams played against one another.*

age (**ages**) *n* Your **age** is the number of years that you have lived. عمر

aged *adj* You use **aged** followed by a number to say how old someone is. عمر کا

age limit (**age limits**) *n* An **age limit** is the oldest or youngest age at which you are allowed under particular regulations to do something. عمر کی قید

agency (**agencies**) *n* An **agency** is a business which provides services for a person or another business. ایجنسی

agenda (**agendas**) *n* An **agenda** is a list of items to be discussed at a meeting. ایجنڈا

agent (**agents**) *n* An **agent** is someone who arranges work or business for someone else. دلال

aggressive *adj* An **aggressive** person behaves angrily or violently towards other people. جارح

AGM (**AGMs**) *abbr* The **AGM** of a company or organization is a meeting which it holds once a year in order to discuss the previous year's activities and accounts. **AGM** is an abbreviation for 'Annual General Meeting'. سالانہ اجلاس عام

ago *adv* You use **ago** to talk about a time in the past. قبل، پہلے

agree (**agrees, agreeing, agreed**) *v* If you **agree** with someone, you have the same opinion about something. راضی ہونا

agreed *adj* If people are **agreed** on something, they have reached a joint decision on it or have the same opinion about it. رضامند

agreement (**agreements**) *n* An **agreement** is a decision that two or more people, groups, or countries have made together. قرارنامہ

agricultural *adj* **Agricultural** means involving or relating to agriculture. زراعتی

agriculture *n* **Agriculture** is farming and the methods used to look after crops and animals. زراعت

ahead *adv* Someone who is **ahead** of another person is in front of them. آگے

aid *n* **Aid** is money, equipment, or services that are provided for people, countries, or organizations who need them but cannot provide them for themselves. امداد

AIDS *n* **AIDS** is an illness which destroys the natural system of protection that the body has against disease. **AIDS** is an abbreviation for 'acquired immune deficiency syndrome'. ایڈز

aim (**aims, aiming, aimed**) *n* The **aim** of something that you do is the purpose for which you do it. ارادہ ▷ *v* If you **aim** for something or **aim** to do it, you plan or hope to achieve it. ارادہ کرنا

air *n* **Air** is the mixture of gases which forms the earth's atmosphere and which we breathe. ہوا

airbag (**airbags**) *n* An **airbag** is a safety device in a car which automatically fills with air if the car crashes, and is designed to protect the people in the car when they are thrown forward in the crash. ہوا بھرا تھیلا

air-conditioned *adj* If a room is **air-conditioned**, the air in it is kept cool and dry by means of a special machine. ایر کنڈیشنڈ

air conditioning *n* **Air conditioning** is a method of providing buildings and vehicles with cool air. ایر کنڈیشنگ

aircraft (**aircraft**) *n* An **aircraft** is a vehicle which can fly, for example an aeroplane or a helicopter. طیارہ

air force (**air forces**) *n* An **air force** is the part of a country's military organization that is concerned with fighting in the air. فضائیہ فوج

air hostess (**air hostesses**) *n* An **air hostess** is a woman whose job is to look after passengers in an aircraft. (*old-fashioned*) ہوائی میزبان (عورتیں)

airline (**airlines**) *n* An **airline** is a company which provides regular services carrying people or goods in aeroplanes. ادارہ طیران

airmail *n* **Airmail** is the system of sending letters, parcels, and goods by air. ہوائی ڈاک

airport (**airports**) *n* An **airport** is a place where aircraft land and take off, usually with a lot of buildings and facilities. ہوائی اڈہ

airsick *adj* If you are **airsick**, you are sick or nauseated from travelling in an aircraft. ہوائی سفر کا بیمار

airspace *n* A country's **airspace** is the part of the sky that is over that country and is considered to belong to that country. ہوائی فضا

airtight *adj* If a container is **airtight**, its lid fits so tightly that no air can get in or out. ہوا بند

air traffic controller (**air traffic controllers**) *n* An **air traffic controller** is someone whose job is to organize the routes that aircraft should follow, and to tell pilots by radio which routes they should take. ایر ٹریفک کنٹرولر

aisle (**aisles**) *n* An **aisle** is a long narrow gap that people can walk along between rows of seats in a public building such as a church, or between rows of shelves in a supermarket. بغلی راستہ

alarm *n* **Alarm** is a feeling of fear or anxiety that something unpleasant or dangerous might happen. انتباہ

alarm clock (**alarm clocks**) *n* An **alarm clock** is a clock that you can set to make a noise so that it wakes you up at a particular time. الارم گھڑی

alarming *adj* Something that is **alarming** makes you feel afraid or anxious that something unpleasant or dangerous might happen. پریشان کن

Albania *n* **Albania** is a republic in south-east Europe, on the Balkan Peninsula. البانیہ

Albanian (**Albanians**) *adj* **Albanian** means belonging or relating to Albania, its people, language, or culture. البانی ▷ *n* An **Albanian** is a person who comes from Albania. البانیائی ▷ *n* **Albanian** is the language spoken by people who live in Albania. البانی

album (**albums**) *n* An **album** is a CD, record, or cassette with music on it. البم

alcohol *n* Drinks that can make people drunk, such as beer, wine, and whisky, can be referred to as **alcohol**. الکحل

alcohol-free *adj* Beer or wine which is **alcohol-free** contains only a trace of alcohol. الکحل سے پاک

alcoholic (**alcoholics**) *adj* **Alcoholic** drinks contain alcohol. الکحل آمیز ▷ *n* An **alcoholic** is someone who is addicted to alcohol. الکحل زدہ

alert (**alerts, alerting, alerted**) *adj* If you are **alert**, you are paying full attention to things around you and are ready to deal with anything that might happen. خبردار ▷ *vt* If you **alert** someone to a situation, especially a dangerous or unpleasant situation, you tell them about it. خبردار کرنا

Algeria *n* **Algeria** is a republic in north-west Africa, on the Mediterranean. الجیریا

Algerian (**Algerians**) *adj* **Algerian** means belonging or relating to Algeria, or its people or culture. الجزائری ▷ *n* An **Algerian** is an Algerian citizen or a person of Algerian origin. الجیریائی

alias *prep* You use **alias** when you are mentioning another name that someone, especially a criminal or an actor, is known by. عرف *...the defendant Pericles Pericleous, alias Peter Smith.*

alibi (**alibis**) *n* If you have an **alibi**, you can prove that you were somewhere else when a crime was committed. عذر عدم موجودگی

alien (**aliens**) *n* An **alien** is someone who is not a legal citizen of the country in which they live. (*formal*) پردیسی

alive *adj* If people or animals are **alive**, they are living. زندہ

all *det* You use **all** to talk about everything, everyone, or the whole of something. سبھی، تمام *Did you eat all of it?* ▷ *pron* You use **all** to talk about everything, everyone, or the whole of something. سبھی *We make our own hair-care products, all based on herbal recipes.*

Allah *n* **Allah** is the name of God in Islam. اللہ

allegation (**allegations**) *n* An **allegation** is a statement saying that someone has done something wrong. الزام

alleged *adj* An **alleged** fact has been stated but has not been proved to be true. (*formal*) مبینہ

allergic *adj* If you are **allergic** to something, or have an **allergic** reaction to it, you become ill or get a rash when you eat it, smell it, or touch it. الرجی زدہ

allergy (**allergies**) *n* If you have a particular **allergy**, you become ill or get a rash when you eat, smell, or touch something that does not normally make people ill. الرجی

alley (**alleys**) *n* An **alley** or **alleyway** is a narrow passage or street with buildings or walls on both sides. تنگ راستہ

alliance (**alliances**) *n* An **alliance** is a group of countries or political parties that are formally united and working together because they have similar aims. اتحاد

alligator (**alligators**) *n* An **alligator** is a large reptile with short legs, a long tail and very powerful jaws. گھڑیال

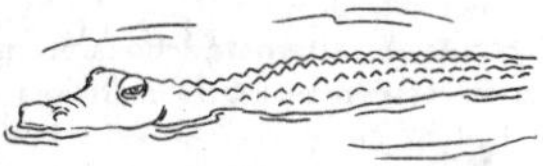

allow (**allows, allowing, allowed**) *vt* If someone **is allowed** to do something, it is all right for them to do it. اجازت دینا
all right *adv* If something goes **all right**, it happens in a satisfactory manner. (*informal*) بالکل ٹھیک ▷ *adj* If you say that something is **all right**, you mean that it is good enough. (*informal*) اچھا، اچھی، ٹھیک
ally (**allies**) *n* An **ally** is a country, organization, or person that helps and supports another. اتحادی
almond (**almonds**) *n* An **almond** is a kind of pale oval nut. بادام
almost *adv* **Almost** means very nearly. زیادہ تر
alone *adj* When you are **alone**, you are not with any other people. تنہا
along *prep* If you walk **along** a road or other place, you move towards one end of it. کے ساتھ ساتھ پر *We walked along the street.* ▷ *adv* If you bring something **along** when you go somewhere, you bring it with you. ساتھ
aloud *adv* When you speak or read **aloud**, you speak so that other people can hear you. زور سے
alphabet (**alphabets**) *n* The **alphabet** is the set of letters in a fixed order which is used for writing the words of a language. حروف تہجی
Alps *npl* The **Alps** are a mountain range in south central Europe. آلپس
already *adv* You use **already** to show that something has happened before the present time. پہلے سے
also *adv* You use **also** to give more information about something. بھی
altar (**altars**) *n* An **altar** is a holy table in a church or temple. مقدس چبوترہ
alter (**alters, altering, altered**) *v* If something **alters,** or if you alter it, it changes. بدلنا
alternate *adj* **Alternate** actions, events, or processes regularly occur after each other. باری باری
alternative (**alternatives**) *adj* An alternative plan or offer is different from the one that you already have, and can be done or used instead. متبادل
n If one thing is an **alternative** to another, the first can be found, used, or done instead of the second. بدل
alternatively *adv* You use **alternatively** to introduce a suggestion or to mention something different from what has just been stated. متبادل طور پر
although *conj* You use **although** to add information that changes what you have already said. کے باوجود *They all play basketball, although on different teams.*
conj You use **although** to start talking about an idea that is not what you would expect. حالانکہ، اگرچہ *I can remember seeing it on TV, although I was only six.*
altitude (**altitudes**) *n* If something is at a particular **altitude**, it is at that height above sea level. سمندر کی سطح سے یا کسی سطح سے بلندی
altogether *adv* If you say that different numbers of people or things add up to something **altogether**, you mean that you have counted all of them. ملا کر، کل ملا کر
aluminium *n* **Aluminium** is a lightweight metal used for making things such as cooking equipment and aircraft parts. المونیم
always *adv* If you **always** do something, you do it every time or all the time. ہمیشہ
Alzheimer's disease *n* **Alzheimer's disease** is a condition in which a person's brain gradually stops working properly. مرض الزائمر
a.m. *abbr* **a.m.** after a number indicates that the number refers to a particular time between midnight and noon. صبح
amateur (**amateurs**) *n* An **amateur** is someone who does a particular activity as a hobby, not as a job. شوقین
amaze (**amazes, amazing, amazed**) *vt* If something **amazes** you, it surprises you very much. حیرت زدہ کرنا

amazed *adj* If you are **amazed**, you are very surprised. حیرت زدہ

amazing *adj* If something is **amazing**, it is very surprising and makes you feel pleasure or admiration. حیرت انگیز

ambassador (**ambassadors**) *n* An **ambassador** is an important official living in a foreign country who represents the government of his or her own country. سفیر

amber *n* **Amber** is a hard yellowish-brown substance used for making jewellery. عنبر

ambition (**ambitions**) *n* If you have an **ambition** to achieve something, you want very much to achieve it. عزم

ambitious *adj* Someone who is **ambitious** wants to be successful, rich, or powerful. با عزم

ambulance (**ambulances**) *n* An **ambulance** is a vehicle for taking people to and from hospital. ایمبولنس

amenities *npl* **Amenities** are things such as shopping centres or sports facilities that are for people's convenience or enjoyment. آسائشیں

America *n* **America** is the **American** continent, including North, South, and Central America. امریکہ

American (**Americans**) *adj* **American** means belonging or relating to the United States of America, or to its people or culture. امریکی ▷ *n* An American is a person who comes from the United States of America. امریکی

American football *n* **American football** is a game similar to rugby that is played by two teams of eleven players using an oval-shaped ball. امریکی فٹبال

among *prep* Someone or something that is **among** a group of things or people has them around them. بیچ میں *There were children sitting among adults.* ▷ *prep* If something happens among a group of people, it happens in that group. درمیان *Discuss it among yourselves.*

amount (**amounts**) *n* An **amount** of something is how much of it you have, need, or get. مقدار

amp (**amps**) *n* An amp is a unit which is used for measuring electric current. ایمپیر

amplifier (**amplifiers**) *n* An **amplifier** is an electronic device in a radio or stereo system, which causes sounds or signals to become louder. ایمپلی فایر

amuse (**amuses, amusing, amused**) *vt* If something **amuses** you, it makes you want to laugh or smile. جی بہلانا - دل خوش کرنا

amusement arcade (**amusement arcades**) *n* An **amusement arcade** is a place where you can play games on machines which work when you put money in them. تفریح گاہ

an *det* An means the same as a, but you use an before words that begin with the sound of a, e, i, o, or u. کوئی، کوئی ایک *He started eating an apple.*

anaemic *adj* Someone who is **anaemic** suffers from a medical condition in which there are too few red cells in their blood, making them feel tired and look pale. انیمیا کا مریض

anaesthetic (**anaesthetics**) *n* **Anaesthetic** is a substance used to stop you feeling pain during an operation. بیہوشی آور

analyse (**analyses, analysing, analysed**) *vt* If you analyse something, you consider it or examine it in order to understand it or to find out what it consists of. تجزیہ کرنا

analysis (**analyses**) *n* **Analysis** is the process of considering something or

a

examining it in order to understand it or to find out what it consists of. تجزیہ

ancestor (**ancestors**) *n* Your **ancestors** are the people from whom you are descended. آباؤاجداد

anchor (**anchors**) *n* An **anchor** is a heavy hooked object at the end of a chain that is dropped from a boat into the water to make the boat stay in one place. لنگر

anchovy (**anchovies**) *n* **Anchovies** are small fish that live in the sea. They are often eaten salted. سمورہ

ancient *adj* Ancient means very old, or having existed for a long time. قدیم

and *conj* You use **and** to join two or more words or ideas. اور *She and her husband have already gone.*

Andes *npl* The **Andes** are a major mountain system of South America. اینڈیز

Andorra *n* **Andorra** is a small, mountainous country in south-west Europe, between France and Spain. اندورا

angel (**angels**) *n* **Angels** are spiritual beings that some people believe are God's messengers and servants in heaven. فرشتہ

anger *n* Anger is the strong emotion that you feel when you think someone has behaved in an unfair, cruel, or unacceptable way. غصہ

angina *n* **Angina** is severe pain in the chest and left arm, caused by heart disease. انجائنا (سینے کا درد)

angle (**angles**) *n* An **angle** is the difference in direction between two lines or surfaces. Angles are measured in degrees. زاویہ

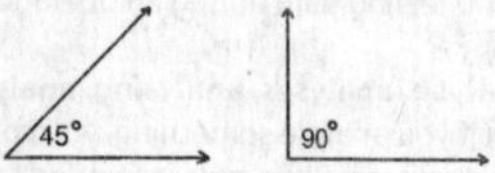

angler (**anglers**) *n* An **angler** is someone who fishes with a fishing rod as a hobby. بنسی باز

angling *n* **Angling** is the activity of fishing with a fishing rod. بنسی بازی

Angola *n* **Angola** is a republic in south-west Africa, on the Atlantic. انگولا

Angolan (**Angolans**) *adj* **Angolan** means belonging or relating to Angola or its people. انگولائی ▷ *n* An **Angolan** is someone who comes from Angola. انگولائی

angry (**angrier, angriest**) *adj* When you are **angry**, you feel strong emotion about something that you consider unfair, cruel, or insulting. ناراض

animal (**animals**) *n* Any living creature other than a human being can be referred to as an **animal**. جانور

aniseed *n* **Aniseed** is a substance made from the seeds of the anise plant. It is used as a flavouring in sweets, drinks, and medicine. سونف

ankle (**ankles**) *n* Your **ankle** is the joint where your foot joins your leg. ٹخنہ

anniversary (**anniversaries**) *n* An **anniversary** is a date which is remembered or celebrated because a special event happened on that date in a previous year. سالگرہ

announce (**announces, announcing, announced**) *n* If you announce something, you tell people about it publicly or officially. اعلان کرنا

announcement (**announcements**) *n* An **announcement** is a public statement which gives information about something that has happened or that will happen. اعلان

annoy (**annoys, annoying, annoyed**) *vt* If someone annoys you, they make you quite angry and impatient. ناراض کرنا

annoying *adj* An annoying person or action makes you feel quite angry and impatient. اشتعال انگیز

annual *adj* Annual means happening or done once every year. سالانہ

annually *adv* If something happens annually, it happens once every year. سالانہ

anonymous *adj* If you remain **anonymous** when you do something, you do not let people know that you were the person who did it. گمنام

anorak (**anoraks**) *n* An anorak is a warm waterproof jacket, usually with a hood. انورک (برساتی جیکٹ)

anorexia *n* **Anorexia** or **anorexia** nervosa is an illness in which a person refuses to eat enough because they have a fear of becoming fat. عدم اشتہا

anorexic *adj* If someone is **anorexic**, they are suffering from anorexia and so are very thin. عدم اشتہا کا مریض

another *det* You use **another** to mean one more. دوسرا، ایک اور *She ate another cake.*

answer (**answers, answering, answered**) *n* An **answer** is something that you say or write when you answer someone. جواب ▷ *v* When you **answer** someone who has asked you something, you say something back to them. جواب دینا

answering machine (**answering machines**) *n* An **answering machine** is a device which records telephone messages while you are out. فون پیغامات ریکارڈ کرنے والی مشین، آنسرنگ مشین

answerphone (**answerphones**) *n* An **answerphone** is a device which you connect to your telephone and which records telephone calls while you are out. آنسر فون

ant (**ants**) *n* Ants are small crawling insects that live in large groups. چیونٹی

antagonize (**antagonizes, antagonizing, antagonized**) *vt* If you **antagonize** someone, you make them feel hostile towards you. دشمن بنانا

Antarctic *n* The **Antarctic** is the area around the South Pole. انٹارکٹک

Antarctica *n* **Antarctica** is a continent around the South Pole. It is extremely cold and there is very little light in winter and very little darkness in summer. انٹارکٹکا

antelope (**antelopes, antelope**) *n* An **antelope** is an animal like a deer, with long legs and horns, that lives in Africa or Asia. Antelopes are graceful and can run fast. بارہ سنگھا

antenatal *adj* **Antenatal** means relating to the medical care of women when they are expecting a baby. قبل از ولادت

anthem (**anthems**) *n* An **anthem** is a song or hymn written for a special occasion. ترانہ

anthropology *n* Anthropology is the study of people, society, and culture. بشریات

antibiotic (**antibiotics**) *n* **Antibiotics** are drugs that are used in medicine to kill bacteria and to cure infections. انٹی بایوٹک

antibody (**antibodies**) *n* **Antibodies** are substances which your body produces in order to fight diseases. ضد جسم

anticlockwise *adv* If something is moving **anticlockwise**, it is moving in the opposite direction to the direction in which the hands of a clock move. گھڑی کی الٹی سمت

antidepressant (**antidepressants**) *n* An antidepressant is a drug which is used to treat people who are suffering from depression. دافع افسردگی

antidote (**antidotes**) *n* An **antidote** is a chemical substance that controls the effect of a poison. تریاق

antifreeze *n* **Antifreeze** is a liquid which is added to water to stop it freezing. It is used in car radiators in cold weather. دافع انجماد

antihistamine (**antihistamines**) *n* An **antihistamine** is a drug that is used to treat allergies. الرجی مخالف دوا

antiperspirant (**antiperspirants**) *n* An **antiperspirant** is a substance that you put on your skin to stop you from sweating. پسینہ مخالف

antique (**antiques**) *n* An **antique** is an old object which is valuable because of its beauty or rarity. نوادرات

a

antique shop (**antique shops**) *n* An **antique shop** is a shop where antiques are sold. نوادرات کی دوکان

antiseptic (**antiseptics**) *n* **Antiseptic** kills harmful bacteria. دافع عفونت

anxiety (**anxieties**) *n* **Anxiety** is a feeling of nervousness or worry. اضطراب

any *det* You use **any** to mean some of a thing. کچھ *Is there any juice left?* ▷ *pron* **Any** is used in negative sentences to show that no person or thing is involved. کوئی *The children needed new clothes and we couldn't afford any.* ▷ *det* You use **any** to show that it does not matter which one. کوئی *Take any book you want.*

anybody *pron* You use **anybody** to talk about a person, when it does not matter which one. کوئی شخص *Is there anybody there?*

anyhow *adv* You use **anyhow** to give the idea that something is true even though other things have been said. کسی طرح

anymore *adv* If something does not happen or is not true **anymore**, it has stopped happening or is no longer true. مزید نہ ہونا

anyone *pron* You use **anyone** to talk about a person, when it does not matter who. کوئی بھی *Don't tell anyone.*

anything *pron* You use **anything** to talk about a thing, when it does not matter which one. کوئی چیز *I can't see anything.*

anytime *adv* You use **anytime** to mean a point in time that is not fixed. کسی وقت

anyway *adv* You use **anyway** or anyhow to give the idea that something is true even though other things have been said. کسی طرح

anywhere *adv* You use **anywhere** to talk about a place, when it does not matter which one. کہیں بھی

apart *adv* When things are **apart**, there is a space or a distance between them. الگ ▷ *adv* If you take something **apart**, you take it to pieces. الگ کرنا

apart from *prep* You use **apart from** when you are giving an exception to a general statement. سوائے *The room was empty apart from one man sitting beside the fire.*

apartment (**apartments**) *n* An **apartment** is a set of rooms for living in, usually on one floor of a large building. گھر، رہائش

aperitif (**aperitifs**) *n* An **aperitif** is an alcoholic drink that you have before a meal. اشتا آور سیال

aperture (**apertures**) *n* An **aperture** is a narrow hole or gap. (*formal*) سوراخ

apologize (**apologizes, apologizing, apologized**) *vi* When you **apologize** to someone, you say that you are sorry that you have hurt them or caused trouble for them. معافی مانگنا

apology (**apologies**) *n* An **apology** is something that you say or write in order to tell someone that you are sorry that you have hurt them or caused trouble for them. معذرت

apostrophe (**apostrophes**) *n* An apostrophe is the mark' that shows that one or more letters have been removed from a word, as in 'isn't'. It is also added to nouns to show possession, as in 'the girl's doll'. علامت تخفیف حروف

appalling *adj* Something that is **appalling** is so bad that it shocks you. خوفناک

apparatus (**apparatuses**) *n* The **apparatus** of an organization or system is its structure and method of operation. ڈھانچہ

apparent *adj* An **apparent** situation seems to be the case, although you cannot be certain that it is. واضح

apparently *adv* You use **apparently** to refer to something that seems to be the case although it may not be. واضح طور پر

appeal (**appeals, appealing, appealed**) *n* An **appeal** is a serious and urgent request.

درخواست ▷ *vi* If you **appeal** to someone to do something, you make a serious and urgent request to them. درخواست کرنا

appear (**appears, appearing, appeared**) *vt* If something **appears** to be the way you describe it, it seems that way. ظاہر ہونا

appearance (**appearances**) *n* When someone makes an **appearance** at a public event or in a broadcast, they take part in it. ظہور

appendicitis *n* **Appendicitis** is an illness in which a person's appendix is infected and painful. بڑی آنت کا درد

appetite (**appetites**) *n* Your **appetite** is your desire to eat. بھوک

applaud (**applauds, applauding, applauded**) *v* When a group of people **applaud** or **applaud** someone, they clap their hands to show that they have enjoyed a performance. داد دینا

applause *n* **Applause** is the noise made by a group of people clapping their hands to show approval. داد

apple (**apples**) *n* An **apple** is a round fruit with a smooth skin and firm white flesh. سیب

apple pie (**apple pies**) *n* An **apple pie** is a kind of pie made with apples. ایپل پائی

appliance (**appliances**) *n* An **appliance** is a device such as a vacuum cleaner that does a particular job in your home. (*formal*) مشین

applicant (**applicants**) *n* An **applicant** for a job or position is someone who applies for it. درخواست دہندہ

application (**applications**) *n* An **application** for something such as a job or a place at a college is a formal written request to be given it. درخواست

application form (**application forms**) *n* An **application form** is a formal written request for something such as a job or membership of an organization. درخواست فارم

apply (**applies, applying, applied**) *v* If you **apply** for something or to something, you ask to be allowed to have it or do it. درخواست دینا

appoint (**appoints, appointing, appointed**) *vt* If you **appoint** someone to a job or post, you formally choose them for it. مقرر کرنا

appointment (**appointments**) *n* The **appointment** of a person to a particular job is the choice of that person to do it. تقرری

appreciate (**appreciates, appreciating, appreciated**) *vt* If you **appreciate** something, you like it because you recognize its good qualities. ستائش کرنا

apprehensive *adj* Someone who is apprehensive is afraid that something bad may happen. خائف

apprentice (**apprentices**) *n* An **apprentice** is a person who works with someone in order to learn their skill. کارآموز

approach (**approaches, approaching, approached**) *v* When you **approach** something, you get closer to it. پہنچنا

appropriate *adj* Something that is **appropriate** is suitable or acceptable for a particular situation. موزوں

approval *n* If a plan or request gets someone's **approval**, they agree to it. منظوری

approve (**approves, approving, approved**) *vi* If you **approve** of something or someone, you like them or think they are good. منظور کرنا

approximate *adj* **Approximate** figures are close to the correct figure, but are not exact. قریب قریب

approximately *adv* **Approximately** means close to, around, or roughly. تقریباً

apricot (**apricots**) *n* An **apricot** is a small, soft, round fruit with yellow-orange flesh and a stone inside. خوبانی

April (**Aprils**) *n* **April** is the fourth month of the year in the Western calendar. اپریل

April Fools' Day *n* In the West, **April Fools' Day** is the 1st of April, the day on which people traditionally play tricks on each other. یکم اپریل

apron (**aprons**) *n* An **apron** is a piece of clothing that you put on over the front of your clothes to prevent them from getting dirty. لبادہ

aquarium (**aquariums, aquaria**) *n* An **aquarium** is a building, often in a zoo, where fish and underwater animals are kept. ماہی خانہ

Aquarius *n* **Aquarius** is one of the twelve signs of the zodiac. Its symbol is a person pouring water. People who are born between 20th January and 18th February come under this sign. دلو

Arab (**Arabs**) *adj* **Arab** means belonging or relating to Arabs or to their countries or customs. عرب ▷ *n* **Arabs** are people who speak Arabic and who come from the Middle East and parts of North Africa. عربی

Arabic *n* **Arabic** is a language that is spoken in the Middle East and in parts of North Africa. عربی زبان ▷ *adj* Something that is **Arabic** belongs or relates to the language, writing, or culture of the Arabs. عربی

arbitration *n* **Arbitration** is the judging of a dispute between people or groups by someone who is not involved. ثالثی

arch (**arches**) *n* An **arch** is a structure which is made when two columns join at the top in a curve. محراب

archaeologist (**archaeologists**) *n* An **archaeologist** is a person who studies the past by examining the remains of things such as buildings and tools. ماہر آثار قدیمہ

archaeology *n* **Archaeology** is the study of the past by examining the remains of things such as buildings and tools. علم آثار قدیمہ

architect (**architects**) *n* An **architect** is a person who designs buildings. معمار۔ ماہر تعمیرات

architecture *n* **Architecture** is the art of designing and constructing buildings. فن تعمیر

archive (**archives**) *n* **Archives** are collections of documents that contain information about the history of an organization or group of people. محافظ خانہ

Arctic *n* The **Arctic** is the area of the world around the North Pole. It is extremely cold and there is very little light in winter and very little darkness in summer. علاقہ قطب شمالی

Arctic Circle *n* The **Arctic Circle** is an imaginary line drawn around the northern part of the world at approximately 66° North. دائرہ قطب شمالی

Arctic Ocean *n* The **Arctic Ocean** is the ocean surrounding the North Pole, north of the Arctic Circle. بحر قطب شمالی

area (**areas**) *n* An **area** is a particular part of a city, a country, or the world. علاقہ

Argentina *n* **Argentina** is a republic in southern South America. ارجنٹینا

Argentinian (**Argentinians**) *adj* **Argentinian** means belonging or relating to Argentina or its people. ارجنٹینیائی ▷ *n* An **Argentinian** is someone who comes from Argentina . ارجنٹینیائی

argue (**argues, arguing, argued**) *vi* If you **argue** with someone, you disagree with them about something, often angrily. بحث کرنا

argument (**arguments**) *n* If people have an **argument**, they disagree with each other, often angrily. دلیل

Aries *n* **Aries** is one of the twelve signs of the zodiac. Its symbol is a ram. People who are born between 21st March and 19th April come under this sign. برج حمل

arm (**arms**) *n* Your **arms** are the two parts of your body between your shoulders and your hands. بازو

armchair (**armchairs**) *n* An **armchair** is a comfortable chair with a support on each side for your arms. آرام کرسی

armed *adj* Someone who is armed is carrying a weapon. مسلح

Armenia *n* **Armenia** is a republic in north-west Asia. آرمینیا

Armenian (**Armenians**) *adj* **Armenian** means of or relating to Armenia, its inhabitants, their language, or the Armenian Church. آرمینیائی ⊳ *n* An **Armenian** is a native or inhabitant of Armenia or an Armenian-speaking person elsewhere. آرمینیائی ⊳ *n* **Armenian** is the language spoken by people who live in Armenia. آرمینیائی زبان

armour *n* In former times, **armour** was special metal clothing that soldiers wore for protection in battle. زرہ

armpit (**armpits**) *n* Your **armpits** are the areas of your body under your arms where your arms join your shoulders. بغل

army (**armies**) *n* An **army** is a large organized group of people who are armed and trained to fight. فوج

aroma (**aromas**) *n* An **aroma** is a strong pleasant smell. خوشبو

aromatherapy *n* **Aromatherapy** is a type of treatment which involves massaging the body with special fragrant oils. خوشبو سے علاج

around *adv* **Around** means surrounding, or on all sides of. گھیرے ہوئے ⊳ *prep* Things or people that are **around** a place or object surround it or are on all sides of it. اطراف *There were lots of people around her.* ⊳ *prep* You use **around** to say that something is in every part of a place. ارد گرد *His toys lay around the room.* ⊳ *prep* **Around** means near to something. آس پاس، قریب *We left around noon.*

arrange (**arranges, arranging, arranged**) *v* If you **arrange** something, you make plans for it to happen. انتظام کرنا ⊳ *vt* If you **arrange** things somewhere, you put them in a way that looks tidy or pretty. ترتیب دینا

arrangement (**arrangements**) *n* **Arrangements** are plans and preparations which you make so that something can happen. بندوبست

arrears *npl* **Arrears** are amounts of money that someone owes. If someone is in **arrears** with regular payments, they have not paid them. بقایا

arrest (**arrests, arresting, arrested**) *n* An **arrest** is the act of taking a person into custody, especially under lawful authority. گرفتاری ⊳ *vt* If the police **arrest** you, they take charge of you and take you to a police station, because they believe you may have committed a crime. گرفتار کرنا

arrival (**arrivals**) *n* Your **arrival** at a place is the act of arriving there. آمد

arrive (**arrives, arriving, arrived**) *vi* When you **arrive** at a place, you reach it at the end of a journey. آنا

arrogant *adj* If you say that someone is **arrogant**, you disapprove of them because they behave as if they are better than other people. مغرور

arrow (**arrows**) *n* An **arrow** is a long, thin stick with a sharp point at one end. تیر ⊳ *n* An **arrow** is a sign that shows you which way to go. تیر کا نشان

arson *n* **Arson** is the crime of deliberately setting fire to a building or vehicle. آگ زنی

art *n* **Art** is paintings, drawings, and sculpture which are beautiful or which express an artist's ideas. فنون لطیف

artery (**arteries**) *n* Your **arteries** are the tubes that carry blood from your heart to the rest of your body. شریان

art gallery (**art galleries**) *n* An art gallery is a building where paintings and other works of art are shown to the public. آرٹ گیلری

arthritis *n* **Arthritis** is a condition in which the joints in someone's body are swollen and painful. گٹھیا

artichoke (**artichokes**) *n* An **artichoke** or a globe artichoke is a round vegetable with thick green leaves arranged like the petals of a flower. فرشوف، ایک مخلوط پودا جو اونٹ کٹارے سے ملتا جلتا ہے

article (**articles**) *n* An **article** is a piece of writing in a newspaper or magazine. مضمون

artificial *adj* **Artificial** objects, materials, or situations do not occur naturally and are created by people. مصنوعی

artist (**artists**) *n* An **artist** is someone who draws, paints, or produces other works of art. فنکار

artistic *adj* Someone who is **artistic** is good at drawing or painting, or arranging things in a beautiful way. فنی

art school *n* An **art school** is a college that specializes in art. آرٹ اسکول

as *conj* If one thing happens **as** a different thing happens, it happens at the same time. جیسے *We shut the door behind us as we entered.* ▷ *prep* You use **as** when you are talking about somebody's job. بطور *He works as a doctor.*

asap *abbr* **Asap** is an abbreviation for 'as soon as possible'. حتی الامکان جلد سے جلد

as ... as *adv* You use the structure **as ... as** when you are comparing things, or emphasizing how large or small something is. اتنا۔ اتنا

ashamed *adj* If someone is **ashamed** of something or someone, they feel embarrassed about it or guilty because of it. شرمندہ

ashtray (**ashtrays**) *n* An **ashtray** is a small dish in which people put the ash from their cigarettes and cigars. خاکستر دان

Ash Wednesday *n* **Ash Wednesday** is the first day of Lent. ایش بدھ (ایسٹر چلہ کا پہلا دن)

Asia *n* **Asia** is the largest of the continents, bordering on the Arctic Ocean, the Pacific Ocean, the Indian Ocean, and the Mediterranean and Red Seas in the west. ایشیا

Asian (**Asians**) *adj* **Asian** means belonging or relating to Asia. ایشیائی ▷ *n* An **Asian** is a person who comes from a country or region in Asia. ایشیائی

aside *adv* If you move something **aside**, you move it to one side of you. ایک طرف کرنا، کنارے کرنا

ask (**asks, asking, asked**) *vt* If you **ask** someone a question, you say that you want to know something. پوچھنا

ask for *v* If you **ask for** something, you say that you want it. طلب کرنا *She asked for some sweets.*

asleep *adj* Someone who is **asleep** is sleeping. خوابیدہ

asparagus *n* **Asparagus** is a vegetable with green shoots that you cook and eat. مارچوبہ، ناگ دون

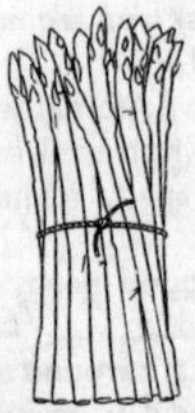

aspect (**aspects**) *n* An **aspect** of something is one of the parts of its character or nature. پہلو

aspirin (**aspirins, aspirin**) *n* **Aspirin** is a mild drug which reduces pain and fever. اسپرن

assembly (**assemblies**) *n* An **assembly** is a group of people gathered together for a particular purpose. اجلاس، اجتماع

asset (**assets**) *n* If something that you have is an **asset**, it is useful to you. اثاثہ

assignment (**assignments**) *n* An **assignment** is a piece of work that you are given to do, as part of your job or studies. تفویض

assistance *n* If you give someone **assistance**, you help them. اعانت

assistant (**assistants**) *n* Someone's **assistant** is a person who helps them in their work. معاون

associate (**associates**) *adj* **Associate** is used before a rank or title to indicate a slightly different or lower rank or title. رفیق کار ▷ *n* Your **associates** are your business colleagues. رفیق کار

association (**associations**) *n* An **association** is an official group of people who have the same occupation, aim, or interest. وابستگی

assortment (**assortments**) *n* An **assortment** is a group of similar things that have different sizes, colours, or qualities. تقسیم کاری

assume (**assumes, assuming, assumed**) *vt* If you **assume** that something is true, you suppose that it is true, sometimes wrongly. فرض کرنا

assure (**assures, assuring, assured**) *vt* If you **assure** someone that something is true or will happen, you tell them that it is the case, to make them less worried. یقین دلانا

asthma *n* **Asthma** is an illness which affects the chest and makes breathing difficult. دمہ

astonish (**astonishes, astonishing, astonished**) *vt* If someone or something **astonishes** you, they surprise you very much. حیرت زدہ کرنا

astonished *adj* If you are **astonished** by something, you are very surprised about it. حیرت زدہ

astonishing *adj* Something that is **astonishing** is very surprising. تحیر آمیز

astrology *n* **Astrology** is the study of the movements of the planets, sun, moon, and stars in the belief that they can influence people's lives. علم نجوم

astronaut (**astronauts**) *n* An **astronaut** is a person who travels in a spacecraft. خلا باز

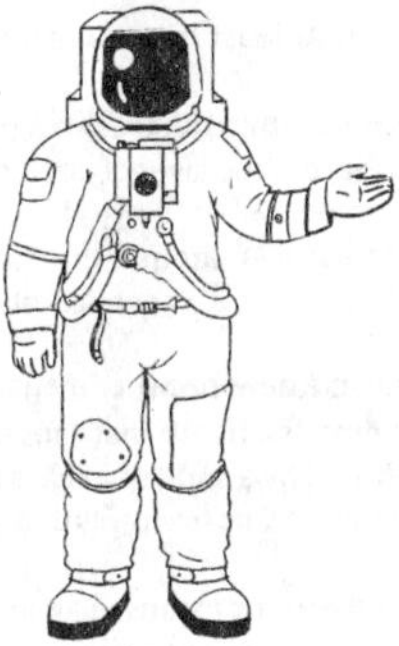

astronomy *n* **Astronomy** is the scientific study of the stars, planets, and other natural objects in space. علم افلاک

asylum (**asylums**) *n* If a government gives a person from another country **asylum**, they allow them to stay, usually because they are unable to return home safely for political reasons. پناہ

asylum seeker (**asylum seekers**) *n* An **asylum seeker** is a person who is trying to get asylum in a foreign country. پناہ گزیں

at *prep* You use **at** to say where or when something happens or where it is. بوقت، بمقام *I'll meet you at the information desk at seven o'clock.*

atheist (**atheists**) *n* An **atheist** is a person who believes that there is no God. منکر خدا

athlete (**athletes**) *n* An **athlete** is a person who takes part in athletics competitions. کھیل کود میں حصہ لینے والا

athletic *adj* **Athletic** means relating to athletes and athletics. ایتھلیٹک

athletics *npl* **Athletics** consists of sports such as running, the high jump, and the javelin. کھیل کود

Atlantic Ocean *n* The **Atlantic Ocean** is the second largest ocean in the world. بحر اوقیانوس

atlas (**atlases**) *n* An **atlas** is a book of maps. اٹلس، خریطہ

at least *adv* **At least** means not less than. کم از کم

atmosphere (**atmospheres**) *n* A planet's **atmosphere** is the layer of air or other gas around it. فضا

atom (**atoms**) *n* An **atom** is the smallest possible amount of a chemical element. ذرہ، جوہر

atom bomb (**atom bombs**) *n* An **atom bomb** is a bomb that causes an explosion by a sudden release of energy that results from splitting atoms. جوہری بم

atomic *adj* **Atomic** means relating to atoms or to the power produced by splitting atoms. جوہری

attach (**attaches, attaching, attached**) *vt* If you **attach** something to an object, you join it or fasten it to the object. جوڑنا

attached *adj* If you are **attached** to someone or something, you care deeply about them. منسلک

attachment (**attachments**) *n* An **attachment** to someone or something is a love or liking for them. انسلاک

attack (**attacks, attacking, attacked**) *n* An **attack** is the act or an instance of attacking. حملہ ▷ *v* To **attack** a person or place means to try to hurt or damage them using physical violence. حملہ کرنا

attempt (**attempts, attempting, attempted**) *n* If you make an **attempt** to do something, you try to do it, often without success. کوشش ▷ *vt* If you **attempt** to do something, especially something difficult, you try to do it. کوشش کرنا

attend (**attends, attending, attended**) *n* If you **attend** a meeting or other event, you are at it. حاضری دینا

attendance *n* Someone's **attendance** at an event or an institution is the fact that they are present at the event or go regularly to the institution. حاضری

attention *n* If something has your **attention** or if you are paying **attention** to it, you have noticed it and are interested in it. توجہ

attic (**attics**) *n* An **attic** is a room at the top of a house, just below the roof. اٹاری

attitude (**attitudes**) *n* Your **attitude** to something is the way you think and feel about it. رجحان

attract (**attracts, attracting, attracted**) *vt* If something **attracts** people or animals, it has features that cause them to come to it. راغب کرنا

attraction (**attractions**) *n* **Attraction** is a feeling of liking someone. کشش

attractive *adj* An **attractive** person or thing is pleasant to look at. پرکشش

aubergine (**aubergines**) *n* An **aubergine** is a vegetable with a smooth purple skin. بیگن

auburn *adj* **Auburn** hair is reddish brown. سرخ بھورا

auction (**auctions**) *n* An **auction** is a sale where goods are sold to the person who offers the highest price. نیلامی

audience (**audiences**) *n* The **audience** is all the people who are watching or listening to a play, concert, film, or programme. ناظرین، سامعین

audit (**audits, auditing, audited**) *n* An **audit** is an inspection, correction, and verification of business accounts, conducted by an independent qualified accountant. احتساب ▷ *vt* When an accountant **audits** an organization's accounts, he or she examines the accounts officially in order to make sure that they have been done correctly. محاسبہ کرنا

audition (**auditions**) *n* An **audition** is a short performance given by an actor, dancer, or musician so that someone can decide if they are good enough to be in a play, film, or orchestra. آڈیشن

auditor (**auditors**) *n* An **auditor** is an accountant who officially examines the accounts of organizations. محتسب

August (**Augusts**) *n* **August** is the eighth month of the year in the Western calendar. اگست

aunt (**aunts**) *n* Your **aunt** is the sister of your mother or father, or the wife of your uncle. چچی، خالہ، پھوپی

auntie (**aunties**) *n* Someone's **auntie** is the sister of their mother or father, or the wife of their uncle. (*informal*) چچی، خالہ، پھوپی

au pair (**au pairs**) *n* An **au pair** is a young person who lives with a family in a foreign country in order to learn their language and help around the house. طالبِ لسان بعوض گھریلو کام کاج

austerity *n* **Austerity** is a situation in which people's living standards are reduced because of economic difficulties. سادگی

Australasia *n* **Australasia** is Australia, New Zealand, and neighbouring islands in the South Pacific Ocean. آسٹریلیشیا

Australia *n* **Australia** is a country located between the Indian Ocean and the Pacific. آسٹریلیا

Australian (**Australians**) *adj* **Australian** means belonging or relating to Australia, or to its people or culture. آسٹریلیائی ▷ *n* An **Australian** is someone who comes from Australia. آسٹریلیائی

Austria *n* **Austria** is a republic in central Europe. آسٹریا

Austrian (**Austrians**) *adj* **Austrian** means belonging or relating to Austria, or to its people or culture. آسٹریائی ▷ *n* An **Austrian** is a person who comes from Austria. آسٹریلیائی

authentic *adj* If something is **authentic**, it is genuine or accurate. مستند

author (**authors**) *n* The **author** of a piece of writing is the person who wrote it. مصنف

authorize (**authorizes, authorizing, authorized**) *vt* If someone **authorizes** something, they give their official permission for it to happen. اختیار دینا

autobiography (**autobiographies**) *n* Your **autobiography** is an account of your life, which you write yourself. خودنوشت سوانح حیات

autograph (**autographs**) *n* An **autograph** is the signature of someone famous which is specially written for a fan to keep. دستی تحریر

automatic *adj* An **automatic** machine or device is one which has controls that enable it to perform a task without needing to be constantly operated by a person. خودکار

automatically *adv* If you do something **automatically**, you do it without thinking about it. خودبخود

autonomous *adj* An **autonomous** country, organization, or group governs or controls itself rather than being controlled by anyone else. خودمختاری

autonomy *n* If a country, person, or group has **autonomy**, they control themselves rather than being controlled by others. خودمختار نظام

autumn (**autumns**) *n* Autumn is the season between summer and winter. خزاں

availability *n* The **availability** of something is the ease with which you can find it or obtain it. دستیابی

available *adj* If something is **available**, you can use it or obtain it. میسر

avalanche (**avalanches**) *n* An **avalanche** is a large mass of snow or rock that falls down the side of a mountain. برفانی تودہ

avenue (**avenues**) *n* An **avenue** is a wide road, with shops or houses on each side. اوینیو

average (**averages**) *adj* If you describe a figure as **average**, you mean that it represents a numerical average. اوسط ▷ *n* An **average** is the result that you get when you add two or more numbers together and divide the total by the number of numbers you added together. اوسط

avocado (**avocados**) *n* An **avocado** is a fruit in the shape of a pear with a dark green skin and a large stone inside it. ناشپاتی جیسا پھل

avoid (**avoids, avoiding, avoided**) *vt* If you **avoid** something unpleasant that might happen, you take action in order to prevent it from happening. ٹالنا

awake (**awakes, awaking, awoke, awoken**) *adj* If you are **awake**, you are not sleeping. بیدار ▷ *v* When you **awake**, or when something **awakes** you, you wake up. (*literary*) جاگنا، جگانا

award (**awards**) *n* An **award** is a prize or certificate you get for doing something well. انعام

aware *adj* If you are **aware** of a fact or situation, you know about it. باخبر

away *adv* If someone moves **away** from a place, they move so that they are not there any more. دور ▷ *adv* If you put something **away**, you put it where it should be. جگہ پر رکھنا

away match (**away matches**) *n* When a sports team plays an **away match**, it plays on its opponents' ground. مقابل کے میدان پر میچ

awful *adj* If you say that someone or something is **awful**, you dislike that person or thing or you think that they are not very good. ناگوار

awfully *adv* You use **awfully** to emphasize how much of a quality someone or something has. ناگوار انداز میں

awkward *adj* An **awkward** situation is embarrassing and difficult to deal with. بدوضع، بے ڈول

axe (**axes**) *n* An **axe** is a tool used for chopping wood. It consists of a blade attached to the end of a long handle. کلہاڑی

axle (**axles**) *n* An **axle** is a rod connecting a pair of wheels on a car or other vehicle. ایکسل (پہیوں کے بیچ کی سلاخ)

Azerbaijan *n* **Azerbaijan** is a republic in north-west Asia. آذربائجان

Azerbaijani (**Azerbaijanis**) *adj* **Azerbaijani** means belonging or relating to Azerbaijan. آذربائجانی ▷ *n* An **Azerbaijani** is a native or inhabitant of **Azerbaijan**. آذربائجانی

b

BA (**BAs**) *abbr* A **BA** is a first degree in an arts or social science subject. **BA** is an abbreviation for 'Bachelor of Arts'. بی اے

baby (**babies**) *n* A **baby** is a very young child that cannot yet walk or talk. بچہ

baby milk *n* **Baby milk** is a powder which you mix with water to make artificial milk for babies. بچے کا دودھ

baby's bottle (**babies' bottles**) *n* A **baby's bottle** is a drinking container used by babies. It has a special rubber part at the top through which they can suck their drink. بچے کی بوتل

babysit (**babysits, babysitting, babysat**) *v* If you **babysit** for someone or **babysit** their children, you look after their children while they are out. بچہ کھلائی

babysitter (**babysitters**) *n* A **babysitter** is a person who looks after someone's children while they are out. بچہ نگراں

babysitting *n* **Babysitting** is the action of looking after someone's children while they are out. بچہ نگرانی

baby wipe (**baby wipes**) *n* A **baby wipe** is a disposable moistened medicated paper towel, usually supplied in a plastic drum or packet, used for cleaning babies. بچہ کا تولیہ

bachelor (**bachelors**) *n* A **bachelor** is a man who has never married. کنوارہ

back (**backs, backing, backed**) *adj* **Back** is used to refer to the part of something that is farthest from the front. پشت ▷ *adv* If you move **back**, you move away from the way you are facing. پیچھے ▷ *n* Your **back** is the part of your body from your neck to your bottom. پیٹھ ▷ *vi* If a building **backs** onto something, the **back** of it faces that thing. عقب میں ▷ *n* The **back** of something is the side or part of it that is farthest from the front. پیچھے

backache (**backaches**) *n* **Backache** is a dull pain in your back. پیٹھ درد

backbone (**backbones**) *n* Your **backbone** is the column of small linked bones along the middle of your back. ریڑھ کی ہڈی

backfire (**backfires, backfiring, backfired**) *vi* If a plan **backfires**, it has the opposite result to the one that was intended. الٹ جانا

background (**backgrounds**) *n* Your **background** is the kind of family you come from and the kind of education you have had. پس منظر

backing (**backings**) *n* **Backing** is money, resources, or support given to a person or organization. حمایت

back out *v* If you **back out**, you decide not to do something that you previously agreed to do. واپس ہونا *They backed out of the project.*

backpack (**backpacks**) *n* A **backpack** is a bag with straps that go over your shoulders, so that you can carry things on your back when you are walking or climbing. پشتی بیگ

backpacker (**backpackers**) *n* A **backpacker** is a person who goes travelling with a backpack. پٹھو لادے مسافر

backpacking *n* If you go **backpacking**, you go travelling with a backpack. پٹھو لادے سفر

back pain *n* **Back pain** is pain that you feel in your back. پیٹھ درد

backside (**backsides**) *n* Your **backside** is the part of your body that you sit on. (*informal*) پیچھے کی سمت

backslash (**backslashes**) *n* A **backslash** is the mark. پیچھے کی طرف جھکی آڑی لکیر

backstroke *n* **Backstroke** is a swimming stroke that you do on your back. پیٹھ کے بل تیرنا

back up (**backups**) *v* If someone or something **backs up** a statement, they show that it is true. تائید کرنا *He didn't have any proof to back up his story.*
▷ *n* **Backup** consists of extra equipment or people that you can get help or support from if necessary. محفوظ وسائل

backwards *adv* If you move **backwards**, you move in the direction behind you. پیچھے کی طرف ▷ *adv* If you do something **backwards**, you do it the opposite of the usual way. الٹی طرف

bacon *n* **Bacon** is salted or smoked meat taken from the back or sides of a pig. سور کا بھنا ہوا گوشت یا نمکین گوشت

bacteria *npl* **Bacteria** are very small organisms which can cause disease. جرثومہ

bad (**worse, worst**) *adj* Something that is **bad** is not nice or good. خراب ▷ *adj* Someone who is **bad** does things they should not do. خراب، بدمعاش

badge (**badges**) *n* A **badge** is a small piece of metal or cloth showing a design or words, which you attach to your clothes. بلا

badger (**badgers**) *n* A **badger** is a wild animal with a white head with two wide black stripes on it. بجو

badly *adv* If you do something **badly**, you do it with very little success or effect. برے طریقے سے

badminton *n* **Badminton** is a game played on a rectangular court by two or four players. They hit a feathered object called a shuttlecock across a high net. بیڈمنٹن

bad-tempered *adj* If you are **bad-tempered**, you are not cheerful and get angry easily. بدمزاج

baffled *adj* If you are **baffled** by something, you cannot understand or explain it. بھونچکا

bag (**bags**) *n* A **bag** is a container made of paper, plastic, or leather which you use to carry things. تھیلا

baggage *n* Your **baggage** consists of the suitcases and bags that you take with you when you travel. سامان سفر

baggy (**baggier, baggiest**) *adj* **Baggy** clothes hang loosely on your body. ڈھیلا لباس

bagpipes *npl* **Bagpipes** are a musical instrument that are played by blowing air through a pipe into a bag, and then squeezing the bag to force the air out through other pipes. مشکی باجا

Bahamas *npl* The **Bahamas** are a group of over 700 coral islands in the Caribbean. بہاماس

Bahrain *n* **Bahrain** is a country on the Persian Gulf that consists of several islands. بحرین

bail *n* **Bail** is a sum of money that an arrested person or someone else puts forward as a guarantee that the arrested person will attend their trial in a law court. If the arrested person does not attend it, the money is lost. زرضمانت

bake (**bakes, baking, baked**) *vi* If you **bake**, you spend some time preparing and mixing together ingredients to make bread, cakes, pies, or other food which is cooked in the oven. سینکنا

baked *adj* **Baked** food is cooked in the oven. سینکا ہوا

baked potato (**baked potatoes**) *n* A

baked potato is a large potato that has been baked with its skin on. بھونا ہوا آلو

baker (**bakers**) *n* A **baker** is a person whose job is to bake and sell bread and cakes. بیکری والا

bakery (**bakeries**) *n* A **bakery** is a building where bread and cakes are baked, or the shop where they are sold. بیکری

baking *n* **Baking** is the activity of cooking bread or cakes in an oven. بھوننا، سینکنا

baking powder (**baking powders**) *n* **Baking powder** is an ingredient used in cake making. It causes cakes to rise when they are in the oven. خمیر

balance *n* **Balance** is the steadiness that someone or something has when they are balanced on something. توازن

balanced *adj* A **balanced** account or report is fair and reasonable. متوازن

balance sheet (**balance sheets**) *n* A **balance sheet** is a written statement of the amount of money and property that a company or person has, including amounts of money that are owed or are owing. بیلنس شیٹ

balcony (**balconies**) *n* A **balcony** is a platform on the outside of a building with a wall or railing around it. بالکنی

bald (**balder, baldest**) *adj* Someone who is **bald** has little or no hair on the top of their head. گنجا

Balkan *adj* **Balkan** means of or relating to the Balkan Peninsula or the Balkan Mountains, or to the Balkan States or their inhabitants. بلقانی

ball (**balls**) *n* A **ball** is a round object used in games such as football. گیند ▷ *n* A **ball** is a large formal dance. بال رقص

ballerina (**ballerinas**) *n* A **ballerina** is a woman ballet dancer. بیلے رقاصہ

ballet *n* **Ballet** is a type of artistic dancing with carefully planned movements. بیلے

ballet dancer (**ballet dancers**) *n* A **ballet dancer** is a dancer who does ballet, especially as a profession. بیلے رقاص

ballet shoes *npl* **Ballet shoes** are special soft, light shoes that ballet dancers wear. بیلے جوتے

balloon (**balloons**) *n* A **balloon** is a small, thin, rubber bag that becomes larger when you blow air into it. غبارہ

ballpoint (**ballpoints**) *n* A **ballpoint** or a **ballpoint** pen is a pen with a very small metal ball at the end which transfers the ink from the pen onto a surface. بال پوئنٹ پین

ballroom dancing *n* **Ballroom dancing** is a type of dancing in which a man and a woman dance together using fixed sequences of steps and movements. بال روم رقص

bamboo (**bamboos**) *n* **Bamboo** is a tall tropical plant with hard hollow stems. بانس

ban (**bans, banning, banned**) *n* A **ban** is an official ruling that something must not be done, shown, or used. پابندی ▷ *vt* To **ban** something means to state officially that it must not be done, shown, or used. پابندی لگانا

banana (**bananas**) *n* An **ally** is a country, organization, or person that helps and supports another. کیلا

band (**bands**) *n* A **band** is a group of people who play music together. بینڈ، سازندہ جماعت ▷ *n* A **band** is a narrow strip of material that you put around something. رکاوٹ

bandage (**bandages, bandaging, bandaged**) *n* A **bandage** is a long strip of cloth that is tied around a wounded part of someone's body in order to protect or support it. مرہم پٹی ▷ *vt* If you **bandage** a wound or part of someone's body, you tie a bandage round it. پٹی باندھنا

bang (**bangs, banging, banged**) *n* A **bang** is a sudden loud noise such as an explosion. دھماکہ ▷ *v* If you **bang** something such as a door, or if it bangs, it closes suddenly with a loud noise. دھماکہ کرنا

Bangladesh *n* **Bangladesh** is a republic in South Asia, formerly the Eastern Province of Pakistan. بنگلہ دیش

Bangladeshi (**Bangladeshis**) *adj* **Bangladeshi** means belonging to or relating to Bangladesh, or to its people or culture. بنگلہ دیشی ▷ *n* The **Bangladeshis** are the people who come from Bangladesh. بنگلہ دیشی

banister (**banisters**) *n* A **banister** is a rail supported by posts and fixed along the side of a staircase. ریلنگ

banjo (**banjos**) *n* A **banjo** is a musical instrument that looks like a guitar with a circular body, a long neck, and four or more strings. بنجو

bank (**banks**) *n* A **bank** is the ground beside a river. کنارہ ▷ *n* A **bank** is a place where people can keep their money. بینک

bank account (**bank accounts**) *n* A **bank account** is an arrangement with a bank which allows you to keep your money in the bank and to take some out when you need it. بینک کھاتہ

bank balance (**bank balances**) *n* Your **bank balance** is the amount of money that you have in your bank account at a particular time. بینک میں میزان

bank charges *npl* **Bank charges** are an amount of money that you have to pay to your bank, for example, if you have spent more money than you have in your account. بینک کو اخراجات کے عوض ادا کی جانے والی رقم

banker (**bankers**) *n* A **banker** is someone involved in banking at a senior level. بینک کار

bank holiday (**bank holidays**) *n* A **bank holiday** is a public holiday. (30) جون بنکوں کی عام تعطیل

banknote (**banknotes**) *n* A **banknote** is a piece of paper money. کاغذی نوٹ

bankrupt *adj* People or organizations that go **bankrupt** do not have enough money to pay their debts. دیوالیہ

bank statement (**bank statements**) *n* A **bank statement** is a printed document showing all the money paid into and taken out of a bank account. بینک کا گوشوارہ

banned *adj* If something is **banned**, it has been stated officially that it must not be done, shown, or used. ممنوعہ

bar (**bars**) *n* A **bar** is a long, thin piece of wood or metal. چھڑ ▷ *n* A **bar** is a place where people buy and drink alcoholic drinks. بار - سلاخ

Barbados *n* **Barbados** is an island in the Caribbean, in the east Lesser Antilles. بارباڈوس

barbaric *adj* **Barbaric** behaviour is extremely cruel. وحشیانہ

barbecue (**barbecues**) *n* A **barbecue** is a grill used to cook food outdoors. باربی کیو

barbed wire *n* **Barbed wire** is strong wire with sharp points sticking out of it, which is used to make fences. کانٹے دار تار

barber (**barbers**) *n* A **barber** is a man whose job is cutting men's hair. نائی

bare (**barer, barest, bares, baring, bared**) *adj* If a part of your body is **bare**, it is not covered by any clothes. ننگا ▷ *adj* If something is **bare**, it has nothing on top of it or inside it. کھلا ▷ *vt* If you **bare** something, you show it. برہنہ کرنا

barefoot *adj* If you are **barefoot** or **barefooted**, you are wearing nothing on your feet. ننگے پیر ▷ *adv* If you do something **barefoot**, you do it while wearing nothing on your feet. ننگے پیروں

barely *adv* You use **barely** to say that something is only just true or possible. بمشکل

bargain (**bargains**) *n* Something that is a **bargain** is good value, usually because it has been sold at a lower price than normal. مول بھاؤ

barge (**barges**) *n* A **barge** is a narrow boat with a flat bottom, used for carrying heavy loads. چلی سپاٹ پیندے کی مال بردار کشتی

bark (**barks, barking, barked**) *vi* When a dog **barks**, it makes a short, loud noise. بھونکنا

barley *n* **Barley** is a crop which has seeds that are used in the production of food, beer, and whisky. جو

barn (**barns**) *n* A **barn** is a building on a farm in which crops or animal food are kept. باڑا

barrel (**barrels**) *n* A **barrel** is a large round container for liquids or food. Barrels are usually wider in the middle than at the top or bottom. بیرل

barrier (**barriers**) *n* A **barrier** is something such as a law or policy that makes it difficult or impossible for something to happen. رکاوٹ

base (**bases**) *n* The **base** of something is its lowest edge or part, or the part at which it is attached to something else. اساس

baseball *n* **Baseball** is a game that is played with a bat and a ball on a large field by two teams of nine players. Players must hit the ball and run around four bases to score. بیس بال

baseball cap (**baseball caps**) *n* A **baseball cap** is a close-fitting thin cap with a deep peak. بیس بال ٹوپی

based *adj* If one thing is **based** on another, the first thing is developed from the second one. مبنی

basement (**basements**) *n* The **basement** of a building is an area partly or completely below ground level, with a room or rooms in it. تہہ خانہ

bash (**bashes, bashing, bashed**) *n* A **bash** is a party or celebration. (*informal*) جشن
▷ *vt* If you **bash** someone or something, you hit them hard in a rough way. (*informal*) کاری ضرب لگا

basic *adj* You use **basic** to describe things, activities, and principles that are very important or necessary, and on which others depend. بنیادی

basically *adv* You use **basically** for emphasis when you are stating an opinion, or when you are making an important statement about something. بنیادی طور پر

basics *npl* The **basics** of something are its simplest, most important elements, ideas, or principles, in contrast to more complicated or detailed ones. بنیادی حقائق

basil *n* **Basil** is a strong-smelling and strong-tasting herb that is used in cooking, especially with tomatoes. تلسی

basin (**basins**) *n* A **basin** is a deep bowl that you use for holding liquids, or for mixing food in. تسلا

basis (**bases**) *n* If something happens or is done on a particular **basis**, it happens or is done in that way. بنیاد

basket (**baskets**) *n* A **basket** is a container made of thin strips of cane, metal or plastic woven together. ٹوکری

basketball *n* **Basketball** is a game in which two teams of five players each try to throw a large ball through a round net hanging from a high metal ring. باسکیٹ بال

Basque (**Basques**) *adj* **Basque** means relating to, denoting, or characteristic of the Basques or their language. باسکی
▷ *n* The **Basques** are a people of unknown origin living around the western Pyrenees in France and Spain. باسکی
▷ *n* **Basque** is the language spoken by the Basque people. باسکی زبان

bass (**basses**) *n* A **bass** is a man with a deep singing voice. بھاری آواز والا گلوکار

bass drum (**bass drums**) *n* A **bass drum** is a large shallow drum of low and indefinite pitch. بھاری شوردار ڈھول

bassoon (**bassoons**) *n* A **bassoon** is a large musical instrument of the woodwind family that is shaped like a tube and played by blowing into a curved metal pipe. پائپ باجہ

bat (**bats**) *n* A **bat** is a special stick that you use to hit a ball in some games. بلا
▷ *n* A **bat** is a small animal that looks like a mouse with wings. **Bats** come out to fly at night. چمگادڑ

bath (**baths**) *n* A **bath** is a container which you fill with water and sit in while you wash your body. غسل ٹب

bathe (**bathes, bathing, bathed**) *vi* When you **bathe** in a sea, river, or lake, you swim or play there. (*formal*) نہانا

bathing suit (**bathing suits**) *n* A **bathing suit** is a piece of clothing which people wear when they go swimming. لباس غسل

bathrobe (**bathrobes**) *n* A **bathrobe** is a loose piece of clothing made of the same material as towels. You wear it before or after you have a bath or a swim. بعد غسل لباس

bathroom (**bathrooms**) *n* A **bathroom** is a room in a house that contains a bath or shower, a washbasin, and sometimes a toilet. غسل خانہ

baths *npl* A **baths** is a public building containing a swimming pool, and sometimes other facilities that people can use to have a wash or a bath. حمام

bath towel (**bath towels**) *n* A **bath towel** is a very large towel used for drying your body after you have had a bath or shower. غسل تولیہ

bathtub (**bathtubs**) *n* A **bathtub** is a container which you fill with water and sit in while you wash your body. غسل ٹب

batter *n* **Batter** is a mixture of flour, eggs, and milk used to make pancakes. آٹا دودھ انڈے کا گھول

battery (**batteries**) *n* **Batteries** are the devices that you put in electrical items to provide the power that makes them work. بیٹری

battle (**battles**) *n* In a war, a **battle** is a fight between armies or between groups of ships or planes. لڑائی

battleship (**battleships**) *n* A **battleship** is a very large, heavily armoured warship. بڑا جنگی جہاز

bay (**bays**) *n* A **bay** is a part of a coastline where the land curves inwards. خلیج

bay leaf (**bay leaves**) *n* A **bay leaf** is a leaf of an evergreen tree that can be dried and used as a herb in cooking. تیزپتہ

BC *abbr* You use **BC** in dates to indicate a number of years or centuries before the year in which Jesus Christ is believed to have been born. قبل مسیح

be (**am, are, is, being, was, were, been**) *v* You use **be** to say what a person or thing is like. ہونا *She is very young.* ▷ *v* You use **be** to say that something is there. موجود ہونا *There is a tree in the garden.*

beach (**beaches**) *n* A **beach** is an area of sand or pebbles by the sea. ساحل

bead (**beads**) *n* **Beads** are small pieces of coloured glass, wood, or plastic with a hole through the middle which are used for jewellery or decoration. منکا

beak (**beaks**) *n* A bird's **beak** is the hard curved or pointed part of its mouth. چونچ

beam (**beams**) *n* A **beam** of light is a line of light that shines from an object such as a torch or the sun. شعاع۔کرن

bean (**beans**) *n* **Beans** are the pods of a climbing plant, or the seeds that the pods contain, which are eaten as a vegetable. پھلی یا پھلی کے دانے

beansprouts *npl* **Beansprouts** are small, long, thin shoots grown from beans. انکرائے دانے

bear (**bears**) *n* A **bear** is a big, strong animal with thick fur and sharp claws. بھالو

bear (**bears, bearing, bore, borne**) *vt* If you **bear** something somewhere, you carry it there. (*literary*) بوجھ اٹھانا

beard (**beards**) *n* A man's **beard** is the hair that grows on his chin and cheeks. داڑھی

bearded (**adj**) *n* A **bearded** man has a beard. داڑھی والا

bear up *v* If you **bear up** when experiencing problems, you remain cheerful and show courage in spite of them. برداشت کرنا *How's she bearing up?*

beat (**beats, beating, beaten**) *n* A **beat** is a regular sound or rhythm. بیٹ ▷ *vt* If you **beat** something, you keep hitting it. مارنا ▷ *vt* If you **beat** someone in a game or a competition, you do better than they do. شکست دینا، ہرانا

beautiful *adj* **Beautiful** means attractive to look at. خوبصورت

beautifully *adv* If you do something **beautifully**, you do it in a beautiful manner. خوبصورتی سے

beauty *n* **Beauty** is the state or quality of being beautiful. خوبصورتی

beauty salon (**beauty salons**) *n* A **beauty salon** is a place where women can go to have beauty treatments, for example to have their hair, nails or make-up done. بیوٹی سیلون

beauty spot (**beauty spots**) *n* A **beauty spot** is a place in the country that is popular because of its beautiful scenery. حسین مقام

beaver (**beavers**) *n* A **beaver** is a furry animal like a large rat with a big flat tail. اود بلاؤ

because *conj* You use **because** to say why something happens. کیوں کہ *I went to bed because I was tired.*

become (**becomes, becoming, became**) *v* If one thing **becomes** another thing, it starts to be that thing. ہونا

bed (**beds**) *n* A **bed** is a piece of furniture that you lie on when you sleep. بستر

bed and breakfast *n* **Bed and breakfast** is a system of accommodation in a hotel or guest house in which you pay for a room for the night and for breakfast the following morning. The abbreviation 'B&B' is also used. بستر مع ناشتہ

bedclothes *npl* **Bedclothes** are the sheets and covers which you put on a bed. چادریں غلاف

bedding *n* **Bedding** consists of sheets, blankets, and other covers used on beds. سامان بستر

bed linen *n* **Bed linen** is sheets and pillowcases. چادر اور تکیے غلاف

bedroom (**bedrooms**) *n* A **bedroom** is a room which is used for sleeping in. خواب گاہ

bedside lamp (**bedside lamps**) *n* A **bedside lamp** is a lamp that you have next to your bed. چراغ بستر

bedside table (**bedside tables**) *n* A **bedside table** is a small table usually with shelves or drawers, that you have next to your bed. بستر میز

bedsit (**bedsits**) *n* A **bedsit** is a room you rent which you use for both living in and sleeping in. بیٹھک

bedspread (**bedspreads**) *n* A **bedspread** is a decorative cover which is put over a bed, on top of the sheets and blankets. پلنگ پوش

bedtime *n* Your **bedtime** is the time when you usually go to bed. سونے کا وقت

bee (**bees**) *n* A **bee** is an insect with a yellow-and-black striped body that makes a buzzing noise as it flies. Bees make honey. شہد کی مکھی

beech (**beeches**) *n* A **beech** or a **beech** tree is a tree with a smooth grey trunk. تناور درخت

beef *n* **Beef** is the meat of a cow, bull, or ox. بڑے کا گوشت

beefburger (**beefburgers**) *n* A **beefburger** is minced meat which has been shaped into a flat circle. کباب

beeper (**beepers**) *n* A **beeper** is a portable device that makes a beeping noise, usually to tell you to phone someone or to remind you to do something. (*informal*) یاد دلانے والا بیپر

beer (**beers**) *n* **Beer** is a bitter alcoholic drink made from grain.

beetle (**beetles**) *n* A **beetle** is an insect with a hard covering to its body. بھنورا

beetroot (**beetroots**) *n* **Beetroot** is a dark red root vegetable which can be cooked or pickled. چقندر

before *adv* You use **before** when you are talking about a previous time. قبل
▷ *conj* If you do something **before** someone else, you do it when they have not yet done it. پہلے *Before I got to the*

b

ball, someone else kicked it away. ▷ *prep* If one thing happens **before** another thing, it happens earlier than it. قبل، پہلے *My birthday is just before his.*

beforehand *adv* If you do something **beforehand**, you do it earlier than a particular event. پہلے سے ہی

beg (**begs, begging, begged**) *v* If you **beg** someone to do something, you ask them anxiously or eagerly to do it. مانگنا

beggar (**beggars**) *n* A **beggar** is someone who lives by asking people for money or food. بھکاری

begin (**begins, beginning, began, begun**) *vt* If you **begin** to do something, you start to do it. شروع کرنا

beginner (**beginners**) *n* A **beginner** is someone who has just started learning to do something and cannot do it well yet. مبتدی

beginning (**beginnings**) *n* The **beginning** of something is the first part of it. شروعات

behave (**behaves, behaving, behaved**) *vi* The way you **behave** is the way that you do and say things. سلوک کرنا ▷ *vt* If you **behave** yourself, you are good. تمیز سے پیش آنا

behaviour *n* A person's **behaviour** is the way they behave. برتاؤ

behind (**behinds**) *adv* **Behind** means in or to a position further back. پیچھے ▷ *n* Your **behind** is the part of your body that you sit on. پشت ▷ *prep* If something is **behind** another thing, it is at the back of it. پیچھے *He stood behind his desk.*

beige *adj* Something that is **beige** is pale brown in colour. شتری خاکستری رنگ

Beijing *n* **Beijing** is the capital of the People's Republic of China. بیجنگ

Belarus *n* **Belarus** is a republic in eastern Europe. بیلاروس

Belarussian (**Belarussians**) *adj* **Belarussian** means of, relating to, or characteristic of Belarus, its people, or their language. بیلاروسی ▷ *n* A **Belarussian** is a native or inhabitant of Belarus. بیلاروسی ▷ *n* **Belarussian** is the official language of Belarus. بیلاروسی زبان

Belgian (**Belgians**) *adj* **Belgian** means belonging or relating to Belgium or to its people. بیلجین ▷ *n* A **Belgian** is a native or inhabitant of Belgium. بیلجین

Belgium *n* **Belgium** is a country in north-west Europe. بیلجیم

belief (**beliefs**) *n* **Belief** is a feeling of certainty that something exists, is true, or is good. عقیدہ

believe (**believed, believing, believes**) *vt* If you **believe** that something is true, you think that it is true. (*formal*) عقیدہ رکھنا ▷ *vi* If you **believe** in things such as God, fairies, or miracles, you are sure that they exist or happen. اعتقاد رکھنا

bell (**bells**) *n* A **bell** is a device that makes a ringing sound which attracts people's attention. گھنٹی

belly (**bellies**) *n* A person's or animal's **belly** is their stomach or abdomen. پیٹ، پیڑو

belly button (**belly buttons**) *n* Your **belly button** is the small round thing in the centre of your stomach. (*informal*) ناف

belong (**belongs, belonging, belonged**) *vi* If something **belongs** somewhere, that is where it should be. پر ہونا، اس جگہ پر ہونا ▷ *vi* If you **belong** to a group of people, you are one of them. وابستہ ہونا، متعلق ہونا، کا ہونا

belongings *npl* Your **belongings** are the things that you own. مقبوضات

belong to *v* If something **belongs to** you, you own it. متعلق ہونا، کا ہونا، وابستہ ہونا *The house had belonged to her family for three or four generations.*

below *adv* **Below** means at or to a lower position or place. نیچے کو ▷ *prep* If something is **below** another thing, it is lower down than it. نیچے *His shoes were below his bed.*

belt (**belts**) *n* A **belt** is a strip of leather or cloth that you fasten round your waist. پیٹی

bench (**benches**) *n* A **bench** is a long seat of wood or metal. بینچ

bend (**bends, bending, bent**) *n* A **bend** in a road, river, or pipe is a curved part in it. موڑ ▷ *vi* When you **bend**, you move the top part of your body downwards and forwards. موڑنا

bend down *v* When you **bend down**, you move the top part of your body downwards and forwards. جھکنا *He bent down to tie his laces.*

bend over *v* When you **bend over**, you move the top part of your body downwards and forwards. بل کھانا *I bent over and kissed her cheek.*

beneath *prep* If something is **beneath** another thing, it is below it. نیچے *The dog was beneath the table.*

benefit (**benefits, benefiting, benefited**) *n* The **benefit** of something is the help that you get from it or the advantage that results from it. فائدہ ▷ *v* If you **benefit** from something or if it benefits you, it helps you or improves your life. فائدہ اٹھانا

bent *adj* Something that is **bent** is not straight. خمیدہ ▷ *adj* If you say that someone in a position of responsibility is **bent**, you mean that they are dishonest or do illegal things. جانبدار

beret (**berets**) *n* A **beret** is a circular, flat hat that is made of soft material and has no brim. گول ہیٹ

berry (**berries**) *n* **Berries** are small round fruit that grow on a bush or a tree. بیر

berth (**berths**) *n* A **berth** is a bed on a boat or train, or in a caravan. نشست

beside *prep* If something is **beside** another thing, it is next to it. بغل *He sat down beside me.*

besides *adv* You use **besides** when you want to give another reason for something. اسی طرح ▷ *prep* **Besides** means as well as. اس کے علاوہ *Besides being tall, they're strong and clever.*

best *adj* If you say that something is **best**, you mean that it is better than all the others. بہترین ▷ *adv* You use **best** to say that something is better than all the others. بہتر طور پر

best-before date (**best-before dates**) *n* The **best-before date** on a food container is the date by which the food should be used before it starts to decay. تاریخ سالمیت

best man *n* The **best man** at a wedding is the man who assists the bridegroom. بہترین شخص

bestseller (**bestsellers**) *n* A **bestseller** is a book of which a very large number of copies have been sold. بسیار فروش

bet (**bets, betting**) *n* A **bet** is an agreement between two parties that a sum of money will be paid by the loser to the party who correctly predicts the outcome of an event. سٹہ ▷ *v* If you **bet** on the result of a horse race, football game, or other event, you give someone a sum of money which they give you back with extra money if the result is what you predicted, or which they keep if it is not. سٹہ لگانا

betray (**betrays, betraying, betrayed**) *vt* If you **betray** someone who trusts you, you do something which hurts and disappoints them. اعتماد توڑنا

better *adj* You use **better** to mean that a thing is very good compared to another thing. بہتر ▷ *adv* You use **better** to mean that someone or something does something very well compared to another person or thing. بہتر ▷ *adj* If you feel **better**, you do not feel ill any more. اچھا، صحت مند

between *prep* If you are **between** two things, one of them is on one side of you and the other is on the other side. درمیان *She stood between her two brothers.*

bewildered *adj* If you are **bewildered**, you are very confused and cannot understand something or decide what you should do. متذبذب

beyond *prep* Something that is **beyond**

a place is on the other side of it, or farther away than it. آگے *On his right was a garden, and beyond it there was a large house.*

biased *adj* Someone or something that is **biased** towards one thing is more concerned with it than with other things. جانبدار

bib (**bibs**) *n* A **bib** is a piece of cloth or plastic which is worn by very young children to protect their clothes while they are eating. بالا پوش

Bible *n* The **Bible** is the sacred book of the Christian religion. انجیل

bicarbonate of soda *n* **Bicarbonate of soda** is a white powder which is used in baking to make cakes rise, and also as a medicine for your stomach. کھانے کا سوڈا

bicycle (**bicycles**) *n* A **bicycle** is a vehicle with two wheels which you ride by sitting on it and pushing two pedals with your feet. سائیکل

bicycle pump (**bicycle pumps**) *n* A **bicycle pump** is a hand pump for pumping air into the tyres of a bicycle. سائیکل پمپ

bid (**bids, bade, bidden**) *n* If you make a **bid** for something that is being sold, you say that you will pay a certain amount of money for it. بولی لگانا ▷ *v* If you **bid** for something that somebody is selling, you offer to pay a price that you think is fair. بولی لگانا

bifocals *npl* **Bifocals** are glasses with lenses made in two halves. The top part is for looking at things some distance away, and the bottom part is for reading and looking at things that are close. دورپاس لینس چشمہ

big (**bigger, biggest**) *adj* A person or thing that is **big** is large in size. بڑی

bigheaded *adj* If you describe someone as **bigheaded**, you disapprove of them because they think they are very clever and know everything. مغرور

bike (**bikes**) *n* A **bike** is a vehicle with two wheels which you ride by sitting on it and pushing two pedals with your feet. (*informal*) بائک

bikini (**bikinis**) *n* A **bikini** is a two-piece swimming costume worn by women. نسوانی لباس غسل

bilingual *adj* **Bilingual** means involving or using two languages. دو لسانی

bill (**bills**) *n* A **bill** is a written statement of money that you owe for goods or services. بل ▷ *n* In parliament, a **bill** is a formal statement of a proposed new law that is discussed and then voted on. قانونی مسودہ

billiards *npl* **Billiards** is a game played on a large table, in which you use a long stick called a cue to hit small heavy balls against each other or into pockets around the sides of the table. بلیرڈ

billion (**billions**) *num* A **billion** is the number 1,000,000,000. بلین

bin (**bins**) *n* A **bin** is a container that you put rubbish in. کوڑے دان

bingo *n* **Bingo** is a game in which players aim to match the numbers that someone calls out with the numbers on a card that they have been given. بنگو

binoculars *npl* **Binoculars** consist of two small telescopes joined together side by side, which you look through in order to see things that are a long way away. دوربین

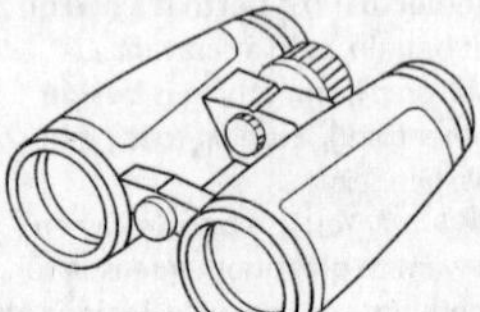

biochemistry *n* **Biochemistry** is the study of the chemical processes that happen in living things. حیاتیاتی کیمیا

biodegradable *adj* Something that is

biodegradable breaks down or decays naturally without any special scientific treatment, and can therefore be thrown away without causing pollution. قابل بازاحیاء

biography (**biographies**) *n* A **biography** of a person is an account of their life, written by someone else. آپ بیتی

biological *adj* **Biological** is used to describe processes and states that occur in the bodies and cells of living things. حیاتیاتی

biology *n* **Biology** is the science concerned with the study of living things. حیاتیات

biometric *adj* **Biometric** tests and devices use biological information about a person to create a detailed record of their personal characteristics. بایومیٹرک

birch (**birches**) *n* A **birch** is a tall tree with thin branches. برچ

bird (**birds**) *n* A **bird** is a creature with feathers and wings. چڑیا

bird flu *n* **Bird flu** is a virus which can be transmitted from chickens, ducks, and other birds to people. برڈفلو

bird of prey (**birds of prey**) *n* A **bird of prey** is a bird such as an eagle or a hawk that kills and eats other birds and animals. شکاری پرندہ

birdwatching *n* **Birdwatching** is the activity of watching and studying wild birds in their natural surroundings. پرندہ بینی

Biro® (**Biros**) *n* A **Biro** is a pen with a small metal ball at its tip. بائرو®

birth (**births**) *n* When a baby is born, you refer to this event as its **birth**. پیدائش

birth certificate (**birth certificates**) *n* Your **birth certificate** is an official document which gives details of your birth, such as the date and place of your birth, and the names of your parents. سندپیدائش

birthday (**birthdays**) *n* Your **birthday** is the anniversary of the date on which you were born. یوم پیدائش

birthplace (**birthplaces**) *n* Your **birthplace** is the place where you were born. (*written*) جائے پیدائش

biscuit (**biscuits**) *n* A **biscuit** is a small flat cake that is crisp and usually sweet. بسکٹ

bit (**bits**) *n* A **bit** of something is a small amount of it, or a small part of it. ٹکڑا

bitch (**bitches**) *n* A **bitch** is a female dog. کتیا

bite (**bites, biting, bit, bitten**) *n* A **bite** of something, especially food, is the action of biting it. لقمہ ▷ *v* If you **bite** something, you use your teeth to cut into it, for example in order to eat it or break it. If an animal or person **bites** you, they use their teeth to hurt or injure you. کاٹنا

bitter (**bitterest**) *adj* In a **bitter** argument, people argue very angrily. تیکھا

black (**blacker, blackest**) *adj* Something that is **black** is of the darkest colour that there is, the colour of the sky at night when there is no light at all. کالا

blackberry (**blackberries**) *n* A **blackberry** is a small dark purple fruit. بلیک بیری

BlackBerry® (**Blackberries**) *n* A **BlackBerry** is a mobile computing device that allows you to send and receive email. بلیک بیری®

blackbird (**blackbirds**) *n* A **blackbird** is a common European bird. The male has black feathers and a yellow beak, and the female has brown feathers. عام یوروپین پرندہ

blackboard (**blackboards**) *n* A **blackboard** is a dark-coloured board which teachers write on with chalk. تختہ سیاہ

black coffee (**black coffees**) *n* **Black coffee** has no milk or cream added to it. کالی کافی

blackcurrant (**blackcurrants**) *n* **Blackcurrants** are very small, dark purple fruits that grow in bunches. کالا بیلنگی پھل

black ice *n* **Black ice** is a thin, transparent layer of ice on a road or path that is very difficult to see. نادیدہ برف کی پرت

blackmail (**blackmails, blackmailing, blackmailed**) *n* **Blackmail** is the action of threatening to reveal a secret about someone, unless they do something you tell them to do, such as giving you money. بلیک میل ▷ *vt* If one person **blackmails** another person, they use **blackmail** against them. بلیک میل کرنا

blackout (**blackouts**) *n* A **blackout** is a period of time during a war in which the buildings in an area are made dark for safety reasons. اندھیرا

bladder (**bladders**) *n* Your **bladder** is the part of your body where urine is held until it leaves your body. مثانہ

blade (**blades**) *n* The **blade** of a knife, axe, or saw is the sharp edge of it that is used for cutting. دھار

blame (**blames, blaming, blamed**) *vt* If you **blame** a person or thing for something bad, you believe or say that they are responsible for it or that they caused it. الزام دینا ▷ *n* The **blame** for something bad that has happened is the responsibility for causing it or letting it happen. الزام

blank (**blanks**) *adj* Something that is **blank** has nothing on it. خالی ▷ *n* A **blank** is a space which is left in a piece of writing or on a printed form for you to fill in particular information. خالی جگہ

blank cheque (**blank cheques**) *n* If someone is given a **blank cheque**, they are given the authority to spend as much money as they need or want. سادہ چیک

blanket (**blankets**) *n* A **blanket** is a large piece of thick cloth, especially one which you put on a bed to keep you warm. کمبل

blast (**blasts**) *n* A **blast** is a big explosion. دھماکہ

blatant *adj* If you describe something you think is bad as **blatant**, you mean that it is very obvious. واضح

blaze (**blazes**) *n* A **blaze** is a large fire in which things are damaged. آگ

blazer (**blazers**) *n* A **blazer** is a kind of jacket. بلیزر

bleach *n* **Bleach** is a chemical that is used to make cloth white, or to clean things thoroughly. بلیچ

bleached *adj* Something that is **bleached** has been made lighter in colour. بلیچ کیا ہوا

bleak (**bleaker, bleakest**) *adj* If a situation is **bleak**, it is bad, and seems unlikely to improve. مایوس کن

bleed (**bleeds, bleeding, bled**) *vi* When you **bleed**, you lose blood from your body as a result of injury or illness. خون بہنا

blender (**blenders**) *n* A **blender** is an electrical kitchen appliance used for mixing liquids and soft foods together or turning fruit or vegetables into liquid. جوس کی مشین

bless (**blesses, blessing, blessed**) *vt* When a priest **blesses** people or things, he or she asks for God's favour and protection for them. برکت کی دعا دینا

blind (**blinds**) *adj* Someone who is **blind** is unable to see because their eyes are damaged. نابینا

blindfold (**blindfolds, blindfolding, blindfolded**) *n* A **blindfold** is a strip of cloth that is tied over someone's eyes so that they cannot see. نگاہ پوش ▷ *vt* If you **blindfold** someone, you tie a strip of cloth over their eyes. آنکھوں پر پٹی باندھنا

blink (**blinks, blinking, blinked**) *v* When you **blink** or when you **blink** your eyes, you shut your eyes and very quickly open them again. پلک جھپکنا

bliss *n* **Bliss** is a state of complete happiness. برکت

blister (**blisters**) *n* A **blister** is a painful swelling containing clear liquid on the surface of your skin. آبلہ

blizzard (**blizzards**) *n* A **blizzard** is a storm in which snow falls heavily and there are strong winds. برفانی طوفان

block (**blocks, blocking, blocked**) *n* A **block** of a substance is a large rectangular piece of it. تختہ ▷ *n* In a town, a **block** is a group of buildings with streets on all four sides. بلاک ▷ *n* A **block** is an obstruction or hindrance. رکاوٹ ▷ *vt* To **block** a road or channel means to put something across or in it so that nothing can go through it or along it. رکاوٹ ڈالنا

blockage (**blockages**) *n* A **blockage** in a pipe or tunnel is something that is blocking it. رکاوٹ

blocked *adj* If something is **blocked**, it is completely closed so that nothing can get through it. بند

blog (**blogs, blogging, blogged**) *v* When you **blog**, you update a website containing a diary or journal. بلوگ پر لکھنا

bloke (**blokes**) *n* A **bloke** is a man. (*informal*) شخص

blonde (**blonder, blondest**) *adj* Someone who has **blonde** hair has pale-coloured hair. ہلکے بھورے بالوں والی خاتون

blood *n* **Blood** is the red liquid that flows inside your body. خون

blood group (**blood groups**) *n* Someone's **blood group** is the type of blood that they have in their body. There are four main types: A, B, AB, and O. خون کی اقسام

blood poisoning *n* **Blood poisoning** is a serious illness resulting from an infection in your blood. خون کی زہر آلودگی

blood pressure *n* Your **blood pressure** is a measure of the force with which blood is pumped around your body. فشار خون

blood test (**blood tests**) *n* A **blood test** is a medical examination of a sample of your blood. خون جانچ

blossom (**blossoms, blossoming, blossomed**) *n* **Blossom** is the flowers that appear on a tree before the fruit. موسم بہار ▷ *vi* If someone or something **blossoms**, they develop good, attractive, or successful qualities. بہار آنا

blouse (**blouses**) *n* A **blouse** is a kind of shirt worn by girls or women. بلاوز

blow (**blowing, blew, blows**) *n* Someone receives a **blow** when someone or something hits them. دھکہ ▷ *vi* When the wind **blows**, it moves the air. بہنا ▷ *vt* When you **blow**, you push air out of your mouth. پھونک مارنا

blow-dry *n* A **blow-dry** is a method of styling the hair while drying it with a hand-held hairdryer. خشک کر کے بال سنوارنا

blow up *v* If someone blows something up, or if it **blows up**, it is destroyed by an explosion. اڑا دینا (دھماکے سے) *Their boat blew up.*

blue (**bluer, bluest**) *adj* Something that is **blue** is the colour of the sky on a sunny day. نیلا

blueberry (**blueberries**) *n* A blueberry is a small dark blue fruit that is found in North America. نیلے بیر

blues *npl* The **blues** is a type of music which was developed by African-American musicians in the southern United States. It is characterized by a slow tempo and a strong rhythm. موسیقی

bluff (**bluffs, bluffing, bluffed**) *n* A **bluff** is an attempt to make someone believe that you will do something when you do not really intend to do it. دھوکہ ▷ *v* If you **bluff**, you try to make someone believe that you will do something although you do not really intend to do it, or that you know something when you do not really know it. دھوکہ دینا

blunder (**blunders**) *n* A **blunder** is a stupid or careless mistake. فاش غلطی

blunt (**blunter, bluntest**) *adj* If you are **blunt**, you say exactly what you think without trying to be polite. منہ پھٹ

blush (**blushes, blushing, blushed**) *vi* When you **blush**, your face becomes redder than usual because you are ashamed or embarrassed. شرمانا

blusher (**blushers**) *n* **Blusher** is a coloured substance that women put on their cheeks. غازہ

board (**boards**) *n* The **board** of a company or organization is the group of people who control it. بورڈ ▷ *n* A **board** is a flat piece of wood, plastic, or cardboard which is used for a particular purpose. تختہ

boarder (**boarders**) *n* A **boarder** is a pupil who lives at school during the term. اقامتی مدرسے کا طالب علم

board game (**board games**) *n* A **board game** is a game such as chess or backgammon, which people play by moving small objects around on a board. بساطی کھیل

boarding school (**boarding schools**) *n* A **boarding school** is a school where the pupils live during the term. اقامتی اسکول

boast (**boasts, boasting, boasted**) *vi* If someone **boasts** about something that they have done or that they own, they talk about it very proudly, in a way that other people may find irritating or offensive. ڈینگ مارنا

boat (**boats**) *n* A **boat** is something in which people can travel across water. ناؤ

body (**bodies**) *n* Your **body** is all your physical parts, including your head, arms, and legs. جسم

bodybuilding *n* **Bodybuilding** is the activity of doing special exercises regularly in order to make your muscles grow bigger. جسم بنانا

bodyguard (**bodyguards**) *n* Someone's **bodyguard** is the person or group of people employed to protect them. محافظ

bog (**bogs**) *n* A **bog** is a wet muddy area of land. پوکھر

boil (**boils, boiling, boiled**) *vt* When you **boil** food, you cook it in water that is boiling. ابالنا ▷ *vi* When water **boils**, it becomes very hot, and you can see bubbles in it and steam coming from it. ابلنا، کافی گرم ہونا

boiled *adj* Food that is **boiled** is cooked in boiling water. ابلا ہوا

boiled egg (**boiled eggs**) *n* A **boiled egg** is an egg that has been cooked in its shell in boiling water. ابلا انڈا

boiler (**boilers**) *n* A **boiler** is a device which burns fuel to provide hot water. پانی ابالنے کا آلہ

boiling *adj* Something that is **boiling** is very hot. ابلتی ہوئی

boil over *v* When a liquid that is being heated **boils over**, it rises and flows over the edge of the container. ابال آنا *Heat the liquid in a large, wide container so it doesn't boil over.*

Bolivia *n* **Bolivia** is an inland republic in central South America. بولیویا

Bolivian (**Bolivians**) *adj* **Bolivian** means belonging or relating to Bolivia or its people. بولیویائی ▷ *n* A **Bolivian** is a person who comes from Bolivia. بولیویائی

bolt (**bolts**) *n* A **bolt** is a long metal object which screws into a nut and is used to fasten things together. بولٹ (نٹ)

bomb (**bombs, bombing, bombed**) *n* A **bomb** is a device which explodes, damaging a large area or killing people. بم ▷ *vt* When a place is **bombed**, it is attacked with **bombs**. بم باری کرنا

bombing (**bombings**) *n* **Bombing** is the action of attacking a place with bombs. بم باری کرنا

bond (**bonds**) *n* A **bond** between people is a close link between them, for example feelings of love, or a special agreement. بندھن

bone (**bones**) *n* Your **bones** are the hard parts inside your body which together form your skeleton. ہڈی

bone dry *adj* If you say that something is **bone dry**, you are emphasizing that it is very dry indeed. بہت خشک

bonfire (**bonfires**) *n* A **bonfire** is a fire built outdoors, usually to burn rubbish. آگ

bonnet (**bonnets**) *n* The **bonnet** of a car is the metal cover over the engine at the front. انجن کا ڈھکن

bonus (**bonuses**) *n* A **bonus** is an amount

of money that is added to someone's pay, usually because they have worked very hard. اضافی تنخواہ

book (**books, booking, booked**) *n* A **book** consists of pieces of paper, usually with words printed on them, which are fastened together and fixed inside a cover of strong paper or cardboard. کتاب ▷ *vt* When you **book** something such as a hotel room or a ticket, you arrange to have it or use it at a particular time. بکنگ کرنا

bookcase (**bookcases**) *n* A **bookcase** is a piece of furniture with shelves for books. کتاب کا خانہ

booking (**bookings**) *n* A **booking** is the arrangement that you make when you book something such as a hotel room, a table at a restaurant, a theatre seat, or a place on public transport. بکنگ کرنا

booklet (**booklets**) *n* A **booklet** is a small paperback book, containing information on a particular subject. کتابچہ

bookmark (**bookmarks**) *n* A **bookmark** is a narrow piece of card or cloth that you put between the pages of a book so that you can find a particular page easily. نشان کتاب

bookshelf (**bookshelf**) *n* A **bookshelf** is a shelf on which you keep books. کتاب کا خانہ

bookshop (**bookshops**) *n* A **bookshop** is a shop where books are sold. کتاب کی دکان

boost (**boosts, boosting, boosted**) *vt* If one thing **boosts** another, it causes it to increase, improve, or be more successful. قوی کرنا

boot (**boots**) *n* **Boots** are strong heavy shoes that cover your whole foot and the lower part of your leg. بوٹ (جوتے)

booze *n* **Booze** is alcoholic drink. (*informal*) بوز (الکحل والی شراب)

border (**borders**) *n* The **border** between two countries is the dividing line between them. سرحد

bore (**bores, boring, bored**) *vt* If someone or something **bores** you, you find them dull and uninteresting. بیزار ہونا

bored *adj* If you are **bored**, you feel tired and impatient because you are not interested in something or because you have nothing to do. بے زار

boredom *n* **Boredom** is the state of being bored. بے زاری

boring *adj* If you say that someone or something is **boring**, you think that they are very dull and uninteresting. بے زار کن

born *adj* You use **born** to describe someone who has a natural ability to do a particular activity or job. For example, a **born** cook has a natural ability to cook well. پیدائشی

borrow (**borrows, borrowing, borrowed**) *vt* If you **borrow** something that belongs to someone else, you take it, usually with their permission, intending to return it. ادھار لینا

Bosnia *n* **Bosnia** is a region of central Bosnia-Herzegovina. بوسنیا

Bosnia-Herzegovina *n* **Bosnia-Herzegovina** is a country in south-west Europe, which was part of Yugoslavia until 1991. بوسنیا اور ہرزیگووینا

Bosnian (**Bosnians**) *adj* **Bosnian** means of or relating to Bosnia or its inhabitants. بوسنیائی ▷ *n* A **Bosnian** is a native or inhabitant of Bosnia. بوسنیائی

boss (**bosses**) *n* Your **boss** is the person in charge of the organization or department where you work. باس۔ سرغنہ

boss around *v* If you say that someone **bosses** you **around**, you mean that they keep telling you what to do in a way that is irritating. باس گیری کرنا، حکم چلانا

bossy *adj* If someone is **bossy**, they enjoy telling people what to do. حکم چلانے والا

both *det* You use **both** to mean two people or two things together. دونوں *He put both books in the drawer.* ▷ *pron* You use **both** when you are saying that something is true about two people or things. دونوں *The woman and her friend, both aged 50, were arrested.*

bother (**bothers, bothering, bothered**) *v* If you do not **bother** to do something or if you do not **bother** with it, you do not do it, consider it, or use it because you think it is unnecessary or because you are too lazy. خاطر میں لانا

Botswana *n* **Botswana** is a republic in southern Africa. بوتسوانا

bottle (**bottles**) *n* A **bottle** is a glass or plastic container in which drinks and other liquids are kept. بوتل

bottle bank (**bottle banks**) *n* A **bottle bank** is a large container into which people can put empty bottles so that the glass can be used again. بوتل بینک

bottle-opener (**bottle-openers**) *n* A **bottle-opener** is a metal device for removing caps or tops from bottles. بوتل کشا

bottom (**bottoms**) *adj* The **bottom** thing is the lowest one. نیچے کا ▷ *n* The **bottom** of something is its lowest part. نچلا حصہ، پیندا ▷ *n* Your **bottom** is the part of your body that you sit on. چوتڑ، سرین

bounce (**bounces, bouncing, bounced**) *v* When an object such as a ball **bounces** or when you **bounce** it, it moves upwards from a surface or away from it immediately after hitting it. اچھلنا

boundary (**boundaries**) *n* The **boundary** of an area of land is an imaginary line that separates it from other areas. حد

bouquet (**bouquets**) *n* A **bouquet** is a bunch of flowers arranged in an attractive way. گلدستہ

bow (**bows**) *n* A **bow** is a long, curved piece of wood with a string stretched between the two ends, that is used to send arrows through the air. کمان ▷ *n* A **bow** is a knot that you use to tie laces and ribbons. کمان ▷ (**bows, bowing, bowed**) *vi* When you **bow**, you bend your body towards someone as a polite way of saying hello or thanking them. جھکنا

bowels *npl* Your **bowels** are the tubes in your body through which digested food passes from your stomach to your anus. آنتیں

bowl (**bowls**) *n* A **bowl** is a circular container with a wide uncovered top that is used for mixing and serving food. بڑا پیالا

bowling *n* **Bowling** is a game in which you roll a heavy ball down a narrow track towards a group of wooden objects and try to knock down as many of them as possible. بال لڑھکانا

bowling alley (**bowling alleys**) *n* A **bowling alley** is a building which contains several tracks for bowling. بولنگ ایلی

bow tie (**bow ties**) *n* A **bow tie** is a tie in the form of a bow. Bow ties are worn by men, especially for formal occasions. کمان نما ٹائی

box (**boxes**) *n* A **box** is a square or rectangular container with stiff sides and sometimes a lid. بکس

boxer (**boxers**) *n* A **boxer** is someone who takes part in the sport of boxing. مکے باز

boxer shorts *npl* **Boxer shorts** are loose-fitting men's underpants that are shaped like the shorts worn by boxers. مکہ بازی جانگھیہ

boxing *n* **Boxing** is a sport in which two people wearing padded gloves fight, using only their hands. مکے بازی

box office (**box offices**) *n* The **box office** in a theatre or cinema is the place where the tickets are sold. باکس آفس

boy (**boys**) *n* A **boy** is a male child. لڑکا

boyfriend (**boyfriends**) *n* Someone's **boyfriend** is the man or boy with whom they are having a romantic relationship. محبوب

bra (**bras**) *n* A **bra** is a piece of underwear that a woman wears to support her breasts. پستان پوش

brace (**braces**) *n* A **brace** is a device attached to a person's leg to strengthen or support it. پٹی

bracelet(bracelets) *n* A **bracelet** is a piece of jewellery that you wear round your wrist. بازوبند

braces *npl* **Braces** are a pair of straps that you wear over your shoulders to prevent your trousers from falling down. تسمہ

brackets *npl* **Brackets** are a pair of written marks that you place round a word, expression, or sentence in order to indicate that you are giving extra information. قوسین

brain(brains) *n* Your **brain** is the organ inside your head that controls your body's activities and enables you to think and to feel things. مغز

brainy(brainier, brainiest) *adj* Someone who is **brainy** is clever and good at learning. (*informal*) ذہین

brake(brakes, braking, braked) *n* A vehicle's **brakes** are devices that make it go slower or stop. بریک ▷ *v* When a vehicle or its driver **brakes**, or when a driver **brakes** a vehicle, the driver makes it slow down or stop by using the brakes. بریک لگا

brake light(brake lights) *n* A **brake light** is a red light attached to the rear of a motor vehicle that lights up when the brakes are applied, serving as a warning to following drivers. بریک لائٹ

bran *n* **Bran** consists of small brown flakes that are left when wheat grains have been used to make white flour. چھلکا

branch(branches) *n* The **branches** of a tree are the parts that grow out from its trunk. شاخ

brand(brands) *n* A **brand** of a product is the version made by one particular manufacturer. برانڈ

brand name(brand names) *n* A product's **brand name** is the name the manufacturer gives it and under which it is sold. برانڈ نام

brand-new *adj* Something that is **brand-new** is completely new. بالکل نئی

brandy(brandies) *n* **Brandy** is a strong alcoholic drink. برانڈی

brass *n* **Brass** is a yellow metal made from copper and zinc. پیتل

brass band(brass bands) *n* A **brass band** is a band that is made up of brass and percussion instruments. پیتل کا باجہ

brat(brats) *n* If you call a child a **brat**, you disapprove of their bad or annoying behaviour. (*informal*) چھوکرا

brave(braver, bravest) *adj* Someone who is **brave** is willing to do dangerous things, and does not show fear in difficult or dangerous situations. بہادر

bravery *n* **Bravery** is brave behaviour or the quality of being brave. بہادری

Brazil *n* **Brazil** is a country in South America. برازیل

Brazilian(Brazilians) *adj* **Brazilian** means belonging or relating to Brazil, or to its people or culture. برازیلی ▷ *n* A **Brazilian** is a person who comes from Brazil. برازیلی

bread *n* **Bread** is a food made from flour, water, and often yeast. روٹی

bread bin(bread bins) *n* A **bread bin** is a wooden, metal, or plastic container for storing bread. روٹی دان

breadcrumbs *npl* **Breadcrumbs** are tiny pieces of dry bread. They are used in cooking. روٹی کے چھوٹے ٹکڑے

bread roll(bread rolls) *n* A **bread roll** is a small piece of bread that is round or long and is made to be eaten by one person. بریڈ رول

break(breaks, breaking, broke, broken) *n* A **break** is the result of breaking. رکاوٹ ▷ *v* When something **breaks**, or when you **break** it, it goes into pieces. ٹوٹنا ▷ *v* If a machine **breaks**, or if you **break** it, it stops working. ٹوٹنا

break down(breakdowns) *v* If a machine or a vehicle **breaks down**, it stops working. ناکارہ ہونا *Their car broke down.* ▷ *n* The **breakdown** of a system, plan, or discussion is its failure or ending. ناکامی

breakdown truck (**breakdown trucks**) *n* A **breakdown truck** is a truck which is used to pull broken or damaged cars and other vehicles. ٹوٹی کاریں کھینچنے والا ٹرک

breakdown van (**breakdown vans**) *n* A **breakdown van** is a motor vehicle which is used to pull broken or damaged vehicles. ٹوٹی گاڑیاں ہٹانے والی وین

breakfast (**breakfasts**) *n* **Breakfast** is the first meal of the day, which is usually eaten early in the morning. ناشتہ

break in (**break-ins**) *v* If someone **breaks in**, they get into a building by force. بہ زور گھسنا *The robbers broke in and stole a valuable painting.* ▷ *n* When there is a **break-in**, someone gets into a building by force. جبری داخلہ

break up *v* When something **breaks up** or when you **break** it up, it separates or is divided into several smaller parts. ٹوٹنا *Break up the chocolate and melt it.*

breast (**breasts**) *n* A woman's **breasts** are the two soft round pieces of flesh on her chest that can produce milk to feed a baby. پستان

breast-feed (**breast-feeds, breast-feeding, breast-fed**) *v* When a woman **breast-feeds**, or **breast-feeds** her baby, she feeds her baby with milk from her breasts, rather than from a bottle. پستان سے دودھ پلانا

breaststroke *n* **Breaststroke** is a swimming stroke which you do lying on your front, and making circular movements with your arms and legs. چھاتی کے بل تیرنا

breath (**breaths**) *n* Your **breath** is the air which you take into and let out of your lungs when you breathe. سانس

Breathalyser® (**Breathalysers**) *n* A **Breathalyser** is a bag or electronic device that the police use to test whether a driver has drunk too much alcohol. بریدالیزر®

breathe (**breathes, breathing, breathed**) *v* When people or animals **breathe**, they take air into their lungs and let it out again. سانس لینا

breathe in *v* When you **breathe in**, you take some air into your lungs. سانس اندر لینا *She breathed in deeply.*

breathe out *v* When you **breathe out**, you send air out of your lungs through your nose or mouth. سانس خارج کرنا *Breathe out and bring your knees in toward your chest.*

breathing *n* **Breathing** is the passage of air into and out of the lungs to supply the body with oxygen. تنفس

breed (**breeds, breeding, bred**) *n* A **breed** of animal is a particular type of it. پیداوار ▷ *vt* If you **breed** animals or plants, you keep them for the purpose of producing more animals or plants. پیدا کرنا

breeze (**breezes**) *n* A **breeze** is a gentle wind. نرم ہوا

brewery (**breweries**) *n* A **brewery** is a place where beer is made. بیر کارخانہ

bribe (**bribes, bribing, bribed**) *vt* If one person **bribes** another, they give them a **bribe**. رشوت دینا

bribery *n* **Bribery** is the action of giving someone a bribe. رشوت

brick (**bricks**) *n* **Bricks** are rectangular blocks of baked clay used for building walls. اینٹ

bricklayer (**bricklayers**) *n* A **bricklayer** is a person whose job is to build walls using bricks. معمار

bride (**brides**) *n* A **bride** is a woman who is getting married or who has just got married. دلہن

bridegroom (**bridegrooms**) *n* A **bridegroom** is a man who is getting married. دولہا

bridesmaid (**bridesmaids**) *n* A **bridesmaid** is a woman or a girl who helps a bride on her wedding day. دلہن کی سہیلی

bridge (**bridges**) *n* A **bridge** is a structure built over a river, road, or railway so that people or vehicles can cross from one side to the other. پل، رسیوں سے سہارا دینا

brief (**briefer, briefest**) *adj* Something that is **brief** lasts for only a short time. مختصر

briefcase (**briefcases**) *n* A **briefcase** is a case for carrying documents. بریف کیس

briefing (**briefings**) *n* A **briefing** is a meeting at which information or instructions are given to people. ہدایت

briefly *adv* Something that happens **briefly** happens for a very short period of time. مختصراً

briefs *npl* Men's or women's underpants can be referred to as briefs. زیر جامے

bright (**brighter, brightest**) *adj* A **bright** colour is very easy to see. چمکیلا، بھڑکیلا ▷ *adj* Something that is **bright** shines with a lot of light. چمکدار

brilliant *adj* If you describe people or ideas as **brilliant**, you mean that they are extremely clever. ذہین

bring (**brings, bringing, brought**) *vt* If you **bring** something, you take it with you when you go somewhere. لانا

bring back *v* If something **brings back** a memory, it makes you start thinking about it. واپس لانا

bring forward *v* If you **bring forward** an event, you arrange for it to take place at an earlier time than had been planned. رونما کرنا *He had to bring forward an 11 o'clock meeting.*

bring up *v* If you **bring up** a child, you look after it until it is grown up. پالنا *She brought up four children.*

Britain *n* **Britain** is the island consisting of England, Scotland, and Wales, which together with Northern Ireland makes up the United Kingdom. برطانیہ

British *adj* **British** means belonging or relating to Great Britain. برطانوی ▷ *npl* The **British** are the people who come from Great Britain. برطانوی

broad (**broader, broadest**) *adj* Something that is **broad** is wide. وسیع

broadband *n* **Broadband** is a method of sending many electronic messages at the same time by using a wide range of frequencies. براڈبینڈ

broad bean (**broad beans**) *n* **Broad beans** are flat round beans that are light green in colour and are eaten as a vegetable. گول دانے

broadcast (**broadcasts, broadcasting**) *n* A **broadcast** is something that you hear on the radio or see on television. نشریہ ▷ *v* To **broadcast** a programme means to send it out by radio waves, so that it can be heard on the radio or seen on television. نشر کرنا

broad-minded *adj* Someone who is **broad-minded** does not disapprove of actions or attitudes that many other people disapprove of. کشادہ ذہن

broccoli *n* **Broccoli** is a vegetable with green stalks and green or purple flower buds. بروکولی

brochure (**brochures**) *n* A **brochure** is a booklet with pictures that gives you information about a product or service. بروشر

broke *adj* If you are **broke**, you have no money. (*informal*) قلاش

broken *adj* A **broken** line is not continuous but has gaps in it. ٹوٹی ہوئی

broken down *adj* A **broken down** vehicle or machine no longer works because it has something wrong with it. ناکارہ

broker (**brokers**) *n* A **broker** is a person whose job is to buy and sell shares, foreign money, or goods for other people. دلال

bronchitis *n* **Bronchitis** is an illness like a very bad cough, in which your bronchial tubes become sore and infected. کھانسی

bronze *n* **Bronze** is a yellowish-brown metal made from copper and tin. کانسہ

brooch (**brooches**) *n* A **brooch** is a small piece of jewellery which can be pinned on a dress, blouse, or coat. بکدار زیور

broom (**brooms**) *n* A **broom** is a long-handled brush which is used to sweep the floor. جھاڑو

broth (**broths**) *n* **Broth** is a kind of soup. It usually has vegetables or rice in it. شوربہ

brother (**brothers**) *n* Your **brother** is a boy or a man who has the same parents as you. بھائی

brother-in-law (**brothers-in-law**) *n* Someone's **brother-in-law** is the brother of their husband or wife, or the man who is married to their sister. سالا، بہنوئی

brown (**browner, brownest**) *adj* Something that is **brown** is the colour of earth or of wood. بھورا

brown bread *n* **Brown bread** is made from grains that have not had their outer layers removed. بھوری روٹی

brown rice *n* **Brown rice** is unpolished rice, in which the grains retain the outer yellowish-brown layer (bran). بھورا چاول

browse (**browses, browsing, browsed**) *vi* If you **browse** in a shop, you look at things in a fairly casual way, in the hope that you might find something you like. تلاش کرنا

browser (**browsers**) *n* A **browser** is a piece of computer software that you use to search for information on the Internet. براؤزر

bruise (**bruises**) *n* A **bruise** is an injury which appears as a purple or dark mark on your body. خراش

brush (**brushes, brushing, brushed**) *n* A **brush** is an object with a large number of bristles fixed to it. You use brushes for painting, for cleaning things, and for tidying your hair. برش ▷ *vt* If you **brush** something or **brush** something such as dirt off it, you clean it or tidy it using a brush. برش کرنا

Brussels sprouts *npl* **Brussels sprouts** are vegetables that look like tiny cabbages. گوبھی نما سبزی

brutal *adj* A **brutal** act or person is cruel and violent. سفاک

bubble (**bubbles**) *n* **Bubbles** are small balls of air or gas in a liquid. بلبلہ

bubble bath *n* **Bubble bath** is a liquid that smells nice and makes a lot of bubbles when you add it to your bath water. بلبلہ کار

bubble gum *n* **Bubble gum** is a sweet substance similar to chewing gum. You can blow it out of your mouth so it makes the shape of a bubble. بل گم

bucket (**buckets**) *n* A **bucket** is a deep round metal or plastic container with a handle. بالٹی

buckle (**buckles**) *n* A **buckle** is a piece of metal or plastic attached to one end of a belt or strap, which is used to fasten it. بکوا

Buddha *n* **Buddha** is the title given to Gautama Siddhartha, the religious teacher and founder of Buddhism. بدھ

Buddhism *n* **Buddhism** is a religion which teaches that the way to end suffering is by overcoming your desires. بودھ مذہب

Buddhist (**Buddhists**) *adj* **Buddhist** means relating or referring to Buddhism. بودھ ▷ *n* A **Buddhist** is a person whose religion is Buddhism. بودھ

budgerigar (**budgerigars**) *n* **Budgerigars** are small, brightly-coloured birds from Australia. آسٹریلیائی چڑیا

budget (**budgets**) *n* Your **budget** is the amount of money that you have available to spend. The **budget** for something is the amount of money that a person, organization, or country has available to spend on it. بجٹ

budgie (**budgies**) *n* **Budgies** are small, brightly-coloured birds from Australia. (*informal*) بجی

buffalo (**buffaloes, buffalo**) *n* A **buffalo** is a wild animal like a large cow with long curved horns. بھینس

buffet (**buffets**) *n* A **buffet** is a meal of cold food at a special occasion. Guests usually help themselves to the food. بوفے

buffet car (**buffet cars**) *n* On a train, the **buffet car** is the carriage where food is sold. بوفے کار

bug (**bugs**) *n* A **bug** is a tiny insect, especially one that causes damage. (*informal*) کیڑا

bugged *adj* If a place or a telephone is **bugged**, tiny microphones have been hidden in it which transmit what people are saying. مصنوعی جاسوس کیڑا

buggy (**buggies**) *n* A **buggy** is a small folding seat with wheels, which a young child can sit in and which can be pushed around. بگھی

build (**builds, building, built**) *vt* If you **build** a structure, you make it by joining things together. بنانا

builder (**builders**) *n* A **builder** is a person whose job is to build or repair buildings. عمارت ساز

building (**buildings**) *n* A **building** is a structure with a roof and walls, such as a house. عمارت

building site (**building sites**) *n* A **building site** is an area of land on which a building or a group of buildings is in the process of being built or altered. مقام تعمیر

bulb (**bulbs**) *n* A **bulb** is an onion-shaped root that grows into a plant. بلب نما بیج ▷ *n* A **bulb** is the glass part of an electric lamp which gives out light when electricity passes through it. بلب

Bulgaria *n* **Bulgaria** is a republic in south-east Europe, on the Balkan Peninsula on the Black Sea. بلغاریا

Bulgarian (**Bulgarians**) *adj* **Bulgarian** means belonging or relating to Bulgaria, or to its people, language, or culture. بلغاریائی ▷ *n* A **Bulgarian** is a person who comes from Bulgaria. بلغاریائی ▷ *n* Bulgarian is the main language spoken by people who live in Bulgaria. بلغاری زبان

bulimia *n* **Bulimia** or bulimia nervosa is a mental illness in which a person eats very large amounts and then makes themselves vomit. بولیمیا

bull (**bulls**) *n* A **bull** is a male animal of the cow family. سانڈ

bulldozer (**bulldozers**) *n* A **bulldozer** is a large tractor with a broad metal blade at the front, used for moving earth or knocking down buildings. بلڈوزر

bullet (**bullets**) *n* A **bullet** is a small piece of metal which is fired from a gun. بلیٹ

bulletin board (**bulletin boards**) *n* A **bulletin board** is a board which is usually attached to a wall in order to display notices giving information about something. بلیٹن بورڈ

bully (**bullies, bullying, bullied**) *n* A **bully** is someone who uses their strength or power to hurt or frighten other people. وحشی ▷ *vt* If someone **bullies** you, they use their strength or power to hurt or frighten you. متوحش کرنا

bum (**bums**) *n* Your **bum** is the part of your body which you sit on. (*informal*) سرین

bum bag (**bum bags**) *n* A **bum bag** consists of a small bag attached to a belt which you wear round your waist. You use it to carry things such as money and keys. کمر بیگ

bumblebee (**bumblebees**) *n* A **bumblebee** is a large hairy bee. بالدار شہد کی مکھی

bump (**bumps**) *n* A **bump** is an accidental knock or collision. حادثاتی ٹکراو

bumper (**bumpers**) *n* **Bumpers** are bars at the front and back of a vehicle which protect it if it bumps into something. ٹکر-روک

bump into *v* If you **bump into** someone you know, you meet them by chance. (*informal*) اچانک مل جانا *I bumped into a friend of yours today.*

bumpy (**bumpier, bumpiest**) *adj* A **bumpy** road or path has a lot of bumps on it. دھچکے دار

bun (**buns**) *n* A **bun** is a small round cake. جوڑا بنا

bunch (**bunches**) *n* A **bunch** of things is a group of them. (*informal*) گچھا

bungalow (**bungalows**) *n* A **bungalow** is a house with only one storey. بنگلہ

bungee jumping *n* If someone goes **bungee jumping**, they jump from a high place such as a bridge or cliff with a long piece of strong elastic cord tied around their ankle connecting them to the bridge or cliff. بنجی چھلانگ

bunion (**bunions**) *n* A **bunion** is a large painful lump on the first joint of a person's big toe. پیر کے انگوٹھے کے جوڑ پر گانٹھ

bunk (**bunks**) *n* A **bunk** is a bed fixed to a wall, especially in a ship or caravan. دیواری پلنگ

bunk beds *npl* **Bunk beds** are two beds fixed one above the other in a frame. تلے اوپر پلنگ

buoy (**buoys**) *n* A **buoy** is a floating object that shows ships and boats where they can go and warns them of danger. بہتا نشان

burden (**burdens**) *n* Something that is a **burden** causes you a lot of worry or hard work. بوجھ

bureaucracy (**bureaucracies**) *n* A **bureaucracy** is an administrative system operated by a large number of officials. نوکر شاہی

bureau de change (**bureaux de change**) *n* A **bureau de change** is a place where foreign currencies can be exchanged. مقام زر مبادلہ

burger (**burgers**) *n* A **burger** is a flat round mass of meat or vegetables, which is grilled or fried. برگر

burglar (**burglars**) *n* A **burglar** is a thief who breaks into houses and steals things. نقب زن

burglar alarm (**burglar alarms**) *n* A **burglar alarm** is an electric device that makes a bell ring loudly if someone tries to enter a building by force. نقب زن الارم

burglary (**burglaries**) *n* If someone commits a **burglary**, they enter a building by force and steal things. نقب زنی

burgle (**burgles, burgling, burgled**) *vt* If a house is **burgled**, someone breaks in and steals things. نقب لگانا

Burmese *n* A **Burmese** is a person who comes from Myanmar. برمی ▷ *n* **Burmese** is the main language spoken by the people who live in Myanmar. برمی زبان

burn (**burns, burning, burned, burnt**) *n* A **burn** is an injury caused by fire or something very hot. جلا ہوا ▷ *vi* If something is **burning**, it is on fire. جلنا ▷ *vt* If you **burn** something, you destroy it or damage it with fire. جلانا ▷ *vt* If you **burn** yourself, you touch something that is hot and get hurt. جلانا

burn down *v* If a building **burns down** or if someone **burns** it **down**, it is completely destroyed by fire. جلا ڈالنا *Anarchists burnt down a restaurant.*

burp (**burps, burping, burped**) *n* A **burp** is a noise someone makes because air from their stomach has been forced up through their throat. ڈکار ▷ *vi* When someone **burps**, they make a noise because air from their stomach has been forced up through their throat. ڈکار لینا

burst (**bursts, bursting**) *v* When something **bursts** or when you **burst** it, it suddenly splits open, and air or some other substance comes out. پھٹنا

bury (**buries, burying, buried**) *vt* If you **bury** something, you put it into a hole in the ground and cover it up, often in order to hide it. دفنانا

bus (**buses**) *n* A **bus** is a large motor vehicle which carries passengers. بس

bus conductor (**bus conductors**) *n* A **bus conductor** is the person whose job is to sell tickets to the passengers. بس کنڈکٹر

bush (**bushes**) *n* A **bush** is a dense cluster of shrubs. جھاڑی ▷ *n* A **bush** is a plant which is like a very small tree. چھوٹا پودا

business *n* **Business** is work relating to the production, buying, and selling of goods or services. تجارت

businessman (**businessmen**) *n* A businessman is a man who works in business. تاجر

businesswoman (**businesswomen**) *n* A **businesswoman** is a woman who works in business. تاجرہ

busker (**buskers**) *n* A **busker** is a person who sings or plays music for money in streets and other public places. پیشہ ور سازندہ گلوکار

bus station (**bus stations**) *n* A **bus station** or coach **station** is a place where buses or coaches start a journey. بس اڈہ

bus stop (**bus stops**) *n* A **bus stop** is a place on a road where buses stop to let passengers on and off. بس اسٹاپ

bust (**busts**) *n* A **bust** is a statue of someone's head and shoulders. سر اور کاندھوں کا مجسمہ

bus ticket (**bus tickets**) *n* A **bus ticket** is a small, official piece of paper or card which shows that you have paid for a journey on a bus. بس ٹکٹ

busy (**busier, busiest**) *adj* If you are **busy**, you have a lot of things to do. مصروف ▷ *adj* A **busy** place is full of people. بھیڑ بھرا، مصروف

busy signal (**busy signals**) *n* A **busy signal** is a repeated single note heard on a telephone when the number called is already in use. مصروف سگنل

but *conj* You use **but** to say something that is different than what you have just said. لیکن *Heat the milk until it is very hot but not boiling.*

butcher (**butchers**) *n* A **butcher** is a shopkeeper who sells meat. قصاب ▷ *n* A **butcher** or a **butcher's** is a shop where meat is sold. قصائی کی دکان

butter *n* **Butter** is a yellowish substance made from cream which you spread on bread or use in cooking. مکھن

buttercup (**buttercups**) *n* A **buttercup** is a small plant with bright yellow flowers. پیلے پھول والا پودا

butterfly (**butterflies**) *n* A **butterfly** is an insect with large colourful wings and a thin body. تتلی

buttocks *npl* Your **buttocks** are the two rounded fleshy parts of your body that you sit on. سرین

button (**buttons**) *n* **Buttons** are small hard objects sewn on to pieces of clothing, which you use to fasten the clothing. بٹن

buy (**buys, buying, bought**) *vt* If you **buy** something, you obtain it by paying money for it. خریدنا

buyer (**buyers**) *n* A **buyer** is a person who is buying something or who intends to buy it. خریدار

buyout (**buyouts**) *n* A **buyout** is the buying of a company, especially by its managers or employees. کمپنی خرید (بذریعہ ملازمین)

by *prep* If something is done **by** a person or thing, that person or thing does it. ذریعہ *Dinner was cooked by the children.*

bye! *excl* **Bye!** is another way of saying goodbye. (*informal*) خدا حافظ!

bye-bye! (**bypasses**) *n* Bye-bye! is another way of saying goodbye. خدا حافظ!

bypass (**bypasses**) *excl* A **bypass** is a surgical operation performed on or near the heart, in which the flow of blood is redirected so that it does not flow through a part of the heart that is diseased or blocked. بائی پاس

C

cab (**cabs**) *n* A **cab** is a taxi. ٹیکسی
cabbage (**cabbages**) *n* A **cabbage** is a round vegetable with green leaves. بند گوبھی
cabin (**cabins**) *n* A **cabin** is a small room in a ship or boat, or one of the areas inside a plane. کیبن
cabin crew (**cabin crews**) *n* The **cabin crew** on an aircraft are the people whose job is to look after the passengers. جہاز کا عملہ
cabinet (**cabinets**) *n* A **cabinet** is a cupboard used for storing things or for displaying objects in. الماری
cable (**cables**) *n* A **cable** is a thick wire which is used to carry electricity or electronic signals. کیبل
cable car (**cable cars**) *n* A **cable car** is a vehicle for taking people up mountains or steep hills. It is pulled by a moving cable. کیبل کار
cable television *n* **Cable television** is a television system in which signals are sent along wires rather than by radio waves. کیبل ٹیلیویژن
cactus (**cactuses, cacti**) *n* A **cactus** is a desert plant with a thick stem, often with spikes. کیکٹس
cadet (**cadets**) *n* A **cadet** is a young person who is being trained in the armed forces or police. کیڈیٹ
cafeteria (**cafeterias**) *n* A **cafeteria** is a self-service restaurant in a large shop or workplace. کیفے ٹیریا۔ قہوہ خانہ
caffeine *n* **Caffeine** is a chemical substance found in coffee, tea, and cocoa, which makes you more active. کیفین
café (**cafés**) *n* A **café** is a place where simple meals, snacks, and drinks are sold. کیفے
cage (**cages**) *n* A **cage** is a structure of wire or metal bars in which birds or animals are kept. پنجرہ
cagoule (**cagoules**) *n* A **cagoule** is a lightweight usually knee-length type of anorak. کوہپیمائی کا لباس
cake (**cakes**) *n* A **cake** is a sweet food made by baking a mixture of flour, eggs, sugar, and fat. کیک
calcium *n* **Calcium** is a soft white element found in bones and teeth, and also in limestone, chalk, and marble. کیلشیم
calculate (**calculates, calculating, calculated**) *vt* If you **calculate** a number or amount, you work it out by doing some arithmetic. حساب کرنا
calculation (**calculations**) *n* A **calculation** is something that you think about and work out mathematically. حساب
calculator (**calculators**) *n* A **calculator** is a small electronic device used for doing mathematical calculations. کیلکولیٹر
calendar (**calendars**) *n* A **calendar** is a chart or device which displays the date and the day of the week, and often the whole of a particular year. کلینڈر
calf (**calves**) *n* A **calf** is a young cow. بچھڑا ▷ *n* Your **calves** are the thick parts at the backs of your legs, between your ankles and your knees. پنڈلی
call (**calls, calling, called**) *n* When you make a telephone **call**, you telephone someone. فون کرنا ▷ *vt* If you **call** someone something, you give them a name. پکارنا، نام دینا ▷ *v* If you **call** something, you say it in a loud voice. پکارنا ▷ *v* If you **call** someone, you talk to them on the telephone. فون پر بات کرنا

call back *v* If you **call** someone **back**, you telephone them again or in return for a telephone call that they have made to you earlier. واپس کال کرنا *OK. I'll call you back around three o'clock.*

call box (**call boxes**) *n* A **call box** is a small shelter in the street in which there is a public telephone. کال بکس

call centre (**call centres**) *n* A **call centre** is an office where people work answering or making telephone calls for a company. کال سینٹر

call for *v* If you **call for** someone or something, you go to collect them. ---- کے لئے پکارنا *I shall be calling for you at seven o'clock.*

call off *v* If you **call off** an event, you cancel it. ملتوی کرنا *The wedding was called off.*

calm (**calmer, calmest**) *adj* A **calm** person does not show or feel any worry, anger, or excitement. پر سکون

calm down *v* If you **calm down** or if someone calms you down, you become less upset or excited. پر سکون ہونا *I'll try a herbal remedy to calm him down.*

calorie (**calories**) *n* A **calorie** is a unit of measurement for the energy value of food. کیلوری

Cambodia *n* **Cambodia** is a country in south-east Asia. کمبوڈیا

Cambodian (**Cambodians**) *adj* **Cambodian** means of or relating to Cambodia or its inhabitants. کمبوڈیائی ▷ *n* A **Cambodian** is a native or nhabitant of Cambodia. کمبوڈیائی

camcorder (**camcorders**) *n* A **camcorder** is a portable video camera. ویڈیو کیمرا

camel (**camels**) *n* A **camel** is a desert animal with one or two humps on its back. اونٹ

camera (**cameras**) *n* A **camera** is a piece of equipment for taking photographs or for making a film. کیمرا

cameraman (**cameramen**) *n* A **cameraman** is a person who operates a television or film camera. کیمرا مین

camera phone (**camera phones**) *n* A **camera phone** is a mobile phone that can also take photographs. کیمرا فون

Cameroon *n* **Cameroon** is a republic in West Africa, on the Gulf of Guinea. کیمیرون

camp (**camps, camping, camped**) *n* A **camp** is a place where people live or stay in tents or caravans. کیمپ ▷ *vi* If you **camp** somewhere, you stay there in a tent or caravan. ٹھہرنا۔ ٹھہرانا

campaign (**campaigns**) *n* A **campaign** is a planned set of activities that people carry out over a period of time in order to achieve something such as social or political change. مہم

camp bed (**camp beds**) *n* A **camp bed** is a small bed that you can fold up. کیمپ بستر

camper (**campers**) *n* A **camper** is a person who goes camping. کیمپ والا

camping *n* **Camping** is the action of staying in a tent or caravan. قیام

campsite (**campsites**) *n* A **campsite** or a **camping site** is a place where people who are on holiday can stay in tents. مقام کیمپ

campus (**campuses**) *n* A **campus** is the area of land containing the main buildings of a college or university. کیمپس

can *v* If you **can** do something, you are able to do it. سکنا، کرنے کے قابل ہونا *I can swim.* ▷ (**cans**) *n* A **can** is a metal container for food or drink. ڈبہ، ٹن

Canada *n* **Canada** is a country in North America. کینیڈا

Canadian (**Canadians**) *adj* **Canadian** means belonging or relating to Canada, or to its people or culture. کینیڈین ▷ *n* A **Canadian** is a Canadian citizen, or a person of Canadian origin. کینیڈین

canal (**canals**) *n* A **canal** is a long, narrow, man-made stretch of water. نہر

Canaries *npl* The **Canaries** are a group of islands in the Atlantic, off the northwest coast of Africa. کینیریز

canary (**canaries**) *n* **Canaries** are small yellow birds which sing beautifully. بلبل زرد

cancel (**cancels, cancelling, cancelled**) *v* If you **cancel** an order or an arrangement, you stop it from happening. رد کرنا

cancellation (**cancellations**) *n* **Cancellation** is the fact or an instance of cancelling. منسوخی

Cancer *n* **Cancer** is one of the twelve signs of the zodiac. Its symbol is a crab. People who are born between the 21st of June and the 22nd of July come under this sign. برج سرطان

cancer (**cancers**) *n* **Cancer** is a serious illness in which abnormal body cells increase, producing growths. سرطان

candidate (**candidates**) *n* A **candidate** is someone who is being considered for a position. امیدوار

candle (**candles**) *n* A **candle** is a stick of hard wax with a piece of string called a wick through the middle. You light the wick so the candle produces light. موم بتی

candlestick (candlesticks) *n* A **candlestick** is a narrow object with a hole at the top which holds a candle. موم بتی دان

candyfloss *n***Candyfloss** is a large pink or white mass of sugar threads that is eaten from a stick. It is sold at fairs or other outdoor events. بڑھیا کا کاتہ

canister (**canisters**) *n* A **canister** is a metal container. کنستر

canned *adj* **Canned** music, laughter, or applause on a television or radio programme has been recorded beforehand and is added to the programme to make it sound as if there is a live audience. پیوست کردہ

canoe (**canoes**) *n* A **canoe** is a small narrow boat that you row using a paddle. ناؤ

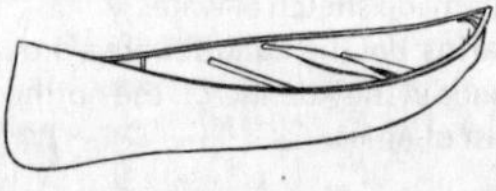

canoeing *n* **Canoeing** is the sport of using and racing a canoe. ناؤ دوڑ

can opener (**can openers**) *n* A **can opener** is a tool that is used for opening cans of food. ڈبہ کھولنے کا اوزار

canteen (**canteens**) *n* A **canteen** is a place in a factory, office, or shop where the workers can have meals. کینٹین

canter (**canters, cantering, cantered**) *vi* When a horse **canters** it moves at a speed that is slower than a gallop but faster than a trot. پویہ چلنا چلانا

canvas (**canvases**) *n* **Canvas** is strong heavy cloth used for making tents, sails, and bags. کینوس

canvass (**canvasses, canvassing, canvassed**) *vi* If you **canvass** for a person or political party, you try to persuade people to vote for them. مائل کرنا

cap (**caps**) *n* A **cap** is a soft flat hat usually worn by men or boys. ٹوپی

capable *adj* If you are **capable** of doing something, you are able to do it. کے قابل

capacity (**capacities**) *n* Your **capacity** for something is your ability to do it, or the amount of it that you are able to do. صلاحیت

capital (**capitals**) *n* **Capital** is money that you use to start a business. سرمایہ
▷ *n* The **capital** of a country is the main city, where the country's leaders work دارالسلطنت، دارالحکومت، راجدھانی ▷ *n* A **capital** is a big letter of the alphabet, for example A or R. انگریزی کا بڑا حروف

capitalism *n* **Capitalism** is an economic and political system in which property, business, and industry are owned by private individuals and not by the state. سرمایہ داری

capital punishment *n* **Capital punishment** is the legal killing of a person who has committed a serious crime. موت کی سزا

Capricorn *n* **Capricorn** is one of the twelve signs of the zodiac. Its symbol is a goat. People who are born between the 22nd of December and the 19th of January come under this sign. برج جدی

capsize (**capsizes, capsizing, capsized**) *v* If you **capsize** a boat or if it **capsizes**, it turns upside down in the water. الٹ جانا

capsule (**capsules**) *n* A **capsule** is a small container with powdered or liquid medicine inside, which you swallow whole. کیپسول

captain (**captains**) *n* In the army, navy, and some other armed forces, a **captain** is an officer of middle rank. کپتان

caption (**captions**) *n* The **caption** of a picture consists of the words printed underneath. مختصر عنوان

capture (**captures, capturing, captured**) *vt* If you **capture** someone or something, you catch them and keep them somewhere so that they cannot leave. گرفتار کرنا

car (**cars**) *n* A **car** is a motor vehicle with room for a small number of passengers. کار

carafe (**carafes**) *n* A **carafe** is a glass container in which you serve water or wine. جام

caramel (**caramels**) *n* A **caramel** is a chewy sweet food made from sugar, butter, and milk. سوختہ شکر

carat (**carats**) *n* A **carat** is a unit equal to 0.2 grams used for measuring the weight of diamonds and other precious stones. قیراط

caravan (**caravans**) *n* A **caravan** is a vehicle without an engine that can be pulled by a car or van. It contains beds and cooking equipment so that people can live or spend their holidays in it. کارواں

carbohydrate (**carbohydrates**) *n* **Carbohydrates** are energy-giving substances found in foods such as sugar and bread. کاربوہائڈریٹ

carbon *n* **Carbon** is a chemical element that diamonds and coal are made of. کاربن

carbon footprint (**carbon footprints**) *n* Your **carbon footprint** is a measure of the amount of carbon dioxide released into the atmosphere by your activities over a particular period. کاربن فٹ پرنٹ

carburettor (**carburettors**) *n* A **carburettor** is the part of an engine, usually in a car, in which air and petrol are mixed together to form a vapour which can be burned. کاربوریٹر

card (**cards**) *n* A **card** is a folded piece of stiff paper that has a picture on the front and a message inside. You send **cards** to people at special times, like birthdays. کارڈ، تاش کے پتے ▷ *n* **Card** is stiff paper. کارڈ، موٹا سخت کاغذ ▷ *n* **Cards** are pieces of stiff paper with numbers or pictures on them that you use for playing games. تاش

cardboard *n* **Cardboard** is thick stiff paper used to make boxes and other containers. کارڈبورڈ

cardigan (**cardigans**) *n* A **cardigan** is a knitted woollen garment that fastens at the front. کارڈیگن (سویٹر)

cardphone (**card phones**) *n* A **cardphone** is a public telephone operated by the insertion of a phonecard instead of coins. کارڈفون

care (**cares, caring, cared**) *n* **Care** is very careful attention. نگہداشت ▷ *vi* If you **care** about something, you think that it is important. خیال رکھنا ▷ *vi* If you **care** for a person or an animal, you look after them. دیکھ بھال کرنا، نگہداشت کرنا

career (**careers**) *n* Your **career** is your job or profession. پیشہ

careful *adj* If you are **careful**, you pay attention to what you are doing in order to avoid damage or mistakes. محتاط

carefully *adv* If you do something **carefully**, you pay attention to what you are doing, in order to avoid damage or mistakes. ہوشیاری سے

careless *adj* If you are **careless**, you do not pay enough attention to what you are doing, and so you make mistakes. لاپرواہ

caretaker (**caretakers**) *n* A **caretaker** is someone who looks after a building and the area around it. نگراں

car ferry *n* A **car ferry** is a boat that transports vehicles and passengers, usually across rivers or short stretches of sea. کار ڈھونے والی ناؤ

cargo (**cargoes**) *n* The **cargo** of a ship or plane is the goods that it is carrying. مال بردار جہاز

car hire *n* **Car hire** is the activity or process of hiring a car. کارکرایہ پر لینا

Caribbean *adj* **Caribbean** means belonging or relating to the Caribbean Sea and its islands, or to its people. کیریبیائی ⊳ *n* The **Caribbean** is the sea which is between the West Indies, Central America and the north coast of South America. کیریبیائی

caring *adj* A **caring** person is affectionate, helpful, and sympathetic. شفیق

car insurance *n* **Car insurance** is an arrangement in which you pay money to a company, and they pay money to you if you have an accident in your car or if your car is stolen. کار بیمہ

car keys *npl* **Car keys** are a set of keys that you use to lock and unlock a car and to start and stop its engine. کار کی چابیاں

carnation (**carnations**) *n* A **carnation** is a plant with white, pink, or red flowers. گلنار

carnival (**carnivals**) *n* A **carnival** is a public festival with music, processions, and dancing. کارنیوال

carol (**carols**) *n* **Carols** are Christian religious songs that are sung at Christmas. مذہبی گیت

car park (**car parks**) *n* A **car park** is an area or building where people can leave their cars. کارپارک مقام

carpenter (**carpenters**) *n* A **carpenter**is a person whose job is making and repairing wooden things. بڑھئی

carpentry *n* **Carpentry** is the activity of making and repairing wooden things. بڑھئی گیری

carpet (**carpets**) *n* A **carpet** is a thick covering for a floor or staircase, made of wool or a similar material. قالین

car rental *n* **Car rental** is the activity or process of renting a car. کارکرایہ پر دینا

carriage (**carriages**) *n* A **carriage** is one of the separate sections of a train that carries passengers. ڈبے

carrier bag (**carrier bags**) *n* A **carrier bag** is a paper or plastic bag with handles. کاغذی، پلاسٹک بیگ

carrot (**carrots**) *n* **Carrots** are long, thin, orange-coloured vegetables that grow under the ground. گاجر

carry (**carries, carrying, carried**) *vt* If you **carry** something, you take it with you, holding it so that it does not touch the ground. لے جانا

carrycot (**carrycots**) *n* A **carrycot** is a small bed for babies which has handles so it can be carried. پالنا

carry on *v* If you **carry on** doing something, you continue to do it. جاری رکھنا *The assistant carried on talking.*

carry out *v* If you **carry out** a threat, task, or instruction, you do it or act according to it. انجام دینا *The police carried out the arrests.*

cart (**carts**) *n* A **cart** is an old-fashioned wooden vehicle, usually pulled by an animal. گاڑی

carton (**cartons**) *n* A **carton** is a plastic or cardboard container in which food or drink is sold. کارٹن

cartoon (**cartoons**) *n* A **cartoon** is a funny drawing. کارٹون ⊳ *n* A **cartoon** is a film that uses drawings, not real people or things. کارٹون فلم

cartridge (**cartridges** *n* In a gun, a **cartridge** is a tube containing a bullet and an explosive substance. کارتوس

carve (**carves, carving, carved**) *v* If you **carve** an object, you cut it out of stone or wood. You **carve** wood or stone in order to make the object. تراشنا

car wash (**car washes**) *n* A **car wash** is a place with special equipment, where you can pay to have your car washed. کار دھلائی

case (**cases**) *n* A **case** is a particular situation, especially one that you are using as an example. معاملہ ▷ *n* A **case** is a container that is used to hold or carry something. خول

cash *n* **Cash** is money, especially money in the form of notes and coins. نقدی

cash dispenser (**cash dispensers**) *n* A **cash dispenser** is a machine built into the wall of a bank or other building, which allows people to take out money from their bank account using a special card. نقدی تقسیم کار مشین

cashew (**cashews**) *n* A **cashew** or a **cashew nut** is a curved nut that you can eat. کاجو

cashier (**cashiers**) *n* A **cashier** is the person that customers pay money to or get money from in a shop or bank. خزانچی

cashmere *n* **Cashmere** is a kind of very fine soft wool. کشمیرا

cash register (**cash registers**) *n* A **cash register** is a machine in a shop, pub, or restaurant that is used to add up and record how much money people pay, and in which the money is kept. کیش رجسٹر

casino (**casinos**) *n* A **casino** is a place where people play gambling games. جواگھر

casserole (**casseroles**) *n* A **casserole** is a meal made by cooking food in liquid in an oven. کیسرول (کھانا)

cassette (**cassettes**) *n* A **cassette** is a small, flat, rectangular, plastic container with magnetic tape inside, which is used for recording and playing back sounds. کیسیٹ

cast (**casts**) *n* The **cast** of a play or film is all the people who act in it. کاسٹ (تمام اداکار)

castle (**castles**) *n* A **castle** is a large building with thick, high walls that was built in the past to protect people during wars and battles. محل

casual *adj* If you are **casual**, you are relaxed and not very concerned about what is happening. اتفاقیہ

casually *adv* If you do something **casually**, you do it in a relaxed and unconcerned way. اتفاقی طور پر

casualty (**casualties**) *n* A **casualty** is a person who is injured or killed in a war or accident. زخم خوردگی، ہلاکت

cat (**cats**) *n* A **cat** is a small furry animal with a tail, whiskers, and sharp claws. بلی

catalogue (**catalogues**) *n* A **catalogue** is a list of things, such as the goods you can buy from a company. کٹیلاگ

catalytic converter (**catalytic converters**) *n* A **catalytic converter** is a device which is fitted to a car's exhaust to reduce the pollution coming from it. کیٹیلیٹک کنورٹر

cataract (**cataracts**) *n* A **cataract** is a large waterfall or rapids. جھرنا ▷ *n* A **cataract** is a layer that has grown over a person's eye that prevents them from seeing properly. موتیابند

catarrh *n* **Catarrh** is a medical condition in which a lot of mucus is produced in your nose and throat. You may get catarrh when you have a cold. ناک بہنا

catastrophe (**catastrophes**) *n* A **catastrophe** is an unexpected event that causes great suffering or damage. غیر متوقع آفت

catch (**catches, catching, caught**) *vt* If you **catch** a person or animal, you capture them. پکڑنا ▷ *vt* If you **catch** something that is moving, you take hold of it while it is in the air. ہوا میں پکڑنا ▷ *vt* If you **catch** a bus or a train, you get on it. پکڑنا ▷ *vt* If you **catch** an illness, you become ill with it. مبتلا ہونا

catching *adj* If an illness or a disease is

catching, it is easily passed on or given to someone else. متعدی

catch up *v* If you **catch up** with someone, you reach them by moving faster than them. گرفت میں لینا I ran faster to catch up with him.

category (**categories**) *n* If people or things are divided into **categories**, they are divided into groups according to their qualities and characteristics. زمرہ

catering *n* **Catering** is the activity or business of providing food for people. کیٹرنگ

caterpillar (**caterpillars**) *n* A **caterpillar** is a small worm-like animal that eventually develops into a butterfly or moth. لاروا

cathedral (**cathedrals**) *n* A **cathedral** is a large important Christian church which has a bishop in charge of it. اہم کلیسہ

cattle *npl* **Cattle** are cows and bulls. مویشی

Caucasus *n* The **Caucasus** is a mountain range in south-west Russia. کاکیش

cauliflower (cauliflowers) *n* A **cauliflower** is a large, round, white vegetable surrounded by green leaves. پھول گوبھی

cause (**causes, causing, caused**) *n* The **cause** of an event is the thing that makes it happen. وجہ ▷ *n* A **cause** is an aim which a group of people supports or is fighting for. مقصد ▷ *vt* To **cause** something, usually something bad, means to make it happen. سبب بننا

caution *n* **Caution** is great care taken in order to avoid danger. تنبیہ

cautious *adj* A **cautious** person acts very carefully in order to avoid danger. محتاط

cautiously *adv* If you do something **cautiously**, you do it very carefully in order to avoid possible danger. احتیاط سے

cave (**caves**) *n* A **cave** is a large hole in the side of a cliff or hill, or under the ground. غار

CCTV *abbr* **CCTV** is an abbreviation for 'closed-circuit television'. سی سی ٹی وی

CD (**CDs**) *n* A **CD** is a small shiny disc on which music or information is stored. **CD** is an abbreviation for 'compact disc'. سی ڈی

CD burner (**CD burners**) *n* A **CD burner** is a piece of computer equipment that you use for copying data from a computer onto a CD. سی ڈی برنر

CD player (**CD players**) *n* A **CD player** is a machine on which you can play CDs. سی ڈی پلیئر

CD-ROM (**CD-ROMs**) *n* A **CD-ROM** is a disc which can be read by a computer, and on which a large amount of data is stored. سی ڈی روم

ceasefire (**ceasefires**) *n* A **ceasefire** is an arrangement in which countries at war agree to stop fighting for a time. فائر بندی

ceiling (**ceilings**) *n* A **ceiling** is the top inside surface of a room. چھت

celebrate (**celebrates, celebrating, celebrated**) *v* If you **celebrate**, or **celebrate** something, you do something enjoyable because of a special occasion. جشن منانا

celebration (**celebrations**) *n* A **celebration** is a special enjoyable event that people organize because something pleasant has happened or because it is someone's birthday or anniversary. جشن

celebrity (**celebrities**) *n* A **celebrity** is someone who is famous. اہم شخصیت

celery *n* **Celery** is a vegetable with long pale green stalks. اجوائن

cell (**cells**) *n* A **cell** is the smallest part of an animal or plant. Animals and plants are made up of millions of cells. خلیہ

cellar (**cellars**) *n* A **cellar** is a room underneath a building. تہ خانہ

cello (**cellos**) *n* A **cello** is a musical instrument that looks like a large violin. You hold it upright and play it sitting down. سیلو (باجہ)

cement *n* **Cement** is a grey powder which is mixed with sand and water in order to make concrete. سیمنٹ

cemetery (**cemeteries**) *n* A **cemetery** is a place where dead people are buried. قبرستان

census (**censuses**) *n* A **census** is an official survey of the population of a country. مردم شماری

cent (**cents**) *n* A **cent** is a small unit of money in many countries. سینٹ (سکہ)

centenary (**centenaries**) *n* A **centenary** is the one hundredth anniversary of an event. صدی

centimetre (**centimetres**) *n* A **centimetre** is a unit of length equal to ten millimetres or one-hundredth of a metre. سینٹی میٹر

central *adj* Something that is **central** is in the middle of a place or area. مرکزی

Central African Republic *n* The **Central African Republic** is a country of central Africa. وسط افریقی جمہوریہ

Central America *n* **Central America** is an area joining the continents of North and South America, extending from the south border of Mexico to the north-west border of Colombia. وسطی امریکہ

central heating *n* **Central heating** is a heating system in which water or air is heated and passed round a building through pipes and radiators. مرکزی حرارت

centre (**centres**) *n* The **centre** of something is the middle of it. مرکز

century (**centuries**) *n* A **century** is one hundred years. صدی

CEO (**CEOs**) *abbr* **CEO** is an abbreviation for 'chief executive officer'. سربراہ عامل افسر

ceramic *adj* **Ceramic** means of, relating to, or made of clay that has been heated to a very high temperature so that it becomes hard. چینی مٹی

cereal (**cereals**) *n* A **cereal** is a food made from grains that you eat with milk for breakfast. اناج، سیریل ▷ *n* A **cereal** is a kind of plant, for example wheat or rice. The seeds of **cereals** are used for food. اناج کا پودا

ceremony (**ceremonies**) *n* A **ceremony** is a formal event such as a wedding or a coronation. تقریب

certain *adj* If you are **certain** about something, you know it is true. پریقین

certainly *adv* You can use **certainly** to emphasize what you are saying. یقین سے

certainty (**certainties**) *n* **Certainty** is the state of having no doubts at all. تیقن

certificate (**certificates**) *n* A **certificate** is an official document which states that particular facts are true, or which you receive when you have successfully completed a course of study or training. سند

Chad *n* **Chad** is a republic in north central Africa. چاڈ

chain (**chains**) *n* A **chain** consists of metal rings connected together in a line. زنجیر

chair (**chairs**) *n* A **chair** is a piece of furniture for one person to sit on, with a back and four legs. کرسی

chairlift (**chairlifts**) *n* A **chairlift** is a line of chairs that hang from a moving cable and carry people up and down a mountain or ski slope. کرسی لفٹ

chairman (**chairmen**) *n* The **chairman** of a meeting or organization is the person in charge of it. چیرمین

chalk *n* **Chalk** is soft white rock. کھریا

challenge (**challenges, challenging, challenged**) *n* A **challenge** is something new and difficult which requires great effort and determination. مسابقت ▷ *vt* If you **challenge** ideas or people, you question their truth, value, or authority. دعوت مبارزت دینا

challenging *adj* A **challenging** job or activity requires great effort and determination. محنت طلب

chambermaid (**chambermaids**) *n* A **chambermaid** is a woman who cleans and tidies the bedrooms in a hotel. صفائی والی

champagne (**champagnes**) *n* **Champagne** is an expensive French sparkling white wine. شیمپین

champion (**champions**) *n* A **champion** is someone who has won the first prize in a competition. چمپین

championship (**championships**) *n* A **championship** is a competition to find the best player or team in a particular sport. چمپین شپ

chance (**chances**) *n* If there is a **chance** of something happening, it is possible that it will happen. موقع

change (**changes, changing, changed**) *n* If there is a **change** in something, it becomes different. تبدیلی ▷ *vi* When you **change**, you put on different clothes. لباس تبدیل کرنا ▷ *v* When you **change** something, or when it **changes**, it becomes different. تبدیل کرنا ▷ *n* **Change** is the money that you get back when you pay too much for something. تبادلہ، مبادلہ

changeable *adj* Someone or something that is **changeable** is likely to change many times. قابل تبدیل

changing room (**changing rooms**) *n* A **changing room** is a room where you can change your clothes and usually have a shower, for example at a sports centre. لباس تبدیل کرنے کا کمرہ

channel (**channels**) *n* A **channel** is a wavelength on which television programmes are broadcast. چینل

chaos *n* **Chaos** is a state of complete disorder and confusion. افراتفری

chaotic *adj* If a situation is **chaotic**, it is in a state of disorder and confusion. افرا تفری والی

chap (**chaps**) *n* A **chap** is a man or boy. (*informal*) لڑکا

chapel (**chapels**) *n* A **chapel** is a part of a Christian church which has its own altar and which is used for private prayer. چیپل

chapter (**chapters**) *n* A **chapter** is one of the parts that a book is divided into. باب

character (**characters**) *n* Your **character** is the kind of person you are. عادات و خصلت ▷ *n* A **character** is a person in a story or a film. کردار

characteristic (**characteristics**) *n* A **characteristic** is a quality or feature that is typical of someone or something. خاصیت

charcoal *n* **Charcoal** is a black substance used as a fuel and for drawing, obtained by burning wood without much air. چارکول

charge (**charges, charging, charged**) *n* A **charge** is an amount of money that you have to pay for a service. مزدوری ▷ *n* A **charge** is a formal accusation that someone has committed a crime. الزام ▷ *n* An electrical **charge** is an amount of electricity that is held in or carried by something. توانائی (کام کرنے کے لئے) ▷ *v* If you **charge** someone an amount of money, you ask them to pay that amount for something. فیس ▷ *vt* When the police **charge** someone, they formally accuse them of having done something illegal. الزام لگانا ▷ *vt* To **charge** a battery means to pass an electrical current through it to make it more powerful or to make it last longer. توانائی دینا

charger (**chargers**) *n* A **charger** is a device used for charging or recharging batteries. چارجر

charity (**charities**) *n* A **charity** is an organization which raises money to help people who are ill, disabled, or poor. خیراتی ادارہ

charity shop (**charity shops**) *n* A **charity shop** is a shop that sells used goods cheaply and gives its profits to a charity. عطائی سامان کی دوکان

charm (**charms**) *n* **Charm** is the quality of being attractive and pleasant. کشش

charming *adj* If someone or something is **charming**, they are very pleasant and attractive. پرکشش

chart (**charts**) *n* A **chart** is a diagram or graph which displays information. خاکہ

chase (**chases, chasing, chased**) *n* A **chase** is the act of chasing someone. تعاقب ▷ *vt* If you **chase** someone, you run after them or follow them in order to catch them or force them to leave a place. تعاقب کرنا

hat (**chats, chatting, chatted**) *n* A **chat** is informal conversation or talk conducted in an easy familiar manner. غپ شپ ▷ *vi* When people **chat**, they talk to each other in an informal and friendly way. غپ شپ کرنا

hatroom (**chatrooms**) *n* A **chatroom** is a site on the Internet, or another computer network, where users have group discussions by electronic mail, typically about one subject. غپ شپ کا کمرہ

hat show (**chat shows**) *n* A **chat show** is a television or radio show in which an interviewer and his or her guests talk in a friendly, informal way about different topics. بات چیت کا شو

hauffeur (**chauffeurs**) *n* A **chauffeur** is a person whose job is to drive and look after another person's car. شوفر

hauvinist (**chauvinists**) *n* A **chauvinist** is a man who believes that men are naturally better and more important than women. شاؤنی

heap (**cheaper, cheapest**) *adj* **Cheap** goods or services cost less money than usual or than you expected. سستی

heat (**cheats, cheating, cheated**) *n* Someone who is a **cheat** does not obey a set of rules which they should be obeying. دھوکہ باز ▷ *vi* When someone **cheats**, they do not obey a set of rules which they should be obeying, for example in a game or exam. دھوکہ دینا

hechnya *n* **Chechnya** is a republic that is part of south Russia. چیچنیا

heck (**checks, checking, checked**) *n* A **check** is a control, especially a rapid or informal one, designed to ensure accuracy, progress, etc. معائنہ ▷ *v* If you **check** something such as a piece of information or a document, you make sure that it is correct or satisfactory. معائنہ کرنا

hecked *adj* Something that is **checked** has a pattern of small squares, usually of two colours. خانے دار

check in (**check-ins**) *v* When you **check in** or **check into** a hotel or clinic, you arrive and go through the necessary procedures before staying there. آنا *He checked in at the hotel and asked to see the manager.*

check out (**checkouts**) *v* When you **check out** of a hotel, you pay the bill and leave. بل ادائیگی کا کاؤنٹر *They packed and checked out of the hotel.* ▷ *n* In a supermarket, a **checkout** is a counter where you pay for your goods. روانگی

check-up (**check-ups**) *n* A **check-up** is a routine examination by a doctor or dentist. جانچنا

cheek (**cheeks**) *n* Your **cheeks** are the sides of your face below your eyes. گال

cheekbone (**cheekbones**) *n* Your **cheekbones** are the two bones in your face just below your eyes. گال کی ہڈیاں

cheeky (**cheekier, cheekiest**) *adj* Someone who is **cheeky** is rude to someone they ought to respect, but often in a charming or amusing way. گستاخ

cheer (**cheers, cheering, cheered**) *n* A **cheer** is a shout or cry of approval, encouragement, etc. نعرہ تحسین ▷ *v* When people **cheer**, they shout loudly to show their approval or to encourage someone who is doing something such as taking part in a game. نعرہ مارنا

cheerful *adj* A **cheerful** person is happy. خوش باش

cheerio! *excl* People sometimes say '**Cheerio!**' as a way of saying goodbye. (*informal*) چیریو، مرحبا!

cheers! *excl* **Cheers!** is a word that people say to each other as they lift up their glasses to drink. چیرس، مرحبا!

cheese (**cheeses**) *n* **Cheese** is a solid food made from milk. پنیر

chef (**chefs**) *n* A *chef* is a cook in a restaurant or hotel. شیف، باورچی

C

chemical (**chemicals**) *n* **Chemicals** are substances that are used in or made by a chemical process. کیمیکل

chemist (**chemists**) *n* A **chemist** is a specially qualified person who prepares and sells medicines. کیمسٹ ▷ *n* A **chemist** or a **chemist's** is a place where medicines are sold or given out. دوافروش

chemistry *n* (**Chemistry**) is the scientific study of the characteristics and composition of substances. کیمیا

cheque (**cheques**) *n* A **cheque** is a printed form on which you write an amount of money and say who it is to be paid to. Your bank then pays the money to that person from your account. چیک

chequebook (**chequebooks**) *n* A **chequebook** is a book containing detachable blank cheques and issued by a bank or building society to holders of cheque accounts. چیک بک

cherry (**cherries**) *n* **Cherries** are small, round fruit with red or black skins. چیری

chess *n* **Chess** is a game for two people played on a board with 64 black and white squares. Each player has 16 pieces including a King. The aim is to trap your opponent's King. شطرنج

chest (**chests**) *n* Your **chest** is the top part of the front of your body. سینہ ▷ *n* A **chest** is a large heavy box, used for storing things. بھاری بکس

chestnut (**chestnuts**) *n* A **chestnut** or **chestnut tree** is a tall tree with broad leaves. اخروٹ

chest of drawers (**chests of drawers**) *n* A **chest of drawers** is a low, flat piece of furniture with drawers in which you keep clothes and other things. دراز

chew (**chews, chewing, chewed**) *v* When you **chew** food, you break it up with your teeth and make it easier to swallow. چبا

chewing gum *n* **Chewing gum** is a kind of sweet that you can chew for a long time. You do not swallow it. چیونگم

chick (**chicks**) *n* A **chick** is a baby bird. چوزہ

chicken (**chickens**) *n* A **chicken** is a bird that is kept on a farm for its eggs and meat. مرغ ▷ *n* **Chicken** is the meat that comes from chickens. مرغ کا گوشت

chickenpox *n* **Chickenpox** is a disease which gives you a high temperature and red spots that itch. چیچک

chickpea (**chickpeas**) *n* **Chickpeas** are hard round seeds that look like pale-brown peas. They can be cooked and eaten. مصری چنا

chief (**chiefs**) *adj* **Chief** is used in the job titles of the most senior worker or workers of a particular kind in an organization. خاص ▷ *n* The **chief** of an organization or department is its leader or the person in charge of it. سرغنہ

child (**children**) *n* A **child** is a human being who is not yet an adult. بچہ

childcare *n* **Childcare** refers to looking after children. نگہداشت طفل

childhood (**childhoods**) *n* A person's **childhood** is the time when they are a child. بچپن

childish *adj* **Childish** means relating to or typical of a child. بچگانہ

childminder (**childminders**) *n* A **childminder** is someone whose job it is to look after children when the children's parents are away or are at work. Childminders usually work in their own homes. نگران اطفال

Chile *n* **Chile** is a republic in South America, on the Pacific. چلی

Chilean (**Chileans**) *adj* **Chilean** means of or relating to Chile or its inhabitants. چلین ▷ *n* A **Chilean** is a native or inhabitant of Chile. چلین

chill (**chills, chilling, chilled**) *v* To **chill** something means to make it cold. ٹھنڈا کرنا

chilli (**chillies, chillis**) *n* **Chillies** are small red or green seed pods with a hot, spicy taste. مرچ

chilly(**chillier, chilliest**) *adj* **Chilly** means uncomfortably cold. ٹھنڈی

chimney(**chimneys**) *n* A **chimney** is a pipe above a fireplace or furnace through which smoke can go up into the air. چمنی

chimpanzee(**chimpanzees**) *n* A **chimpanzee** is a kind of small African ape. چمپینزی

chin(**chins**) *n* Your **chin** is the part of your face below your mouth and above your neck. ٹھوڑی

China *n* (**China**) is a republic in East Asia. چین

china *n* (**China**) or **china clay** is a very thin clay used to make cups, plates, and ornaments. چینی مٹی

Chinese(**Chinese**) *adj* **Chinese** means relating to or belonging to China, or its people, languages, or culture. چینی ▷ *n* The **Chinese** are the people who come from China. چینی ▷ *n* The languages that are spoken in China, especially Mandarin, are often referred to as **Chinese.** چینی زبان

chip(**chips, chipping, chipped**) *n* A **chip** is a small piece which has been broken off something. پارچہ ▷ *n* A **chip** is a very small part that controls a piece of electronic equipment. چپ، پارچہ ▷ *vt* If you **chip** something, you break a small piece off it by accident. توڑنا

chips *npl* **Chips** or potato **chips** are thin pieces of potato fried in hot oil. چپ، آلو کے پتلے تلے ہوئے قتلے

chiropodist(**chiropodists**) *n* A **chiropodist** is a person whose job is to treat and care for people's feet. پیروں سے متعلق بیماری کا ڈاکٹر

chisel(**chisels**) *n* A **chisel** is a tool that has a long metal blade with a sharp edge at the end. It is used for cutting and shaping wood and stone. بسولہ

chives *npl* **Chives** are long, thin, hollow green leaves which are cut into small pieces and added to food to give it a flavour similar to onions. بوٹی کی پتیاں

chlorine *n* **Chlorine** is a gas that is used to disinfect water and to make cleaning products. کلورین

chocolate(**chocolates**) *n* **Chocolate** is a sweet food made from cocoa beans. چاکلیٹ

choice(**choices**) *n* If there is a **choice** of things, there are several of them and you can choose the one you want. پسند

choir(**choirs**) *n* A **choir** is a group of people who sing together. گلوکار لوگ

choke(**chokes, choking, choked**) *v* When you **choke** or when something **chokes** you, you cannot breathe properly or get enough air into your lungs. دم گھٹنا

cholesterol *n* **Cholesterol** is a substance that exists in the fat, tissues, and blood of all animals. Too much cholesterol in a person's blood can cause heart disease. کولیسٹرول

choose(**chooses, choosing, chose, chosen**) *v* If you *choose* someone or something from all the people or things that are available, you decide to have that person or thing. چننا

chop(**chops, chopping, chopped**) *n* A **chop** is a small piece of meat cut from the ribs of a sheep or pig. ٹکڑا ▷ *vt* If you **chop** something, you cut it into pieces with a knife or axe. ٹکڑے کرنا

chopsticks *npl* **Chopsticks** are a pair of thin sticks which people in Asia use to eat their food. چوپ اسٹک (جوڑا)

chosen *adj* Something that is **chosen** has been selected or picked out. چنا ہوا

Christ *n* **Christ** is one of the names of Jesus, whom Christians believe to be the son of God and whose teachings are the basis of Christianity. مسیح

Christian(**Christians**) *adj* **Christian** means relating to Christianity or Christians. مسیحی ▷ *n* A **Christian** is someone who follows the teachings of Jesus Christ. عیسائی

Christianity *n* **Christianity** is a religion

C

based on the teachings of Jesus Christ. مسیحیت
Christmas (**Christmases**) *n* **Christmas** is the period around the 25th of December when Christians celebrate the birth of Jesus Christ. کرسمس
Christmas card (**Christmas cards**) *n* **Christmas cards** are cards with greetings, which people send to their friends and family at Christmas. کرسمس کارڈ
Christmas Eve *n* **Christmas Eve** is the 24th of December. کرسمس کی شام
Christmas tree (**Christmas trees**) *n* A **Christmas tree** is a real or artificial fir tree, which people put in their houses at Christmas and decorate with lights and balls. کرسمس کا پیڑ
chrome *n* **Chrome** is a hard silver-coloured metal, used to coat other metals. کروم دھات
chronic *adj* A **chronic** illness lasts for a very long time. دیرینہ
chrysanthemum (**chrysanthemums**)*n* A **chrysanthemum** is a large garden flower with many long, thin petals. گل داؤدی
chubby (**chubbier, chubbiest**) *adj* A **chubby** person is rather fat. موٹا
chunk (**chunks**) *n* A **chunk** of something is a thick solid piece of it. بڑا ٹکڑا
church (**churches**) *n* A **church** is a building in which Christians worship. گرجا
cider (**ciders**) *n* **Cider** is an alcoholic drink made from apples. سیب کی شراب
cigar (**cigars**) *n* **Cigars** are rolls of dried tobacco leaves which people smoke. سگار
cigarette (**cigarettes**) *n* **Cigarettes** are small tubes of paper containing tobacco which people smoke. سگریٹ
cigarette lighter (**cigarette lighters**) *n* A **cigarette lighter** is a device which produces a small flame when you press a switch and which you use to light a cigarette or cigar. سگریٹ لائٹر
cinema (**cinemas**) *n* A **cinema** is a place where people go to watch films. سنیما
cinnamon *n* **Cinnamon** is a spice used for flavouring sweet food. دارچینی
circle (**circles**) *n* A **circle** is a round shape. Every part of its edge is the same distance from the centre. دائرہ
circuit (**circuits**) *n* An electrical **circuit** is a complete route which an electric current can flow around. سرکٹ
circular *adj* Something that is **circular** is shaped like a circle. مدور
circulation *n* The **circulation** of something is the passing of it around, or the spreading of it among a group of people. دوران
circumstances *npl* Your **circumstances** are the conditions of your life, especially the amount of money that you have. حالات
circus (**circuses**) *n* A **circus** is a travelling show performed in a large tent, with performers such as clowns and trained animals. سرکس
citizen (**citizens**) *n* If someone is a **citizen** of a country, they are legally accepted as belonging to that country. شہری
citizenship *n* If you have **citizenship** of a country, you are legally accepted as belonging to it. شہریت
city (**cities**) *n* A **city** is a large town. شہر
city centre (**city centres**) *n* The **city centre** is the busiest part of a city, where most of the shops and businesses are. مرکز شہر
civilian (**civilians**) *adj* In a military situation, **civilian** is used to describe people or things that are not military. غیر فوجی ▷ *n* A **civilian** is anyone who is not a member of the armed forces. عام شہری
civilization (**civilizations**) *n* A **civilization** is a human society with its own social organization and culture. تہذیب
civil rights *npl* **Civil rights** are the rights that people have to equal treatment and equal opportunities, whatever their race, sex, or religion. دیوانی حقوق

civil servant (**civil servants**) *n* A **civil servant** is a person who works in the Civil Service. دیوانی ملازم
civil war (**civil wars**) *n* A **civil war** is a war which is fought between different groups of people living in the same country. خانہ جنگی
claim (**claims, claiming, claimed**) *n* A **claim** is something which someone says which they cannot prove and which may be false. دعوی ▷ *vt* If you say that someone **claims** that something is true, you mean they say that it is true but you are not sure whether or not they are telling the truth. دعوی کرنا
claim form (**claim forms**) *n* A **claim form** is a formal written request to the government, an insurance company, or another organization for money that you think you are entitled to according to their rules. دعوی فارم
clap (**claps, clapping, clapped**) *v* When you **clap**, you hit your hands together to show appreciation or attract attention. تالی بجانا
clarify (**clarifies, clarifying, clarified**) *vt* To **clarify** something means to make it easier to understand. (*formal*) وضاحت کرنا
clarinet (**clarinets**) *n* A **clarinet** is a wind instrument with a single reed in its mouthpiece. الغوزہ
clash (**clashes, clashing, clashed**) *vi* When people **clash**, they fight, argue, or disagree with each other. متصادم ہونا
clasp (**clasps**) *n* A **clasp** is a small metal fastening. دھاتی پیچ
class (**classes**) *n* A **class** is a group of pupils or students who are taught together. درجہ
classic (**classics**) *adj* A **classic** example of something has all the features which you expect that kind of thing to have. اعلی درجہ کے ▷ *n* A **classic** is a piece of writing, film, or piece of music of high quality that has become a standard against which similar things are judged. بلند درجہ
classical *adj* You use **classical** to describe something that is traditional in form, style, or content. عالیشان
classmate (classmates) *n* Your **classmates** are students in the same class as you at school or college. کلاس کا ساتھی
classroom (classrooms) *n* A **classroom** is a room in a school where lessons take place. کلاس روم
classroom assistant (**classroom assistants**) *n* A classroom assistant is a person whose job is to help a schoolteacher in the classroom. استاد کا معاون
clause (**clauses**) *n* A **clause** is a section of a legal document. شق
claustrophobic *adj* You describe a place or situation as **claustrophobic** when it makes you feel uncomfortable and unhappy because you are enclosed or restricted. بند جگہوں سے خوفزدہ
claw (**claws**) *n* The **claws** of a bird or animal are the thin curved nails on its feet. پنجہ
clay *n* **Clay** is a type of earth that is soft when it is wet and hard when it is baked dry. مٹی
clean (**cleaner, cleanest, cleans, cleaning, cleaned**) *adj* Something that is **clean** does not have any dirt or marks on it. صاف ▷ *vt* When you **clean** something, you take all the dirt off it. صفائی کرنا
cleaner (**cleaners**) *n* A **cleaner** is someone who is employed to clean the rooms and furniture inside a building or someone whose job is to clean a particular type of thing. صفائی کار
cleaning *n* **Cleaning** is the action of making something clean. صفائی کرنا
cleaning lady (**cleaning ladies**) *n* A **cleaning lady** is a woman who is employed to clean the rooms and furniture inside a building. صفائی والی

C

cleanser (**cleansers**) *n* A **cleanser** is a liquid or cream that you use for cleaning something, especially your skin. کلینزر

cleansing lotion (**cleansing lotions**) *n* **Cleansing lotion** is a liquid or cream that you use for cleaning your skin. صفائی کا لوشن

clear (**clearer, clearest, clears, clearing, cleared**) *adj* If something is **clear**, it is easy to understand, to see, or to hear. واضح ▷ *adj* If something like glass or plastic is **clear**, you can see through it. شفاف ▷ *adj* If a place is **clear**, it does not have anything there that you do not want. صاف ▷ *vt* When you **clear** a place, you take away all the things you do not want there. صاف کرنا

clearly *adv* **Clearly** means in a manner that is easy to understand, see, or hear. صاف طور پر

clear off *v* If you tell someone to **clear off**, you are telling them in a rude way to go away. (*informal*) دفع کرنا, *The boys told me to clear off.*

clear up *v* When you **clear up**, or when you **clear** a place **up**, you tidy a place and put things away. صفائی کرنا *I cleared up my room.*

clementine (**clementines**) *n* A **clementine** is a fruit that looks like a small orange. سنترے کی نسل کا ایک پھل

clever (**cleverer, cleverest**) *adj* A **clever** person is intelligent and able to understand things easily or to plan things well. چالاک

click (**clicks, clicking, clicked**) *n* A **click** is a short, light often metallic sound. کلک ▷ *v* If something **clicks** or if you **click** it, it makes a short, sharp sound. کلک کرنا

client (**clients**) *n* A **client** is someone for whom a professional person or organization is providing a service or doing some work. موکل

cliff (**cliffs**) *n* A **cliff** is a high area of land with a very steep side, especially one next to the sea. ٹیلا

climate (**climates**) *n* The **climate** of a place is the general weather conditions that are typical of it. آب وہوا

climate change *n* **Climate change** is change that is taking place in the Earth's climate that is believed to be the result of human activity. تبدیلی آب وہوا

climb (**climbs, climbing, climbed**) *v* If you **climb** something such as a tree, mountain, or ladder, or **climb** up it, you move towards the top of it. If you **climb** down it, you move towards the bottom of it. چڑھنا

climber (**climbers**) *n* A **climber** is someone who climbs rocks or mountains as a sport. چڑھنے والا

climbing *n* **Climbing** is the activity of climbing rocks or mountains. چڑھائی

clinic (**clinics**) *n* A **clinic** is a building where people receive medical advice or treatment. مطب

clip (**clips**) *n* A **clip** is a small metal or plastic device that is used for holding things together. کلپ

clippers *npl* **Clippers** are a tool used for cutting small amounts from something, especially from someone's hair or nails. قینچی

cloakroom (**cloakrooms**) *n* A **cloakroom** is a small room in a public building where people can leave their coats. امانت خانہ

clock (**clocks**) *n* A **clock** is an instrument, for example in a room or on the outside of a building, that shows you what the time is. گھڑی

clockwise *adv* When something is moving **clockwise**, it is moving in a circle in the same direction as the hands on a clock. گھڑی کی سوئیوں کی سمت میں

clog (**clogs**) *n* **Clogs** are heavy leather or wooden shoes with thick wooden soles. بھاری کاٹھ لیدر جوتا

clone (**clones, cloning, cloned**) *n* If someone or something is a **clone** of another person or thing, they are so similar to this person or thing that they seem to be exactly the same as them. ہمزاد ▷ *vt* If you **clone** an animal or plant, you produce it artificially from a cell of another animal or plant, so that it is exactly the same as the original. ہمزاد بنانا

close (**closer, closest, closes, closing, closed**) *adj* If something is **close** to another thing, it is near it. قریب ہونا ▷ *adv* **Close** means near to something else. نزدیک ▷ *vt* When you **close** something, you shut it. بند کرنا

close by *adj* Something that is **close by** is near to you. نزدیک

closed *adj* A **closed** group of people does not welcome new people or ideas from outside. بند

closely *adv* **Closely** means near to something else. قریب سے

closing time (**closing times**) *n* **Closing time** is the time when something such as a shop, library, or pub closes and people have to leave. بند کرنے کا وقت

closure (**closures**) *n* The **closure** of a business or factory is the permanent shutting of it. بندی

cloth (**cloths**) *n* **Cloth** is material that is used to make things like clothes and curtains. کپڑا ▷ *n* A **cloth** is a piece of material that you use to clean something. صافی، پونچھا

clothes *npl* **Clothes** are the things that people wear, such as shirts, coats, trousers, and dresses. کپڑے

clothes line (**clothes lines**) *n* A **clothes line** is a thin rope on which you hang washing so that it can dry. الگنی

clothes peg (**clothes pegs**) *n* A **clothes peg** is a small device which you use to fasten clothes to a washing line. الگنی کلپ

clothing *n* **Clothing** is the clothes people wear. لباس

cloud (**clouds**) *n* A **cloud** is a mass of water vapour that is seen as a white or grey mass in the sky. بادل

cloudy (**cloudier, cloudiest**) *adj* If it is **cloudy**, there are a lot of clouds in the sky. ابر آلود

clove (**cloves**) *n* **Cloves** are small dried flower buds used as a spice. لونگ

clown (**clowns**) *n* A **clown** is a performer who wears funny clothes and bright make-up, and does silly things to make people laugh. مسخرہ

club (**clubs**) *n* A **club** is an organization of people who are all interested in a particular activity. کلب ▷ *n* A **club** is a thick, heavy stick that can be used as a weapon. چھڑی

club together *v* If people **club together** to do something, they all give money towards the cost of it. ساتھ آنا *For my thirtieth birthday, my friends clubbed together and bought me a watch.*

clue (**clues**) *n* A **clue** to a problem, mystery, or puzzle is something that helps you find the answer. سراغ

clumsy (**clumsier, clumsiest**) *adj* A **clumsy** person moves or handles things in an awkward way. بے ڈھنگا

clutch (**clutches**) *n* If you are in another person's **clutches**, that person has control over you. پنجہ

clutter *n* **Clutter** is a lot of unnecessary or useless things in an untidy state. فضول بکھراہٹ

coach (**coaches**) *n* A **coach** is someone who trains a person or team of people in a particular sport. تربیت کار ▷ *n* A **coach** is a large comfortable bus that carries passengers on long journeys. کوچ (گاڑی)

coal *n* **Coal** is a hard black substance taken from underground and burned as fuel. کوئلہ

coarse (**coarser, coarsest**) *adj* **Coarse** things have a rough texture. بھدی

coast (**coasts**) *n* The **coast** is an area of land next to the sea. ساحل

coastguard (**coastguards**) *n* A **coastguard** is an official who watches the sea near a coast, in order to get help when it is needed and to prevent smuggling. ساحل کا محافظ

coat (**coats**) *n* A **coat** is a piece of clothing with long sleeves worn over your other clothes when you go outside. کوٹ

coathanger (**coat hangers**) *n* A **coathanger** is a curved piece of wood, metal, or plastic that you hang a piece of clothing on. کوٹ ہینگر

cobweb (**cobwebs**) *n* A **cobweb** is the fine net that a spider makes in order to catch insects. مکڑی کا جالہ

cock (**cocks**) *n* A **cock** is an adult male chicken. مرغا

cockerel (**cockerels**) *n* A **cockerel** is a young male chicken. نوجوان مرغا

cockpit (**cockpits**) *n* The **cockpit** in a small plane or racing car is the part where the pilot or driver sits. کاک پٹ

cockroach (**cockroaches**) *n* A **cockroach** is a large brown insect that is often found in dirty or damp places. کاکروچ

cocktail (**cocktails**) *n* A **cocktail** is an alcoholic drink containing several ingredients. کاکٹیل

cocoa *n* **Cocoa** is a brown powder used in making chocolate. کوکو(آسفوف، مشروب)

coconut (**coconuts**) *n* A **coconut** is a very large nut with a hairy shell, white flesh, and milky juice inside. ناریل

cod (**cods, cod**) *n* A **cod** is a large sea fish with white flesh. کوڈ مچھلی

code (**codes**) *n* A **code** is a set of rules about how people should behave. قانون

coeliac *adj* **Coeliac** means of or relating to the abdomen. پیڑو والے حصے میں، کا

coffee (**coffees**) *n* **Coffee** is the roasted beans of the coffee plant. کافی، قہوہ

coffee bean (**coffee beans**) *n* **Coffee beans** are small dark-brown beans that are roasted and ground to make coffee. They are the seeds of the coffee plant. کافی کے دانے

coffeepot (**coffeepots**) *n* A **coffeepot** is a tall narrow pot with a spout and a lid, in which coffee is made or served. قہوہ دانی

coffee table (**coffee tables**) *n* A **coffee table** is a small low table in a living room. کافی کی میز

coffin (**coffins**) *n* A **coffin** is a box in which a dead body is buried or cremated. تابوت

coin (**coins**) *n* A **coin** is a small piece of metal used as money. سکہ

coincide (**coincides, coinciding, coincided**) *vi* If one event **coincides** with another, they happen at the same time. اتفاق ہونا

coincidence (**coincidences**) *n* A **coincidence** happens when two or more things occur at the same time by chance. اتفاق

Coke® (**Cokes**) *n* **Coke** is a sweet, brown, non-alcoholic fizzy drink. کوک

colander (**colanders**) *n* A **colander** is a container in the shape of a bowl with holes in it which you wash or drain food in. چھلنی، چھلنی

cold (**colder, coldest, colds**) *adj* If something is **cold**, it is not hot. ٹھنڈا
▷ *n* When you have a **cold**, you sneeze and cough a lot, and you have a sore throat. نزلہ زکام میں مبتلا ہونا
adj If you are **cold**, you do not feel comfortable because you are not warm enough. سردی لگنا، ٹھنڈک محسوس کرنا

cold sore (**cold sores**) *n* **Cold sores** are small sore spots that sometimes appear on or near someone's lips and nose when they have a cold. ٹھنڈی دانے

coleslaw *n* **Coleslaw** is a salad of chopped raw cabbage, carrots, onions, and sometimes other vegetables, usually with mayonnaise. سلاد

collaborate (**collaborates, collaborating, collaborated**) *vi* When people **collaborate**, they work together on a particular project. اشتراک کرنا

collapse (**collapses, collapsing,**

collapsed) *vi* If a building or other structure **collapses**, it falls down very suddenly. ڈھے جانا

collar (**collars**) *n* The **collar** of a shirt or jacket is the part that goes around your neck. کالر ⊳ *n* A **collar** is a band that goes around the neck of a dog or cat. گریباں

collarbone (**collarbones**) *n* Your **collarbones** are the two long bones which run from your throat to your shoulders. ہنسلی کی ہڈی

colleague (**colleagues**) *n* Your **colleagues** are the people you work with, especially in a professional job. رفیق کار

collect (**collects, collecting, collected**) *vt* If you **collect** things, you bring them together. جمع کرنا ⊳ *vt* If you **collect** someone from a place, you go there and take them away. لے جانا

collection (**collections**) *n* A **collection** of things is a group of similar things that you have deliberately acquired, usually over a period of time. مجموعہ

collective (**collectives**) *adj* **Collective** means shared by or involving every member of a group of people. اجتماعی ⊳ *n* A **collective** is a business or farm whose employees share the decision-making and the profits. مشترک

collector (**collectors**) *n* A **collector** is a person who collects things of a particular type as a hobby. جمع کرنے والا

college (**colleges**) *n* A **college** is an institution where students study after they have left school. کالج

collide (**collides, colliding, collided**) *vi* If people or vehicles **collide**, they bump into each other. ٹکرانا

collie (**collies**) *n* A **collie** or a **collie dog** is a dog with long hair and a long, narrow nose. لمبے بال والا کتا

colliery (**collieries**) *n* A **colliery** is a coal mine. کوئلے کی کان

collision (**collisions**) *n* A **collision** occurs when a moving object hits something. ٹکر

Colombia *n* **Colombia** is a republic in north-west South America. کولمبیا

Colombian (**Colombians**) *adj* **Colombian** means belonging or relating to Colombia or its people or culture. کولمبیائی ⊳ *n* A **Colombian** is a Colombian citizen, or a person of Colombian origin. کولمبیائی

colon (**colons**) *n* A **colon** is the punctuation mark:. کولن

colonel (**colonels**) *n* A **colonel** is a senior officer in an army, air force, or the marines. کرنل

colour (**colours**) *n* The **colour** of something is the appearance that it has as a result of reflecting light. Red, blue, and green are colours. رنگ

colour-blind *adj* Someone who is **colour-blind** cannot see the difference between colours, especially between red and green. رنگ کا اندھاپن

colourful *adj* Something that is **colourful** has bright colours. رنگین

colouring *n* Someone's **colouring** is the colour of their hair, skin, and eyes. رنگ

column (**columns**) *n* A **column** is a tall solid cylinder, especially one supporting part of a building. ستون

coma (**comas**) *n* If someone is in a **coma**, they are deeply unconscious. کوما، دماغی موت

comb (**combs, combing, combed**) *n* A **comb** is a flat piece of plastic or metal with narrow pointed teeth along one side, which you use to tidy your hair. کنگھا ⊳ *vt* When you **comb** your hair, you tidy it using a comb. کنگھی کرنا

combination (**combinations**) *n* A **combination** is a mixture of things. امتزاج

combine (**combines, combining, combined**) *v* If you **combine** two or more things, or if they **combine**, they exist or join together. ملانا

come (**comes, coming, came**) *vi* When you **come** to a place, you move towards it or arrive there. آنا

come back *v* If someone **comes back**

to a place, they return to it. واپس آنا *I came back to my hometown and decided to be a photographer.*

comedian (**comedians**) *n* A **comedian** is an entertainer whose job is to make people laugh by telling jokes. مسخرہ

come down *v* If the cost, level, or amount of something **comes down**, it becomes less than it was before. نیچے آنا *The price of petrol is coming down.*

comedy *n* **Comedy** consists of types of entertainment that are intended to make people laugh. مزاحیہ

come from *v* If someone or something **comes from** a particular place or thing, that place or thing is their origin or source. سے آنا *Half the students come from abroad.*

come in *v* If information or a report **comes in**, you receive it. اندر آنا *Reports are now coming in of trouble at the event.*

come out *v* When a new product **comes out**, it becomes available to the public. باہر آنا *The actor has a new movie coming out.*

come round *v* When someone who is unconscious **comes round** or **comes around**, they recover consciousness. ہوش میں آنا *When I came round I was on the kitchen floor.*

comet (**comets**) *n* A **comet** is an object that travels around the sun leaving a bright trail behind it. دمدار ستارہ

come up *v* If someone **comes up** to you, they walk over to you. اوپر آنا *Her cat came up and rubbed itself against their legs.*

comfortable *adj* You describe things such as furniture as **comfortable** when they make you feel physically relaxed. آرام دہ

comic (**comics**) *n* A **comic** is an entertainer who tells jokes in order to make people laugh. مزاحیہ

comic book (**comic books**) *n* A **comic book** is a magazine that contains stories told in pictures. مزاحیہ کتاب

comic strip (**comic strips**) *n* A **comic strip** is a series of drawings that tell a story, especially in a newspaper or magazine. مزاح کا تصویری سلسلہ

coming *adj* A **coming** event or time will happen soon. آنے والا

comma (**commas**) *n* A **comma** is the punctuation mark ,. کوما (،)

command (**commands**) *n* If you give someone a **command** to do something, you order them to do it. (*written*) حکم

comment (**comments, commenting, commented**) *n* A **comment** is something that you say which expresses your opinion of something or which gives an explanation of it. تبصرہ ▷ *v* If you **comment** on something, you give your opinion about it or you give an explanation for it. تبصرہ کرنا

commentary (**commentaries**) *n* A **commentary** is a spoken description of an event that is broadcast on radio or television while it is taking place. زبانی تبصرہ

commentator (**commentators**) *n* A **commentator** is a broadcaster who gives a commentary on an event. کمنٹری کرنے والا، تبصرہ کرنے والا

commercial (**commercials**) *n* A **commercial** is an advertisement broadcast on television or radio. تجارتی

commercial break (**commercial breaks**) *n* A **commercial break** is the interval during a commercial television programme, or between programmes, during which advertisements are shown. تجارتی وقفہ

commission (**commissions**) *n* A **commission** is a piece of work that someone is asked to do and is paid for. کمیشن

commit (**commits, committing, committed**) *vt* If someone **commits** a crime or a sin, they do something illegal or bad. ارتکاب کرنا

committee (**committees**) *n* A **committee** is a group of people who represent a

larger group or organization and make decisions for them. کمیٹی
common (**commoner, commonest**) *adj* If something is **common**, it is found in large numbers or it happens often. عمومی
common sense *n* **Common sense** is the natural ability to make good judgements and behave sensibly. عمومی شعور
communicate (**communicates, communicating, communicated**) *vi* If you **communicate** with someone, you give them information, for example by speaking, writing, or sending radio signals. بات کرنا
communication *n* **Communication** is the act of sharing or exchanging information with someone, for example by speaking, writing, or sending radio signals. مواصلت
communion *n* **Communion** with nature or with a person is the feeling that you are sharing thoughts or feelings with them. ہم آہنگی
communism *n* **Communism** is the political belief that all people are equal and that workers should control the means of producing things. اشتراکیت
communist (**communists** *adj* **Communist** means relating to communism. اشتراکی ▷ *n* A **communist** is someone who believes in communism. کمیونسٹ
community (**communities**) *n* The **community** is all the people who live in a particular area or place. فرقہ
commute (**commutes, commuting, commuted**) *vi* If you **commute**, you travel a long distance to work every day. سفر کرنا
commuter (**commuters**) *n* A **commuter** is a person who travels a long distance to work every day. مسافر
compact *adj* Something that is **compact** is small or takes up very little space. کمپیکٹ (چھوٹی)
compact disc (**compact discs**)*n* **Compact discs** are small discs on which sound, especially music, is recorded. The abbreviation 'CD' is also used. کمپیکٹ ڈسک
companion (**companions**) *n* A **companion** is someone who you spend time with or travel with. ساتھی
company (**companies**) *n* A **company** is a business organization that makes money by selling goods or services. کمپنی
company car (**company cars**) *n* A **company car** is a car which an employer gives to an employee to use as their own. کمپنی کار
comparable *adj* Something that is **comparable** to something is roughly similar, for example in amount or importance. قابل موازنہ
comparatively *adv* **Comparatively** means compared to something else. تقابلی طور پر
compare (**compares, comparing, compared**) *vt* If you **compare** things, you consider them and discover the differences or similarities between them. تقابل کرنا
comparison (**comparisons**) *n* When you make a **comparison** between two or more things, you discover the differences or similarities between them. موازنہ
compartment (**compartments**) *n* A **compartment** is one of the separate sections of a railway carriage. خانہ
compass (**compasses**) *n* A **compass** is an instrument that you use for finding directions. It has a dial and a magnetic needle that always points to the north. سمت نما

C

compatible *adj* If things, systems, or ideas are **compatible**, they work well together or can exist together successfully. مطابقت پذیر

compensate (**compensates, compensating, compensated**) *vt* If someone **is compensated** for something unpleasant which has happened to them, they receive compensation for it. ہرجانہ دینا

compensation (**compensations**) *n* **Compensation** is money that someone who has undergone loss or suffering claims from the person or organization responsible. ہرجانہ

compere (**comperes**) *n* A **compere** is the person who introduces the people taking part in a radio or television show or a live show. میزبانی

compete (**competes, competing, competed**) *vi* If one person or organization **competes** with another for something, they try to get that thing for themselves and stop the other getting it. مقابلہ کرنا

competent *adj* Someone who is **competent** is efficient and effective. باصلاحیت

competition (**competitions**) *n* **Competition** is a situation in which two or more people or groups are trying to get something which not everyone can have. مقابلہ

competitive *adj* **Competitive** situations or activities are ones in which people compete with each other. مقابلہ آرا

competitor (**competitors**) *n* A company's **competitors** are other companies that sell similar kinds of goods or services. مقابل

complain (**complains, complaining, complained**) *v* If you **complain** about something, you say you are not satisfied with it. شکایت کرنا

complaint (**complaints**) *n* A **complaint** is a statement of dissatisfaction about a situation. شکایت

complementary *adj* If two different things are **complementary**, they form a complete unit when they are brought together, or they combine well with each other. (*formal*) تکمیلی

complete *adj* You use **complete** to emphasize that something is as great in extent, degree, or amount as it possibly can be. مکمل

completely *adv* **Completely** means as much in extent, degree, or amount as possible. مکمل طور پر

complex (**complexes**) *adj* **Complex** things have many different parts and are hard to understand. پیچیدہ ▷ *n* A **complex** is a group of buildings used for a particular purpose. مجموعہ

complexion (**complexions**) *n* Your **complexion** is the natural colour or condition of the skin on your face. جلدی رنگ

complicated *adj* Something that is **complicated** has many parts and is therefore difficult to understand. الجھے ہوئے، پیچیدہ

complication (**complications**) *n* A **complication** is a problem or difficulty. پیچیدگی

compliment (**compliments, complimenting, complimented**) *n* A **compliment** is a polite remark that you say to someone to show that you like their appearance, appreciate their qualities, or approve of what they have done. تعریف، تحسین ▷ *vt* If you **compliment** someone, you say something nice about them. خوبی بیان کرنا

complimentary *adj* If you are **complimentary** about something, you express admiration for it. تعریفی

component (**components**) *n* The **components** of something are its parts. پرزہ

composer (**composers**) *n* A **composer** is a person who writes music. موسیقار

composition (**compositions**) *n* The **composition** of something is the things that it consists of and the way that they are arranged. دھن

comprehension *n* **Comprehension** is the ability to understand something or the process of understanding something. (*formal*) فہم

comprehensive *adj* Something that is **comprehensive** includes everything necessary or relevant. جامع

compromise (**compromises, compromising, compromised**) *n* A **compromise** is a situation in which people accept something slightly different from what they really want. سمجھوتا ▷ *vi* If you **compromise** with someone, you reach an agreement with them in which you both give up something that you originally wanted. You can also say that two people or groups **compromise**. سمجھوتا کرنا

compulsory *adj* If something is **compulsory**, you must do it because a law or someone in authority says you must. لازمی

computer (**computers**) *n* A **computer** is an electronic machine which makes quick calculations and deals with large amounts of information. کمپیوٹر

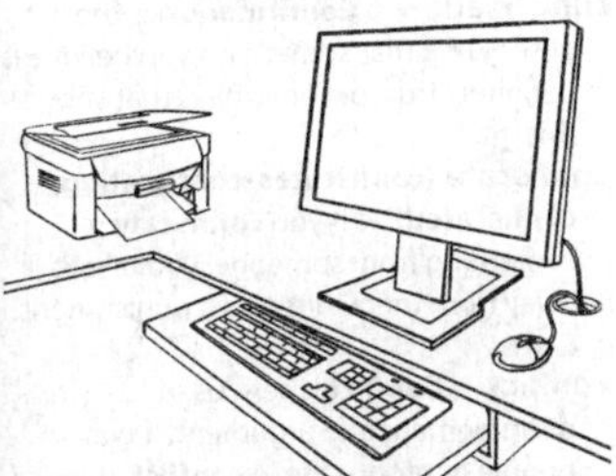

computer game (**computer games**) *n* A **computer game** is a game that you play on a computer or on a small portable piece of electronic equipment. کمپیوٹر کھیل

computer science *n* **Computer science** is the study of computers and their application. کمپیوٹر سائنس

computing *n* **Computing** is the activity of using a computer and writing programs for it. حساب کتاب کرنا

concentrate (**concentrates, concentrating, concentrated**) *vi* If you **concentrate** on something, you give it all your attention. یکسو ہونا

concentration *n* **Concentration** on something involves giving all your attention to it. یکسوئی

concern (**concerns**) *n* **Concern** is worry about a situation. تشویش

concerned *adj* If you are **concerned** about something, you are worried about it. وابستہ

concerning *prep* You use **concerning** to show what a piece of information is about. (*formal*) متعلق *Contact the teacher for more information concerning the class.*

concert (**concerts**) *n* A **concert** is a performance of music. محفل موسیقی

concerto (**concerti, concertos**) *n* A **concerto** is a piece of music for a solo instrument and an orchestra. اکیلے شخص کی موسیقی

concession (**concessions**) *n* If you make a **concession** to someone, you agree to let them do or have something, especially in order to end an argument or conflict. رعایت

concise *adj* Something that is **concise** gives all the necessary information in a very brief form. اختصاری، جامع

conclude (**concludes, concluding, concluded**) *vt* If you **conclude** that something is true, you decide that it is true using the facts you know. نتیجہ نکالنا

conclusion (**conclusions**) *n* When you

C

come to a **conclusion**, you decide that something is true after you have thought about it carefully. نتیجہ

concrete *n* **Concrete** is a substance used for building. It is made from cement, sand, small stones, and water. ٹھوس، پختہ

concussion *n* If you suffer **concussion** after you hit your head, you lose consciousness or feel sick or confused. دماغی صدمہ

condemn (**condemns, condemning, condemned**) *vt* If you **condemn** something, you say that it is bad and unacceptable. ملامت کرنا

condensation *n* **Condensation** consists of small drops of water which form when warm water vapour or steam touches a cold surface such as a window. عمل تکثیف

condition (**conditions**) *n* The **condition** of someone or something is the state they are in. حالت

conditional *adj* If a situation or agreement is **conditional** on something, it will only happen if this thing happens. مشروط

conditioner (**conditioners**) *n* A **conditioner** is a substance which you can put on your hair after you have washed it to make it softer. سنوارنے والا

condom (**condoms**) *n* A **condom** is a rubber covering which a man wears on his penis as a contraceptive. کنڈوم، مانع حمل

conduct (**conducts, conducting, conducted**) *vt* When you **conduct** an activity or task, you organize it and carry it out. چلانا

conductor (**conductors**) *n* A **conductor** is a person who stands in front of an orchestra or choir and directs its performance. چلانے والا

cone (**cones**) *n* A **cone** is a shape with a circular base and smooth curved sides ending in a point at the top. مخروط

conference (**conferences**) *n* A **conference** is a meeting, often lasting a few days, which is organized on a particular subject. کانفرنس

confess (**confesses, confessing, confessed**) *v* If you **confess** to doing something wrong or something that you are ashamed of, you admit that you did it. اعتراف کرنا

confession (**confessions**) *n* A **confession** is a signed statement by someone in which they admit that they have committed a particular crime. اعتراف

confetti *npl* **Confetti** is small pieces of coloured paper that people throw over the bride and bridegroom at a wedding. رنگین کاغذ کے ٹکڑے

confidence *n* If you have **confidence** in someone, you feel you can trust them. اعتماد ▷ *n* If you have **confidence**, you feel sure about your abilities, qualities, or ideas. خود اعتمادی ▷ *n* If you tell someone something in **confidence**, you tell them a secret. راز

confident *adj* If you are **confident** about something, you are certain that it will happen in the way you want it to. پر یقین

confidential *adj* Information that is **confidential** is meant to be kept secret. رازدارانہ

confirm (**confirms, confirming, confirmed**) *vt* If something **confirms** what you believe, it shows that it is definitely true. تصدیق کرنا

confirmation *n* **Confirmation** is the act of showing that something you believe is definitely true, or something that shows this. تصدیق

confiscate (**confiscates, confiscating, confiscated**) *vt* If you **confiscate** something from someone, you take it away from them, often as a punishment. ضبط کرنا

conflict *n* **Conflict** is serious disagreement and argument. If two people or groups are in **conflict**, they have had a serious disagreement and have not yet reached agreement. جھگڑا

confuse (**confuses, confusing, confused**) *vt* If you **confuse** two things, you get them mixed up, so that you think one is the other. متذبذب ہونا

confused *adj* If you are **confused**, you do not know what to do or you do not understand what is happening. متذبذب

confusing *adj* Something that is **confusing** makes it difficult for people to know what to do or what is happening. الجھن آمیز

confusion *n* If there is **confusion** about something, the facts are not clear. تذبذب

congestion *n* If there is **congestion** in a place, the place is extremely crowded and blocked with traffic or people. جام

Congo *n* The **Congo** is a republic in south central Africa. کانگو

congratulate (**congratulates, congratulating, congratulated**) *vt* If you **congratulate** someone, you express pleasure for something good that has happened to them, or you praise them for something they have achieved. مبارکباد دینا

congratulations *npl* You say '**congratulations**' to someone in order to congratulate them. مبارکباد

conifer (**conifers**) *n* **Conifers** are a group of trees and shrubs, for example pine trees and fir trees, that grow in cooler areas of the world. They have fruit called cones, and very thin leaves called needles which they do not normally lose in winter. سرد علاقوں کے درخت

conjugation (**conjugations**) *n* A **conjugation** is one of the different forms of a verb. The form can change according to the number of people it refers to, or according to whether it refers to the past, present, or future. گردان (تصریف) فعل کا صیغہ

conjunction (**conjunctions**) *n* A **conjunction** of two or more things is the occurrence of them at the same time or place. (*formal*) اتصال

conjurer (**conjurers**) *n* A **conjurer** is a person who entertains people by doing magic tricks. مداری

connection (**connections**) *n* A **connection** is a relationship between two people, groups, or things. جوڑ

conquer (**conquers, conquering, conquered**) *vt* If one country or group of people **conquers** another, they take complete control of their land. جیتنا

conscience (**consciences**) *n* Your **conscience** is the part of your mind that tells you if what you are doing is wrong. If you have a **guilty conscience**, or if you have something **on** your **conscience**, you feel guilty because you know you have done something wrong. ضمیر

conscientious *adj* Someone who is **conscientious** is very careful to do their work properly. باضمیر

conscious *adj* If you are **conscious** of something, you notice it or are aware of it. ہوشمند

consciousness *n* Your **consciousness** consists of your mind, thoughts, beliefs, and attitudes. ہوش و شعور

consecutive *adj* **Consecutive** periods of time or events happen one after the other without interruption. سلسلے وار

consensus *n* A **consensus** is general agreement amongst a group of people. اتفاق رائے

consequence (**consequences**) *n* The **consequences** of something are the results or effects of it. نتیجہ

consequently *adv* **Consequently** means as a result. (*formal*) نتیجے کے طور پر

conservation *n* **Conservation** is the preservation and protection of the environment. تحفظ

conservative *adj* Someone who is **conservative** has right-wing views. قدامت پرست

conservatory (**conservatories**) *n* A **conservatory** is a glass room built onto a house. حفاظت خانہ، پود گھر

C

consider (**considers, considering, considered**) *vt* If you **consider** a person or thing to be something, this is your opinion of them. سمجھنا

considerate *adj* A **considerate** person pays attention to the needs, wishes, or feelings of other people. بامروت

considering *prep* You use **considering** to show that you haven't forgotten an important fact. زیر غور *Considering the time, I think we'll have to wait until tomorrow.*

consistent *adj* A **consistent** person always behaves or responds in the same way. بااصول

consist of *v* Something that **consists of** particular things or people is formed from them. مشتمل ہونا *The cabin consisted of two small rooms.*

consonant (**consonants**) *n* A **consonant** is a sound such as 'p' or 'f' which you pronounce by stopping the air flowing freely through your mouth. حرف صامت

conspiracy (**conspiracies**) *n* **Conspiracy** is the secret planning by a group of people to do something wrong or illegal. سازش

constant *adj* Something that is **constant** happens all the time or is always there. مستقل

constantly *adv* If something happens **constantly**, it happens all the time. مستقلاً

constipated *adj* Someone who is **constipated** has difficulty in getting rid of solid waste from their body. قبض زدہ

constituency (**constituencies**) *n* A **constituency** is an area, and the people who live in it. In an election, the people in the constituency choose one person for the government. انتخابی علاقہ

constitution (**constitutions**) *n* The **constitution** is the laws of a country or organization. دستور

construct (**constructs, constructing, constructed**) *vt* If you **construct** something, you build, make, or create it. تعمیر کرنا

construction (**constructions**) *n* **Construction** is the building or creating of something. تعمیر

constructive *adj* A **constructive** discussion, comment, or approach is useful and helpful. تعمیری

consul (**consuls**) *n* A **consul** is a government official who lives in a foreign city and looks after all the people there who are from his or her own country. قونصل

consulate (**consulates**) *n* A **consulate** is the place in a city where a foreign government official works and looks after all the people there who are from his or her own country. سفارت خانہ

consult (**consults, consulting, consulted**) *v* If you **consult** someone or something, you refer to them for advice or information. You can also *consult* with someone. مشورہ کرنا

consultant (**consultants**) *n* A **consultant** is an experienced doctor specializing in one area of medicine. صلاحکار

consumer (**consumers**) *n* A **consumer** is a person who buys things or uses services. صارف

contact (**contacts, contacting, contacted**) *n* **Contact** involves meeting or communicating with someone. رابطہ ▷ *vt* If you **contact** someone, you telephone them or write to them. رابطہ کرنا

contact lenses *npl* **Contact lenses** are small lenses that you put on your eyes to help you to see better. کانٹیکٹ لینس

contagious *adj* A **contagious** disease can be caught by touching people or things that are infected with it. متعدی

contain (**contains, containing, contained**) *vt* If something such as a box or a room **contains** things, those things are in it. رکھنا

container (**containers**) *n* A **container** is something such as a box or bottle that is used to hold things. ڈبہ

contemporary *adj* **Contemporary**

means existing now or at the time you are talking about. ہم زمانہ
contempt *n* If you have **contempt** for someone or something, you have no respect for them. تحقیر
content (**contents**) *n* The **content** of a piece of writing, speech, or television programme is its subject and the ideas expressed in it. مواد
content *adj* If you are **content**, you are happy. مطمئن
contents *npl* The **contents** of a container such as a bottle, box, or room are the things inside it. مشمولات
contest (**contests**) *n* A **contest** is a competition or game. مقابلہ
contestant (**contestants**) *n* A **contestant** in a competition or quiz is a person who takes part in it. مقابل
context (**contexts**) *n* The **context** of an idea or event is the general situation in which it occurs. سیاق و سباق
continent (**continents**) *n* A **continent** is a very large area of land, such as Africa or Asia, that consists of several countries. براعظم
continual *adj* **Continual** means happening without stopping, or happening again and again. تسلسل سے
continually *adv* If something happens **continually**, it happens without stopping, or happens again and again. مسلسل
continue (**continues, continuing, continued**) *vt* If you **continue** to do something, you do not stop doing it. جاری رکھنا ▷ *vi* If something **continues**, it does not stop. جاری رہنا
continuous *adj* A **continuous** process or event continues for a period of time without stopping. لگاتار
contraception *n* Methods of preventing pregnancy are called **contraception**. امتناع حمل
contraceptive (**contraceptives**) *n* A **contraceptive** is a device or pill used to prevent pregnancy. مانع حمل
contract (**contracts**) *n* A **contract** is a legal agreement, usually between two companies or between an employer and employee, which involves doing work for a stated sum of money. ٹھیکہ
contractor (**contractors**) *n* A **contractor** is a person or company that works for other people or companies. ٹھیکے دار
contradict (**contradicts, contradicting, contradicted**) *vt* If you **contradict** someone, you say or suggest that what they have just said is wrong. تردید کرنا
contradiction (**contradictions**) *n* A **contradiction** is an aspect of a situation which appears to conflict with other aspects, so that they cannot all exist or be successful. تضاد
contrary *n* You use **on the contrary** when you are contradicting what has just been said. برعکس
contrast (**contrasts**) *n* A **contrast** is a great difference between two or more things. تخالف
contribute (**contributes, contributing, contributed**) *vi* If you **contribute** to something, you say or do something to help make it successful. عطا کرنا
contribution (**contributions**) *n* If you make a **contribution** to something, you do something to help make it successful or to produce it. عطیہ
control (**controls, controlling, controlled**) *n* **Control** of an organization, place, or system is the power to make all the important decisions about the way that it is run. قابو ▷ *vt* The people who **control** an organization or place have the power to take all the important decisions about the way that it is run. قابو کرنا
controversial *adj* Someone or something that is **controversial** causes intense public argument, disagreement, or disapproval. متنازع فیہ

convenient *adj* Something that is **convenient** is easy, useful, or suitable for a particular purpose. سہولت بخش
conventional *adj* **Conventional** people behave in a way that is accepted as normal in their society. روایتی
conversation (**conversations**) *n* If you have a **conversation** with someone, you talk to each other, usually in an informal situation. گفتگو
convert (**converts, converting, converted**) *v* To **convert** one thing into another means to change it into a different shape or form. بدلنا
convertible (**convertibles**) *adj* **Convertible** money can be easily exchanged for other forms of money. قابل بدل ▷ *n* A **convertible** is a car with a soft roof that can be folded down or removed. کھولنے اور بند کرنے والی چھت گاڑی
conveyor belt (**conveyor belts**) *n* A **conveyor belt** or a **conveyor** is a continuously moving strip which is used in factories to move objects along. ترسیل پٹی
convict (**convicts, convicting, convicted**) *vt* If someone **is convicted** of a crime, they are found guilty of it in a law court. سزا سنایا جانا
convince (**convinces, convincing, convinced**) *vt* If someone or something **convinces** you of something, they make you believe that it is true or that it exists. قائل کرنا
convincing *adj* If someone or something is **convincing**, you believe them. قابل قبول
convoy (**convoys**) *n* A **convoy** is a group of vehicles or ships travelling together. قافلہ
cook (**cooks, cooking, cooked**) *n* A **cook** is a person whose job is to prepare and cook food. باورچی ▷ *v* When you **cook**, or **cook** a meal, you prepare and heat food so it can be eaten. پکانا
cookbook (**cookbooks**) *n* A **cookbook** is a book that contains recipes for preparing food. پکوان کتابچہ
cooker (**cookers**) *n* A **cooker** is a large metal device used for cooking food using gas or electricity. کوکر
cookery *n* **Cookery** is the activity of preparing and cooking food. پکانے کا فن
cookery book (**cookery books**) *n* A **cookery book** is a book that contains recipes for preparing food. پکوانوں کی کتاب
cooking *n* **Cooking** is the act of preparing and heating food so it can be eaten. پکانے کا عمل
cool (**cooler, coolest**) *adj* Something that is **cool** has a low temperature but is not cold. ٹھنڈا ▷ *adj* If you say that someone is **cool**, you mean that they are fashionable and attractive. (*informal*) فیشن پرست
cooperation *n* **Cooperation** is the action of working together with or helping someone. تعاون
cop (**cops**) *n* A **cop** is a policeman or policewoman. (*informal*) پولس والا
cope (**copes, coping, coped**) *vi* If you **cope** with a problem, task, or difficult situation, you deal with it successfully. نمٹنا
copper (**coppers**) *n* **Copper** is a soft reddish-brown metal. تانبہ
copy (**copies, copying, copied**) *n* If you make a **copy** of something, you produce something that looks like the original thing. نقل ▷ *n* A **copy** of a book, newspaper, or record is one of many identical ones that have been printed or produced. نقل ▷ *vt* If you **copy** something, you produce something that looks like the original thing. نقل کرنا
copyright (**copyrights**) *n* If someone has the **copyright** on a piece of writing or music, it is illegal to reproduce or perform it without their permission. حق اشاعت
coral (**corals**) *n* **Coral** is a hard substance formed from the skeletons of very small sea animals. مونگا

cordless *adj* A **cordless** telephone or piece of electric equipment is operated by a battery fitted inside it and is not connected to the electricity mains. بے تار

corduroy *n Corduroy* is thick cotton cloth with parallel raised lines on the outside. کورڈرائی، ڈوریا گری

core (**cores**) *n* The **core** of a fruit is the central part containing seeds or pips. مرکز

coriander *n* **Coriander** is a plant with seeds that are used as a spice and leaves that are used as a herb. دھنیا

cork *n* **Cork** is a soft light substance which forms the bark of a Mediterranean tree. کاگ

corkscrew (**corkscrews**) *n* A **corkscrew** is a device for pulling corks out of bottles. ڈھکن کھولنے کا آلہ

corn *n* **Corn** refers to crops such as wheat and barley, or their seeds. مکئی

corner (**corners**) *n* A **corner** is a place where two sides or edges of something meet, or where a road meets another road. کونہ

cornet (**cornets**) *n* A **cornet** is a musical instrument of the brass family that looks like a small trumpet. پیتل کا ساز

cornflakes *npl* **Cornflakes** are small flat pieces of maize that are eaten with milk as a breakfast cereal. مکئی کے پھوٹے

cornflour *n* **Cornflour** is a fine white powder made from maize and is used to make sauces thicker. مکئی کا آٹا

corporal (**corporals**) *n* A **corporal** is a non-commissioned officer in the army or United States Marines. کارپورل

corporal punishment *n* **Corporal punishment** is the punishment of people by hitting them. جسمانی سزا

corpse (**corpses**) *n* A **corpse** is a dead body. لاش

correct (**corrects, correcting, corrected**) *adj* Something that is **correct** is accurate and has no mistakes. (*formal*) صحیح ▷ *vt* If you **correct** a mistake, problem, or fault, you put it right. صحیح کرنا

correction (**corrections**) *n* A **correction** is something which puts right something that is wrong. صحیح

correctly *adv* If you do something **correctly**, you do it in the correct way. صحیح طور پر

correspondence *n* **Correspondence** is the act of writing letters to someone. خط وکتابت

correspondent (**correspondents**) *n* A **correspondent** is a television or newspaper reporter. نامہ نگار

corridor (**corridors**) *n* A **corridor** is a long passage in a building or train, with rooms on one or both sides. گلیارا

corrupt *adj* A **corrupt** person behaves in a way that is morally wrong, especially by doing illegal things for money. بدعنوان

corruption *n* **Corruption** is dishonesty and illegal behaviour by people in positions of power. بدعنوانی

cosmetics *npl* **Cosmetics** are substances such as lipstick or face powder. زیبائشی سامان

cosmetic surgery *n* **Cosmetic surgery** is surgery done to make a person look more attractive. آرائشی سرجری

cost (**costs, costing**) *n* The **cost** of something is the amount of money needed to buy, do, or make it. لاگت ▷ *vt* If something **costs** a particular amount of money, you can buy, do, or make it for that amount. قیمت ہونا

Costa Rica *n* **Costa Rica** is a republic in Central America. کوستاریکا

cost of living *n* The **cost of living** is the average amount of money that people need to spend on food, housing, and clothing. گزربسر کی لاگت

costume (**costumes**) *n* An actor's or performer's **costume** is the set of clothes they wear while they are performing. پوشاک

cosy (**cosier, cosiest**) *adj* A **cosy** house or room is comfortable and warm. گرم اور آرام دہ
cot (**cots**) *n* A **cot** is a bed for a baby, with bars or panels round it so that the baby cannot fall out. پلنگڑی، کھٹولا
cottage (**cottages**) *n* A **cottage** is a small house, usually in the country. جھونپڑا
cottage cheese *n* **Cottage cheese** is a soft, white, lumpy cheese made from sour milk. کاٹج پنیر
cotton (**cottons**) *n* **Cotton** is a kind of cloth that is made from the **cotton** plant. سوتی ⊳ *n* **Cotton** is thread that you use to sew with. سوتی دھاگہ
cotton bud (**cotton buds**) *n* A *cotton bud* is a small stick with a ball of cotton wool at each end, which people use, for example, for applying make-up. کپاس لگی سلائی
cotton wool *n* **Cotton wool** is soft fluffy cotton, often used for applying creams to your skin. روئی
couch (**couches**) *n* A **couch** is a long soft piece of furniture for sitting or lying on. پلنگ
couchette (**couchettes**) *n* A **couchette** is a bed on a train or a boat which is either folded against the wall or used as an ordinary seat during the day. ریل یا جہاز کی نشست
cough (**coughs, coughing, coughed**) *n* A **cough** is an act, instance, or sound of coughing. کھانسی ⊳ *vi* When you **cough**, you force air out of your throat with a sudden, harsh noise. You often cough when you are ill, or when you are nervous or want to attract someone's attention. کھانسنا
cough mixture (**cough mixtures**) *n* **Cough mixture** is a liquid medicine that you take when you have a cough. کھانسی کا آمیزہ
could *v* If you say you **could** do something, you mean that you were able to do it. کر سکتا، کرنے کے قابل ہونا *I could see through the window.*
council (**councils**) *n* A **council** is a group of people elected to govern a town or other area. مجلس، کونسل
council house (**council houses**) *n* A **council house** is a house that is owned by a local council and that people can rent at a low cost. کونسل ہاؤس
councillor (**councillors**) *n* A **councillor** is a member of a local council. کونسلر
count (**counts, counting, counted**) *vi* When you **count**, you say numbers in order, one after the other. گنتی کرنا ⊳ *vt* When you **count** all the things in a group, you add them up to see how many there are. شمار کرنا، گنتی کرنا
counter (**counters**) *n* In a shop, a **counter** is a long flat surface at which customers are served. کاؤنٹر
count on *v* If you **count on** someone or something, you rely on them to support you. گنتے بانا *I can always count on you to cheer me up.*
country (**countries**) *n* A **country** is a part of the world with its own people and laws. ملک ⊳ *n* The **country** is land that is away from towns and cities. There are farms and woods in the **country**. دیہی علاقہ
countryside *n* The **countryside** is land away from towns and cities. مضافات
couple (**couples**) *n* A couple is two people who are married or who are having a romantic relationship. جوڑا ⊳ *det* A couple of people or things means two or around two of them. دو، ایک *Things should get better in a couple of days.*
courage *n* **Courage** is the quality shown by someone who does something difficult or dangerous, even though they may be afraid. ہمت
courageous *adj* Someone who is **courageous** does something difficult or dangerous, even though they may be afraid. ہمت ور
courgette (**courgettes**) *n* **Courgettes** are long thin green vegetables. کورجیٹ (سبزی)

courier (**couriers**) *n* A **courier** is a person who is paid to take letters and parcels direct from one place to another. کوریر

course (**courses**) *n* The **course** of a vehicle is the route along which it is travelling. نصاب

court (**courts**) *n* A **court** is a place where a judge and a group of people (= a jury) decide if someone has done something wrong. عدالت ▷ *n* A **court** is an area for playing a game such as tennis. کورٹ

courtyard (**courtyards**) *n* A **courtyard** is a flat open area of ground surrounded by buildings or walls. آنگن

cousin (**cousins**) *n* Your **cousin** is the child of your uncle or aunt. چچازاد بھائی یا بہن

cover (**covers, covering, covered**) *n* A **cover** is something that you put over another thing. خول، ڈھکن ▷ *vt* If you **cover** something, you put another thing over it. ڈھکنا

cover charge (**cover charges**) *n* A **cover charge** is a sum of money that you must pay in some restaurants and nightclubs in addition to the money that you pay there for your food and drink. کور چارج (ریستوراں میں)

cow (**cows**) *n* A **cow** is a large female animal kept on farms for its milk. گائے

coward (**cowards**) *n* A **coward** is someone who is easily frightened and avoids dangerous or difficult situations. بزدل

cowardly *adj* Someone who is **cowardly** is easily frightened and so avoids doing dangerous or difficult things. بزدلانہ

cowboy (**cowboys**) *n* A **cowboy** is a male character in a western. مغربی لوک کہانیوں کا کردار

crab (**crabs**) *n* A **crab** is a sea creature with a flat round body covered by a shell, and five pairs of legs with claws on the front pair. کیکڑا

crack (**cracks, cracking, cracked**) *n* A **crack** is a very narrow gap between two things. دراز ▷ *n* A **crack** is a line on the surface of something when it is slightly damaged. شگاف ▷ *v* If something **cracks** or if you **crack** it, it becomes damaged, and lines appear on the surface where it has broken. شگاف پڑنا

crack down on *v* If people in authority **crack down on** a group of people, they become stricter in making the group obey rules or laws. دھاوا بولنا، گرفت کرنا *The police are cracking down on motorists who drive too fast.*

cracked *adj* An object that is **cracked** has lines on its surface because it is damaged. شگاف دار

cracker (**crackers**) *n* A **cracker** is a thin crisp savoury biscuit. خستہ (بسکٹ)

cradle (**cradles**) *n* A **cradle** is a baby's bed with high sides. پالنا

craft (**craft**) *n* You can refer to a boat, a spacecraft, or an aircraft as a **craft**. جہاز

craftsman (**craftsmen**) *n* A **craftsman** is a man who makes things skilfully with his hands. دست کار

cram (**crams, cramming, crammed**) *v* If you **cram** things or people into a place, or if they **cram** it, there are so many of them in it at one time that it is completely full. ٹھونسنا

crammed *adj* If a place is **crammed** with things or people, it is very full of them. ٹھنسا ہوا

cranberry (**cranberries**) *n* **Cranberries** are red berries with a sour taste. They are often used to make a sauce or jelly that you eat with meat. کروندا

crane (**cranes**) *n* A **crane** is a large bird with a long neck and long legs. **Cranes** live near water. سارس، بگلا ▷ *n* A **crane** is a tall machine that can lift very heavy things. کرین

crash (**crashes, crashing, crashed**) *n* A **crash** is an accident when a vehicle hits something. ٹکر ▷ *vt* If you **crash** a moving vehicle, it hits something. ٹکرانا ▷ *vi* If a moving vehicle **crashes**, it hits something. ٹکرانا ▷ *n* A **crash** is a sudden, loud noise. تیز آواز

crawl (**crawls, crawling, crawled**) *vi* When you **crawl**, you move forward on your hands and knees. رینگنا

crayfish (**crayfish**) *n* A **crayfish** is a small shellfish with five pairs of legs which lives in rivers and streams. You can eat some types of crayfish. کرے مچھلی

crayon (**crayons**) *n* A **crayon** is a rod of coloured wax used for drawing. رنگین مومی پینسل

crazy (**crazier, craziest**) *adj* If you describe someone or something as **crazy**, you think they are very foolish or strange. (*informal*) جنونی

cream *adj* Something that is **cream** in colour is yellowish-white. کریم رنگ کا ▷ *n* **Cream** is a thick liquid that is produced from milk. You can use it in cooking or put it on fruit or puddings. بالائی

crease (**creases**) *n* **Creases** are lines that are made in cloth or paper when it is crushed or folded. سلوٹ

creased *adj* If something such as cloth or paper is **creased**, there are lines in it because it has been crushed or folded. سلوٹدار

create (**creates, creating, created**) *vt* To **create** something means to cause it to happen or exist. تخلیق کرنا

creation (**creations**) *n* The **creation** of something is the act of bringing it into existence. تخلیق

creative *adj* A **creative** person has the ability to invent and develop original ideas, especially in art. تخلیقی

creature (**creatures**) *n* You can refer to any living thing that is not a plant as a **creature**. جاندار

crèche (**crèches**) *n* A **crèche** is an establishment where preschool children are looked after in the daytime, enabling their parents to work full time. دارالصبیان

credentials *npl* Your **credentials** are your previous achievements, training, and general background, which indicate that you are qualified to do something. اسنادِ اعتبار

credible *adj* **Credible** means able to be trusted or believed. قابل اعتبار

credit *n* **Credit** is a system where you pay for goods or services several weeks or months after you have received them. ساکھ

credit card (**credit cards**) *n* A **credit card** is a plastic card that you use to buy goods on credit. کریڈٹ کارڈ

creep (**creeps, creeping, crept**) *vi* If you **creep** somewhere, you move in a very slow and quiet way. دھیرے دھیرے چلنا ▷ *vi* If an animal **creeps**, it moves along close to the ground. رینگنا

crematorium (**crematoria, crematoriums**) *n* A **crematorium** is a building in which the bodies of dead people are burned. شمشان

cress *n* **Cress** is a plant with small green leaves that are used in salads or to decorate food. بطور سلاد استعمال ہونے والا پودا

crew (**crews**) *n* The **crew** of a ship, an aircraft, or a spacecraft consists of the people who work on it and operate it. **Crew** can take the singular or plural form of the verb. عملہ

crew cut (**crew cuts**) *n* A **crew cut** is a man's hairstyle in which his hair is cut very short. بال چھوٹے تراشنے کا اسٹائل

cricket (**crickets**) *n* **Cricket** is a game where two teams take turns to hit a ball with a bat and run up and down. کرکٹ ▷ *n* A **cricket** is a small jumping insect that rubs its wings together to make a high sound. جھینگر

crime (**crimes**) *n* A **crime** is an illegal action or activity for which a person can be punished by law. جرم

criminal (**criminals**) *adj* **Criminal** means connected with crime. مجرمانہ ▷ *n* A **criminal** is a person who has committed a crime. مجرم

crisis (**crises**) *n* A **crisis** is a situation in which something or someone is affected by one or more very serious problems. بحران

crisp (**crisper, crispest**) *adj* **Crisp** food is pleasantly hard and crunchy. خستہ

crisps *npl* **Crisps** are very thin slices of fried potato that are eaten cold as a snack. آلو چپس

crispy (**crispier, crispiest**) *adj* Food that is **crispy** is pleasantly hard, or has a pleasantly hard surface. خستہ

criterion (**criteria**) *n* A **criterion** is a factor on which you judge or decide something. کسوٹی، معیار

critic (**critics**) *n* A **critic** is a person who writes reviews and expresses opinions about books, films, music, and art. نکتہ چیں، نقاد

critical *adj* A **critical** time or situation is extremely important. بحرانی

criticism (**criticisms**) *n* **Criticism** is the action of expressing disapproval of something or someone. نکتہ چینی

criticize (**criticizes, criticizing, criticized**) *vt* If you **criticize** someone or something, you express your disapproval of them by saying what you think is wrong with them. نکتہ چینی کرنا

Croatia *n* **Croatia** is a republic in south-east Europe. کروشیا

Croatian (**Croations**) *adj* **Croatian** means of, relating to, or characteristic of Croatia, its people, or their language. کروشیائی ▷ *n* A **Croatian** is a native or inhabitant of Croatia. کروشیائی ▷ *n* **Croatian** is the language that is spoken in Croatia. کروشیائی زبان

crochet (**crochets, crocheting, crocheted**) *v* If you **crochet**, you make cloth by using a needle with a small hook at the end. کروشیا

crocodile (**crocodiles**) *n* A **crocodile** is a large reptile with a long body. Crocodiles live in rivers. مگرمچھ

crocus (**crocuses**) *n* **Crocuses** are small white, yellow, or purple flowers that grow in the early spring. جنس زعفران، سوسنی جنس کا پھول

crook (**crooks**) *n* A **crook** is a criminal or a dishonest person. (*informal*) بے ایمان

crop (**crops**) *n* **Crops** are plants such as wheat and potatoes that are grown in large quantities for food. فصل

cross (**crosser, crossest, crosses, crossing, crossed**) *adj* If you are **cross**, you feel angry about something. غصہ ▷ *n* A **cross** is a mark that you write. It looks like **X** or +. صلیب ▷ *vt* If you **cross** something, you go from one side of it to the other. پار کرنا

cross-country *n* **Cross-country** is the sport of running, riding, or skiing across open countryside. کھلے میدانوں میں کھیل کود کا مقابلہ

crossing (**crossings**) *n* A **crossing** is a boat journey to the other side of a sea. ندی پار ناو کا سفر

cross out *v* If you **cross out** words, you draw a line through them. کاٹنا *He crossed out her name and added his own.*

crossroads (**crossroads**) *n* A **crossroads** is a place where two roads meet and cross. چوراہا

crossword (**crosswords**) *n* A **crossword** or a **crossword puzzle** is a word game in which you work out answers to clues, and write the answers in the white squares of a pattern of black and white squares. پہیلی

crouch down *v* If you **are crouching down**, your legs are bent under you so that you are close to the ground and leaning forward slightly. زمین بوس ہونا *He crouched down and reached under the mattress.*

crow (**crows**) *n* A **crow** is a large black bird which makes a loud harsh noise. کوا

crowd (**crowds**) *n* A **crowd** is a large group of people who have gathered together. بھیڑ

crowded *adj* A **crowded** place is full of people or things. بھیڑ بھاڑ

crown (**crowns**) *n* A **crown** is a circular ornament, usually made of gold and jewels, which a king or queen wears on their head at official ceremonies. تاج

crucial *adj* Something that is **crucial** is extremely important. فیصلہ کن

crucifix (**crucifixes**) *n* A **crucifix** is a cross with a figure of Christ on it. صلیب مع مسیح

crude (**cruder, crudest**) *adj* Something that is **crude** is simple and not sophisticated. خام

cruel (**crueller, cruellest**) *adj* Someone who is **cruel** deliberately causes pain or distress. ظالم

cruelty (**cruelties**) *n* **Cruelty** is behaviour that deliberately causes pain or distress to people or animals. ظالمانہ

cruise (**cruises**) *n* A **cruise** is a holiday spent on a ship or boat which visits a number of places. ناو یا جہاز پر چھٹی

crumb (**crumbs**) *n* **Crumbs** are tiny pieces that fall from bread, biscuits, or cake when you cut or eat them. روٹی کے پارچے

crush (**crushes, crushing, crushed**) *vt* To **crush** something means to press it very hard so that its shape is destroyed or so that it breaks into pieces. کچلنا

crutch (**crutches**) *n* A **crutch** is a stick which someone with an injured foot or leg uses to support them when walking. بیساکھی

cry (**cries, crying, cried**) *n* A **cry** is a loud sound that you make with your voice. چیخ ⊳ *vi* When you **cry**, tears come from your eyes. People **cry** when they are sad or hurt. رونا

crystal (**crystals**) *n* A **crystal** is a piece of a mineral that has formed naturally into a regular symmetrical shape. بلور

cub (**cubs**) *n* A **cub** is a young wild animal such as a lion, wolf, or bear. شیر کا بچہ

Cuba *n* **Cuba** is a republic and the largest island in the Caribbean, at the entrance to the Gulf of Mexico. کیوبا

Cuban (Cubans) *adj* **Cuban** means belonging or relating to Cuba, or to its people or culture. کیوبائی ⊳ *n* A **Cuban** is a Cuban citizen, or a person of Cuban origin. کیوبائی

cube (**cubes**) *n* A **cube** is a solid shape with six square surfaces which are all the same size. مکعب

cubic *adj* **Cubic** is used to express units of volume. مکعبی

cuckoo (**cuckoos**) *n* A **cuckoo** is a grey bird which makes an easily recognizable sound consisting of two quick notes. کوئل

cucumber (**cucumbers**) *n* A **cucumber** is a long dark green vegetable. کھیرا

cuddle (**cuddles, cuddling, cuddled**) *n* A **cuddle** is a close embrace, especially when prolonged. آغوش ⊳ *vt* If you **cuddle** someone, you put your arms round them and hold them close as a way of showing your affection. آغوش میں لینا

cue (**cues**) *n* A **cue** is something said or done by a performer that is a signal for another performer to begin speaking or to begin doing something. سراغ

cufflinks *npl* **Cufflinks** are small decorative objects used for holding together shirt cuffs around the wrist. کف لنک

culprit (**culprits**) *n* The person who committed a crime or did something wrong can be referred to as the **culprit**. بدمعاش

cultural *adj* **Cultural** means relating to the arts generally, or to the arts and customs of a particular society. ثقافتی

culture (**cultures**) *n* **Culture** consists of activities such as the art, music, literature, and theatre. تہذیب

cumin *n* **Cumin** is a sweet-smelling spice, and is popular in cooking. زیرہ

cunning *adj* A **cunning** person is clever and deceitful. عیار

cup (**cups**) *n* A **cup** is a small round container with a handle, which you drink from. پیالی

cupboard (**cupboards**) *n* A **cupboard** is a piece of furniture with doors at the front and usually shelves inside. الماری

curb (**curbs**) *n* A **curb** is something that restrains or holds something else back. رکاوٹ

cure (**cures, curing, cured**) *n* A **cure** for an illness is a medicine or other treatment that cures the illness. شفا ▷ *vt* If a doctor or a medical treatment **cures** someone, or **cures** their illness, they make the person well again. شفایاب ہونا

curfew (**curfews**) *n* A **curfew** is a law stating that people must stay inside their houses after a particular time at night. کرفیو

curious *adj* If you are **curious** about something, you are interested in it and want to learn more about it. متجسس

curl (**curls**) *n* **Curls** are lengths of hair shaped in curves and circles. خم

curler (**curlers**) *n* **Curlers** are small plastic or metal tubes that women roll their hair round in order to make it curly. چھلہ کار

curly (**curlier, curliest**) *adj* **Curly** hair is full of curls. خم دار

currant (**currants**) *n* **Currants** are small dried black grapes, used especially in cakes. کشمش

currency (**currencies**) *n* The money used in a country is referred to as its **currency**. کرنسی

current (**currents**) *adj* Something that is **current** is happening, being done, or being used at the present time. حالات حاضرہ ▷ *n* A **current** is a steady, continuous, flowing movement of water or air. بہاؤ ▷ *n* An electric **current** is electricity flowing through a wire or circuit. کرنٹ

current account (**current accounts**) *n* A **current account** is a bank account which you can take money out of at any time. چالو کھاتہ

current affairs *npl* **Current affairs** are political events and problems which are discussed in the media. موجودہ معاملات

currently *adv* **Currently** means at the present time. فی الحال

curriculum (**curriculums, curricula**) *n* A **curriculum** is all the different courses of study that are taught in a school, college, or university. نصاب

curriculum vitae *n* A **curriculum vitae** is a brief written account of your personal details, your education, and jobs you have had, which you send when you are applying for a job. The abbreviation 'CV' is also used. سوانحی خاکہ

curry (**curries**) *n* **Curry** is an Asian dish made with hot spices. کڑھی

curry powder (**curry powders**) *n* **Curry powder** is a powder made from a mixture of spices. It is used in cooking, especially when making curry. کڑھی سفوف

curse (**curses**) *n* A **curse** is rude or offensive language which someone uses, usually because they are angry. (*written*) بد دعا

cursor (**cursors**) *n* On a computer screen, the **cursor** is a small, movable shape which indicates where anything typed by the user will appear. کرسر (کمپیوٹر میں)

curtain (**curtains**) *n* **Curtains** are hanging pieces of material which you can pull across a window to keep light out or prevent people from looking in. پردہ

cushion (**cushions**) *n* A **cushion** is a fabric case filled with soft material, which you put on a seat to make it more comfortable. گدا

custard *n* **Custard** is a sweet yellow sauce made from milk and eggs or from milk and a powder. It is eaten with puddings. کسٹرڈ

custody *n* **Custody** is the legal right to look after a child, especially the right given to a child's father or mother when they get divorced. تحویل

custom (**customs**) *n* A **custom** is an activity, a way of behaving, or an

C

event which is usual or traditional in a particular society or in particular circumstances. رواج

customer (**customers**) *n* A **customer** is someone who buys goods or services, especially from a shop. خریدار، صارف

customized *adj* Something that is **customized** has had its appearance or features changed to suit someone's tastes or needs. حسب ضرورت

customs *npl* **Customs** is the official organization responsible for collecting taxes on goods coming into a country and preventing illegal goods from being brought in. محکمہ کسٹم

customs officer (**customs officers**) *n* A **customs officer** is a person who works for the official organization responsible for collecting taxes on goods coming into a country and preventing illegal goods from being brought in. کسٹم آفیسر

cut (**cuts, cutting**) *n* A **cut** is a place on your skin where something sharp has gone through it. کٹنے کا زخم ▷ *v* If you **cut** something, you use a knife or scissors to divide it into pieces. کاٹنا ▷ *vt* If you **cut** yourself, something sharp goes through your skin and blood comes out. کاٹ لینا

cutback (**cutbacks**) *n* A **cutback** is a reduction in something. کٹوتی

cut down *v* If you **cut down** on something, you use or do less of it. کمی کرنا *He cut down on coffee.*

cute (**cuter, cutest**) *adj* **Cute** means pretty or attractive. (*informal*) پیارا

cutlery *n* The knives, forks, and spoons that you eat with are referred to as **cutlery**. چھری چمچ کانٹے

cutlet (**cutlets**) *n* A **cutlet** is a small piece of meat which is usually fried or grilled. کباب

cut off *v* If you **cut** something **off**, you remove it with a knife or a similar tool. کاٹ پھینکنا *She cut off a large piece of meat.*

cutting (**cuttings**) *n* A **cutting** is a piece of writing cut from a newspaper or magazine. تراشہ (اخبار کا)

cut up *v* If you **cut** something **up**, you cut it into several pieces. ٹکڑے کاٹنا *Halve the tomatoes, then cut them up.*

CV (**CVs**) *abbr* Your **CV** is a brief written account of your personal details, your education, and jobs you have had, which you send when you are applying for a job. **CV** is an abbreviation for 'curriculum vitae'. سوانحی خاکہ

cybercafé (**cybercafés**) *n* A **cybercafé** is a café where people can pay to use the Internet. سائبر کیفے

cybercrime *n* **Cybercrime** is the illegal use of computers and the Internet. سائبر جرائم

cycle (**cycles, cycling, cycled**) *n* A **cycle** is a bicycle. بائیسکل (دو پہیہ) ▷ *n* A **cycle** is a series of events or processes that is continually repeated, always in the same order. دور ▷ *vi* If you **cycle**, you ride a bicycle. سائکل چلانا

cycle lane (**cycle lanes**) *n* A **cycle lane** is a part of a road or path that only bicycles are allowed to use. سڑک کا حصہ صرف سائکلوں کے لئے

cycle path (**cycle paths**) *n* A **cycle path** is a special path on which people can travel by bicycle separately from motor vehicles. سائکل کا راستہ

cycling *n* **Cycling** is the action of riding a cycle. سائکل کی سواری

cyclist (**cyclists**) *n* A **cyclist** is someone who rides a bicycle. سائکل سوار

cyclone (**cyclones**) *n* A **cyclone** is a violent tropical storm. گردابی طوفان

cylinder (**cylinders**) *n* A **cylinder** is a shape or container with flat circular ends and long straight sides. سلنڈر

cymbals (**cymbals**) *npl* **Cymbals** are flat circular brass objects that are used as musical instruments. You hit two cymbals together to make a loud noise. جھانج مجیرے

Cypriot (**Cypriots**) *adj* **Cypriot** means belonging or relating to Cyprus, or to its people or culture. قبرص سے متعلق ⊳ *n* A **Cypriot** is a Cypriot citizen, or a person of Cypriot origin. قبرص کا باشندہ

Cyprus *n* **Cyprus** is an island in the East Mediterranean. قبرص

cyst (**cysts**) *n* A **cyst** is a growth containing liquid that appears inside your body or under your skin. گانٹھ

cystitis *n* **Cystitis** is a bladder infection. مثانے کی سوزش

Czech (**Czechs**) *adj* **Czech** means belonging or relating to the Czech Republic, or to its people, language, or culture. چیکوسلواکیا سے متعلق ⊳ *n* A **Czech** is a person who comes from the Czech Republic. چیک باشندہ ⊳ *n* **Czech** is the language spoken in the Czech Republic. چیک زبان

Czech Republic *n* The **Czech Republic** is a country in central Europe. چیک جمہوریہ

d

dad (**dads**) *n* Your **dad** is your father. You can call your dad 'Dad'. (*informal*) ابا

daddy (**daddies**) *n* Children often call their father **daddy**. (*informal*) ابا

daffodil (**daffodils**) *n* A **daffodil** is a yellow flower that blooms in the spring. نرگس

daft (**dafter, daftest**) *adj* **Daft** means stupid and not sensible. بے وقوفانہ

daily *adj* (**Daily**) means of or occurring every day or every weekday. روزانہ ⊳ *adv* If something happens **daily**, it happens every day. روزانہ

dairy (**dairies**) *n* A **dairy** is a shop or company that sells milk, butter, and cheese. ڈیری

dairy produce *n* **Dairy produce** is foods such as butter and cheese that are made from milk. ڈیری مصنوع

dairy products *npl* **Dairy products** are foods such as butter and cheese that are made from milk. ڈیری مصنوعات

daisy (**daisies**) *n* A **daisy** is a small wild flower with a yellow centre and white petals. گل داؤدی

dam (**dams**) *n* A **dam** is a wall built across a river to stop the flow of the water and make a lake. باندھ

damage (**damages, damaging, damaged**) *n* **Damage** is injury or harm that is caused to something. نقصان ⊳ *vt*

If you **damage** something, you injure or harm it. نقصان کرنا
damp (**damper, dampest**) *adj* **Damp** means slightly wet. نم
dance (**dances, dancing, danced**) *n* A **dance** is a series of steps and rhythmic movements which you do to music. It is also a piece of music which people can dance to. رقص ▷ *vi* When you **dance**, you move around in time to music. رقص کرنا
dancer (**dancers**) *n* A **dancer** is a person who is dancing, or who earns money by dancing. رقاص
dancing *n* When people dance for enjoyment or to entertain others, you can refer to this activity as **dancing**. رقص
dandelion (dandelions) *n* A **dandelion** is a wild plant which has yellow flowers first, then a fluffy ball of seeds. شیر دندان
dandruff *n* **Dandruff** is small white pieces of dead skin in someone's hair, or fallen from someone's hair. روسی
Dane (Danes)*n* A **Dane** is a person who comes from Denmark. ڈنمارکی
danger *n* **Danger** is the possibility that someone may be harmed or killed. خطرہ
dangerous *adj* If something is **dangerous**, it may hurt or harm you. خطرناک
Danish *adj* **Danish** means relating to or belonging to Denmark, or to its people, language, or culture. ڈینش ▷ *n* **Danish** is the language spoken in Denmark. ڈینش
dare (**dares, daring, dared**) *vt* If you **dare** to do something, you are brave enough to do it. ہمت کرنا *Most people don't dare to argue with him.*
daring *adj* A **daring** person does things which might be dangerous or shocking. ہمتی
dark (**darker, darkest**) *adj* When it is **dark**, there is no light or not much light. اندھیرا ▷ *n* The **dark** is the lack of light in a place. اندھیرا ▷ *adj* A **dark** colour is not pale. گہرا
darkness *n* **Darkness** is the lack of light in a place. اندھیرا
darling (**darlings**) *n* You call someone **darling** if you love them or like them very much. پیاری
dart (darts) *n* A **dart** is a small, narrow object with a sharp point which you can throw or shoot. ڈارٹ
darts *npl* **Darts** is a game in which you throw darts at a round board with numbers on it. ڈارٹ شوٹنگ
dash (**dashes, dashing, dashed**) *vi* If you **dash** somewhere, you run or go there quickly and suddenly. وارد ہونا
dashboard (**dashboards**) *n* The **dashboard** in a car is the panel facing the driver's seat where most of the instruments and switches are. ڈیش بورڈ
data *npl* You can talk about information as **data**, especially when it is in the form of facts or numbers. مفروضات
database (**databases**) *n* A **database** is a collection of data stored in a computer in a way that makes it easy to obtain. ڈاٹابیس
date (**dates**) *n* A date is a particular day or year, for example 7th June 2010, or 1066. تاریخ
daughter daughters *n* Your **daughter** is your female child. بیٹی
daughter-in-law (**daughters-in-law**) *n* Your **daughter-in-law** is the wife of your son. بہو
dawn (**dawns**) *n* **Dawn** is the time of day when light first appears in the sky, before the sun rises. طلوع
day (**days**) *n* A **day** is the length of time between one midnight and the next. There are twenty-four hours in a **day**, and seven **days** in a week. روز، دن ▷ *n* **Day** is the time when there is light outside. دن
day return (**day returns**) *n* A **day return** is a train or bus ticket which allows you to go somewhere and come back on

the same day for a lower price than an ordinary return ticket. واپسی ٹکٹ
daytime *n* **Daytime** is the part of a day when it is light. دن کا وقت
dead *adj* A person, animal, or plant that is **dead** is no longer living. مردہ ▷ *adv* **Dead** means 'precisely' or 'exactly'. دقیق
dead end (**dead ends**) *n* If a street is a **dead end**, there is no way out at one end of it. بند سرا
deadline (**deadlines**) *n* A **deadline** is a time or date before which a particular task must be finished or a particular thing must be done. مقررہ وقت
deaf (**deafer, deafest**) *adj* Someone who is **deaf** is unable to hear anything or is unable to hear very well. بہرا
deafening *adj* A **deafening** noise is a very loud noise. بہرہ کرنے والی آواز
deal (**deals, dealing, dealt**) *n* If you make a **deal**, you agree to do something with somebody. معاہدہ ▷ *v* If you **deal** playing cards, you give them out to the players in a game of cards. بانٹنا، تقسیم کرنا
dealer (**dealers**) *n* A **dealer** is a person whose business involves buying and selling things. سوداگر
deal with *v* When you **deal with** a situation or problem, you do what is necessary to achieve the result you want. نپٹنا *How do you deal with an uninvited guest?*
dear (**dearer, dearest**) *adj* You use **dear** to describe someone or something that you feel affection for. عزیز ▷ *adj* Something that is **dear** costs a lot of money. (*informal*) قیمتی، مہنگی
death (**deaths**) *n* **Death** is the end of the life of a person or animal. موت
debate (**debates, debating, debated**) *n* A **debate** is a discussion about a subject on which people have different views. بحث ▷ *vt* When people **debate** a topic, they discuss it fairly formally, putting forward different views. You can also say that one person **debates** a topic with another person. بحث کرنا
debit (**debits, debiting, debited**) *n* A **debit** is a record of the money taken from your bank account. کسی کھاتے سے نکالی رقم کا اندراج ▷ *vt* When your bank **debits** your account, money is taken from it and paid to someone else. ادھار کھاتے میں اندراج کرنا
debit card (**debit cards**) *n* A **debit card** is a bank card that you can use to pay for things. When you use it, the money is taken out of your bank account immediately. ڈیبٹ کارڈ
debt (**debts**) *n* A **debt** is a sum of money that you owe someone. قرض
decade (**decades**) *n* A **decade** is a period of ten years, especially one that begins with a year ending in 0, for example 2000 to 2009. دہائی
decaffeinated coffee (**decaffeinated coffees**) *n* **Decaffeinated coffee** has had most of the caffeine removed from it. کیفین نکالی ہوئی کافی
decay (**decays, decaying, decayed**) *vi* When something such as a dead body, a dead plant, or a tooth **decays**, it is gradually destroyed by a natural process. سڑنا
deceive (**deceives, deceiving, deceived**) *vt* If you **deceive** someone, you make them believe something that is not true. دھوکہ دینا
December (**Decembers**) *n* **December** is the twelfth and last month of the year in the Western calendar. دسمبر
decent *adj* **Decent** means acceptable in standard or quality. شائستہ
decide (**decides, deciding, decided**) *vt* If you **decide** to do something, you choose to do it. فیصلہ کرنا
decimal *adj* A **decimal** system involves counting in units of ten. اعشاریہ
decision (**decisions**) *n* When you make a **decision**, you choose what should be done or which is the best of various alternatives. فیصلہ
decisive *adj* If a fact, action, or event is

d

decisive, it makes it certain that there will be a particular result. فیصلہ کن

deck (**decks**) *n* A **deck** on a bus or ship is a downstairs or upstairs area. عرشہ

deckchair (**deckchairs**) *n* A **deckchair** is a simple chair with a folding frame, and a piece of canvas as the seat and back. Deckchairs are usually used on the beach, on a ship, or in the garden. عرشہ پر رکھی کرسی

declare (**declares, declaring, declared**) *vt* If you **declare** that something is the case, you say that it is true in a firm, deliberate way. (*written*) اعلان کرنا

decorate (**decorates, decorating, decorated**) *vt* If you **decorate** something, you make it more attractive by adding things to it. سجانا

decorator decorators *n* A **decorator** is a person whose job is to paint houses or put wallpaper up. سجانے والا

decrease (**decreases, decreasing, decreased**) *n* A **decrease** is a reduction in the quantity or size of something. تخفیف ▷ *v* When something **decreases**, or when you **decrease** it, it becomes less in quantity, size, or intensity. گھٹنا

dedicated *adj* If you describe a person as **dedicated**, you mean that they are devoted to a particular purpose or cause. وقف

dedication *n* **Dedication** is the state of being devoted to a particular purpose or cause. وقف

deduct (**deducts, deducting, deducted**) *vt* When you **deduct** an amount from a total, you subtract it from the total. منفی کرنا

deep (**deeper, deepest**) *adj* If something is **deep**, it extends a long way down from the ground or from the top surface of something. گہرا

deep-fry (**deep-fries, deep-frying, deep-fried**) *vt* If you **deep-fry** food, you fry it in a large amount of fat or oil. خوب تلنا

deeply *adv* **Deeply** means seriously, strongly, or to a great degree. گہرائی سے

deer (**deer**) *n* A **deer** is a large wild animal. Male deer usually have large, branching horns. ہرن

defeat (**defeats, defeating, defeated**) *n* **Defeat** is the state of being beaten in a battle, game, or contest, or of failing to achieve what you wanted to. شکست ▷ *vt* If you **defeat** someone, you win a victory over them in a battle or contest. ہرانا

defect (**defects**) *n* A **defect** is a fault or imperfection in a person or thing. نقص

defence *n* **Defence** is action taken to protect someone or something from attack. دفاع

defend (**defends, defending, defended**) *vt* If you **defend** someone or something, you take action to protect them. دفاع کرنا

defendant (**defendants**) *n* The **defendant** in a trial is the person accused of a crime. مدعی

defender (**defenders**) *n* If you are a **defender** of a particular thing or person that has been criticized or attacked, you support that thing or person in public. مدعا علیہ، حامی

deficit (**deficits**) *n* A **deficit** is the amount by which something is less than the amount that is needed. گھاٹا

define (**defines, defining, defined**) *vt* If you **define** something, you say exactly what it is or exactly what it means. تعریف کرنا

definite *adj* If something is **definite**, it is firm and clear, and unlikely to be changed. یقینی

definitely *adv* You use **definitely** to emphasize that something is the case and will not change. یقیناً

definition (**definitions**) *n* A **definition** of a word or term is a statement giving its meaning, especially in a dictionary. تعریف

degree (**degrees**) *n* You use **degree** to indicate the extent to which something happens or is the case. درجہ، ڈگری

degree Celsius (**degrees Celsius**) *n* A

degree Celsius is a unit of measurement on the Celsius scale that is used to measure temperatures. ڈگری سیلسیس، حرارت ناپنے کا پیمانہ

degree centigrade (**degrees centigrade**) *n* A **degree centigrade** is a unit of measurement on the centigrade scale that is used to measure temperatures. ڈگری سینٹی گریڈ

degree Fahrenheit (**degrees Fahrenheit**) *n* A **degree Fahrenheit** is a unit of measurement on the Fahrenheit scale that is used to measure temperatures. ڈگری فارن ہائٹ

dehydrated *adj* When something such as food is **dehydrated**, all the water is removed from it, often in order to preserve it. بے آب

delay (**delays, delaying, delayed**) *n* If there is a **delay**, something does not happen until later than planned or expected. تاخیر ▷ vt If you **delay** doing something, you do not do it until a later time. تاخیر کرنا

delayed *adj* If a person or thing is **delayed**, they are made late. متاخر

delegate (**delegates, delegating, delegated**) *n* A **delegate** is a person chosen to vote or make decisions on behalf of a group of people, especially at a conference or meeting. مندوب، ڈیلیگیٹ ▷ *vt* If you **delegate** duties, responsibilities, or power to someone, you give them those duties or responsibilities or that power, so that they can act on your behalf. مندوب بنانا، اختیار دینا

delete (**deletes, deleting, deleted**) *vt* If you **delete** something that has been written down or stored in a computer, you cross it out or remove it. مٹانا

deliberate *adj* If something that you do is **deliberate**, you intended to do it. ارادتاً

deliberately *adv* If you do something **deliberately**, you intended to do it. ارادی طور پر

delicate *adj* Something that is **delicate** is small and beautifully shaped. نازک

delicatessen (**delicatessens**) *n* A **delicatessen** is a shop that sells unusual or foreign foods. انوکھے کھانوں کی دوکان

delicious *adj* **Delicious** food or drink has an extremely pleasant taste. لذیذ

delight *n* **Delight** is a feeling of very great pleasure. سرور

delighted *adj* If you are **delighted**, you are extremely pleased and excited about something. مسرور

delightful *adj* Someone or something that is **delightful** is very pleasant. مسرور کن

deliver (**delivers, delivering, delivered**) *vt* If you **deliver** something somewhere, you take it there. سونپنا

delivery (**deliveries**) *n* **Delivery** is the act of bringing of letters, parcels, or goods to someone's house or office. سپردگی

demand (**demands, demanding, demanded**) *n* A **demand** is a firm request for something. مطالبہ ▷ *vt* If you **demand** something such as information or action, you ask for it in a very forceful way. مطالبہ کرنا

demanding *adj* A **demanding** job requires a lot of time, energy, or attention. وقت طلب

demo (**demos**) *n* A **demo** is a march or gathering by a group of people to show their opposition to something or their support for something. (*Informal*) نمائش

democracy *n* **Democracy** is a political system in which people choose their government by voting for them in elections. جمہوریت

democratic *adj* A **democratic** country, organization, or system is governed by representatives who are elected by the people. جمہوری

demolish (**demolishes, demolishing, demolished**) *vt* When a building is **demolished**, it is knocked down, often because it is old or dangerous. منہدم کرنا

d

demonstrate (**demonstrates, demonstrating, demonstrated**) *vt* To **demonstrate** a fact or theory means to make it clear to people. مظاہرہ کرنا

demonstration (**demonstrations**) *n* A **demonstration** of something is the act of making it clear to people. مظاہرہ

demonstrator (**demonstrators**) *n* **Demonstrators** are people who are marching or gathering somewhere to show their opposition to something or their support for something. مظاہرین

denim *n* **Denim** is a thick cotton cloth used to make clothes. Jeans are made from denim. ڈینم (جینس کا کپڑا)

denims *npl* **Denims** are casual trousers made of denim. ڈینم پتلون

Denmark *n* **Denmark** is a kingdom in north Europe, between the Baltic and the North Sea. ڈنمارک

dense (**denser, densest**) *adj* Something that is **dense** contains a lot of things or people in relation to its size. گھنا

density (**densities**) *n* The **density** of something is the extent to which it fills a place. گھناپن

dent (**dents, denting, dented**) *n* A **dent** is a hollow in the surface of something which has been caused by hitting or pressing it. کھڈا ▷ *vt* If you **dent** something, you damage it by hitting or pressing it, causing a hollow dip to form in it. کھڈا کرنا

dental *adj* **Dental** is used to describe things relating to teeth. دندانی

dental floss *n* **Dental floss** is a type of thread that is used to clean the gaps between your teeth. دندانی ریشمی دھاگہ

dentist (dentists) *n* A **dentist** is a person qualified to treat people's teeth. معالج دندان

dentures *npl* **Dentures** are artificial teeth. نقلی دانت

deny (**denies, denying, denied**) *vt* If you **deny** something, you say that it is not true. انکار کرنا

deodorant (**deodorants**) *n* **Deodorant** is a substance that you put on your body to reduce or hide the smell of perspiration. ڈیوڈرینٹ

depart (**departs, departing, departed**) *vi* To **depart** from a place means to leave it and start a journey to another place. روانہ ہونا

department (**departments**) *n* A **department** is one of the sections of a large shop or organization such as a university. شعبہ

department store (**department stores**) *n* A **department store** is a large shop which sells many different kinds of goods. بڑی دوکان

departure (**departures**) *n* **Departure** is the act of leaving a place or a job. روانگی

departure lounge (**departure lounges**) *n* In an airport, the **departure lounge** is the place where passengers wait before they get onto their plane. مقام انتظار (روانگی سے پہلے)

depend (**depends, depending, depended**) *vi* If you say that one thing **depends** on another, you mean that the first thing will be affected or decided by the second. منحصر ہونا

deport (**deports, deporting, deported**) *vt* If a government **deports** someone, it sends them out of the country. ملک بدر کرنا

deposit (**deposits**) *n* A **deposit** is a sum of money given as part payment for something, or as security when you rent something. ضمانتی رقم

depressed *adj* If you are **depressed**, you are sad and feel you cannot enjoy anything, because your situation is difficult and unpleasant. افسردہ

depressing *adj* Something that is **depressing** makes you feel sad and disappointed. افسردہ کن

depression depressions *n* **Depression** is a mental state in which someone feels unhappy and has no energy or enthusiasm. افسردگی

depth (**depths**) *n* The **depth** of something such as a hole is the distance between its top and bottom surfaces. گہرائی

deputy head (**deputy heads**) *n* The **deputy head** of a school is the second most important person after the head teacher. ڈپٹی سربراہ

descend (**descends, descending, descended**) *v* If you **descend**, or if you **descend** something, you move downwards. (*formal*) اترنا

describe (**describes, describing, described**) *vt* If you **describe** someone or something, you say what they are like. بیان کرنا

description (**descriptions**) *n* A **description** of someone or something is a statement which explains what they are or what they look like. بیان، حلیہ

desert (**deserts**) *n* A **desert** is a large area of land, usually in a hot region, which has almost no water, rain, trees, or plants. ریگستان

desert island (**desert islands**) *n* A **desert island** is a small tropical island, where nobody lives. ویران جزیرہ

deserve (**deserves, deserving, deserved**) *vt* If you say that someone **deserves** something, you mean that they should have it or do it because of their qualities or actions. مستحق ہونا

design (**designs, designing, designed**) n **Design** is the process and art of planning and making detailed drawings of something. نقشہ ▷ *vt* When someone **designs** a garment, building, machine, or other object, they plan it and make a detailed drawing of it from which it can be built or made. ڈیزائن کرنا

designer (**designers**) *n* A **designer** is a person whose job involves planning the form of a new object. نقشہ بنانے والا

desire (**desires, desiring, desired**) *n* A **desire** is a strong wish to do or have something. خواہش ▷ vt If you **desire** something, you want it. خواہش کرنا

desk (desks) *n* A **desk** is a table which you sit at in order to write or work. لکھنے کی میز

despair *n* **Despair** is the feeling that everything is wrong and that nothing will improve. پریشانی

desperate *adj* If you are **desperate**, you are in such a bad situation that you will try anything to change it. پریشان

desperately *adv* If you do something **desperately**, you are in such a bad situation that you are willing to try anything to achieve it. پریشانی میں

despise (**despises, despising, despised**) *vt* If you **despise** someone or something, you hate them very much. نفرت کرنا

despite (**prep**) If you say that one thing is true **despite** another thing, it's a surprise to you that the first thing is true. باوجود *The party was fun, despite the rain.*

dessert (**desserts**) *n* **Dessert** is something sweet, such as fruit or a pudding, that you eat at the end of a meal. بعد طعام میٹھا

dessert spoon (**dessert spoons**) *n* A **dessert spoon** is a spoon which is midway between the size of a teaspoon and a tablespoon. You use it to eat desserts. میٹھا کھانے کا چمچ

destination (**destinations**) *n* Your **destination** is the place you are going to. منزل

destiny (**destinies**) *n* A person's **destiny** is everything that happens to them during their life, including what will happen in the future. تقدیر

destroy (**destroys, destroying, destroyed**) *vt* To **destroy** something means to cause so much damage to it that it is completely ruined or does not exist any more. برباد کرنا

destruction *n* **Destruction** is the act of destroying something, or the state of being destroyed. تخریب

detached house (**detached houses**) *n* A

detached house is one that is not joined to any other house. غیر متصل گھر

detail (**details**) *n* The **details** of something are its small, individual features or elements. If you examine or discuss something **in detail**, you examine all these features. تفصیل

detailed *adj* A **detailed** report or plan contains a lot of details. مفصل

detective (**detectives**) *n* A **detective** is someone whose job is to discover the facts about a crime or other situation. سراغ رساں

detention (**detentions**) *n* **Detention** is the arrest or imprisonment of someone, especially for political reasons. گرفتاری

detergent (detergents) *n* **Detergent** is a chemical substance used for washing things such as clothes or dishes. ڈٹرجنٹ، کپڑے صاف کرنے کا مادہ

deteriorate (**deteriorates, deteriorating, deteriorated**) *vi* If something **deteriorates**, it becomes worse. ابتر ہونا

determined *adj* If you are **determined** to do something, you have made a firm decision to do it and will not let anything stop you. ثابت قدم

detour (**detours**) *n* If you make a **detour** on a journey, you go by a route which is not the shortest way. لمبا راستہ

devaluation (**devaluations**) *n* **Devaluation** is an official reduction in the value of a currency. گراوٹ

devastated *adj* If you are **devastated** by something, you are very shocked and upset by it. تباہ

devastating *adj* You describe something as **devastating** when it is very damaging or upsetting. تباہ کن

develop (**develops, developing, developed**) *vt* When someone **develops** something, the thing grows or changes over a period of time and usually becomes more advanced or complete. فروغ دینا ▷ *vi* When someone or something **develops**, the person or thing grows or changes over a period of time and usually becomes more advanced or complete. نشو نما پا

developing country (**developing countries**) *n* A **developing country** is a poor country that does not have many industries. ترقی پذیر ملک

development *n* **Development** is the gradual growth or formation of something. ترقی

device (**devices**) *n* A **device** is an object that has been made for a particular purpose. آلہ

Devil *n* In Christianity, Judaism, and Islam, the **Devil** is the most powerful evil spirit. شیطان

devise (**devises, devising, devised**) *vt* If you **devise** something, you have the idea for it and design it. وضع کرنا

devoted *adj* If you are **devoted** to someone or something, you care about them or love them very much. نہایت وفادار

diabetes *n* **Diabetes** is a condition in which someone's body is unable to control the level of sugar in their blood. ذیابیطس

diabetic (**diabetics**) *adj* **Diabetic** means of, relating to, or having diabetes. ذیابیطس سے متعلق ▷ *n* A **diabetic** is a person who suffers from diabetes. ذیابیطس کا مریض

diagnosis (**diagnoses**) *n* **Diagnosis** is identifying what is wrong with someone who is ill or with something that is not working properly. تشخیص

diagonal *adj* A **diagonal** line or movement goes in a slanting direction. وتری

diagram (**diagrams**) *n* A **diagram** is a drawing which is used to explain something. خاکہ

dial (**dials, dialling, dialled**) *v* If you **dial**, or if you **dial** a number, you turn the dial or press the buttons on a telephone. ڈائیل کرنا

dialect (**dialects**) *n* A **dialect** is a form of a language spoken in a particular area. لہجہ

dialling code (**dialling codes**) *n* A **dialling code** for a particular city or region is the series of numbers that you have to dial before a particular telephone number if you are making a call to that place from a different area. ڈائل کوڈ

dialling tone (dialling tones) *n* The **dialling tone** is the noise which you hear when you pick up a telephone receiver and which means that you can dial the number you want. ڈائل ٹون

dialogue (**dialogues**) *n* **Dialogue** is communication or discussion between people or groups. مکالمہ

diameter (**diameters**) *n* The **diameter** of a circle or sphere is the length of a straight line through the middle of it. قطر

diamond (**diamonds**) *n* A **diamond** is a kind of jewel that is hard, clear, and shiny. ہیرا ▷ *n* A **diamond** is a shape with four straight sides. چوکور

diarrhoea *n* When someone has **diarrhoea**, a lot of liquid waste material comes out of their bowels because they are ill. اسہال، دست

diary (**diaries**) *n* A **diary** is a notebook with a separate space for each day of the year. روزنامچہ

dice (**dice, die**) *npl* **Dice** are small cubes with one to six spots on each face, used in games. پانسہ

dictation *n* **Dictation** is the speaking or reading aloud of words for someone else to write down. املا

dictator (**dictators**) *n* A **dictator** is a ruler who has complete power in a country; used showing disapproval. آمر

dictionary (**dictionaries**) *n* A **dictionary** is a book in which the words and phrases of a language are listed, usually in alphabetical order, together with their meanings or their translations in another language. لغت

die (**dies, dying, died**) *vi* When people, animals, or plants **die**, they stop living. مرنا

diet (**diets, dieting, dieted**) *n* Your **diet** is the type and range of food that you regularly eat. غذا ▷ *vi* If you are **dieting**, you eat special kinds of food or you eat less food than usual because you are trying to lose weight. مخصوص غذا کھانا

difference (**differences**) *n* The **difference** between things is the way in which they are different from each other. فرق

different *adj* If two things are **different**, they are not like each other. مختلف

difficult *adj* If something is **difficult**, it is not easy to do or to understand. مشکل

difficulty (**difficulties**) *n* A **difficulty** is a problem. دشواری

dig (**digs, digging, dug**) *v* When people or animals **dig**, they make a hole in the ground or in a pile of stones or debris. کھودنا

digest (**digests, digesting, digested**) *v* When food **digests** or when you **digest** it, it passes through your body to your stomach. Your stomach removes the substances that your body needs and gets rid of the rest. ہضم ہونا

digestion *n* **Digestion** is the process of digesting food. ہاضمہ

digger (**diggers**) *n* A **digger** is a machine that is used for digging. کھودنے والی مشین

digital *adj* **Digital** systems record or transmit information in the form of thousands of very small signals. ہندسی، ڈیجیٹل

d

digital camera (**digital cameras**) *n* A **digital camera** is a camera that produces digital images that can be stored on a computer. ڈیجیٹل کیمرا

digital radio *n* **Digital radio** is radio in which the signals are transmitted in digital form and decoded by the radio receiver. ڈیجیٹل ریڈیو

digital television *n* **Digital television** is television in which the signals are transmitted in digital form and decoded by the television receiver. ڈیجیٹل ٹیلیویژن

digital watch (**digital watches**) *n* A **digital watch** gives information by displaying numbers rather than by having a pointer which moves round a dial. ڈیجیٹل گھڑی

dignity *n* If someone behaves with **dignity**, they are serious, calm, and controlled. وقار

dilemma (**dilemmas**) *n*A **dilemma** is a difficult situation in which you have to choose between two or more alternatives. مشکل صورت حال

dilute (**dilutes, diluting, diluted**) *v* If a liquid is **diluted**, it is mixed with water or another liquid, and becomes weaker. رقیق بنانا ▷ *adj* A **dilute** liquid is very thin and weak, usually because it has had water added to it. رقیق کردہ

dim (**dimmer, dimmest**) *adj* **Dim** light is not bright. You can also say that something is **dim** when the light is not bright enough to see very well. مدھم

dimension (**dimensions**) *n* A particular **dimension** of something is a particular aspect of it. بعد

diminish (**diminishes, diminishing, diminished**) *v* When something **diminishes**, its importance, size, or intensity is reduced. گھٹنا

din *n* A **din** is a very loud and unpleasant noise that lasts for some time. تیز شور

diner (**diners**) *n* A **diner** is a small cheap restaurant that is open all day. US سستا ریستراں

dinghy (**dinghies**) *n* A **dinghy** is a small boat that you sail or row. چھوٹی ناو

dining car (**dining cars**) *n* A **dining car** is a carriage on a train where passengers can have a meal. ڈائننگ کار

dining room (**dining rooms**) *n* The **dining room** is the room in a house or hotel where people have their meals. کمرۂ طعام

dinner (**dinners**) *n* **Dinner** is the main meal of the day, eaten in the evening. عشائیہ

dinner jacket (**dinner jackets**) *n* A **dinner jacket** is a jacket, usually black, worn by men for formal social events. ڈنر جیکٹ

dinner party (**dinner parties**) *n* A **dinner party** is a social event where a small group of people are invited to have dinner and spend the evening at someone's house. عشائیہ تقریب

dinner time *n* **Dinner time** is the period of the day when most people have their main meal of the day, usually in the evening. وقت عشائیہ

dinosaur (dinosaurs) *n* **Dinosaurs** were large reptiles which lived in prehistoric times. ڈائناسور

dip (**dips, dipping, dipped**) *n* A **dip** is a thick creamy sauce. You dip pieces of raw vegetable or biscuits into the sauce and then eat them. غوطی ساس ▷ *vt* If you **dip** something into a liquid, you put it in and then quickly take it out again. ڈبونا

diploma (**diplomas**) *n* A **diploma** is a qualification which may be awarded to a student by a university, college, or high school. ڈپلوما

diplomat (diplomats) *n* A **diplomat** is a senior official, usually based at an embassy, who negotiates with another country on behalf of his or her own country. سفیر

diplomatic *adj* **Diplomatic** means relating to diplomacy and diplomats. سفارتی

dipstick (dipsticks) *n* A **dipstick** is a metal rod with marks along one end. It is used to measure the amount of liquid in a container, especially the amount of oil in a car engine. سطح ناپکار

direct (**directs, directing, directed**) *adj* **Direct** means moving towards a place or object, without changing direction and without stopping, for example in a journey. براہ راست ▷ *vt* If you **direct** something at a particular thing, you aim or point it at that thing. رخ کرنا

direct debit (**direct debits**) *n* If you pay a bill by **direct debit**, you give permission for the company who is owed money to transfer the correct amount from your bank account into theirs, usually every month. براہ راست نکاسی

direction (**directions**) *n* A **direction** is the way that you go to get to a place. سمت

directions *npl* **Directions** are words or pictures that show you how to do something, or how to get somewhere. ہدایت

directly *adv* If you go somewhere **directly**, you go there without changing direction and without stopping. بلا رکاوٹ

director (**directors**) *n* The **director** of a play, film, or television programme is the person who decides how it will appear on stage or screen, and who tells the actors and technical staff what to do. ہدایت کار

directory (**directories**) *n* A **directory** is a book which gives lists of information such as people's names, addresses, and telephone numbers. ڈائرکٹری

directory enquiries *npl* **Directory enquiries** is a service which you can telephone to find out someone's telephone number. ڈائرکٹری انکوائری

dirt *n* If there is **dirt** on something, there is dust, mud, or a stain on it. گندگی

dirty (**dirtier, dirtiest**) *adj* If something is **dirty**, it is marked or covered with stains, spots, or mud, and needs to be cleaned. گندا

disability (**disabilities**) *n* A **disability** is a physical or mental condition that restricts the way someone can live their life. معذوری

disabled *adj* Someone who is disabled has an illness, injury, or condition that tends to restrict the way that they can live their life, especially by making it difficult for them to move about. معذور

disadvantage (**disadvantages**) *n* A **disadvantage** is a part of a situation which causes problems. نقصان

disagree (**disagrees, disagreeing, disagreed**) *vi* If you **disagree** with someone, you have a different opinion to them about something. متفق نہ ہونا

disagreement (**disagreements**) *n* **Disagreement** means objecting to something. عدم اتفاق

disappear (**disappears, disappearing, disappeared**) *vi* If someone or something **disappears**, they go where they cannot be seen or found. غائب ہونا

disappearance (**disappearances**) *n* If you refer to someone's **disappearance**, you are referring to the fact that nobody knows where they have gone. غیر موجودگی

disappoint (**disappoints, disappointing, disappointed**) *vt* If things or people **disappoint** you, they are not as good as you had hoped, or do not do what you hoped they would do. مایوس کرنا

disappointed *adj* If you are **disappointed**, you are sad because something has not happened or because something is not as good as you hoped it would be. مایوس

disappointing *adj* Something that is **disappointing** is not as good or as large as you hoped it would be. مایوس کن

disappointment *n* **Disappointment** is the state of feeling sad because something has not happened or because something is not as good as you hoped it would be. مایوسی

d

disaster (**disasters**) *n* A **disaster** is a very bad accident such as an earthquake or a plane crash. بلا، حادثہ

disastrous *adj* Something that is **disastrous** has extremely bad consequences and effects or is very unsuccessful. تباہ کن

disc (**discs**) *n* A **disc** is a flat, circular shape or object. ڈسک (طشت نما)

discipline *n* **Discipline** is the practice of making people obey rules or standards of behaviour, and punishing them when they do not. نظم و ضبط کی تربیت

disc jockey (**disc jockeys**) *n* A **disc jockey** is someone who plays and introduces pop records on the radio or at a club. ڈسک جوکی (رکارڈ بجانے والا)

disclose (**discloses, disclosing, disclosed**) *vt* If you **disclose** new or secret information, you tell it to someone. فاش کرنا

disco (discos) *n* A **disco** is a place or event where people dance to pop music. ڈسکو (محفل رقص)

disconnect (**disconnects, disconnecting, disconnected**) *vt* To **disconnect** a piece of equipment means to detach it from its source of power. منقطع کرنا

discount (**discounts**) *n* A **discount** is a reduction in the price of something. چھوٹ دینا

discourage (**discourages, discouraging, discouraged**) *vt* If someone or something **discourages** you, they cause you to lose your enthusiasm about doing something. ہمت توڑنا

discover (**discovers, discovering, discovered**) *vt* If you **discover** something that you did not know about before, you become aware of it or learn of it. دریافت کرنا

discretion *n* **Discretion** is the quality of behaving in a quiet and controlled way without attracting attention or giving away private information. (*formal*) صوابدید

discrimination *n* **Discrimination** is the practice of treating one person or group of people less fairly or less well than other people or groups. امتیاز

discuss (**discusses, discussing, discussed**) *vt* If people **discuss** something, they talk about it, often in order to reach a decision. مباحثہ کرنا

discussion (**discussions**) *n* If there is **discussion** about something, people talk about it, often in order to reach a decision. مباحثہ

disease (**diseases**) *n* A **disease** is an illness which affects people, animals, or plants. بیماری

disgraceful *adj* If you say that something is **disgraceful**, you disapprove of it strongly. بے وقعت

disguise (**disguises, disguising, disguised**) *vt* If you **disguise** yourself, you put on clothes which make you look like someone else or alter your appearance in other ways, so that people will not recognize you. بہروپ بھرنا

disgusted *adj* If you are **disgusted**, you have a strong feeling of dislike or disapproval. بیزار

disgusting *adj* If you say that something is **disgusting**, you think it is extremely unpleasant or unacceptable. نفرت انگیز

dish (**dishes**) *n* A **dish** is a shallow container used for cooking or serving food. طشتری، تھالی

dishcloth (**dishcloths**) *n* A **dishcloth** is a cloth used to dry dishes after they have been washed. برتن پونچھنے کا کپڑا

dishonest *adj* If you say someone is **dishonest**, you mean that they are not honest and you cannot trust them. بے ایمان

dish towel (**dish towels**) *n* A **dish towel** is a cloth used to dry dishes after they have been washed. طشت تولیہ

dishwasher (**dishwashers**) *n* A **dishwasher** is an electrically operated machine that washes and dries plates, saucepans, and cutlery. طشت دھونے والا

disinfectant (disinfectants) *n* **Disinfectant** is a substance that kills germs. جراثیم ربا

disk (**disks**) *n* In a computer, the **disk** is the part where information is stored. ڈسک (ہارڈ ڈسک)

disk drive (disk drives) *n* The **disk drive** on a computer is the part that contains the hard disk or into which a disk can be inserted. ڈسک ڈرائو

diskette (diskettes) *n* A **diskette** is a small magnetic disk that used to be used for storing computer data and programs. ڈسکیٹ (مقناطیسی ڈسک)

dislike (**dislikes, disliking, disliked**) *vt* If you **dislike** someone or something, you consider them to be unpleasant and do not like them. ناپسند کرنا

dismal *adj* Something that is **dismal** is depressingly bad. مایوس کن

dismiss (dismisses, dismissing, dismissed) *vt* If you **dismiss** something, you decide that it is not important enough for you to think about. مسترد کرنا

disobedient *adj* If you are **disobedient**, you deliberately do not do what someone in authority tells you to do, or what a rule or law says that you should do. نافرمان

disobey (**disobeys, disobeying, disobeyed**) *v* When someone **disobeys** a person or an order, they deliberately do not do what they have been told to do. نافرمانی کرنا

dispenser (**dispensers**) *n* A **dispenser** is a machine or container from which you can get things. تقسیم کار

display (**displays, displaying, displayed**) *n* **Display** is the act of exhibiting or showing something. نمائش ▷ *vt* If you **display** something that you want people to see, you put it in a particular place, so that people can see it easily. نمائش کرنا

disposable *adj* **Disposable** things are designed to be thrown away after use. قابل ضیاع

disqualify (**disqualifies, disqualifying, disqualified**) *vt* When someone is **disqualified** from an event or an activity, they are officially stopped from taking part in it. نااہل قرار دینا

disrupt (**disrupts, disrupting, disrupted**) *vt* If someone or something **disrupts** an event or process, they cause problems that prevent it from continuing normally. درہم برہم کرنا

dissatisfied *adj* If you are **dissatisfied** with something, you are not content or pleased with it. غیر مطمئن

dissolve (**dissolves, dissolving, dissolved**) *v* If a substance **dissolves** in liquid, or if you **dissolve** a substance, it mixes with the liquid, becoming weaker until it finally disappears. تحلیل ہونا

distance (**distances**) *n* The **distance** between two places is the amount of space between them. فاصلہ

distant *adj* **Distant** means far away. دور کا

distillery (**distilleries**) *n* A **distillery** is a place where whisky or a similar strong alcoholic drink is made by a process of distilling. شراب کی بھٹی

distinction (**distinctions**) *n* A **distinction** is a difference between similar things. امتیاز

distinctive *adj* Something that is **distinctive** has special qualities that make it easily recognizable. امتیازی

distinguish (**distinguishes, distinguishing, distinguished**) *v* If you can **distinguish** one thing from another, you can see or understand the difference between them. تفریق کرنا

distract (**distracts, distracting, distracted**) *vt* If something **distracts** you, or if it **distracts** your attention, it stops you concentrating. توجہ ہٹانا

distribute (**distributes, distributing, distributed**) *vt* If you **distribute** things, you hand them or deliver them to a number of people. تقسیم کرنا

distributor (**distributors**) *n* A **distributor** is a company that supplies goods to shops or other businesses. تقسیم کار

district (**districts**) *n* A **district** is an area of a town or country. ضلع

disturb (**disturbs, disturbing, disturbed**) *vt* If you **disturb** someone, you interrupt what they are doing and cause them inconvenience. خلل ڈالنا

ditch (**ditches, ditching, ditched**) *n* A **ditch** is a long narrow channel cut into the ground at the side of a road or field. خندق، کھائی ▷ *vt* If you **ditch** something, you get rid of it. پیچھا چھڑانا

dive (**dives, diving, dived**) *n* A **dive** is a headlong plunge into water, especially one of several formalized movements made as a sport. سر کے بل غوطہ لگانا ▷ *vi* If you **dive** into some water, you jump in head-first with your arms held straight above your head. غوطہ لگانا

diver (**divers**) *n* A **diver** is a person who swims under water using special breathing equipment. غوطہ خور

diversion (**diversions**) *n* A **diversion** is a special route arranged for traffic when the normal route cannot be used. انحراف

divide (**divides, dividing, divided**) *vt* If you **divide** something, you make it into smaller pieces. تقسیم کرنا ▷ *vt* When you **divide** numbers, you see how many times one number goes into another number. تقسیم کرنا

diving *n* **Diving** is the activity of working or looking around underwater, using special breathing equipment. غوطہ خوری

diving board (**diving boards**) *n* A **diving board** is a board high above a swimming pool from which people can dive into the water. غوطہ لگانے کا تختہ

division *n* The **division** of something is the act of separating it into two or more different parts. تقسیم

divorce (**divorces**) *n* A **divorce** is the formal ending of a marriage by law. طلاق

divorced *adj* Someone who is **divorced** from their former husband or wife has separated from them and is no longer legally married to them. مطلقہ

DIY *abbr* **DIY** is the activity of making or repairing things in your home. **DIY** is an abbreviation for 'do-it-yourself'. اپنے خود سے کریں

dizzy (**dizzier, dizziest**) *adj* If you feel **dizzy**, you feel that you are losing your balance and are about to fall. سرگراں

DJ (**DJs**) *abbr* A **DJ** is someone who plays and introduces pop records on the radio or at a club. ڈی جے (پوپ موسیقی بجانے والا)

DNA *n* **DNA** is a chemical that is found in all living cells. It contains genetic information. **DNA** is an abbreviation for 'deoxyribonucleic acid'. ڈی اوکسی رائبو نیوکلے ایسڈ

do (**does, doing, did, done**) *vt* If you **do** something, you spend some time on it or finish it. کرنا *I tried to do some work.*

dock (**docks**) *n* A **dock** is an enclosed area of water where ships are loaded, unloaded, or repaired. بندرگاہ، گودی

doctor (**doctors**) *n* A **doctor** is someone who is qualified in medicine and treats people who are ill. ڈاکٹر

document (**documents**) *n* A **document**

is an official piece of paper with writing on it. دستاویز

documentary (**documentaries**) *n* A **documentary** is a radio or television programme or a film which provides factual information about a particular subject. دستاویزی فلم

documentation *n* **Documentation** consists of documents which provide a record of something. دستاویز بندی

documents *npl* **Documents** are official pieces of paper with writing on them. دستاویزات

dodge (**dodges, dodging, dodged**) *vi* If you **dodge** somewhere, you move there suddenly to avoid being hit, caught, or seen. بچ نکلنا

dog (**dogs**) *n* A **dog** is an animal that is often kept as a pet or used to guard or hunt things. کتا

dole *n* The **dole** is money that is given regularly by the government to people who are unemployed. خیرات

doll (**dolls**) *n* A **doll** is a child's toy which looks like a small person or baby. گڑیا

dollar (**dollars**) *n* The **dollar** is a unit of money in the USA, Canada, and some other countries. It is represented by the symbol $. ڈالر

dolphin (**dolphins**) *n* A **dolphin** is a mammal with fins and a pointed nose which lives in the sea. ڈولفن مچھلی

domestic *adj* **Domestic** political activities and situations happen or exist within one particular country. گھریلو

Dominican Republic *n* The **Dominican Republic** is a republic in the Caribbean, on the eastern side of the island of Hispaniola. ڈومنیکن جمہوریہ

domino (**dominoes**) *n* A **domino** is a small rectangular block marked with two groups of spots on one side. **Dominoes** are used for playing various games. ڈومینو (لکڑی کے مستطیل ٹکڑوں سے کھیل)

dominoes *npl* **Dominoes** is a game played using small rectangular blocks, called **dominoes**, which are marked with two groups of spots on one side. ڈومینوز (جمع)

donate (**donates, donating, donated**) *vt* If you **donate** something to a charity or other organization, you give it to them. عطیہ دینا

done *adj* A task that is **done** has been completed. کیا ہوا

donkey (**donkeys**) *n* A **donkey** is an animal like a small horse with long ears. گدھا

donor (**donors**) *n* A **donor** is someone who gives a part of their body or some of their blood to be used by doctors to help a person who is ill. عطیہ کنندہ

door (**doors**) *n* A **door** is a swinging or sliding piece of wood, glass, or metal, which is used to open and close the entrance to a building, room, cupboard, or vehicle. دروازہ

doorbell (doorbells) *n* A **doorbell** is a bell on the outside of a house which you can ring so that the people inside know that you want to see them. دروازے کی گھنٹی

door handle (**door handles**) *n* A **door handle** is a small round object or a lever that is attached to a door and is used for opening and closing it. دروازے کا دستہ

doorman (**doormen**) *n* A **doorman** is a man who stands at the door of a club, prevents unwanted people from coming In, and makes people leave if they cause trouble. دربان

doorstep (**doorsteps**) *n* A **doorstep** is a step on the outside of a building, in front of a door. چوکھٹ

dormitory (**dormitories**) *n* A **dormitory** is a large bedroom where several people sleep. اجتماعی خوابگاہ

dose (**doses**) *n* A **dose** of a medicine or drug is a measured amount of it. خوراک

dot (**dots**) *n* A **dot** is a very small round mark. نقطہ

double (**doubles, doubling, doubled**)

adj You use **double** to describe a pair of similar things. دوگنا ▷ *v* When something **doubles** or when you **double** it, it becomes twice as great in number, amount, or size. دوگنا ہو جانا

double bass (**double basses**) *n* A **double bass** is the largest instrument in the violin family. You play it standing up. ڈبل باس (ساز)

double glazing *n* If someone has **double glazing** in their house, their windows are fitted with two layers of glass. People put in double glazing in order to keep buildings warmer or to keep out noise. دوہرے قلعی والی

doubt (**doubts, doubting, doubted**) *n* If you feel **doubt** or **doubts** about something, you feel uncertain about it. شک ▷ *vt* If you **doubt** something, or if you **doubt** whether something is true or possible, you believe that it is probably not true, genuine, or possible. شک کرنا

doubtful *adj* Something that is **doubtful** seems unlikely or uncertain. مشکوک

dough *n* **Dough** is a mixture of flour and water, and sometimes also sugar and fat, which can be cooked to make bread, pastry, and biscuits. گندھا آٹا

doughnut (**doughnuts**) *n* A **doughnut** is a lump or ring of sweet dough cooked in hot fat. ڈونٹ

do up *v* If you **do** something **up**, you fasten it. (کسنا (ٹانٹ کرنا *She did up the buttons.*

dove (doves) *n* A **dove** is a white bird that looks like a pigeon. فاختہ

do without *v* If you **do without** something, you manage or survive in spite of not having it. کے بغیر کرنا *We can't do without the help of your organisation.*

down *adv* When something moves **down**, it goes from a higher place to a lower place. نیچے

download (**downloads**) *vt* To **download** data means to transfer it to or from a computer along a line such as a telephone line, a radio link, or a computer network. ڈاؤن لوڈ کرنا

downpour (**downpours**) *n* A **downpour** is a heavy fall of rain. موسلا دھار

Down's syndrome *n* **Down's syndrome** is a condition that some people are born with. People who have Down's syndrome have a flat forehead and sloping eyes and lower than average intelligence. ڈاؤنس سنڈروم (بیماری)

downstairs *adj* **Downstairs** means situated on the ground floor of a building or on a lower floor than you are. نچلی منزل ▷ *adv* If you go **downstairs** in a building, you go down a staircase towards the ground floor. فرش کی طرف

doze (**dozes, dozing, dozed**) *vi* When you **doze**, you sleep lightly or for a short period, especially during the daytime. اونگھنا

dozen (**dozens**) *num* A **dozen** means twelve. درجن

doze off *v* If you **doze off**, you fall into a light sleep. ہلکی نیند سونا *She dozed off for a few moments.*

drab (**drabber, drabbest**) *adj* Something that is **drab** is dull and not attractive or exciting. بھدی

draft (**drafts**) *n* A **draft** is an early version of a letter, book, or speech. مسودہ

drag (**drags, dragging, dragged**) *vt* If you **drag** something or someone somewhere, you pull them there with difficulty. گھسیٹنا

dragon (**dragons**) *n* In stories and legends, a **dragon** is an animal like a big lizard. It has wings and claws, and breathes out fire. اژدہا

dragonfly (**dragonflies**) *n* A **dragonfly** is a brightly coloured insect with a long thin body and two sets of wings. کابلی مکھی

drain (**drains, draining, drained**) *n* A **drain** is a pipe that carries water or sewage away from a place, or an opening in a surface that leads to the pipe. نالی ▷ *v*

If you **drain** a liquid from a place or object, you remove the liquid by causing it to flow somewhere else. If a liquid **drains** somewhere, it flows there. نکاسی کرنا

draining board (**draining boards**) *n* The **draining board** is the place on a sink unit where things such as cups, plates, and cutlery are put to drain after they have been washed. برتنوں کو دھوکر بہانے کا بورڈ

drainpipe (**drainpipes**) A **drainpipe** is a pipe attached to the side of a building, through which rainwater flows from the roof into a drain. نکاسی پائپ

drama (**dramas**) *n* A **drama** is a serious play for the theatre, television, or radio. ڈراما

dramatic *adj* A **dramatic** change is sudden and noticeable. ڈرامائی

drastic *adj* A **drastic** course of action is extreme and is usually taken urgently. شدید

draught (**draughts**) *n* A **draught** is an unwelcome current of air coming into a room or vehicle. ہوا کا جھونکا

draughts *npl* **Draughts** is a game for two people, played with 24 round pieces on a board. چوپڑ

draw (**draws, drawing, drew, drawn**) *v* When you **draw**, or when you **draw** something, you use pens, pencils, or crayons to make a picture. تصویر بنانا ▷ *vi* In a game, if one person or team **draws** with another one, or if two people or teams **draw**, they finish with the same number of points. مقابلے میں برابری پر رہنا ▷ *v* You can use **draw** to indicate that someone or something moves somewhere or is moved there. کھینچنا

drawback (**drawbacks**) *n* A **drawback** is an aspect of something that makes it less acceptable. خامی

drawer (**drawers**) *n* A **drawer** is a part of a desk or other piece of furniture that is shaped like a rectangular box. You pull it towards you to open it. دراز

drawing (drawings) *n* A **drawing** is a picture or plan made by means of lines on a surface, especially one made with a pencil or pen without the use of colour. خاکہ

drawing pin (**drawing pins**) *n* A **drawing pin** is a short pin with a broad, flat top which is used for fastening papers or pictures to a board, wall, or other surface. ڈرائنگ پن

dreadful *adj* If you say that something is **dreadful**, you mean that it is very unpleasant or very poor in quality. ناگوار

dream (**dreams, dreaming, dreamed, dreamt**) *n* A **dream** is an imaginary series of events that you experience in your mind while you are asleep. خواب ▷ *v* When you **dream**, you experience imaginary events in your mind while you are asleep. خواب دیکھنا

drench (**drenches, drenching, drenched**) *vt* To **drench** something or someone means to make them completely wet. بھگونا

dress (**dresses, dressing, dressed**) *n* A **dress** is something a girl or a woman can wear. It covers the body and part of the legs. لباس ▷ *vi* When you **dress**, you put on clothes. لباس پہننا

dressed *adj* If you are **dressed**, you are wearing clothes rather than being naked. ملبوس

dresser (**dressers**) *n* A **dresser** is a chest of drawers, sometimes with a mirror on the top. دراز

dressing gown (**dressing gowns**) *n* A **dressing gown** is a loose-fitting coat worn over pyjamas or other night clothes. ڈریسنگ گاؤن

dressing table (**dressing tables**) *n* A **dressing table** is a small table in a bedroom with drawers and a mirror. سنگار میز

dress up *v* If you **dress up**, you put on different clothes, in order to look smarter or to disguise yourself. لبس زیب تن کرنا *You do not need to dress up for dinner.*

d

dried *adj* **Dried** food or milk has had all the water removed from it so that it will last for a long time. خشک کردہ

drift (**drifts, drifting, drifted**) *n* A **drift** is a movement away from somewhere or something, or a movement towards somewhere or something different. انحراف ▷ *vi* When something **drifts** somewhere, it is carried there by the wind or by water. بھٹکنا

drill (**drills, drilling, drilled**) *n* A **drill** is a tool for making holes. ڈرل (سوراخ کرنے کا آلہ) ▷ *v* When you **drill** into something or **drill** a hole in it, you make a hole using a drill. سوراخ کرنا

drink (**drinks, drinking, drank, drunk**) *n* A **drink** is an amount of a liquid which you drink. مشروب ▷ *v* When you **drink**, or **drink** a liquid, you take it into your mouth and swallow it. پینا

drink-driving *n* **Drink-driving** is the offence of driving a car after drinking more than the amount of alcohol that is legally allowed. نشے میں گاڑی چلانا

drinking water *n* **Drinking water** is water which it is safe to drink. پینے کا پانی

drip (**drips, dripping, dripped**) *n* A **drip** is a small individual drop of a liquid. بوند ▷ *vi* When liquid **drips** somewhere, it falls in small drops. بوندیں گرنا

drive (**drives, driving, drove, driven**) *n* A **drive** is a journey in a vehicle such as a car. موٹر کا سفر ▷ *v* When someone **drives** a vehicle, they make it go where they want. گاڑی چلانا

driver (**drivers**) *n* The **driver** of a vehicle is the person who is driving it. ڈرائیور

driveway (**driveways**) *n* A **driveway** is a private road that leads from a public road to a house or garage. ذاتی سڑک

driving instructor (**driving instructors**) *n* A **driving instructor** is someone who teaches a people to drive a vehicle. ڈرائیونگ استاد

driving lesson (**driving lessons**) *n* A **driving lesson** is a one of a course of lessons during which a person is taught how to do drive a vehicle. ڈرائیونگ کا سبق

driving licence (**driving licences**) *n* A **driving licence** is a card showing that you are qualified to drive. ڈرائیونگ لائسنس

driving test (**driving tests**) *n* A **driving test** is a test that must be passed before you are qualified to drive a vehicle. ڈرائیونگ ٹیسٹ

drizzle *n* **Drizzle** is light rain falling in fine drops. پھوار

drop (**drops, dropping, dropped**) *n* If there is a **drop** in something, it quickly becomes less. گراوٹ ▷ *v* If a level or amount **drops** or if someone or something **drops** it, it quickly becomes less. گرنا

drought (**droughts**) *n* A **drought** is a long period of time during which no rain falls. قحط سالی

drown (**drowns, drowning, drowned**) *v* When someone **drowns**, or when they are **drowned**, they die because they have gone under water and cannot breathe. ڈوبنا

drowsy (**drowsier, drowsiest**) *adj* If you are **drowsy**, you feel sleepy and cannot think clearly. نیم خوابیدہ

drug (**drugs**) *n* A **drug** is a chemical substance given to people to treat or prevent an illness or disease. دوا

drum (**drums**) *n* A **drum** is a musical instrument consisting of a skin stretched tightly over a round frame. ڈھول

drummer (**drummers**) *n* A **drummer** is a person who plays a drum or drums in a band or group. ڈھولی

drunk (**drunks**) *adj* If someone is **drunk**, they have consumed too much alcohol. نشہ میں دھت ▷ *n* A **drunk** is someone who is drunk or who often gets drunk. نشہ باز

dry (**drier, dryer, driest, dries, drying, dried**) *adj* If something is **dry**, it has no

water or other liquid on it or in it. خشک
▷ *v* When you **dry** something, or when it **dries**, it becomes dry. خشک کرنا

dry cleaner (**dry cleaners**) *n* A **dry cleaner** or a **dry cleaner's** is a shop where things can be dry-cleaned. ڈرائی کلینر کی دکان

dry-cleaning *n* **Dry-cleaning** is the action or work of dry-cleaning things such as clothes. ڈرائی کلینگ

dryer (**dryers**) *n* A **dryer** is a machine for drying things, for example clothes or people's hair. خشک کار

dual carriageway (**dual carriageways**) *n* A **dual carriageway** is a road which has two lanes of traffic travelling in each direction with a strip of grass or concrete down the middle to separate the two lots of traffic. دہری آمدورفت والی سڑک

dubbed *adj* If a film or soundtrack in a foreign language is **dubbed**, a new soundtrack is added with actors giving a translation. ترجمہ کیا ہوا

dubious *adj* You describe something as **dubious** when you think it is not completely honest, safe, or reliable. مبہم

duck (**ducks**) *n* A **duck** is a common water bird with short legs and a large flat beak. بطخ

due *adj* If something is **due** at a particular time, it is expected to happen or to arrive at that time. لازم، واجب

due to *prep* If something is **due to** another thing, it is a result of that thing. وجہ سے *He couldn't do the job, due to pain in his hands.*

dull (**duller, dullest**) *adj* Something that is **dull** is not interesting. بیزارکن، پھیکا ▷ *adj* A **dull** colour is not bright. مدھم، ہلکا

dumb *adj* Someone who is **dumb** is completely unable to speak. گونگا

dummy (**dummies**) *n* A **dummy** is a model of a person, often used to display clothes. نقل، مجسمہ

dump (**dumps, dumping, dumped**) *n* A **dump** is a site provided for people to leave their rubbish. گھورا ▷ *vt* If something is **dumped** somewhere, it is put there because it is no longer wanted or needed. (*informal*) گھورے میں پھینکنا

dumpling (**dumplings**) *n* **Dumplings** are small lumps of dough that are cooked and eaten, either with meat and vegetables or as part of a sweet pudding. باڑی

dungarees *npl* **Dungarees** are a one-piece garment consisting of trousers, a piece of cloth which covers your chest, and straps which go over your shoulders. کام کے وقت پہنا جانے والا لباس

dungeon (**dungeons**) *n* A **dungeon** is a dark underground prison in a castle. جیل تہ خانہ (قلعہ میں)

duration *n* The **duration** of an event or state is the time that it lasts. مدت

during *prep* If something happens **during** a period of time, it happens between the beginning and the end of that period. دوران *Storms are common during the winter.*

dusk *n* **Dusk** is the time just before night when it is not yet completely dark. شام

dust (**dusts, dusting, dusted**) *n* **Dust** consists of very small dry particles of earth, sand, or dirt. دھول ▷ *v* When you **dust** or **dust** furniture or other objects, you remove dust from them using a dry cloth. دھول جھاڑنا

dustbin (**dustbins**) *n* A **dustbin** is a large container for rubbish. کوڑے دان

dustman (**dustmen**) *n* A **dustman** is a person whose job is to empty the rubbish from people's dustbins and take it away to be disposed of. صفائی والا

d

dustpan (**dustpans**) *n* A **dustpan** is a small flat container made of metal or plastic. You hold it flat on the floor and put dirt and dust into it using a brush. کوڑے کا برتن

dusty (**dustier, dustiest**) *adj* Something that is **dusty** is covered with dust. دھول بھرا

Dutch *adj* **Dutch** means relating to or belonging to the Netherlands, or to its people, language, or culture. ڈچ (نیدرلینڈ) ▷ *n* **Dutch** is the language spoken in the Netherlands. ڈچ زبان

Dutchman (**Dutchmen**) *n* A **Dutchman** is a man who is a native of the Netherlands. نیدرلینڈ کا شہری

Dutchwoman (**Dutchwomen**) *n* A **Dutchwoman** is a woman who is a native of the Netherlands. ڈچ خاتون

duty (**duties**) *n* **Duty** is the work that you have to do as your job. فریضہ

duty-free *adj* **Duty-free** goods are sold at airports or on planes or ships at a cheaper price than usual because they are not taxed. بغیر ٹیکس ▷ *n* **Duty-free** is goods sold at airports or on planes or ships at a cheaper price than usual because they are not taxed. بغیر ٹیکس سامان

duvet (**duvets**) *n* A **duvet** is a large cover filled with feathers or similar material, which you use to cover yourself in bed. نرم لحاف

DVD (**DVDs**) *n* A **DVD** is a disc similar to a compact disc on which a film or music is recorded. **DVD** is an abbreviation for 'digital video disc' or 'digital versatile disc'. ڈیجیٹل ویڈیو ڈسک (ڈی وی ڈی)

DVD burner (**DVD burners**) *n* A **DVD burner** is a piece of computer equipment that you use for copying data from a computer onto a DVD. ڈی وی ڈی برنر

DVD player (**DVD players**) *n* A **DVD player** is a machine for playing DVDs. ڈی وی ڈی پلیئر

dwarf (**dwarves**) *n* In children's stories, a **dwarf** is an imaginary creature that is like a small man. Dwarves often have magical powers. بونا

dye (**dyes, dyeing, dyed**) *n* **Dye** is a substance which is used to dye something. رنگ ▷ *vt* If you **dye** something, you change its colour by soaking it in a special liquid. رنگنا

dynamic *adj* A **dynamic** person is full of energy; used showing approval. متحرک

dyslexia *n* If someone suffers from **dyslexia**, they have difficulty with reading because of a slight disorder of their brain. ڈسلیکسیا (پڑھنے میں دشواری کی بیماری)

dyslexic (**dyslexics**) *adj* If someone is **dyslexic**, they have difficulty with reading because of a slight disorder of their brain. ڈسلیکسک (پڑھنے میں دشواری)

e

each *det* **Each** thing or person in a group means every member as an individual. ہر ایک *Each book is beautifully illustrated. A waiter came in with a glass of water.* ▷ *pron* **Each** means every one. ہر ایک *He gave each of us a book.*

eagle (eagles) *n* An **eagle** is a large bird that hunts and kills small animals for food. باز

ear (ears) *n* Your **ears** are the two parts of your body with which you hear ounds. کان

earache (earaches) *n* **Earache** is a pain in the inside part of your ear. کان درد

eardrum (eardrums) *n* Your **eardrums** are the thin pieces of tightly stretched skin inside each ear, which vibrate when sound waves reach them. کان کی جھلی

earlier *adv* **Earlier** is used to refer to a point or period in time before the present or before the one you are talking about. ---سے قبل

early (earlier, earliest) *adj* If you are **early**, you arrive before the time that you were expected to come. پہلے، جلدی ▷ *adv* **Early** means before the usual time that a particular event or activity happens. جلدی ▷ *adj* **Early** means near the first part of something. نزدیک

earn (earns, earning, earned) *vt* If you **earn** money, you receive it in return for work that you do. کمانا

earnings *npl* Your **earnings** are the money that you earn by working. کمائی

earphones *npl* **Earphones** are a small piece of equipment which you wear over or inside your ears so that you can listen to a radio or MP3 player without anyone else hearing. ایئر فون

earplugs *npl* **Earplugs** are small pieces of a soft material which you put into your ears to keep out noise, water, or cold air. ایئر پلگ

earring (earrings) *n* **Earrings** are pieces of jewellery which you attach to your ears. کان کی بالی / بالا

earth *n* The **earth** is the planet that we live on. زمین ▷ *n* **Earth** is the soil that plants growin. مٹی

earthquake(earthquakes) *n* An **earthquake** is a shaking of the ground caused by movement of the earth's crust. زلزلہ

easily *adv* You use **easily** to emphasize that something is very likely to happen, or is certainly true. آسانی سے

east *adj* The east edge, corner, or part of a place or country is the part which is towards the east. مشرقی ▷ *adv* If you go **east**, you travel towards the east. مشرق کو ▷ *n* The **east** is the direction in which you look to see the sun rise. مشرق

eastbound *adj* **Eastbound** roads or vehicles lead to or are travelling towards the east. مشرق کی طرف

Easter (Easters) *n* **Easter** is a Christian festival and holiday, when the resurrection of Jesus Christ is celebrated. ایسٹر

Easter egg (Easter eggs) *n* An **Easter egg** is an egg made of chocolate that is given as a present at Easter. In some countries, **Easter eggs** are hidden and children then look for them. ایسٹر بیضہ

eastern *adj* **Eastern** means in or from the east of a region or country. مشرقی

easy (**easier, easiest**) *adj* If a job or action is easy, you can do it without difficulty. آسان

easy chair (**easy chairs**) *n* An **easy chair** is a large, comfortable padded chair. آرام کرسی

easy-going *adj* If you describe someone as **easy-going**, you approve of the fact that that they are not easily worried or upset. خوش مزاج

eat (**eats, eating, ate, eaten**) *v* When you **eat**, you chew and swallow food. کھانا

e-book (**e-books**) *n* An **e-book** is a book which is produced for reading on a computer screen. **E-book** is an abbreviation for 'electronic book'. الیکٹرانک کتاب

eccentric *adj* If you say that someone is **eccentric**, you mean that they behave in a strange way, and have habits or opinions that are different from those of most people. عجیب

echo *adj* An **echo** is a sound caused by a noise being reflected off a surface such as a wall. بازگشت

ecofriendly *adj* **Ecofriendly** products or services are less harmful to the environment than other similar products or services. ماحول دوست

ecological *adj* **Ecological** means involved with or concerning ecology. ماحولیاتی

ecology *n* **Ecology** is the study of the relationship between living things and their environment. ماحولیات

e-commerce (**allies**) *n* **E-commerce** is the buying, selling, and ordering of goods and services using the Internet. انٹرنیٹ پر تجارت

economic *adj* **Economic** means concerned with the organization of the money, industry, and trade of a country, region, or society. معاشیات

economical *adj* Something that is **economical** does not require a lot of money to operate. کفایتی

economics *npl* **Economics** is the study of the way in which money, industry, and trade are organized in a society. معاشیات

economist (**economists**) *n* An **economist** is a person who studies, teaches, or writes about economics. ماہر معاشیات

economize (**economizes, economizing, economized**) *vi* If you **economize**, you save money by spending it very carefully. کفایت شعاری سے خرچ کرنا

economy (**economies**) *n* The **economy** of a country or region is the system by which money, industry, and trade are organized. معیشت

economy class *n* **Economy class** is a class of travel in aircraft, providing less luxurious accommodation than first class at a lower fare. کفایتی درجہ

ecstasy (**ecstasies**) *n* **Ecstasy** is a feeling of great happiness. لطف کا نقطہ عروج

Ecuador *n* **Ecuador** is a republic in South America, on the Pacific. اکواڈور جمہوریہ

eczema *n* **Eczema** is a skin condition which makes your skin itch and become sore and broken. داد

edge (**edges**) *n* The **edge** of something is the place or line where it stops, or the part of it that is furthest from the middle. کنارا

edgy (**edgier, edgiest**) *adj* If you feel **edgy**, you are nervous and anxious. دھاردار

edible *adj* If something is **edible**, it is safe to eat. کھانے لائق

edition (**editions**) *n* An **edition** is a particular version of a book, magazine, or newspaper that is printed at one time. شمارہ

editor (**editors**) *n* An **editor** is a person in charge of a newspaper or magazine, or a section of a newspaper or magazine, who makes decisions concerning the contents. مدیر

educated *adj* **Educated** people have reached a high standard of learning. تعلیم یافتہ

education (**educations**) *n* **Education** means learning and teaching. تعلیم

educational *adj* **Educational** matters or institutions are concerned with or relate to education. تعلیمی

eel (**eels**) *n* An **eel** is a fish with a long, thin body. بام مچھلی

effect (**effects**) *n* An **effect** is a change, reaction, or impression that is caused by something or is the result of something. اثر

effective *adj* Something that is **effective** produces the intended results. اثردار

effectively *adv* If you do something **effectively**, you do it well and produce the results that were intended. اثردار طریقے سے

efficient *adj* Something or someone that is **efficient** does a job successfully, without wasting time or energy. باصلاحیت

efficiently *adv* If you do something **efficiently**, you do it successfully, ithout wasting time or energy. قابلیت کے ساتھ

effort (**efforts**) *n* If you make an **effort** to do something, you try hard to do it. کوشش

e.g. *abbr* **e.g.** is an abbreviation that means 'for example'. It is used before a noun, or to introduce another sentence. مثلاً

egg (**eggs**) *n* An **egg** is the rounded object produced by a female bird from which a baby bird later emerges. Reptiles, fish, and insects also produce eggs. انڈا

eggcup (**eggcups**) *n* An **eggcup** is a small container in which you put a boiled egg while you eat it. بیضہ دان

egg white (**egg whites**) *n* An **egg white** is the clear liquid part of an egg, which becomes white when you cook it. بیضوی سفید

egg yolk (**egg yolks**) *n* An **egg yolk** is the yellow part in the middle of the egg. انڈے کی زردی

Egypt *n* **Egypt** is a republic in north-east Africa, on the Mediterranean and Red Sea. مصر

Egyptian (**Egyptians**) *adj* **Egyptian** means belonging or relating to Egypt or to its people, language, or culture. مصری ▷ *n* The **Egyptians** are the people who come from Egypt. مصری شہری

eight *num* **Eight** is the number 8. آٹھ

eighteen (**eighteens**) *num* **Eighteen** is the number 18. اٹھارہ

eighteenth *adj* The **eighteenth** item in a series is the one that you count as number eighteen. اٹھارہواں

eighth (**eighths**) *adj* The **eighth** item in a series is the one that you count as number eight. آٹھواں ▷ *n* An **eighth** is one of eight equal parts of something. آٹھواں حصہ

eighty *num* **Eighty** is the number 80. اسی

Eire *n* **Eire** is the Gaelic name for Ireland. آیرلینڈ (آریوں کا ملک)

either *adv* You use **either** in negative sentences to mean also. بھی ▷ *det* **Either** means each. ہر ▷ *pron* You can use **either** when there are two things to choose from. دونوں میں سے ▷ *det* **Either** means one of two things or people. کوئی ایک

either ... or *conj* You use **either** in front of the first of two or more alternatives, when you are stating the only possibilities or choices that there are. The other alternatives are introduced by **or**. یا تو ۔ ۔ ۔ یا

elastic *n* **Elastic** is a rubber material that stretches when you pull it and returns to its original size when you let it go. لچیلا

elastic band (**elastic bands**) *n* An **elastic band** is a thin circle of very stretchy rubber that you can put around things in order to hold them together. لچکدار بینڈ (چھلا)

Elastoplast® (**Elastoplasts**) *n* **Elastoplast** is a type of sticky tape that you use to

e

cover small cuts on your body. •الاسٹوپلاسٹ (کٹے ہوئے پر مرہم)

elbow (**elbows**) *n* Your **elbow** is the joint where your arm bends in the middle. کہنی

elder *adj* The **elder** of two people is the one who was born first. بڑا

elderly *adj* You use **elderly** as a polite way of saying that someone is old. عمر رسیدہ

eldest *adj* The **eldest** person in a group is the one who was born before all the others. سب سے بڑا

elect (**elects, electing, elected**) *vt* When people **elect** someone, they choose that person to represent them, by voting. چننا

election (**elections**) *n* An **election** is a process in which people vote to choose a person or group of people to hold an official position. چناؤ

electorate (**electorates**) *n* The **electorate** of a country is the people there who have the right to vote in an election. رائے دہندگان

electric *adj* An **electric** device works by means of electricity. برقی

electrical *adj* **Electrical** devices work by means of electricity. برقیاتی

electric blanket (**electric blankets**) *n* An **electric blanket** is a blanket with wires inside it which carry an electric current that keeps the blanket warm. برقی کمبل

electrician (**electricians**) *n* An **electrician** is a person whose job is to install and repair electrical equipment. بجلی مستری

electricity *n* **Electricity** is a form of energy used for heating and lighting, and to provide power for machines. بجلی

electric shock (**electric shocks**) *n* If you get an **electric shock**, you get a sudden painful feeling when you touch something which is connected to a supply of electricity. برقی جھٹکا

electronic *adj* An **electronic**device has transistors, silicon chips, or valves which control and change the electric current passing through it. الیکٹرانک

electronics *npl* You can refer to electronic devices, or the part of a piece of equipment that consists of electronic devices, as the **electronics**. برقیات

elegant *adj* If you describe a person or thing as **elegant**, you think they are pleasing and graceful in appearance or style. شستہ

element (**elements**) *n* An **element** of something is one of the parts which make up the whole thing. عنصر

elephant (**elephants**) *n* An **elephant** is a very large animal with a long trunk. ہاتھی

eleven *num* **Eleven** is the number 11. گیارہ

eleventh *adj* The **eleventh** item in a series is the one that you count as number eleven. گیارہواں

eliminate (**eliminates, eliminating, eliminated**) *vt* To **eliminate** something means to remove it completely. نکال دینا

elm (**elms**) *n* An **elm** is a tree with broad leaves which it loses in autumn. بوقیراس

else *adv* You use **else** after words such as 'someone', and 'everyone', and after question words like 'what', to talk about another person, place, or thing. اور

elsewhere *adv* **Elsewhere** means in other places or to another place. کہیں اور

email (**emails, emailed, emailing**) *n* **Email** is a system of sending written messages electronically from one computer to another. **Email** is an abbreviation of 'electronic mail'. ای میل ▷ *v* If you **email** a person, you contact them by electronic mail. ای میل کرنا

email address (**email addresses**) *n* Your **email address** is the combination of letters, numbers, and symbols that people use for sending email to you. ای میل پتہ

embankment (**embankments**) *n* An **embankment** is a thick wall built of earth, often supporting a railway line or road. پشتہ، بند

embarrassed *adj* A person who is

embarrassed feels shy, ashamed, or guilty about something. شرمسار

embarrassing *adj* Something that is **embarrassing** makes you feel shy or ashamed. شرمناک

embassy (embassies) *n* An **embassy** is a group of officials, headed by an ambassador, who represent their government in a foreign country. سفارت خانہ

embroider (embroiders, embroidering, embroidered) *vt* If cloth is **embroidered** with a design, the design is stitched into it. کشیدہ کاری کرنا

embroidery (embroideries) *n* **Embroidery** consists of designs sewn onto cloth. کشیدہ کاری

emergency (emergencies) *n* An **emergency** is an unexpected and serious situation such as an accident, which must be dealt with quickly. ہنگامی صورت حال

emergency exit (emergency exits) *n* The **emergency exit** in a building or on a vehicle is a special doorway that is to be used only in an emergency. ہنگامی نکاسی

emergency landing (emergency landings) *n* An **emergency landing** is an occasion when a plane is forced to land, for example, because of a technical problem or bad weather. ہنگامی لینڈنگ (اترنا)

emigrate (emigrates, emigrating, emigrated) *vi* If you **emigrate**, you leave your own country to live in another. ترک وطن کرنا

emotion (emotions) *n* An **emotion** is a feeling such as happiness, love, fear, anger, or hatred, which can be caused by the situation that you are in or the people you are with. جذبہ

emotional *adj* **Emotional** means relating to emotions and feelings. جذباتی

emperor (emperors) *n* An **emperor** is a man who rules an empire. شہنشاہ

emphasize (emphasizes, emphasizing, emphasized) *vt* To **emphasize** something means to indicate that it is particularly important or true, or to draw special attention to it. زور دینا

empire (empires) *n* An **empire** is a group of countries controlled by one powerful country. سلطنت

employ (employs, employing, employed) *vt* If a person or company **employs** you, they pay you to work for them. ملازم رکھنا

employee (employees) *n* An **employee** is a person who is paid to work for a company or organization. ملازم

employer (employers) *n* Your **employer** is the organization or person that you work for. آجر

employment *n* If you are in **employment**, you have a paid job. ملازمت

empty (emptier, emptiest, empties, emptying, emptied) *adj* An **empty** place, vehicle, or container has no people or things in it. خالی ▷ *vt* If you **empty** a container, or if you **empty** something out of it, you remove its contents. خالی کرنا

enamel *n* **Enamel** is a substance which can be heated and put onto metal in order to decorate or protect it. مینا کاری

encourage (encourages, encouraging, encouraged) *vt* If you **encourage** someone, you give them confidence, for example by letting them know that what they are doing is good. ہمت افزائی کرنا

encouragement (encouragements) *n* **Encouragement** is the activity of encouraging someone. ہمت افزائی

encouraging *adj* Something that is **encouraging** gives you hope or confidence. ہمت افزا

encyclopaedia (encyclopaedias) *n* An **encyclopaedia** is a book, set of books, or CD-ROM in which many facts are arranged for reference. قاموس

end (ends, ending, ended) *n* The **end** of something is the last part of it. سرا، اختتامی حصہ

endanger (endangers, endangering, endangered) *vt* To **endanger**

something or someone means to put them in a situation where they might be harmed or destroyed. خطرے میں ڈالنا

ending *n* An **ending** is an act of bringing to or reaching an end. خاتمہ

endless *adj* If you describe something as **endless**, you mean that it lasts so long that it seems as if it will never end. غیر مختتم

enemy (**enemies**) *n* Your **enemy** is someone who intends to harm you. دشمن

energetic *adj* An **energetic** person has a lot of energy. توانا

energy *n* If you have **energy**, you have the strength to move around a lot and do things. توانائی ▷ *n* **Energy** is the power that makes machines work. توانائی

engaged *adj* Someone who is **engaged in or on** a particular activity is doing it or involved with it. مشغول

engaged tone (**engaged tones**) *n* An **engaged tone** is a repeated single note heard on a telephone when the number called is already in use. مصروف ٹون

engagement (**engagements**) *n* An **engagement** is an arrangement that you have made to do something at a particular time. مصروفیت

engagement ring (**engagement rings**) *n* An **engagement ring** is a ring worn by a woman when she is engaged to be married. منگنی کی انگوٹھی

engine (**engines**) *n* An **engine** is a machine that makes things like cars and planes move. انجن ▷ *n* An **engine** is the front part of a train that pulls it along. انجن

engineer (**engineers**) *n* An **engineer** is a person who designs, builds, and repairs machines, or structures such as roads, railways, and bridges. مہندس، انجینئر

engineering *n* **Engineering** is the work of designing and constructing machines or structures such as roads and bridges. انجینئرنگ

England *n* **England** is the largest division of Great Britain, bordering on Scotland and Wales. انگلینڈ

English *adj* **English** means belonging or relating to England. انگریز ▷ *n* **English** is the language spoken in Great Britain and Ireland, the United States, Canada, Australia, and many other countries. انگریزی زبان

Englishman (**Englishmen**) *n* An **Englishman** is a man who comes from England. انگریز

Englishwoman (**Englishwomen**) *n* An **Englishwoman** is a woman who comes from England. انگریز خاتون

engrave (**engraves, engraving, engraved**) *vt* If you **engrave** something with a design or words, you cut the design or words into its surface. نقش نگاری کرنا

enjoy (**enjoys, enjoying, enjoyed**) *vt* If you **enjoy** something, it gives you pleasure and satisfaction. لطف اندوز ہونا

enjoyable *adj* Something that is **enjoyable** gives you pleasure. لطیف

enlargement *n* The **enlargement** of something is the process or result of making it bigger. اضافہ، توسیع

enormous *adj* **Enormous** means extremely large in size, amount, or degree. عظیم

enough *det* If you have **enough** of something, you have as much as you need. کافی، حسب ضرورت ▷ *pron* **Enough** means as much as is needed or required. کفایت

enquire (**enquired, enquiring, enquires**) *v* If you **enquire** about something, you ask for information about it. معلوم کرنا

enquiry (**enquiries**) *n* An **enquiry** is a question which you ask in order to get information. پوچھ تاچھ

ensure (**ensures, ensuring, ensured**) *vt* To **ensure** that something happens means to make certain that it happens. یقینی بنانا

enter (**enters, entering, entered**) *v* When you **enter** a place, you come or go into it. داخل ہونا

entertain (**entertains, entertaining, entertained**) *v* If you **entertain**, or **entertain** people, you do something that amuses or interests them. دل بہلانا
entertainer (**entertainers**) *n* An **entertainer** is a person whose job is to entertain audiences, for example by telling jokes, singing, or dancing. دل بہلانے والا
entertaining *adj* Something that is **entertaining** is amusing or interesting. تفریحی
enthusiasm *n* **Enthusiasm** is great eagerness to do something or to be involved in something. ولولہ
enthusiastic *adj* If you are **enthusiastic** about something, you show how much you like or enjoy it by the way that you behave and talk. پرجوش، جوشیلا
entire *adj* You use **entire** when you want to emphasize that you are referring to the whole of something. سب، سارا
entirely *adv* **Entirely** means completely. مکمل طور پر، پوری طرح سے
entrance (**entrances**) *n* The **entrance** of a place is the way you get into it. دروازہ
entrance fee (**entrance fees**) *n* An **entrance fee** is a sum of money which you pay before you go into somewhere such as a cinema or museum, or which you have to pay in order to join an organization or institution. داخلہ فیس
entry (**entries**) *n* An **entry** is something that you complete in order to take part in a competition, for example the answers to a set of questions. اندراج
entry phone (**entry phones**) *n* An **entry phone** is a type of telephone on the wall next to the entrance to a building enabling a person inside the building to speak to a person outside before opening the door. دروازہ کا فون
envelope (**envelopes**) *n* An **envelope** is the rectangular paper cover in which you send a letter through the post. لفافہ
envious *adj* If you are **envious** of someone else, you envy them. حاسد
environment (**environments**) *n* Someone's **environment** is their surroundings, especially the conditions in which they grow up, live, or work. ماحول
environmental *adj* **Environmental** means concerned with the protection of the natural world of land, sea, air, plants, and animals. ماحولیاتی
environmentally friendly *adj* **Environmentally friendly** products do not harm the environment. ماحولیاتی طور پر سازگار
envy (**envies, envying, envied**) *n* **Envy** is the feeling you have when you wish you could have the same thing or quality that someone else has. حسد، رشک ▷ *vt* If you **envy** someone, you wish that you had the same things or qualities that they have. رشک کرنا
epidemic (**epidemics**) *n* If there is an **epidemic** of a particular disease somewhere, it spreads quickly to a very large number of people there. وبائی
episode (**episodes**) *n* You can refer to an event or a short period of time as an **episode** if you want to suggest that it is important or unusual, or has some particular quality. واقعہ، سلسلے کا جزو
equal (**equals, equalling, equalled**) *adj* If two things are **equal**, or if one thing is **equal** to another, they are the same in size, number, or value. مساوی ▷ *vt* To **equal** something or someone means to be as good or as great as them. برابر کرنا
equality *n* **Equality** is a situation or state where all the members of a society or group have the same status, rights, and opportunities. برابری
equalize (**equalizes, equalizing, equalized**) *vt* To **equalize** a situation means to give everyone the same rights or opportunities. مساوی کرنا
equation (**equations**) *n* An **equation** is a mathematical statement saying that

two amounts or values are the same, for example 6x4=12x2. مساوات

equator *n* **The equator** is an imaginary line round the middle of the earth, halfway between the North and South poles. خط استوا

Equatorial Guinea *n* **Equatorial Guinea** is a republic of West Africa. استوائی گنی

equipment *n* **Equipment** consists of the things such as tools or machines which are used for a particular purpose. ساز و سامان

equipped *adj* If someone or something is **equipped**, they are provided with the tools or equipment that are needed. ساز و سامان سے لیس

equivalent *n* If one amount or value is the **equivalent** of another, they are the same. برابر

erase (**erases, erasing, erased**) *vt* If you **erase** a thought or feeling, you destroy it completely so that you can no longer remember it or feel it. مٹا

Eritrea *n* **Eritrea** is a small country in north-east Africa, on the Red Sea. اریٹریا

error (**errors**) *n* An **error** is a mistake. غلطی

escalator (**escalators**) *n* An **escalator** is a moving staircase. رواں زینہ

escape (**escapes, escaping, escaped**) *n* Someone's **escape** is the act of getting away from a particular place or situation. چھٹکارا ▷ *vi* If you **escape** from a place, you succeed in getting away from it. بچ نکلنا

escort (**escorts, escorting, escorted**) *vt* If you **escort** someone somewhere, you accompany them there, usually in order to make sure that they leave a place or get to their destination. بحفاظت لے جانا

especially *adv* You use **especially** to emphasize that what you are saying applies more to one person or thing than to any others. خاص طور سے

espionage *n* **Espionage** is the activity of finding out the political, military, or industrial secrets of your enemies or rivals by using spies. جاسوسی

essay (**essays**) *n* An **essay** is a piece of writing on a particular subject. مضمون

essential *adj* Something that is **essential** is absolutely necessary. لازمی

estate (**estates**) *n* An **estate** is a large area of land in the country owned by one person or organization. جاگیر

estate agent (**estate agents**) *n* An **estate agent** is someone who works for a company selling houses and land. جائداد دلال

estate car (**estate cars**) *n* An **estate** car is a car with a long body, a door at the rear, and space behind the back seats. ریاستی کار

estimate (**estimates, estimating, estimated**) *n* An **estimate** is an approximate calculation of a quantity or value. تخمینہ ▷ *vt* If you **estimate** a quantity or value, you make an approximate judgment or calculation of it. تخمینہ لگانا

Estonia *n* **Estonia** is a republic in north-east Europe, on the Gulf of Finland and the Baltic. اسٹونیا

Estonian (**Estonians**) *adj* **Estonian** means of, relating to, or characteristic of Estonia, its people, or their language. اسٹونیائی ▷ *n* An **Estonian** is a native or inhabitant of Estonia. اسٹونیائی باشندہ ▷ *n* **Estonian** is the official language of Estonia. اسٹونیائی زبان

etc *abbr* **etc** is used at the end of a list to show that you have not given a full list. **etc** is a written abbreviation for 'etcetera'. وغیرہ

eternal *adj* Something that is **eternal** lasts for ever. دائمی
eternity *n* **Eternity** is time without an end, or a state of existence outside time, especially the state which some people believe they will pass into after they have died. دوام
ethical *adj* **Ethical** means relating to beliefs about right and wrong. اخلاقی
Ethiopia *n* **Ethiopia** is a state in north-east Africa, on the Red Sea. ایتھوپیا
Ethiopian (**Ethiopians**) *adj* **Ethiopian** means belonging or relating to Ethiopia, or to its people, language, or culture. ایتھیوپیائی ▷ *n* An **Ethiopian** is an Ethiopian citizen, or a person of Ethiopian origin. ایتھیوپیائی باشندہ
ethnic *adj* **Ethnic** means relating to different racial or cultural groups of people. نسلی
EU *abbr* **The EU** is an organization of European countries which have joint policies on matters such as trade, agriculture, and finance. **EU** is an abbreviation of 'European Union'. یوروپین یونین
euro (**euros**) *n* The **euro** is a unit of currency that is used by the member countries of the European Union which have joined the European Monetary union. یورو
Europe *n* **Europe** is the second smallest continent in the world, situated between western Asia and the Atlantic Ocean. یوروپ
European (**Europeans**) *adj* **European** means coming from or relating to Europe. یوروپین ▷ *n* A **European** is a person who comes from Europe. یوروپیائی
European Union *n* **The European Union** is an organization of European countries which have joint policies on matters such as trade, agriculture, and finance. یوروپی یونین
evacuate (**evacuates, evacuating, evacuated**) *v* If people **are evacuated** from a place, they move out of it because it has become dangerous. نکالنا
eve (**eves**) *n* The **eve** of an event is the day before it, or the period of time just before it. پہلے کی شام
even *adj* Something that is **even** is flat and smooth. ہموار ▷ *adv* You use **even** to suggest that what comes just after or just before it in the sentence is surprising. بھی ▷ *adj* An **even** number is a number that you can divide by two, with nothing left over. جفت عدد، برابر
evening (**evenings**) *n* The **evening** is the part of each day between the end of the afternoon and the time when you go to bed. شام
evening class (**evening classes**) *n* An **evening class** is a course for adults that is taught in the evening rather than during the day. شام کی کلاس
evening dress *n* **Evening dress** consists of the formal clothes that people wear to formal occasions in the evening. شام کا لباس
event (**events**) *n* An **event** is something that happens. واقعہ
eventful *adj* If you describe an event or a period of time as **eventful**, you mean that a lot of interesting, exciting, or important things have happened during it. واقعات سے پر
eventually *adv* **Eventually** means in the end, especially after a lot of delays, problems, or arguments. آخر کار
ever *adv* **Ever** means at any time. کبھی
every *adj* You use **every** to mean all the people or things in a group. سبھی
everybody *pron* **Everybody** means all the people in a group, or all the people in the world. ہر کوئی
everyone *pron* **Everyone** means all the people in a group, or all the people in the world. ہر ایک
everything *pron* **Everything** means all of something. سب کچھ
everywhere *adv* **Everywhere** means in every place. ہر جگہ
evidence *n* **Evidence** is anything that

makes you believe that something is true or exists. ثبوت

evil *adj* If an act or a person is **evil**, they are morally very bad. شیطانی

evolution *n* **Evolution** is a process in which animals and plants slowly change over many years. ارتقاء

ewe (**ewes**) *n* A **ewe** is an adult female sheep. بھیڑ

exact *adj* Something that is **exact** is correct, accurate, and complete in every way. ٹھیک ٹھیک

exactly *adv* **Exactly** means in an exact manner, accurately or precisely. ٹھیک طور پر

exaggerate (**exaggerates, exaggerating, exaggerated**) *v* If you **exaggerate**, or **exaggerate** something, you make the thing that you are talking about seem bigger or more important than it actually is. مبالغہ کرنا

exaggeration *n* **Exaggeration**, or an **exaggeration**, is the act of saying that something is bigger, worse, or more important than it really is. مبالغہ

exam (**exams**) *n* An **exam** is a formal test taken to show your knowledge of a subject. امتحان

examination (**examinations**) *n* An **examination** is a formal test taken to show your knowledge of a subject. امتحان

examine (**examines, examining, examined**) *vt* If you **examine** something, you look at it or consider it carefully. جانچنا

examiner (**examiners**) *n* An **examiner** is a person who sets or marks an exam. ممتحن

example (**examples**) *n* An **example** is something which represents or is typical of a particular group of things. مثال

excellent *adj* Something that is **excellent** is very good indeed. بہت خوب

except *prep* You use **except** or **except for** to show that you are not counting something or somebody. سوائے

exception (**exceptions**) *n* An **exception** is a situation, thing, or person that is not included in a general statement. مستثنیٰ

exceptional *adj* You use **exceptional** to describe someone or something that ha a particular quality to an unusually high degree. استثنائی

excess baggage *n* On an aeroplane journey, **excess baggage** is luggage tha is larger or weighs more than your ticket allows, so that you have to pay extra to take it on board. فاضل سامان

excessive *adj* If something is **excessive**, i is too great in amount or degree. حد سے زیادہ

exchange (**exchanges, exchanging, exchanged**) *vt* If two or more people **exchange** things of a particular kind, they give them to each other at the sam time. ادلا بدلی کرنا

exchange rate (**exchange rates**) *n* The **exchange rate** of a country's unit of currency is the amount of another country's currency that you get in exchange for it. زرمبادلہ کی شرح

excited *adj* If you are **excited**, you are looking forward to something eagerly. مشتعل

exciting *adj* Something that is **exciting** makes you feel very happy or enthusiastic. اشتعال انگیز

exclamation mark (**exclamation marks**) *n* An **exclamation mark** is the punctuation mark! فجائی نشان

exclude (**excludes, excluding, excluded**) *vt* If you **exclude** someone from a place or activity, you prevent them from entering it or taking part in it. خارج کرنا

excluding *prep* You use **excluding** before mentioning a person or thing to show that you are not including them in your statement. بغیر

exclusively *adv* **Exclusively** is used to refer to situations or activities that involve only the thing or things mentioned, and nothing else. کام طور پر، بلا شرکت غیرے

excuse (**excuses, excusing, excused**) *n* An **excuse** is a reason which you give in order to explain why something has been done or has not been done, or to avoid doing something. عذر ▷ *vt* To **excuse** someone or to **excuse** their behaviour means to provide reasons for their actions, especially when other people disapprove of these actions. معذرت کرنا

execute (**executes, executing, executed**) *vt* To **execute** someone means to kill them as a punishment. سزائے موت دینا

execution (**executions**) *n* **Execution** is the act or process of killing someone as a punishment. سزائے موت

executive (**executives**) *n* An **executive** is someone employed by a company at a senior level. عامل

exercise (**exercises**) *n* When you do **exercise**, you move your body so that you can keep healthy and strong. ورزش، کثرت ▷ *n* An **exercise** is something you do to practise what you have learnt. مشق

exhaust (**exhausts**) *n* The **exhaust** or the **exhaust pipe** is the pipe which carries the gas out of the engine of a vehicle. دھواں نکاسی پیپ

exhausted *adj* If you are **exhausted**, you are very tired. تھکا ہوا

exhaust fumes *npl* **Exhaust fumes** are the gas or steam that is produced when the engine of a vehicle is running. باقی دھواں، بخارات

exhibition (**exhibitions**) *n* An **exhibition** is a public display of art, products, skills, activities, etc. نمائش

ex-husband (**ex-husbands**) *n* A woman's **ex-husband** was once her husband but is no longer her husband. سابق شوہر

exile *n* If someone is living in **exile**, they are living in a foreign country because they cannot live in their own country, usually for political reasons. جلا وطن

exist (**exists, existing, existed**) *vi* If something **exists**, it is present in the world as a real thing. وجود میں ہونا

exit (**exits**) *n* An **exit** is a doorway through which you can leave a public building. نکاسی

exotic *adj* Something that is **exotic** is unusual and interesting, usually because it comes from another country. غیر ملکی، بیرونی

expect (**expects, expecting, expected**) *vt* If you **expect** something to happen, you believe that it will happen. توقع کرنا

expedition (**expeditions**) *n* An **expedition** is a journey made for a particular purpose such as exploration. مہم

expel (**expels, expelling, expelled**) *vt* If someone **is expelled** from a school or organization, they are officially told to leave because they have behaved badly. نکالنا

expenditure (**expenditures**) *n* **Expenditure** is the spending of money on something, or the money that is spent on something. خرچ، صرفہ

expenses *npl* Your **expenses** are the money you spend while doing something in the course of your work, which will be paid back to you afterwards. اخراجات

expensive *adj* If something is **expensive**, it costs a lot of money. مہنگا

experience (**experiences**) *n* **Experience** is knowledge or skill in a particular job or activity, which you have gained from doing that job or activity. تجربہ

experienced *adj* If you describe someone as **experienced**, you mean that they have been doing a particular job or activity for a long time, and therefore know a lot about it or are very skilful at it. تجربہ کار

experiment (**experiments**) *n* An **experiment** is a scientific test which is done to discover what happens to something in particular conditions. تجربہ

expert (**experts**) *n* An **expert** is a person

e

who is very skilled at doing something or who knows a lot about a particular subject. ماہر

expire (**expires, expiring, expired**) *vi* When something such as a contract or a visa **expires**, it comes to an end or is no longer valid. ختم ہونا

expiry date (**expiry dates**) *n* The **expiry date** of an official document or agreement is the date after which it is no longer valid. تاریخ اختتام

explain (**explains, explaining, explained**) *vt* If you **explain** something, you give details about it or describe it so that it can be understood. تشریح کرنا، وضاحت کرنا

explanation (**explanations**) *n* If you give an **explanation**, you give reasons why something happened, or describe something in detail. تشریح، وضاحت

explode (**explodes, exploding, exploded**) *vi* If something such as a bomb **explodes**, it bursts with great force. دھاکے سے پھٹنا

exploit(**exploits, exploiting, exploited**) *vt* If someone **exploits** you, they unfairly use your work or ideas and give you little in return. استحصال کرنا

exploitation *n* **Exploitation** is the act of treating someone unfairly by using their work or ideas and giving them little in return. استحصال

explore (**explores, exploring, explored**) *v* If you **explore**, or **explore** a place, you travel around it to find out what it is like. دریافتی سیاحت کرنا

explorer (**explorers**) *n* An **explorer** is someone who travels to places about which very little is known, in order to discover what is there. دریافتی سیاح

explosion (**explosions**) *n* An **explosion** is a sudden violent burst of energy, for example one caused by a bomb. دھاکہ

explosive (**explosives**) *n* An **explosive** is a substance or device that can cause an explosion. دھاکہ خیز اشیاء

export (**exports, exporting, exported**) *n* **Export** is the selling of products or raw materials to another country. برآمد ▷ *v* To **export** products or raw materials means to sell them to another country. برآمد کرنا

express (**expresses, expressing, expressed**) *vt* When you **express** an idea or feeling, you show what you think or feel. اظہار کرنا

expression (**expressions**) *n* The **expression** of ideas or feelings is the showing of them through words, actions or art. اظہار

extension (**extensions**) *n* An **extension** is a new room or building which is added to an existing building. توسیع

extension cable (**extension cables**) *n* An **extension cable** is an electrical cable that is connected to the cable on a piece of equipment in order to make it reach further. توسیعی کیبل

extensive *adj* Something that is **extensive** covers a large area. وسیع

extensively *adv* If you travel **extensively** you cover a large physical area. وسیع پیمانے پر

extent *n* The **extent** of a situation is how great, important, or serious it is. وسعت، حد

exterior *adj* You use **exterior** to refer to the outside parts of something, or to things that are outside something. باہری

external *adj* **External** means happening, coming from, or existing outside a place, person, or area of activity. بیرونی

extinct *adj* If a species of animals is **extinct**, it no longer has any living members. نایاب

extinguisher (**extinguishers**) *n* An **extinguisher** is a metal cylinder which contains water or chemicals at high pressure which can put out fires. بجھانے والا

extortionate *adj* If you describe something such as a price as **extortionate**, you are emphasizing that it is much greater than it should be. استحصالی

extra *adj* You use **extra** to describe an

amount, person, or thing that is added to others of the same kind, or that can be added to others of the same kind. فاضل ▷ *adv* You can use **extra** in front of adjectives and adverbs to emphasize the quality that they are describing. زائد

xtraordinary *adj* An **extraordinary** person or thing has some extremely good or special quality. غیر معمولی

xtravagant *adj* Someone who is **extravagant** spends more money than they can afford or uses more of something than is reasonable. فضول خرچ

xtreme *adj* **Extreme** means very great in degree or intensity. انتہائی

xtremely *adv* You use **extremely** in front of adjectives and adverbs to emphasize that the specified quality is present to a very great degree. انتہائی طور پر

xtremism *n* **Extremism** is the behaviour or beliefs of people who try to bring about political change by using violent or extreme methods. انتہاپسندی

xtremist (**extremists**) *n* If you describe someone as an **extremist**, you disapprove of them because they try to bring about political change by using violent or extreme methods. انتہاپسند

x-wife (**ex-wives**) *n* A man's **ex-wife** was once his wife but is no longer his wife. سابقہ بیوی

ye (**eyes**) *n* Your **eyes** are the parts of your body with which you see. آنکھ

yebrow (**eyebrows**) *n* Your **eyebrows** are the lines of hair which grow above your eyes. ابرو

ye drops *npl* **Eye drops** are a kind of medicine that you put in your eyes one drop at a time. بوند کی شکل میں ڈالنے والی آنکھ کی دوا

yelash (**eyelashes**) *n* Your **eyelashes** are the hairs which grow on the edges of your eyelids. پلکوں کے بال

yelid (**eyelids**) *n* Your **eyelids** are the two flaps of skin which cover your eyes when they are closed. پلک

eyeliner (**eyeliners**) *n* **Eyeliner** is a special kind of pencil which some women use on the edges of their eyelids next to their eyelashes in order to look more attractive. کاجل پینسل

eye shadow (**eye shadows**) *n* **Eye shadow** is a substance which you can paint on your eyelids in order to make them a different colour. آئی شیڈو

eyesight *n* Your **eyesight** is your ability to see. بینائی

e

f

fabric (**fabrics**) *n* **Fabric** is cloth. سوتی کپڑا

fabulous *adj* You use **fabulous** to emphasize how wonderful or impressive you think something is. (*informal*) حیرت انگیز

face (**faces, facing, faced**) *n* Your **face** is the front part of your head. چہرہ ▷ *vt* To **face** a particular direction means to look directly in that direction. رخ کرنا

face cloth (**face cloths**) *n* A **face cloth** is a small cloth made of towelling which you use for washing yourself. چہرہ صاف کرنے کا تولیہ

facial (**facials**) *adj* **Facial** is used to describe things that relate to your face. چہرے سے متعلق ▷ *n* A **facial** is a sort of beauty treatment in which someone's face is massaged, and creams and other substances are rubbed into it. فیشل (چہرے کا مساج)

facilities *npl* **Facilities** are buildings, equipment, or services that are provided for a particular purpose. سہولیات

fact (**facts**) *n* **Facts** are pieces of information which can be proved to be true. حقیقت

factory (**factories**) *n* A **factory** is a large building where machines are used to make goods in large quantities. کارخانہ

fade (**fades, fading, faded**) *v* When something **fades**, or when something **fades** it, it slowly becomes less intense in brightness, colour, or sound. دھندلانا

fail (**fails, failing, failed**) *v* If you **fail** or **fail** to do something that you were trying to do, you do not succeed in doing it. ناکام ہونا

failure (**failures**) *n* **Failure** is a lack of success in doing or achieving something. ناکامی

faint (**fainter, faintest, faints, fainting, fainted**) *adj* Something that is **faint** is not strong or intense. نحیف ▷ *vi* If you **faint**, you lose consciousness for a short time, especially because you are hungry, or because of pain, heat, or shock. بیہوش ہونا

fair (**fairer, fairest, fairs**) *adj* If something is **fair**, it seems right because it is the same for everyone. منصفانہ ▷ *adj* **Fair** hair is pale yellow in colour. ہلکے پیلے رنگ کا ▷ *n* A **fair** is a place where you can play games to win prizes, and you can ride on special, big machines for fun. نمائش، میلا

fairground (**fairgrounds**) *n* A **fairground** is a part of a park or field where people pay to ride on various machines for amusement or try to win prizes in games. میلا گاہ، نمائش گاہ

fairly *adv* **Fairly** means to quite a large degree. نمایاں طور پر

fairness *n* **Fairness** is the quality of being reasonable, right, and just. منصف مزاجی

fairy (**fairies**) *n* A **fairy** is an imaginary creature with magical powers. پری

fairy tale (**fairy tales**) *n* A **fairy tale** is a story for children involving magical events and imaginary creatures. الف لیلوی داستان

faith *n* If you have **faith** in someone or something, you feel confident about their ability or goodness. اعتماد، عقیدہ

faithful *adj* If you are **faithful** to a person, organization, or idea, you remain firm in your support for them. وفادار

faithfully *adv* If you do something **faithfully**, you remain firm in your support for a person, organization, or idea. وفادارانہ طور پر

ake (**fakes**) *adj* A **fake** fur or a **fake** painting, for example, is a fur or painting that has been made to look valuable or genuine, usually in order to deceive people. فرضی، نقلی ▷ *n* A **fake** is an object, person, or act that is not genuine. بناوٹی

ll (**falls, falling, fell, fallen**) *n* A **fall** is an act of falling. گراوٹ ▷ *vi* If a person or thing **falls**, they move towards the ground suddenly by accident. گرنا

all down *v* If a person or thing **falls down**, they move from an upright position, so that they are lying on the ground. گر پڑنا *He fell down the stairs.*

all for *v* If you **fall for** someone, you are strongly attracted to them and start loving them. عشق کا شکار ہونا، دام میں پھنسنا *I fell for him right away.*

all out *v* If a person's hair or a tooth **falls out**, it becomes loose and separates from their body. ٹوٹ کر گرنا

lse *adj* If something is **false**, it is incorrect, untrue, or mistaken. غلط

lse alarm (**false alarms**) *n* When you think something dangerous is about to happen, but then discover that you were mistaken, you can say that it was a **false alarm**. جھوٹا الارم

me *n* If you achieve **fame**, you become very well known. شہرت

miliar *adj* If someone or something is **familiar** to you, you recognize them or know them well. مقبول، جانا پہچانا

mily (**families**) *n* A **family** is a group of people who are related to each other, especially parents and their children. خاندان

mine (**famines**) *n* A **famine** is a serious shortage of food in a country, which may cause many deaths. قحط

mous *adj* Someone or something that is **famous** is very well known. مشہور

n (**fans**) *n* If you are a **fan** of someone or something, you admire them and are very interested in them. شائق، شوقین

fanatic (**fanatics**) *n* If you describe someone as a **fanatic**, you disapprove of them because you consider their behaviour or opinions to be very extreme. جنونی

fan belt (**fan belts**) *n* In a car engine, the **fan belt** is the belt that drives the fan which keeps the engine cool. پنکھے کی بیلٹ (کار میں)

fancy (**fancies, fancying, fancied, fancier, fanciest**) *vt* If you **fancy** something, you want to have it or do it. (*informal*) تصور کرنا، تمنا کرنا ▷ *adj* Something that is **fancy** is special and not ordinary. عمدہ ترین، خصوصی

fancy dress *n* **Fancy dress** is clothing that you wear for a party at which everyone tries to look like a famous person or a person from a story, from history, or from a particular profession. رواجی لباس

fantastic *adj* If you say that something is **fantastic**, you are emphasizing that you think it is very good. (*informal*) شاندار

FAQ (**FAQs**) *abbr* **FAQ** is used especially on websites to refer to questions about a particular topic. **FAQ** is an abbreviation for 'frequently asked questions'. متعدد بار پوچھے گئے سوالات

far (**farther, farthest**) *adj* You use **far** to refer to the part that is the greatest distance from the centre. زیادہ دور ▷ *adv* If something is **far** away, it is a long way away. دور

fare (**fares**) *n* The **fare** is the money that you pay for a journey by bus, taxi, train, boat, or aeroplane. کرایہ

Far East *n* In the West, the expression '**The Far East**' is used to refer to all the countries of Eastern Asia, including China and Japan. بعید مشرق

farewell! *excl* **Farewell!** means the same as goodbye! الوداع

farm (**farms**) *n* A **farm** is an area of land consisting of fields and buildings, where crops are grown or animals are raised. فارم (کھیت مع گھر)

farmer (**farmers**) *n* A **farmer** is a person who owns or manages a farm. دہقان، کسان

farmhouse (**farmhouses**) *n* A **farmhouse** is the main house on a farm, usually where the farmer lives. فارم ہاؤس (فارم کا گھر)

farming *n* **Farming** is the activity of growing crops or keeping animals on a farm. کھیتی باڑی

Faroe Islands *npl* The **Faroe Islands** are a group of 21 islands in the North Atlantic, between Iceland and the Shetland Islands. جزائر فارو

fascinating *adj* If you find something **fascinating**, you find it extremely interesting. دلفریب

fashion *n* **Fashion** is the area of activity that involves styles of clothing and appearance. فیشن

fashionable *adj* Something that is **fashionable** is popular or approved of at a particular time. فیشن ایبل، فیشن پرست

fast (**faster, fastest**) *adj* **Fast** means happening, moving, or doing something at great speed. You also use **fast** in questions or statements about speed. تیز ▷ *adv* You use **fast** to say that something happens without any delay. تیزی سے

fat (**fatter, fattest, fats**) *adj* A **fat** person has a lot of flesh on their body and weighs too much. موٹا ▷ *n* **Fat** is a substance in many foods which your body uses to produce energy. چربی

fatal *adj* A **fatal** action has undesirable results. مہلک

fate *n* **Fate** is a power that some people believe controls everything that happens. تقدیر

father (**fathers**) *n* Your **father** is your male parent. باپ

father-in-law (**fathers-in-law**) *n* Your **father-in-law** is the father of your husband or wife. سسر

fault *n* If a bad or undesirable situation is your **fault**, you caused it or are responsible for it. قصور

faulty *adj* A **faulty** machine or piece of equipment is not working properly. ناقص

fauna *npl* Animals, especially those in a particular area, can be referred to as **fauna**. چرند پرند (حیوانات)

favour *n* If you regard something or someone with **favour**, you like or support them. طرفداری

favourite (**favourites**) *adj* Your **favourite** thing or person of a particular type is the one you like most. پسندیدہ ▷ *n* A **favourite** is a person or thing regarded with especial preference or liking. پسند

fax (**faxes, faxing, faxed**) *n* A **fax** or a **fax machine** is a piece of equipment used to send and receive documents electronically along a telephone line. فیکس (تحریری ترسیل) ▷ *vt* If you **fax** a document, you send a document from one fax machine to another. فیکس کرنا

fear (**fears, fearing, feared**) *n* **Fear** is the unpleasant feeling of worry that you get when you think that you are in danger or that something horrible is going to happen. خوف ▷ *vt* If you **fear** something unpleasant, you are worried that it might happen, or might have happened. ڈرنا

feasible *adj* If something is **feasible**, it can be done, made, or achieved. قابل عمل

feather (**feathers**) *n* A bird's **feathers** are the light soft things covering its body. پنکھ

feature (**features**) *n* A particular **feature** of something is an interesting or important part or characteristic of it. فیچر (نمایاں حصہ)

February (**Februaries**) *n* **February** is the second month of the year in the Western calendar. فروری

fed up *adj* Someone who is **fed up** is bored or annoyed. (*informal*) بیزار

fee (**fees**) *n* A **fee** is a sum of money that

you pay to be allowed to do something. فیس، حق خدمت

eed (**feeds, feeding, fed**) *vt* If you **feed** a person or animal, you give them food. کھلانا، پلانا

eedback *n* When you get **feedback** on your work or progress, someone tells you how well or badly you are doing. فیڈبیک، تعامل

eel (**feels, feeling, felt**) *v* The way you **feel**, for example happy or sad, or cold or tired, is how you are at the time. احساس ▷ *vt* If you **feel** something, you touch it with your hand to see what it is like. محسوس کرنا

eeling (**feelings**) *n* A **feeling** is an emotion. جذبہ، احساس

eet *npl* Your **feet** are the parts of your body that are at the ends of your legs, and that you stand on. پیر

elt *n* **Felt** is a type of thick cloth made from wool or other fibres packed tightly together. نمدا

elt-tip (**felt-tips**) *n* A **felt-tip** or a **felt-tip pen** is a pen which has a piece of fibre at the end that the ink comes through. پین جس کے نب میں روشنائی نمدے سے آتی ہے

emale (**females**) *adj* Someone who is **female** is a woman or a girl. زنانہ، نسوانی ▷ *n* Women and girls are sometimes referred to as **females** when they are being considered as a type. زن، خاتون

eminine *adj* **Feminine** means relating to women or considered typical of or suitable for them. نسوانی

eminist (**feminists**) *n* A **feminist** is a person who believes that women should have the same rights and opportunities as men. حامیٔ نسواں

ence (**fences**) *n* A **fence** is a barrier made of wood or wire supported by posts. جنگلا، باڑا

ennel *n* **Fennel** is a plant with a crisp rounded base and feathery leaves. It can be eaten as a vegetable or the leaves can be used as a herb. بوٹی (پودا)، سویا

fern (**ferns**) *n* A **fern** is a plant with long stems, thin leaves, and no flowers. بے پھول پودا

ferret (**ferrets**) *n* A **ferret** is a small, fierce animal which hunts rabbits and rats. فیریٹ (چوہا، خرگوش یا بلی نما جانور)

ferry (**ferries**) *n* A **ferry** is a boat that carries passengers or vehicles across a river or a narrow stretch of sea. گھاٹ کی کشتی

fertile *adj* Land or soil that is **fertile** is able to support a large number of strong healthy plants. زرخیز

fertilizer (**fertilizers**) *n* **Fertilizer** is a substance that you spread on the ground to make plants grow more successfully. کھاد

festival (**festivals**) *n* A **festival** is an organized series of events and performances. تہوار

fetch (**fetches, fetching, fetched**) *vt* If you **fetch** something or someone, you go and get them from where they are. جاکر لانا

fever (**fevers**) *n* If you have a **fever**, your temperature is higher than usual because you are ill. بخار، حرارت

few *det* A **few** means some, but not many. چند، تھوڑا *She gave me a few sweets.* ▷ *pron* You use a **few** to refer to a small number of things or people. کچھ *The doctors are all busy and a few work more than 100 hours a week.*

fewer (**fewest**) *adj* You use **fewer** to indicate that you are talking about a number of people or things that is smaller than another number. نسبتاً تھوڑے

fiancé (**fiancés**) *n* A woman's **fiancé** is the man she is engaged to and will marry. منگیتر (مرد)

fiancée (**fiancées**) *n* A man's **fiancé** is the woman he is engaged to and will marry. منگیتر (خاتون)

fibre (**fibres**) *n* A **fibre** is a thin thread of a natural or artificial substance, especially one used to make cloth or rope. ریشہ

fibreglass *n* **Fibreglass** is plastic strengthened with short, thin threads of glass. فائبر شیشہ

fiction *n* **Fiction** is stories about imaginary people and events. تصور، تخیل

field (**fields**) *n* A **field** is an enclosed area of land where crops are grown or animals are kept. کھیت

fierce (**fiercer, fiercest**) *adj* A **fierce** animal or person is very aggressive or angry. شدید

fifteen *num* **Fifteen** is the number 15. پندرہ

fifteenth *adj* The **fifteenth** item in a series is the one that you count as number fifteen. پندرہواں

fifth *adj* The **fifth** item in a series is the one that you count as number five. پانچواں

fifty *num* **Fifty** is the number 50. پچاس

fifty-fifty *adj* If a division or sharing of something such as money or property between two people is **fifty-fifty**, each person gets half of it. (*informal*) نصف ۔ نصف ▷ *adv* If something such as money or property is divided or shared **fifty-fifty** between two people, each person gets half of it. (*informal*) نصف ۔ نصف حاصل کرنا

fig (**figs**) *n* A **fig** is a soft sweet fruit full of tiny seeds. Figs grow on trees in hot countries. انجیر

fight (**fights, fighting, fought**) *n* A **fight** against something is an attempt to stop it. لڑائی ▷ *v* If you **fight** something unpleasant, you try in a determined way to prevent it or stop it happening. لڑنا

fighting *n* **Fighting** is a battle, struggle, or physical combat. لڑائی، جنگ

figure (**figures**) *n* A **figure** is a particular amount expressed as a number, especially a statistic. عدد

figure out *v* If you **figure out** a solution to a problem or the reason for something, you succeed in solving it or understanding it. (*informal*) حل کرنا *His parents could not figure out how to start their new computer.*

Fiji *n* **Fiji** is an independent republic, consisting of 844 islands in the south-west Pacific. فجی (جمہوریہ ۸۴۴ جزائر)

file (**files, filing, filed**) *n* A **file** is a box or folder in which documents are kept. فائل ▷ *n* A **file** is a tool with rough surfaces, used for smoothing and shaping hard materials. ریتی ▷ *vt* If you **file** a document, you put it in the correct file. فائل میں رکھنا ▷ *vt* If you **file** an object, you smooth or shape it with a file. ریتنا

Filipino (**Filipinos**) *adj* **Filipino** means belonging or relating to the Philippines, or to its people or culture. فلپائنی ▷ *n* A **Filipino** is a person who comes from the Philippines. فلپائنی باشندہ

fill (**fills, filling, filled**) *v* If you **fill** a container or area, or if it **fills**, an amount of something enters it that is enough to make it full. بھرنا

fillet (**fillets, filleting, filleted**) *n* A **fillet** of fish or meat is a piece that has no bones in it. بے ہڈی گوشت ▷ *vt* When you **fillet** fish or meat, you prepare it by taking the bones out. گوشت سے ہڈی نکالنا

fill in *v* When you **fill in** a form, you write information in the spaces on it. خانہ پری کرنا *Fill in the coupon and send it to the address shown.*

fill up *v* If you **fill** a container **up**, you keep putting or pouring something into it until it is full. منہ تک بھرنا *Filling up your car's petrol tank these days is very expensive.*

film (**films**) *n* A **film** consists of moving pictures that have been recorded so that they can be shown in a cinema or on television. فلم (سنیما)

film star (**film stars**) *n* A **film star** is a famous actor or actress who appears in films. فلم اسٹار (اداکار)

filter (**filters, filtering, filtered**) *n* A **filter** is a device through which a substance is passed when it is being filtered. فلٹر (چھنے

والا) ⊳ *vt* To **filter** a substance, or to **filter** particles out of a substance, means to pass it through a device which removes the particles from it. چھاننا

lthy (**filthier, filthiest**) **adj** Something that is **filthy** is very dirty indeed. غلیظ

nal (**finals**) *adj* In a series of events, things, or people, the **final** one is the last one, or the one that happens at the end. (فاءنل) آخری ⊳ *n* A **final** is the last game or contest in a series, which decides the overall winner. فائنل (فیصلہ کن)

inalize (**finalizes, finalizing, finalized**) *vt* If you **finalize** something that you are arranging, you complete the arrangements for it. آخری نتیجہ تک پہنچنا، پہنچانا

inally *adv* If something **finally** happens, it happens after a long delay. آخر کار

inance (**finances, financing, financed**) *n* **Finance** is funds provided to pay for a project or a purchase, or the provision of these funds. رقم، مال ⊳ *vt* When someone **finances** something such as a project or a purchase, they provide the money that is needed to pay for them. رقم، مال دینا

inancial *adj* **Financial** means relating to or involving money. مالی، رقوماتی

inancial year (**financial years**) *n* A **financial year** is a period of twelve months, used by government, business, and other organizations in order to calculate their budgets, profits, and losses. مالی سال

nd (**finds, finding, found**) *vt* If you **find** someone or something, you see them or learn where they are. پانا

ind out *v* If you **find** something **out**, you learn it, often by making an effort to do so. دریافت کرنا، معلوم کرنا *They wanted to find out the truth.*

ine (**finer, finest, fines**) *adj* When the weather is **fine**, it is dry and sunny. اچھا ہونا ⊳ *adj* If you say that you are **fine**, you mean that you are well or happy. ٹھیک ہونا ⊳ *adj* Something that is **fine** is very thin. باریک ⊳ *n* A **fine** is money that a person is ordered to pay because they have done something wrong. جرمانہ

finger (**fingers**) *n* Your **fingers** are the four long moveable parts at the end of your hands. انگلی

fingernail (**fingernails**) *n* Your **fingernails** are the hard areas on the ends of your fingers. انگلی کے ناخن

fingerprint (**fingerprints**) *n* **Fingerprints** are marks made by a person's fingers which show the lines on the skin. Everyone's fingerprints are different, so they can be used to identify criminals. انگلیوں کے نشان

finish (**finishes, finishing, finished**) *n* **The finish** of something is the end of it or the last part of it. آخر ⊳ *vt* When you **finish** doing or dealing with something, you do or deal with the last part of it, so that there is no more for you to do or deal with. ختم کرنا

finished *adj* If you are **finished with** something, you are no longer doing it or interested in it. خاتم

Finland *n* **Finland** is a republic in north Europe, on the Baltic Sea. فن لینڈ

Finn (**Finns**) *n* The **Finns** are the people of Finland. فنی باشندے

Finnish *adj* **Finnish** means belonging or relating to Finland or to its people, language, or culture. فنی ⊳ *n* **Finnish** is the language spoken in Finland. فنی زبان

fire *n* **Fire** is the hot, bright flames that come from something that is burning. آگ

fire alarm (**fire alarms**) *n* A **fire alarm** is a device that makes a noise, for example with a bell, to warn people when there is a fire. فایر الارم

fire brigade (**fire brigades**) *n* **The fire brigade** is an organization which has the job of putting out fires. فایر برگید

fire escape (**fire escapes**) *n* A **fire escape** is a metal staircase on the outside of a building, which can be used to escape from the building if there is a fire. دھاتی سیڑھی

fire extinguisher (**fire extinguishers**) *n* A **fire extinguisher** is a metal cylinder which contains water or chemicals at high pressure which can put out fires. آگ بجھانے والا

fireman (**firemen**) *n* A **fireman** is a person whose job is to put out fires. فائر مین

fireplace (**fireplaces**) *n* In a room, the **fireplace** is the place where a fire can be lit. آتش دان

firewall (**firewalls**) *n* A **firewall** is a computer system or program that automatically prevents an unauthorized person from gaining access to a computer when it is connected to a network such as the Internet. کمپیوٹر کا حفاظتی نظام

fireworks *npl* **Fireworks** are small objects that are lit to entertain people on special occasions. They burn in a bright, attractive, and often noisy way. آتشبازی

firm (**firmer, firmest, firms**) *adj* Something that is **firm** is fairly hard and does not change much in shape when it is pressed. مضبوط ▷ *n* A **firm** is a business selling or producing something. فرم (تجارتی ادارہ)

first *adj* If a person or thing is **first**, they come before all the others. پہلے ▷ *adv* If you do something **first**, you do it before anyone else does, or before you do anything else. اولاً ▷ *n* An event that is described as a **first** has never happened before. پہلی بار

first aid *n* **First aid** is medical treatment given as soon as possible to a sick or injured person. فرسٹ ایڈ (ابتدائی طبی علاج)

first-aid kit (**first-aid kits**) *n* A **first-aid kit** is a bag or case containing basic medical supplies that are designed to be used on someone who is injured or who suddenly becomes ill. فرسٹ ایڈ کٹ

first-class *adj* Something or someone that is **first-class** is of the highest quality or standard. اول درجے کا

firstly *adv* You use **firstly** when you are about to mention the first in a series of items. اولین طور پر

first name (**first names**) *n* Your **first name** is the first of the names that you were given when you were born, as opposed to your family name. پہلا نام

fir tree fir trees *n* A **fir** or a **fir tree** is a tall pointed tree. صنوبر کا درخت

fiscal *adj* **Fiscal** means related to government money or public money, especially taxes. عوامی مالیاتی

fiscal year (**fiscal years**) *n* The **fiscal year** is a twelve-month period beginning and ending in April, which governments and businesses use to plan their finances. مالیاتی سال

fish (**fish, fishes, fishing, fished**) *n* A **fish** is a creature with a tail and fins that lives in water. مچھلی ▷ *vi* If you **fish**, you try to catch fish. مچھلی مارنا

fisherman (**fishermen**) *n* A **fisherman** is a person who catches fish as a job or for sport. مچھیرا، ماہیگیر

fishing *n* **Fishing** is the sport or business of catching fish. ماہیگیری

fishing boat (**fishing boats**) *n* A **fishing boat** is a boat that is used in the business of catching fish. ماہیگیری ناو

fishing rod (**fishing rods**) *n* A **fishing rod** is a long, thin pole which has a line and hook attached to it and which is used for catching fish. بنسی

fishing tackle *n* **Fishing tackle** consists of all the equipment that is used in the sport of fishing, such as fishing rods, lines, hooks, and bait. ڈوری بنسی

fishmonger (**fishmongers**) *n* A **fishmonger** is a shopkeeper who sells fish. ماہی فروش

fist (**fists**) *n* You refer to someone's hand as their **fist** when they have bent their fingers towards their palm. مٹھی

fit (**fitter, fittest, fits, fitting, fitted**) *adj* If something is **fit** for a particular purpose, it is suitable for that purpose. فٹ، مناسب ▷ *n* If something is a good **fit**, it fits well. مناسب ▷ *v* If something **fits** you, it is the right size and shape for you. مناسب ہونا، موزوں ہونا

fit in *v* If you manage to **fit** a person or task **in**, you manage to find time to deal with them. - - - کے قابل ہونا *I find that I just can't fit in the housework.*

fitted carpet (**fitted carpets**) *n* A **fitted carpet** is cut to the same shape as a room so that it covers the floor completely. فٹ کی ہوئی قالین

fitted kitchen (**fitted kitchens**) *n* A **fitted kitchen** is a kitchen with units that are attached to the wall. جڑا ہوا کچن (دیوار سے)

fitted sheet (**fitted sheets**) *n* A **fitted sheet** is a bedsheet with the corners sewn so that they fit over the corners of the mattress and do not have to be folded. کونے سلی چادر

fitting room (**fitting rooms**) *n* A **fitting room** is a room or cubicle in a shop where you can put on clothes to see how they look. فٹنگ روم (درزی کے ہاں)

five *num* **Five** is the number 5. پانچ

fix (**fixes, fixing, fixed**) *vt* If you **fix** something to another thing, you join them together. لگانا، نصب کرنا ▷ *vt* If you **fix** something that is broken, you mend it. ٹھیک کرنا

fixed *adj* You use **fixed** to describe something which stays the same and does not vary. فکس کیا ہوا

fizzy (**fizzier, fizziest**) *adj* **Fizzy** drinks are full of little bubbles of gas. بلبلے دار مشروب

flabby (**flabbier, flabbiest**) *adj* **Flabby** people are rather fat, with loose flesh over their bodies. تھل تھل بدن

flag (**flags**) *n* A **flag** is a piece of coloured cloth used as a sign for something or as a signal. پرچم، جھنڈا

flame (**flames**) *n* A **flame** is a hot bright stream of burning gas that comes from something that is burning. لپٹ

flamingo (**flamingos, flamingoes**) *n* A **flamingo** is a bird with pink feathers, long thin legs, a long neck, and a curved beak. Flamingos live near water in warm countries. سارس

flammable *adj* **Flammable** chemicals, gases, cloth, or other things catch fire and burn easily. آتشی اشیاء

flan (**flans**) *n* A **flan** is a food that has a base and sides of pastry or sponge cake. The base is filled with fruit or savoury food. فلان (کیک)

flannel (**flannels**) *n* A **flannel** is a small cloth that you use for washing yourself. فلالین

flap (**flaps, flapping, flapped**) *v* If something that is attached at one end **flaps**, or if you **flap** it, it moves quickly up and down or from side to side. پھڑپھڑانا

flash (**flashes, flashing, flashed**) *n* A **flash** of light is a sudden, short burst of it. فلیش (کیمرا میں) ▷ *v* If a light **flashes**, or if you **flash** a light, it shines brightly and suddenly. فلیش مارنا

flask (**flasks**) *n* A **flask** is a bottle used for carrying alcoholic or hot drinks around with you. تھرموس

flat (**flatter, flattest, flats**) *adj* Something that is **flat** is level and smooth. ہموار ▷ *n* A **flat** is a set of rooms for living in, that is part of a larger building. فلیٹ (گھر)

flat-screen *adj* A **flat-screen** television set or computer monitor has a slim flat screen. چپٹا اسکرین (کمپیوٹر، ٹی وی)

flatter (**flatters, flattering, flattered**) *vt* If someone **flatters** you, they praise you in an exaggerated way that is not sincere. خوشامد کرنا

flattered *adj* If you are **flattered** by something that has happened, you are pleased about it because it makes you feel important. جس کی خوشامد کی گئی ہو

flavour (**flavours**) *n* The **flavour** of a food or drink is its taste. ذائقہ، فلیور

flavouring (**flavourings**) *n* **Flavourings** are substances that are added to food or drink to give it a particular taste. مسالہ

flaw (**flaws**) *n* A **flaw** in something such as a theory is a mistake in it. نقص

flea (**fleas**) *n* A **flea** is a small jumping insect that sucks human or animal blood. پسو

flea market (**flea markets**) *n* A **flea market** is an outdoor market which sells cheap used goods and sometimes also very old furniture. استعمال شدہ سامان کی دوکان

flee (**flees, fleeing, fled**) *v* If you **flee**, you escape from something or someone by running away. (*written*) فرار ہونا

fleece (**fleeces**) *n* A sheep's **fleece** is its coat of wool. بھیڑ کی اون

fleet (**fleets**) *n* A **fleet** is an organized group of ships. جہازی بیڑہ

flex (**flexes**) *n* A **flex** is an electric cable containing wires that is connected to an electrical appliance. بجلی آلہ سے جڑا کیبل

flexible *adj* A **flexible** object or material can be bent easily without breaking. لچکدار

flexitime *n* **Flexitime** is a system that allows employees to vary the time that they start or finish work, provided that an agreed total number of hours are spent at work. مختلف الاوقاتی کام کے گھنٹے

flight (**flights**) *n* A **flight** is a journey made by flying, usually in an aeroplane. پرواز

flight attendant (**flight attendants**) *n* On an aeroplane, the **flight attendants** are the people whose job is to look after the passengers and serve their meals. پرواز خادم

fling (**flings, flinging, flung**) *vt* If you **fling** something or someone somewhere, you throw them there suddenly, using a lot of force. پھینک دینا

flip-flops *npl* **Flip-flops** are open shoes which are held on your feet by a strap that goes between your toes. ہوائی چپل

flippers *npl* **Flippers** are flat pieces of rubber that you can wear on your feet to help you swim more quickly, especially underwater. فلپرس (تیراکی جوتے)

flirt (**flirts, flirting, flirted**) *n* A **flirt** is someone who flirts a lot. تفریحاً محبت ▷ *vi* If you **flirt** with someone, you behave as if you are sexually attracted to them, in a playful or not very serious way. تفریحاً عشق جتانا

float (**floats, floating, floated**) *n* A **float** is a light object that is used to help someone or something float in water. تیراک چیز ▷ *vi* If something **floats** in a liquid, it stays on top of it. تیرنا ▷ *vi* If something **floats** in the air, it moves slowly through it. ہوا میں تیرنا، جھولنا

flock (**flocks**) *n* A **flock** of birds, sheep, or goats is a group of them. **Flock** can take the singular or plural form of the verb. جھنڈ

flood (**floods, flooding, flooded**) *n* If there is a **flood**, a large amount of water covers an area which is usually dry. سیلاب ▷ *vt* If something such as a river or a burst pipe **floods** an area that is usually dry, it becomes covered with water. سیلاب آنا ▷ *vi* If an area that is usually dry **floods**, it becomes covered with water. پانی بھر جانا

flooding *n* If **flooding** occurs, an area of land that is usually dry is covered with water after heavy rain or after a river or lake flows over its banks. باڑھ

floodlight (**floodlights**) *n* **Floodlights** are powerful lamps which are used to light sports grounds and the outsides of public buildings. تیزلائٹ (کھیل کے میدان میں)

floor (**floors**) *n* A **floor** is the part of a room that you walk on. فرش ▷ *n* A **floor** of a building is all the rooms in it that are at the same height. منزل

flop (**flops**) *n* If something is a **flop**, it is completely unsuccessful. ناکامی

floppy disk (**floppy disks**) *n* A **floppy disk** is a small magnetic disk that used to be used for storing computer data and programs. فلوپی ڈسک

flora *npl* You can refer to plants as **flora**, especially the plants growing in a particular area. (*formal*) نباتات

florist (**florists**) *n* A **florist** is a shopkeeper who sells flowers and indoor plants. گلفروش

flour (**flours**) *n* **Flour** is a white or brown powder that is made by grinding grain. It is used to make bread, cakes, and pastry. آٹا

flow (**flows, flowing, flowed**) *vi* If a liquid, gas, or electrical current **flows** somewhere, it moves there steadily and continuously. بہنا

flower (**flowers, flowering, flowered**) *n* A **flower** is the brightly coloured part of a plant which grows at the end of a stem. پھول ▷ *vi* When a plant or tree **flowers**, its flowers appear and open. پھول آنا، بہار آنا

flu *n* **Flu** is an illness caused by a virus. The symptoms are like those of a bad cold, but more serious. فلو

fluent *adj* Someone who is **fluent** in a particular language can speak it easily and correctly. خوش اسلوب

fluorescent *adj* A **fluorescent** surface or colour has a very bright appearance when light is directed onto it. چمکدار

flush (**flushes, flushing, flushed**) *n* A **flush** is a rosy colour, especially in the cheeks. سرخی، تمتاہٹ ▷ *vi* If you **flush**, your face goes red because you are hot or ill, or because you are feeling a strong emotion such as embarrassment or anger. تمتانا

flute (**flutes**) *n* A **flute** is a musical wind instrument consisting of a long tube with holes in it. You play it by blowing over a hole at one end while holding it sideways. بانسری

fly (**flies, flying, flew, flown**) *n* A **fly** is a small insect with two thin, clear wings. مکھی ▷ *vi* When a bird or aeroplane **flies**, it moves through the air. اڑنا

fly away *v* When something such as a bird, insect, or aircraft **flies away**, it leaves a place by moving through the air. اڑ جانا *With a flap and a screech, the falcon flew away.*

foal foals *n* A **foal** is a very young horse. نو عمر گھوڑا

focus (**foci, focuses, focusing, focused**) *n* The **focus** of something is the main topic or main thing that it is concerned with. توجہ مرکوز کرنا ▷ *v* If you **focus** on a particular topic, or if your attention **is focused** on it, you concentrate on it and deal with it. توجہ مرکوز کرنا

foetus (**foetuses**) *n* A **foetus** is an unborn animal or human being in its later stages of development. جنین

fog (**fogs**) *n* When there is **fog**, there are tiny drops of water in the air which form a thick cloud and make it difficult to see things. کہرا

foggy (**foggier, foggiest**) *adj* When it is **foggy**, there is fog. کہرآلود

fog light (**fog lights**) *n* A **fog light** is a very bright light on the front or back of a car to help the driver to see or be seen in fog. کہرے میں دیکھنے میں مدد کرنے والی تیز لائٹ

foil *n* **Foil** is metal that is as thin as paper. It is used to wrap food in. دھاتی کاغذ

fold (**folds, folding, folded**) *n* A **fold** in a piece of paper or cloth is a bend that you make in it when you put one part of it over another part and press the edge. سلوٹ، تہ ▷ *vt* If you **fold** something such as a piece of paper or cloth, you bend it so that one part covers another part, often pressing the edge so that it stays in place. تہ کرنا

folder (**folders**) *n* A **folder** is a thin piece of cardboard in which you can keep loose papers. فولڈر، کاغذ رکھنے کی فائل

folding *adj* A **folding** piece of furniture, bicycle, etc. can be folded, so that it can be carried or stored in a small space. تہدار

folklore *n* **Folklore** consists of the traditional stories, customs, and habits of a particular community or nation.

کسی فرقے یا قوم کی روایتی داستانیں، لباس اور عادتیں

folk music *n* **Folk music** is music which is traditional or typical of a particular community or nation. عوامی موسیقی

follow (**follows, following, followed**) *v* If you **follow** someone who is going somewhere, you move along behind them. تعاقب کرنا

following *adj* The **following** day, week, or year is the day, week, or year after the one you have just talked about. آنے والے

food (**foods**) *n* **Food** is what people and animals eat. کھانا، خوراک

food poisoning *n* If you get **food poisoning**, you become ill because you have eaten food that has gone bad. کھانا زہریلا ہونا

food processor (**food processors**) *n* A **food processor** is a piece of electrical equipment that is used to mix, chop, or beat food, or to make it into a liquid. فوڈ پروسیسر (برقی آلہ)

fool (**fools, fooling, fooled**) *n* If you call someone a **fool**, you are indicating that you think they are not sensible and show a lack of good judgement. بیوقوف ▷ *vt* If someone **fools** you, they deceive or trick you. بیوقوف بنانا

foot (**feet**) *n* Your **feet** are the parts of your body that are at the ends of your legs, and that you stand on. پیر

football (**footballs**) *n* **Football** is a game played by two teams of eleven people who kick a ball and try to score goals by getting the ball into a net. فٹبال ▷ *n* A **football** is the ball that you use to play football. بال

footballer (**footballers**) *n* A **footballer** is a person who plays football. فٹبالر

football match (**football matches**) *n* A **football match** is an organized game that is played between two football teams. فٹبال میچ

football player (**football players**) *n* A **football player** is a person who plays football, especially as a profession. فٹبال کھلاڑی

footpath (**footpaths**) *n* A **footpath** is a path for people to walk on. فٹ پاتھ

footprint (**footprints**) *n* A **footprint** is the mark of a person's foot or shoe left on a surface. پیر یا جوتے کا نشان

footstep (**footsteps**) *n* A **footstep** is the sound made by someone's feet touching the ground when they are walking or running. قدموں کی آواز

for *prep* If something is **for** someone, they will have it or use it. کے لئے *These flowers are for you.* ▷ *prep* You use **for** when you are talking about the way in which you use something. کیلئے *This knife is for cutting bread.* ▷ *prep* If someone does something **for** you, they do it so that you do not have to do it. کیلئے *I held the door open for the next person.*

forbid (**forbids, forbidding, forbade, forbidden**) *vt* If you **forbid** someone to do something, or if you **forbid** an activity, you order that it must not be done. منع کرنا

forbidden *adj* If something is **forbidden**, you are not allowed to do it or have it. ممنوع

force (**forces, forcing, forced**) *n* **Force** is power or strength. طاقت، زور ▷ *vt* If something or someone **forces** you to do something, they make you do it, even though you do not want to. زور ڈالنا

forecast (**forecasts**) *n* A **forecast** is a statement of what is expected to happen in the future, especially in relation to a particular event or situation. پیشین گوئی

foreground *n* The **foreground** of a picture is the part that seems nearest to you. قریب دکھنے والا حصہ (تصویر میں)

forehead (**foreheads**) *n* Your **forehead** is the flat area at the front of your head above your eyebrows and below where your hair grows. پیشانی

foreign *adj* Something that is **foreign** comes from or relates to a country that is not your own. بیرونِ ملک

foreigner (**foreigners**) *n* A **foreigner** is someone who belongs to a country that is not your own. غیر ملکی

foresee (**foresees, foreseeing, foresaw, foreseen**) *vt* If you **foresee** something, you expect and believe that it will happen. پیش بینی کرنا

forest (**forests**) *n* A **forest** is a large area where trees grow close together. جنگل

forever *adv* Something that will happen or continue **forever** will always happen or continue. ہمیشہ کے لیے

forge (**forges, forging, forged**) *vt* If someone **forges** banknotes, documents, or paintings, they make false copies of them in order to deceive people. جعل سازی کرنا

forgery *n* **Forgery** is the crime of making fake banknotes, documents, or paintings. جعل سازی

forget (**forgets, forgetting, forgot, forgotten**) *vt* If you **forget** something, or if you **forget** how to do something, you cannot think of it or think of how to do it, although you knew in the past. بھولنا

forgive (**forgives, forgiving, forgave, forgiven**) *vt* If you **forgive** someone who has done something wrong, you stop being angry with them. معاف کر دینا

forgotten *adj* Something that is **forgotten** is no longer remembered or thought about by people. بھولی ہوئی

fork (**forks**) *n* A **fork** is an implement that you use when you are eating food. It consists of three or four long thin points on the end of a handle. کانٹا

form (**forms**) *n* A **form** of something is a type or kind of it. قسم

formal *adj* **Formal** speech or behaviour is very correct and serious rather than relaxed and friendly, and is used especially in official situations. باقاعدہ

formality *n* **Formality** is speech or behaviour which is correct and serious, rather than relaxed and friendly, and is used especially in official situations. باضابطگی

format (**formats, formatting, formatted**) *n* The **format** of something is the way it is arranged and presented. فورمیٹ (ترتیب) ▷ *vt* To **format** a computer disk means to run a program so that the disk can be written on. فورمیٹ کرنا (کمپیوٹر کو)

former *adj* You use **former** when you are talking about someone or something in the past. سابق

formerly *adv* If something happened or was **formerly** true, it happened or was true in the past. سابقہ طور پر

formula (**formulae, formulas**) *n* A **formula** is a plan that is made as a way of dealing with a problem. فورمولا

fort (**forts**) *n* A **fort** is a strong building that is used as a military base. قلع

fortnight (**fortnights**) *n* A **fortnight** is a period of two weeks. پندرہ دن

fortunate *adj* If someone or something is **fortunate**, they are lucky. خوش قسمت

fortunately *adv* **Fortunately** is used to introduce or indicate a statement about an event or situation that is good. خوش قسمتی سے

fortune (**fortunes**) *n* You can refer to a large sum of money as a **fortune** or a small **fortune** to emphasize how large it is. مقدر

forty *num* **Forty** is the number 40. چالیس

forward (**forwards, forwarding, forwarded**) *adv* If you move or look

forward, you move or look in a direction that is in front of you. آگے ▷ *vt* If a letter or message **is forwarded** to someone, it is sent to the place where they are, after having been sent to a different place earlier. آگے بھیجنا

forward slash (**forward slashes**) *n* A **forward slash** is the sloping line (/) that separates letters, words, or numbers. ترچھی لائن

foster (**fosters, fostering, fostered**) *vt* If you **foster** a child, you take him or her into your family as a foster child. پالنا، پرورش کرنا

foster child (**foster children**) *n* A **foster child** is a child looked after temporarily or brought up by people other than its parents. منہ بولا بچہ

foul (**fouler, foulest, fouls**) *adj* If you describe something as **foul**, you mean it is dirty and smells or tastes unpleasant. غلیظ، گندا ▷ *n* In sports such as football, a **foul** is an action that is against the rules. خلاف قاعدہ

foundations *npl* The **foundations** of a building or other structure are the layer of bricks or concrete below the ground that it is built on. بنیادیں

fountain (**fountains**) *n* A **fountain** is an ornamental feature in a pool which consists of a jet of water that is forced up into the air by a pump. فوارہ

fountain pen (**fountain pens**) *n* A **fountain pen** is a pen which uses ink that you have drawn up inside it from a bottle. فاؤنٹین پین

four *num* **Four** is the number 4. چار

fourteen *num* **Fourteen** is the number 14. چودہ

fourteenth *adj* The **fourteenth** item in a series is the one that you count as number fourteen. چودہواں

fourth *adj* The **fourth** item in a series is the one that you count as number four. چوتھا

four-wheel drive (**four-wheel drives**) *n* A **four-wheel drive** is a vehicle in which all four wheels receive power from the engine. چوپہیہ گاڑی (سب پہیوں کو انجن سے راست توانائی ملتی ہے)

fox (**foxes**) *n* A **fox** is a wild animal which looks like a dog and has reddish-brown fur and a thick tail. لومڑی

fracture (**fractures**) *n* A **fracture** is a crack or break in something. ہڈی ٹوٹ جانا

fragile *adj* If you describe a situation as **fragile**, you mean that it is weak or uncertain, and unlikely to be able to resist strong pressure or attack. غیر یقینی

frail (**frailer, frailest**) *adj* Someone who is **frail** is not very strong or healthy. کمزور

frame (**frames**) *n* The **frame** of a picture or mirror is the part around its edges. چوکھٹا

France *n* **France** is a republic in western Europe, between the English Channel, the Mediterranean, and the Atlantic. فرانس

frankly *adv* You use **frankly** when you are expressing an opinion or feeling to emphasize that you mean what you are saying. صاف طور پر

frantic *adj* If someone is **frantic**, they are behaving in a desperate, wild, and disorganized way, because they are frightened, worried, or in a hurry. بدحواس

fraud (**frauds**) *n* **Fraud** is the crime of gaining money by a trick or lying. فریب، دھوکہ

freckles *npl* If someone has **freckles**, they have small light brown spots on their skin. لسن، جھائیاں

free (**freer, freest, frees, freeing, freed**) *adj* If you are **free**, you can do what you like or go where you like. آزاد ▷ *adj* If something is **free**, you can have it without paying any money for it. مفت ▷ *vt* If you **free** someone of something unpleasant, you remove it from them. آزاد کرنا

freedom (**freedoms**) *n* **Freedom** is the state of being allowed to do what you want. آزادی

free kick (**free kicks**) *n* In a game of football, when there is a **free kick**, the ball is given to a member of one side to kick because a member of the other side has broken a rule. فری کک (فٹبال میں)

freelance *adj* Someone who does **freelance** work or who is, for example, a **freelance** journalist or photographer is not employed by one organization, but is paid for each piece of work they do by the organization they do it for. آزاد (صحافی) ▷ *adv* If someone works **freelance**, they are not employed by one organization, but are paid for each piece of work they do by the organization they do it for. آزادانہ طور پر

freeze (**freezes, freezing, froze, frozen**) *vi* When water **freezes**, it is so cold that it becomes ice. جمنا ▷ *vt* If you **freeze** food, you make it very cold so that it will not go bad. منجمد کرنا

freezer (**freezers**) *n* A **freezer** is a fridge in which the temperature is kept below freezing point so that you can store food inside it for long periods. جمانے والا (فرج)

freezing *adj* Something that is **freezing** is very cold. انجمادی

freight *n* **Freight** is the movement of goods by lorries, trains, ships, or aeroplanes. بار برداری

French *adj* **French** means belonging or relating to France, or to its people, language, or culture. فرانسیسی ▷ *n* **French** is the language spoken by people who live in France and in parts of some other countries, including Belgium, Canada, and Switzerland. فرانسیسی زبان

French beans *npl* **French beans** are narrow green beans that are eaten as a vegetable. They grow on a tall climbing plant and are the cases that contain the seeds of the plant. فرینچ بینس (پھلی کے دانے)

French horn (**French horns**) *n* A **French horn** is a musical instrument shaped like a long round metal tube with one wide end, which is played by blowing into it. فرینچ ہورن (موسیقی ساز)

Frenchman (**Frenchmen**) *n* A **Frenchman** is a man who comes from France. فرانسیسی (شخص)

Frenchwoman (**Frenchwomen**) *n* A **Frenchwoman** is a woman who comes from France. فرانسیسی خاتون

frequency *n* The **frequency** of an event is the number of times it happens. فریکوینسی (ہونے کی شرح)

frequent *adj* If something is **frequent**, it happens often. کثیر الوقوع

fresh (**fresher, freshest**) *adj* A **fresh** thing or amount replaces or is added to an existing thing or amount. تازہ ▷ *adj* If food is **fresh**, it has been picked or made a short time ago. تازہ ▷ *adj* **Fresh** water has no salt in it. The water in rivers is **fresh**. تازہ ▷ *adj* **Fresh** air is clean and cool. تازہ

freshen up *v* If you **freshen** something **up**, you make it clean and pleasant in appearance or smell. تازہ کرنا، ہونا
A thorough brushing helps to freshen up your mouth.

freshwater fish (**freshwater fish, freshwater fishes**) *n* A **freshwater fish** lives in water that is not salty. غیر نمکین پانی کی مچھلی

fret (**frets, fretting, fretted**) *vi* If you **fret** about something, you worry about it. فکر مند ہونا

Friday (**Fridays**) *n* **Friday** is the day after Thursday and before Saturday. جمعہ

fridge (**fridges**) *n* A **fridge** is a large metal container for storing food at low temperatures to keep it fresh. فرج

fried *adj* If food is **fried**, it is cooked in a pan containing hot fat. تلا ہوا

friend (**friends**) *n* A **friend** is someone who you know well and like, but who is not related to you. دوست

friendly (**friendlier, friendliest**) *adj* A **friendly** person is kind and pleasant. دوستانہ

friendship (**friendships**) *n* A **friendship** is a relationship or state of friendliness between two people who like each other. دوستی

fright *n* **Fright** is a sudden feeling of fear. ڈر

frighten (**frightens, frightening, frightened**) *vt* If something or someone **frightens** you, they cause you to suddenly feel afraid or anxious. ڈرانا، ڈرنا

frightened *adj* If you are **frightened**, you feel anxious or afraid. ڈرا ہوا

frightening *adj* If something is **frightening**, it makes you feel afraid or anxious. ڈراونا

fringe (**fringes**) *n* A **fringe** is hair which is cut so that it hangs over your forehead. ماتھے کی زلف

frog (**frogs**) *n* A **frog** is a small creature with smooth skin, big eyes, and long back legs which it uses for jumping. مینڈک

from *prep* If something comes **from** a person, they give it to you or send it to you. بطرف، منجانب *I received a letter from him yesterday.* ▷ *prep* If someone or something moves **from** a place, they leave it. سے *Everyone watched as she ran from the room.* ▷ *prep* You use **from** to say what somebody used to make something. سے *This bread is made from white flour.*

front (**fronts**) *adj* **Front** is used to refer to the side or part of something that is towards the front or nearest to the front. سامنے ▷ *n* The **front** of something is the part of it that faces you, or that faces forward, or that you normally see or use. مقابل

frontier (**frontiers**) *n* A **frontier** is a border between two countries. سرحد

frost (**frosts**) *n* When there is **frost** or a **frost**, the temperature outside falls below freezing point and the ground becomes covered in ice crystals. انجماد

frosty (**frostier, frostiest**) *adj* If the weather is **frosty**, the temperature is below freezing. انجمادی

frown (**frowns, frowning, frowned**) *vi* When someone **frowns**, their eyebrows become drawn together, because they are annoyed, worried, or puzzled, or because they are concentrating. تیوری چڑھانا

frozen *adj* If the ground is **frozen**, it has become very hard because the weather is very cold. جما ہوا

fruit (**fruit, fruits**) *n* **Fruit** is something which grows on a tree or bush and which contains seeds or a stone covered by edible flesh. Apples, oranges, and bananas are all fruit. پھل

fruit juice *n* **Fruit juice** is the liquid that can be obtained from a fruit and drunk. پھل کا رس (جوس)

fruit salad (**fruit salads**) *n* **Fruit salad** is a mixture of pieces of different kinds of fruit. It is usually eaten as a dessert. پھلوں کا سلاد

frustrated *adj* If you are **frustrated**, you are upset or angry because you are unable to do anything about a situation. شکست خوردہ

fry (**fries, frying, fried**) *vt* When you **fry** food, you cook it in a pan containing hot fat. تلنا

frying pan (**frying pans**) *n* A **frying pan** is a flat metal pan with a long handle, in which you fry food. تلنے کا مخصوص برتن

fuel (**fuels**) *n* **Fuel** is a substance such as coal, oil, or petrol that is burned to provide heat or power. ایندھن

fulfil (**fulfils, fulfills, fulfilling, fulfilled**) *vt* If you **fulfil** a promise, dream, or ambition, you do what you said or hoped you would do. پورا کرنا (وعدہ، خواب۔۔۔)

full (**fuller, fullest**) *adj* Something that is **full** contains as much of a substance or as many objects as it can. لبریز

full moon *n* You use **full moon** to describe one of the four phases of the moon, occurring when the earth lies between the sun and the moon so that the moon is visible as a fully illuminated disc. مکمل چاند

full stop (**full stops**) *n* A **full stop** is the punctuation mark . which you use at the end of a sentence when it is not a question or exclamation. وقف لازم

full-time *adj* **Full-time** work or study involves working or studying for the whole of each normal working week rather than for part of it. کل وقتی
adv If you do something **full-time**, you do it for the whole of each normal working week. کل وقتی

fully *adv* **Fully** means to the greatest degree or extent possible. پوری طرح، مکمل طور پر

fumes *npl* **Fumes** are unpleasantly strong or harmful gases or smells. بخارات

fun *adj* If someone is **fun**, you enjoy their company. If something is **fun**, you enjoy doing it. تفریحی ▷ *n* You refer to an activity or situation as **fun** if you think it is pleasant and enjoyable. تفریح

funds *npl* **Funds** are amounts of money that are available to be spent. رقومات

funeral (**funerals**) *n* A **funeral** is a ceremony for the burial or cremation of someone who has died. تجہیز و تکفین

funeral parlour (**funeral parlours**) *n* A **funeral parlour** is a place where dead people are prepared for burial or cremation. تکفین گھر

funfair (**funfairs**) *n* A **funfair** is an event held in a park or field at which people pay to ride on various machines for amusement or try to win prizes in games. تفریحی میلا

funnel (**funnels**) *n* A **funnel** is an object with a wide top and a tube at the bottom, which is used to pour substances into a container. قیف

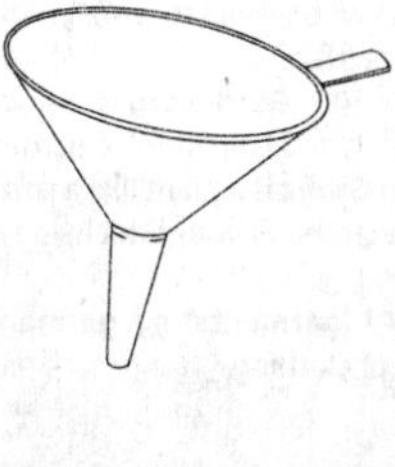

funny (**funnier, funniest**) *adj* If something is **funny**, it makes you laugh. پر مزاح، ہنسانے والا ▷ *adj* **Funny** means strange. عجیب

fur *n* **Fur** is the thick hair that grows on the bodies of many animals, such as rabbits and bears, and is sometimes used to make clothes or rugs. پشم، بال

fur coat (**fur coats**) *n* A **fur coat** is a coat made from real or artificial fur. بالدار کوٹ

furious *adj* If someone is **furious**, they are extremely angry. غضبناک، طیش میں

furnished *adj* A **furnished** room or house is available to be rented together with the furniture in it. آراستہ (ساز و سامان فرنیچر سے)

furniture *n* **Furniture** consists of large movable objects such as tables, chairs, or beds that are used in a room for sitting or lying on, or for putting things on or in. فرنیچر، کرسی میز وغیرہ

further (**furthest**) *adj* A **further** thing or amount is an additional one. مزید، آگے کی
adv **Further** means to a greater degree or extent. بڑی حد تک

further education *n* **Further education** is the education of people who have left school but who are not at a university or a college of education. اسکول سے آگے کی تعلیم (ہائر سیکنڈری)

fuse (**fuses**) *n* In an electrical appliance, a **fuse** is a wire safety device which melts and stops the electric current if there is a fault. فیوز

fuse box (**fuse boxes**) *n* The **fuse box** is the box that contains the fuses for all the electric circuits in a building. It is usually fixed to a wall. فیوز بکس

fuss *n* **Fuss** is anxious or excited behaviour which serves no useful purpose. افراتفری

fussy (**fussier, fussiest**) *adj* Someone who is **fussy** is very concerned with unimportant details and is difficult to please. فضولیات پر توجہ دینے والا

future *adj* **Future** things will happen or exist after the present time. آئندہ

g

Gabon *n* **Gabon** is a republic in west central Africa, on the Atlantic. گبون

gain (**gains, gaining, gained**) *n* A **gain** is an improvement or increase. نفع، ماحصل ▷ *vt* If you **gain** something, you acquire it. حاصل کرنا

gale (**gales**) *n* A **gale** is a very strong wind. جھکڑ

gall bladder (**gall bladders**) *n* Your **gall bladder** is the organ in your body which contains bile and is next to your liver. پت

gallery (**galleries**) *n* A **gallery** is a place that has permanent exhibitions of works of art in it. گیلری

gallop (**gallops, galloping, galloped**) *n* A **gallop** is a ride on a horse that is galloping. سرپٹ ▷ *vi* When a horse **gallops**, it runs very fast. سرپٹ دوڑانا

gallstone (**gallstones**) *n* A **gallstone** is a small, painful lump which can develop in your gall bladder. سنگ مثانہ

Gambia *n* **Gambia** is a republic in West Africa. گیمبیا

gamble (**gambles, gambling, gambled**) *v* If you **gamble** on something, you take a risk because you hope that something good will happen. جوا کھیلنا، اندھا جوکھم اٹھانا

gambler (**gamblers**) *n* A **gambler** is someone who gambles regularly, for example in card games or horse racing. جواری

gambling *n* **Gambling** is the act or activity of betting money, for example in card games or on horse racing. قماربازی

game (**games**) *n* A **game** is something you play that has rules, for example football. کھیل، گیم ▷ *n* Children play a **game** when they pretend to be other people. گیم، کھیل

games console (**games consoles**) *n* A **games console** is an electronic device used for playing computer games on a television screen. گیمس کنسول (ٹی وی پر کمپیوٹر گیم کھلانے والا)

gang (**gangs**) *n* A **gang** is a group of people who join together for some purpose, often criminal. گروہ

gangster (**gangsters**) *n* A **gangster** is a member of a group of violent criminals. مجرم گروہ کا رکن

gap (**gaps**) *n* A **gap** is a space between two things or a hole in something solid. شگاف

garage (**garages**) *n* A **garage** is a building where you keep a car. گیراج، کار کھڑی کرنے کی جگہ ▷ *n* A **garage** is a place where you can get your car repaired. گیراج، کار مرمت کرنے کی جگہ

garden (**gardens**) *n* A **garden** is an area of land next to a house, with plants, trees, and grass. باغیچہ

garden centre (**garden centres**) *n* A **garden centre** is a large shop, usually with an outdoor area, where you can buy things for your garden such as plants and gardening tools. باغبانی کی اشیاء فروخت کرنے کی بڑی دوکان

gardener (**gardeners**) *n* A **gardener** is a person who is paid to work in someone else's garden. مالی

gardening *n* **Gardening** is the activity of planning and cultivating a garden. باغبانی

garlic *n* **Garlic** is a plant like a small onion, with a strong flavour, which you use in cooking. لہسن

garment (**garments**) *n* A **garment** is a piece of clothing. کپڑا، لباس

gas (**gases**) *n* A **gas** is any substance that is neither liquid nor solid. گیس

gas cooker (**gas cookers**) *n* A **gas cooker** is a large metal device for cooking food using gas. گیس کوکر

gasket (**gaskets**) *n* A **gasket** is a flat piece of soft material that you put between two joined surfaces in a pipe or engine in order to make sure that gas and oil cannot escape. نمدہ

gate (**gates**) *n* A **gate** is a structure like a door that you use to enter a field, a garden, or the area around a building. پھاٹک

gateau (**gateaux**) *n* A **gateau** is a very rich, elaborate cake, especially one with cream in it. گیٹیو (مرغن کیک)

gather (**gathers, gathering, gathered**) *v* When people **gather** somewhere, or if someone **gathers** them there, they come together in a group. اکٹھا کرنا

gauge (**gauges, gauging, gauged**) *n* A **gauge** is a device that measures the amount or quantity of something and shows the amount measured. ناپ، پیمانہ ▷ *vt* If you **gauge** something, you measure it or judge it. ناپنا، ناپنا

gaze (**gazes, gazing, gazed**) *vi* An **ally** is If you **gaze** at someone or something, you look steadily at them for a long time. گھورنا، ٹکٹکی لگا کر دیکھنا

gear (**gears**) *n* A **gear** is a piece of machinery, for example in a car or on a bicycle, which helps to control its movement. گیئر (رفتار کنٹرول) ▷ *n* The **gear** for a particular activity is the equipment and special clothes that you use. لباس و سامان

gearbox (**gearboxes**) *n* A **gearbox** is the system of gears in an engine or vehicle. گیئر بکس (انجن میں)

gear lever (**gear levers**) *n* A **gear lever** or a **gear stick** is the lever that you use to change gear in a car or other vehicle. گیئر لیور (ہتھہ)

gel (**gels**) *n* **Gel** is a smooth, soft, jelly-like substance, especially one used to keep your hair in a particular style. جیل (لیدار مادہ)

gem (**gems**) *n* A **gem** is a jewel. جواہر، نگینہ

Gemini *n* **Gemini** is one of the twelve signs of the zodiac. Its symbol is a pair of twins. People who are born approximately between 21st May and 20th June come under this sign. برج جیمینی

gender (**genders**) *n* A person's **gender** is the fact that they are male or female. صنف

gene (**genes**) *n* A **gene** is the part of a cell in a living thing which controls its physical characteristics, growth, and development. جین

general (**generals**) *adj* If you talk about the **general** situation somewhere or talk about something in **general** terms, you are describing the situation as a whole rather than part of it. عام ▷ *n* A **general** is a senior officer in the armed forces, usually in the army. جنرل

general anaesthetic (**general anaesthetics**) *n* A **general anaesthetic** is a substance that doctors use to stop you feeling pain during an operation. It causes you to lose consciousness. بیہوشی آور

general election (**general elections**) *n* A **general election** is a time when people choose a new government. عام انتخابات

generalize (**generalizes, generalizing, generalized**) *v* If you **generalize**, you say something that is usually, but not always, true. عمومی بنانا

general knowledge *n* **General knowledge** is knowledge about many different things, as opposed to detailed knowledge about one particular subject. عمومی معلومات

generally *adv* You use **generally** to summarize a situation, activity, or idea without referring to the particular details of it. عام طور پر

generation (**generations**) *n* A **generation** is all the people in a group or country who are of a similar age,

g

especially when they are considered as having the same experiences or attitudes. نسل
generator (**generators**) *n* A **generator** is a machine which produces electricity. جنریٹر (بجلی پیدا کرنے والا)
generosity *n* If you refer to someone's **generosity**, you mean that they are generous, especially in doing or giving more than is usual or expected. فراخ دلی
generous *adj* A **generous** person gives more of something, especially money, than is usual or expected. فراخ دل
genetic *adj* You use **genetic** to describe something that is related to genetics or genes. جینیاتی
genetically-modified *adj* **Genetically-modified** plants and animals have had one or more genes changed. The abbreviation **GM** is often used. جینیاتی طور پر تبدیل شدہ
genetics *n* **Genetics** is the study of how characteristics are passed from one generation to another by means of genes. علم جینیات
genius *n* **Genius** is very great ability or skill in something. عبقری
gentle (**gentler, gentlest**) *adj* A **gentle** person is kind, mild, and calm. شریف
gentleman (**gentlemen**) *n* A **gentleman** is a man from a family of high social standing. نیک شخص
gently *adv* If you do something **gently** you do it in a kind, mild, and calm manner. نرمی سے
gents *n* The **gents** is a public toilet for men. مردوں کا
genuine *adj* Something that is **genuine** is real and exactly what it appears to be. اصلی
geography *n* **Geography** is the study of the countries of the world and things such as the land, oceans, weather, towns, and population. جغرافیہ
geology *n* **Geology** is the study of the earth's structure, surface, and origins. علم ارضیات
Georgia *n* **Georgia** is a state of the southeastern United States, on the Atlantic. جارجیا ریاست ▷ *n* **Georgia** is a republic in north-west Asia, on the Black Sea. جارجیا جمہوریہ
Georgian (**Georgians**) *adj* **Georgian** means belonging to or connected with the republic of Georgia, in north-west Asia, or to its people, language, or culture. جارجیائی ▷ *n* A **Georgian** is a person who comes from the republic of Georgia, in north-west Asia. جارجیائی شخص
geranium (**geraniums**) *n* A **geranium** is a plant with red, pink, or white flowers. جریشیم (سرخ، گلابی، سفید پھول والا پودا)
gerbil (**gerbils**) *n* A **gerbil** is a small, furry animal. جربل (روئیں دار جانور)
geriatric *adj* **Geriatric** is used to describe things relating to the illnesses and medical care of old people. بوڑھوں کی طبی نگہداشت سے وابستہ چیزیں (جریاٹرک)
germ (**germs**) *n* A **germ** is a very small organism that causes disease. جرثومہ
German (**Germans**) *adj* **German** means belonging or relating to Germany, or to its people, language, or culture. جرمن ▷ *n* A **German** is a person who comes from Germany. جرمن ▷ *n* **German** is the language spoken in Germany, Austria, and parts of Switzerland. جرمن زبان
German measles *n* **German measles** is a disease which causes you to have a cough, a sore throat, and red spots on your skin. جرمن خسرہ
Germany *n* **Germany** is a country in central Europe. جرمنی
gesture (**gestures**) *n* A **gesture** is a movement that you make with a part of your body, especially your hands, to express emotion or information. وضع
get (**gets, getting, got**) *v* You can use **get** to mean the same as 'become'. بننا ▷ *vi* If you **get** somewhere, you arrive there.

پہنچنا ▷ *vt* If you **get** something, someone gives it to you. پانا، حاصل ہونا ▷ *vt* If you **get** something, you go to where it is and bring it back. لانا، حاصل کرنا

get away *v* If you **get away**, you succeed in leaving a place or situation that you do not want to be in. فرار ہونا

get back *v* If you **get** something **back** after you have lost it or after it has been taken from you, you have it again. واپس پانا

get in *v* When a train, bus, or plane **gets in**, it arrives. آنا

get into *v* If you **get into** an activity, you start doing it or being involved in it. داخل ہونا

get off *v* If someone who has broken a law or rule **gets off**, they are not punished, or only slightly punished. سستے چھوٹ جانا

get on *v* If you **get on** with someone, you have a friendly relationship with them. تعلق ہو جانا

get out *v* If you **get out**, you leave a place because you want to escape from it, or because you are made to leave it. نکل جانا

get over *v* If you **get over** an unpleasant experience or an illness, you recover from it. قابو پانا، پیچھے چھوڑ دینا

get together *v* When people **get together**, they meet in order to discuss something or to spend time together. ساتھ آنا، مجتمع ہونا

get up *v* If you are sitting or lying and then **get up**, you rise to a standing position. اٹھنا

Ghana *n* **Ghana** is a republic in West Africa, on the Gulf of Guinea. گھانا

Ghanaian (Ghanaians) *adj* **Ghanaian** means belonging or relating to Ghana, or to its people, language or culture. گھانائی ▷ *n* **Ghanaians** are people who are Ghanaian. گھانائی

ghost (ghosts) *n* A **ghost** is the spirit of a dead person that someone believes they can see or feel. بھوت

giant (giants) *adj* You use **giant** to describe something that is much larger or more important than most other things of its kind. بہت بڑا ▷ *n* A large successful organization or country can be referred to as a **giant**. عظیم (سالک یا رتبہ میں)

gift (gifts) *n* A **gift** is something that you give someone as a present. تحفہ

gifted *adj* A **gifted** person has a natural ability for doing most things or for doing a particular activity. خداداد صلاحیت والا

gift voucher (gift vouchers) *n* A **gift voucher** is a card or piece of paper that you buy at a shop and give to someone, which entitles the person to exchange it for goods worth the same amount. گفٹ واچر

gigantic *adj* If you describe something as **gigantic**, you are emphasizing that it is extremely large in size, amount, or degree. عظیم، ضخیم

giggle (giggles, giggling, giggled) *vi* If someone **giggles**, they laugh in a childlike way, because they are amused, nervous, or embarrassed. کھلکھلانا

gin (gins) *n* **Gin** is a colourless alcoholic drink. جن (الکحلی مشروب)

ginger *adj* **Ginger** is used to describe things that are orangey-brown in colour. نارنجی بھورا ▷ *n* **Ginger** is the root of a plant that is used to flavour food. It has a sweet spicy flavour. ادرک

giraffe (giraffes) *n* A **giraffe** is a large African animal with a very long neck, long legs, and dark patches on its body. زراف

girl (girls) *n* A **girl** is a female child. لڑکی

girlfriend (girlfriends) *n* Someone's **girlfriend** is a girl or woman with whom they are having a romantic relationship. محبوبہ

give (gives, giving, gave, given) *vt* If you **give** someone something, you let them have it to keep. دینا، دے

give back *v* If you **give** something **back**, you return it to the person who gave it to you. لوٹانا

give in *v* If you **give in**, you admit that you are defeated or that you cannot do something. ہتھیار ڈالنا، جھک جانا

give out *v* If you **give out** a number of things, you distribute them among a group of people. تقسیم کر دینا

give up *v* If you **give up** something, you stop doing it or having it. چھوڑ دینا، ترک کر دینا

glacier (**glaciers**) *n* A **glacier** is a huge mass of ice which moves very slowly, often down a mountain. برفانی تودہ

glad *adj* If you are **glad** about something, you are happy and pleased about it. خوش

glamorous *adj* If you describe someone or something as **glamorous**, you mean that they are more attractive, exciting, or interesting than ordinary people or things. بھڑکیلا

glance (**glances, glancing, glanced**) *n* A **glance** is a quick look at someone or something. ایک نظر ▷ *vi* If you **glance** at something or someone, you look at them very quickly and then look away again immediately. ایک نظر ڈالنا

gland (**glands**) *n* **Glands** are organs in your body that produce chemical substances which your body needs in order to function. غدود

glare (**glares, glaring, glared**) *vi* If you **glare** at someone, you look at them with an angry expression on your face. غصے سے گھورنا

glaring *adj* If you describe something bad as **glaring**, you mean that it is very obvious. فاش، صریح (غلطی)

glass (**glasses**) *n* **Glass** is a hard, clear material that is used to make things like windows and bottles. It is quite easy to break **glass**. شیشہ، بلور ▷ *n* A **glass** is a container made from **glass** that you can drink out of. گلاس

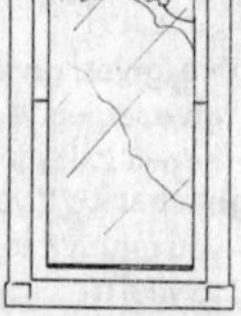

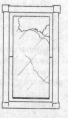

glasses *npl* **Glasses** are two lenses in a frame that some people wear in front of their eyes in order to see better. چشمہ

glider (**gliders**) *n* A **glider** is an aircraft without an engine which flies by floating on the air. گلائڈر

gliding *n* **Gliding** is the sport or activity of flying in a glider. گلائڈنگ

global *adj* **Global** means concerning or including the whole world. عالمی، آفاقی

globalization *n* **Globalization** is the idea that the world is developing a single economy as a result of improved technology and communications. عالم گیر

global warming *n* The problem of the gradual rise in the earth's temperature is referred to as **global warming**. عالمی حدت

globe (**globes**) *n* You can refer to the Earth as the **globe**. کرہ ارض

gloomy (**gloomier, gloomiest**) *adj* If a place is **gloomy**, it is almost dark so that you cannot see very well. تقریباً تاریک

glorious *adj* If you describe something as **glorious**, you are emphasizing that it is very beautiful or wonderful. شاندار

glory *n* **Glory** is fame and admiration that you get for an achievement. شان

glove (**gloves**) *n* **Gloves** are pieces of clothing which cover your hand and wrist and have individual sections for each finger. دستانہ

glove compartment (**glove compartments**) *n* The **glove compartment** in a car is a small cupboard or shelf below the front windscreen. کار میں دراز

glucose *n* **Glucose** is a type of sugar. گلوکوز

glue (**glues, glueing, gluing, glued**) *n* **Glue** is a sticky substance used for joining things together. گوند، سریش ▷ *vt* If you **glue** one object to another, you stick them together, using glue. چپکانا

gluten *n* **Gluten** is a substance found in cereal grains such as wheat. گلوٹن

GM *abbr* **GM** crops have had one or more

genes changed, for example in order to make them resist pests better. **GM** is an abbreviation for 'genetically modified'. جینیاتی طور پر تبدیل شدہ

go (**goes, going, went, gone**) *vi* If you **go** somewhere, you move there from another place. جانا ▷ *v* If you say that something is **going** to happen, you mean that it will happen. جانا

go after *v* If you **go after** something, you try to get it, catch it, or hit it. پیچھا کرنا

go ahead *v* If someone **goes ahead** with something, they begin to do it or make it. آگے بڑھنا

goal (**goals**) *n* In games such as football or hockey, the **goal** is the space into which the players try to get the ball in order to score. گول، ہدف

goalkeeper (**goalkeepers**) *n* A **goalkeeper** is the player in a sports team whose job is to guard the goal. گول کیپر

goat (**goats**) *n* A **goat** is an animal which is a bit bigger than a sheep and has horns. بکری

go away *v* If you **go away**, you leave a place or a person's company. چلے جانا

go back *v* If something **goes back** to a particular time in the past, it was made or started at that time. ماضی میں جانا

go by *v* If you say that time **goes by**, you mean that it passes. گزرنا

God *n* The name **God** is given to the spirit or being who is worshipped as the creator and ruler of the world, especially by Christians, Jews, and Muslims. اللہ، رب، خالق کائنات

godfather *n* A powerful man who is at the head of a criminal organization is sometimes referred to as a **godfather**. مجرموں کے گروہ کا سرغنہ

go down *v* If a price, level, or amount **goes down**, it becomes lower than it was. نیچے جانا

goggles *npl* **Goggles** are large glasses that fit closely to your face around your eyes to protect them, for example in a laboratory. رنگین چشمہ

go in *v* If the sun **goes in**, it becomes covered by a cloud. اندر جانا

gold (**golds**) *n* **Gold** is a valuable yellow-coloured metal used for making jewellery, and as an international currency. سونا

golden *adj* Something that is **golden** is bright yellow. سنہری

goldfish (**goldfish, goldfishes**) *n* A **goldfish** is a small orange-coloured fish. نارنجی مچھلی

gold-plated *adj* Something that is **gold-plated** is covered with a very thin layer of gold. سنہری ملمع

golf *n* **Golf** is a game in which you use long sticks called clubs to hit a ball into holes that are spread out over a large area of grassy land. گولف (کھیل)

golf club (**golf clubs**) *n* A **golf club** is a long, thin, metal stick with a piece of wood or metal at one end that you use to hit the ball in golf. گولف کلب (اسٹک) ▷ *n* A **golf club** is a social organization which provides a golf course and a clubhouse for its members. گولف کلب (کلب)

golf course (**golf courses**) *n* A **golf course** is an area of land where people play golf. گولف کورس

gone *adj* Someone or something that is **gone** is no longer present or no longer exists. گزرا ہوا

good (**better, best**) *adj* If you say that something is **good**, you like it. اچھا ▷ *adj* If you are **good**, you behave well. اچھا ▷ *adj* If you are **good** at something, you do it well. ماہر ہونا

goodbye! *excl* You say '**goodbye**!' to someone when you or they are leaving, or at the end of a telephone conversation. خدا حافظ

good-looking (**better-looking, best-looking**) *adj* A **good-looking** person has an attractive face. جاذب نظر

good-natured *adj* A **good-natured** person or animal is naturally friendly and does not get angry easily. نیک

goods *npl* **Goods** are things that are made to be sold. مال

go off *v* If an explosive device or a gun **goes off**, it explodes or fires. چھوٹ جانا، چلے جانا

google (**googles, googling, googled**) *v* If you **google** someone or something, you search the Internet for information about them, especially using the website Google®. گوگل پر تلاش کرنا

go on *v* If you **go on** doing something, or **go on with** an activity, you continue to do it. جاری رکھنا

goose (**geese**) *n* A **goose** is a large bird similar to a duck, with a long neck. ہنس

gooseberry (**gooseberries**) *n* A **gooseberry** is a small green fruit that has a sharp taste and is covered with tiny hairs. گوزبیری (روئیں دار پھل)

goose pimples *npl* If you get **goose pimples**, the hairs on your skin stand up so that it is covered with tiny bumps. بالدار دانے

go out *v* When you **go out**, you do something enjoyable away from your home, for example you go to a restaurant or the cinema. باہر جانا

go past *v* If you **go past** someone or something, you go near them and keep moving, so that they are then behind you. پیچھے چھوڑ کر گزر جانا

gorgeous *adj* Someone or something that is **gorgeous** is extremely pleasant or attractive. زرق برق، ٹھاٹھ دار

gorilla (**gorillas**) *n* A **gorilla** is a very large ape. گوریلا

go round *v* If you **go round** to someone's house, you visit them at their house. دورہ لگانا

gossip (**gossips, gossiping, gossiped**) *n* **Gossip** is informal conversation, often about other people's private affairs. گپ شپ ▷ *vi* If you **gossip** with someone, you talk informally with them, especially about other people or local events. گپ شپ کرنا

go through *v* If you **go through** a difficult experience or period of time, you experience it. گزرنا

go up *v* If a price, amount, or level **goes up**, it becomes higher or greater than it was. اونچا ہونا

government (**governments**) *n* The **government** of a country is the group of people who are responsible for running it. حکومت

GP (**GPs**) *abbr* A **GP** is a doctor who treats all types of illness, instead of specializing in one area of medicine. **GP** is an abbreviation for 'general practitioner'. طبیب (جنرل فریشنر)

GPS (**GPSs**) *abbr* **GPS** is a system that uses signals from satellites to find out the position of an object. **GPS** is an abbreviation for 'global positioning system'. سٹلائٹ سگنل پر مبنی شناخت کا نظام

grab (**grabs, grabbing, grabbed**) *vt* If you **grab** something, you take it or pick it up roughly. ہتھیانا

graceful *adj* Someone or something that is **graceful** moves in a smooth and elegant way that is attractive to watch. شاندار

grade (**grades**) *n* The **grade** of a product is its quality. گریڈ (درجہ)

gradual *adj* A **gradual** change or process happens in small stages over a long period of time, rather than suddenly. تدریجی

gradually *adv* If something changes or is done **gradually**, it changes or is done in small stages over a long period of time, rather than suddenly. بتدریج

graduate (**graduates**) *n* A **graduate** is a student who has completed a course at a college or university. گریجویٹ

graduation *n* **Graduation** is the successful completion of a course of study at a university, college, or school, for which you receive a degree or diploma. گریجویشن

graffiti *npl* **Graffiti** is words or pictures that are written or drawn in public places, for example on walls or trains. عمارات وغیرہ پر لکھی تحریر

grain (**grains**) *n* A **grain** is the seed of a cereal plant, for example rice or wheat. اناج ▷ *n* A **grain** of something, for example sand or salt, is a tiny piece of it. چھوٹا ٹکڑا

gram (**grams**) *n* A **gram** or **gramme** is a unit of weight equal to one thousandth of a kilogram. گرام

grammar *n* **Grammar** is the ways that words can be put together in order to make sentences. قواعد لسان

grammatical *adj* **Grammatical** is used to describe something relating to grammar. لسانی قواعد

grand (**grander, grandest**) *adj* If you describe a building or landscape as **grand**, you mean that it is splendid or impressive. عظیم

grandchild (**grandchildren**) *n* Someone's **grandchild** is the child of their son or daughter. پوتے پوتیاں

granddad (**granddads**) *n* Your **granddad** is your grandfather. You can call your granddad 'Granddad'. دادا

granddaughter (**granddaughters**) *n* Someone's **granddaughter** is the daughter of their son or daughter. پوتی

grandfather (**grandfathers**) *n* Your **grandfather** is the father of your father or mother. You can call your grandfather 'Grandfather'. دادا، نانا

grandma (**grandmas**) *n* Your **grandma** is your grandmother. You can call your grandma 'Grandma'. دادی

grandmother (**grandmothers**) *n* Your **grandmother** is the mother of your father or mother. You can call your grandmother 'Grandmother'. دادی، نانی

grandpa (**grandpas**) *n* Your **grandpa** is your grandfather. You can call your grandpa 'Grandpa'. دادا

grandparents *npl* Your **grandparents** are the parents of your father or mother. دادا، دادی، نانا، نانی

grandson (**grandsons**) *n* Someone's **grandson** is the son of their son or daughter. پوتا، نواسا

granite *n* Granite is a very hard rock used in building. گرینائٹ (سخت چٹان)

granny (**grannies**) *n* Some people refer to or address their grandmother as **granny**. دادی، نانی

grant (**grants**) *n* A **grant** is an amount of money that the government or other institution gives to a person or an organization for a particular purpose. امداد، گرانٹ

grape (**grapes**) *n* **Grapes** are small green or purple fruit that grow in bunches. انگور

grapefruit (**grapefruit, grapefruits**) *n* A **grapefruit** is a large, round, yellow fruit that has a sharp taste. چکوترہ

graph (**graphs**) *n* A **graph** is a mathematical diagram which shows the relationship between two or more sets of numbers or measurements. گراف

graphics *npl* **Graphics** are drawings and pictures that are composed using simple lines and sometimes strong colours. خاکے، گرافکس

grasp (**grasps, grasping, grasped**) *vt* If you **grasp** something, you take it in your hand and hold it very firmly. گرفت میں لینا، ہڑپ لینا

grass (**grasses**) *n* **Grass** is a very common green plant with narrow leaves that forms a layer covering an area of ground. گھاس ▷ *n* A **grass** is someone who tells the police or other authorities about criminal activities that they know about. مخبر

grasshopper (**grasshoppers**) *n* A **grasshopper** is an insect with long back legs that jumps high into the air and makes a high, vibrating sound. ٹڈا، جھینگر

grate (**grates, grating, grated**) *vt* When you **grate** food, you shred it into very small pieces using a tool called a grater. کدوکش کرنا

grateful *adj* If you are **grateful** for something that someone has given you or done for you, you are pleased and wish to thank them. شکرگزار

grave (**graves**) *n* A **grave** is a place where a dead person is buried. قبر

gravel *n* **Gravel** consists of very small stones. کنکر

gravestone (**gravestones**) *n* A **gravestone** is a large stone with words carved into it, which is placed on a grave. کتبہ

graveyard (**graveyards**) *n* A **graveyard** is an area of land where dead people are buried. قبرستان

gravy *n* **Gravy** is a sauce made from the juices that come from meat when it cooks. شوربہ

grease *n* **Grease** is a thick substance used to oil the moving parts of machines. گریس (چکناہٹ)

greasy (**greasier, greasiest**) *adj* Something that is **greasy** is covered with grease or contains a lot of grease. گریسی (چکنا)

great (**greater, greatest**) *adj* **Great** means very large. عظیم، کافی بڑا، عظیم الشان ▷ *adj* **Great** means very important. عظیم، بڑا ▷ *n* A **grass** is someone who tells the police or other authorities about criminal activities that they know about. مخبر

Great Britain *n* **Great Britain** is the island consisting of England, Scotland, and Wales, which together with Northern Ireland makes up the United Kingdom. برطانیہ عظمی

great-grandfather (**great-grandfathers**) *n* Your **great-grandfather** is the father of your grandmother or grandfather. پردادا

great-grandmother (**great-grandmothers**) *n* Your **great-grandmother** is the mother of your grandmother or grandfather. پرنانی

Greece *n* **Greece** is a republic in south-east Europe. یونان

greedy (**greedier, greediest**) *adj* Someone who is **greedy** wants more of something than is necessary or fair. لالچی

Greek (**Greeks**) *adj* **Greek** means belonging or relating to Greece, or to its people, language, or culture. یونانی ▷ *n* A **Greek** is a person who comes from Greece. یونانی ▷ *n* **Greek** is the language spoken in Greece. یونانی زبان

green (**greener, greenest, greens**) *adj* Something that is **green** is the colour of grass or leaves. ہرا ▷ *adj* If you say that someone is **green**, you mean that they have had very little experience of life or a particular job. اناڑی، ناتجربہ کار ▷ *n* **Greens** are members of political movements concerned with the protection of the environment. گرین (سیاسی رکن)

greengrocer *n* A **greengrocer** or a **greengrocer's** is a shop that sells fruit and vegetables. پھل سبزی فروش

greenhouse (**greenhouses**) *n* A **greenhouse** is a glass building in which you grow plants that need to be protected from bad weather. گرین ہاوس (نباتی شیش گھر)

Greenland *n* **Greenland** is a large island, lying mostly within the Arctic Circle. گرین لینڈ

green salad (**green salads**) *n* A **green salad** is a salad made mainly with lettuce and other green vegetables. سبزی سلاد

greet (**greets, greeting, greeted**) *vt* When you **greet** someone, you say something friendly such as 'hello' when you meet them. سلام دعا کرنا

greeting (**greetings**) *n* A **greeting** is something friendly that you say or do when you meet someone. تہنیت

greetings card (**greetings cards**) *n* A **greetings card** is a folded card with a picture on the front and greetings inside that you give or send to someone, for example on their birthday. تہنیت نامہ

grey (**greyer, greyest**) *adj* Something that is **grey** is the colour of ashes or of clouds on a rainy day. خاکستری رنگ

grey-haired *adj* A **grey-haired** person has grey hair. خاکستری رنگین

grid (**grids**) *n* A **grid** is a pattern of straight lines that cross over each other to form squares. جال

grief *n* **Grief** is extreme sadness. ملال

grill (**grills, grilling, grilled**) *n* A **grill** is a part of a cooker where food is grilled. سیخ ▷ *vt* If you **grill** food, you cook it using strong heat directly above or below it. سیخ پر پکانا

grilled *adj* If food is **grilled**, it is cooked using strong heat directly above or below it. راست آگ پر پکایا ہوا

grim (**grimmer, grimmest**) *adj* A situation or news that is **grim** is unpleasant. ناشاد، بے مہر

grin (**grins, grinning, grinned**) *n* A **grin** is a broad smile. مسکراہٹ ▷ *vi* When you **grin**, you smile broadly. مسکرانا

grind (**grinds, grinding, ground**) *vt* When something such as corn or coffee **is ground**, it is crushed until it becomes a fine powder. پیسنا

grip (**grips, gripping, gripped**) *vt* If you **grip** something, you take hold of it with your hand and continue to hold it firmly. پکڑنا

gripping *adj* If something is **gripping**, it holds your interest or attention. پرکشش، جکڑنے والی

grit *n* **Grit** consists of tiny pieces of stone, often put on roads in winter to make them less slippery. کنکر، سنگریزہ

groan (**groans, groaning, groaned**) *vi* If you **groan**, you make a long, low sound because you are in pain, or because you are upset or unhappy about something. کراہ

grocer (**grocers**) *n* A **grocer** is a shopkeeper who sells foods such as flour, sugar, and tinned foods. پنساری ▷ *n* A **grocer** or a **grocer's** is a small shop that sells foods such as flour, sugar, and canned goods. کریانہ دوکان

groceries *npl* **Groceries** are foods you buy at a grocer's or at a supermarket. اشیاء خورد و نوش

groom (**grooms**) *n* A **groom** is a man who is getting married. دولہا

grope (**gropes, groping, groped**) *vi* If you **grope** for something that you cannot see, you search for it with your hands. ٹٹولنا

gross (**grosser, grossest**) *adj* You use **gross** to emphasize the degree to which something is unacceptable or unpleasant. ناشائستہ

grossly *adv* **Grossly** means in a manner that is unacceptable or unpleasant to a very great degree. ناشائستگی سے

ground (**grounds, grounding, grounded**) *n* **The ground** is the surface of the earth or the floor of a room. فرش ▷ *vi* If an argument, belief, or opinion is **grounded** in something, that thing is used to justify it. بنیاد، دلیل پر مبنی ہونا

ground floor (**ground floors**) *n* The **ground floor** of a building is the floor that is level or almost level with the ground outside. فرشی منزل

group (**groups**) *n* A **group** of people or things is a number of them together in one place at one time. گروہ

grouse (**grouses, grouse**) *n* A **grouse** is a complaint. شکایت ▷ *n* **Grouse** are small fat birds which are often shot for sport and can be eaten. یوروپی چڑیا

grow (**grows, growing, grew, grown**) *vt* When you **grow** something, you cause it to develop or increase in size or length. اگانا ▷ *vi* When something or someone **grows**, they develop and increase in size or intensity. نشوونما ہونا

g

growl (**growls, growling, growled**) *vi* When a dog or other animal **growls**, it makes a low noise in its throat, usually because it is angry. غرانا
grown-up (**grown-ups**) *n* Children, or people talking to children, often refer to adults as **grown-ups**. عمر رسیدہ، بالغ نظر
growth *n* The **growth** of something such as an industry, organization, or idea is its development in size, wealth, or importance. بالیدگی
grow up *v* When someone **grows up**, they gradually change from being a child into being an adult. بالغ ہونا
grub (**grubs**) *n* A **grub** is an insect which has just hatched from its egg. لاروا (کیڑے کا)
grudge (**grudges**) *n* If you have a **grudge** against someone, you have unfriendly feelings towards them because they have harmed you in the past. تلخی کینہ بغض
gruesome *adj* Something that is **gruesome** is horrible and shocking. خوفناک
grumpy (**grumpier, grumpiest**) *adj* If you say that someone is **grumpy**, you think they are bad-tempered and miserable. بدمزاج، چڑچڑا
guarantee (**guarantees, guaranteeing, guaranteed**) *n* Something that is a **guarantee** of something else makes it certain that it will happen or that it is true. ضمانت ▷ *vt* If one thing **guarantees** another, the first is certain to cause the second thing to happen. ضمانت دینا، لینا
guard (**guards, guarding, guarded**) *n* A **guard** is someone such as a soldier, police officer, or prison officer who is guarding a particular place or person. محافظ ▷ *vt* If you **guard** a place, person, or object, you watch them carefully, either to protect them or to stop them from escaping. حفاظت کرنا
Guatemala *n* **Guatemala** is a republic in Central America. گواٹے مالا جمہوریہ
guess (**guesses, guessing, guessed**) *n* A **guess** is an attempt to give an answer or provide an opinion when you do not know if it is true. اندازہ ▷ *v* If you **guess** something, you give an answer or provide an opinion when you do not know if it is true. اندازہ کرنا
guest (**guests**) *n* A **guest** is someone who has been invited to stay in your home, attend an event, or appear on a radio or television show. مہمان
guesthouse (**guesthouses**) *n* A **guesthouse** is a small hotel. مہمان خانہ، ہوٹل
guide (**guides**) *n* A **guide** is a book hat gives you information or instructions to help you do or understand something. گائیڈ (رہنما کتاب)
guidebook (**guidebooks**) *n* A **guidebook** is a book that gives tourists information about a town, area, or country. رہنما کتابچہ
guide dog (**guide dogs**) *n* A **guide dog** is a dog that has been trained to lead a blind person. رہنما کتا
guided tour (**guided tours**) *n* If someone takes you on a **guided tour** of a place, they show you the place and tell you about it. ٹور مع گائیڈ
guilt *n* **Guilt** is an unhappy feeling that you have because you have done something bad. احساس جرم
guilty (**guiltier, guiltiest**) *adj* If you feel **guilty**, you feel unhappy because you have done something bad or have failed to do something which you should have done. قصوروار
Guinea *n* **Guinea** is a republic in West Africa, on the Atlantic. گنی جمہوریہ
guinea pig (**guinea pigs**) *n* If someone is used as a **guinea pig** in an experiment, a drug or other treatment is tested for the first time on them. تختۂ مشق، بلی کا بکرہ ▷ *n* A **guinea pig** is a small furry animal without a tail. امریکی چوہا
guitar (**guitars**) *n* A **guitar** is a wooden musical instrument with six strings which are plucked or strummed. گٹار
Gulf States (**npl**) *n* The **Gulf States** are

the oil-producing states around the Persian Gulf: Iran, Iraq, Kuwait, Saudi Arabia, Bahrain, Qatar, the United Arab Emirates, and Oman. خلیجی ریاستیں

gum *n* **Gum** is a substance, often mint-flavoured, which you chew for a long time but do not swallow. چیونگم

gun (**guns**) *n* A **gun** is a weapon from which bullets or pellets are fired. بندوق

gust (**gusts**) *n* A **gust** is a short, strong, sudden rush of wind. جھکڑ

gut (**guts**) *n* A person's or animal's **guts** are all their internal organs. آنت

guy (**guys**) *n* A **guy** is a man. شخص

Guyana *n* **Guyana** is a republic in north-east South America, on the Atlantic. گیانا جمہوریہ

gym (**gyms**) *n* A **gym** is a club or room, usually containing special equipment, where people can exercise. جم (کسرت گھر)

gymnast (**gymnasts**) *n* A **gymnast** is someone who is trained in gymnastics. جمناسٹ

gymnastics *npl* **Gymnastics** consists of physical exercises that develop your strength, co-ordination, and agility. جمناسٹک ورزش

gynaecologist (**gynaecologists**) *n* A **gynaecologist** is a doctor who specialises in women's diseases and medical conditions. ماہر امراض نسواں

gypsy (**gypsies**) *n* A **gypsy** is a member of a race of people who travel from place to place in caravans, rather than living in one place. خانہ بدوش

h

habit (**habits**) *n* A **habit** is something that you do often or regularly. عادت

hack (**hacks, hacking, hacked**) *v* If you **hack** something or **hack** at it, you cut it with strong, rough strokes using a sharp tool such as an axe or knife. سختی سے کاٹنا

hacker (**hackers**) *n* A computer **hacker** is someone who tries to break into computer systems, especially in order to get secret information. (کمپیوٹر/انٹرنٹ) چور، ہیکر

haddock (**haddock**) *n* A **haddock** is a type of sea fish. سمندری مچھلی

haemorrhoids *npl* **Haemorrhoids** are painful swellings that can appear in the veins inside the anus. بواسیری مسے

haggle (**haggles, haggling, haggled**) *vi* If you **haggle**, you argue about something before reaching an agreement, especially about the cost of something. مول بھاؤ کرنا

hail *n* **Hail** consists of tiny balls of ice that fall like rain from the sky. اولا ▷ **hails, hailing, hailed** *vt* If a person or event **is hailed** as important or successful, they are praised publicly. خیر مقدم کرنا

hair (**hairs**) *n* Your **hair** is the mass of fine thread-like strands that grow on your head. بال

hairband (**hairbands**) *n* A **hairband** is a strip of fabric or curved plastic worn by women in their hair, that fits closely over the top of the head and behind the ears. ہیر بینڈ

hairbrush (**hairbrushes**) *n* A **hairbrush** is a brush that you use to brush your hair. بالوں کا برش

haircut (**haircuts**) *n* If you have a **haircut**, someone cuts your hair for you. بال تراشی، حجامت

hairdo (**hairdos**) *n* A **hairdo** is the style in which your hair has been cut and arranged. بال تراشی کا اسٹائل

hairdresser (**hairdressers**) *n* A **hairdresser** is a person who cuts, washes, and styles people's hair. حجام ▷ *n* A **hairdresser** or a **hairdresser's** a place where you can get your hair cut, washed, and shaped. نائی کی دوکان

hairdryer (**hairdryers**) *n* A **hairdryer** is a machine that you use to dry your hair. بال سکھانے کا آلہ، ہیر ڈرایر

hair gel (**hair gels**) *n* **Hair gel** is a thick substance like jelly that you use to keep your hair in a particular style. بالوں کی جیل

hairgrip (**hairgrips**) *n* A **hairgrip** is a small piece of metal or plastic bent back on itself, which you use to hold your hair in position. بال باندھنے والا کلپ

hair spray (**hairsprays**) *n* **Hair spray** is a sticky substance that you spray out of a can onto your hair in order to hold it in place. بالوں کا اسپرے

hairstyle (**hairstyles**) *n* Your **hairstyle** is the style in which your hair has been cut or arranged. بالوں کا اسٹائل

hairy (**hairier, hairiest**) *adj* Someone or something that is **hairy** is covered with a lot of hair. بال دار

Haiti *n* **Haiti** is a republic in the Caribbean, on the western side of the island of Hispaniola. ہیٹی

half (**halves**) *adj* **Half** means being a half or approximately a half. آدھا ▷ *adv* You use **half** to say that something is only partly the case. نصف، آدھا ▷ *n* A **half** is one of two equal parts that make up a whole thing. آدھا

half board *n* If you stay at a hotel and have **half board**, your breakfast and evening meal are included in the price of your stay at the hotel, but not your lunch. ایسا ہوٹل جس میں صبح کا ناشتہ اور شام کے کھانے کی قیمت کرایہ میں شامل ہو

half-hour (**half-hours**) *n* A **half-hour** is a period of 30 minutes. آدھا گھنٹہ

half-price *adj* If something is **half-price**, it costs only half what it usually costs. آدھی قیمت ▷ *adv* If you do something **half-price** or if you buy or sell something **half-price**, it costs only half what it usually costs. آدھی قیمت پر

half-term (**half-terms**) *n* **Half-term** is a short holiday in the middle of a school term. اسکولی میعاد کے درمیان قلیل چھٹی

half-time *n* In sport, **half-time** is the short rest period between the two parts of a game. اسکول دن کے درمیان چھٹی کا وقفہ

halfway *adv* **Halfway** means in the middle of a place or in between two points, at an equal distance from each of them. آدھے راستے میں

hall (**halls**) *n* In a house or flat, the **hall** is the area just inside the front door. ہال

hallway (**hallways**) *n* A **hallway** is the entrance hall of a house or other building. داخلہ ہال

halt (**halts**) *n* A **halt** is an interruption or end to activity, movement or progress. رکاوٹ، وقفہ

hamburger (**hamburgers**) *n* A s**hamburger** is a flat round mass of minced beef, fried and eaten in a bread roll. ہیمبرگر

hammer (**hammers**) *n* A **hammer** is a tool used for hitting things. It consists of a heavy piece of metal at the end of a handle. ہتھوڑا

hammock (**hammocks**) *n* A **hammock** is a piece of strong cloth or netting which is hung between two supports and used as a bed. جالیدار کپڑا

hamster (**hamsters**) *n* A **hamster** is a small furry animal which is similar to a mouse. ہیمسٹر (چوہے جیسا بالدار جانور)

hand (**hands, handing, handed**) *n* Your **hands** are the parts of your body that are at the ends of your arms, and that you use to hold things. A **hand** has four fingers and a thumb. ہاتھ ▷ *vt* If you **hand** something to someone, you pass it to them. ہاتھ سے دینا

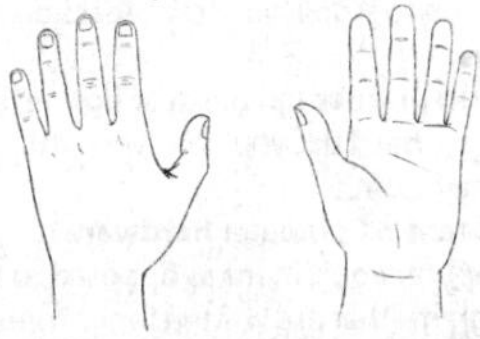

handbag (**handbags**) *n* A **handbag** is a small bag used by women to carry things such as money and keys. دستی بیگ

handball *n* **Handball** is a team sport in which the players try to score goals by throwing or hitting a large ball with their hand. ہینڈ بال (کھیل)

handbook (**handbooks**) *n* A **handbook** is a book giving advice or instructions on how to do a practical task. کتابچہ

handbrake (**handbrakes**) *n* In a vehicle, the **handbrake** is a brake which the driver operates with his or her hand, for example when parking. دستی بریک

handcuffs *npl* **Handcuffs** are two metal rings linked by a short chain which are locked round a prisoner's wrists. ہتھکڑی

handkerchief (**handkerchiefs**) *n* A **handkerchief** is a small square of fabric which you use for blowing your nose. رومال

handle (**handles, handling, handled**) *n* A **handle** is the part of something, for example a tool or a bag, that you use to hold it. ہتھا ▷ *vt* If you **handle** a situation, you deal with it. سلجھانا، مشکل حل کرنا ▷ *n* A **handle** is something that is joined to a door, a window, or a drawer, that you use to open and close it. ہینڈل، دستہ

handlebars *npl* The **handlebars** of a bicycle consist of a curved metal bar with handles at each end which are used for steering. سائکل کے ہینڈلوں کے بیچ مڑا ہوا حصہ

hand luggage *n* When you travel by air, your **hand luggage** is the luggage you have with you in the plane, rather than the luggage that is carried in the hold. دستی سامان

handmade *adj* If something is **handmade**, it is made without using machines. ہاتھ کا بنا ہوا

hands-free *adj* A **hands-free** phone or other device can be used without being held in your hand. ہاتھ آزاد رکھنے والا

hands-free kit (**hands-free kits**) *n* A **hands-free kit** is equipment that enables you to use your mobile phone, for example while driving, without holding it in your hand. ہینڈ فری کٹ (آلہ جن سے ہاتھ آزاد رہتے ہیں)

handsome *adj* A **handsome** man has an attractive face. خوب رو

handwriting *n* Your **handwriting** is your style of writing with a pen or pencil. تحریر

handy (**handier, handiest**) *adj* Something that is **handy** is useful. سہل، مفید

hang (**hangs, hanging, hung**) *vt* If you **hang** something somewhere, you fix the top of it to something so that it does not touch the ground. لٹکانا ▷ *vi* If something **hangs** somewhere, it is attached at the top so it does not touch the ground. لٹکنا

hanger (**hangers**) *n* A **hanger** is a curved piece of metal, plastic or wood used for hanging clothes on. ہینگر (کپڑے لٹکانے والا)

hang-gliding *n* **Hang-gliding** is the activity of flying from high places in a type of glider made from a large piece of cloth fixed to a frame. The pilot hangs underneath the glider. معلق گلائڈنگ

hang on *v* If you ask someone to **hang on**, you mean you want them to wait for a moment. انتظار کرانا *Hang on a second. I'll come with you.*

hangover (**hangovers**) *n* A **hangover** is a headache and feeling of sickness that you have after drinking too much alcohol. نشہ کا خمار

hang up *v* If you **hang up** or you **hang up** the phone, you end a phone call. فون رکھ دینا *Don't hang up!*

hankie (**hankies**) *n* A **hankie** is a small square of fabric which you use for blowing your nose. رومال

happen (**happens, happening, happened**) *vi* When something **happens**, it occurs or is done without being planned. ہونا

happily *adv* You can add **happily** to a statement to show that you are glad that something happened or is true. خوشی خوشی

happiness *n* **Happiness** is feelings of joy or contentment. خوشی

happy (**happier, happiest**) *adj* Someone who is **happy** has feelings of joy or contentment. خوش

harassment *n* **Harassment** is behaviour which is intended to trouble or annoy someone, for example repeated attacks on them or attempts to cause them problems. ہراسانی

harbour (**harbours**) *n* A **harbour** is an area of deep water which is protected from the sea by land or walls, so that boats can be left there safely. بندرگاہ

hard (**harder, hardest**) *adj* If something is **hard**, you have to try a lot to do it or to understand it. سخت، دشوار ▷ *adj* Something that is **hard** is solid, and it is not easy to bend it or break it. سخت ▷ *adv* If you work **hard**, you work with a lot of effort. سختی سے

hardboard *n* **Hardboard** is a material which is made by pressing very small pieces of wood very closely together to form a thin, slightly flexible sheet. ہارڈبورڈ

hard disk (**hard disks**) *n* A **hard disk** is a hard plastic disk inside a computer on which data and programs are stored. ہارڈ ڈسک (کمپیوٹر میں)

hardly *adv* You use **hardly** to say that something is almost, or only just, true. مشکل سے ▷ *adv* When you say things like **hardly ever** and **hardly any**, you mean almost never or almost none. شاید ہی، نہیں کے برابر

hard shoulder (**hard shoulders**) *n* The **hard shoulder** is the area at the side of a motorway or other road where you are allowed to stop if your car breaks down. سڑک کا کنارا

hard up (**harder up, hardest up**) *adj* If you are **hard up**, you have very little money. تنگ دست

hardware *n* Computer **hardware** is computer equipment as opposed to the programs that are written for it. Printers and monitors are computer hardware. ہارڈویئر (کمپیوٹر میں)

hare (**hares**) *n* A **hare** is an animal like a large rabbit, but with longer ears and legs. خرگوش

harm (**harms, harming, harmed**) *vt* To **harm** a person or animal means to cause them physical injury, usually on purpose. نقصان پہنچانا، مضروب کرنا

harmful *adj* Something that is **harmful** has a bad effect on someone or something else. نقصاندہ

harmless *adj* Something that is **harmless** does not have any bad effects. بے ضرر

harp (**harps**) *n* A **harp** is a large musical instrument consisting of a triangular frame with vertical strings which you pluck with your fingers. باجہ

harsh (**harsher, harshest**) *adj* **Harsh** climates or living conditions are very difficult for people, animals, and plants to exist in. سخت، کھردرا

harvest (**harvests, harvesting, harvested**) *n* **The harvest** is the gathering of a crop. فصل ▷ *vt* When you **harvest** a crop, you gather it in. فصل اگانا

hastily *adv* If you do something **hastily**, you do it in a hurry, without planning or preparation. جلدی سے

hat (**hats**) *n* A **hat** is a covering that you wear on your head. ٹوپی

hatchback (**hatchbacks**) *n* A **hatchback** is a car with an extra door at the back which opens upwards. پشت میں ایک فاضل دروازے والی کار

hate (**hates, hating, hated**) *vt* If you **hate** someone or something, you have an extremely strong feeling of dislike for them. نفرت کرنا

hatred *n* **Hatred** is an extremely strong feeling of dislike for someone or something. نفرت

haunted *adj* A **haunted** building or other place is one where a ghost regularly appears. آسیب زدہ

have (**has, having, had**) *v* You use **have** and **has** with another verb to form the present perfect. رکھنا *Alex hasn't left yet.* ▷ *v* When you **have** something, you feel it, or it happens to you. مبتلا ہونا *I have a bad cold.*

have to *v* You use **have to** when you are saying that something is necessary, obligatory, or must happen. If you do not **have to** do something, it is not necessary or obligatory for you to do it. لازمی طور پر *He had to go to Germany.*

hawthorn (**hawthorns**) *n* A **hawthorn** is a small tree which has sharp thorns and produces white or pink flowers. تھوہر

hay *n* **Hay** is grass which has been cut and dried so that it can be used to feed animals. سوکھی گھاس

hay fever *n* If someone suffers from **hay fever**, they have an allergy to pollen which makes their nose, throat, and eyes become red and swollen. تپ کاہی

haystack (**haystacks**) *n* A **haystack** is a large, solid pile of hay, often covered with a straw roof to protect it, which is left in the field until it is needed. گھاس کا انبار

hazard warning lights *npl* The **hazard warning lights** on a motor vehicle are small lights set to flash all at the same time to indicate that the vehicle is stopped and blocking the traffic. خطرے کی خبر دینے والی لائٹیں

hazelnut (**hazelnuts**) *n* **Hazelnuts** are nuts from a hazel tree, which can be eaten. گری (سخت چھلکے دار)

he *pron* You use **he** to talk about a man, a boy, or a male animal. وہ (مذکر)

head (**heads, heading, headed**) *n* The **head** of something is the person who is its leader. سربراہ، صدر، قائد ▷ *n* Your **head** is the part of your body at the top that has your eyes, ears, nose, mouth, and brain in it. سر ▷ *vt* If someone or something **heads** a line, they are at the front of it. رہنمائی کرنا

headache (**headaches**) *n* If you have a **headache**, you have a pain in your head. سر درد

headlight (**headlights**) *n* A vehicle's **headlights** are the large bright lights at the front. ہیڈلائٹ

headline (**headlines**) *n* A **headline** is the title of a newspaper story, printed in large letters at the top of it. سرخی

head office (**head offices**) *n* The **head office** of a company is its main office. صدر دفتر

headphones *npl* **Headphones** are small speakers which you wear over your ears in order to listen to music or other sounds without other people hearing. ہیڈ فون (اسپیکر)

headquarters *npl* The **headquarters** of an organization are its main offices. **Headquarters** can take the singular or plural form of the verb. صدر مرکز

headroom *n* **Headroom** is the amount of space below a roof or bridge. چھت یا پل کے نیچے کا رقبہ

h

headscarf (**headscarves**) *n* A **headscarf** is a piece of cloth which some women wear around their heads, for example to keep their hair neat, or as part of their religious beliefs. سرپوش

headteacher (**headteachers**) *n* A **headteacher** is a teacher who is in charge of a school. ہیڈ ماسٹر

heal (**heals, healing, healed**) *vi* When an injury such as a broken bone **heals**, it becomes healthy and normal again. مندمل ہونا

health *n* Your **health** is the condition of your body. صحت

healthy (**healthier, healthiest**) *adj* Someone who is **healthy** is well and strong and is not often ill. صحت مند ▷ *adj* Something that is **healthy** is good for you. صحت بخش

heap (**heaps**) *n* A **heap** of things is a messy pile of them. ڈھیر

hear (**hears, hearing, heard**) *v* When you **hear** sounds, you are aware of them because they reach your ears. سننا

hearing (**hearings**) *n* **Hearing** is the sense which makes it possible for you to be aware of sounds. سماعت

hearing aid (**hearing aids**) *n* A **hearing aid** is a device which people with hearing difficulties wear in their ear to enable them to hear better. سماعتی آلہ

heart (**hearts**) *n* Your **heart** is the organ in your chest that pumps the blood around your body. دل

heart attack (**heart attacks**) *n* If someone has a **heart attack**, their heart begins to beat irregularly or stops completely. دل کا صدمہ، ہارٹ اٹیک

heartbroken *adj* Someone who is **heartbroken** is extremely sad and upset. دل شکستہ

heartburn *n* **Heartburn** is a painful burning sensation in your chest, caused by indigestion. سوزش دل

heat (**heats, heating, heated**) *n* **Heat** is warmth or the quality of being hot. گرمی ▷ *vt* When you something, you raise its temperature, for example by using a flame or a special piece of equipment. گرم کرنا

heater (**heaters**) *n* A **heater** is a piece of equipment which is used to warm a place or to heat water. ہیٹر

heather *n* **Heather** is a low spreading plant with small purple, pink, or white flowers that grows wild on hills or moorland. ہیتھر (پودا)

heating *n* **Heating** is the process or equipment involved in keeping a building warm. حرارت

heat up *v* When you **heat** something **up**, especially food which has already been cooked and allowed to go cold, you make it hot. گرم کرنا (ٹھنڈے کھانے کو)

heaven *n* In some religions, **heaven** is said to be the place where God lives and where good people go when they die. جنت

heavily *adv* You can use **heavily** to indicate that something is great in amount, degree, or intensity. شدید طور پر

heavy (**heavier, heaviest**) *adj* Something that is **heavy** weighs a lot. بھاری

hedge (**hedges**) *n* A **hedge** is a row of bushes along the edge of a garden, field, or road. جھاڑی

hedgehog (**hedgehogs**) *n* A **hedgehog** is a small brown animal with sharp spikes covering its back. چھوٹا بھورا جانور

heel (**heels**) *n* Your **heel** is the back part of your foot, just below your ankle. ایڑی

height (**heights**) *n* The **height** of a person or thing is their measurement from bottom to top. قد

heir (**heirs**) *n* Someone's **heir** is the person who will inherit their money, property, or title when they die. وارث

heiress (**heiresses**) *n* An **heiress** is a woman who will inherit property, money, or a title. وارث (خاتون)

helicopter (**helicopters**) *n* A **helicopter** is an aircraft with no wings. It hovers or moves vertically and horizontally by means of large overhead blades which rotate. ہیلی کاپٹر

hell *n* According to some religions, **hell** is the place where the Devil lives, and where wicked people are sent to be punished when they die. جہنم

hello! *excl* You say '**hello!**' to someone when you meet them. ہلو

helmet (**helmets**) *n* A **helmet** is a hard hat which you wear to protect your head. ہیلمیٹ

help (**helps, helping, helped**) *excl* You shout '**help!**' when you are in danger in order to attract someone's attention so that they can come and rescue you. بچاؤ ▷ *n* **Help** is the act of helping. مدد ▷ *v* If you **help** someone, you make something easier for them to do, for example by doing part of their work or by giving them advice or money. مدد کرنا

helpful *adj* If someone is **helpful**, they help you by doing work for you or by giving you advice or information. مددگار

helpline (**helplines**) *n* A **helpline** is a special telephone service that people can call to get advice about a particular subject. ہیلپ لائن (ٹیلیفون خدمت)

hen (**hens**) *n* A **hen** is a female chicken. مرغی

hen night (**hen nights**) *n* A **hen night** is a party for a woman who is getting married very soon, to which only women are invited. خاتون کی شادی سے پہلے کی پارٹی

hepatitis *n* **Hepatitis** is a serious disease which affects the liver. ہیپاٹائٹس

her *det* You use **her** to say that something belongs to a woman or a girl. اس کا (خاتون کا) ▷ *pron* You use **her** to talk about a woman or a girl. اس کو (خاتون کو)

herbal tea (**herbal teas**) *n* **Herbal tea** is tea made from or using herbs. جڑی بوٹی والی چائے

herbs *npl* **Herbs** are plants whose leaves are used in cookery to add flavour to food, or as a medicine. جڑی بوٹیاں

here *adv* **Here** means the place where you are. یہاں

hereditary *adj* A **hereditary** characteristic or illness is passed on to a child from its parents before it is born. موروثی

heritage (**heritages**) *n* A country's **heritage** consists of all the qualities and traditions that have continued over many years, especially when they are considered to be of historical importance. وراثت

hernia (**hernias**) *n* A **hernia** is a medical condition in which one of your internal organs sticks through a weak point in the surrounding tissue. ہرنیا (فوطوں میں پانی بھر جانا)

hero (**heroes**) *n* The **hero** of a book, play, or film is the main male character, who usually has good qualities. ہیرو (مرکزی کردار)

heroine (**heroines**) *n* The **heroine** of a book, play, or film is its main female character, who usually has good qualities. ہیروئن (خاتون مرکزی کردار)

heron (**herons**) *n* A **heron** is a large bird which has long legs and a long beak, and which eats fish. لمبی ٹانگیں اور چونچ والا پرندہ

herring (**herring, herrings**) *n* A **herring** is a long silver-coloured fish. چاندی رنگ کی مچھلی

hers *pron* You use **hers** to say that something belongs to a woman or a girl. اس کی (خاتون کی)

herself *pron* You use **herself** when you want to say that something a woman or a girl does has an effect on her. وہ (خاتون) خود *She pulled herself out of the water.*

hesitate (**hesitates, hesitating, hesitated**) *vi* If you **hesitate**, you pause slightly while you are doing something or just before you do it, usually because you are uncertain, embarrassed, or worried. ہچکچانا

HGV *abbr* An **HGV** is a large vehicle such

as a lorry. **HGV** is an abbreviation for 'heavy goods vehicle'. لاری جیسی بڑی گاڑی

hi! *excl* In informal situations, you say '**hi!**' to greet someone. ہائے

hiccups *npl* When you have **hiccups**, you make repeated sharp sounds in your throat, often because you have been eating or drinking too quickly. ہچکیاں

hidden *adj* Something that is **hidden** is not easily noticed. چھپی ہوئی

hide (**hides, hiding, hid, hidden**) *vt* If you **hide** something, you put it where no one can see it or find it. چھپانا ▷ *vi* If you **hide**, you go somewhere where people cannot easily find you. چھپنا ▷ *vt* If you **hide** what you feel, you do not let people know about it. چھپانا، پردہ پوشی کرنا

hide-and-seek *n* **Hide-and-seek** is a children's game in which one player covers his or her eyes until the other players have hidden themselves, and then he or she tries to find them. لکا چھپی

hideous *adj* If you say that someone or something is **hideous**, you mean that they are extremely unpleasant or ugly. کریہہ

hifi (**hifis**) *n* A **hifi** is a set of equipment on which you play CDs and tapes, and which produces stereo sound of very good quality. ہائی فائی

high (**higher, highest**) *adj* Something that is **high** is tall or is a long way above the ground. اونچا ▷ *adv* If items are piled **high**, they are arranged in a tall pile. اونچائی میں ▷ *adj* **High** means great in amount or strength. اونچا ▷ *adj* A **high** sound or voice goes up a long way. بلند

highchair (**highchairs**) *n* A **highchair** is a chair with long legs for a small child to sit in while they are eating. اونچی کرسی

higher education *n* **Higher education** is education at universities and colleges. اعلیٰ تعلیم

high-heeled *adj* **High-heeled** shoes are women's shoes that have high heels. اونچی ایڑی والے جوتے

high heels *npl* You can refer to women's shoes that have high heels as **high heels**. اونچی ایڑی

high jump *n* The **high jump** is an athletics event which involves jumping over a raised bar. اونچی کود، جست

highlight (**highlights, highlighting, highlighted**) *n* The **highlights** of an event, activity, or period of time are the most interesting or exciting parts of it. سرخی ▷ *vt* If you **highlight** a point or problem, you draw attention to it. سرخی لگانا، واضح کرنا

highlighter (**highlighters**) *n* A **highlighter** is a pen with brightly coloured ink that is used to mark parts of a document. الفاظ نمایاں کرنے والی قلم

high-rise (**high-rises**) *n* A **high-rise** is a modern building which is very tall and has many levels or floors. اونچی جدید عمارت

high season *n* The **high season** is the time of year when a place has most tourists or visitors. سیاحوں کا موسم

Highway Code *n* **The Highway Code** is an official book which contains the rules which tell people how to use public roads safely. محکمہ ٹرانسپورٹ کی کتاب (برطانیہ میں)

hijack (**hijacks, hijacking, hijacked**) *vt* If someone **hijacks** a plane or other vehicle, they illegally take control of it by force while it is travelling from one place to another. اغوا کرنا

hijacker (**hijackers**) *n* A **hijacker** is a person who hijacks a plane or other vehicle. اغوا کار

hike (**hikes**) *n* A **hike** is a long walk in the country, especially one that you go on for pleasure. طویل چہل قدمی

hiking *n* **Hiking** is the activity of going on long walks in the country, especially for pleasure. پیدل سفر

hilarious *adj* If something is **hilarious**, it is extremely funny. نہایت مضحکہ خیز

hill (**hills**) *n* A **hill** is an area of land that is higher than the land that surrounds it, but not as high as a mountain. پہاڑی

hill-walking *n* **Hill-walking** is the activity of walking through hilly country for pleasure. پہاڑی علاقے میں چلنا

him *pron* You use **him** to talk about a man or a boy. اس کو (مرد کو)

himself *pron* You use **himself** when you want to say that something a man or a boy does has an effect on him. وہ (مرد) خود *He fell and hurt himself.*

Hindu (**Hindus**) *adj* **Hindu** is used to describe things that belong or relate to Hinduism. ہندو (غیر مسلم) ▷ *n* A **Hindu** is a person who believes in Hinduism. ہندو (کثیر العقیدہ)

Hinduism *n* **Hinduism** is an Indian religion, which has many gods and teaches that people have another life on earth after they die. ہندو مذہب

hinge (**hinges**) *n* A **hinge** is a moveable joint made of metal, wood, or plastic that joins two things so that one of them can swing freely. قبضہ

hint (**hints, hinting, hinted**) *n* A **hint** is a suggestion about something that is made in an indirect way. اشارہ ▷ *vi* If you **hint** at something, you suggest it in an indirect way. اشارہ کرنا

hip (**hips**) *n* Your **hips** are the two areas or bones at the sides of your body between the tops of your legs and your waist. سرین

hippie (**hippies**) *n* In the 1960s and 1970s, **hippies** were people who rejected conventional society and tried to live a life based on peace and love. ہپی (مغربی تہذیب کے باغی)

hippo (**hippos**) *n* A **hippo** is a hippopotamus. گینڈا

hippopotamus (**hippopotami, hippopotamuses**) *n* A **hippopotamus** is a very large African animal with short legs and thick, hairless skin. Hippopotamuses live in and near rivers. گینڈا

hire (**hires, hiring, hired**) *n* You use **hire** to refer to the activity or business of hiring something. کرایہ ▷ *vt* If you **hire** someone, you employ them or pay them to do a particular job for you. کرایہ پر لینا

his *det* You use **his** to say that something belongs to a man or a boy. اس کا *He showed me his new football.* ▷ *pron* You use **his** to say that something belongs to a man or a boy. اس (مرد) کی *He listened to the advice, but the decision was his.*

historian (**historians**) *n* A **historian** is a person who specializes in the study of history and who writes about it. مؤرخ

historical *adj* **Historical** people, situations, or things existed in the past and are considered to be a part of history. تاریخی

history (**histories**) *n* You can refer to the events of the past as **history**. You can also refer to the past events which concern a particular topic or place as its **history**. تاریخ

hit (**hits, hitting**) *n* A **hit** is the act of a moving object touching another object very quickly or hard. قابل حرکت چیز سے مارنے کا عمل ▷ *vt* If you **hit** something, you touch it with a lot of strength. مارنا، ٹھوکر لگانا

hitch (**hitches**) *n* A **hitch** is a slight problem. معمولی دشواری

hitchhike (**hitchhikes, hitchhiking, hitchhiked**) *vi* If you **hitchhike**, you travel by getting free lifts from passing vehicles. مفت لفٹ لیکر سفر کرنا

hitchhiker (**hitchhikers**) *n* A **hitchhiker** is someone who travels somewhere by getting free lifts from passing vehicles. مفت لفٹ لیکر سفر کرنے والا

hitchhiking *n* **Hitchhiking** is the activity or process of travelling by getting lifts from passing vehicles without paying. مفت لفٹ لیکر سفر

HIV-negative *adj* If someone is **HIV-negative**, they are not infected with the HIV virus, which reduces the ability of people's bodies to fight illness and which can cause AIDS. ایچ آئی وی منفی

HIV-positive *adj* If someone is **HIV-positive**, they are infected with the HIV virus, which reduces the ability of people's bodies to fight illness, and they may develop AIDS. ایچ آئی وی مثبت
hobby (**hobbies**) *n* A **hobby** is something that you enjoy doing in your spare time, for example reading or playing tennis. شوق
hockey *n* **Hockey** is a sport played between two teams of 11 players who use long curved sticks to hit a small ball and try to score goals. ہاکی
hold (**holds, holding, held**) *vt* When you **hold** something, you have it in your hands or your arms. پکڑنا ▷ *vt* If something **holds** an amount of something, then that is how much it has room for inside. گنجائش ہونا
holdall (**holdalls**) *n* A **holdall** is a strong bag which you use to carry your clothes and other things, for example when you are travelling. بستر بند
hold on *v* If you **hold on** or **hold onto** something, you keep your hand firmly round something. پکڑے رکھنا *He held on to a coffee cup.*
hold up (**hold-ups**) *v* If someone or something **holds** you **up**, they delay you. اونچا اٹھانا *Why were you holding everyone up?* ▷ *n* A **hold-up** is a situation in which someone is threatened with a weapon in order to make them hand over money or valuables. جمود
hole (**holes**) *n* A **hole** is an opening or hollow space in something. سوراخ
holiday (**holidays**) *n* A **holiday** is a period of time during which you relax and enjoy yourself away from home. چھٹی
Holland *n* **Holland** is another name for the Netherlands. ہالینڈ
hollow *adj* Something that is **hollow** has a hole or space inside it. کھوکھلا
holly (**hollies**) *n* **Hollies** are a group of evergreen trees and shrubs which have hard, shiny, prickly leaves, and also have bright red berries in winter. سدا بہار درخت اور جھاڑیوں کا مجموعہ
holy (**holier, holiest**) *adj* Something that is **holy** is considered to be special because it relates to God or to a particular religion. مقدس
home (**homes**) *adv* **Home** means to or at the place where you live. گھر کے طور پر ▷ *n* Your **home** is the place where you live. گھر
home address (**home addresses**) *n* Your **home address** is the address of your house or flat. گھر کا پتہ
homeland (**homelands**) *n* Your **homeland** is your native country. مادر وطن
homeless *adj* **Homeless** people have nowhere to live. بے گھر
home-made *adj* **Home-made** things are made in someone's home, rather than in a shop or factory. گھر کا بنا
home match (**home matches**) *n* When a sports team plays a **home match**, they play a game on their own ground, rather than on the opposing team's ground. اپنے میدان میں کھیلا گیا میچ
homeopathic *adj* **Homeopathic** means relating to or used in homeopathy. ہومیوپیتھک
homeopathy *n* **Homeopathy** is a way of treating illness in which the patient is given very small amounts of a drug which would produce symptoms of the illness if taken in large quantities. ہومیوپیتھی
home page (**home pages**) *n* On the Internet, a person's or organization's **home page** is the main page of information about them. ہوم پیج
homesick *adj* If you are **homesick**, you feel unhappy because you are away from home and are missing your family and friends. گھر کی یاد سے پریشان
homework *n* **Homework** is school work given to pupils to do at home. گھر کا کام (ہوم ورک)
Honduras *n* **Honduras** is a republic in Central America. ہونڈوراس

honest *adj* If you describe someone as **honest**, you mean that they always tell the truth, and do not try to deceive people or break the law. ایماندار

honestly *adv* If you do something **honestly**, you are truthful, and do not try to deceive people or break the law. ایماندارای سے

honesty *n* **Honesty** is the quality of being honest. ایمانداری

honey (**honeys**) *n* **Honey** is a sweet, sticky, edible substance made by bees. شہد

honeymoon (**honeymoons**) *n* A **honeymoon** is a holiday taken by a couple who have just married. ایام عسل

honeysuckle (**honeysuckles**) *n* **Honeysuckle** is a climbing plant with sweet-smelling yellow, pink, or white flowers. چڑھتی بیل

honour (**honours**) *n* **Honour** means doing what you believe to be right and being confident that you have done what is right. عزت

hood (**hoods**) *n* A **hood** is a part of some pieces of clothing which covers your head. سرپوش

hook (**hooks**) *n* A **hook** is a bent piece of metal or plastic that is used for catching or holding things, or for hanging things up. ہک

hooray! *excl* People sometimes shout '**hooray!**' when they are very happy and excited about something. ہرے!

Hoover® (**hoovers**) *n* A **Hoover** is an electric machine which sucks up dust and dirt from carpets. ہوور®

hoover (**hoovers, hoovering, hoovered**) *v* If you **hoover** a carpet, you clean it using a vacuum cleaner. دھول مٹی صاف کرنا

hop (**hops, hopping, hopped**) *vi* If you **hop**, you jump on one foot. آدمی کا ایک پیر پہ کودنا ▷ *vi* When animals or birds **hop**, they jump with two feet together. جانور اور پرندوں کا دو پیر پہ کودنا

hope (**hopes, hoping, hoped**) *n* **Hope** is a feeling of desire and expectation that things will go well in the future. امید ▷ *v* If you **hope** that something is true, or if you **hope** for something, you want it to be true or to happen, and you usually believe that it is possible or likely. امید کرنا

hopeful *adj* If you are **hopeful**, you are fairly confident that something that you want to happen will happen. پرامید

hopefully *adv* **Hopefully** is often used when mentioning something that you hope and are fairly confident will happen. امید کے ساتھ

hopeless *adj* If you feel **hopeless**, you feel desperate because there seems to be no possibility of success. ناامید

horizon *n* The **horizon** is the distant line where the sky seems to touch the land or the sea. افق

horizontal *adj* Something that is **horizontal** is flat and parallel with the ground. افقی

hormone (**hormones**) *n* A **hormone** is a chemical, usually occurring naturally in your body, that stimulates certain organs of your body. ہارمون

horn (**horns**) *n* On a vehicle such as a car, the **horn** is the device that makes a loud noise. ہارن ▷ *n* A **horn** is one of the hard bones with sharp points that grow out of some animals' heads. Goats and bulls have **horns**. سینگ ▷ *n* A **horn** is an instrument that you blow into to make music. ہارن

horoscope (**horoscopes**) *n* Your **horoscope** is a forecast of events which some people believe will happen to you in the future, based on the position of the stars when you were born. کنڈلی

horrendous *adj* Something that is **horrendous** is very bad or unpleasant. دہشت ناک

horrible *adj* If you say that someone or something is **horrible**, you mean that

h

they are very unpleasant. ڈراؤنا
horrifying *adj* If you describe something as **horrifying**, you mean that it is shocking or disgusting. خوفناک
horror *n* **Horror** is a strong feeling of alarm caused by something extremely unpleasant. ڈر
horror film (**horror films**) *n* A **horror film** is a film that is intended to be very frightening. ڈراونی فلم
horse (**horses**) *n* A **horse** is a large animal which people can ride. گھوڑا
horse racing *n* **Horse racing** is a sport in which horses ridden by people called jockeys run in races, sometimes jumping over fences. گھڑدوڑ
horseradish *n* **Horseradish** is a small white vegetable that is the root of a crop. It has a very strong sharp taste and is often made into a sauce. مولی
horse riding *n* **Horse riding** is the activity of riding a horse, especially for enjoyment or as a form of exercise. گھڑسواری
horseshoe (**horseshoes**) *n* A **horseshoe** is a piece of metal shaped like a U which is fixed to a horse's hoof. نال
hose (**hoses**) *n* A **hose** is a long, flexible pipe through which water is carried in order to do things such as put out fires or water gardens. ہوز(لمبا لچکدار پائپ)
hosepipe (**hosepipes**) *n* A **hosepipe** is a hose that people use to water their gardens or wash their cars. آبپاشی یا دھلائی کے لئے لمبا لچکدار پائپ
hospital (**hospitals**) *n* A **hospital** is a place where people who are ill are looked after by doctors and nurses. ہسپتال
hospitality *n* **Hospitality** is friendly, welcoming behaviour towards guests or strangers. مہمان نوازی
host (**hosts**) *n* The **host** at a party is the person who has invited everybody. میزبان ▷ *n* A **host** of things is a lot of them. بڑی مقدار میں سامان
hostage (**hostages**) *n* A **hostage** is someone who has been captured by a person or organization and who may be killed or injured if people do not do what that person or organization demands. یرغمال
hostel (**hostels**) *n* A **hostel** is a large house where people can stay cheaply for a short time. ہاسٹل
hostile *adj* If someone is **hostile** to another person or to an idea or suggestion, they show their dislike for them in an aggressive way. باغی
hot (**hotter, hottest**) *adj* If something is **hot**, it has a high temperature. گرم
hot dog (**hot dogs**) *n* A **hot dog** is a long bread roll with a sausage in it. لمبا بریڈرول
hotel (**hotels**) *n* A **hotel** is a building where people stay, paying for their rooms and meals. ہوٹل
hot-water bottle (**hot-water bottles**) *n* A **hot-water bottle** is a rubber container that you fill with hot water and put in a bed to make it warm. گرم پانی کی بوتل
hour (**hours**) *n* An **hour** is a period of sixty minutes. گھنٹہ
hourly *adj* An **hourly** event happens once every hour. گھنٹے کے اعتبار سے ▷ *adv* If something happens **hourly**, it happens once every hour. ہر گھنٹے
house (**houses**) *n* A **house** is a building in which people live. گھر
household (**households**) *n* A **household** is all the people in a family or group who live together in a house. گھرانہ
housewife (**housewives**) *n* A **housewife** is a married woman who does not have a paid job, but instead looks after her home and children. خاتون خانہ
house wine (**house wines**) *n* A restaurant's **house wine** is the cheapest wine it sells, which is not listed by name on the wine list. کسی ریستراں کی سب سے سستی شراب
housework *n* **Housework** is the work such as cleaning and cooking that you do in your home. گھریلو کام

hovercraft (**hovercraft**) *n* A **hovercraft** is a vehicle that can travel across land and water. It floats above the land or water on a cushion of air. ہوا اور پانی پر چلنے والی گاڑی

how *adv* You use the word **how** when you ask about the way that something happens or the way that you do something. کیسے، کس طرح ▷ *adv* You use **how** when you ask about an amount. کتنے، کتنا

however *adv* You use **however** when you are saying something that somebody might not expect because of what you have just said. پھر بھی، باوجود اس کے

howl (**howls, howling, howled**) *vi* If an animal such as a wolf or a dog **howls**, it makes a long, loud, crying sound. جانور کا آواز کرنا

HQ (**HQs**) *abbr* The **HQ** of an organization is the centre or building from which its operations are directed. **HQ** is an abbreviation for 'headquarters'. ہیڈ کوارٹر (صدر مرکز)

hubcap (**hubcaps**) *n* A **hubcap** is a metal or plastic disc that covers and protects the centre of a wheel on a car, truck, or other vehicle. کار کے پہیے کی مرکزی ٹوپی

hug (**hugs, hugging, hugged**) *n* If you give someone a **hug**, you put your arms around them and hold them tightly, for example because you like them or are pleased to see them. معانقہ ▷ *vt* When you **hug** someone, you put your arms around them and hold them tightly, for example because you like them or are pleased to see them. You can also say that two people **hug** each other or that they **hug**. معانقہ کرنا، گلے لگانا

huge (**huger, hugest**) *adj* Something that is **huge** is extremely large in size, amount, or degree. بڑی، دیو ہیکل

hull (**hulls**) *n* The **hull** of a boat is the main part of its body. ناو کا ڈھانچہ

hum (**hums, humming, hummed**) *vi* If something **hums**, it makes a low continuous noise. بھنبھناہٹ

human *adj* **Human** means relating to or concerning people. انسانی

human being (**human beings**) *n* A **human being** is a man, woman, or child. انسان

humanitarian *adj* If a person or society has **humanitarian** ideas or behaviour, they try to avoid making people suffer or they help people who are suffering. انسانیت نواز

human rights *npl* **Human rights** are basic rights which many societies believe that all people should have. انسانی حقوق

humble (**humbler, humblest**) *adj* A **humble** person is not proud and does not believe that they are better than other people. نرم خو

humid *adj* You use **humid** to describe an atmosphere or climate that is very damp, and usually very hot. مرطوب

humidity *n* **Humidity** is dampness in the air. رطوبت

humorous *adj* If someone or something is **humorous**, they are amusing, especially in a clever or witty way. مزاحیہ

humour *n* You can refer to the amusing things that people say as their **humour**. مزاح

hundred *num* A **hundred** is the number 100. سو

Hungarian (**Hungarians**) *adj* **Hungarian** means belonging or relating to Hungary, or to its people, language, or culture. ہنگریائی ▷ *n* A **Hungarian** is a person who comes from Hungary. ہنگری کا باشندہ

Hungary *n* **Hungary** is a republic in central Europe. ہنگری

hunger *n* **Hunger** is the feeling of weakness or discomfort that you get when you need something to eat. بھوک

hungry (**hungrier, hungriest**) *adj* When you are **hungry**, you want food. بھوکا

hunt (**hunts, hunting, hunted**) *vi* If you **hunt** for something, you try to find it. تلاش کرنا ▷ *v* When animals **hunt**, they chase another animal to kill it for food. شکار کرنا

hunter (**hunters**) *n* A **hunter** is a person who hunts wild animals for food or as a sport. شکاری

hunting *n* **Hunting** is the chasing and killing of wild animals by people or other animals, for food or as a sport. شکار کا عمل

hurdle (**hurdles**) *n* A **hurdle** is a difficulty that you must overcome in order to achieve something. مشکل

hurricane (**hurricanes**) *n* A **hurricane** is a very violent storm with strong winds. گردابی طوفان

hurry (**hurries, hurrying, hurried**) *n* If you are in a **hurry** to do something, you need or want to do something quickly. If you do something in a **hurry**, you do it quickly or suddenly. جلدی ▷ *vi* If you **hurry** somewhere, you go there quickly. جلدی کرنا

hurry up *v* If you tell someone to **hurry up**, you are telling them to do something more quickly. جلدی کرو *Hurry up with that coffee, will you.*

hurt (**hurts, hurting, hurt**) *adj* If you are **hurt**, you have been injured. زخمی ▷ *vt* If you **hurt** yourself or **hurt** a part of your body, you feel pain because you have injured yourself. ضرب لگنا

husband (**husbands**) *n* A woman's **husband** is the man she is married to. شوہر

hut (**huts**) *n* A **hut** is a small, simple building, often made of wood, mud, or grass. جھونپڑی

hyacinth (**hyacinths**) *n* A **hyacinth** is a plant with a lot of small, sweet-smelling flowers growing closely around a single stem. It grows from a bulb and the flowers are usually blue, pink, or white. خوشبودار پھول کا پودا (سنبل)

hydrogen *n* **Hydrogen** is a colourless gas that is the lightest and most common element in the universe. ہائڈروجن

hygiene *n* **Hygiene** is the practice of keeping yourself and your surroundings clean, especially in order to prevent the spread of disease. حفظان صحت

hypermarket (**hypermarkets**) *n* A **hypermarket** is a very large supermarket. بہت بڑا سپر مارکیٹ

hyphen (**hyphens**) *n* A **hyphen** is the punctuation sign (-) used to join words together to make a compound. ہائفن (-) خط ربط

i

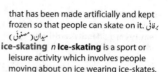

I *pron* You use **I** to talk about yourself. میں *I like cats.*

ice *n* **Ice** is frozen water. برف، آئس

iceberg (**icebergs**) *n* An **iceberg** is a large, tall piece of ice floating in the sea. برفانی تودہ

icebox (**allies iceboxes**) *n* An **icebox** is a container which is kept cool so that the food and drink inside stays fresh. (old-fashioned) برف بکس

ice cream (**ice creams**) *n* **Ice cream** is a very cold sweet food made from frozen milk, fats, and sugar. آئس کریم

ice cube (**ice cubes**) *n* An **ice cube** is a small square block of ice that you put into a drink in order to make it cold. آئس کیوب (مکعبی شکل میں)

ice hockey *n* **Ice hockey** is a game like hockey played on ice. آئس ہوکی

Iceland *n* **Iceland** is an island republic in the North Atlantic, regarded as part of Europe. آئس لینڈ جمہوریہ

Icelandic *adj* **Icelandic** means belonging or relating to Iceland, or to its people, language, or culture. آئس لینڈ سے متعلق
▷ *n* **Icelandic** is the official language of Iceland. آئس لینڈ کی زبان

ice lolly (**ice lollies**) *n* An **ice lolly** is a piece of flavoured ice or ice cream on a stick. آئس لولی (لولی پوپ)

ice rink (**ice rinks**) *n* An **ice rink** is a level area of ice, usually inside a building, that has been made artificially and kept frozen so that people can skate on it. برفانی میدان (مصنوئی)

ice-skating *n* **Ice-skating** is a sport or leisure activity which involves people moving about on ice wearing ice-skates. آئس اسکیٹنگ

icing *n* **Icing** is a sweet substance made from powdered sugar that is used to cover and decorate cakes. مسفوف شکر (کیک پر لگانے کا عمل)

icing sugar *n* **Icing sugar** is very fine white sugar that is used for making icing and sweets. برف نما شکر

icon (**icons**) *n* If you describe something or someone as an **icon**, you mean that they are important as a symbol of something. نشان، علامت

icy (**icier, iciest**) *adj* **Icy** air or water is extremely cold. برفانی

ID card *abbr* An **ID card** is a card with a person's name, photograph, date of birth, and other information on it. شناختی کارڈ

idea (**ideas**) *n* An **idea** is a plan or suggestion. خیال

ideal *adj* The **ideal** person or thing for a particular purpose is the best one for it. مثالی

ideally *adv* If you say that **ideally** a particular thing should happen or be done, you mean that this is what you would like to happen or be done, but you know that this may not be possible or practical. مثال کے طور پر

identical *adj* Things that are **identical** are exactly the same. یکساں

identification *n* When someone asks you for **identification**, they are asking to see something such as a passport which proves who you are. شناخت

identify (**identifies, identifying, identified**) *vt* If you can **identify** someone or something, you can recognize them and say who or what they are. شناخت کرنا

identity (**identities**) *n* Your **identity** is who you are. شناخت

identity card (**identity cards**) *n* An **identity card** is a card with a person's name, photograph, date of birth, and other information about them on it. شناختی کارڈ

identity theft *n* **Identity theft** is the crime of getting personal information about another person without their knowledge, for example in order to gain access to their bank account. شناخت کی چوری

ideology (**ideologies**) *n* An **ideology** is a set of beliefs, especially the political beliefs on which people, parties, or countries base their actions. نظریہ

idiot (**idiots**) *n* If you call someone an **idiot**, you mean that they are very stupid. بیوقوف

idiotic *adj* If you call someone or something **idiotic**, you mean that they are very stupid or silly. بیوقوفانہ

idle *adj* If you describe someone as **idle** you disapprove of them not doing anything when they should be doing something. سست، کام چور

i.e. *abbr* **i.e.** is used to introduce a word or sentence which makes what you have just said clearer or gives details. مثلاً

if *conj* You use **if** to talk about things that might happen, or that might have happened. اگر *You can go if you want. If he was there, I didn't see him.*

ignition (**ignitions**) *n* In a car, the **ignition** is the mechanism which ignites the fuel and starts the engine, usually operated by turning a key. اگنیشن (چنگاری پیدا کرنے والا)

ignorance *n* **Ignorance** of something is lack of knowledge about it. غفلت

ignorant *adj* If you refer to someone as **ignorant**, you mean that they do not know much because they are not well educated. If someone is **ignorant** of a fact, they do not know it. غافل

ignore (**ignores, ignoring, ignored**) *vt* If you **ignore** someone or something, you deliberately take no notice of them. نظرانداز کرنا

ill *adj* Someone who is **ill** is suffering from a disease or a health problem. بیمار

illegal *adj* If something is **illegal**, the law says that it is not allowed. غیرقانونی

illegible *adj* Writing that is **illegible** is so unclear that you cannot read it. غیرواضح

illiterate *adj* Someone who is **illiterate** cannot read or write. ناخواندہ

illness (**illnesses**) *n* **Illness** is the fact or experience of being ill. بیماری

ill-treat (**ill-treats, ill-treating, ill-treated**) *vt* If someone **ill-treats** you, they treat you badly or cruelly. برا برتاؤ کرنا

illusion (**illusions**) *n* An **illusion** is something that appears to exist or to be a particular thing but in reality does not exist or is something else. دھوکہ، بہروپ

illustration (**illustrations**) *n* An **illustration** of something is a clear example of it. عکس

image (**images**) *n* If you have an **image** of someone or something, you have a picture or idea of them in your mind. شبیہ

imaginary *adj* An **imaginary** person, place, or thing exists only in your mind or in a story, and not in real life. خیالی

imagination (**imaginations**) *n* Your **imagination** is your ability to form pictures or ideas in your mind of new, exciting, or imaginary things. تخیل

imagine (**imagines, imagining, imagined**) *vt* If you **imagine** a situation, your mind forms a picture or idea of it. خیال کرنا، تصور کرنا

imitate (**imitates, imitating, imitated**) *vt* If you **imitate** someone, you copy what they do or produce. نقل کرنا

imitation (**imitations**) *n* An imitation of something is a copy of it. نقل

immature *adj* Something that is **immature** is not yet fully developed. ناپختہ

immediate *adj* An **immediate** result, action, or reaction happens or is done without any delay. فوری

immediately *adv* If something happens

immediately, it happens without any delay. فوری طور پر

immigrant (**immigrants**) *n* An **immigrant** is a person who has come to live in a country from another country. مہاجر

immigration *n* **Immigration** is the fact or process of people coming into a country in order to live and work there. ترک وطن

immoral *adj* If you describe someone or their behaviour as **immoral**, you mean that their behaviour is bad or wrong. غیر اخلاقی

immune system (**immune systems**) *n* Your **immune system** consists of all the cells and processes in your body which protect you from illness and infection. نظام مدافعت

impact (**impacts**) *n* The **impact** that something has on a situation, process, or person is a sudden and powerful effect that it has on them. اثر، تاثر

impartial *adj* If you are **impartial**, you are able to act fairly because you are not personally involved in a situation. غیر جانبدار

impatience *n* **Impatience** is annoyance caused by having to wait too long for something. بے صبری

impatient *adj* If you are **impatient**, you are annoyed because you have had to wait too long for something. بے صبر

impatiently *adv* If you do something **impatiently**, you do it in an annoyed manner because you have had to wait too long for something. بے صبری سے

impersonal *adj* If you describe a place, organization, or activity as **impersonal**, you feel that the people there see you as unimportant or unwanted. پرایا، غیر مانوس

import (**imports, importing, imported**) *n* **Imports** are products or raw materials bought from another country for use in your own country. درآمد ▷ *vt* When a country or organization **imports** a product, they buy it from another country for use in their own country. درآمد کرنا

importance *n* The **importance** of something is its quality of being significant, valued, or necessary in a particular situation. اہمیت

important *adj* If something is **important**, people care about it and think about it a lot. اہم، ضروری ▷ *adj* If someone is **important**, people pay a lot of attention to what they say and do. اہم

impossible *adj* Something that is **impossible** cannot be done or cannot happen. ناممکن

impractical *adj* If an idea or course of action is **impractical**, it is not sensible or practical. ناقابل عمل

impress (**impresses, impressing, impressed**) *v* If someone or something **impresses** you, you feel great admiration for them. متاثر کرنا

impressed *adj* If you are **impressed** by something or someone, you feel great admiration for them. متاثر

impression (**impressions**) *n* Your **impression** of someone or something is what you think they are like. Your **impression** of a situation is what you think is going on. تاثر

impressive *adj* **Impressive** is used to describe people or things which impress you. اثر دار

improve (**improves, improving, improved**) *v* If something **improves**, or if you **improve** it, it gets better. سدھارنا

improvement (**improvements**) *n* If there is an **improvement** in something, it becomes better. If you make improvements to something, you make it better. سدھار، اصلاح

in *prep* **In** means not outside. اندر *The juice is in the fridge.* ▷ *prep* You also use **in** to say when something happens. میں *He was born in winter.*

i

inaccurate *adj* If a statement or measurement is **inaccurate**, it is not accurate or correct. غیر صحیح
inadequate *adj* If something is **inadequate**, there is not enough of it or it is not good enough. ناکافی
inadvertently *adv* If you do something **inadvertently**, you do it without realizing what you are doing. انجانے طور پر
inbox (**inboxes**) *n* On a computer, your **inbox** is the part of your mailbox which stores emails that have arrived for you. ان باکس، ای میل اسٹور
incentive (**incentives**) *n* An **incentive** is something that encourages you to do something. مراعات
inch (**inches**) *n* An **inch** is a unit of length, equal to 2.54 centimetres. انچ
incident (**incidents**) *n* An **incident** is an event, especially one involving something unpleasant. (*formal*) واقعہ
include (**includes, including, included**) *vt* If something **includes** something else, it has it as one of its parts. شامل کرنا
included *adj* You use **included** to emphasize that a person or thing is part of the group of people or things that you are talking about. مشمول
including *prep* You use **including** to talk about people or things that are part of a group. بشمول *Nine people were hurt, including both drivers.*
inclusive *adj* If a price is **inclusive**, it includes all the charges connected with the goods or services offered. If a price is **inclusive** of postage and packing, it includes the charge for this. بہ معیت
income (**incomes**) *n* The **income** of a person or organization is the money that they earn or receive. آمدنی
income tax (**income taxes**) *n* **Income tax** is a part of your income that you have to pay regularly to the government. انکم ٹیکس
incompetent *adj* If you describe someone as **incompetent**, you are criticizing them because they cannot do their job or a task properly. کم صلاحیت
incomplete *adj* Something that is **incomplete** is not yet finished, or does not have all the parts or details that it needs. نامکمل
inconsistent *adj* If you describe someone as **inconsistent**, you are criticizing them for not behaving in the same way every time a similar situation occurs. بے ہنگم
inconvenience (**inconveniences**) *n* If someone or something causes **inconvenience**, they cause problems or difficulties. زحمت، دشواری
inconvenient *adj* Something that is **inconvenient** causes problems or difficulties for someone. دشوارگزار
incorrect *adj* Something that is **incorrect** is wrong or untrue. غیر صحیح
increase (**increases, increasing, increased**) *n* If there is an **increase** in the number, level, or amount of something, it becomes greater. اضافہ ▷ *v* If something **increases** or you **increase** it, it becomes greater in number, level, or amount. اضافہ کرنا
increasingly *adv* You use **increasingly** to indicate that a situation or quality is becoming greater, stronger, or more common. اضافی طور پر
incredible *adj* If you describe someone or something as **incredible**, you like them very much or are impressed by them, because they are extremely or unusually good. حیرت ناک
indecisive *adj* If you are **indecisive**, you find it difficult to make decisions. ڈھلمل یقین، فیصلہ لینے میں کمزور
indeed *adv* You use **indeed** to emphasize your agreement with something that has just been said. واقعی، حقیقتاً
independence *n* A person's **independence** is their ability to do things without relying on other people. آزادی (خود مختاری)

independent *adj* Someone who is **independent** does not rely on other people. خود مختار

index (indices, indexes) *n* An **index** is an alphabetical list at the back of a book saying where particular things are mentioned in the book. اشاریہ ▷ *v* An **index** is a system by which changes in the value of something can be recorded, measured, or interpreted. تحقی

index finger (index fingers) *n* Your **index finger** is the finger that is next to your thumb. شہادت کی انگلی

India *n* **India** is a republic in south Asia. ہندوستان

Indian (Indians) *adj* **Indian** means belonging or relating to India, or to its people or culture. ہندوستانی ▷ *n* An **Indian** is an Indian citizen, or a person of Indian origin. ہندوستانی

Indian Ocean *n* The **Indian Ocean** is an ocean bordered by Africa in the west, Asia in the north, and Australia in the east, and merging with the Antarctic Ocean in the south. بحر ہند

indicate (indicates, indicating, indicated) *vt* If one thing **indicates** another, the first thing shows that the second is true or exists. اشارہ کرنا

indicator (indicators) *n* An **indicator** is a measurement or value which gives you an idea of what something is like. اشاریہ

indigestion *n* If you have **indigestion**, you have pains in your stomach that are caused by difficulties in digesting food. بد ہضمی

indirect *adj* An **indirect** result or effect is not caused immediately and obviously by a thing or person, but happens because of something else that they have done. بالواسطہ

indispensable *adj* If someone or something is **indispensable**, they are absolutely essential and other people or things cannot function without them. ناگزیر

individual *adj* **Individual** means relating to one person or thing, rather than to a large group. فرد

Indonesia *n* **Indonesia** is a republic in south-east Asia. انڈونیشیا

Indonesian (Indonesians) *adj* **Indonesian** means belonging or relating to Indonesia, or to its people or culture. انڈونیشیائی ▷ *n* An **Indonesian** is an Indonesian citizen, or a person of Indonesian origin. انڈونیشیائی

indoor *adj* **Indoor** activities or things are ones that happen or are used inside a building, rather than outside. اندرونِ دروازہ

indoors *adv* If something happens **indoors**, it happens inside a building. اندرونی طور پر

industrial *adj* **Industrial** means relating to industry. صنعتی

industrial estate (industrial estates) *n* An **industrial estate** is an area which has been specially planned for a lot of factories. صنعتی اسٹیٹ (جائداد)

industry *n* **Industry** is the work and processes involved in making things in factories. صنعت

inefficient *adj* A person, organization, system, or machine that is **inefficient** does not work in the most economical way. بے صلاحیت

inevitable *adj* If something is **inevitable**, it is certain to happen and cannot be prevented or avoided. ناگزیر

inexpensive *adj* Something that is **inexpensive** does not cost much. سستا

inexperienced *adj* If you are **inexperienced**, you have little or no experience of a particular activity. ناتجربہ کار

infantry *n* The **infantry** are the soldiers in an army who fight on foot. پیادہ فوج

infant school (infant schools) *n* An **infant school** is a school for children between the ages of five and seven. اطفال اسکول

infection (infections) *n* An **infection** is a

disease caused by germs. آلودگی،چھوت

infectious *adj* If you have an **infectious** disease, people near you can catch it from you. آلودہ، متعدی

inferior (**inferiors**) *adj* Something that is **inferior** is not as good as something else. کمتر ▷ *n* If one person is regarded as another person's **inferior**, they are considered to have less ability, status, or importance. چھوٹا

infertile *adj* Someone who is **infertile** is unable to produce babies. بانجھ

infinitive (**infinitives**) *n* The **infinitive** of a verb is its base form or simplest form, such as 'do', 'take', and 'eat'. The infinitive is often used with 'to' in front of it. فعل کی حالت (جانا، کھانا وغیرہ)

infirmary (**infirmaries**) *n* Some hospitals are called **infirmaries**. بیمار گھر (ہسپتال)

inflamed *adj* If part of your body is **inflamed**, it is red or swollen because of an infection or injury. سوزش زدہ

inflammation (**inflammations**) *n* An **inflammation** is a swelling in your body that results from an infection or injury. (*formal*) سوزش

inflatable *adj* An **inflatable** object is one that you fill with air when you want to use it. ہوا بھری / بھرا ہوا

inflation *n* **Inflation** is a general increase in the prices of goods and services in a country. افراطِ زر

inflexible *adj* Something or someone that is **inflexible** cannot or will not change or be altered, even if the situation changes. بے لچک

influence (**influences, influencing, influenced**) *n* **Influence** is the power to make other people agree with your opinions or make them do what you want. اثر ▷ *vt* If you **influence** someone, you use your power to make them agree with you or do what you want. اثر ڈالنا

influenza *n* **Influenza** is an illness caused by a virus. The symptoms are like those of a bad cold, but more serious. (*formal*) انفلوئنزا

inform (**informs, informing, informed**) *vt* If you **inform** someone of something, you tell them about it. مطلع کرنا

informal *adj* You use **informal** to describe behaviour, speech, or situations that are relaxed and casual rather than correct and serious. غیر رسمی

information *n* If you have **information** about a particular thing, you know something about it. معلومات

information office (**information offices**) *n* An **information office** is an **office** where you can go to get information. معلومات دفتر

informative *adj* Something that is **informative** gives you useful information. معلوماتی

infrastructure (**infrastructures**) *n* The **infrastructure** of a country or society consists of the basic facilities such as transport, communications, power supplies, and buildings, which enable it to function properly. بنیادی سہولیات

infuriating *adj* Something that is **infuriating** annoys you very much. طیش آمیز

ingenious *adj* Something that is **ingenious** is very clever and involves new ideas or equipment. مدبر، سلیقہ مند

ingredient (**ingredients**) *n* **Ingredients** are the things that are used to make something, especially all the different foods you use when you are cooking a particular dish. عنصر، جزو

inhabitant (**inhabitants**) *n* The **inhabitants** of a place are the people who live there. باشندہ

inhaler (**inhalers**) *n* An **inhaler** is a small device that helps you to breathe more easily if you have asthma or a bad cold. You put it in your mouth and breathe in deeply, and it sends a small amount of a drug into your lungs. انہیلر (بند ناک کھولنے والا)

inherit (**inherits, inheriting, inherited**) *vt* If you **inherit** money or property, you receive it from someone who has died. وارث ہونا

inheritance (**inheritances**) *n* An **inheritance** is money or property which you receive from someone who is dead. وراثت

inhibition (**inhibitions**) *n* **Inhibitions** are feelings of embarrassment that make it difficult for you to behave naturally. جھجک

initial (**initials, initialling, initialled**) *adj* You use **initial** to describe something that happens at the beginning of a process. ابتدائی ▷ *vt* If someone **initials** an official document, they write their initials on it, for example to show that they have seen it or that they accept or agree with it. مخفف حروف

initially *adv* **Initially** means in the early stages of a process or situation. ابتدائی طور پر

initials *npl* **Initials** are the capital letters which begin each word of a name. نام کے ابتدائی حروف

initiative (**initiatives**) *n* An **initiative** is an important act intended to solve a problem. پیشقدمی، پہلا قدم

inject (**injects, injecting, injected**) *vt* To **inject** someone with a substance such as a medicine, or to **inject** it into them, means to use a needle and a syringe to put it into their body. سوئی لگانا

injection (**injections**) *n* If you have an **injection**, someone puts a medicine into your body using a needle and a syringe. انجکشن

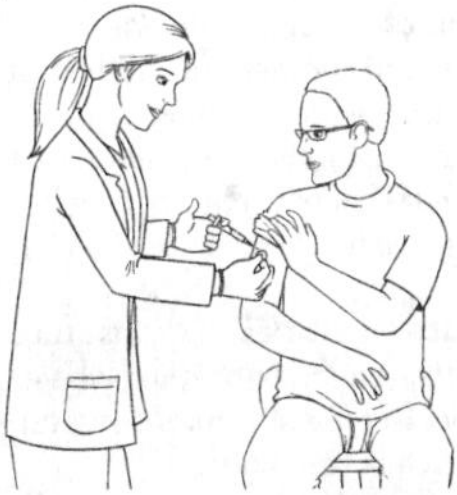

injure (**injures, injuring, injured**) *vt* If you **injure** a person or animal, you damage some part of their body. زخمی کرنا، ضرب لگانا

injured *adj* An **injured** person or animal has physical damage to part of their body, usually as a result of an accident or fighting. زخمی

injury (**injuries**) *n* An **injury** is damage done to a person's body. ضرب، زخم، ضرر

injury time *n* **Injury time** is the period of time added to the end of a football game because play was stopped during the match when players were injured. فٹ بال میچ کیدوران چوٹ لگنے پر کھیل میں خلل پڑنے پر دیا جانے والا اضافی وقت

injustice (**injustices**) *n* **Injustice** is unfairness in a situation. ناانصافی

ink (**inks**) *n* **Ink** is the coloured liquid used for writing or printing. روشنائی

in-laws *npl* Your **in-laws** are the parents and close relatives of your husband or wife. سسرالی رشتے دار

inmate (**inmates**) *n* The **inmates** of a prison or a psychiatric hospital are the prisoners or patients who are living there. مقیم

inn (**inns**) *n* An **inn** is a small hotel or a pub, usually an old one. (old-fashioned) سرائے

inner *adj* The **inner** parts of something are the parts which are contained or enclosed inside the other parts, and which are closest to the centre. اندرونی

inner tube (**inner tubes**) *n* An **inner tube** is a rubber tube containing air which is inside a car tyre or a bicycle tyre. سائکل / کار کے پہیہ کا ٹیوب، اندرونی ٹیوب

innocent *adj* If someone is **innocent**, they did not commit a crime which they have been accused of. بے قصور

innovation (**innovations**) *n* An **innovation** is a new thing or new method of doing something. ایجاد

innovative *adj* Something that is **innovative** is new and original. اختراعی

inquest (**inquests**) *n* An **inquest** is an official inquiry into the cause of someone's death. تفتیش قتل

inquire (**inquires, inquiring, inquired**) *v* If you **inquire** about something, you ask for information about it. (*formal*) پوچھنا، دریافت کرنا

inquiries office (**inquiries offices**) *n* An **inquiries office** is an office where you can go or call to get information. پوچھ تاچھ دفتر

inquiry (**inquiries**) *n* An **inquiry** is a question which you ask in order to get information. پوچھ گچھ

inquiry desk (**enquiry desks**) *n* The place in a hotel, hospital, airport, or other building where you obtain information is called the **inquiry desk**. پوچھ تاچھ ڈیسک

inquisitive *adj* An **inquisitive** person likes finding out about things, especially secret things. متجسس

insane *adj* Someone who is **insane** has a mind that does not work in a normal way, with the result that their behaviour is very strange. پاگل، دیوانہ

inscription (**inscriptions**) *n* An **inscription** is a piece of writing carved into a surface, or written on a book or photograph. نقش

insect (**insects**) *n* An **insect** is a small creature with six legs. Most insects have wings. کیڑا، حشرہ

insecure *adj* If you feel **insecure**, you feel that you are not good enough or are not loved. غیر محفوظ

insensitive *adj* If you describe someone as **insensitive**, you mean that they are not aware of other people's feelings or problems. بے حس

inside (**insides**) *adv* **Inside** also means indoors. گھر کے اندر ▷ *n* The **inside** of something is the area that its sides surround. اندرون ▷ *prep* If something is **inside** another thing, it is in it. اندر

insincere *adj* If you say that someone is **insincere**, you are being critical of them because they say things they do not really mean, usually pleasant, admiring, or encouraging things. غیر مخلص

insist (**insists, insisting, insisted**) *v* If you **insist** that something should be done, you say very firmly that it must be done. اصرار کرنا

insomnia *n* Someone who suffers from **insomnia** finds it difficult to sleep. بے خوابی

inspect (**inspects, inspecting, inspected**) *vt* If you **inspect** something, you examine it or check it carefully. معائنہ کرنا

inspector (**inspectors**) *n* An **inspector** is someone whose job is to inspect things. معائنہ کار، انسپکٹر

instability (**instabilities**) *n* **Instability** is a lack of stability in a place, situation, or person. بے ثباتی، ناپائداری

instalment (**instalments**) *n* If you pay for something in **instalments**, you pay small sums of money at regular intervals over a period of time. قسط

instance (**instances**) *n* An **instance** is a particular example or occurrence of something. مثال

instant *adj* You use **instant** to describe something that happens immediately. فوری

instantly *adv* If something happens **instantly**, it happens immediately. فی الفور

instead *adv* If you do not do something, but do something else **instead**, you do the second thing and not the first thing. بجائے

instead of *prep* If you do one thing **instead of** another, you do the first thing and not the second thing. باوجودیکہ

instinct (**instincts**) *n* An **instinct** is the natural tendency that a person has to behave or react in a particular way. جبلت، وجدان

institute (**institutes**) *n* An **institute** is an organization or building where a particular type of work is done, especially research or teaching. ادارہ

institution (**institutions**) *n* An **institution** is a large organization such as a parliament, a school, or a bank. ادارہ

instruct (**instructs, instructing, instructed**) *vt* If you **instruct** someone to do something, you formally tell them to do it. (*formal*) ہدایت دینا

instructions *npl* **Instructions** are clear and detailed information on how to do something. ہدایات

instructor (**instructors**) *n* An **instructor** is a teacher, especially of driving, skiing, or swimming. معلم

instrument (**instruments**) *n* An **instrument** is a tool that you use to do something. آلہ، اوزار ▷ *n* An **instrument** is also something, for example a piano or a guitar, that you use to make music. آلہ موسیقی

insufficient *adj* Something that is **insufficient** is not enough for a particular purpose. (*formal*) ناکافی

insulation *n* **Insulation** is a thick layer of material used to insulate something. غلاف

insulin *n* **Insulin** is a substance that most people produce naturally in their body and which controls the level of sugar in their blood. If your body does not produce enough insulin, then it develops a disease called diabetes. انسولین

insult (**insults, insulting, insulted**) *n* An **insult** is a rude remark or action which offends someone. بے عزتی ▷ *vt* If you **insult** someone, you offend them by being rude to them. بے عزتی کرنا

insurance *n* **Insurance** is an arrangement in which you pay money regularly to a company, and they pay money to you if something unpleasant happens to you, for example if your property is stolen. بیمہ

insurance certificate (**insurance certificates**) *n* An **insurance certificate** is a certificate that shows that a person or organization has insurance. بیمہ سند

insurance policy (**insurance policies**) *n* An **insurance policy** is a written contract between a person and an insurance company. بیمہ پالیسی

insure (**insures, insuring, insured**) *v* If you **insure** yourself or your property, you pay money to an insurance company so that if you become ill or if your property is stolen, the company will pay you a sum of money. بیمہ کرنا،کرانا

insured *adj* If someone or their property is **insured**, they pay money to an insurance company so that, if they become ill or if their property is damaged or stolen, the company will pay them a sum of money. بیمہ شدہ

intact *adj* Something that is **intact** is complete and has not been damaged or spoilt. ثابت

intellectual (**intellectuals**) *adj* **Intellectual** means involving a person's ability to think and to understand ideas and information. دانشور ▷ *n* An **intellectual** is someone who spends a lot of time studying and thinking about complicated ideas. دانشور

intelligence *n* Your **intelligence** is your ability to understand and learn things. دانائی

intelligent *adj* An **intelligent** person has the ability to think, understand, and learn things quickly and well. عاقل

intend *v* If you **intend** to do something, you have decided or planned to do it. ارادہ رکھنا

intense *adj* Something that is **intense** is very great in strength or degree. شدید

intensive *adj* An **intensive** activity involves the concentration of energy or people on one particular task. شدید

intensive care unit (**intensive care units**) *n* The intensive care unit is the part of a hospital that provides continuous care and attention, often using special equipment, for people who are very seriously ill or injured. نگہداشت یونٹ، انتہائی

i

intention (**intentions**) *n* An **intention** is an idea or plan of what you are going to do. ارادہ

intentional *adj* Something that is **intentional** is deliberate. بالارادہ

intercom (**intercoms**) *n* An **intercom** is a small box with a microphone which is connected to a loudspeaker in another room. You use it to talk to the people in the other room. انٹرکام

interest (**interests, interesting, interested**) *n* If you have an **interest** in something, you want to learn or hear more about it. دلچپی ▷ *n* **Interest** is extra money that you receive if you have invested a sum of money. سود ▷ *vt* If something **interests** you, you want to learn more about it or to continue doing it. دلچسپ لگنا

interested *adj* If you are **interested** in something, you think it is important and you are keen to learn more about it or spend time doing it. خواہاں

interesting *adj* If you find something **interesting**, it attracts you or holds your attention. دلچسپ

interest rate (**interest rates**) *n* The **interest rate** is the amount of interest that must be paid. It is expressed as a percentage of the amount that is borrowed or gained as profit. شرح سود

interior (**interiors**) *n* The **interior** of something is the inside or central part of it. اندرون

interior designer (**interior designers**) *n* An **interior designer** is a person who is employed to design the decoration for the inside of people's houses. اندرون تزئین کار

intermediate *adj* An **intermediate** stage or level is one that occurs between two other stages or levels. درمیانی

internal *adj* You use **internal** to describe things that exist or happen inside a place or organization. اندرونی

international *adj* **International** means between or involving different countries. بین الاقوامی

Internet *n* The **Internet** is the computer network which allows computer users to connect with computers all over the world, and which carries email. انٹرنیٹ

Internet café (**Internet cafés**) *n* An **Internet café** is a café with computers where people can pay to use the Internet. انٹرنیٹ کیفے

Internet user (**Internet users**) *n* An **Internet user** is a person who uses the Internet. انٹرنیٹ صارف

interpret (**interprets, interpreting, interpreted**) *vt* If you **interpret** something in a particular way, you decide that this is its meaning or significance. ترجمانی کرنا

interpreter (**interpreters**) *n* An **interpreter** is a person whose job is to translate what someone is saying into another language. مترجم

interrogate (**interrogates, interrogating, interrogated**) *vt* If someone, especially a police officer, **interrogates** someone, they question him or her for a long time, in order to get information from you. تفتیش کرنا

interrupt (**interrupts, interrupting, interrupted**) *v* If you **interrupt** someone who is speaking, you say or do something that causes them to stop. رکاوٹ ڈالنا

interruption (**interruptions**) *n* An **interruption** is something such as an action, comment, or question, that causes someone or something to stop. رکاوٹ

interval (**intervals**) *n* The **interval** between two events or dates is the period of time between them. وقفہ

interview (**interviews, interviewing, interviewed**) *n* An **interview** is a formal meeting at which someone is asked questions in order to find out if they are suitable for a job or a course of study. انٹرویو ▷ *vt* If you are **interviewed** for a particular job or course of study, someone asks you questions about yourself to find out if you are suitable for it. انٹرویو لینا

interviewer (**interviewers**) *n* An **interviewer** is a person who is asking someone questions at an interview. انٹرویو کرنے والا

intimate *adj* If two people have an **intimate** friendship, they are very good friends. گہری / گہرے

intimidate (**intimidates, intimidating, intimidated**) *vt* To **intimidate** someone means to frighten them, sometimes as a deliberate way of making them do something. دھمکانا

into *prep* If you put one thing **into** another thing, you put the first thing inside the second thing. اندر *Put the apples into a dish.* ▷ *prep* If you go **into** a place or a vehicle, you move from being outside it to being inside it. اندر جانا *He got into the car and started the engine.*

intolerant *adj* If you describe someone as **intolerant**, you disapprove of the fact that they do not accept behaviour and opinions that are different from their own. غیر متحمل

intranet (**intranets**) *n* An **intranet** is a network of computers, similar to the Internet, within a company or organization. انٹرانیٹ

introduce (**introduces, introducing, introduced**) *vt* To **introduce** something means to cause it to enter a place or exist in a system for the first time. تعارف کروانا

introduction (**introductions**) *n* The **introduction** of something is the act of causing it to enter a place or exist in a system for the first time. تعریف

intruder (**intruders**) *n* An **intruder** is a person who enters a place without permission. گھس بیٹھیا

intuition (**intuitions**) *n* Your **intuition** or your **intuitions** are feelings you have that something is true even when you have no evidence or proof of it. الہام

invade (**invades, invading, invaded**) *v* To **invade** a country means to enter it by force with an army. حملہ کرنا

invalid (**invalids**) *n* An **invalid** is someone who is very ill or disabled and needs to be cared for by someone else. ناکارہ

invent (**invents, inventing, invented**) *vt* If you **invent** something, you are the first person to think of it or make it. ایجاد کرنا

invention (**inventions**) *n* An **invention** is a machine or system that has been invented by someone. ایجاد، دریافت

inventor (**inventors**) *n* An **inventor** is a person who has invented something, or whose job is to invent things. موجد

inventory (**inventories**) *n* An **inventory** is a written list of all the objects in a place. فہرست (کل چیزوں کی)

inverted commas *npl* **Inverted commas** are the punctuation marks (' ') or (" ") which are used in writing to show where speech or a quotation begins and ends. الٹا کوما

invest (**invests, investing, invested**) *v* If you **invest** in something, or if you **invest** a sum of money, you use your money in a way that you hope will increase its value, for example by buying shares or property. سرمایہ لگانا

investigation (**investigations**) *n* An **investigation** is a careful search or examination in order to discover facts, etc. تفتیش

investment *n* **Investment** is the activity of investing money. سرمایہ

investor (**investors**) *n* An **investor** is a person or organization that buys stocks or shares, or pays money into a bank in order to receive a profit. سرمایہ کار

invigilator (**invigilators**) *n* An **invigilator** supervises the people who are taking

i

an examination in order to ensure that it starts and finishes at the correct time, and that there is no cheating. ممتحن

invisible *adj* If something is **invisible**, you cannot see it, because it is hidden or because it is very small or faint. نادیدہ

invitation (**invitations**) *n* An **invitation** is a written or spoken request to come to an event such as a party or a meeting. دعوت

invite (**invites, inviting, invited**) *vt* If you **invite** someone to something such as a party or a meal, you ask them to come to it. دعوت دینا

invoice (**invoices, invoicing, invoiced**) *n* An **invoice** is an official document that lists goods or services that you have received and says how much money you owe for them. بل ▷ *vt* If you **invoice** someone, you send them an invoice. بل بھیجنا

involve (**involves, involving, involved**) *vt* If an activity **involves** something, that thing is a necessary part of it. ملوث کرنا

iPod® (**iPods**) *n* An **iPod** is a portable MP3 player that can play music downloaded from the Internet. آئی پوڈ (ٹریڈ مارک)

IQ (**IQs**) *abbr* Your **IQ** is your level of intelligence, as indicated by a special test. **IQ** is an abbreviation for 'Intelligence Quotient'. آئی کیو (دانش پیماں)

Iran *n* **Iran** is a republic in south-west Asia, between the Caspian Sea and the Persian Gulf. ایران

Iranian (**Iranians**) *adj* **Iranian** means belonging or relating to Iran, or to its people or culture. ایرانی ▷ *n* An **Iranian** is an Iranian citizen, or a person of Iranian origin. ایرانی

Iraq *n* **Iraq** is a republic in south-west Asia, on the Persian Gulf. عراق

Iraqi (**Iraqis**) *adj* **Iraqi** means belonging or relating to Iraq, or to its people or culture. عراقی ▷ *n* An **Iraqi** is an Iraqi citizen, or a person of Iraqi origin. عراقی

Ireland *n* **Ireland** is an island off north-west Europe, to the west of Great Britain. آئیرلینڈ

iris (**irises**) *n* The **iris** is the round coloured part of a person's eye. پتلی

Irish *adj* **Irish** means belonging or relating to Ireland, or to its people, language, or culture. **Irish** sometimes refers to the whole of Ireland, and sometimes only to the Republic of Ireland. آئیرلینڈ کا ▷ *n* **Irish** is a Celtic language spoken in Ireland. آئیرلینڈ کی زبان

Irishman (**Irishmen**) *n* An **Irishman** is a man who is an Irish citizen or is of Irish origin. آئیرلینڈ کا آدمی

Irishwoman (**Irishwomen**) *n* An **Irishwoman** is a woman who is an Irish citizen or is of Irish origin. آئیرلینڈ کی عورت

iron (**irons, ironing, ironed**) *n* **Iron** is a strong, hard, grey metal. لوہا، فولاد ▷ *n* An **iron** is a piece of equipment with a flat bottom that gets hot. You move the bottom over clothes to make them smooth. استری ▷ *v* If you **iron** clothes, you make them smooth using an iron. استری کرنا

ironic *adj* When you make an **ironic** remark, you say something that you do not mean, as a joke. طنزیہ

ironing *n* **Ironing** is the act of removing the creases from clothes using an iron. استری کرنے کا عمل

ironing board (**ironing boards**) *n* An **ironing board** is a long narrow board covered with cloth on which you iron clothes. استری بورڈ (تختہ)

ironmonger (**ironmongers**) *n* An **ironmonger's** or an **ironmonger's** is a shop where articles for the house and garden such as tools, nails, and building supplies are sold. لوہے کا سامان بیچنے والے

irony *n* **Irony** is a form of humour which involves saying things that you do not mean. طنز

irregular *adj* If events or actions occur at

irregular intervals, the periods of time between them are of different lengths. بے ترتیب

irrelevant *adj* If you say that something is **irrelevant**, you mean that it is not important to or not connected with the present situation or discussion. غیر وابستہ

irresponsible *adj* If you describe someone as **irresponsible**, you are criticizing them because they do things without properly considering their possible consequences. غیر ذمہ دار

irritable *adj* If you are **irritable**, you are easily annoyed. تنک مزاج

irritating *adj* Something that is **irritating** keeps annoying you. برہمی

Islam *n* **Islam** is the religion of the Muslims, which teaches that there is only one God and that Mohammed is His prophet. (اسلام (دینِ فطرت

Islamic *adj* **Islamic** means belonging or relating to Islam. اسلامی

island (**islands**) *n* An **island** is a piece of land that is completely surrounded by water. جزیرہ

isolated *adj* If someone or something is **isolated** they are separate from other people or things of the same kind, either physically or socially. الگ تھلگ، تنہا

ISP *ISPs* An ISP is a company that provides Internet and email services. ISP is an abbreviation for 'Internet service provider'. انٹرنیٹ سروس پرووائڈر

Israel *n* **Israel** is a republic in south-west Asia, on the Mediterranean Sea. اسرائیل

Israeli (**Israelis**) *adj* **Israeli** means belonging or relating to Israel, or to its people or culture. اسرائیلی ⊳ *n* An **Israeli** is a person who comes from Israel. اسرائیلی باشندہ

issue (**issues, issuing, issued**) *n* An **issue** is an important subject that people are arguing about or discussing. موضوعِ بحث ⊳ *vt* If someone **issues** a statement, they make it formally or publicly. جاری کرنا

IT *abbr* **IT** is the theory and practice of using computers to store and analyze information. **IT** is an abbreviation for 'information technology'. اطلاعاتی ٹیکنالوجی

it *pron* You use **it** to talk about a thing or an animal. (یہ (بے جان کے لئے *This is a good book - have you read it?*

Italian (**Italians**) *adj* **Italian** means belonging or relating to Italy, or to its people, language, or culture. اطالوی ⊳ *n* An **Italian** is a person who comes from Italy. اطالوی ⊳ *n* **Italian** is the language spoken in Italy, and in parts of Switzerland. اطالوی زبان

Italy *n* **Italy** is a republic in southern Europe. اٹلی

itch (**itches, itching, itched**) *vi* When a part of your body **itches**, you have an unpleasant feeling on your skin that makes you want to scratch. کھجلی

itchy *adj* If a part of your body or something you are wearing is **itchy**, you have an unpleasant feeling on your skin that makes you want to scratch. (*informal*) خارشی

item *items* An **item** is one of a collection or list of objects. شئ

itinerary (**itineraries**) *n* An **itinerary** is a plan of a journey, including the route and the places that will be visited. سفری منصوبہ (جگہوں اور روٹ کی وضاحت کے ساتھ)

its *det* You use **its** to say that something belongs to a thing or an animal. اس کا *The lion lifted its head.*

itself *pron* You use **itself** to talk about something that you have just talked about. بذاتِ خود *The kitten washed itself, then lay down by the fire.*

ivory (**ivories**) *n* **Ivory** is a valuable type of bone, which forms the tusks of an elephant. ہاتھی دانت

ivy *n* **Ivy** is an evergreen plant that grows up walls or along the ground. آئوی (سدا بہار بیل)

i

j

jab (**jabs**) *n* A **jab** is an injection to prevent illness. حفاظتی انجکشن

jack (**jacks**) *n* A **jack** is a device for lifting a heavy object such as a car off the ground. جیک (اوپر اٹھانے والا آلہ)

jacket (**jackets**) *n* A **jacket** is a short coat. جیکیٹ

jacket potato (**jacket potatoes**) *n* A **jacket potato** is a large potato that has been baked with its skin on. بڑا چھلکے سمیت بھنا آلو

jackpot (**jackpots**) *n* A **jackpot** is a large sum of money which is the most valuable prize in a game or lottery. لاٹری کا بڑا داو

jail (**jails, jailing, jailed**) *n* A **jail** is a building where criminals are kept in order to punish them. قید خانہ ▷ *vt* If someone is **jailed**, they are put in jail. قید کرنا

jam (**jams**) *n* **Jam** is a food that you spread on bread, made by cooking fruit with a large amount of sugar. جام (بریڈ والا)

Jamaican (**Jamaicans**) *adj* **Jamaican** means belonging or relating to Jamaica or to its people or culture. جمیکن ▷ *n* A **Jamaican** is a person who comes from Jamaica. جمیکا کا باشندہ

jam jar (**jam jars**) *n* A **jam jar** is a glass container for jam, etc. جام جار (مرتبان)

jammed *adj* If a place is **jammed**, a lot of people are packed tightly together there and can hardly move. ٹھسا ٹھس بھرا

janitor (**janitors**) *n* A **janitor** is a person whose job is to look after a building. دربان، نگہبان

January (**Januaries**) *n* **January** is the first month of the year in the Western calendar. جنوری

Japan *n* **Japan** is an archipelago and empire in east Asia, extending between the Sea of Japan and the Pacific. جاپان

Japanese (**japanese**) *adj* **Japanese** means belonging or relating to Japan, or to its people, language, or culture. جاپانی ▷ *n* The **Japanese** are the people of Japan. جاپانی ▷ *n* **Japanese** is the language spoken in Japan. جاپانی زبان

jar (**jars**) *n* A **jar** is a glass container with a lid, used for storing food. مرتبان

jaundice *n* **Jaundice** is an illness that makes your skin and eyes become yellow. یرقان

javelin (**javelins**) *n* A **javelin** is a long spear that is thrown in sports competitions. نیزہ

jaw (**jaws**) *n* Your **jaw** is the part of your face below your mouth and cheeks. جبڑا

jazz *n* **Jazz** is a style of music invented by black American musicians in the early part of the twentieth century. It has very strong rhythms and the musicians often improvise. جاز (موسیقی)

jealous *adj* If someone is **jealous**, they feel angry because they think that another person is trying to take away someone or something that they love. حاسد

jeans *npl* **Jeans** are casual trousers that are usually made of strong blue denim. جینس (پتلون)

Jehovah's Witness (**Jehovah's Witnesses**) *n* A **Jehovah's Witness** is a member of a religious organization which accepts some Christian ideas and believes that the world is going to end very soon. جہواس وٹنس (یہودی فرقہ)

jelly (**jellies**) *n* **Jelly** is a transparent food made from gelatine, fruit juice, and sugar, which is eaten as a dessert. جیلی (شفاف مٹھائی)

jellyfish (**jellyfish**) *n* A **jellyfish** is a sea creature that has a clear soft body and can sting you. جیلی فش (آبی جاندار)

jersey (**jerseys**) *n* A **jersey** is a knitted piece of clothing that covers the upper part of your body and your arms. old-fashioned جرسی (پوری آستین کا سویٹر)

Jesus *n* Jesus or Jesus Christ is the name of the man who Christians believe was the son of God, and whose teachings are the basis of Christianity. عیسیٰ مسیح (پیغمبر خدا)

jet (**jets**) *n* A **jet** is an aeroplane that is powered by jet engines. جیٹ (ہوائی جہاز)

jetlag *n* If you are suffering from **jetlag**, you feel tired and slightly confused after a long journey by aeroplane. چلنے سے تھکان کا عارضہ

jetty (**jetties**) *n* A **jetty** is a wide stone wall or wooden platform where boats stop to let people get on and off, or to load or unload goods. جٹی، جیٹی

Jew (**Jews**) *n* A **Jew** is a person who believes in and practises the religion of Judaism. یہودی

jewel (**jewels**) *n* A **jewel** is a valuable stone, like a diamond. نگینہ، جڑاؤ پتھر ⊳ *n* **Jewels** are things made with valuable stones, that you wear to decorate your body. زیور

jeweller (**jewellers**) *n* A **jeweller** is a person who makes, sells, and repairs jewellery and watches. جوہری ⊳ *n* A **jeweller** or a **jeweller's** is a shop that sells jewellery and watches. زیورات کی دوکان

jewellery *n* **Jewellery** consists of ornaments that people wear such as rings and bracelets. زیورات، جواہرات

Jewish *adj* **Jewish** means belonging or relating to the religion of Judaism or to Jews. یہود کا

jigsaw (**jigsaws**) *n* A **jigsaw** or **jigsaw puzzle** is a picture on cardboard or wood that has been cut up into odd shapes and which has to be put back together again. آڑا کٹا معا (تصویر کے ٹکڑے جوڑنا)

job (**jobs**) *n* A **job** is the work that someone does to earn money. ملازمت

job centre (**job centres**) *n* A **job centre** is a place where people who are looking for work can go to get advice on finding a job, and to look at advertisements placed by people who are looking for new employees. ملازمت کا مرکز

jobless *adj* Someone who is **jobless** does not have a job, but would like one. بیروزگار

jockey (**jockeys**) *n* A **jockey** is someone who rides a horse in a race. جوکی (پیشہ ور گھڑسوار)

jog (**jogs, jogging, jogged**) *vi* If you **jog**, you run slowly, often as a form of exercise. آہستہ دوڑنا

jogging *n* **Jogging** is the act of running at a slow regular pace as part of an exercise routine. آہستہ دوڑ

join (**joins, joining, joined**) *v* When things **join**, or you **join** them, they come together. جوڑنا، ملانا ⊳ *v* If you **join** a group of people, you become one of the group. شامل ہونا

joiner (**joiners**) *n* A **joiner** is a person who makes wooden window frames, door frames, doors, and cupboards. بڑھئی، جوڑنے والا

joint (**joints**) *adj* **Joint** means shared by or belonging to two or more people. مشترکہ ⊳ *n* A **joint** is a place where two things meet or are fixed together. دو چیزوں کو ملانے والا، جوڑ ⊳ *n* A **joint** is a fairly large piece of meat which is suitable for roasting. گوشت کا بڑا ٹکڑا

joint account (joint accounts) *n* A **joint account** is a kind of bank account registered in the name of two or more people. مشترکہ کھاتہ

joke (jokes, joking, joked) *n* A **joke** is something that is said or done to make you laugh, for example a funny story. لطیفہ ▷ *vi* If you **joke**, you tell funny stories or say amusing things. مذاق کرنا

jolly (jollier, jolliest) *adj* A **jolly** person is happy and cheerful. مذاقیہ

Jordan *n* **Jordan** is a kingdom in south-west Asia. اردن

Jordanian (Jordanians) *adj* **Jordanian** means belonging or relating to the country of Jordan, or to its people or culture. اردنی ▷ *n* A **Jordanian** is a Jordanian citizen, or a person of Jordanian origin. اردنی

jot down *v* If you **jot** something **down**, you write it down in the form of a short informal note. جلدی سے لکھنا *Keep a notebook nearby to jot down queries.*

jotter (jotters) *n* A **jotter** is a small book for writing notes in. نوٹ بک

journalism *n* **Journalism** is the job of collecting news and writing about it for newspapers, magazines, television, or radio. صحافت

journalist (journalists) *n* A **journalist** is a person whose job is to collect news, and write about it in newspapers or magazines or talk about it on television or radio. صحافی

journey (journeys) *n* When you make a **journey**, you travel from one place to another. سفر

joy *n* **Joy** is a feeling of great happiness. لطف

joystick (joysticks) *n* In some computer games, the **joystick** is the lever which the player uses in order to control the direction of the things on the screen. جوئے اسٹک (کمپیوٹر کھیل میں کنٹرول لیور)

judge (judges, judging, judged) *n* A **judge** is the person in a court of law who decides how the law should be applied, for example how criminals should be punished. قاضی، منصف ▷ *vt* If you **judge** a competition, you decide who or what is the winner. فیصلہ کرنا، انصاف کرنا

judo *n* **Judo** is a sport or martial art in which two people wrestle and try to throw each other to the ground. جوڈو

jug (jugs) *n* A **jug** is a container which is used for holding and pouring liquids. جگ

juggler (jugglers) *n* A **juggler** is someone who juggles in order to entertain people. مداری

juice (juices) *n* **Juice** is the liquid that can be obtained from a fruit. رس، جوس

July (Julys) *n* **July** is the seventh month of the year in the Western calendar. جولائی

jumbo jet (jumbo jets) *n* A **jumbo jet** or a **jumbo** is a very large jet aeroplane. بڑا جہاز

jump (jumps, jumping, jumped) *v* If you **jump**, you bend your knees, push against the ground with your feet, and move quickly upwards into the air. جست لگانا، کودنا

jumper (jumpers) *n* A **jumper** is a knitted piece of clothing which covers the upper part of your body and your arms. جمپر

jump leads *npl* **Jump leads** are two thick wires that can be used to start a car when its battery does not have enough power. The jump leads are used to connect the battery to the battery of another car that is working properly. دوسری کار کی بیٹری سے جڑنے والے دو موٹے تار

junction (junctions) *n* A **junction** is a place where roads or railway lines join. مقام اتصال (جنکشن)

June (Junes) *n* **June** is the sixth month of the year the Western calendar. جون

jungle (jungles) *n* A **jungle** is a forest in a tropical country where tall trees and other plants grow very closely together. جنگل

junior *adj* A **junior** official or employee

holds a low-ranking position in an organization or profession. جونیئر

junk *n* **Junk** is an amount of old or useless things. فضول

junk mail *n* **Junk mail** is advertisements and publicity materials that you receive through the post or by email which you have not asked for and which you do not want. فضول کے ای میل

jury (**juries**) *n* In a court of law, the **jury** is the group of people who have been chosen from the general public to listen to the facts about a crime and to decide whether the person accused is guilty or not. شورای، جیوری

just *adv* If you **just** did something, you did it a very short time ago. بس ابھی، ٹھیک

justice *n* **Justice** is fairness in the way that people are treated. عدل

justify (**justifies, justifying, justified**) *vt* If someone or something **justifies** a particular decision, action, or idea, they show or prove that it is reasonable or necessary. صحیح ٹھہرانا، توجیہ کرنا

k

kangaroo (**kangaroos**) *n* A **kangaroo** is a large Australian animal. Female kangaroos carry their babies in a pocket on their stomachs. کنگارو

karaoke *n* **Karaoke** is a form of entertainment in which a machine plays the tunes of songs, and people take it in turns to sing the words. کراوکے

karate *n* **Karate** is a martial art in which people fight using their hands, elbows, feet, and legs. کراٹے (خالی ہاتھ)

Kazakhstan *n* **Kazakhstan** is a republic in central Asia. قزاقستان

kebab (**kebabs**) *n* A **kebab** is pieces of meat or vegetables grilled on a long thin stick, or slices of grilled meat served in pitta bread. کباب

keen (**keener, keenest**) *adj* If you are **keen** on doing something, you very much want to do it. If you are **keen** that something should happen, you very much want it to happen. شائق

keep (**keeps, keeping, kept**) *v* If someone **keeps** still or warm, they stay like that. رکھنا ▷ *vi* If someone **keeps** away from a place, they do not go near it. رکھنا ▷ *vt* If you **keep** doing something, you do it many times or you do it some more. جاری رکھنا، برقرار رکھنا ▷ *vt* When you **keep** something, you store it somewhere. حفاظت سے رکھنا

keep-fit *n* **Keep-fit** is the activity of

keeping your body in good condition by doing special exercises. فٹ رکھنے والی (ورزش)

keep out *v* If you **keep out** of something, you avoid getting involved in it. ملوث نہ ہونا *They have kept out of the debate so far.*

keep up *v* If someone or something **keeps up** with another person or thing, the first one moves or progresses as fast as the second. برقرار رکھنا *She shook her head and started to walk on. He kept up with her.*

kennel (**kennels**) *n* A **kennel** is a small hut made for a dog to sleep in. کتا گھر

Kenya *n* **Kenya** is a republic in East Africa, on the Indian Ocean. کینیا

Kenyan (**Kenyans**) *adj* **Kenyan** means belonging or relating to Kenya, or to its people or culture. کینیائی ▷ *n* A **Kenyan** is a Kenyan citizen, or a person of Kenyan origin. کینیائی

kerb (**kerbs**) *n* The **kerb** is the raised edge of a pavement which separates it from the road. سڑک سے جڑا فٹ پاتھ کا اونچا کنارا

kerosene *n* **Kerosene** is a strong-smelling liquid which is used as a fuel in heaters, lamps, and engines. (*US*) مٹی کا تیل

ketchup *n* **Ketchup** is a thick, cold sauce, usually made from tomatoes, that is sold in bottles. چٹنی

kettle (**kettles**) *n* A **kettle** is a covered container that you use for boiling water. کیتلی

key (**keys**) *n* The **keys** on a computer or instrument are the buttons that you press on it. کلید، کمپیوٹر وغیرہ کے کی بورڈ پر موجود کلیدیں ▷ *n* A **key** is a piece of metal that opens or closes a lock. چابی، کنجی

keyboard (**keyboards**) *n* The **keyboard** of a computer is the set of keys that you press in order to operate it. کی بورڈ

keyring (**keyrings**) *n* A **keyring** is a metal ring which you use to keep your keys together. You pass the ring through the holes in your keys. چھلہ، کی رنگ

kick (**kicks, kicking, kicked**) *n* A **kick** is a forceful hit made with your foot. لات ▷ *v* If you **kick** someone or something, you hit them forcefully with your foot. لات مارنا

kick off (**kick-offs**) *v* If an event, game, series, or discussion **kicks off**, or if someone **kicks** it **off**, it begins. شروع کرنا *The Mayor kicked off the party.* ▷ *n* In football or rugby, **kick-off** is the time at which a particular match starts. شروعات

kid (**kids, kidding, kidded**) *n* You can refer to a child as a **kid**. (*informal*) بچہ ▷ *vi* If you are **kidding**, you are saying something that is not really true, as a joke. (*informal*) بچکانہ بات کرنا

kidnap (**kidnaps, kidnapping, kidnapped**) *vt* To **kidnap** someone is to take them away illegally and by force, and usually to hold them prisoner in order to demand something from their family, employer, or government. اغوا کرنا

kidney (**kidneys**) *n* Your **kidneys** are the two organs in your body that filter waste matter from your blood and send it out of your body in your urine. گردہ

kill (**kills, killing, killed**) *v* If a person, animal, or other living thing is **killed**, something or someone causes them to die. مارنا، قتل کرنا

killer (**killers**) *n* A **killer** is a person who has killed someone. قاتل

kilo (**kilos**) *n* A **kilo** is a metric unit of weight. One kilogram is a thousand grams, and is equal to 2.2 pounds. کلو (باٹ)

kilometre (**kilometres**) *n* A **kilometre** is a metric unit of distance or length. One kilometre is a thousand metres, and is equal to 0.62 miles. کلومیٹر

kilt (**kilts**) *n* A **kilt** is a skirt with a lot of vertical folds, traditionally worn by Scottish men. Kilts can also be worn by women and girls. اسکرٹ (لہنگا)

kind (**kinder, kindest, kinds**) *adj* Someone who is **kind** is friendly and helps you. مہربان، رحم دل ▷ *n* A **kind** of thing is a type or sort of that thing. قسم

kindly *adv* If you do something **kindly**, you do it in a gentle, caring, and helpful way. رحدلانہ طور پر

kindness *n* **Kindness** is the quality of being gentle, caring, and helpful. رحم

king (**kings**) *n* A **king** is a man who is a member of the royal family of his country, and who is the head of state of that country. بادشاہ

kingdom (**kingdoms**) *n* A **kingdom** is a country or region that is ruled by a king or queen. بادشاہت

kingfisher (**kingfishers**) *n* A **kingfisher** is a brightly-coloured bird which lives near rivers and lakes and catches fish. کنگ فشر (مچھلی پکڑنے والی چڑیا)

kiosk (**kiosks**) *n* A **kiosk** is a small shop in a public place such as a street or station. It sells things such as snacks or newspapers which you buy through a window. کیوسک (کھڑکی سے بیچنے کی دوکان)

kipper (**kippers**) *n* A **kipper** is a fish, usually a herring, which has been preserved by being hung in smoke. دھوئیں میں سکھائی مچھلی

kiss (kisses, kissing, kissed) *n* A **kiss** is the act of touching somebody with your lips to show affection or to greet them. بوسہ ▷ *v* If you **kiss** someone, you touch them with your lips to show affection, or to greet them or say goodbye. چومنا

kit (**kits**) *n* A **kit** is a group of items that are kept together because they are used for similar purposes. کٹ (کسی پیشہ سے جڑے سامان کا تھیلا)

kitchen (**kitchens**) *n* A **kitchen** is a room used for cooking and related jobs such as washing dishes. باورچی خانہ

kite (**kites**) *n* A **kite** is an object consisting of a light frame covered with paper or cloth, which you fly in the air at the end of a long string. پتنگ

kitten (**kittens**) *n* A **kitten** is a very young cat. بلی کا بچہ

kiwi (**kiwis**) *n* A **kiwi**, or **kiwi fruit**, is a fruit with a brown hairy skin and green flesh. کیوی (بھورا روئیں دار چھلکا اور ہرا مغز)

km/h *abbr* **Km/h** is a written abbreviation for 'kilometres per hour'. کلومیٹر فی گھنٹہ

knee (**knees**) *n* Your **knee** is the place where your leg bends. گھٹنا

kneecap (**kneecaps**) *n* Your **kneecaps** are the bones at the front of your knees. گھٹنے کی کٹوری

kneel (**kneels, kneeling, kneeled, knelt**) *vi* When you **kneel**, you bend your legs so that your knees are touching the ground. دوزانو ہونا

kneel down *v* When you **kneel down**, you bend your legs so that your knees are touching the ground. گھٹنوں کے بل زمین پر چلنا *She kneeled down beside him.*

knickers *npl* **Knickers** are a piece of underwear worn by women and girls which have holes for the legs and elastic around the top. نیکر (زیر جامہ)

knife (**knives**) *n* A **knife** is a tool consisting of a sharp flat piece of metal attached to a handle, used to cut things or as a weapon. چاقو، چھری

knit (**knits, knitting, knitted**) *v* When someone **knits** something, they make it from wool or a similar thread using knitting needles or a machine. بننا

knitting *n* **Knitting** is something, such as an article of clothing, that is being knitted. بنائی

knitting needle (**knitting needles**) *n* **Knitting needles** are thin plastic or metal rods which you use when you are knitting. بننے کی سلائیاں

knob (**knobs**) *n* A **knob** is a round handle or switch. گھنڈی، ہینڈل، ہتھہ

knock (**knocks, knocking, knocked**) *n* A **knock** is the act or sound of something being hit, such as a door or window, to attract someone's attention. دستک ▷ *vi* If you **knock** on something such as a door or window, you hit it, usually several times, to attract someone's attention. دستک دینا

knock down *v* To **knock down** a building or part of a building means to demolish or destroy it. گرا دینا *Why doesn't he just knock the wall down?*

knock out *v* To **knock** someone **out** means to cause them to become unconscious. بےہوش کر دینا *I nearly knocked him out.*

knot (**knots**) *n* If you tie a **knot** in a piece of string, rope, cloth, or other material, you pass one end or part of it through a loop and pull it tight. گرہ، گانٹھ

know (**knows, knowing, knew, known**) *vt* If you **know** something, you have that information in your mind. جاننا، معلوم ہونا ▷ *vt* If you **know** a person, you have met them and spoken to them. جاننا

know-all (**know-alls**) *n* If you say that someone is a **know-all**, you are critical of them because they think that they know a lot more than other people. (*informal*) سب جاننا

know-how *n* **Know-how** is knowledge of the methods or techniques of doing something. (*informal*) تکنیک

knowledge *n* **Knowledge** is information and understanding about a subject, which someone has in their mind. علم، معلومات

knowledgeable *adj* A **knowledgeable** person knows a lot about many different things or a lot about a particular subject. عالم، جانکار

known *adj* You use **known** to describe someone or something that is clearly recognized by or familiar to all people, or to a particular group of people. شناسا

Koran *n* The **Koran** is the sacred book on which the religion of Islam is based. قرآن

Korea *n* **Korea** is a former country in East Asia, now divided into two separate countries, North Korea and South Korea. کوریا

Korean (**Koreans**) *adj* **Korean** means belonging or relating to North or South Korea, or to their people, language, or culture. کوریائی ▷ *n* A **Korean** is a North or South Korean citizen, or a person of North or South Korean origin. کوریائی ▷ *n* **Korean** is the language spoken by people who live in North and South Korea. کوریائی

kosher *adj* Something, especially food, that is **kosher** is approved of or allowed by the laws of Judaism. کھانے کے لئے پاک (یہودیت کے مطابق)

Kosovo *n* **Kosovo** is a disputed territory in south-east Europe. It is a self-declared independent state, but the Constitution of Serbia considers it to be an autonomous province of Serbia. کوسوو

Kuwait *n* **Kuwait** is a state on the north-west coast of the Persian Gulf. کویت

Kuwaiti (**Kuwaitis**) *adj* **Kuwaiti** means belonging or relating to Kuwait, or to its people or culture. کویتی ▷ *n* A **Kuwaiti** is a Kuwaiti citizen, or a person of Kuwaiti origin. کویتی

Kyrgyzstan *n* **Kyrgyzstan** is a republic in central Asia. کرغزستان

l

lab (**labs**) *n* A **lab** is a building or room when scientific experiments and research are performed. لیب، تجربہ گاہ

label (**labels**) *n* A **label** is a piece of paper or plastic that is attached to an object in order to give information about it. لیبل

laboratory (**laboratories**) *n* A **laboratory** is a building or room where scientific experiments and research are performed. تجربہ گاہ، لیباریٹری

labour *n* **Labour** is very hard work. محنت

labourer (**labourers**) *n* A **labourer** is a person who does a job which involves a lot of hard physical work. مزدور

lace (**laces**) *n* **Lace** is a pretty cloth that has patterns of holes in it. لیس، زریں چمکدار پٹی
▷ *n* **Laces** are like pieces of string for fastening shoes. فیتہ

lack *n* If there is a **lack** of something, there is not enough of it, or there is none at all. کمی

lacquer (**lacquers**) *n* **Lacquer** is a special type of liquid which is put on wood or metal to protect it and make it shiny. لاکھ کاروغن، وارنش

lad (**lads**) *n* A **lad** is a boy or young man. (*informal*) لڑکا

ladder (**ladders**) *n* A **ladder** is a piece of equipment used for climbing up something such as a wall. It consists of two long pieces of wood or metal with steps fixed between them. سیڑھی

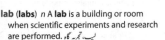

ladies *n* Some people refer to a public toilet for women as the **ladies.** خواتین کا

ladle (**ladles**) *n* A **ladle** is a large, round, deep spoon with a long handle, used for serving soup, stew, or sauce. ڈوئی

lady (**ladies**) *n* You can use **lady** when you are referring to a woman, especially when you are showing politeness or respect. خاتون

ladybird (**ladybirds**) *n* A **ladybird** is a small round beetle that is red with black spots. سیاہ چتی والا بادامی بھونرا

lag behind *vi* If you **lag behind** someone or something, you make slower progress than them. پیچھے رہ جانا *He now lags 10 points behind the champion.*

lager (**lagers**) *n* **Lager** is a kind of pale beer. پرانی بیئر

lagoon (**lagoons**) *n* A **lagoon** is an area of calm sea water that is separated from the ocean by sand or rock. بحری جھیل

laid-back *adj* If you describe someone as **laid-back**, you mean that they behave in a relaxed way as if nothing ever worries them. (*informal*) سرد مہری والا

lake (**lakes**) *n* A **lake** is a large area of fresh water, surrounded by land. جھیل

lamb (**lambs**) *n* A **lamb** is a young sheep. بھیڑ کا بچہ

lame (**lamer, lamest**) *adj* A **lame** person or animal cannot walk properly because an injury or illness has damaged one or both of their legs. لنگڑا

lamp (**lamps**) *n* A **lamp** is a light that works by using electricity or by burning oil or gas. چراغ، بلب

lamppost (**lampposts**) *n* A **lamppost** is a tall metal or concrete pole that is fixed beside a road and has a light at the top. چراغ کا کھمبا

lampshade (**lampshades**) *n* A **lampshade** is a covering that is fitted round or over an electric light bulb in order to protect it or decorate it, or to make the light less harsh. بلب کا سایہ

land (**lands, landing, landed**) *n* **Land** is an area of ground. زمین ▷ *v* When something **lands**, it comes down to the ground after moving through the air. اترا

landing (**landings**) *n* In a house or other building, the **landing** is the area at the top of the staircase which has rooms leading off it. زمین پر اترنے کا عمل

landlady (**landladies**) *n* Someone's **landlady** is the woman who allows them to live or work in a building which she owns, in return for rent. مکان مالکن

landlord (**landlords**) *n* Someone's **landlord** is the man who allows them to live or work in a building which he owns, in return for rent. مکان مالک

landmark (**landmarks**) *n* A **landmark** is a building or feature which is easily noticed and can be used to judge your position or the position of other buildings or features. نشان منزل

landowner (**landowners**) *n* A **landowner** is a person who owns land, especially a large amount of land. زمین کا مالک

landscape (**landscapes**) *n* The **landscape** is everything that you can see when you look across an area of land, including hills, rivers, buildings, and trees. ارضی منظر

landslide (**landslides**) *n* If an election is won by a **landslide**, it is won by a large number of votes. بڑے پیمانے پر

lane (**lanes**) *n* A **lane** is a type of road, especially in the country. گلی

language (**languages**) *n* A **language** is a system of sounds and written symbols used by the people of a particular country, area, or tribe to communicate with each other. زبان

language laboratory (**language laboratories**) *n* A **language laboratory** is a classroom equipped with tape recorders or computers where people can practise listening to and talking foreign languages. لینگویج لیبارٹری

language school (**language schools**) *n* A **language school** is a private school where a foreign language is taught. لینگویج اسکول

lanky (**lankier, lankiest**) *adj* If you describe someone as **lanky**, you mean that they are tall and thin and move rather awkwardly. لمبا تراشیدہ جسم والا

Laos *n* **Laos** is a republic in south-east Asia. لاؤس

lap (**laps**) *n* Your **lap** is the flat area formed by your thighs when you are sitting down. گود

laptop (**laptops**) *n* A **laptop** or a **laptop computer** is a small computer that you can carry around with you. لیپ ٹاپ

larder (**larders**) *n* A **larder** is a room or large cupboard in a house, usually near the kitchen, in which food is kept. نعمت خانہ

large (**larger, largest**) *adj* A **large** thing or person is big or bigger than usual. بڑا، جسم

largely *adv* You use **largely** to say that a statement is mostly but not completely true. بڑے پیمانے پر

laryngitis *n* **Laryngitis** is an infection of the throat in which your larynx becomes swollen and painful, making it difficult to speak. ورم نرخرہ

laser (**lasers**) *n* A **laser** is a narrow beam of concentrated light produced by a special machine. لیزر (شعاعی بیم)

lass (**lasses**) *n* A **lass** is a young woman or girl. دوشیزہ، لڑکی

last (**lasts, lasting, lasted**) *adj* The **last** thing is the one before this one. آخری ▷ *adj* The **last** thing or person comes after all the others. آخری، اختتامی ▷ *adv* Something **last** happened on the most recent occasion on which it happened. آخرش ▷ *v* If an event or situation **lasts** for a particular length of time, it continues for that length of time. آخر ہونا، اخیر ہونا

lastly *adv* You use **lastly** when you want to make a final point that is connected with the ones you have already mentioned. آخر میں

late (**later, latest**) *adj* **Late** means after the usual time that something happens. آخری ▷ *adj* You use **late** when you are talking about someone who is dead. مرحوم ▷ *adv* **Late** also means after the proper time. تاخیر سے ▷ *adv* **Late** means near the end of a period of time. دیر

lately *adv* **Lately** means recently. فی الحال

later *adv* You use **later** to refer to a time or situation that is after the one that you have been talking about or after the present one. پہلے، بعد والا

Latin *n* **Latin** is the language which the ancient Romans used to speak. لاطینی

Latin America *n* You can use **Latin America** to refer to the countries of South America, Central America, and Mexico. لاطینی امریکہ

Latin American *adj* **Latin American** means belonging or relating to the countries of South America, Central America, and Mexico. **Latin American** also means belonging or relating to the people or culture of these countries. لاطینی امریکی

latitude (**latitudes**) *n* The **latitude** of a place is its distance from the Equator. عرض البلد

Latvia *n* **Latvia** is a republic in north-east Europe, on the Gulf of Riga and the Baltic Sea. لٹویا (ایک ملک)

Latvian (**Latvians**) *adj* **Latvian** means belonging to or relating to Latvia, its people, or their language. لٹویائی ▷ *n* A **Latvian** is a person from Latvia. لٹویا کا شہری ▷ *n* **Latvian** is the language spoken in Latvia. لٹویا کی زبان

laugh (**laughs, laughing, laughed**) *n* A **laugh** is the act of making a sound while smiling and showing that you are happy or amused. ہنسی ▷ *vi* When you **laugh**, you smile and make a sound because something is funny. ہنسنا

laughter *n* **Laughter** is the sound of people laughing. ہنسی

launch (**launches, launching, launched**) *vt* To **launch** a rocket, missile, or satellite means to send it into the air or into space. جاری کرنا، بھیجنا

Launderette® (**Launderettes**) *n* A **Launderette** is a place where people can pay to use machines to wash and dry their clothes. لانڈری•

laundry *n* **Laundry** is used to refer to clothes, sheets, and towels that are about to be washed, are being washed, or have just been washed. کپڑے دھونے کا عمل

lava *n* **Lava** is the very hot liquid rock that comes out of a volcano. لاوا

lavatory (**lavatories**) *n* A **lavatory** is a toilet. بیت الخلاء

lavender *n* **Lavender** is a garden plant with sweet-smelling purple flowers. لوینڈر

law *n* The **law** is a system of rules that a society or government develops to deal with things like crime. قانون

lawn (**lawns**) *n* A **lawn** is an area of grass that is kept cut short and is usually part of a garden or park. گھاس کا میدان

lawnmower (**lawnmowers**) *n* A **lawnmower** is a machine for cutting grass on lawns. گھاس کاٹنے کی مشین

law school (**law schools**) *n* **Law school** is an institution that trains people to become lawyers. قانون پڑھانے والا ادارہ

lawyer (**lawyers**) *n* A **lawyer** is a person who is qualified to advise people about the law and represent them in court. وکیل (قانون داں)

laxative (**laxatives**) *n* A **laxative** is food or medicine that you take to make you go to the toilet. ملین

lay (**lays, laying, laid**) *vt* When you **lay** something somewhere, you put it down so that it lies there. رکھنا، پھیلانا ▷ *vt* When a bird **lays** an egg, it pushes an egg out of its body. انڈے دینا

layby (**laybys**) *n* A **layby** is a short strip of road by the side of a main road, where cars can stop for a while. ٹریفک نشان والی پٹی

layer (**layers**) *n* A **layer** of a material or substance is a quantity or flat piece of it that covers a surface or that is between two other things. پرت

lay off *v* If workers are **laid off** by their employers, they are told to leave their jobs, usually because there is no more work for them to do. برطرف کرنا (کام نہ ہونے کے سبب) *They did not sell a single car for a month and had to lay off workers.*

layout (**layouts**) *n* The **layout** of a garden, building, or piece of writing is the way in which the parts of it are arranged. لے آؤٹ (خاکہ)

lazy (**lazier, laziest**) *adj* If someone is **lazy**, they do not want to work or make an effort. سست

lead (**leads, leading, led**) *vt* If you **lead** someone to a place, you take them there. رہنمائی کرنا ▷ *n* The **lead** in a play, film, or show is the most important role in it. لیڈ رول، مرکزی کردار ▷ *n* If you are in the **lead** in a race or competition, you are winning. آگے ہونا، بڑھت حاصل کرنا

lead *n* Lead is a soft, grey, heavy metal. سیسہ

leader (**leaders**) *n* The **leader** of an organization or a group of people is the person who is in charge of it. رہنما

lead-free *adj* Something such as petrol or paint which is **lead-free** is made without lead, or has no lead added to it. سیسہ سے پاک

lead singer (**lead singers**) *n* The **lead singer** of a pop group is the person who sings most of the songs. رہنما گلوکار

leaf (**leaves**) *n* A **leaf** is one of the parts of a tree or plant that is flat, thin, and usually green. پتہ، پتی

leaflet (**leaflets**) *n* A **leaflet** is a little book or a piece of paper containing information about a particular subject. کتابچہ

league (**leagues**) *n* A **league** is a group of people, clubs, or countries that have joined together for a particular purpose. لیگ

leak (**leaks, leaking, leaked**) *n* A **leak** is a crack, hole, or other gap that a substance such as a liquid or gas can pass through. شگاف ▷ *vi* If a container **leaks**, there is a hole or crack in it which lets a substance such as liquid or gas escape. You can also say that a container **leaks** a substance such as liquid or gas. رسنا

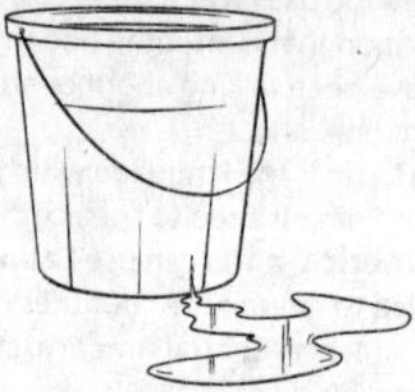

lean (**leans, leaning, leaned, leant**) *vi* When you **lean** in a particular direction, you bend your body in that direction. جھکنا

lean forward *v* When you **lean forward**, you bend your body forwards. آگے کی طرف جھکنا *He leaned forward to give her a kiss.*

lean on *v* If you **lean on** someone, you depend on them for support and help. انحصار کرنا *You can lean on me.*

lean out *v* When you **lean out**, you bend your body outwards. باہر کی طرف جھکنا *He opened the window and leaned out.*

leap (**leaps, leaping, leaped, leapt**) *vi* If you **leap**, you jump high in the air or jump a long distance. اچھلنا، جست لگانا

leap year (**leap years**) *n* A **leap year** is a year which has 366 days. The extra day is the 29th February. There is a leap year every four years in the Western calendar. لیپ سال

learn (**learns, learning, learned, learnt**) *v* When you **learn**, you obtain knowledge or a skill through studying or training. سیکھنا، علم حاصل کرنا

learner (**learners**) *n* A **learner** is someone who is learning about a particular subject or how to do something. متعلم

learner driver (**learner drivers**) *n* A **learner driver** is a person who is learning to drive a car. متعلم ڈرائیور

lease (**leases, leasing, leased**) *n* A **lease** is a legal agreement under which someone pays money to another person in exchange for the use of a building or piece of land for a specified period of time. پٹہ ▷ *vt* If you **lease** property or something such as a car, or if someone **leases** it to you, they allow you to use it in return for regular payments of money. پٹہ پر دینا، لینا

least *adj* You use the **least** to mean a smaller amount than any other thing or person, or the smallest amount possible. کمتر (رقم وغیرہ)

leather (**leathers**) *n* **Leather** is treated animal skin which is used for making shoes, clothes, bags, and furniture. چمڑا

leave (**leaves, leaving, left**) *n* **Leave** is a period of time when you are not working at your job, because you are on holiday or vacation. چھٹی ▷ *v* When you **leave** a place, you go away from it. روانہ ہونا، روانگی ▷ *vt* If you **leave** something somewhere, you do not bring it with you. چھوڑنا

leave out *v* If you **leave** someone or something **out** of something such as an activity or a collection, you do not include them in it. باہر نکالنا *I never left him out of my team.*

Lebanese (**Lebanese**) *adj* **Lebanese** means belonging or relating to Lebanon, or to its people or culture. لبنانی ▷ *n* A **Lebanese** is a Lebanese citizen, or a person of Lebanese origin. لبنانی

Lebanon *n* **Lebanon** is a republic in west Asia, on the Mediterranean. لبنان

lecture (**lectures, lecturing, lectured**) *n* A **lecture** is a talk that someone gives in order to teach people about a particular subject, usually at a university. خطبہ ▷ *vi* If you **lecture** on a particular subject, you give a lecture or a series of lectures about it. خطبہ دینا، تقریر کرنا

lecturer (**lecturers**) *n* A **lecturer** is a teacher at university or college. خطیب، مقرر، لیکچرر

leek (**leeks**) *n* **Leeks** are long green and white vegetables which smell like onions. آل کی پیاز

left *adj* If there is a certain amount of something **left**, it remains when the rest has gone or been used. باقی

left *adv* If you are facing north and you turn **left**, you will be facing west. بائیں ▷ *n* The **left** is one side of something. For example, on a page, English writing begins on the left. بائیں

left-hand *adj* **Left-hand** describes the position of something when it is on the left side. بایاں ہاتھ

left-hand drive (**left-hand drives**) *n* A **left-hand drive** is a vehicle which has the steering wheel on the left side, and is designed to be used in countries where people drive on the right-hand side of the road. بائیں جانب ڈرائیونگ

left-handed *adj* Someone who is **left-handed** finds it easier to use their left hand rather than their right hand for activities such as writing and throwing a ball. بائیں ہاتھ سے کام کرنے والا

left luggage *n* **Left luggage** is used to refer to luggage that people leave at a special place in a railway station or an airport, and which they collect later. چھوڑا ہوا سامان

left-luggage office (**left-luggage offices**) *n* A **left-luggage office** is a special place in a railway station or an airport, where you can leave luggage and collect it later. سامان رکھنے کا دفتر

leftovers *npl* You can refer to food that has not been eaten after a meal as **leftovers**. باقیات

left-wing *adj* **Left-wing** people have political ideas that are based on socialism. بایاں بازو

leg (**legs**) *n* A person's or animal's **legs** are

the long parts of their body that they use for walking and standing. ٹانگ ▷ *n* The **legs** of a table or chair are the long parts that it stands on. پائے

legal *adj* **Legal** is used to describe things that relate to the law. قانونی

legend (**legends**) *n* A **legend** is a very old and popular story that may be based on real events. روایتی داستان

leggings *npl* **Leggings** are tight trousers that are made out of a fabric which stretches easily. ساق پوش (لچکیلے کپڑے کے پائجامے)

legible *adj* **Legible** writing is clear enough to read. پڑھنے لائق، صاف دید

legislation *n* **Legislation** consists of a law or laws passed by a government. (*formal*) قانون سازی

leisure *n* **Leisure** is the time when you do not have to work and can do things that you enjoy. خالی وقت

leisure centre (**leisure centres**) *n* A **leisure centre** is a large public building containing different facilities for leisure activities, such as a sports hall, a swimming pool, and rooms for meetings. خالی وقت گزارنے کا مرکز

lemon (**lemons**) *n* A **lemon** is a sour yellow citrus fruit. لیموں

lemonade (**lemonades**) *n* **Lemonade** is a clear, sweet, fizzy drink, or a drink that is made from lemons, sugar, and water. لیموں کا مشروب

lend (**lends, lending, lent**) *vt* When people or organizations such as banks **lend** you money, they give it to you and you agree to pay it back at a future date, often with an extra amount as interest. ادھار دینا

length (**lengths**) *n* The **length** of something is the amount that it measures from one end to the other. لمبائی

lens (**lenses**) *n* A **lens** is a thin, curved piece of glass or plastic in something such as a camera or pair of glasses which makes things appear larger or clearer. محدب عدسہ

Lent *n* **Lent** is the period of forty days before Easter, during which some Christians give up something that they enjoy. ایسٹر سے پہلے چالیس دنوں کی مدت

lentils *npl* **Lentils** are a type of dried seed used in cooking. مسور

Leo *n* **Leo** is one of the twelve signs of the zodiac. Its symbol is a lion. People who are born between approximately the 23rd of July and the 22nd of August come under this sign. برج اسد

leopard (**leopards**) *n* A **leopard** is a type of large wild cat from Africa or Asia. Leopards have yellow fur and black spots. چیتا، تیندوا

leotard (**leotards**) *n* A **leotard** is a tight-fitting piece of clothing, covering the body but not the legs, that some people wear when they practise dancing or do exercise. دھڑ کا چست لباس (ایک ہی ٹکڑے میں)

less *adv* You use **less** to talk about a smaller amount. کم ▷ *pron* You use **less** to talk about a smaller amount of something. کم *Borrowers are spending less and saving more.* ▷ *adj* **Less** means a smaller amount. کم، تھوڑا

lesson (**lessons**) *n* A **lesson** is a fixed period of time during which people are taught something. سبق

let (**lets, letting**) *vt* If you **let** someone do something, you allow them to do it. اجازت دینا

let down *v* If you **let** someone **down**, you disappoint them, usually by not doing something that you said you would do. مایوس کرنا *Don't worry, I won't let you down.*

let in *v* If an object **lets in** something such as air or water, it allows air or water to get into it or pass through it. آنے دینا *There is no glass in the front door to let in light.*

letter (**letters**) *n* **Letters** are written symbols that represent the sounds in a language. حرف ▷ *n* A **letter** is a message on paper that you post to someone. خط

letterbox (**letterboxes**) *n* A **letterbox** is a

rectangular hole in a door through which letters are delivered. لیٹرباکس

lettuce (**lettuces**) *n* A **lettuce** is a plant with large green leaves that you eat in salads. کاہو، سلاد

leukaemia *n* **Leukaemia** is a serious disease of the blood. لیوکیمیا (خون کی کمی یا بیماری)

level (**levels**) *adj* If one thing is **level** with another thing, it is at the same height. سطح ▷ *n* A **level** is a point on a scale, for example a scale of amount, importance, or difficulty. سطح (ناپنے کا نشان)

level crossing (**level crossings**) *n* A **level crossing** is a place where a railway line crosses a road. ریلوے پھاٹک

lever (**levers**) *n* A **lever** is a handle or bar that you pull or push to operate a piece of machinery. ہتھہ، دستہ

liar (**liars**) *n* A **liar** is someone who tells lies. جھوٹا

liberal *adj* Someone who has **liberal** views believes people should have a lot of freedom in deciding how to behave and think. آزاد خیال

liberation *n* The **liberation** of a place or the people in it means the freeing of them from the political or military control of another country, area, or group of people. آزادی، حریت

Liberia *n* **Liberia** is a republic in West Africa, on the Atlantic. لائبیریا

Liberian (**Liberians**) *adj* **Liberian** means belonging or relating to Liberia, its people, or its culture. لائبیریائی ▷ *n* A **Liberian** is a person who comes from Liberia, or a person of Liberian origin. لائبیریائی

Libra *n* **Libra** is one of the twelve signs of the zodiac. Its symbol is a pair of scales. People who are approximately born between the 23rd of September and the 22nd of October come under this sign. برج میزان

librarian (**librarians**) *n* A **librarian** is a person who works in, or is in charge of a library. لائبریرین

library (**libraries**) *n* A public **library** is a building where things such as books, newspapers, videos, and music are kept for people to read, use, or borrow. لائبریری

Libya *n* **Libya** is a republic in North Africa, on the Mediterranean. لیبیا

Libyan (**Libyans**) *adj* **Libyan** means belonging or relating to Libya, or to its people or culture. لیبیائی ▷ *n* A **Libyan** is a Libyan citizen, or a person of Libyan origin. لیبیائی

lice *npl* **Lice** are small insects that live on the bodies of people or animals. جوں، لیکھ

licence (**licences**) *n* A **licence** is an official document which gives you permission to do, use, or own something. لائسنس

lick (**licks, licking, licked**) *vt* When people or animals **lick** something, they move their tongue across its surface. چاٹنا

lid (**lids**) *n* A **lid** of a container is the top which you open to reach inside. ڈھکن

lie (**lies, lying, lay, lain**) *n* A **lie** is something you say that is not true. جھوٹ بولنا. ▷ *vi* When you **lie** somewhere, your body is flat, and you are not standing or sitting. لیٹنا

Liechtenstein *n* **Liechtenstein** is a small mountainous country in central Europe on the Rhine. لیشٹنسٹائن

lie-in (**lie-ins**) *n* If you have a **lie-in**, you rest by staying in bed later than usual in the morning. (*informal*) بستر میں لیٹنا

lieutenant (**lieutenants**) *n* A **lieutenant** is a junior officer in the army, navy, or air force. لیفٹیننٹ

life (**lives**) *n* **Life** is the quality which people, animals, and plants have when they are not dead. زندگی

lifebelt (**lifebelts**) *n* A **lifebelt** is a large ring, usually made of a light substance such as cork, which someone who has fallen into deep water can use to float. تیراکی بیلٹ (ہوا بھری پٹی)

lifeboat (**lifeboats**) *n* A **lifeboat** is a boat

used to rescue people who are in danger at sea. ناو(ڈوبنے والوں کو بچانے کے لئے)

lifeguard (**lifeguards**) *n* A **lifeguard** is a person who works at a beach or swimming pool and rescues people when they are in danger of drowning. جان محافظ(ڈوبنے والوں کو بچانے والا)

life jacket (**life jackets**) *n* A **life jacket** is a sleeveless jacket which keeps you floating in water. تیراکی جیکیٹ

life-saving *adj* A **life-saving** drug, operation, or action is one that saves someone's life or is likely to save their life. جان بچانے والی

lifestyle (**lifestyles**) *n* Your **lifestyle** is the way you live, for example the things you normally do. معیار زندگی

lift (**lifts, lifting, lifted**) *n* If you give someone a **lift**, you drive them from one place to another. اپنے ساتھ سوار کر لینا ▷ *n* A **lift** is a device that carries people or goods up and down inside tall buildings. لفٹ (برقی کیبن) ▷ *vt* If you **lift** something, you move it to another position, especially upwards. اٹھانا

light (**lighter, lightest, lights, lighting, lit, lighted**) *adj* Something that is **light** is not heavy. ہلکا / ہلکی ہونا ▷ *adj* If a place is **light**, it is bright because of the sun or lamps. روشن ہونا ▷ *n* **Light** is the bright energy that comes from the sun, that lets you see things. روشنی ▷ *vt* When you **light** a fire, it starts burning. جلانا ▷ *n* A **light** is something, like a lamp, that allows you to see. روشنی ▷ *adj* A **light** colour is pale. ہلکا / ہلکی

light bulb (**light bulbs**) *n* A **light bulb** is the round glass part of an electric light or lamp which light shines from. روشنی کا بلب

lighter (**lighters**) *n* A **lighter** is a small device that produces a flame that is used to light cigarettes. لائٹر(شعلہ پیدا کرنے والا آلہ)

lighthouse (**lighthouses**) *n* A **lighthouse** is a tower near or in the sea which contains a powerful flashing lamp to guide ships or to warn them of danger. روشنی کا مینار

lighting *n* The **lighting** in a place is the way that it is lit. روشنی

lightning *n* **Lightning** is the bright flashes of light in the sky that you see during a thunderstorm. بجلی

like (**likes, liking, liked**) *prep* If things or people are **like** each other, they are almost the same. پسند کرنا *He's very funny, like my uncle.* ▷ *vt* If you **like** something, you think it is nice or interesting. پسند کرنا ▷ *v* What something or someone is **like** is how they seem to you. جیسا ہونا

likely (**likelier, likeliest**) *adj* You use **likely** to indicate that something is probably true or will probably happen in a particular situation. امکان

lilac (**lilacs, lilac**) *adj* Something that is **lilac** is pale pinkish-purple in colour. نیل ▷ *n* A **lilac** is a small tree with pleasant-smelling purple, pink, or white flowers. نیل، لیلیک پودا

lily (**lilies**) *n* A **lily** is a plant with large sweet-smelling flowers. سوسن، للی

lily of the valley (**lilies of the valley, lily of the valley**) *n* **Lily of the valley** are small plants with large leaves and small, white, bell-shaped flowers. سوسن کا پودا

lime (**limes**) *n* A **lime** is a small, round citrus fruit with green skin. ترش ▷ *n* **Lime** is a substance containing calcium. It is found in soil and water. چونا

limestone (**limestones**) *n* **Limestone** is a white rock which is used for building and making cement. چونا پتھر

limit (**limits**) *n* A **limit** is the greatest amount, extent, or degree of something that is possible. حد

limousine (**limousines**) *n* A **limousine** is a large and very comfortable car. Limousines are usually driven by a chauffeur and are used by very rich or important people. لیموزین

limp (**limps, limping, limped**) *vi* If a

person or animal **limps**, they walk with difficulty or in an uneven way because one of their legs or feet is hurt. لنگڑا کر چلنا
line (**lines**) *n* A **line** is a long, thin mark or shape. خط
linen *n* **Linen** is a kind of cloth that is made from a plant called flax. لینن
liner (**liners**) *n* A **liner** is a large passenger ship. بڑا مسافر بردار جہاز (بحری)
linguist (**linguists**) *n* A **linguist** is someone who is good at speaking or learning foreign languages. ماہرِ لسانیات
linguistic *adj* **Linguistic** abilities or ideas relate to language. لسانی
lining (**linings**) *n* The **lining** of a piece of clothing or a curtain is a material attached to the inside of it in order to make it thicker or warmer. دھاریوں کو موٹا کرنیوالا مادہ
link (**links, linking, linked**) *n* If there is a **link** between two things or situations, there is a relationship between them, for example because one thing causes or affects the other. ربط ▷ *vt* If someone or something **links** two things or situations, there is a relationship between them, for example because one thing causes or affects the other. ربط کرنا، جوڑنا
lino *n* **Lino** is a floor covering which is made of cloth covered with a hard shiny substance. فرشپوش
lion (**lions**) *n* A **lion** is a large wild member of the cat family that is found in Africa. Lions have yellowish fur, and male lions have long hair on their head and neck. شیر
lioness (**lionesses**) *n* A **lioness** is a female lion. شیرنی
lip (**lips**) *n* Your **lips** are the two outer parts of the edge of your mouth. ہونٹ
lip-read (**lip-reads, lip-reading**) *vi* If someone can **lip-read**, they are able to understand what someone else is saying by looking at the way the other person's lips move as they speak, without actually hearing any of the words. بدبدانا
lip salve (**lip salves**) *n* **Lip salve** is an oily substance that is put on cracked or dry lips to help them heal. ہونٹ تر، خشک یا پھٹے ہونٹوں کا لوشن
lipstick (**lipsticks**) *n* **Lipstick** is a coloured substance which women put on their lips. ہونٹوں کی سرخی، لپسٹک
liqueur (**liqueurs**) *n* A **liqueur** is a strong sweet alcoholic drink. الکحلی مشروب
liquid (**liquids**) *n* A **liquid** is a substance such as water which is not solid and which can be poured. سیال
liquidizer (**liquidizers**) *n* A **liquidizer** is an electric machine that you use to turn solid food into liquid. مائع کار مشین
list (**lists, listing, listed**) *n* A **list** is a set of things which all belong to a particular category, written down one below the other. فہرست ▷ *vt* To **list** a set of things means to write them or say them one after another, usually in a particular order. فہرست بنانا
listen (**listens, listening, listened**) *vi* If you **listen** to someone who is talking or to a sound, you give your attention to them. سننا ▷ *vi* If you **listen** to someone, you do what they advise you to do, or you believe them. بغور سننا
listener (**listeners**) *n* People who listen to the radio are often referred to as **listeners**. سامع
literally *adv* You can use **literally** to emphasize a statement. واقعی
literature *n* Novels, plays, and poetry are referred to as **literature**. ادب
Lithuania *n* **Lithuania** is a republic in north-east Europe, on the Baltic Sea. لتھوانیا
Lithuanian (**Lithuanians**) *adj* **Lithuanian** means belonging or relating to Lithuania, or to its people, language, or culture. لتھوانیائی ▷ *n* A **Lithuanian** is a person who comes from Lithuania. لتھوانیائی ▷ *n* **Lithuanian** is the language spoken in Lithuania. لتھوانیائی
litre (**litres**) *n* A **litre** is a metric unit of

volume. It is equal to approximately 1.76 British pints or 2.11 American pints. لیٹر

litter (litters) *n* **Litter** is rubbish which is left lying around outside. کوڑا کرکٹ ▷ *n* A **litter** is a group of animals born to the same mother at the same time. ایک ہی وقت پیدا جانوروں کے بچے (ایک ہی ماں سے)

litter bin (litter bins) *n* A **litter bin** is a container, usually in a street, park, or public building, into which people can put rubbish. کوڑا دان

little (littler, littlest) *adj* A person or thing that is **little** is small in size. چھوٹا، چھوٹی

live (lives, living, lived) *adj* **Live** animals or plants are alive, rather than being dead or artificial. زندہ ▷ *vi* You **live** in the place where your home is. رہنا ▷ *vi* To **live** means to be alive. زندہ رہنا

lively (livelier, liveliest) *adj* You can describe someone as **lively** when they behave in an enthusiastic and cheerful way. زندہ دل

live on *v* If you **live on** a particular amount of money, or if you **live off** it, you have that amount of money to buy things. گزارہ کرنا *Most students are unable to live on that amount of money.*

liver (livers) *n* Your **liver** is a large organ in your body which cleans your blood. جگر

living *n* The work that you do for a **living** is the work that you do to earn the money that you need. روزی

living room (living rooms) *n* The **living room** in a house is the room where people sit and relax. بیٹھک

lizard (lizards) *n* A **lizard** is a reptile with short legs and a long tail. چھپکلی

load (loads, loading, loaded) *n* A **load** is something, usually large or heavy, which is being carried. بوجھ، گٹھر ▷ *vt* If you **load** a vehicle, you put something on it. بار کرنا، لادنا

loaf (loaves) *n* A **loaf** of bread is bread in a shape that can be cut into slices. ڈبل روٹی

loan (loans, loaning, loaned) *n* A **loan** is a sum of money that you borrow. قرض ▷ *vt* If you **loan** something to someone, you lend it to them. قرض دینا

loathe (loathes, loathing, loathed) *vt* If you **loathe** something or someone, you dislike them very much. سخت نفرت کرنا

lobster (lobsters) *n* A **lobster** is a sea creature with a hard shell, two large claws, and eight legs. جھینگا

local *adj* **Local** means existing in or belonging to the area where you live, or to the area that you are talking about. مقامی

local anaesthetic (local anaesthetics) *n* A **local anaesthetic** is a substance used by a doctor to stop you feeling pain, which affects only a small area of your body. مقامی بیہوشی آور

location (locations) *n* A **location** is a place, especially the place where something happens or is situated. جگہ، مقام

lock (locks, locking, locked) *n* The **lock** on something such as a door is the device which fastens it when you turn a key in it. تالا ▷ *n* A **lock** of hair is a small bunch of hairs on your head that grow together in the same direction. خدارلٹ ▷ *vt* When you **lock** something, you fasten it by means of a key. تالا لگانا

locker (lockers) *n* A **locker** is a small cupboard for someone's personal belongings, for example in a changing room. تالیدار درازیا الماری

locket (lockets) *n* A **locket** is a piece of jewellery containing something such as a picture, which you wear on a chain around your neck. لاکیٹ (زیور)

lock out *v* If someone **locks** you **out** of a place, they prevent you entering it by locking the doors. تالا بندی *They had had a row, and she had locked him out of the apartment.*

locksmith (locksmiths) *n* A **locksmith** is a person whose job is to make or repair locks. تالا مستری

lodger (**lodgers**) *n* A **lodger** is a person who pays money to live in someone else's house. لاج میں رہنے والا
loft (**lofts**) *n* A **loft** is the space inside the sloping roof of a building. عمارت کی چھت کی ڈھلان میں مقام
log (**logs**) *n* A **log** is a thick piece of wood cut from a branch or trunk of a tree. گیلی لکڑی کا کندہ، لٹھہ
logical *adj* In a **logical** argument, each step or point must be true if the step before it is true. منطقی
log in *v* If you **log in** or **log on**, you type your name and a password so that you can start using a computer or a website. کمپیوٹر اسٹارٹ کرنا *She turned on her computer and logged in.*
logo (**logos**) *n* The **logo** of an organization is the special design that it puts on all its products. لوگو
log out *v* If you **log out** or **log off**, you stop using a computer or website by clicking on an instruction. کمپیوٹر بند کرنا *I logged off and went out for a walk.*
lollipop (**lollipops**) *n* A **lollipop** is a sweet consisting of a hard disc or ball of a sugary substance on the end of a stick. لالی پوپ
lolly (**lollies**) *n* A **lolly** is a sweet consisting of a hard disc or ball of a sugary substance on the end of a stick. لالی پوپ
London *n* **London** is the capital city of the United Kingdom. لندن
loneliness *n* **Loneliness** is the unhappiness that is felt by someone because they do not have any friends or do not have anyone to talk to. تنہائی
lonely (**lonelier, loneliest**) *adj* A **lonely** person is unhappy because they are alone, or because they do not have any friends. اکیلا
lonesome *adj* Someone who is **lonesome** is unhappy because they do not have any friends or do not have anyone to talk to. مایوس، اداس
long (**longer, longest, longs, longing, longed**) *adj* Something that is **long** takes a lot of time. طویل، لمبا ▷ *adj* Something that is **long** measures a great distance from one end to the other. طویل، لمبا ▷ *adv* **Long** means a great amount of time. لمبی مدت ▷ *v* If you **long** for something, you want it very much. لمبا کرنا، بڑھانا
longer *adv* **Longer** means for a greater amount of time. لمبے عرصے کا
longitude (**longitudes**) *n* The **longitude** of a place is its distance to the west or east of a line passing through Greenwich in England. طول البلد
long jump *n* The **long jump** is an athletics contest which involves jumping as far as you can from a marker which you run up to. اونچی کود
loo (**loos**) *n* A **loo** is a toilet. (*informal*) بیت الخلاء
look (**looks, looking, looked**) *n* A **look** is the act of directing your eyes so that you can see something. نگاہ ▷ *vi* When you **look** at something, you turn your eyes so that you can see it. دیکھنا ▷ *v* You use **look** when you describe how a person seems. نظر آنا
look after *v* If you **look after** someone or something, you keep them healthy, safe, or in good condition. پرورش کرنا، دیکھ بھال کرنا *I love looking after the children.*
look at *vi* If you **look at** a book, newspaper, or magazine, you read it fairly quickly or read part of it. نظر ڈالنا *You've just got to look at the last bit of Act Three.*
look for *v* If you **look for** something, for example something that you have lost, you try to find it. تلاش کرنا *I'm looking for my keys.*
look round *v* If you **look round** a place, or if you **look around** it, you walk round it and look at the different parts of it. اطراف کا جائزہ لینا *We went to look round the show homes.*

look up *v* If you **look up** a piece of information, you find it out by looking in a book or list. (دیکھنا (تحریر میں *I looked your address up in your file.*

loose (**looser, loosest**) *adj* Something that is **loose** moves when it should not. ڈھیلا ▷ *adj* **Loose** clothes are rather large and are not tight. ڈھیلا ڈھالا

lorry (**lorries**) *n* A **lorry** is a large vehicle used to transport goods by road. لاری، ٹرک

lorry driver (**lorry drivers**) *n* A **lorry driver** is someone who drives a lorry as their job. لاری ڈرائور

lose (**loses, losing, lost**) *v* If you **lose** a game, you do not win it. ہارجانا ▷ *vt* If you **lose** something, you do not know where it is. کھونا

loser (**losers**) *n* The **losers** of a contest or struggle are the people who are defeated. شکست خوردہ، ہارا ہوا

loss (**losses**) *n* **Loss** is the fact of no longer having something or of having less of it than before. نقصان

lost *adj* If you are **lost**, you do not know where you are or you are unable to find your way. کھویا ہوا

lot (**lots**) *n* A **lot** of something, or **lots** of something, is a large amount of it. کافی، بہت زیادہ

lotion (**lotions**) *n* A **lotion** is a liquid that you use to clean, improve, or protect your skin or hair. مرہم

lottery (**lotteries**) *n* A **lottery** is a type of gambling in which people bet on a number or a series of numbers being chosen as the winner. Lotteries usually offer large cash prizes and are often organized so that a percentage of the profits is donated to good causes. لاٹری

loud (**louder, loudest**) *adj* If a noise is **loud**, the level of sound is very high and it can be easily heard. Someone or something that is **loud** produces a lot of noise. تیزآواز، شور

loudly *adv* If you do something **loudly**, you produce a lot of noise. زور سے

loudspeaker (**loudspeakers**) *n* A **loudspeaker** is a piece of equipment, for example part of a radio, through which sound comes out. لاؤڈاسپیکر

lounge (**lounges**) *n* A **lounge** is a room in a house, or in a hotel, where people sit and relax. بیٹھک خانہ

lousy (**lousier, lousiest**) *adj* If you describe something as **lousy**, you mean that it is of very bad quality. (*informal*) گھٹیا

love (**loves, loving, loved**) *n* **Love** is the very strong warm feeling that you have when you care very much about someone, or you have strong romantic feelings for them. پیار ▷ *vt* If you **love** someone, you care very much about them. پیار کرنا، محبت کرنا خیال رکھنا ▷ *vt* If you **love** something, you like it very much. محبت کرنا، پیار کرنا

lovely (**lovelier, loveliest**) *adj* If you describe someone or something as **lovely**, you mean that they are very beautiful or that you like them very much. پیارا

low (**lower, lowest**) *adj* Something that is **low** is close to the ground. نیچے / پست ہونا ▷ *adj* A **low** number is a small number. چھوٹا، کمتر، کم ▷ *adv* If someone or something does something **low**, they do it close to the ground. نچائی پر

low-alcohol *adj* **Low-alcohol** beer or wine contains only a small amount of alcohol. کم الکحل والا

lower (**lowers, lowering, lowered**) *adj* You can use **lower** to refer to the bottom one of a pair of things. زیریں ▷ *vt* If you **lower** something, you move it slowly downwards. نیچے کرنا، نیچے اتارنا

low-fat *adj* **Low-fat** food and drinks contain only a very small amount of fat. کم روغنی

low season *n* The **low season** is the time of year when a place receives the fewest visitors, and fares and holiday accommodation are often cheaper. جب سب سے کم سیاح آئے ہوں

loyalty (**loyalties**) *n* **Loyalty** is behaviour in which you stay firm in your friendship or support for someone or something. وفاداری

luck *n* **Luck** is success or good things that happen to you, which do not come from your own abilities or efforts. قسمت

luckily *adv* You add **luckily** to your statement to indicate that you are glad that something happened or is the case. قسمت سے

lucky (**luckier, luckiest**) *adj* If someone is **lucky**, they are in a very desirable situation. قسمت والا

lucrative *adj* A **lucrative** business or activity earns you a lot of money. نفع بخش

luggage *n* **Luggage** consists of the suitcases and bags that you take when you travel. سامان، اسباب

luggage rack (**luggage racks**) *n* A **luggage rack** is a shelf for putting luggage on, on a vehicle such as a train or bus. سامان رکھنے کی دراز یا آلماری

lukewarm *adj* **Lukewarm** water is only slightly warm. ہلکا گرم

lullaby (**lullabies**) *n* A **lullaby** is a quiet song which is intended to be sung to babies and young children to help them go to sleep. لوری (بچہ کو سلانے کے لئے گایا جانے والا گیت)

lump (**lumps**) *n* A **lump** is a solid piece of something. ڈھیر، ڈھیلا

lunatic (**lunatics**) *n* If you describe someone as a **lunatic**, you think they behave in a dangerous, stupid, or annoying way. (*informal*) پاگل

lunch (**lunches**) *n* **Lunch** is a meal that you have in the middle of the day. دوپہر کا کھانا (ظہرانہ)

lunch break (**lunch breaks**) *n* Your **lunch break** is the period in the middle of the day when you stop work in order to have a meal. لنچ کا وقفہ

lunchtime (**lunchtimes**) *n* **Lunchtime** is the period of the day when people have their lunch. لنچ کا وقت

lung (**lungs**) *n* Your **lungs** are the two organs inside your chest which you use for breathing. پھیپھڑا

lush (**lusher, lushest**) *adj* **Lush** fields or gardens have a lot of very healthy grass or plants. طراوت دار، گھنا

Luxembourg *n* **Luxembourg** is a small country in Western Europe. لگزمبرگ (ایک ملک کا نام ہے)

luxurious *adj* Something that is **luxurious** is very comfortable and expensive. پر تعیش

luxury *n* **Luxury** is very great comfort, especially among beautiful and expensive surroundings. عیش و عشرت

lyrics *npl* The **lyrics** of a song are its words. گیت کے بول

m

mac (**macs**) *n* A **mac** is a raincoat, especially one made from a particular kind of waterproof cloth. میکنتوش برساتی

macaroni *npl* **Macaroni** is a kind of pasta made in the shape of short hollow tubes. کھوکھلے ٹیوب کی شکل میں سیو (پاستا)

machine (**machines**) *n* A **machine** is a piece of equipment which uses electricity or an engine in order to do a particular kind of work. مشین

machine gun (**machine guns**) *n* A **machine gun** is a gun which fires a lot of bullets very quickly one after the other. مشین گن

machinery *n* **Machinery** is machines in general, or machines that are used in a factory. مشینری

machine washable *adj* **Machine washable** clothes are suitable for washing in a washing machine. واشنگ مشین میں دھونے کے لائق کپڑے

mackerel (**mackerel**) *n* A **mackerel** is a sea fish with a dark, patterned back. اسقری مچھلی

mad (**madder, maddest**) *adj* Someone who is **mad** has a mental illness which makes them behave in strange ways. پاگل ▷ *adj* You can say that someone is **mad** when they are very angry. (*informal*) غصہ میں پاگل

Madagascar *n* **Madagascar** is an island republic in the Indian Ocean, off the east coast of Africa. میڈاگاسکر

madam *n* **Madam** is a formal and polite way of addressing a woman. محترمہ، مادام

madly *adv* If you do something **madly**, you do it in a fast, excited, or eager way. مجنونانہ

madman (**madmen**) *n* A **madman** is a man who is insane. پاگل آدمی

madness *n* If you describe a decision or an action as **madness**, you think it is very foolish. پاگلپن

magazine (**magazines**) *n* A **magazine** is a weekly or monthly publication which contains articles, stories, photographs, and advertisements. رسالہ ▷ *n* In an automatic gun, the **magazine** is the part that contains the bullets. میگزین

maggot (**maggots**) *n* **Maggots** are tiny creatures that look like very small worms and turn into flies. سڑاندہ کا کیڑا جو مکھی بن جاتا ہے

magic *n* **Magic** is the power to use supernatural forces to make impossible things happen, such as making people disappear or controlling events in nature. جادو ▷ *adj* You use **magic** to describe something that does things, or appears to do things, by magic. جادوئی

magical *adj* Something that is **magical** seems to use magic or to be able to produce magic. جادوئی، ساحرانہ

magician (**magicians**) *n* A **magician** is a person who entertains people by doing magic tricks. جادوگر، ساحر

magistrate (**magistrates**) *n* A **magistrate** is a person who is appointed to act as a judge in law courts which deal with minor crimes or disputes. مجسٹریٹ

magnet (**magnets**) *n* A **magnet** is a piece of iron which attracts iron or steel towards it. مقناطیس

magnetic *adj* If something is **magnetic**, it has the power of a magnet or functions like a magnet. مقناطیسی

magnificent *adj* Something or someone

that is **magnificent** is extremely good, beautiful, or impressive. شاندار

magnifying glass (**magnifying glasses**) *n* A **magnifying glass** is a piece of glass which makes objects appear bigger than they actually are. اشیا کو بڑا کر کے دکھانے والا شیشہ

magpie (**magpies**) *n* A **magpie** is a black and white bird with a long tail. چتلا کوا

mahogany *n* **Mahogany** is a dark reddish-brown wood that is used to make furniture. موگنی لکڑی

maid (**maids**) *n* A **maid** is a woman who works as a servant in a hotel or private house. خاتون خدمتگار، نوکرانی

maiden name (**maiden names**) *n* A married woman's **maiden name** is her parents' surname, which she used before she got married and started using her husband's surname. متزوج خاتون کا شادی سے پہلے کا نام

mail (**mails, mailing, mailed**) *n* **Mail** is the letters and parcels that are delivered to you. ڈاک ▷ *vt* If you **mail** something, you post it. ڈاک بھیجنا

mailing list (**mailing lists**) *n* A **mailing list** is a list of names and addresses that a company or organization keeps, so that they can send people information or advertisements. ڈاک فہرست

main *adj* The **main** thing is the most important one. خاص، اہم

main course (**main courses**) *n* The **main course** is the most important dish of a meal. رئیسی غذا

mainland *n* The **mainland** is the large main part of a country, in contrast to the islands around it. مرکزی خطہ

mainly *adv* You use **mainly** to say that a statement is true in most cases or to a large extent. عموماً

main road (**main roads**) *n* A **main road** is an important road that leads from one town or city to another. شاہراہ

maintain (**maintains, maintaining, maintained**) *vt* If you **maintain** something, you continue to have it, and do not let it stop or grow weaker. برقرار رکھنا

maintenance *n* The **maintenance** of a building, road, vehicle, or machine is the process of keeping it in good condition. دیکھ ریکھ

maize *n* **Maize** is a tall plant which produces corn. مکئی

majesty (**majesties**) *n* You use majesty in expressions such as Your **Majesty** or Her **Majesty** when you are addressing or referring to a King or Queen. شان

major *adj* You use **major** to describe something that is more important, serious, or significant than other things. بڑی

majority *n* The **majority** of people or things in a group is more than half of them. اکثریت

make (**makes, making, made**) *n* The **make** of a product is the name of the company that made it. بناوٹ ▷ *vt* You can use **make** to show that a person does or says something. کرنا ▷ *vt* If you **make** something, you put it together or build it from other things. بنانا ▷ *vt* If you **make** a person do something, they must do it. کہنا، مجبور کرنا

makeover (**makeovers**) *n* If a person or room is given a **makeover**, their appearance is improved, usually by an expert. نیاپن

maker (**makers**) *n* The **maker** of something is the person or company that makes it. بنانے والا

make up *v* The people or things that **make up** something are the members or parts that form that thing. بناؤ سنگار کرنا *Women officers make up 13 per cent of the police force.* ▷ *n* **Make-up** consists of things such as lipstick or eye shadow which you can put on your face to make yourself look more attractive. زیبائشی سامان، میک اپ کا سامان

malaria *n* **Malaria** is a serious disease caught from mosquitoes. ملیریا

Malawi *n* **Malawi** is a republic in east central Africa. ملاوی جمہوریہ

Malaysia *n* **Malaysia** is a federation in South-East Asia. ملیشیا

Malaysian (**Malaysians**) *adj* **Malaysian** means belonging or relating to Malaysia, or to its people or culture. ملیشیائی ▷ *n* A **Malaysian** is a person who comes from Malaysia. ملیشیائی

male (**males**) *adj* Someone who is **male** is a man or a boy. مرد ▷ *n* Men and boys are sometimes referred to as **males** when they are being considered as a type. مذکر

malicious *adj* **Malicious** talk or behaviour is intended to harm people or their reputation, or to embarrass or upset them. بد خواہ

malignant *adj* A **malignant** tumour or disease is serious, spreads rapidly to other parts of the body, and may cause death. آلودہ، جان لیوا

malnutrition *n* If someone is suffering from **malnutrition**, they are physically weak and extremely thin because they have not eaten enough food or had a balanced diet. قلت تغذیہ

Malta *n* **Malta** is a republic occupying the islands of Malta, Gozo, and Comino, in the Mediterranean. مالٹا

Maltese (**Maltese**) *adj* **Maltese** means belonging or relating to Malta, or to its people, language, or culture. مالٹیز ▷ *n* A **Maltese** is a person who comes from Malta. مالٹائی ▷ *n* **Maltese** is a language spoken in Malta. مالٹائی زبان

malt whisky (**malt whiskies**) *n* **Malt whisky** or **malt** is whisky that is made from malt. مالٹ وہسکی

mammal (**mammals**) *n* **Mammals** are animals such as dogs and humans that give birth to babies rather than laying eggs, and feed their young with milk. پستان دار جانور (پستان سے دودھ پلانے والے)

mammoth (**mammoths**) *adj* You can use **mammoth** to emphasize that a task is very great and needs a lot of effort to achieve. بڑی، عظیم ▷ *n* A **mammoth** was a prehistoric animal like a large elephant with long curling tusks. عظیم الجثہ ہاتھی (ناپید)

man (**men**) *n* A **man** is an adult male human. آدمی

manage (**manages, managing, managed**) *vt* If you **manage** an organization, business, or system, or the people who work in it, you are responsible for controlling them. انتظام کرنا

manageable *adj* Something that is **manageable** is of a size, quantity, or level of difficulty that people are able to deal with. قابل انتظام

management (**managements**) *n* **Management** is the control and organizing of something. انتظامیہ

manager (**managers**) *n* A **manager** is the person responsible for running part of or the whole of a business organization. منتظم

manageress (**manageresses**) *n* The **manageress** of a shop, restaurant, or other small business is the woman who is responsible for running it. منتظمہ

managing director (**managing directors**) *n* The **managing director** of a company is the senior working director, and is in charge of the way the company is managed. مینیجنگ ڈائریکٹر

mandarin (**mandarins**) *n* Journalists sometimes use **mandarin** to refer to someone who has an important job working for a government department. اعلیٰ افسر ▷ *n* A **mandarin** or a **mandarin orange** is a small orange whose skin comes off easily. موٹے چھلکے کی نارنگی

mangetout (**mangetout, mangetouts**) *n* **Mangetout** are a type of pea whose pods are eaten as well as the peas inside them. ایک قسم کی مٹر جسے چھلکے کے ساتھ کھاتے ہیں

mango (**mangoes, mangos**) *n* A **mango**

is a large, sweet yellowish fruit which grows in hot countries. آم

mania (**manias**) *n* If you say that a person or group has a **mania** for something, you mean that they enjoy it very much or devote a lot of time to it. دیوانگی

maniac (**maniacs**) *n* A **maniac** is a mad person who is violent and dangerous. دیوانہ

manicure (**manicures, manicuring, manicured**) *n* A **manicure** is the cosmetic procedure of having the skin on your hands softened and your nails cut and polished. ہاتھوں اور ناخنوں کی صفائی ⊳ *vt* If you **manicure** your hands or nails, you care for them by softening your skin and cutting and polishing your nails. ہاتھوں اور ناخنوں کی صفائی کرنا

manipulate (**manipulates, manipulating, manipulated**) *vt* If you say that someone **manipulates** people or events, you disapprove of them because they control or influence them to produce a particular result. چالاکی سے کام نکالنا

mankind *n* You can refer to all human beings as **mankind** when you are considering them as a group. نسل انسانی

man-made *adj* **Man-made** things are created or caused by people, rather than occurring naturally. انسان کا بنایا ہوا

manner *n* The **manner** in which you do something is the way that you do it. طور طریقہ

manners *npl* If someone has good **manners**, they are polite and observe social customs. If someone has bad **manners**, they are impolite and do not observe these customs. اخلاق وعادات

manpower *n* Workers are sometimes referred to as **manpower** when they are being considered as a part of the process of producing goods or providing services. افرادی قوت

mansion (**mansions**) *n* A **mansion** is a very large, expensive house. حویلی، فلیٹوں والی عمارت

mantelpiece (**mantelpieces**) *n* A **mantelpiece** is a shelf over a fireplace. انگیٹھی کا حاشیہ

manual (**manuals**) *n* A **manual** is a book which tells you how to do something or how a piece of machinery works. ہدایتی کتاب

manufacture (**manufactures, manufacturing, manufactured**) *vt* To **manufacture** something means to make it in a factory, usually in large quantities. اشیاء بنانا تیار کرنا (بڑے پیمانے پر)

manufacturer (**manufacturers**) *n* A **manufacturer** is a business that makes goods in large quantities. صنعت کار

manure *n* **Manure** is animal faeces that is spread on the ground in order to improve the growth of plants. کھاد

manuscript (**manuscripts**) *n* A **manuscript** is a handwritten or typed document, especially a writer's first version of a book before it is published. مسودہ (غیر مطبوعہ)

many *det* If there are **many** people or things, there are a lot of them. بہت سارے *Does he have many friends?* ⊳ *pron* **Many** is used to refer to a large number of people or things. بہت۔ متعدد *We thought about the possibilities. There weren't many.*

Maori (**Maoris**) *adj* **Maori** means belonging to or relating to the race of people who have lived in new Zealand and the Cook Islands since before Europeans arrived. ماوری (نیوزیلینڈ کے) لوگ ⊳ *n* The **Maori** or the **Maoris** are people who are Maori. ماوری لوگ ⊳ *n* **Maori** is the language spoken by the Maori people. ماوری (پولینیشین) زبان

map (**maps**) *n* A **map** is a drawing of a particular area, showing its main features as they appear if you looked at them from above. نقشہ

maple (**maples**) *n* A **maple** is a tree with large leaves with five points. میپل (درخت)

m

marathon (**marathons**) *n* A **marathon** is a race in which people run a distance of 26 miles (about 42 km). لمبی دوڑ (20 یا 24 میل) یونانی میراتھن
marble *n* **Marble** is a very hard rock used, for example, to make statues and fireplaces. سنگ مرمر
march (**marches, marching, marched**) *n* A **march** is the action, by a group of soldiers, of walking somewhere with very regular steps, as a group. کوچ، فوجی انداز میں روانگی ▷ *v* When soldiers **march** somewhere, or when a commanding officer **marches** them somewhere, they walk there with very regular steps, as a group. گشت کرنا
March (**Marches**) *n* **March** is the third month of the year in the Western calendar. مارچ
mare (**mares**) *n* A **mare** is an adult female horse. گھوڑی
margarine *n* **Margarine** is a substance similar to butter, made from vegetable oil and sometimes animal fats. مارجرین
margin (**margins**) *n* A **margin** is the difference between two amounts, especially the difference in the number of votes or points between the winner and the loser in a contest. حاشیہ
marigold (**marigolds**) *n* A **marigold** is a type of yellow or orange flower. گیندا
marina (**marinas**) *n* A **marina** is a small harbour for pleasure boats. ساحلی سیرگاہ کا لنگر
marinade (**marinades, marinading, marinaded**) *n* A **marinade** is a sauce of oil, vinegar, and spices, which you soak meat or fish in before cooking it, in order to flavour it. میرینیڈ (ایک قسم چٹنی) ▷ *v* If you **marinade** meat or fish, you keep it in a mixture of oil, vinegar, spices, and herbs, before cooking it, so that it can develop a special flavour. میرینیڈ میں گوشت یا سرکہ ڈبونا
marital (**status**) *n* Your **marital status** is whether you are married, single, or divorced. (*formal*) ازدواجی حیثیت
maritime *adj* **Maritime** means relating to the sea and to ships. بحری
marjoram *n* **Marjoram** is a kind of herb. ایک قسم کی گھاس (مروا)
mark (**marks, marking, marked**) *n* A **mark** is a small dirty area on a surface. دھبہ ▷ *n* A **mark** is a shape that you write or draw. نشان ▷ *vt* If you **mark** something, you write a word or symbol on it. نشان لگانا ▷ *vt* When a teacher **marks** a student's work, the teacher corrects it or gives it a grade. درجہ بندی کرنا
market (**markets**) *n* A **market** is a place where goods are bought and sold, usually in the open air. بازار
marketing *n* **Marketing** is the organization of the sale of a product, for example, deciding on its price, the areas it should be supplied to, and how it should be advertised. مارکیٹنگ
marketplace (**marketplaces**) *n* in business, the **marketplace** refers to the activity of buying and selling products. منڈی
market research *n* **Market research** is the activity of collecting and studying information about what people want, need, and buy. بازار سے متعلق تحقیق
marmalade (**marmalades**) *n* **Marmalade** is a food like jam made from oranges or lemons. نارنگی کا مربہ
maroon *adj* Something that is **maroon** is dark reddish-purple in colour. بادامی قرمزی رنگ
marriage (**marriages**) *n* A **marriage** is the relationship between a husband and wife, or the state of being married. شادی، نکاح
marriage certificate (**marriage certificates**) *n* A **marriage certificate** is a legal document that proves two people are married. سند نکاح
married *adj* If you are **married**, you have a husband or wife. شادی شدہ
marrow (**marrows**) *n* A **marrow** is a long,

thick, green vegetable with soft white flesh that is eaten cooked. سبزی (لمبی سفید مغز)
marry (**marries, marrying, married**) *v* When two people **get married** or **marry**, they become each other's husband and wife during a special ceremony. شادی کرنا
marsh (**marshes**) *n* A **marsh** is a wet muddy area of land. دلدل
martyr (**martyrs**) *n* A **martyr** is someone who is killed or made to suffer greatly because of their religious or political beliefs. شہید
marvellous *adj* If you describe someone or something as **marvellous**, you are emphasizing that they are very good. حیرت انگیز
Marxism *n* **Marxism** is a political philosophy based on the writings of Karl Marx which stresses the importance of the struggle between different social classes. مارکسی نظریہ
marzipan *n* **Marzipan** is a paste made of almonds, sugar, and egg which is sometimes put on top of cakes. بادام کا حلوہ
mascara (**mascaras**) *n* **Mascara** is a substance used to colour eyelashes. مسکارہ
masculine *adj* **Masculine** characteristics or things relate to or are considered typical of men, rather than women. مردانہ
mashed potatoes *npl* **Mashed potatoes** are potatoes that have been boiled and crushed into a soft mass, often with butter and milk. ابال کر کچلے ہوئے آلو
mask (**masks**) *n* A **mask** is something which you wear over your face for protection or to disguise yourself. نقاب، مکھوٹا
masked *adj* Someone who is **masked** is wearing a mask. مکھوٹا لگائے ہوئے
mass (**masses**) *n* A **mass** of something is a large amount of it. ڈھیر، ڈلا
Mass (**masses**) *n* **Mass** is a Christian church ceremony during which people eat bread and drink wine in order to remember the last meal of Jesus Christ. عشائے ربانی کی رسم
massacre (**massacres**) *n* A **massacre** is the killing of many people in a violent and cruel way. قتل عام
massive *adj* Something that is **massive** is very large in size. بہت بڑی
mast (**masts**) *n* The **masts** of a boat are the tall upright poles that support its sails. مستول
master (**masters, mastering, mastered**) *n* A servant's **master** is the man that he or she works for. مالک ▷ *vt* If you **master** something, you manage to learn how to do it properly or understand it completely. مالک ہونا، ماہر ہونا
masterpiece (masterpieces) *n* A **masterpiece** is an extremely good painting, novel, film, or other work of art. شاہکار
mat (**mats**) *n* A **mat** is a small piece of material which you put on a table to protect it from a hot plate or cup. چٹائی
match (**matches, matching, matched**) *n* A **match** is a game of football, cricket, or some other sport. مقابلہ، میچ ▷ *n* If things or people are a good **match**, they look good together or go well together. ملان ▷ *v* If one thing **matches** another, they look good together. مماثل ہونا ▷ *n* A **match** is a small, thin stick that makes a flame when you rub it on a rough surface. ماچس کی تیلی
matching *adj* **Matching** is used to describe things which are of the same colour or design. ملتا جلتا
mate (**mates**) *n* You can refer to someone's friends as their **mates**. informal ساتھی
material (**materials**) *n* A **material** is what something is made of, like rock, glass, or plastic. مادہ ▷ *n* **Material** is cloth. مادہ، میٹریل
maternal *adj* **Maternal** feelings or actions are typical of those of a mother towards her child. مادری
maternity hospital (**maternity hospitals**) *n* A **maternity hospital** is a

m

hospital that provides help and medical care to women when they are pregnant and when they give birth. زچہ ہسپتال

maternity leave *n* **Maternity leave** is a period of paid absence from work, to which a woman is legally entitled during the months immediately before and after childbirth. زچگی کی چھٹیاں

mathematical *adj* Something that is **mathematical** involves numbers and calculations. حسابی

mathematics *npl* **Mathematics** is the study of numbers, quantities, or shapes. ریاضی

maths *npl* Mathematics is usually referred to as **maths**. مضمون حساب

matter (**matters, mattering, mattered**) *n* A **matter** is a task, situation, or event which you have to deal with or think about. معاملہ ▷ *v* If something **matters**, it is important because it has an effect on a situation. اہم ہونا

mattress (**mattresses**) *n* A **mattress** is a large flat pad which is put on a bed to make it comfortable to sleep on. گدا

mature (**maturer, maturest**) *adj* A **mature** person or animal is fully grown. پختہ، بالغ

mature student (**mature students**) *n* A **mature student** is a person who begins their studies at university or college a number of years after leaving school, so that they are older than most of the people they are studying with. پختہ کار طالب علم

Mauritania *n* **Mauritania** is a republic in north-West Africa, on the Atlantic. موریطانیہ جمہوریہ

Mauritius *n* **Mauritius** is an island and state in the Indian Ocean, east of Madagascar. موریشس

mauve *adj* Something that is mauve is of a pale purple colour. ہلکا ارغوانی

maximum *adj* You use **maximum** to describe an amount which is the largest that is possible, allowed, or required. زیادہ سے زیادہ (بڑے سے بڑا) ▷ *n* A **maximum** is the greatest possible amount, degree, etc. زیادہ سے زیادہ (ممکن حد تک)

May (**Mays**) *n* **May** is the fifth month of the year in the Western calendar. مئی

may *v* If you **may** do something, it is possible that you will do it. سکنا *I may come back next year.* ▷ *v* If you **may** do something, you can do it because someone allows you to do it. سکنا *Please may I leave the room?*

maybe *adv* You use **maybe** when you are not sure about something. شاید

mayonnaise *n* **Mayonnaise** is a sauce made from egg yolks, oil, and vinegar, eaten cold. مایونیز (ایک قسم چٹنی)

mayor (**mayors**) *n* The **mayor** of a town or city is the person who has been elected to represent it for a fixed period of time. صدر بلدیہ

maze (**mazes**) *n* A **maze** is a complex system of passages or paths separated by walls or hedges. بھول بھلیاں

me *pron* You use **me** when you are talking about yourself. مجھے *Can you hear me?*

meadow (**meadows**) *n* A **meadow** is a field with grass and flowers growing in it. مرغزار، سبزہ زار

meal (**meals**) *n* A **meal** is an occasion when people eat. کھانا

mealtime (**mealtimes**) *n* **Mealtimes** are occasions when you eat breakfast, lunch, or dinner. کھانے کا وقت

mean (**meaner, meanest, means, meaning, meant**) *adj* Someone who is **mean** is not nice to other people. کمینہ ▷ *vt* If you ask what something **means**, you want to understand it. معنی، مفہوم ▷ *vt* If you **mean** what you are saying, it is not a joke. مطلب ہونا ▷ *vt* If you **mean** to do something, it is not an accident. مقصد ہونا

meaning (**meanings**) *n* The **meaning** of something such as a word, symbol, or gesture is the thing that it refers to or the message that it conveys. معنی، مطلب

means *npl* You can refer to the money that someone has as their **means**. ذرائع وسائل

meantime *adv* In the **meantime** means in the period of time between two events, or while an event is happening. درمیان کا وقت

meanwhile *adv* **Meanwhile** means in the period of time between two events, or while an event is happening. اس دوران

measles *npl* **Measles** is an infectious illness that gives you a high temperature and red spots. خسرہ

measure (**measures, measuring, measured**) *vt* If you **measure** something, you find out its size. پیمائش کرنا، تخمینہ لگانا

measurements *npl* Your **measurements** are the size of your chest, waist, hips, and other parts of your body. پیمائشیں

meat (**meats**) *n* **Meat** is the flesh of a dead animal that people cook and eat. گوشت

meatball (**meatballs**) *n* **Meatballs** are small balls of chopped meat. They are usually eaten with a sauce. کوفتے

Mecca *n* **Mecca** is a city in Saudi Arabia, which is the holiest city in Islam because the Prophet Mohammed was born there. All Muslims face towards Mecca when they pray. مکہ

mechanic (**mechanics**) *n* A **mechanic** is someone whose job is to repair and maintain machines and engines, especially car engines. مستری

mechanical *adj* A mechanical device has moving parts and uses power in order to do a particular task. میکانکی، مبنی بر تکنیک

mechanism (**mechanisms**) *n* A **mechanism** is a part of a machine that does a particular task. میکانیت

medal (**medals**) *n* A **medal** is a small metal disc, given as an award for bravery or as a prize in a sporting event. تمغہ

medallion (**medallions**) *n* A **medallion** is a round metal disc which some people wear as an ornament, especially on a chain round their neck. بڑا تمغہ

media *npl* You can refer to television, radio, and newspapers as the **media**. ذرائع ابلاغ

mediaeval *adj* **Mediaeval** things relate to or date from the period in European history between about 500 AD and about 1500 AD. قرون وسطی کا

medical (**medicals**) *adj* **Medical** means relating to illness and injuries and to their treatment or prevention. طبی ▷ *n* A **medical** is a thorough examination of your body by a doctor. طبی

medical certificate (**medical certificates**) *n* A **medical certificate** is a document stating the result of a satisfactory medical examination. طبی سند

medicine *n* **Medicine** is the treatment of illness and injuries by doctors and nurses. دوا

meditation *n* **Meditation** is the act of remaining in a silent and calm state for a period of time, as part of a religious training, or so that you are more able to deal with the problems of everyday life. مراقبہ

Mediterranean *n* The **Mediterranean** is the sea between southern Europe and north Africa. بحر اوقیانوس ▷ *adj* Something that is **Mediterranean** is characteristic of or belongs to the people or region around the Mediterranean Sea. بحر اوقیانوس کا

medium *adj* You use **medium** to describe something which is average in size, degree, or amount, or approximately half way along a scale between two extremes. اوسط

medium-sized *adj* **Medium-sized** means neither large nor small, but approximately halfway between the two. متوسط درجے کا

meet (**meets, meeting, met**) *vt* If you **meet** someone, you happen to be in the same place as them and start talking to them. You may know the other person,

m

but be surprised to see them, or you may not know them at all. ملنا ▷ *vi* If people **meet**, they happen to be in the same place and start talking to each other. They may know each other, but be surprised to see each other, or they may not know each other at all. ملنا

meeting (**meetings**) *n* A **meeting** is an event at which a group of people come together to discuss things or make decisions. ملاقات

meet up *v* If two or more people **meet up**, they go to the same place, which they have earlier arranged to do, so that they can talk or do something together. ملاقات کرنا *We tend to meet up for lunch once a week.*

mega *adj* Young people sometimes use **mega** in front of nouns in order to emphasize that the thing they are talking about is very good, very large, or very impressive. informal بڑی، کثیر

melody (**melodies**) *n* A **melody** is a tune. formal دھن

melon (**melons**) *n* A **melon** is a large, sweet, juicy fruit with a thick green or yellow skin. خربوزہ

melt (**melts, melting, melted**) *vt* When you **melt** a solid substance, it changes to a liquid because of being heated. پگھلنا ▷ *vi* When a solid substance **melts**, it changes to a liquid because of being heated. پگھلنا

member (**members**) *n* A **member** of a group or organization is one of the people, animals, or things belonging to it. رکن

membership *n* **Membership** is the fact or state of being a member of an organization. رکنیت

membership card (**membership cards**) *n* A **membership card** is a card that proves that you are a member of an organization. رکنیت کارڈ

memento (**mementos, mementoes**) *n* A **memento** is an object which you keep because it reminds you of a person or a special occasion. یادگار، نشانی

memo (**memos**) *n* A **memo** is an official note from one person to another within the same organization. یادداشت

memorial (**memorials**) *n* A **memorial** is a structure built in order to remind people of a famous person or event. یادگار

memorize (**memorizes, memorizing, memorized**) *vt* If you **memorize** something, you learn it so that you can remember it exactly. یاد کرنا

memory (**memories**) *n* Your **memory** is your ability to remember things. حافظہ ▷ *n* A **memory** is something you remember about the past. یادداشت

memory card (**memory cards**) *n* A **memory card** is a type of card containing computer memory that is used in digital cameras and other devices. میموری کارڈ

mend (**mends, mending, mended**) *vt* If you **mend** something that is damaged or broken, you repair it so that it works properly or can be used. سدھارنا، مرمت کرنا

meningitis *n* **Meningitis** is a serious infectious illness which affects your brain and spinal cord. ورم ام دماغ

menopause *n* The **menopause** is the time during which a woman stops menstruating, usually when she is about fifty. سن ایاس

menstruation *n* **Menstruation** is the approximate monthly discharge of blood and cellular debris from the uterus by non-pregnant women from puberty to the menopause. ایام حیض

mental *adj* **Mental** means relating to the mind and the process of thinking. دماغی

mental hospital (**mental hospitals**) *n* A **mental hospital** is a hospital for people who are suffering from mental illness. دماغی ہسپتال

mentality (**mentalities**) *n* Your **mentality**

is your attitudes or ways of thinking. ذہنیت

mention (**mentions, mentioning, mentioned**) *vt* If you **mention** something, you say something about it, usually briefly. ذکر کرنا

menu (**menus**) *n* In a restaurant or café, the **menu** is a list of the available meals and drinks. مینو، طعام نامہ

merchant bank (**merchant banks**) *n* A **merchant bank** is a bank that deals mainly with firms, investment, and foreign trade, rather than with the public. تجارتی بینک

mercury *n* **Mercury** is a silver-coloured liquid metal, used in thermometers. پارہ، سیماب

mercy *n* If someone in authority shows **mercy**, they choose not to harm or punish someone they have power over. رحم

mere (**merest**) *adj* You use **mere** to say that something is small or not important. صرف، محض

merge (**merges, merging, merged**) *v* If one thing **merges** with another, or is **merged** with another, they combine or come together to make one whole thing. You can also say that two things **merge**, or are **merged**. مدغم ہونا

merger (**mergers**) *n* A **merger** is the joining together of two separate companies or organizations so that they become one. ادغام

meringue (**meringues**) *n* **Meringue** is a mixture of beaten egg whites and sugar which is baked in the oven. انڈے کی سفیدی کا کیک

mermaid (**mermaids**) *n* In fairy stories and legends, a **mermaid** is a woman with a fish's tail instead of legs, who lives in the sea. جل پری

merry (**merrier, merriest**) *adj* **Merry** means happy and cheerful. old-fashioned خوش

merry-go-round (**merry-go-rounds**) *n* A **merry-go-round** is a large circular platform at a fairground on which there are model animals or vehicles for people to sit on or in as it turns round. نشستوں کا گھومتا دائرہ

mess *n* If something is a **mess** or in a **mess**, it is dirty or untidy. بےترتیب حالت

mess about *v* If you **mess about**, you spend time doing things without any particular purpose or without achieving anything. بے منصوبہ کام کرنا *The children scribbled with crayons at the table and messed about.*

message (**messages**) *n* A message is a piece of information or a request that you send to someone or leave for them when you cannot speak to them directly. پیغام

messenger (**messengers**) *n* A **messenger** takes a message to someone, or takes messages regularly as their job. پیغامبر

mess up *v* If someone **messes** something **up**, or if they **mess up**, they cause something to fail or be spoiled. informal خراب کرنا *He had messed up his career.*

messy (**messier, messiest**) *adj* A **messy** person or activity makes things dirty or untidy. بے ترتیب، غیر منظم

metabolism (**metabolisms**) *n* Your **metabolism** is the way that chemical processes in your body cause food to be used in an efficient way, for example to give you energy. استحالیت

metal (**metals**) *n* **Metal** is a hard substance such as iron, steel, copper, or lead. دھات

meteorite (**meteorites**) *n* A **meteorite** is a large piece of rock or metal from space that has landed on Earth. حجر شہابی

meter (**meters**) *n* A **meter** is a device that measures and records something such as the amount of gas or electricity that you have used. میٹر

method (**methods**) *n* A **method** is a particular way of doing something. طریقہ، طریق

metre (**metres**) *n* A **metre** is a unit of length equal to 100 centimetres. میٹر
metric *adj* The **metric** system of measurement uses metres, grammes, and litres. پیمانہ
Mexican (**Mexicans**) *adj* **Mexican** means belonging or relating to Mexico, or to its people or culture. میکسیکن ▷ *n* A **Mexican** is a Mexican citizen, or a person of Mexican origin. میکسیکن
Mexico *n* **Mexico** is a republic in north America, on the Gulf of Mexico and the Pacific. میکسکو
microchip (**microchips**) *n* A **microchip** is a small piece of silicon inside a computer, on which electronic circuits are printed. مائکرو چپ (بہت چھوٹا برقی سرکٹ)
microphone (**microphones**) *n* A **microphone** is a device used to record sounds or make them louder. مائکروفون (آوازرساں)

microscope (**microscopes**) *n* A **microscope** is an instrument which magnifies very small objects so that you can study them. مائکروسکوپ (بڑا کرکے دکھانے والا)
microwave (**microwaves**) *n* A **microwave** or a **microwave oven** is an oven which cooks food very quickly by a kind of radiation rather than by heat. مائکروویواوون (برقی بھٹی، چولہا)
mid *adj* **Mid** is used to form nouns or adjectives that refer to the middle part of a particular period of time, or the middle point of a particular place. درمیان
midday *n* **Midday** is twelve o'clock in the middle of the day. نصف النہار
middle (**middles**) *n* The **middle** of something is the part that is farthest from its edges, ends, or outside surface. درمیان
middle-aged *adj* **Middle-aged** people are between the ages of about 40 and 60. ادھیڑ عمر
Middle Ages *npl* In European history, the **Middle Ages** was the period between the end of the Roman Empire in 476 AD and about 1500 AD, especially the later part of this period. تاریخ کا وسطی دور
middle-class *adj* **Middle-class** people are the people in a society who are not working-class or upper-class, for example managers, doctors, and lawyers. درمیانہ طبقہ
Middle East *n* The **Middle East** is the area around the eastern Mediterranean that includes Iran and all the countries in Asia that are to the west and south-west of Iran. مشرق وسطی
midge (**midges**) *n* **Midges** are very small insects which bite. بہت چھوٹے کاٹنے والے کیڑے
midnight *n* **Midnight** is twelve o'clock in the middle of the night. نصف شب
midwife (**midwives**) *n* A **midwife** is a nurse who advises pregnant women and helps them to give birth. دایہ
might *v* You use **might** when something is possible. سکنا *He might win the race.*
migraine (**migraines**) *n* A **migraine** is a very severe headache. تیز سر درد
migrant (**migrants**) *n* A **migrant** is a person who moves from one place to another, especially in order to find work. مہاجر
migration (**migrations**) *n* **Migration** is the act of people moving from one place to another, especially in order to find work. ہجرت
mild (**milder, mildest**) *adj* Something that is **mild** is not very strong or severe. ہلکا
mile (**miles**) *n* A **mile** is a unit of distance

equal to approximately 1.6 kilometres. میل

mileage (**mileages**) *n* **Mileage** refers to a distance that is travelled, measured in miles. فی گھنٹہ رفتار

mileometer (**mileometers**) *n* An **mileometer** is a device that records the number of miles that a bicycle or motor vehicle has travelled. رفتارپیما

military *adj* **Military** means relating to a country's armed forces. فوج

milk (**milks, milking, milked**) *n* **Milk** is the white liquid produced by cows and goats, which people drink and make into butter, cheese, and yoghurt. دودھ ▷ *vt* When someone **milks** a cow or goat, they get milk from it from an organ called the udder, which hangs beneath its body. دودھ دوہنا

milk chocolate *n* **Milk chocolate** is chocolate that has been made with milk. It is lighter in colour and has a creamier taste than plain chocolate. دودھیا چاکلیٹ

milkshake (**milkshakes**) *n* A **milkshake** is a cold drink made by mixing milk with a flavouring or fruit, and sometimes ice cream. ملک شیک (دودھ کے ساتھ رس وغیرہ)

mill (**mills**) *n* A **mill** is a building where grain is crushed to make flour. چکی

millennium (**millenniums, millennia**) *n* A **millennium** is a thousand years. formal ہزارہ

millimetre (**millimetres**) *n* A **millimetre** is a metric unit of length equal to one tenth of a centimetre. ملی میٹر (میٹر کا ہزارواں حصہ)

million (**millions**) *num* A **million** or one **million** is the number 1,000,000. دس لاکھ

millionaire (**millionaires**) *n* A **millionaire** is someone who has money or property worth at least a million pounds or dollars. کروڑپتی

mimic (**mimics, mimicking, mimicked**) *vt* If you **mimic** someone's actions or voice, you imitate them in an amusing or entertaining way. نقل اتارنا

mince *n* **Mince** is meat cut into very small pieces. قیمہ

mind (**minds, minding, minded**) *n* Your **mind** is the part of your brain that thinks, understands, and remembers. دماغ ▷ *vt* If you **mind** something, it annoys you. خیال کرنا

mine (**mines**) *n* A **mine** is a deep hole or tunnel where people go to dig things like gold or diamonds out of rock. کان، کھان ▷ *pron* **Mine** means belonging to me. میرا *That isn't your bag, it's mine.*

miner (**miners**) *n* A **miner** is a person who works underground in mines in order to obtain minerals such as coal, diamonds, or gold. کانکن

mineral (**minerals**) *adj* **Mineral** means of, relating to, or containing minerals. معدنی ▷ *n* A **mineral** is a substance such as tin, salt, or coal that is formed naturally in rocks and in the earth. معدن

mineral water (**mineral waters**) *n* **Mineral water** is water that comes out of the ground naturally and is considered healthy to drink. منرل واٹر (قدرتی پانی)

miniature (**miniatures**) *adj* **Miniature** things are much smaller than other things of the same kind. چھوٹی جسامت والے ▷ *n* A **miniature** is a very small detailed painting, often of a person. مختصر تصویر

minibus (**minibuses**) *n* A **minibus** is a large van which has seats in the back and windows along its sides. چھوٹی بس

minicab (**minicabs**) *n* A **minicab** is a taxi which you have to arrange to pick you up by telephone. چھوٹی ٹیکسی

minimal *adj* Something that is **minimal** is very small in quantity or degree. قلیل

minimize (**minimizes, minimizing, minimized**) *vt* If you **minimize** a risk or problem, you reduce it to the lowest possible level. کم سے کم کرنا

minimum *adj* You use **minimum** to describe an amount which is the smallest that is possible, allowed, or required.

m

اقل ▷ *n* A **minimum** is the least possible amount, degree, or quantity. کم از کم

mining *n* **Mining** is the industry and activities connected with getting valuable or useful minerals from the ground, for example coal, diamonds, or gold. کانکنی

minister *n* A **minister** is a person who is in charge of a government department. وزیر

ministry (**ministries**) *n* A **ministry** is a government department. وزارت

mink (**minks, mink**) *n* A **mink** is a small furry animal with highly valued fur. جھلیدار پیروں فروالا جانور

minor (**minors**) *adj* You use **minor** to describe something that is less important, serious, or significant than other things in a group or situation. مختصر ▷ *n* A **minor** is a person who is still legally a child. In Britain, people are minors until they reach the age of eighteen. نابالغ

minority (**minorities**) *n* If you talk about a **minority** of people or things in a larger group, you are referring to a number of them that forms less than half of the larger group. اقلیتی فرقہ

mint (**mints**) *n* The **mint** is the place where the official coins of a country are made. ٹکسال ▷ *n* **Mint** is a fresh-tasting herb. پودینہ

minus *prep* You use **minus** when you take one number away from another number. گھٹا *Three minus two is one.*

minute (**minutest, minutes**) *adj* Something that is **minute** is very small. معمولی، تھوڑی سی ▷ *n* A **minute** is used for measuring time. There are sixty seconds in one **minute**. منٹ

miracle (**miracles**) *n* If you say that an event or invention is a **miracle**, you mean that it is very surprising and fortunate. کرشمہ

mirror (**mirrors**) *n* A **mirror** is an object made of glass in which you can see your reflection. آئینہ

misbehave (**misbehaves, misbehaving, misbehaved**) *vi* If someone, especially a child, **misbehaves**, they behave in a way that is not acceptable to other people. بدتمیزی کرنا

miscarriage (**miscarriages**) *n* If a woman has a **miscarriage**, she gives birth to a foetus before it is properly formed and it dies. اسقاط حمل

miscellaneous *adj* A **miscellaneous** group consists of many different kinds of things or people that are difficult to put into a particular category. متفرق

mischief *n* **Mischief** is playing harmless tricks on people or doing things you are not supposed to do. شرارت

mischievous *adj* A mischievous person is eager to have fun by embarrassing people or by playing harmless tricks. شرارتی

miser (**misers**) *n* If you say that someone is a **miser**, you disapprove of them because they seem to hate spending money, and to spend as little as possible. کنجوس

miserable *adj* If you are **miserable**, you are very unhappy. قابل رحم

misery (**miseries**) *n* **Misery** is great unhappiness. رنج

misfortune (**misfortunes**) *n* A **misfortune** is something unpleasant or unlucky that happens to someone. بدقسمتی

mishap (**mishaps**) *n* A **mishap** is an unfortunate but not very serious event that happens to you. افسوسناک حادثہ

misjudge (**misjudges, misjudging, misjudged**) *vt* If you say that someone **has misjudged** a person or situation, you mean that they have formed an incorrect idea or opinion about them, and often that they have made a wrong decision as a result of this. غلط فیصلہ کرنا

mislay (**mislays, mislaying, mislaid**) *vt* If you **mislay** something, you put it somewhere and then forget where you have put it. غلط راہ پر ڈالنا

misleading *adj* If you describe something as **misleading**, you mean that it gives you a wrong idea or impression. گمراہ کن

misprint (**misprints**) *n* A **misprint** is a mistake in the way something is printed, for example a spelling mistake. طباعت کی غلطی

miss (**misses, missing, missed**) *v* If you **miss** something that you are trying to hit or catch, you do not manage to hit it or catch it. چھوٹ جانا ▷ *vt* If you **miss** something, you do not notice it. دھیان نہ دینا، چوک جانا ▷ *vt* If you **miss** someone who is not with you, you feel sad that they are not there. کمی محسوس کرنا

Miss (**Misses**) *n* You use **Miss** in front of the name of a girl or unmarried woman when you are speaking to her or referring to her. کنواری

missile (**missiles**) *n* A **missile** is a tube-shaped weapon that moves long distances through the air and explodes when it reaches its target. میزائل

missing *adj* If someone or something is **missing** or has **gone missing**, they are not where you expect them to be, and you cannot find them. گم شدہ

mist (**mists**) *n* **Mist** consists of many tiny drops of water in the air, which make it difficult to see very far. کہرا، دھند

mistake (**mistakes, mistaking, mistook, mistaken**) *n* A **mistake**, you do something which you did not intend to do, or which produces a result that you do not want. غلطی ▷ *vt* If you **mistake** one person or thing **for** another, you wrongly think that they are the other person or thing. غلطی کرنا

mistaken *adj* If you are **mistaken**, or if you have a **mistaken** belief, you are wrong about something. غلط فہمی

mistakenly *adv* If you do or think something **mistakenly**, you do something which you did not intend to do, or you are wrong about something. غلط فہمی سے

mistletoe *n* **Mistletoe** is a plant with pale berries that grows on the branches of some trees. امر بیل

misty *adj* If it is **misty**, there is a lot of mist in the air. کہر آلود

misunderstand (**misunderstands, misunderstanding, misunderstood**) *v* If you **misunderstand** someone or something, you do not understand them properly. غلط سمجھنا

misunderstanding (**misunderstandings**) *n* A **misunderstanding** is a failure to understand something such as a situation or a person's remarks. غلط فہمی

mitten (**mittens**) *n* **Mittens** are gloves which have one section that covers your thumb and another section that covers your four fingers together. دستانہ (ایک ہی خانہ)

mix (**mixes, mixing, mixed**) *n* A **mix** is a powder containing all the substances that you need in order to make something, to which you add liquid. آمیزہ ▷ *v* If two substances **mix**, or if you **mix** one substance with another, they combine to form a single substance. ملانا

mixed *adj* If you have **mixed** feelings about something or someone, you feel uncertain about them because you can see both good and bad points about them. ملی جلی

mixed salad (**mixed salads**) *n* A **mixed salad** is a mixture of raw or cold foods such as lettuce, cucumber, and tomatoes. ملا جلا سلاد

mixer (**mixers**) *n* A **mixer** is a machine used for mixing things together. مکسر

mixture *n* A **mixture** of things consists of several different things together. مرکب

mix up (**mix-ups**) *v* If you **mix up** two things or people, you confuse them, so that you think that one of them is the other one. ضم ہونا *I mixed her up with someone else.* ▷ *n* A **mix-up** is a mistake or a failure in the way that something has been planned. informal خلط

MMS *abbr* **MMS** is a method of sending messages over wireless networks, especially on mobile phones. **MMS** is an abbreviation of 'Multimedia Messaging Service'. MMS

moan (**moans, moaning, moaned**) *vi* If you **moan**, you make a low sound, usually because you are unhappy or in pain. کراہنا

moat (**moats**) *n* A **moat** is a deep, wide channel dug round a place such as a castle and filled with water, in order to protect the place from attack. خندق

mobile *adj* Something or someone that is **mobile** is able to move or be moved easily. متحرک

mobile home (**mobile homes**) *n* A **mobile home** is a large caravan that people live in and that usually remains in the same place, but which can be pulled to another place using a car or van. چلتا پھرتا گھر

mobile number (**mobile numbers**) *n* Someone's **mobile number** is the series of numbers that you dial when you are making a telephone call to their mobile phone. موبائل نمبر

mobile phone (**mobile phones**) *n* A **mobile phone** is a small phone that you can take everywhere with you. موبائل فون

mock (**mocks, mocking, mocked**) *adj* You use **mock** to describe something which is not genuine, but which is intended to be very similar to the real thing. نقلی ▷ *vt* If you **mock** someone, you laugh at them, tease them, or try to make them look foolish. نقل کرنا

mod cons *npl* **Mod cons** are the modern facilities in a house that make it easy and pleasant to live in. informal جدید سہولیات

model (**models, modelling, modelled**) *adj* A **model** wife or a model teacher, for example, is an excellent wife or an excellent teacher. مثالی ▷ *n* A **model** is a small copy of something. نمونہ ▷ *vt* If one thing is **modelled** on another, the first thing is made so that it is like the second thing in some way. اصل کے مطابق بنانا ▷ *n* A **model** is a person whose job is to wear and show new clothes. ماڈل، شخصی نمونہ

modem (**modems**) *n* A **modem** is a device which uses a telephone line to connect computers or computer systems. موڈیم

moderate *adj* **Moderate** political opinions or policies are not extreme. اعتدال پسند

moderation *n* If someone's behaviour shows **moderation**, they act in a way that is reasonable and not extreme. اعتدال پسندی

modern *adj* **Modern** means relating to the present time. جدید

modernize (**modernizes, modernizing, modernized**) *vt* To **modernize** a system means to replace old equipment or methods with new ones. جدید کاری

modern languages *npl* **Modern languages** refers to the modern European languages, for example French, German, and Russian, which are studied at school or university. جدید زبانیں

modest *adj* A **modest** house or other building is not large or expensive. منکسر مزاج

modification (**modifications**) *n* **Modification** is the act of changing something slightly in order to improve it. ترمیم، تبدیلی

modify (**modifies, modifying, modified**) *vt* If you **modify** something, you change it slightly in order to improve it. ترمیم کرنا

module (**modules**) *n* A **module** is one of the units that some university or college courses are divided into. ماڈیول

moist (**moister, moistest**) *adj* Something that is **moist** is slightly wet. نم

moisture *n* **Moisture** is tiny drops of water in the air or on a surface. نمی

moisturizer (**moisturizers**) *n* A **moisturizer** is a cream that you put on your skin to make it feel softer and smoother. نم آور

Moldova *n* **Moldova** is a republic in south-east Europe. مالدووا

Moldovan (**Moldovans**) *adj* **Moldovan** means of or relating to Moldova or its inhabitants. مولڈویائی ▷ *n* A **Moldovan** is a native or inhabitant of Moldova. مولڈویائی

mole (**moles**) *n* A **mole** is a small animal with black fur that lives under the ground. چھچھوندر ▷ *n* A **mole** is a person who works for an organization and gives secret information about it to other people or to its enemies. جاسوس ▷ *n* A **mole** is a natural dark spot on your skin. تل

molecule (**molecules**) *n* A **molecule** is the smallest amount of a chemical substance which can exist. سالمہ

moment (**moments**) *n* A **moment** is a very short period of time. پل، لحہ

momentarily *adv* **Momentarily** means for a short time. written لحاتی طور پر

momentary *adj* Something that is **momentary** lasts for only a very short time. وقتی

momentous *adj* A **momentous** event is very important. بہت اہم

Monaco *n* Monaco is a principality in south-west Europe, on the Mediterranean. فرانسیسی اقلیتی فرقہ (۲۳۰۰۰ لوگ)

monarch (**monarchs**) *n* A **monarch** is a king or queen. بادشاہ

monarchy (**monarchies**) *n* A **monarchy** is a system in which a monarch rules over a country. بادشاہت

monastery (**monasteries**) *n* A **monastery** is a building in which monks live. عیسائی خانقاہ

Monday (**Mondays**) *n* **Monday** is the day after Sunday and before Tuesday. پیر

monetary *adj* **Monetary** means relating to money, or to the money supply. مالی

money *n* **Money** consists of the coins or banknotes that you can spend, or a sum that can be represented by these. رقم

Mongolia *n* **Mongolia** is a republic in east central Asia. منگولیا

Mongolian (**Mongolians**) *adj* **Mongolian** means belonging or relating to Mongolia, or to its people, language, or culture. منگولیائی ▷ *n* A **Mongolian** is a person who comes from Mongolia. منگولیائی ▷ *n* **Mongolian** is the language that is spoken in Mongolia. منگولیائی

mongrel (**mongrels**) *n* A **mongrel** is a dog which is a mixture of different breeds. مخلوط نسل کا (کتا)

monitor (**monitors**) *n* A **monitor** is a machine used to check or record things. مانیٹر

monk (**monks**) *n* A **monk** is a member of a male religious community. بودھ مذہبی پیشوا

monkey (**monkeys**) *n* A **monkey** is an animal with a long tail which lives in hot countries and climbs trees. بندر

monopoly (**monopolies**) *n* If a company, person, or state has a **monopoly** on something such as an industry, they have complete control over it. اجارہ داری

monotonous *adj* Something that is **monotonous** is very boring because it has a regular repeated pattern which never changes. یکسانی، اکتادینے والا

monsoon (**monsoons**) *n* The **monsoon** is the season of very heavy rain in Southern Asia. مانسون

monster (**monsters**) *n* A **monster** is a large imaginary creature that is very frightening. عفریت

month (**months**) *n* A **month** is one of the twelve periods of time that a year is divided into, for example January or February. ماہ

monthly *adj* A **monthly** event or publication happens or appears every month. ماہانہ

monument (**monuments**) *n* A

m

monument is a large structure, usually made of stone, which is built to remind people of an event in history or of a famous person. یادگار (عمارت)

mood (**moods**) *n* Your **mood** is the way you are feeling at a particular time. مزاج

moody (**moodier, moodiest**) *adj* A **moody** person often becomes depressed or angry without any warning. بیزار

moon *n* The **moon** is the object in the sky that goes round the Earth once every four weeks and that you can often see at night as a circle or part of a circle. چاند

moor (**moors, mooring, moored**) *n* A **moor** is an area of high open ground covered mainly with rough grass and heather. بنجر ▷ *v* If you **moor** or **moor** a boat, you attach it to the land with a rope or cable so that it cannot drift away. لنگر ڈال کر روکے رکھنا

mop (**mops**) *n* A **mop** consists of a sponge or many pieces of string attached to a long handle that is used for washing floors. جھاڑو

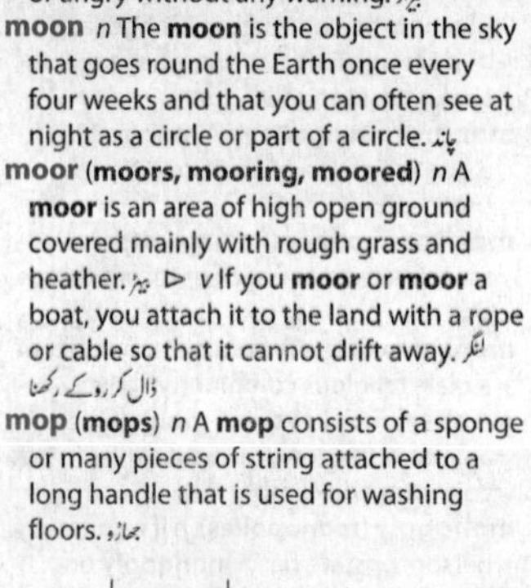

moped (**mopeds**) *n* A **moped** is a kind of motorcycle with a very small engine. موپیڈ (موٹر سائکل کی قسم)

mop up *v* If you **mop up** a liquid, you clean it with a cloth so that the liquid is absorbed. جھاڑنا، صاف کرنا *A waiter mopped up the mess.*

moral (**morals**) *adj* **Moral** means relating to beliefs about what is right or wrong. اخلاقی

morale *n* **Morale** is the amount of confidence and optimism that people have. حوصلہ

morals *npl* **Morals** are principles and beliefs concerning right and wrong behaviour. اخلاق، اطوار

more *det* You use **more** to talk about a greater amount of something. مزید، زیادہ *He has more chips than me.* ▷ *adv* You can use **more** when something continues to happen for a further period of time. مزید ▷ *pron* You use **more** to refer to an additional thing or amount. اضافی *As the amount of work increased, workers ate more.*

morgue (**morgues**) *n* A **morgue** is a building or room where dead bodies are kept before being cremated or buried. مردہ گھر

morning (**mornings**) *n* The **morning** is the part of a day between the time that people wake up and noon. صبح

morning sickness *n* **Morning sickness** is a feeling of sickness that some women have, often in the morning, when they are pregnant. صبح کی کسل مندی

Moroccan (**Moroccans**) *adj* **Moroccan** means belonging or relating to Morocco or to its people or culture. مراقشی ▷ *n* A **Moroccan** is a person who comes from Morocco. مراقشی

Morocco *n* **Morocco** is a kingdom in north-west Africa. مراقش

morphine *n* **Morphine** is a drug used to relieve pain. مارفین

morse code *n* **Morse code** is a code used for sending messages. It represents each letter of the alphabet using short and long sounds or flashes of light, which can be written down as dots and dashes. مورس کوڈ، تار بھیجنے کا طریقہ

mortar (**mortars**) *n* A **mortar** is a short cannon which fires shells high into the air for a short distance. مورٹار ▷ *n* **Mortar** is a mixture of sand, water, and cement, which is put between bricks to make them stay firmly together. ریت پانی سیمنٹ کا آمیزہ

mortgage (**mortgages, mortgaging, mortgaged**) *n* A **mortgage** is a loan of money which you get from a bank in order to buy a house. رہن ▷ *vt* If you **mortgage** your house or land, you use it as a guarantee to a company in order to borrow money from them. گروی رکھنا

mosaic (**mosaics**) *n* A **mosaic** is a design made of small pieces of coloured stone or glass set in concrete or plaster. پچی کاری

Moslem Moslems *adj* **Moslem** means relating to Islam or Moslems. مسلم ▷ *n* A **Moslem** is someone who believes in Islam and lives according to its rules. مسلم

mosque (**mosques**) *n* A **mosque** is a building where Muslims go to worship. مسجد

mosquito (**mosquitoes, mosquitos**) *n* **Mosquitoes** are small flying insects which bite people in order to suck their blood. مچھر

moss (**mosses**) *n* **Moss** is a very small, soft, green plant which grows on damp soil, or on wood or stone. کائی

most *adj* You use **most** to talk about nearly all the people or things in a group. سب سے زیادہ ▷ *adv* The **most** means the largest amount. زیادہ ▷ *pron* **Most** of a group of things or people means nearly all of them. زیادہ تر *Most of the houses here are very old.*

mostly *adv* You use **mostly** to indicate that a statement is true about the majority of a group of things or people, true most of the time, or true in most respects. زیادہ تر

MOT (**MOTs**) *abbr* In Britain, an **MOT** is a test which, by law, must be made each year on all road vehicles that are more than three years old, in order to check that they are safe to drive. ایم او ٹی (سالانہ جانچ برطانیہ میں)

motel (**motels**) *n* A **motel** is a hotel intended for people who are travelling by car. موٹل (جہاں گاڑی والے رات بسر کر سکتے ہیں)

moth (**moths**) *n* A **moth** is an insect like a butterfly, which usually flies about at night. پروانہ، پتنگا

mother (**mothers**) *n* Your **mother** is your female parent. ماں

mother-in-law (**mothers-in-law**) *n* Someone's **mother-in-law** is the mother of their husband or wife. ساس

mother tongue (**mother tongues**) *n* Your **mother tongue** is the language that you learn from your parents when you are a baby. مادری زبان

motionless *adj* Someone or something that is **motionless** is not moving at all. بے حس و حرکت

motivated *adj* If you are **motivated**, you feel enthusiastic and determined to achieve success. تحریک یافتہ

motivation (**motivations**) *n* Your **motivation** for doing something is what causes you to want to do it. تحریک

motive (**motives**) *n* Your **motive** for doing something is your reason for doing it. مقصد

motor (**motors**) *n* A **motor** in a machine, vehicle, or boat is the part that uses electricity or fuel to produce movement, so that the machine, vehicle, or boat can work. موٹر

motorbike (**motorbikes**) *n* A **motorbike** is a two-wheeled vehicle with an engine. موٹر بائک (دو پہیہ)

motorboat (**motorboats**) *n* A **motorboat** is a boat that is driven by an engine. موٹر بوٹ (ناؤ)

motorcycle (**motorcycles**) *n* A **motorcycle** is a two-wheeled vehicle with an engine. موٹر سائکل

m

motorcyclist (**motorcyclists**) *n* A **motorcyclist** is someone who rides a motorcycle. موٹر سائکل سوار

motorist (**motorists**) *n* A **motorist** is someone who drives a car. کار ڈرائیور

motor mechanic (**motor mechanics**) *n* A **motor mechanic** is someone whose job is to repair and maintain car engines. موٹر مستری

motor racing *n* **Motor racing** is the sport of racing fast cars on a special track. موٹر کار ریس

motorway (**motorways**) *n* A **motorway** is a wide road specially built for fast travel over long distances. چوڑی سڑک

mould (**moulds**) *n* A **mould** is a container used to make something into a particular shape. سانچہ ▷ *n* **Mould** is a soft grey, green, or blue substance that sometimes forms in spots on old food or on damp walls or clothes. پھپھوندی

mouldy *adj* Something that is **mouldy** is covered with mould. پھپھوندی لگی ہوئی

mount (**mounts, mounting, mounted**) *vt* To **mount** a campaign or event means to organize it and make it take place. مہم جوئی کرنا

mountain (**mountains**) *n* A **mountain** is a very high area of land with steep sides. پہاڑ، کوہ

mountain bike (**mountain bikes**) *n* A **mountain bike** is a type of bicycle with a strong frame and thick tyres. پہاڑی راستوں کے لئے بائک

mountaineer (**mountaineers**) *n* A **mountaineer** is someone who climbs mountains as a hobby or sport. کوہ پیما

mountaineering *n* **Mountaineering** is the activity of climbing the steep sides of mountains as a hobby or sport. کوہ پیمائی

mountainous *adj* A **mountainous** place has a lot of mountains. پہاڑی سلسلہ

mount up *v* If something **mounts up**, it increases in quantity. چڑھنا، بڑھنا *Her medical bills mounted up.*

mourning *n* **Mourning** is behaviour in which you show sadness about a person's death. ماتم

mouse mice *n* A **mouse** is a small animal with a long tail. چوہا ▷ *n* You use a **mouse** to move things on a computer screen. ماؤس (کمپیوٹر کا)

mouse mat (**mouse mats**) *n* A **mouse mat** is a flat piece of plastic or some other material that you rest the mouse on while using a computer. چوہا گھر

mousse (**mousses**) *n* **Mousse** is a sweet light food made from eggs and cream. انڈے کی سفیدی کی جمی ہوئی ڈش

moustache (**moustaches**) *n* A man's **moustache** is the hair that grows on his upper lip. مونچھ

mouth (**mouths**) *n* Your **mouth** is your lips, or the space behind your lips where your teeth and tongue are. منہ

mouth organ (**mouth organs**) *n* A **mouth organ** is a small musical instrument. You play the harmonica by moving it across your lips and blowing and sucking air through it. ماؤتھ آرگن

mouthwash (**mouthwashes**) *n* **Mouthwash** is a liquid that you put in your mouth and then spit out in order to clean your mouth and make your breath smell pleasant. منہ صفا

move (**moves, moving, moved**) *n* A **move** is an action that you take. حرکت ▷ *vt* When you **move** something, you put it in a different place. منتقل کرنا، حرکت دینا ▷ *vi* If you **move**, you go to live in a different place. منتقل ہونا، گھر بدلنا

move back *v* If you **move back**, you change your position by going in a backward direction. واپس مڑنا *He moved back up the corridor.*

move forward *v* If you **move forward** an event, you arrange for it to take place at an earlier time than had been planned. آگے بڑھنا *He had to move forward an 11 o'clock meeting.*

move in *v* If you **move in** somewhere, or if you **move into** a new house or place, you begin to live in a different house or place. داخل ہونا *A friend has moved in with me to rent my spare room.*

movement (**movements**) *n* **Movement** involves changing position or going from one place to another. نقل و حرکت

movie (**movies**) *n* A **movie** is a motion picture. informal سنیما

moving *adj* If something is **moving**, it makes you feel a strong emotion such as pity. متحرک

mow (**mows, mowing, mowed, mown**) *v* If you **mow** an area of grass, you cut it using a lawnmower or a mower. کاٹنا

mower (**mowers**) *n* A **mower** is a machine for cutting grass, corn, or wheat. گھاس کاٹنے کی مشین

Mozambique *n* **Mozambique** is a republic in south-east Africa. موزمبیق

MP3 player (**MP3 players**) *n* An **MP3 player** is a machine on which you can play music downloaded from the Internet. ایم پی ۳ پلیئر

MP4 player (**MP4 players**) *n* An **MP4 player** is a machine on which you can play music downloaded from the Internet. ایم پی ۴ پلیئر

mph *abbr* **mph** is written after a number to indicate the speed of something such as a vehicle. **mph** is an abbreviation for 'miles per hour'. میل فی گھنٹہ

Mr *n* **Mr** is used before a man's name when you are speaking or referring to him. مسٹر

Mrs *n* **Mrs** is used before the name of a married woman when you are speaking or referring to her. مسز(شادی شدہ عورت کے لیے)

MS *abbr* **MS** is a serious disease of the nervous system, which gradually makes a person weaker, and sometimes affects their sight or speech. **MS** is an abbreviation for 'multiple sclerosis'. ایم ایس (کثیر بافتی تصلب)

Ms *n* **Ms** is used before a woman's name when you are speaking to her or referring to her. If you use **Ms**, you are not specifying if the woman is married or not. مسز(غیر شادی شدہ عورت کے لیے)

much *det* You use **much** to talk about a large amount of something. زیادہ *We don't have much food.* ⊳ *adv* You use **much** with 'so', 'too', and 'very' to mean a very large amount of something. بہت ⊳ *pron* You use **much** to mean a large amount of something. بہت زیادہ *I didn't think much about it then.*

mud *n* **Mud** is a sticky mixture of earth and water. کیچڑ

muddle (**muddles**) *n* A **muddle** is a confused state or situation. گڈمڈ

muddy (**muddier, muddiest**) *adj* Something that is **muddy** contains, or is covered in, mud. کیچڑزدہ

mudguard (**mudguards**) *n* The **mudguards** of a bicycle or other vehicle are curved pieces of metal or plastic above the tyres, which stop mud getting on the rider or vehicle. کیچڑ محافظ (مڈ گارڈ)

muesli (**mueslis**) *n* **Muesli** is a breakfast cereal made from chopped nuts, dried fruit, and grains. خشک میوہ دار ناشتے کا دلیہ

muffler (**mufflers**) *n* A **muffler** is a piece of cloth that you wear round your neck or head, usually to keep yourself warm. old-fashioned گلوبند، مفلر

mug (**mugs, mugging, mugged**) *n* A **mug** is a large deep cup with straight sides. مگ ⊳ *vt* If someone **mugs** you, they attack you in order to steal your money. حملہ کرنا، ڈھانپ لینا

mugger (**muggers**) *n* A **mugger** is a person who attacks someone violently in a street in order to steal money from them. حملہ ور

mugging (**muggings**) *n* A **mugging** is an attack on somebody in order to steal their money. حملہ

mule (**mules**) *n* A **mule** is an animal whose parents are a horse and a donkey. خچر

multinational (**multinationals**) *adj* A **multinational** company has branches or owns companies in many different countries. کثیر ملکی ▷ *n* A **multinational** is a company that has branches or owns companies in many different countries. کثیر ملکی

multiple sclerosis *n* **Multiple sclerosis** is a serious disease of the nervous system. The abbreviation 'MS' is also used. کثیر بافتی تصلب

multiplication *n* **Multiplication** is the process of increasing greatly in number or amount. ضرب

multiply (**multiplies, multiplying, multiplied**) *v* When something **multiplies**, or when you **multiply** it, it increases greatly in number or amount. ضرب دینا

mum (**mums**) *n* Your **mum** is your mother. informal ماں

mummy (**mummies**) *n* Some people, especially young children, call their mother **mummy**. informal ممی ▷ *n* A **mummy** is a dead body which was preserved long ago by being rubbed with oils and wrapped in cloth. مومیائی ہوئی لاش

mumps *n* **Mumps** is a disease usually caught by children. It causes a mild fever and painful swelling of the glands in the neck. گلسوئے

murder (**murders, murdering, murdered**) *n* **Murder** is the crime of deliberately killing a person. قتل ▷ *vt* To **murder** someone means to commit the crime of killing them deliberately. قتل کرنا

murderer (**murderers**) *n* A **murderer** is a person who has murdered someone. قاتل

muscle (**muscles**) *n* Your **muscles** are the parts inside your body that connect your bones, and that help you to move. پٹھا، عضلہ

muscular *adj* **Muscular** means involving or affecting your muscles. عضلاتی

museum (**museums**) *n* A **museum** is a public building where interesting and valuable objects are kept and displayed. عجائب گھر

mushroom (**mushrooms**) *n* **Mushrooms** are fungi with short stems and round tops. You can eat some kinds of mushrooms. کھمبی

music *n* **Music** is the pattern of sounds produced by people singing or playing instruments. موسیقی

musical (**musicals**) *n* A **musical** is a play or film that uses singing and dancing in the story. موسیقی دار ▷ *adj* **Musical** describes things that are concerned with playing or studying music. موسیقارانہ

musical instrument (**musical instruments**) *n* A **musical instrument** is an object such as a piano, guitar, or violin which you play in order to produce music. موسیقی کے سازوسامان

musician (**musicians**) *n* A **musician** is a person who plays a musical instrument as their job or hobby. موسیقار

Muslim (**Muslims**) *adj* **Muslim** means relating to Islam or Muslims. مسلمان یا ان کے مذہب سے متعلق ▷ *n* A **Muslim** is someone who believes in Islam and lives according to its rules. مسلمان، اسلام کا پیرو

mussel (**mussels**) *n* A **mussel** is a kind of shellfish. دو صمامی صدفیہ

must *v* You use **must** to show that you think something is very important. ضروری ہونا *You must tell the police all the facts.*

mustard *n* **Mustard** is a yellow or brown paste made from seeds which tastes spicy. سرسوں، رائی

mutter (**mutters, muttering, muttered**) *v* If you **mutter**, you speak very quietly so that you cannot easily be heard, often because you are complaining about something. بڑبڑانا

mutton *n* **Mutton** is meat from an adult sheep. گوشت (بکری بھیڑ کا)

mutual *adj* You use **mutual** to describe a situation, feeling, or action that is experienced, felt, or done by both of two people mentioned. باہمی
my *det* You use **my** to show that something belongs to you. میرا *I went to sleep in my room.*
Myanmar *n* **Myanmar** is a republic in south-east Asia. میانمار (ملک کا نام)
myself *pron* You use **myself** when the you are talking about yourself. میں خود *I hurt myself when I fell down.*
mysterious *adj* Someone or something that is **mysterious** is strange, not known about, or not understood. پراسرار
mystery (**mysteries**) *n* A **mystery** is something that is not understood or known about. اسرار، (راز)
myth (**myths**) *n* A **myth** is an ancient story about gods and magic. دیومالائی داستان
mythology *n* **Mythology** is a group of myths, especially those from a particular country, religion, or culture. علم الاساطیر

n

naff (**naffer, naffest**) *adj* If you say that something is **naff**, you mean it is very unfashionable or unsophisticated. (*informal*) فرسودہ
nag (**nags, nagging, nagged**) *v* If someone **nags** you, or if they **nag**, they keep asking you to do something you have not done yet or do not want to do. دق کرنا
nail (**nails**) *n* A **nail** is a thin piece of metal. It is flat at one end and it has a point at the other end. کیل، میخ ▷ *n* Your **nails** are the thin hard parts that grow at the ends of your fingers and toes. ناخن
nailbrush (**nailbrushes**) *n* A **nailbrush** is a small brush that you use to clean your nails when washing your hands. ناخن برش
nailfile (**nailfiles**) *n* A **nailfile** is a small strip of rough metal or card that you rub across the ends of your nails to shorten them or shape them. ناخن ریتی
nail polish (**nail polishes**) *n* **Nail polish** is a thick liquid that women paint on their nails. ناخن پالش
nail-polish remover (**nail-polish removers**) *n* **Nail-polish remover** is a solvent used to remove nail polish. ناخن پالش ہٹانے والا
nail scissors *npl* **Nail scissors** are small scissors that you use for cutting your nails. ناخن قینچی

naive *adj* If you describe someone as **naive**, you think they lack experience, causing them to expect things to be uncomplicated or easy, or people to be honest or kind when they are not. سادہ لوح

naked *adj* Someone who is **naked** is not wearing any clothes. ننگا

name (**names**) *n* The **name** of a person, thing, or place is the word or words that you use to identify them. نام

nanny (**nannies**) *n* A **nanny** is a person who is paid by parents to look after their children. آیا

nap (**naps**) *n* If you have a **nap**, you have a short sleep, usually during the day. قیلولہ، جھپکی

napkin (**napkins**) *n* A **napkin** is a small piece of cloth or paper used to protect your clothes when you are eating. چھوٹا تولیہ، دست پاک

nappy (**nappies**) *n* A **nappy** is a piece of thick cloth or paper which is fastened round a baby's bottom in order to absorb its waste. نیپی، نیپکن (بچہ کا جانگھیہ)

narrow (**narrower, narrowest**) *adj* Something that is **narrow** measures a very small distance from one side to the other, especially compared to its length or height. تنگ

narrow-minded *adj* If you describe someone as **narrow-minded**, you are criticizing them because they are unwilling to consider new ideas or other people's opinions. تنگ نظر

nasty (**nastier, nastiest**) *adj* Something that is **nasty** is very unpleasant or unattractive. ناگوار

nation (**nations**) *n* A **nation** is an individual country considered together with its social and political structures. ملک، قوم

national *adj* **National** means relating to the whole of a country, rather than to part of it or to other nations. ملکی، قومی

national anthem (**national anthems**) *n* A **national anthem** is a nation's official song. قومی گیت

nationalism *n* **Nationalism** is the desire for political independence of people who feel they are historically or culturally a separate group within a country. قوم پرستی

nationalist (**nationalists**) *n* A **nationalist** is someone who desires for the group of people to which they belong to gain political independence. قوم پرست

nationality (**nationalities**) *n* If you have the **nationality** of a particular country, you have the legal right to be a citizen of it. شہریت

nationalize (**nationalizes, nationalizing, nationalized**) *vt* If a government **nationalizes** a private industry, that industry becomes owned by the state and controlled by the government. قومیانا

national park (**national parks**) *n* A **national park** is a large area of natural land protected by the government because of its natural beauty, plants, or animals. قومی پارک

native *adj* Your **native** country or area is the country or area where you were born and brought up. ملکی، پیدائشی

native speaker (**native speakers**) *n* A **native speaker** of a language is someone who speaks that language as their first language rather than having learned it as a foreign language. مادری زبان بولنے والا

NATO *abbr* **NATO** is an international organization which consists of the USA, Canada, Britain, and other European countries, all of whom have agreed to support one another if they are attacked. **NATO** is an abbreviation for 'North Atlantic Treaty Organization'. نارتھ اٹلانٹک ٹریٹی اورگنائزیشن

natural *adj* If you say that it is **natural** for someone to act in a particular way, you mean that it is reasonable in the circumstances. فطری، قدرتی

natural gas *n* **Natural gas** is gas which

is found underground or under the sea. It is collected and stored, and piped into people's homes to be used for cooking and heating. قدرتی گیس

naturalist (**naturalists**) *n* A **naturalist** is a person who studies plants, animals, and other living things. فطرت پسند

naturally *adv* You use **naturally** to indicate that you think something is very obvious and not at all surprising in the circumstances. فطری طور پر

natural resources *npl* The **natural resources** of a place are all its land, forests, energy sources, and minerals which exist naturally there and can be used by people. قدرتی وسائل

nature *n* **Nature** refers to all the animals, plants, and other things in the world that are not made by people, and all the events and processes that are not caused by people. فطرت، قدرت

naughty (**naughtier, naughtiest**) *adj* You say that small children are **naughty** when they behave badly. شوخ، شرارتی

nausea *n* **Nausea** is a feeling of sickness and dizziness. متلی

naval *adj* **Naval** people and things belong to a country's navy. بحری

navel (**navels**) *n* Your **navel** is the small hollow just below your waist at the front of your body. ناف

navy (**navies**) *n* A country's (**navy**) is the part of its armed forces that fights at sea. بحریہ ▷ *adj* Something that is **navy** is very dark blue. نیلے رنگ کی

NB *abbr* You write **NB** to draw someone's attention to what you are going to write next. اچھی طرح درج کریں

near (**nearer, nearest**) *adj* **Near** means at or in a place not far away. قریب ▷ *adv* **Near** means at or to a place not far away. قریبی، نزدیکی ▷ *prep* If something is **near** a place, thing, or person, it is not far away from them. قریب *We are very near my house.*

nearby *adj* If something is **nearby**, it is only a short distance away. قریبی ▷ *adv* If something is **nearby**, it is only a short distance away. نزدیک والا

nearly *adv* If something is **nearly** a quantity, it is very close to that quantity but slightly less than it. If something is **nearly** a certain state, it is very close to that state but has not quite reached it. تقریبا

near-sighted *adj* Someone who is **near-sighted** cannot see distant things clearly. US قریب کی نظر والا

neat (**neater, neatest**) *adj* A **neat** place, thing, or person is tidy, smart, and orderly. صاف ستھرا

neatly *adv* **Neatly** means in a tidy or smart manner. صفائی سے

necessarily *adv* If you say that something is **not necessarily** true, you mean that it may not be true or is not always true. ضروری طور پر

necessary *adj* Something that is **necessary** is needed to get a particular result or effect. ضروری

necessity *n* **Necessity** is the need to do something. ضرورت

neck (**necks**) *n* Your **neck** is the part of your body which joins your head to the rest of your body. گردن

necklace (**necklaces**) *n* A **necklace** is a piece of jewellery such as a chain or string of beads, which someone wears round their neck. گلے کا ہار

nectarine (**nectarines**) *n* A **nectarine** is a fruit similar to a peach with a smooth skin. شفتالو

need (**needs, needing, needed**) *n* If you have a **need** for something, you cannot do what you want without it. ضرورت ▷ *vt* If you **need** something, you believe that you must have it or do it. ضرورت ہونا

needle (**needles**) *n* A **needle** is a small very thin piece of metal with a hole at one end and a sharp point at the other, which is used for sewing. سوئی

n

negative (**negatives**) *adj* A fact, situation, or experience that is **negative** is unpleasant, depressing, or harmful. منفی ▷ *n* A **negative** is a word, expression, or gesture that means 'no' or 'not'. نفی

neglect (**neglects, neglecting, neglected**) *n* **Neglect** is the failure to look after someone or something properly. غفلت ▷ *vt* If you **neglect** someone or something, you fail to look after them properly. نظر انداز کرنا

neglected *adj* If someone is **neglected**, they have not been given enough love, attention or support. متروک

negotiate (**negotiates, negotiating, negotiated**) *v* If one person or group **negotiates** with another, they talk about a problem or a situation in order to solve the problem or complete the arrangement. گفت و شنید کرنا

negotiations *npl* **Negotiations** are discussions that take place between people with different interests, in which they try to reach an agreement. گفت و شنید معاملہ داری

negotiator (**negotiators**) *n* **Negotiators** are people who take part in political or financial negotiations. مذاکرات کار

neighbour (**neighbours**) *n* Your **neighbours** are the people who live near you, especially the people who live in the house or flat which is next to yours. پڑوسی

neighbourhood (**neighbourhoods**) *n* A **neighbourhood** is one of the parts of a town where people live. پڑوس

neither *conj* If you say that one person or thing does not do something and **neither** does another, what you say is true of both the people or things that you are mentioning. کسی نے بھی نہیں *I never learned to swim and neither did they.* ▷ *pron* You use **neither** to refer to each of two things or people, when you are making a negative statement that includes both of them. دونوں میں سے کوئی نہیں *They both smiled; neither seemed likely to be aware of my absence for long.* ▷ *adj* **Neither** means not one or the other of two things or people. کوئی بھی نہیں

neither ... nor *conj* You use **neither ... nor** when you are talking about two or more things that are not true or that do not happen. نہ تو نہ ہی *The play was neither as funny nor as exciting as she said it was.*

neon *n* **Neon** is a gas which exists in very small amounts in the atmosphere. نیون گیس

Nepal *n* **Nepal** is a republic in South Asia. نیپال

nephew (**nephews**) *n* Your **nephew** is the son of your sister or brother. بھتیجہ، بھانجہ

nerve (**nerves**) *n* **Nerves** are long thin fibres that transmit messages between your brain and other parts of your body. نس ▷ *n* **Nerve** is the courage you need to do something difficult or dangerous. عصب

nerve-racking *adj* A **nerve-racking** situation or experience makes you feel very tense and worried. اشتعال انگیز

nervous *adj* If you are **nervous**, you are worried and frightened, and show this in your behaviour. حوصلہ شکستہ

nest (**nests**) *n* A **nest** is a place that birds, insects, and other animals make to lay eggs in or give birth to their young in. گھونسلہ

net (**nets**) *n* A **net** is made from pieces of string or rope tied together with holes between them. It is for catching things like fish, or the ball in some sports. جال

netball *n* **Netball** is a game played by two teams of seven players, usually women. Each team tries to score goals by throwing a ball through a net which is at the top of a pole at each end of the court. نیٹ بال

Netherlands *npl* The **Netherlands** is a kingdom in north-west Europe, on the North Sea. نیدرلینڈز (یوروپی ملک)

nettle (**nettles**) *n* A **nettle** is a wild plant with leaves that sting when you touch them. بچھوا

network (**networks**) *n* A **network** of lines, roads, veins, or other long thin things is a large number of them which cross each other or meet at many points. جال (سڑکوں، نسوں وغیرہ کا)

neurotic *adj* If you say that someone is **neurotic**, you mean that they are always frightened or worried about things that you consider unimportant. مضطرب

neutral *adj* A **neutral** person or country does not support anyone in a disagreement, war, or contest. غیر جانب دار ▷ *n* **Neutral** is the position between the gears of a vehicle, in which the gears are not connected to the engine. نیوٹرل غیر (بے رفتاری)

never *adv* **Never** means at no time in the past or future. کبھی نہیں

nevertheless *adv* You use **nevertheless** when saying something that contrasts with what has just been said. (*formal*) تاہم، پھر بھی

new (**newer, newest**) *adj* Something that is **new** was not there before. نیا رنئی ▷ *adj* If something is **new**, nobody has used it before. نیا ▷ *adj* A **new** thing or person is a different one from the one you had before. نیا رنئی

newborn *adj* A **newborn** baby or animal is one that has just been born. نوزائیدہ

newcomer (**newcomers**) *n* A **newcomer** is a person who has recently started a new activity, arrived in a place, or joined an organization. نووارد

news *npl* **News** is information about a recently changed situation or a recent event. خبر

newsagent (**newsagents**) *n* A **newsagent** is the shopkeeper of a shop where newspapers, sweets, soft drinks, and stationery are sold. اخبار کا ایجنٹ

newspaper (**newspapers**) *n* A **newspaper** is a publication consisting of large sheets of folded paper, on which news is printed. اخبار

newsreader (**newsreaders**) *n* A **newsreader** is a person who reads the news on the radio or on television. خبر پڑھنے والا

newt (**newts**) *n* A **newt** is a small creature that has four legs and a long tail and can live on land and in water. آبی چھپکلی

New Year *n* **New Year** or the **New Year** is the time when people celebrate the start of a year. نیا سال

New Zealand *n* **New Zealand** is an island country, with two main islands (the North Island and the South Island), in the south-east Pacific. نیوزی لینڈ (ملک)

New Zealander (**New Zealanders**) *n* A **New Zealander** is a citizen of New Zealand, or a person of New Zealand origin. نیوزی لینڈ کا شہری

next *adj* The **next** thing is the one that comes immediately after this one or after the last one. اگلا، اگلے ▷ *adv* The thing that happens **next** happens immediately after something else. آگے ہونے والی

next of kin *n* Your **next of kin** is your closest relative, especially in official or legal documents. (*formal*) قریب ترین رشتہ دار

next to *prep* If one thing is **next to** another, it is at the side of it. آگے She sat down next to him on the sofa.

Nicaragua *n* **Nicaragua** is a republic in Central America. نکاراگوا

Nicaraguan (**Nicaraguans**) *adj* **Nicaraguan** means belonging or relating to Nicaragua, or to its people or culture. نکاراگوائی ▷ *n* A **Nicaraguan** is a person who comes from Nicaragua. نکاراگوا کا شہری

nice (**nicer, nicest**) *adj* If something is **nice**, you like it. نفیس

nickname (**nicknames**) *n* A **nickname** is an informal name for someone or something. عرفیت

n

nicotine *n* **Nicotine** is an addictive substance in tobacco. نکوٹن (تمباکو کا زہر)

niece (**nieces**) *n* Your **niece** is the daughter of your sister or brother. بھتیجی، بھانجی

Niger *n* **Niger** is a landlocked republic in West Africa. نائجر

Nigeria *n* **Nigeria** is a republic in West Africa, on the Gulf of Guinea. نائجیریائی

Nigerian (**Nigerians**) *adj* **Nigerian** means belonging or relating to Nigeria, its people, or its culture. نائجیریائی ⊳ *n* A **Nigerian** is a Nigerian citizen, or a person of Nigerian origin. نائجیریائی

night (**nights**) *n* The **night** is the part of each period of twenty-four hours when it is dark outside, especially the time when most people are sleeping. رات

nightclub (**nightclubs**) *n* A **nightclub** is a place where people go late in the evening to dance. نائٹ کلب

nightdress (**nightdresses**) *n* A **nightdress** is a sort of loose dress that a woman or girl wears in bed. لباس شب خوابی

nightlife *n* The **nightlife** in a place is the entertainment and social activities that are available at night. شبینہ تفریح گاہیں

nightmare (**nightmares**) *n* A **nightmare** is a very frightening dream. ڈراؤنا خواب یا تجربہ

night school (**night schools**) *n* Someone who goes to **night school** does an educational course in the evenings. شبینہ اسکول

night shift (**night shifts**) *n* If a group of factory workers, nurses, or other people work the **night shift**, they work during the night before being replaced by another group, so that there is always a group working. رات پالی

nil *n* **Nil** means the same as zero. It is often used in scores of sports games. صفر

nine *num* **Nine** is the number 9. نو

nineteen (**nineteens**) *num* **Nineteen** is the number 19. انیس

nineteenth *adj* The **nineteenth** item in a series is the one that you count as number nineteen. انیسواں

ninety *num* **Ninety** is the number 90. نوے

ninth (**ninths**) *adj* The **ninth** item in a series is the one that you count as number nine. نواں ⊳ *n* A **ninth** is one of nine equal parts of something. نواں حصہ

nitrogen *n* **Nitrogen** is a colourless element that has no smell and is usually found as a gas. نائٹروجن گیس

no *det* You use **no** to mean not any or not one person or thing. نہیں *He had no idea where to go.* ⊳ *adv* You use **no** to mean not in any way. منکرانہ طور پر ⊳ *excl* You use **no**! to give a negative response to a question. نہیں

nobody *n* **Nobody** means not one person. کوئی نہیں

nod (**nods, nodding, nodded**) *vi* If you **nod**, you move your head downwards and upwards to show that you are answering 'yes' to a question, or to show agreement, understanding, or approval. سر ہلا کر رضامندی دینا

noise *n* **Noise** is a loud or unpleasant sound. شور

noisy (**noisier, noisiest**) *adj* Someone or something that is **noisy** makes a lot of loud or unpleasant noise. شور کرنے والا

nominate (**nominates, nominating, nominated**) *vt* If someone **is nominated** for a job, position, or prize, their name is formally suggested as a candidate for it. نامزد کرنا

nomination (**nominations**) *n* A **nomination** is an official suggestion of someone for a job, position, or prize. نامزدگی

none *pron* **None** means not one or not any. کوئی نہیں *None of us knew her.*

nonsense *n* If you say that something spoken or written is **nonsense**, you mean that you consider it to be untrue or silly. بکواس، بے معنی

non-smoker (**non-smokers**) *n* A **non-smoker** is someone who does not smoke. غیر تمباکو نوش

non-smoking *adj* A **non-smoking** area in

a public place is an area in which people are not allowed to smoke. غیر تمباکو نوشی

non-stop *adv* If you do something **non-stop**, you continue to do it without any pauses or breaks. بغیر رکے

noodles *npl* **Noodles** are long, thin pieces of pasta. سوئی

noon *n* **Noon** is twelve o'clock in the middle of the day. دوپہر

no one *pron* **No one** means not a single person, or not a single member of a particular group or set. کوئی نہیں *No one can predict what will happen in the months ahead.*

nor *conj* You use **nor** after 'neither' to introduce the second of two things that are not true or that do not happen. نہ ہی *Neither her friends nor her family knew how old she was.*

normal *adj* Something that is **normal** is usual and ordinary, and in accordance with what people expect. معتدل

normally *adv* If you say that something **normally** happens or that you **normally** do a particular thing, you mean that it is what usually happens or what you usually do. معمول کے طور پر

north *adj* The **north** edge, corner, or part of a place or country is the part which is towards the north. شمال *adv* If you go **north**, you travel towards the north. شمالاً ▷ *n* The **north** is the direction on your left when you are looking towards the direction where the sun rises. شمالی سمت

North Africa *n* **North Africa** is the part of Africa between the Mediterranean and the Sahara. شمالی افریقہ

North African (**North Africans**) *adj* **North African** means relating to North Africa or its inhabitants. شمالی افریقی ▷ *n* A **North African** is a native or inhabitant of North Africa. شمالی افریقی

North America *n* **North America** is the third largest continent in the world, and includes Greenland, Canada, the United States, Mexico, and Central America. شمالی امریکہ

North American (**North Americans**) *adj* **North American** means relating to North America or its inhabitants. شمالی امریکی ▷ *n* A **North American** is a native or inhabitant of **North America**. شمالی امریکی

northbound *adj* **Northbound** roads or vehicles lead or are travelling towards the north. شمال طرفی

northeast *n* The **northeast** is the direction which is halfway between north and east. شمال مشرق

northern *adj* **Northern** means in or from the north of a region or country. شمالی

Northern Ireland *n* **Northern Ireland** is that part of the United Kingdom occupying the north-east part of Ireland. شمالی آئرلینڈ

North Korea *n* **North Korea** is a republic in North-East Asia. شمالی کوریا

North Pole *n* The **North Pole** is the place on the surface of the earth which is farthest towards the north. قطب شمالی

North Sea *n* **The North Sea** is the part of the Atlantic between Great Britain and the North European mainland. بحر شمالی

northwest *n* The **northwest** is the direction which is halfway between north and west. شمال مغرب

Norway *n* **Norway** is a kingdom in north-west Europe. ناروے

Norwegian (**Norwegians**) *adj* **Norwegian** means belonging or relating to Norway, or to its people, language, or culture. نارویجین ▷ *n* A **Norwegian** is a person who comes from Norway. نارویجین ▷ *n* **Norwegian** is the language spoken in Norway. نارویجین

nose (**noses**) *n* Your **nose** is the part of your face which sticks out above your mouth. You use it for smelling and breathing. ناک

nosebleed (**nosebleeds**) *n* If someone

n

has a **nosebleed**, blood comes out from inside their nose. نکسیر پھوٹنا

nostril (**nostrils**) *n* Your **nostrils** are the two openings at the end of your nose. نتھنا

nosy (**nosier, nosiest**) *adj* If you describe someone as **nosy**, you mean that they are interested in things which do not concern them. (*informal*) ناک والا، نکو

not *adv* You use **not** or **n't** to show that something is the opposite of true. نہیں

note (**notes**) *n* A **note** is one musical sound. سر (موسیقی کا) ▷ *n* A **note** is a piece of paper money. نوٹ (کرنسی) ▷ *n* A **note** is a short letter or message. نوٹ، یادداشت کیلئے مختصر نکات لکھنا

notebook (**notebooks**) *n* A **notebook** is a small book for writing notes in. نوٹ بک

note down *v* When you **note** something **down**, you write it down so that you have a record of it. اندراج کرنا، درج کرنا *She noted down the names.*

notepad (**notepads**) *n* A **notepad** is a pad of paper that you use for writing notes or letters on. نوٹ پیڈ

notepaper *n* **Notepaper** is paper that you use for writing letters on. کاغذی نوٹ

nothing *n* **Nothing** means not anything. کچھ بھی نہیں

notice (**notices, noticing, noticed**) *n* A **notice** is a sign that gives information or instructions. علامت، نشان ▷ *n* **Notice** is advance warning about something. اطلاع ▷ *vt* If you **notice** something, you suddenly see or hear it. معلوم ہونا، پتہ لگنا

noticeable *adj* Something that is **noticeable** is very obvious, so that it is easy to see or recognize. قابل توجہ

noticeboard (**noticeboards**) *n* A **noticeboard** is a board which is usually attached to a wall in order to display notices giving information about something. اطلاعی تختہ

notify (**notifies, notifying, notified**) *vt* If you **notify** someone of something, you officially inform them of it. (*formal*) مطلع کرنا

nought (**noughts**) *n* **Nought** is the number 0. صفر

noun (**nouns**) *n* A **noun** is a word such as 'car', 'love', or 'man' which is used to refer to a person or thing. اسم

novel novels *n* A **novel** is a book containing a long story about imaginary people and events. ناول

novelist (**novelists**) *n* A **novelist** is a person who writes novels. ناول نگار

November (**Novembers**) *n* **November** is the eleventh month of the year in the Western calendar. نومبر

now *adv* You use **now** to talk about the present time. اب

nowadays *adv* **Nowadays** means at the present time, in contrast with the past. ان دنوں

nowhere *adv* You use **nowhere** to emphasize that a place has more of a particular quality than any other places, or that it is the only place where something happens or exists. کہیں نہیں

nuclear *adj* **Nuclear** means relating to the nuclei of atoms, or to the energy produced when these nuclei are split or combined. نیوکلیائی

nude (**nudes**) *adj* A **nude** person is not wearing any clothes. برہنہ (شخص) ▷ *n* A **nude** is a picture or statue of a person who is not wearing any clothes. برہنہ (تصویر وغیرہ)

nuisance (**nuisances**) *n* If you say that someone or something is a **nuisance**, you mean that they annoy you or cause you problems. مصیبت

numb *adj* If a part of your body is **numb**, you cannot feel anything there. شل

number (**numbers**) *n* A **number** is a word such as 'two', 'nine', or 'twelve', or a symbol such as 1, 3, or 47, which is used in counting something. عدد

number (**plate number plates**) *n* A **number plate** is a sign on the front and back of a vehicle that shows its registration number. نمبر پلیٹ

numerous *adj* If people or things are **numerous**, they exist or are present in large numbers. متعدد

nun (**nuns**) *n* A **nun** is a member of a female religious community. نن (راہبہ)

nurse (**nurses**) *n* A **nurse** is a person whose job is to care for people who are ill. نرس

nursery (**nurseries**) *n* A **nursery** is a place where children who are not old enough to go to school are looked after. نرسری (قبل اسکول)، بچہ خانہ

nursery rhyme (**nursery rhymes**) *n* A **nursery rhyme** is a traditional poem or song for young children. روایتی نظم

nursery school (**nursery schools**) *n* A **nursery school** is a school for very young children. نرسری اسکول

nursing home (**nursing homes**) *n* A **nursing home** is a private hospital for old people. پرائیویٹ ہسپتال

nut (**nuts**) *n* A **nut** is a small piece of metal with a hole through which you put a bolt. Nuts and bolts are used to hold things together such as pieces of machinery. نٹ (بولٹ) ▷ *n* The firm shelled fruit of some trees and bushes are called **nuts**. مغزیات

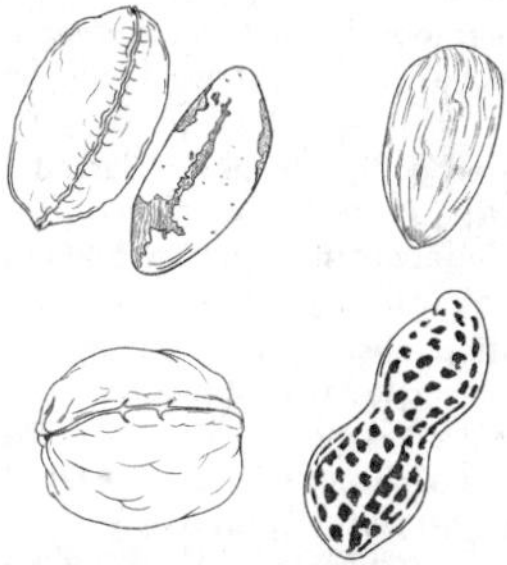

nut allergy (**nut allergies**) *n* If you have a **nut allergy**, you become ill if you eat nuts or come into contact with nuts. مغزیات سے الرجی

nutmeg *n* **Nutmeg** is a spice made from the seed of a tree that grows in hot countries. Nutmeg is usually used to flavour sweet food. جائفل

nutrient (**nutrients**) *n* **Nutrients** are chemical substances that people and animals need from food and plants need from soil. غذائی عنصر

nutrition *n* **Nutrition** is the process of taking and absorbing nutrients from food. تغذیہ

nutritious *adj* **Nutritious** food contains the proteins, vitamins, and minerals which help your body to be healthy. غذائیت بخش

nutter (**nutters**) *n* If you refer to someone as a **nutter**, you mean that they are mad or that their behaviour is very strange. (*informal*) پاگل

nylon *n* **Nylon** is a strong, flexible, artificial material. نائلون، پلاسٹک دھاگہ

O

oak (**oaks**) *n* An **oak** is a large tree with strong, hard wood. شاہ بلوط

oar (**oars**) *n* **Oars** are long poles with flat ends which are used for rowing a boat. چپو

oasis (**oases**) *n* An **oasis** is a small area in a desert where water and plants are found. نخلستان

oath (**oaths**) *n* An **oath** is a formal promise. حلف

oatmeal *n* **Oatmeal** is a kind of flour made by crushing oats. جئی کا آٹا

oats *oats* **Oats** are a cereal crop or its grains, used for making porridge or feeding animals. جئی (جو جیسا)

obedient *adj* An **obedient** person or animal does what they are told to do. فرماں بردار

obese *adj* Someone who is **obese** is extremely fat. موٹا

obey (**obeys, obeying, obeyed**) *v* If you **obey** a rule, instruction, or person, you do what you are told to do. فرماں برداری کرنا

obituary (**obituaries**) *n* Someone's **obituary** is an account of their character and achievements which is published shortly after they have died. خبرِ مرگ (شائع شدہ)

object (**objects**) *n* An **object** is anything that has a fixed shape or form and that is not alive. چیز

objection (**objections**) *n* If you make an **objection** to something, you say that you do not like it or agree with it. اعتراض

objective (**objectives**) *n* Your **objective** is what you are trying to achieve. مقصد

oblong (**oblongs**) *adj* An **oblong** is a shape which has two long sides and two short sides and in which all the angles are right angles. بیضوی

obnoxious *adj* If you describe someone as **obnoxious**, you think that they are very unpleasant. ناپسندیدہ

oboe (**oboes**) *n* An **oboe** is a musical instrument shaped like a tube which you play by blowing through a double reed in the top end. اوبوئے (پھونک والا باجہ)

observant *adj* Someone who is **observant** pays a lot of attention to things and notices more about them than most people do. تیز نگاہ

observatory (**observatories**) *n* An **observatory** is a building with a large telescope from which scientists study the stars and planets. مشاہدہ گاہ

observe (**observes, observing, observed**) *vt* If you **observe** someone or something, you watch them carefully. مشاہدہ کرنا

observer (**observers**) *n* An **observer** is someone who sees or notices something. مشاہد

obsessed *adj* If someone is **obsessed** with a person or thing, they keep thinking about them and find it difficult to think about anything else. فریفتہ

obsession (**obsession**) *n* If you say that someone has an **obsession** with someone or something, you feel they are spending too much of their time thinking about that person or thing. چاہت

obsolete *adj* Something that is **obsolete** is no longer needed because a better thing now exists. متروک

obstacle (**obstacles**) *n* An **obstacle** is something which makes it difficult for you to go forward or do something. رکاوٹ

obstinate *adj* If you describe someone as **obstinate**, you are critical of them because they are very determined to do what they want, and refuse to be persuaded to do something else. ضدی

obstruct (**obstructs, obstructing, obstructed**) *vt* To **obstruct** someone or something means to block their path, making it difficult for them to move forward. رکاوٹ ڈالنا

obtain (**obtains, obtaining, obtained**) *vt* To **obtain** something means to get it or achieve it. (*formal*) حاصل کرنا

obvious *adj* If something is **obvious**, it is easy to see or understand. صاف، واضح

obviously *adv* You use **obviously** when you are stating something that you expect your listener to know already. صاف طور پر

occasion (**occasions**) *n* An **occasion** is a time when something happens. موقع

occasional *adj* **Occasional** means happening sometimes, but not regularly or often. وقتی

occasionally *adv* **Occasionally** means from time to time. وقتی طور پر

occupation (**occupations**) *n* Your **occupation** is your job or profession. پیشہ ▷ *n* The **occupation** of a country is its invasion and control by a foreign army. قبضہ

occupy *vt* The people who **occupy** a building or place are the people who live or work there. قبضہ کرنا

occur (**occurs, occurring, occurred**) *vi* When an event **occurs**, it happens. رونما ہونا

occurrence (**occurrences**) *n* An **occurrence** is something that happens. (*formal*) واقعہ

ocean (**oceans**) *n* The **ocean** is the sea. سمندر

Oceania *n* **Oceania** is the islands of the central and South Pacific, including Melanesia, Micronesia, and Polynesia. سمندری، بحری

October (**Octobers**) *n* **October** is the tenth month of the year in the Western calendar. اکتوبر

octopus (**octopuses**) *n* An **octopus** is a sea creature with eight tentacles. اوکٹوپس (آٹھ ہاتھ والا آبی جندار)

odd (**odder, oddest**) *adj* If something is **odd**, it is strange or unusual. اجنبی، غیر معمولی، مناسب نہ ہونا، بے جوڑ ▷ *adj* You say that two things are **odd** when they do not belong to the same set or pair. بے جوڑ، الگ ▷ *adj* **Odd** numbers, such as three and seventeen, are numbers that cannot be divided by the number two. طاق (عدد)

odour (**odours**) *n* An **odour** is a smell, especially one that is unpleasant. بو، بو

of *prep* You use **of** to show that one thing belongs to another. کا، کی، کے ...*the holiday homes of the rich.* ▷ *prep* You use **of** to talk about amounts. کا *A glass of milk.* ▷ *prep* You use **of** to mean about. کے بارے میں *He was dreaming of her.*

off *prep* If you take something **off** another thing, it is no longer on it. ہٹنا *He took his feet off the desk.* ▷ *adv* When something that uses electricity is **off**, it is not using electricity. بند

offence (**offences**) *n* An **offence** is a crime. جرم

offend (**offends, offending, offended**) *vt* If you **offend** someone, you upset or embarrass them. دل کو ٹھیس پہنچانا

offensive *adj* Something that is **offensive** upsets or embarrasses people because it is rude or insulting. ہتک آمیز

offer (**offers, offering, offered**) *n* An **offer** is something that someone says they will give you or do for you. پیشکش ▷ *vt* If you **offer** something to someone, you ask them if they would like to have it or to use it. پیش کرنا

office (**offices**) *n* An **office** is a room or a part of a building where people work sitting at desks. دفتر

office hours *npl* **Office hours** are the times when an office or similar place is open for business. دفتری اوقات

officer (**officers**) *n* In the armed forces, an **officer** is a person in a position of authority. افسر

official *adj* Something that is **official** is approved by the government or by someone else in authority. دفتری، باضابطہ

off-peak *adv* If things are available **off-peak**, they are available at a time when there is less demand for them, so they are cheaper than usual. جب مانگ نہ ہو

off-season *adj* If something is **off-season** it relates to the time of the year when not many people go on vacation and when things such as hotels and plane tickets are often cheaper. جب موسم نہ ہو ▷ *adv* If something happens **off-season** it happens at the time of the year when not many people go on vacation and when things such as hotels and plane tickets are often cheaper. جب موسم نہ ہو *Visiting hours are more flexible off-season.*

offside *adj* In games such as football or hockey, when an attacking player is **offside**, they have broken the rules by being nearer to the goal than a defending player when the ball is passed to them. ممنوعہ مقام پر

often *adv* If something happens **often**, it happens many times or much of the time. اکثر

oil (**oils, oiling, oiled**) **Oil** is a smooth thick liquid used as a fuel and for lubricating machines. Oil is found underground. تیل ▷ *vt* If you **oil** something, you put oil onto it or into it in order to make it work smoothly or to protect it. تیل ڈالنا، چکنا کرنا

oil refinery (**oil refineries**) *n* An **oil refinery** is a factory where oil is refined. تیل صفا کارخانہ

oil rig (**oil rigs**) *n* An **oil rig** is a structure on land or in the sea that is used when getting oil from the ground. تیل رسنے کے مقام پر بنایا گیا ڈھانچہ

oil slick (**oil slicks**) *n* An **oil slick** is a layer of oil that floats on the sea or on a lake. It is formed when oil accidentally spills out of a ship or container. سمندر پر بہتا تیل

oil well (**oil wells**) *n* An **oil well** is a deep hole which is made in order to get oil out of the ground. تیل کا کنواں

ointment (**ointments**) *n* An **ointment** is a smooth thick substance that is put on sore skin or a wound to help it heal. مرہم

OK! *excl* You can say '**OK!**' to show that you agree to something. ٹھیک ہے!

okay *adj* If you say that something is **okay**, you find it satisfactory or acceptable. (*informal*) اوکے (ٹھیک ہے) ▷ *excl* You can say '**Okay!**' to show that you agree to something. رضامند، ٹھیک

old (**older, oldest**) *adj* An **old** person is someone who has lived for a long time. بوڑھا، بوڑھی، عمر رسیدہ ▷ *adj* An **old** thing is something that somebody made a long time ago. پرانا، پرانی

old-age pensioner (**old-age pensioners**) *n* An **old-age pensioner** is a person who is old enough to receive a pension from their employer or the government. عمر رسیدہ پنشن یافتہ

old-fashioned *adj* Something that is **old-fashioned** is no longer used, done, or believed by most people, because it has been replaced by something that is more modern. پرانی وضع کا

olive (**olives**) *n* **Olives** are small green or black fruit with a bitter taste. زیتون ▷ *n* An **olive** or an **olive tree** is a tree on which olives grow. زیتون کا درخت

olive oil (**olive oils**) *n* **Olive oil** is edible oil obtained by pressing olives. زیتون کا تیل

Oman *n* **Oman** is a country in south-east Arabia, on the Gulf of Oman and the Arabian Sea. عمان

omelette (**omelettes**) *n* An **omelette** is a food made by beating eggs and cooking them in a flat pan. آملیٹ

on *adv* When something that uses electricity is **on**, it is using electricity. چالو، چلتی حالت میں ▷ *prep* If someone or something is **on** a surface, it is resting there. پر (ہونا) *There was a large box on the table.*

on behalf of *n* If you do something **on behalf of** someone, you do it for that person as their representative. منجانب

once *adv* If something happens **once**, it happens one time only. ایک بار

one *num* **One** is the number 1. ایک ▷ *pron* You can use **one** to refer to the first of two or more things. اول *One of the twins was thinner than the other.*

one-off (**one-offs**) *n* A **one-off** is something that is made or happens only once. ایک بار ہونے والی چیز یا واقعہ

one's *det* You use **one's** to show that something belongs to people in general. کا ہونا، کی ملکیت ہونا *It is natural to want to care for one's family and children.*

oneself *pron* Speakers or writers use **oneself** to say things about themselves and about other people. اپنے لئے *To work, one must have time to oneself.*

onion (**onions**) *n* An **onion** is a small round vegetable. It is white with a brown skin, and has a strong smell and taste. پیاز

online *adj* If you are **online**, your computer is connected to the Internet. آن لائن ▷ *adv* If you do something **online**, you do it while connected to a computer or the Internet. آن لائن

onlooker (**onlookers**) *n* An **onlooker** is someone who watches an event take place but does not take part in it. خاموش تماشائی

only *adj* If you talk about the **only** thing or person, you mean that there are no others. صرف، واحد ▷ *adv* You use **only** when you are saying how small or short something is. صرف ▷ *adj* If you are an **only** child, you have no brothers or sisters. اکیلا / اکیلی

on time *adj* If you are **on time**, you are not late. وقت پر

onto *prep* If something moves **onto** a surface, it moves to a place on that surface. کے اوپر *The cat climbed onto her lap.* ▷ *prep* When you get **onto** a bus, train, or plane, you enter it. داخل ہونا، پر چڑھنا *He got onto the plane.*

open (**opens, opening, opened**) *adj* You use **open** to describe something which has been opened. کھلی ▷ *v* When you **open** something, or when it **opens**, you move it or it moves so that it is no longer closed. کھولنا ▷ *v* When a shop or office **opens**, people are able to go in. کھلنا

opening hours *npl* **Opening hours** are the times during which a shop, bank, library, or bar is open for business. کھلنے کے اوقات

opera (**operas**) *n* An **opera** is a musical entertainment. It is like a play, but most of the words are sung. نظم اور موسیقی والا ڈرامہ

operate (**operates, operating, operated**) *v* If you **operate** a business or organization, you work to keep it running properly. If a business or organization **operates**, it carries out its work. چلانا ▷ *vi* When surgeons **operate** on a patient, they cut open the patient's body in order to remove, replace, or repair a diseased or damaged part. جراحی کرنا

O

operating theatre (**operating theatres**) *n* An **operating theatre** is a room in a hospital where surgeons carry out operations. جراحی گھر(آپریشن تھیٹر)

operation (**operations**) *n* An **operation** is a highly organized activity that involves many people doing different things. مہم ▷ *n* If a patient has an **operation**, a surgeon cuts open their body in order to remove, replace, or repair a diseased or damaged part. جراحی(چیر پھاڑ)

operator (**operators**) *n* An **operator** is a person who works at a telephone exchange or on the switchboard of an office or hotel. آپریٹر

opinion (**opinions**) *n* Your **opinion** about something is what you think or believe about it. رائے

opinion poll (**opinion polls**) *n* An **opinion poll** involves asking people for their opinion on a particular subject, especially one concerning politics. رائے شماری

opponent (**opponents**) *n* A politician's **opponents** are other politicians who belong to a different party or have different aims or policies. مخالف، مقابل

opportunity (**opportunities**) *n* An **opportunity** is a situation in which it is possible for you to do something that you want to do. موقع

oppose (**opposes, opposing, opposed**) *vt* If you **oppose** someone or their plans or ideas, you disagree with what they want to do and try to prevent them from doing it. مخالفت کرنا

opposed *adj* If you are **opposed** to something, you disagree with it or disapprove of it. مخالف

opposing *adj* **Opposing** ideas or tendencies are totally different from each other. مخالف

opposite *adj* The **opposite** side or part of something is the side or part that is furthest away from you. مخالف ▷ *adv* If one thing is **opposite** another, it is facing it. مقابل ▷ *prep* If one thing is **opposite** another, it is across from it. سامنے، بالمقابل ▷ *adj* If things are **opposite**, they are as different as they can be. الٹا، معکوس، پیچھے کی طرف کرنا

opposition *n* **Opposition** is strong, angry, or violent disagreement and disapproval. مخالفت

optician (**opticians**) *n* An **optician** is someone whose job involves testing people's eyesight and making and selling glasses and contact lenses. آنکھ کا ماہر

optimism *n* **Optimism** is the feeling of being hopeful about the future or about the success of something. رجائیت

optimist (**optimists**) *n* An **optimist** is someone who is hopeful about the future. رجائیت پسند

optimistic *adj* Someone who is **optimistic** is hopeful about the future or about the success of something. رجائیت پسندی

option (**options**) *n* An **option** is one of two or more things that you can choose between. اختیار

optional *adj* If something is **optional**, you can choose whether or not you do it or have it. اختیاری

opt out *v* If you **opt out** of something, you choose not to be involved in it. چھوڑنا *More and more people are opting out of the urban lifestyle.*

or *conj* You use **or** to show what you can choose or what is possible. یا *You can have tea or coffee.*

oral (**orals**) *adj* **Oral** is used to describe things that involve speaking rather than writing. زبانی، دہنی ▷ *n* An **oral** is an examination, especially in a foreign language, that is spoken rather than written. زبانی اِمتحان

orange (**oranges**) *n* **Orange** is a colour between red and yellow. سنترہ ▷ *n* An

orange is a round fruit with a thick skin and lots of juice. نارنگی (پھل)

orange juice (**orange juices**) *n* **Orange juice** is the liquid that can be obtained from an orange and drunk. سنترے کا رس

orchard (**orchards**) *n* An **orchard** is an area of land on which fruit trees are grown. پھلوں کا باغ

orchestra (**orchestras**) *n* An **orchestra** is a large group of musicians who play a variety of different instruments together. آرکیسٹرا (موسیقی گروپ)

orchid (**orchids**) *n* An **orchid** is a plant with brightly coloured, unusually shaped flowers. اورکیڈ (پودا)

ordeal (**ordeals**) *n* An **ordeal** is an extremely unpleasant and difficult experience. سخت آزمائش

order (**orders, ordering, ordered**) *n* If someone gives you an **order**, they tell you to do something. حکم ▷ *vt* If you **order** someone to do something, you tell them to do it. حکم دینا

order form (**order forms**) *n* An **order form** is a document filled in by customers when ordering goods. آرڈر فارم (خریداری فارم)

ordinary *adj* **Ordinary** people or things are not special or different in any way. معمولی

oregano *n* **Oregano** is a herb that is used in cooking. نازبو

organ (**organs**) *n* An **organ** is a large musical instrument with pipes of different lengths through which air is forced. It has keys and pedals rather like a piano, and is often found in a church. آرگن ▷ *n* An **organ** is a part of your body that has a particular purpose or function, for example your heart or your lungs. عضو

organic *adj* **Organic** food is grown without using chemicals. قدرتی

organism (**organisms**) *n* An **organism** is a living thing. خردحیاتیہ

organization (**organizations**) *n* An **organization** is an official group of people, for example a business or a club. تنظیم

organize (**organizes, organizing, organized**) *vt* If you **organize** an activity or event, you make all the arrangements for it. نظم کرنا

Orient *n* The eastern part of Asia is sometimes referred to as the **Orient**. (*literary, old-fashioned*) مشرقی ایشیا

oriental *adj* You use **oriental** to talk about things that come from places in eastern Asia. استشراقی

origin (**origins**) *n* You can refer to the beginning, cause, or source of something as its **origin** or its **origins**. اصل

original *adj* You use **original** to refer to something that existed at the beginning of a process or activity, or the characteristics that something had when it first existed. اصلی

originally *adv* When you say what happened or was the case **originally**, you are saying what happened or was the case when something began or came into existence, often to contrast it with what happened later. اصل طور پر

ornament (**ornaments**) *n* An **ornament** is an attractive object that you display in your home or garden. زیور

orphan (**orphans**) *n* An **orphan** is a child whose parents are dead. یتیم

ostrich (**ostriches**) *n* An **ostrich** is a very large, long-necked African bird that cannot fly. شتر مرغ

other *adj* **Other** people or things are different people or things. دوسرا

otherwise *adv* You use **otherwise** when stating the general condition or quality of something, when you are also mentioning an exception to this. بصورت دیگر ▷ *conj* You use **otherwise** after stating a situation or fact, to say what

O

the result or consequence would be if this situation or fact was not the case. ورنہ، نہیں تو *I'm lucky that I'm interested in school work; otherwise I'd go mad.* ▷ *adv* You use **otherwise** to say what the result would be if things were different. بصورت دیگر، دوسری صورت میں

otter (**otters**) *n* An **otter** is a small animal with brown fur, short legs, and a long tail. Otters swim well and eat fish. اودبلاؤ (جانور)

ought *vt* If someone **ought to** do something, it is the right thing to do. درست ہونا، مناسب ہونا

ounce (**ounces**) *n* An **ounce** is a unit of weight. There are sixteen ounces in a pound and one ounce is equal to 28.35 grams. اونس

our *det* You use **our** to show that something belongs to you and one or more other people. ہمارا *Our house is near the school.*

ours *pron* You use **ours** when you are talking about something that belongs to you and one or more other people. ہماری. ہمارا *That car is ours.*

ourselves *pron* You use **ourselves** when you are talking about yourself and one or more other people. ہم خود *We sat by the fire to keep ourselves warm.* ▷ *pron* 'We did it **ourselves**' means that you and one or more other people did it without anymore help. ہم بھی *We built the house ourselves.*

out *adj* If a light is **out**, it is no longer shining. غائب ہونا، چلا جانا ▷ *adv* If you are **out**, you are not at home. باہر ▷ *prep* If you go **out** of a place, you leave it. باہر *She ran out of the house.*

outbreak (**outbreaks**) *n* An **outbreak** of something unpleasant is a sudden occurrence of it. وبائی حالت

outcome (**outcomes**) *n* The **outcome** of an action or process is the result of it. نتیجہ

outdoor *adj* **Outdoor** activities or things take place or are used outside, rather than in a building. بیرونی

outdoors *adv* If something happens **outdoors**, it happens outside in the fresh air rather than in a building. بیرونی طور پر

outfit (**outfits**) *n* An **outfit** is a set of clothes. لباس (کسی خاص مقصد کے لئے)

outgoing *adj* **Outgoing** things such as planes, mail, and passengers are leaving or being sent somewhere. باہر جانے والی

outing (**outings**) *n* An **outing** is a short enjoyable trip, usually with a group of people, away from your home, school, or place of work. سفر

outline (**outlines**) *n* An **outline** is a general explanation or description of something. وضاحت یا بیان

outlook (**outlooks**) *n* Your **outlook** is your general attitude towards life. نظریہ

out of date *adj* Something that is **out of date** is old-fashioned and no longer useful. پرانی

out-of-doors *adj* When you are **out-of-doors**, you are not inside a building, but in the open air. کھلے میں

outrageous *adj* If you describe something as **outrageous**, you are emphasizing that it is unacceptable or very shocking. اِشتعال انگیز

outset *n* If something happens at the **outset** of an event, process, or period of time, it happens at the beginning of it. If something happens from the **outset**, it happens from the beginning and continues to happen. شروعات میں

outside (**outsides**) *adj* An **outside** thing surrounds another thing. باہری ▷ *adv* If you are **outside**, you are not in a building. بیرونی طور پر ▷ *n* The **outside** of something is the part that covers the rest of it. باہر کی طرف (پھل) ▷ *prep* If you are **outside** something or somewhere, you are not inside it. باہر کی طرف *The man was waiting outside a shop.*

outsize *adj* **Outsize** or **outsized** things are much larger than usual or much larger than you would expect. معمول سے بڑی جسامت کی

outskirts *npl* **The outskirts** of a city or town are the parts that are farthest from its centre. باہری کنارے پر

outspoken *adj* If you are **outspoken**, you give your opinions about things openly, even if they shock people. منہ پھٹ، کھری کھری سنانے والا

outstanding *adj* If you describe a person or their work as **outstanding**, you think that they are remarkable and impressive. قابل قدر

oval *adj* **Oval** things have a shape that is like a circle but is wider in one direction than the other. بیضوی

ovary (**ovaries**) *n* A woman's **ovaries** are the two organs in her body that produce eggs. بیضہ دانی

oven (**ovens**) *n* An **oven** is a cooker or part of a cooker that is like a box with a door. You cook food inside an oven. اوون

oven glove (**oven gloves**) *n* An **oven glove** is a glove made of thick material, used for holding hot dishes from an oven. گرم چیزیں پکڑنے کے لئے دستانہ

ovenproof *adj* An **ovenproof** dish is one that has been specially made to be used in an oven without being damaged by the heat. جلنے سے محفوظ

over *adj* If something is **over**, it has finished. ختم ہونا ▷ *prep* If one thing is **over** another thing, the first thing is above or higher than the second thing. پر (ہونا)

overall *adv* You use **overall** to indicate that you are talking about a situation in general or about the whole of something. مجموعی طور پر

overalls *npl* **Overalls** consist of a single piece of clothing that combines trousers and a jacket. You wear overalls over your clothes in order to protect them while you are working. لبادے(پینٹ اور جیکیٹ ایک ہی کپڑے میں تراشے ہوئے)

overcast *adj* If it is **overcast**, or if the sky or the day is **overcast**, the sky is completely covered with cloud and there is not much light. بادلوں کی وجہ سے اندھیرا

overcharge (**overcharges, overcharging, overcharged**) *vt* If someone **overcharges** you, they charge you too much for their goods or services. زیادہ معاوضہ بتانا

overcoat (**overcoats**) *n* An **overcoat** is a thick warm coat. اوورکوٹ

overcome (**overcomes, overcoming, overcame**) *vt* If you **overcome** a problem or a feeling, you successfully deal with it and control it. قابو پانا

overdone *adj* If food is **overdone**, it has been spoiled by being cooked for too long. زیادہ کارکردگی سے خراب کر دینا

overdraft (**overdrafts**) *n* If you have an **overdraft**, you have spent more money than you have in your bank account. جمع رقم سے زیادہ

overdrawn *adj* If you are **overdrawn** or if your bank account is **overdrawn**, you have spent more money than you have in your account, and so you are in debt to the bank. جمع رقم سے زیادہ قرض

overdue *adj* If you say that a change or an event is **overdue**, you mean that it should have happened before now. ہونے کو باقی

overestimate (**overestimates, overestimating, overestimated**) *vt* If you **overestimate** someone or something, you think that they are better, bigger, or more important than they really are. اصلیت سے زیادہ اندازہ لگانا

overhead projector (**overhead projectors**) *n* An **overhead projector** is a machine that has a light inside it and makes the writing or pictures on a sheet

O

of plastic appear on a screen or wall. The abbreviation 'OHP' is also used. اوور ہیڈ پروجیکٹر

overheads *npl* The **overheads** of a business are its regular and essential expenses. واجب اخراجات

overlook (**overlooks, overlooking, overlooked**) *vt* If a building or window **overlooks** a place, you can see the place from the building or window. اوپر سے دیکھنا

overrule (**overrules, overruling, overruled**) *vt* If someone in authority **overrules** a person or their decision, they officially decide that the decision is incorrect or not valid. مسترد کرنا

overseas *adv* If something happens or exists **overseas**, it happens or exists abroad. بیرونِ ملک

oversight (**oversights**) *n* In business, **oversight** of a system or process is the responsibility for making sure that it works efficiently and correctly. نگرانی ▷ *n* If there has been an **oversight**, someone has forgotten to do something which they should have done. فروگزاشت / غلطی سے

oversleep (**oversleeps, oversleeping, overslept**) *vi* If you **oversleep**, you sleep longer than you should have done. بسیار خوابی

overtake (**overtakes, overtaking, overtook, overtaken**) *v* If you **overtake** or **overtake** a moving vehicle or person, you pass them because you are moving faster than they are. آگے نکل جانا، جا لینا

overtime *n* **Overtime** is time that you spend doing your job in addition to your normal working hours. اوور ٹائم

overweight *adj* Someone who is **overweight** weighs more than is considered healthy or attractive. موٹاپا

owe (**owes, owing, owed**) *vt* If you **owe** money to someone, they have lent it to you and you have not yet paid it back. قرضدار ہونا

owing to *prep* If something is **owing to** another thing, it is a result of that thing. ۔۔۔ کی وجہ سے، ۔۔۔ کی بنا پر *He was out of work owing to an injury.*

owl (**owls**) *n* An **owl** is a bird with large eyes which hunts small animals at night. الو

own (**owns, owning, owned**) *adj* You use **own** to say that something belongs to you. اپنا، ذاتی ▷ *vt* If you **own** something, it is your property. ملکیت میں ہونا

owner (**owners**) *n* The **owner** of something is the person to whom it belongs. مالک

own up *v* If you **own up** to something wrong that you have done, you admit that you did it. کھلے دل سے اعتراف کرنا *Own up to your failure, but don't dwell on it.*

oxygen *n* **Oxygen** is a colourless gas in the air which is needed by all plants and animals. آکسیجن

oyster (**oysters**) *n* An **oyster** is a large flat shellfish which produces pearls. سیپی

ozone *n* **Ozone** is a form of oxygen. There is a layer of ozone high above the earth's surface. اوزون (آکسیجن کے تین ایٹم والا سالمہ)

ozone layer *n* **The ozone layer** is the area high above the Earth's surface that protects living things from the harmful effects of the sun. اوزون کی پرت (ہوا کے گھیری میں)

p

PA (**PAs**) *abbr* A **PA** is a person who does office work and administrative work for someone. **PA** is an abbreviation for 'personal assistant'. پرسنل اسسٹنٹ

pace (**paces**) *n* The **pace** of something is the speed at which it happens or is done. رفتار

pacemaker (**pacemakers**) *n* A **pacemaker** is a device that is placed inside someone's body in order to help their heart beat in the right way. پیس میکر (آلہ یا مشین)

Pacific Ocean *n* **The Pacific Ocean** is a very large sea to the west of North and South America, and to the east of Asia and Australia. بحر الکاہل

pack (**packs, packing, packed**) *n* A **pack** of things is a collection of them that is sold or given together in a box or bag. مجموعہ ▷ *vt* When you **pack** a bag, you put clothes and other things into it, because you are leaving a place or going on holiday. پیک کرنا

package (**packages**) *n* A **package** is a small parcel. پارسل

packaging *n* **Packaging** is the container or wrappings that something is sold in. پیک کرنے کا ڈبہ یا غلاف

packed *adj* A place that is **packed** is very crowded. پیک کیا ہوا

packed lunch (**packed lunches**) *n* A **packed lunch** is food, for example, sandwiches, which you take to work, to school, or on a trip and eat as your lunch. پیک کیا ہوا کھانا (لنچ)

packet (**packets**) *n* A **packet** is a small box, bag, or envelope in which a quantity of something is sold. پیکیٹ

pad (**pads**) *n* A **pad** is a thick flat piece of a material such as cloth or foam rubber. پیڈ، گدی

paddle (**paddles, paddling, paddled**) *n* A **paddle** is a short oar. You use it to move a small boat through water. پیدل ▷ *vt* If someone **paddles** a boat, they move it using a paddle. پیدل چلانا ▷ *vi* If you **paddle**, you walk in shallow water. پانی پر حرکت کرنا

paddling pool (**paddling pools**) *n* A **paddling pool** is a shallow artificial pool for children to paddle in. کم پانی والا تالاب (بچوں کے لیے)

padlock (**padlocks**) *n* A **padlock** is a lock which is used for fastening two things together. دو چیزوں میں ایک ساتھ تالا

page (**pages, paging, paged**) *n* A **page** is a side of one of the pieces of paper in a book, magazine, or newspaper. صفحہ ▷ *v* If someone **is paged**, they receive a message over a speaker that someone is trying to contact them. زبانی خبر دینا

pager (**pagers**) *n* A **pager** is a small electronic device which gives you a message when someone is trying to contact you. پیجر

paid *adj* **Paid** means to do with the money a worker receives from his or her employer. You can say, for example, that someone is well **paid** when they receive a lot of money for the work that they do. ادا شدہ

pail (**pails**) *n* A **pail** is a bucket, usually made of metal or wood. (*old-fashioned*) بالٹی

pain (**pains**) *n* If you feel **pain**, or if you are in **pain**, you feel great discomfort in a part of your body, because of illness or an injury. درد

painful *adj* If a part of your body is **painful**, it hurts. درد بھرا

painkiller (**painkillers**) *n* A **painkiller** is a drug which reduces or stops physical pain. درد کش

paint (**paints, painting, painted**) *n* **Paint** is a liquid used to decorate buildings, or to make a picture. رنگ ▷ *v* If you **paint** a wall or a door, you cover it with **paint**. رنگ کرنا، رنگنا ▷ *v* If you **paint** something on a piece of paper or cloth, you make a picture of it using **paint**. رنگ سے تصویر بنانا

paintbrush (**paintbrushes**) *n* A **paintbrush** is a brush which you use for painting. رنگ برش

painter (**painters**) *n* A **painter** is an artist who paints pictures. رنگ ساز

painting (**paintings**) *n* A **painting** is a picture which someone has painted. نقاشی

pair (**pairs**) *n* A **pair** of things are two things of the same size and shape that are intended to be used together. جوڑا

Pakistan *n* **Pakistan** is a republic in South Asia, on the Arabian Sea. پاکستان

Pakistani (**Pakistanis**) *adj* **Pakistani** means belonging or relating to Pakistan, or to its people or culture. پاکستانی ▷ *n* A **Pakistani** is a Pakistani citizen, or a person of Pakistani origin. پاکستانی

pal (**pals**) *n* Your **pals** are your friends. (*informal, old-fashioned*) دوست

palace (**palaces**) *n* A **palace** is a very large splendid house, especially the home of a king, queen, or president. محل

pale (**paler, palest**) *adj* Something that is **pale** is not strong or bright in colour. کمزور

Palestine *n* **Palestine** is an area between the Jordan River and the Mediterranean Sea. فلسطین

Palestinian (**Palestinians**) *adj* **Palestinian** means belonging or relating to the region between the River Jordan and the Mediterranean Sea. فلسطینی ▷ *n* A **Palestinian** is an Arab who comes from the region that used to be called Palestine. فلسطینی

palm (**palms**) *n* The **palm** of your hand is the inside part of your hand, between your fingers and your wrist. ہتھیلی ▷ *n* A **palm** or a **palm tree** is a tree that grows in hot countries. It has long leaves at the top, and no branches. تاڑ (پیڑ)

pamphlet (**pamphlets**) *n* A **pamphlet** is a very thin book with a paper cover, which gives information about something. پرچہ

pan (**pans**) *n* A **pan** is a round metal container with a handle, which is used for cooking things, usually on top of a cooker. کڑھائی

Panama *n* **Panama** is a republic in Central America. پناما

pancake (**pancakes**) *n* A **pancake** is a thin, flat, circular piece of cooked batter that is eaten hot, often with a sweet or savoury filling. چپٹا کیک

panda (**pandas**) *n* A **panda** is a large animal with black and white fur which lives in China. پانڈا (جانور)

panic (**panics, panicking, panicked**) *n* **Panic** is a strong feeling of anxiety or fear that makes you act without thinking carefully. خوف وہراس ▷ *v* If you **panic**, or if someone or something **panics** you, you become anxious or afraid, and act without thinking carefully. بغیر سوچے قدم اٹھانا

panther (**panthers**) *n* A **panther** is a large wild animal that belongs to the cat family. Panthers are usually black. تیندوا، گلدار

pantomime (**pantomimes**) *n* A **pantomime** is a funny musical play for children, usually performed at Christmas. موسیقی کھیل (بچوں کے لئے)

pants *npl* **Pants** are a piece of underwear with two holes to put your legs through and elastic round the top. پتلون

paper (**papers**) *n* **Paper** is a material that you write on or wrap things with. کاغذ ▷ *n* A **paper** is a newspaper. اخبار

paperback (**paperbacks**) *n* A **paperback** is a book with a paper cover. پیپر بیک

paperclip (**paperclips**) *n* A **paperclip** is a small piece of bent wire that is used to fasten papers together. پیپر کلپ

paper round (**paper rounds**) *n* A **paper round** is a job of delivering newspapers to houses along a particular route. دائروی روٹ میں اخبار فروشی

paperweight (**paperweights**) *n* A **paperweight** is a small heavy object which you place on papers to prevent them from being disturbed or blown away. پیپر ویٹ

paperwork *n* **Paperwork** consists of the letters, reports, and records which have to be dealt with as the routine part of a job. کاغذی کارروائی

paprika *n* **Paprika** is a red powder used for flavouring meat and other food. رتن جوت

parachute (**parachutes**) *n* A **parachute** is a device which enables a person to jump from an aircraft and float safely to the ground. It consists of a large piece of thin cloth attached to your body by strings. پیراشوٹ

parade (**parades**) *n* A **parade** is a line of people or vehicles moving together through a public place in order to celebrate an important day or event. پریڈ

paradise *n* According to some religions, **paradise** is a wonderful place where people go after they die, if they have led good lives. جنت

paraffin *n* **Paraffin** is a strong-smelling liquid which is used as a fuel in heaters, lamps, and engines. ایندھن

paragraph (**paragraphs**) *n* A **paragraph** is a section of a piece of writing. A paragraph always begins on a new line and contains at least one sentence. پیراگراف

Paraguay *n* **Paraguay** is an inland republic in South America. پیراگوئے

Paraguayan (**Paraguayans**) *adj* **Paraguayan** means of or relating to Paraguay, its people, or its culture. پیراگوائی ▷ *n* A **Paraguayan** is a citizen of Paraguay, or a person of Paraguayan origin. پیراگوائی

parallel *adj* **Parallel** events or situations happen at the same time as one another, or are similar to one another. متوازی

paralysed *adj* If someone or part of their body is **paralysed**, they have no feeling in their body, or in part of their body, and are unable to move. لقوہ زدہ

paramedic (**paramedics**) *n* A **paramedic** is a person whose training is similar to that of a nurse and who helps to do medical work. پیرامیڈک

parcel (**parcels**) *n* A **parcel** is something wrapped in paper, usually so that it can be sent to someone by post. پارسل

pardon (**pardons**) excl You say '**Pardon?**' when you want someone to repeat what they have just said because you have not heard or understood it. معافی چاہتا ہوں! ▷ *n* If someone who has been found guilty of a crime is given a **pardon**, they are officially allowed to go free and are not punished. معافی

parent (**parents**) *n* A **parent** is a father or mother. والدین

park (**parks, parking, parked**) *n* A **park** is a place with grass and trees. People go to **parks** to take exercise or play games. پارک، ٹہلنے یا ورزش کرنے اور کھیلنے کی جگہ ▷ *v* When someone **parks** a car, they leave it somewhere. گاڑی کھڑی کرنا

parking *n* **Parking** is the action of moving a vehicle into a place in a car park or by the side of the road where it can be left. پارکنگ

parking meter (**parking meters**) *n* A **parking meter** is a device which you

p

have to put money into when you park in a parking space. پارکنگ میٹر (وقت درج کرنے والا)

parking ticket (**parking tickets**) *n* A **parking ticket** is a piece of paper with instructions to pay a fine, and is put on your car when you have parked it somewhere illegally. پارکنگ ٹکٹ

parliament (**parliaments**) *n* The **parliament** of a country is the group of people who make or change its laws. پارلیمان

parole *n* If a prisoner is given **parole**, he or she is released before the official end of their prison sentence and has to promise to behave well. پیرول (قیدی کا وقت سے پہلے چھوٹ جانا)

parrot (**parrots**) *n* A **parrot** is a tropical bird with a curved beak and brightly coloured or grey feathers. Parrots can be kept as pets. طوطا

parsley *n* **Parsley** is a small plant with curly leaves used for flavouring or decorating savoury food. پارسلے (اجمود جیسی چیز)

parsnip (**parsnips**) *n* A **parsnip** is a root vegetable similar in shape to a carrot. پارسنپ (ایک قسم کا گاجر)

part (**parts**) *n* **Part** of something is a piece or a section of it. حصہ، جزو

partial *adj* You use **partial** to refer to something that is true or exists to some extent, but is not complete or total. جزوی

participate (**participates, participating, participated**) *vi* If you **participate** in an activity, you are involved in it with other people. حصہ لینا

particular *adj* You use **particular** to emphasize that you are talking about one thing or one kind of thing rather than other similar ones. مخصوص

particularly *adv* You use **particularly** to indicate that what you are saying applies especially to one thing or situation. خاص طور سے

parting (**partings**) *n* **Parting** is the act of leaving a particular person or place. جدائی

partly *adv* You use **partly** to indicate that something is true or exists to some extent, but not completely. جزوی طور پر

partner (**partners**) *n* Your **partner** is the person you are married to or are having a long-term romantic relationship with. ساجھی دار

partridge (**partridges**) *n* A **partridge** is a wild bird with brown feathers, a round body, and a short tail. تیتر

part-time *adj* If someone is a **part-time** worker or has a **part-time** job, they work for only part of each day or week. جزوقتی ▷ *adv* If someone works **part-time**, they work for only part of each day or week. جزوقتی طور پر

part with *v* If you **part with** something that you would prefer to keep, you give it or sell it to someone else. حصہ لگانا، ساجھی کرنا *Think carefully before parting with money.*

party (**parties, partying, partied**) *n* A *party* is a social event at which people enjoy themselves doing things such as eating or dancing. تقریب ▷ *n* A **party** of people is a group of them doing something together, for example travelling. گروہ ▷ *vi* If you **party**, you enjoy yourself doing things with other people such as eating and dancing. دعوت دینا

pass (**passes, passing, passed**) *n* A **pass** is a document that allows you to do something. پاس ▷ *n* A **pass** is a narrow way between two mountains. درہ ▷ *n* A **pass** in an examination, test, or course is a successful result in it. کامیاب ▷ *vt* If you **pass** something to someone, you give it to them. دینا، حوالے کرنا ▷ *vt* When you **pass** someone, you go by them. گزرنا ▷ *v* If you **pass** a test, you do well. پاس کرنا، کامیاب ہونا

passage (**passages**) *n* A **passage** is a long, narrow space between walls or fences connecting one room or place with another. راہداری ▷ *n* A **passage** in a book, speech, or piece of music is a section of it. حصہ

passenger (**passengers**) *n* A **passenger** in a bus, boat, or plane is a person who is travelling in it, but who is not driving it or working on it. سواری

passion fruit (**passion fruit**) *n* A **passion fruit** is a small, round, brown fruit that is produced by certain types of tropical flower. انڈے جیسا پھل

passive *adj* If you describe someone as **passive**, you mean they do not take action but instead let things happen to them. جامد

pass out *v* If you **pass out**, you faint or collapse. مرنا *He felt sick and dizzy and then passed out.*

Passover *n* **Passover** is a Jewish festival beginning in March or April and lasting for seven or eight days. یہودیوں کی عید

passport (**passports**) *n* Your **passport** is an official document which you need to show when you enter or leave a country. پاسپورٹ

password (**passwords**) *n* A **password** is a secret word or phrase that enables you to enter a place or use a computer system. پاس ورڈ (خفیہ شناختی لفظ)

past *adj* **Past** events and things happened or existed before the present time. ماضی کا ▷ *n* The **past** is the period of time before now. ماضی ▷ *prep* You use **past** when you are telling the time. باقی ہونا، بچا ہونا *It was ten past eleven.* ▷ *prep* Something that is **past** a place is on the other side of it. پیچھے *It's just past the school there.*

pasta *n* **Pasta** is a type of food made from a mixture of flour, eggs, and water that is formed into different shapes. Spaghetti and macaroni are types of pasta. پاستہ

paste (**pastes, pasting, pasted**) *n* **Paste** is a soft, wet mixture, which you can spread easily. آمیزہ ▷ *vt* If you **paste** something on to a surface, you stick it with glue. چپکانا ▷ *vt* If you **paste** words or pictures on a computer, you copy them from one place and put them somewhere new. پیسٹ کرنا (کمپیوٹر)

pasteurized *adj* **Pasteurized** milk, cream, or cheese has had bacteria removed from it by a special heating process to make it safer to eat or drink. جراثیم سے پاک

pastime (**pastimes**) *n* A **pastime** is something that you enjoy doing in your spare time. وقت گزاری

pastry *n* **Pastry** is a food made of flour, fat, and water that is used for making pies and flans. پیسٹری (کیک)

patch (**patches**) *n* A **patch** on a surface is a part of it which is different in appearance from the area around it. پیوند

patched *adj* Something that is **patched**</ has been mended by having a piece of material fastened over a hole. پیوند لگا ہوا

paternity leave *n* If a man has **paternity leave**, his employer allows him some time off work because his child has just been born. پدرانہ چھٹی

path (**paths**) *n* A **path** is a strip of ground that people walk along. راستہ (پاتھ)

pathetic *adj* If you describe a person or animal as **pathetic**, you mean that they are sad and weak or helpless, and they make you feel very sorry for them. قابل رحم

patience *n* If you have **patience**, you are able to stay calm and not get annoyed, for example when something takes a long time. صبر

patient (**patients**) *adj* If you are **patient**, you don't get angry quickly. تحمل مزاج، برداشت کرنے والا، صابر ▷ *n* A **patient** is someone that a nurse or a doctor is looking after. مریض

patio (**patios**) *n* A **patio** is a paved area in a garden, where people can sit to eat or relax. باغ میں پٹا ہوا حصہ

patriotic *adj* Someone who is **patriotic** loves their country and feels very loyal towards it. محب وطن

patrol (**patrols**) *n* **Patrol** is the action of moving round an area or building in order to make sure that there is no trouble there. گشت

patrol car (**patrol cars**) *n* A **patrol car** is a police car used for patrolling streets and roads. گشتی کار

pattern (**patterns**) *n* A **pattern** is a particular way in which something is usually or repeatedly done. نمونہ

pause (**pauses**) *n* A **pause** is a short period when something stops before it continues again. رکاوٹ

pavement (**pavements**) *n* A **pavement** is a path with a hard surface by the side of a road. فٹ پاتھ

pavilion (**pavilions**) *n* A **pavilion** is a building on the edge of a sports field where players can change their clothes and wash. پویلین

paw (**paws**) *n* The **paws** of an animal such as a cat, dog, or bear are its feet. پنجہ

pawnbroker (**pawnbrokers**) *n* A **pawnbroker** is a person who will lend you money if you give them something that you own. The pawnbroker can sell that thing if you do not pay back the money before a certain time. گروی رکھ کر قرض دینے والا

pay (**pays, paying, paid**) *n* Your **pay** is the money that you get from your employer as wages or salary. تنخواہ ▷ *v* When you **pay** an amount of money to someone, you give it to them because you are buying something from them or because you owe it to them. ادا کرنا

payable *adj* If an amount of money is **payable**, it has to be paid or it can be paid. قابل ادائیگی

pay back *v* If you **pay back** money that you have borrowed from someone, you give them an equal amount at a later time. واپس لوٹانا *He will have to pay back everything he has stolen.*

payment (**payments**) *n* **Payment** is the act of paying money to someone or of being paid. رقم

payphone (**payphones**) *n* A **payphone** is a telephone which you need to put coins or a card in before you can make a call. Payphones are usually in public places. سکہ والا فون

PC (**PCs**) *n* A **PC** is a computer that is used by one person at a time in a business, a school, or at home. **PC** is an abbreviation for 'personal computer'. پرسنل کمپیوٹر

PDF (**PDFs**) *n* **PDF** files are computer documents which look exactly like the original documents, regardless of which software or operating system was used to create them. **PDF** is an abbreviation for 'Portable Document Format'. پی ڈی ایف (کمپیوٹر فائل)

peace *n* When there is **peace** in a country, it is not involved in a war. امن

peaceful *adj* **Peaceful** means not involving war or violence. پر امن

peach (**peaches**) *n* A **peach** is a soft, round, juicy fruit with sweet yellow flesh and pinky-yellow skin. آڑو، شفتالو

peacock (**peacocks**) *n* A **peacock** is a large bird. The male has a very large tail covered with blue and green spots, which it can spread out like a fan. مور

peak (**peaks**) *n* The **peak** of a process or activity is the point at which it is at its strongest, most successful, or most fully developed. منتہا

peak hours *npl* **Peak hours** are the busiest hours, for example in traffic. مصروف ترین اوقات

peanut (**peanuts**) *n* **Peanuts** are small nuts often eaten as a snack. مونگ پھلی

peanut allergy (**peanut allergies**) *n* If you have a **peanut allergy**, you become ill if you eat peanuts or peanut butter, or come into contact with peanuts or peanut butter. مونگ پھلی سے الرجی

peanut butter *n* **Peanut butter** is a brown paste made out of crushed peanuts which you can spread on bread and eat. مونگ پھلی سے بنا مکھن

pear (**pears**) *n* A **pear** is a juicy fruit which is narrow at the top and wider at the bottom. It has white flesh and green or yellow skin. ناشپاتی

pearl (**pearls**) *n* A **pearl** is a hard, shiny, white, ball-shaped object which grows inside the shell of an oyster. Pearls are used for making jewellery. موتی

peas *npl* **Peas** are small, round, green seeds eaten as a vegetable. مٹر

peat *n* **Peat** is dark decaying plant material which is found in some cool wet regions. It can be burned as a fuel or used as compost. دلدلی کوئلہ

pebble (**pebbles**) *n* A **pebble** is a small stone. گوٹی

peculiar *adj* If you describe someone or something as **peculiar**, you think that they are strange or unusual, often in an unpleasant way. عجیب

pedal (**pedals**) *n* The **pedals** on a bicycle are the two parts that you push with your feet in order to make the bicycle move. پیڈل (سائیکل کا)

pedestrian (**pedestrians**) *n* A **pedestrian** is a person who is walking, especially in a town. پاپیادہ

pedestrian crossing (**pedestrian crossings**) *n* A **pedestrian crossing** is a place where pedestrians can cross a street and where motorists must stop to let them cross. پاپیادہ چوراہا

pedestrianized *adj* A **pedestrianized** area has been made into an area that is intended for pedestrians, not vehicles. علاقہ کو پاپیادہ کے لئے وقف کرنا

pedestrian precinct (**pedestrian precincts**) *n* A **pedestrian precinct** is a street or part of a town where vehicles are not allowed. پاپیادہ علاقہ (گاڑیاں ممنوع)

pedigree *adj* A **pedigree** animal is descended from animals which have all been of a particular breed, and is therefore considered to be of good quality. اچھی نسل کا (جانور)

peel (**peels, peeling, peeled**) *n* The **peel** of a fruit such as a lemon or apple is its skin. چھلکا

vt When you **peel** fruit or vegetables, you remove their skins. چھلکا اتارنا

peg (**pegs**) *n* A **peg** is a small hook or knob on a wall or door which is used for hanging things on. الگنی

Pekinese (**Pekineses**) *n* A **Pekinese** is a type of small dog with long hair, short legs, and a short, flat nose. لمبے بالدار چھوٹا کتا

pelican (**pelicans**) *n* A **pelican** is a type of large water bird. It catches fish and keeps them in the bottom part of its beak which is shaped like a large bag. مچھلی شکاری چڑیا (جسیم)

pelican crossing (**pelican crossings**) *n* A **pelican crossing** is a place pedestrians can cross a busy road. They press a button at the side of the road, which operates traffic lights to stop the traffic. پیلیکن کراسنگ (بٹن دبا کر لائن کلیر کرنا)

pellet (**pellets**) *n* A **pellet** is a small ball of paper, mud, lead, or other material. گولی (آٹے وغیرہ کی)

pelvis (**pelvises**) *n* Your **pelvis** is the wide curved group of bones at the level of your hips. کولے کی ہڈیاں

pen (**pens**) *n* A **pen** is a writing instrument, which you use to write in ink. قلم

penalize (**penalizes, penalizing, penalized**) *vt* If someone is **penalized** for something, they are made to suffer some disadvantage because of it. سزا دینا

penalty (**penalties**) *n* A **penalty** is a punishment for doing something which is against a law or rule. سزا، جرمانہ

pencil (**pencils**) *n* A **pencil** is a thin wooden rod with graphite down the centre which is used for writing or drawing. پنسل

pencil case (**pencil cases**) *n* A **pencil case** is a small bag, etc. for holding pencils and pens. پنسل کیس

p

pencil sharpener (**pencil sharpeners**) *n* A **pencil sharpener** is a small device with a blade inside, used for making pencils sharp. پنسل شارپنر (چھیلنے والا)

pendant (**pendants**) *n* A **pendant** is an ornament on a chain that you wear round your neck. نیکلیس (چین میں لٹکتا پتھر)

penfriend (**penfriends**) *n* A **penfriend** is someone you write friendly letters to and receive letters from, although the two of you may never have met. قلمی دوست

penguin (**penguins**) *n* A **penguin** is a black and white sea bird found mainly in the South Pole. Penguins cannot fly. پینگوئن

penicillin *n* **Penicillin** is a drug that kills bacteria and is used to treat infections. پینیسیلین

peninsula (**peninsulas**) *n* A **peninsula** is a long narrow piece of land that is joined at one part to the mainland and is almost completely surrounded by water. جزیرہ نما

penknife (**penknives**) *n* A **penknife** is a small knife with a blade that folds back into the handle. دستے والا چاقو

penny (**pennies, pence**) *n* In Britain, a **penny** is a coin or an amount which is worth one hundredth of a pound. پینی (سکہ)

pension (**pensions**) *n* A **pension** is a sum of money which a retired, widowed, or disabled person regularly receives from the state or from a former employer. پنشن

pensioner (**pensioners**) *n* A **pensioner** is a person who receives a pension. پنشن یافتہ

pentathlon (**pentathlons**) *n* A **pentathlon** is an athletics competition in which each person must compete in five different events. پہلوانی کا مقابلہ (ہر ایک کو ۵ بار موقع)

penultimate *adj* The **penultimate** thing in a series is the one before the last. (*formal*) آخری سے پہلا

people *npl* **People** are men, women, and children. لوگ

pepper (**peppers**) *n* **Pepper** is a spice with a hot taste which you put on food. کالی مرچ ▷ *n* A **pepper** is a green, red, or yellow vegetable with seeds inside it. مرچ، مرچی

peppermill (**peppermills**) *n* A **peppermill** is a machine for grinding pepper into powder. کالی مرچ کی چکی

peppermint *n* **Peppermint** is a strong fresh-tasting flavouring that is obtained from a plant or made artificially. پیپرمنٹ

per (**prep**) You use **per** to talk about each one of something. For example, if a vehicle is travelling at 40 miles **per** hour, it travels 40 miles each hour. فی *Buses use much less fuel per person than cars.*

per cent *adv* You use **per cent** to talk about amounts. For example, if an amount is 10 per cent (10%) of a larger amount, it is equal to 10 hundredths of the larger amount. فی صد

percentage (**percentages**) *n* A **percentage** is a fraction of an amount expressed as a particular number of hundredths. فی صد

percussion *n* **Percussion** instruments are musical instruments that you hit, such as drums. تھاپ (والے ساز)

perfect *adj* Something that is **perfect** is as good as it can possibly be. مکمل، کامل

perfection *n* **Perfection** is the quality of being perfect. کامل

perfectly *adv* You can use **perfectly** to emphasize an adjective or adverb, especially when you think the person you are talking to might doubt what you are saying. انتہائی طور پر

perform (**performs, performing, performed**) *vt* When you **perform** a task or action, you complete it. مظاہرہ کرنا

performance (**performances**) *n* A **performance** involves entertaining an audience by singing, dancing, or acting. کارکردگی

perfume (**perfumes**) *n* **Perfume** is a pleasant-smelling liquid which women put on their necks and wrists to make themselves smell nice. خوشبو

perhaps *adv* You use **perhaps** when you are not sure about something. شاید

period (**periods**) *n* A particular **period** is a particular length of time. وقفہ، مدت

perjury *n* If someone who is giving evidence in a court of law commits **perjury**, they lie. دروغ حلفی

perm (**perms**) *n* If you have a **perm**, your hair is curled and treated with chemicals so that it stays curly for several months. دیرپا خم (بالوں کے)

permanent *adj* **Permanent** means lasting for ever or occurring all the time. مستقل

permanently *adv* If something lasts or occurs **permanently**, it lasts for ever or occurs all the time. مستقلاً

permission *n* If you give someone **permission** to do something, you tell them that they can do it. اجازت

permit (**permits**) *n* A **permit** is an official document allowing you to do something. پرمٹ (اجازت نامہ)

persecute (**persecutes, persecuting, persecuted**) *vt* If someone is **persecuted**, they are treated cruelly and unfairly, often because of their race or beliefs. ایذا دینا

persevere (**perseveres, persevering, persevered**) *vi* If you **persevere** with something difficult, you continue doing it and do not give up. ثابت قدم رہنا

Persian *adj* Something that is **Persian** belongs or relates to the ancient kingdom of Persia, or sometimes to the modern state of Iran. فارسی

persistent *adj* If something bad is **persistent**, it continues to exist or happen for a long time. ضدی، بار بار ہونے والی

person (**people, persons**) *n* A **person** is a man, woman, or child. شخص

personal *adj* A **personal** opinion, quality, or thing belongs or relates to a particular person. ذاتی

personal assistant (**personal assistants**) *n* A **personal assistant** is a person who does office work and administrative work for someone. The abbreviation 'PA' is also used. ذاتی معاون (پرسنل اسسٹنٹ)

personality (**personalities**) *n* Your **personality** is your whole character and nature. شخصیت

personally *adv* You use **personally** to emphasize that you are giving your own opinion. ذاتی طور پر

personal organizer (**personal organizers**) *n* A **personal organizer** is a book containing personal or business information, which you can add pages to or remove pages from to keep the information up to date. Small computers with a similar function are also called **personal organizers**. ذاتی منتظم

personal stereo (**personal stereos**) *n* A **personal stereo** is a small cassette or CD player with very light headphones, which people carry round so that they can listen to music while doing something else. ذاتی اسٹیریو

personnel *npl* The **personnel** of an organization are the people who work for it. اہلکار

perspective (**perspectives**) *n* A **perspective** is a particular way of thinking about something. زاویہ نگاہ

perspiration *n* **Perspiration** is the liquid that appears on your skin when you are hot or frightened. (*formal*) پسینہ

persuade (**persuades, persuading, persuaded**) *vt* If you **persuade** someone to do a particular thing, you get them to do it, usually by convincing them that it is a good idea. قائل کرنا، منوالینا

persuasive *adj* Someone or something that is **persuasive** is likely to persuade you to do or believe a particular thing. قائل کرنے والا

Peru *n* **Peru** is a republic in western South America, on the Pacific. پیرو

Peruvian (**Peruvians**) *adj* **Peruvian** means belonging or related to Peru, or to its people or culture. پیرودیائی ▷ *n* A **Peruvian** is a citizen of Peru, or a person of Peruvian origin. پیرودیائی

pessimist (**pessimists**) *n* A **pessimist** is someone who thinks that bad things are going to happen. قنوطیت پسند

pessimistic *adj* Someone who is **pessimistic** thinks that bad things are going to happen. قنوطیت پسند

pest (**pests**) *n* A **pest** is an insect or small animal which damages crops or food supplies. کیڑا

pester (**pesters, pestering, pestered**) *vt* If you say that someone **is pestering** you, you mean that they keep asking you to do something, or keep talking to you, and you find this annoying. باتونی

pesticide (**pesticides**) *n* **Pesticides** are chemicals which farmers put on their crops to kill harmful insects. کیڑے مار دوا

pet (**pets**) *n* A **pet** is an animal that you keep in your home to give you company and pleasure. پالتو

petition (**petitions**) *n* A **petition** is a document signed by a lot of people which asks for some official action to be taken. عرضی

petrified *adj* If you are **petrified**, you are extremely frightened. پتھر ہو جانا (خوف یا غم سے)

petrol *n* **Petrol** is a liquid used as a fuel for motor vehicles. پیٹرول

petrol station (**petrol stations**) *n* A **petrol station** is a garage by the side of the road where petrol is sold and put into vehicles. پیٹرول اسٹیشن

petrol tank (**petrol tanks**) *n* The **petrol tank** in a motor vehicle is the container for petrol. پیٹرول کی ٹنکی

pewter *n* **Pewter** is a grey metal made by mixing tin and lead. رانگ، جستہ

pharmacist (**pharmacists**) *n* A **pharmacist** is a person who is qualified to prepare and sell medicines. دوافروش

pharmacy (**pharmacies**) *n* A **pharmacy** is a place where medicines are sold or given out. دوا کی دوکان

PhD (**PhDs**) *n* A **PhD** is a degree awarded to people who have done advanced research. **PhD** is an abbreviation for 'Doctor of Philosophy'. پی ایچ ڈی

pheasant (**pheasants, pheasant**) *n* A **pheasant** is a bird with a long tail. چکور

philosophy *n* **Philosophy** is the study or creation of theories about basic things such as the nature of existence or how people should live. فلسفہ

phobia (**phobias**) *n* A **phobia** is an unreasonably strong fear of something. فوبیا (عارضہ خوف)

phone (**phones, phoning, phoned**) *n* A **phone** is a piece of equipment that you use to talk to someone in another place. فون ▷ *v* When you **phone** someone, you dial their phone number and speak to them by phone. فون کرنا

phone back *v* If you **phone** someone **back**, you telephone them again or in return for a telephone call that they have made to you. واپسی فون کرنا *I'll phone you back later.*

phone bill (**phone bills**) *n* A **phone bill** is an account or bill for the charges for a telephone and line and for calls made from it. فون بل

phonebook (**phonebooks**) *n* A **phonebook** is a book that contains an alphabetical list of the names, addresses, and telephone numbers of the people in a town or area. فون بک

phonebox (**phoneboxes**) *n* A **phonebox** is a small shelter outdoors or in a building in which there is a public telephone. فون باکس

phone call (**phone calls**) *n* If you make a **phone call**, you dial someone's phone number and speak to them by phone. فون کال

phonecard (**phonecards**) *n* A **phonecard**

is a plastic card that you can use instead of money in some public telephones. فون کارڈ

phone number (**phone numbers**) *n* Your **phone number** is the number that other people dial when they want to talk to you on the telephone. فون نمبر

photo (**photos**) *n* A **photo** is a picture that is made using a camera. فوٹو

photo album (**photo albums**) *n* A **photo album** is a book in which you keep photographs that you have collected. فوٹو البم

photocopier (**photocopiers**) *n* A **photocopier** is a machine which quickly copies documents by photographing them. فوٹو کاپی کرنے والی مشین

photocopy (**photocopies, photocopying, photocopied**) *n* A **photocopy** is a document made by a photocopier. فوٹو کاپی ▷ *vt* If you **photocopy** a document, you make a copy of it with a photocopier. نقل تیار کرنا (عکسی)

photograph (**photographs, photographing, photographed**) *n* A **photograph** is a picture that is made using a camera. فوٹو (تصویر) ▷ *vt* When you **photograph** someone or something, you use a camera to obtain a picture of them. فوٹو کھینچنا

photographer (**photographers**) *n* A **photographer** is someone who takes photographs, especially as their job. فوٹوگرافر

photography *n* **Photography** is the skill, job, or process of producing photographs. فوٹوگرافی

phrase (**phrases**) *n* A **phrase** is a short group of words that are used as a unit and whose meaning is not always obvious from the words contained in it. فقرہ

phrasebook (**phrasebooks**) *n* A **phrasebook** is a book used by people travelling to a foreign country. It has lists of useful words and expressions, together with the translation of each word or expression in the language of that country. محاورے کی کتاب

physical (**physicals**) *adj* **Physical** means connected with a person's body, rather than with their mind. جسمانی ▷ *n* A **physical** is a medical examination of the body to diagnose disease or verify fitness. جسمانی

physicist (**physicists**) *n* A **physicist** is a person who studies physics. فزاسسٹ

physics *n* **Physics** is the scientific study of forces such as heat, light, sound, pressure, gravity, and electricity. طبعیات

physiotherapist (**physiotherapists**) *n* A **physiotherapist** is a person whose job is using physiotherapy to treat people. فزیو تھیراپسٹ (جسمانی ورزش سے علاج کرنے والا)

physiotherapy *n* **Physiotherapy** is medical treatment given to people who cannot move a part of their body and involves exercise, massage, or heat treatment. فزیو تھیراپی

pianist (**pianists**) *n* A **pianist** is a person who plays the piano. پیانو بجانے والا

piano (**pianos**) *n* A **piano** is a large musical instrument with a row of black and white keys, which you strike with your fingers. پیانو (ساز)

pick (**picks, picking, picked**) *n* The best things or people in a particular group are the **pick** of that group. منتخب ▷ *vt* If you **pick** someone, you choose them. اٹھانا، لے جانا ▷ *vt* When you **pick** flowers, fruit, or leaves, you take them from a plant or tree. اتارنا، توڑنا

pick on *v* If someone **picks on** you, they repeatedly criticize or attack you unfairly. (*informal*) تنقید کرنا *They were always picking on her.*

pick out *v* If you can **pick out** something or someone, you recognize them when it is difficult to see them. پہچاننا *With my binoculars, I pick out a figure a mile or so away.*

pickpocket (**pickpockets**) *n* A

P

pickpocket is a person who steals things from people's pockets or bags in public places. گرہ کٹ، جیب کترہ

pick up *v* If you **pick** something **up**, you lift it upwards from a surface using your fingers. اٹھانا *Ridley picked up the pencil.*

picnic (**picnics**) *n* When people have a **picnic**, they eat a meal out of doors. پکنک (تفریح)

picture (**pictures**) *n* A **picture** consists of lines and shapes which are drawn, painted, or printed on a surface and show a person, thing, or scene. تصویر

picture frame (**picture frames**) *n* A **picture frame** is the wood, metal, or plastic that is fitted around a picture, especially when it is displayed or hung on a wall. تصویر فریم

picturesque *adj* A **picturesque** place is attractive, interesting, and unspoiled. تصویر نما

pie (**pies**) *n* A **pie** consists of meat, vegetables, or fruit, baked in pastry. شامی کباب، بھجیہ

piece (**pieces**) *n* A **piece** of something is a portion, part, or section of it that has been removed, broken off, or cut off. ٹکڑا

pie chart (**pie charts**) *n* A **pie chart** is a circle divided into sections to show the relative proportions of a set of things. پائی چارٹ

pier (**piers**) *n* A **pier** is a large platform which sticks out into the sea and which people can walk along. گودی

pierce (**pierces, piercing, pierced**) *vt* If a sharp object **pierces** something, or if you **pierce** something with a sharp object, the object goes into it and makes a hole in it. چھیدنا

pierced *adj* If your ears or some other part of your body is **pierced**, you have a small hole made through them so that you can wear a piece of jewellery in them. چھدا ہوا

piercing (**piercings**) *n* A **piercing** is a hole that has been made in part of someone's body that they can put jewellery in. سوراخ (جسم کے کسی حصہ میں)

pig (**pigs**) *n* A **pig** is a farm animal with a pink, white, or black skin. Pigs are kept for their meat, which is called pork, ham, or bacon. سور

pigeon (**pigeons**) *n* A **pigeon** is a grey bird which is often seen in towns. کبوتر

piggybank (**piggybanks**) *n* A **piggybank** is a small container shaped like a pig, with a narrow hole in the top through which to put coins. Children often use piggybanks to save money. سور کی شکل کا ڈبہ (سکے جمع کرنے کے لئے)

pigtail (**pigtails**) *n* If someone has a **pigtail** or **pigtails**, their hair is plaited or braided into one or two lengths. سور کی دم کی طرح چوٹی

pile (**piles**) *n* A **pile** of things is a quantity of them lying on top of one another. ڈھیر

piles *npl* **Piles** are painful swellings that can appear in the veins inside a person's anus. بواسیر

pile-up (**pile-ups**) *n* A **pile-up** is a road accident in which a lot of vehicles crash into each other. حادثہ میں گاڑیوں کا ایک دوسرے پر ڈھیر ہو جانا

pilgrim (**pilgrims**) *n* A **pilgrim** is a person who makes a journey to a holy place. زائرین

pilgrimage (**pilgrimages**) *n* If someone makes a **pilgrimage** to a place, they make a journey there because the place is holy according to their religion, or very important to them personally. مقدس مقامات کو سفر

pill (**pills**) *n* **Pills** are small solid round masses of medicine or vitamins that you swallow. گولی (دوا)

pillar (**pillars**) *n* A **pillar** is a tall solid structure which is usually used to support part of a building. کھمبا

pillow (**pillows**) *n* A **pillow** is a rectangular cushion which you rest your head on when you are in bed. تکیہ

pillowcase (**pillowcases**) *n* A **pillowcase**

is a cover for a pillow, which can be removed and washed. تکیہ کا غلاف

pilot (**pilots**) *n* A **pilot** is a person who is trained to fly an aircraft. پائلٹ

pilot light (**pilot lights**) *n* A **pilot light** is a small gas flame in a cooker, stove, boiler, or fire. It burns all the time and lights the main large flame when the gas is turned fully on. پائلٹ لائٹ

pimple (**pimples**) *n* **Pimples** are small raised spots, especially on the face. مہاسہ

PIN *n* Someone's **PIN** or **PIN number** is a secret number which they can use, for example, with a bank card to withdraw money from a cash machine. **PIN** is an abbreviation for 'personal identification number'. پن (نمبر)

pin (**pins**) *n* **Pins** are very small thin pieces of metal with points at one end, which are used to fasten things together. پن

pinafore (**pinafores**) *n* A **pinafore** or a **pinafore dress** is a sleeveless dress. It is worn over a blouse or sweater. بے آستین لباس (بلاؤز یا سویٹر کے اوپر)

pinch (**pinches, pinching, pinched**) *vt* If you **pinch** a part of someone's body, you take a piece of their skin between your thumb and first finger and give it a short squeeze. چٹکی بھرنا

pine (**pines**) *n* A **pine** or a **pine tree** is a tall tree with long thin leaves which it keeps all year round. اناناس درخت

pineapple (**pineapples**) *n* A **pineapple** is a large oval fruit with sweet, juicy, yellow flesh and thick, brown skin. اناناس

pink (**pinker, pinkest**) *adj* Something that is **pink** is the colour between red and white. گلابی

pint (**pints**) *n* A **pint** is a unit of measurement for liquids. In Britain, it is equal to 568 cubic centimetres or one eighth of an imperial gallon. In America, it is equal to 473 cubic centimetres or one eighth of an American gallon. گیلن کا آٹھواں حصہ

pip (**pips**) *n* **Pips** are the small hard seeds in a fruit such as an apple or orange. پھلوں کے اندر کا سخت بیج

pipe (**pipes**) *n* A **pipe** is a long, round, hollow object through which a liquid or gas can flow. پائپ

pipeline (**pipelines**) *n* A **pipeline** is a large pipe used for carrying oil or gas over a long distance. پائپ لائن

pirate (**pirates**) *n* **Pirates** are sailors who attack other ships and steal property from them. بحری قزاق

Pisces *n* **Pisces** is one of the twelve signs of the zodiac. Its symbol is two fish. People who are born approximately between the 19th of February and the 20th of March come under this sign. برج مچھلی

pistol (**pistols**) *n* A **pistol** is a small handgun. پستول

piston (**pistons**) *n* A **piston** is a cylinder or metal disc that is part of an engine. پسٹن (انجن کا حصہ)

pitch (**pitches, pitching, pitched**) *n* A **pitch** is an area of ground that is marked out and used for playing a game such as football, cricket, or hockey. پچ (کرکٹ کا) ▷ *n* The *pitch* of a sound is how high or low it is. پچ (آواز کی لہر کی ایک حالت) ▷ *vt* If you **pitch** something somewhere, you throw it forcefully while aiming carefully. زور لگا کر پھینکنا

pity (**pities, pitying, pitied**) *n* If you feel **pity** for someone, you feel very sorry for them. رحم ▷ *vt* If you **pity** someone, you feel very sorry for them. رحم کرنا

pixel (**pixels**) *n* A **pixel** is the smallest area on a computer screen which can be given a separate colour by the computer. پکسل

pizza (**pizzas**) *n* A **pizza** is a flat piece of dough covered with tomatoes, cheese, and other savoury food, which is baked in an oven. پزا

place (**places, placing, placed**) *n* A **place** is a building, area, town, or country.

جگہ، مقام ▷ *vt* If you **place** something somewhere, you put it in a particular position. رکھنا ▷ *n* A **place** is where something belongs. جگہ، مقام

placement *n* The **placement** of something is the act of putting it in a particular place. کسی مقام پر رکھنا

place of birth (**places of birth**) *n* Your **place of birth** is the place where you were born. جائے پیدائش

plain (**plainer, plainest, plains**) *adj* A **plain** object, surface, or fabric is entirely in one colour and has no pattern, design, or writing on it. سادہ ▷ *n* A **plain** is a large, flat area of land with very few trees on it. میدانی علاقہ

plain chocolate *n* **Plain chocolate** is dark-brown chocolate that has a stronger and less sweet taste than milk chocolate. سادہ چاکلیٹ

plait (**plaits**) *n* A **plait** is a length of hair that has been twisted over and under two other lengths of hair to make one thick length of hair. چوٹی گوندھے ہوئے بال

plan (**plans, planning, planned**) **n** A **plan** is a method of achieving something that you have worked out in detail beforehand. منصوبہ ▷ *v* If you **plan** what you are going to do, you decide in detail what you are going to do, and you intend to do it. منصوبہ بندی کرنا

plane (**planes**) *n* A **plane** is a vehicle with wings and one or more engines which can fly. ہوائی جہاز ▷ *n* A **plane** is a flat level surface which may be sloping at a particular angle. مکان ▷ *n* A **plane** is a tool that has a flat bottom with a sharp blade in it, used for shaping wood. بسولہ

planet (**planets**) *n* A **planet** is a large, round object in space that moves around a star. The Earth is a planet. کرہ، سیارہ

planning *n* **Planning** is the process of deciding in detail how to do something before you actually start to do it. منصوبہ بندی

plant (**plants, planting, planted**) *n* A **plant** is a factory or a place where power is produced. کارخانہ ▷ *n* A **plant** is a living thing that grows in earth and has a stem, leaves, and roots. پودا ▷ *vt* When you **plant** a seed, plant, or young tree, you put it into earth so that it will grow. بونا

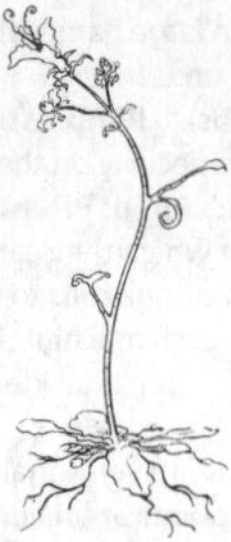

plant pot (**plant pots**) *n* A **plant pot** is a container that is used for growing plants. گملا

plaque (**plaques**) *n* A **plaque** is a flat piece of metal or wood, which is fixed to a wall or monument in memory of a person or event. آرائشی تختی، کتبہ

plasma screen (**plasma screens**) *n* A **plasma screen** is a type of thin television screen or computer screen that produces high-quality images. ٹی وی، کمپیوٹر کا اسکرین

plasma TV (**plasma TVs**) *n* A **plasma TV** is a type of television set with a thin screen that produces high-quality images. پلازمائی وی

plaster (**plasters**) *n* **Plaster** is a paste which people put on walls and ceilings so that they are smooth. پلستر ▷ *n* A **plaster** is a strip of material with a soft part in the middle. You can cover a cut on your body with a **plaster**. پلاسٹر، زخم پر لگانے والی پٹی

plastic (**plastics**) *n* **Plastic** is a light but strong material produced by a chemical process. پلاسٹک

plastic bag (**plastic bags**) *n* A **plastic**

bag is a bag made from a very thin flexible plastic. پلاسٹک کا بیگ

plastic surgery *n* **Plastic surgery** is the practice of performing operations to repair or replace skin which has been damaged, or to improve people's appearance. پلاسٹک سرجری

plate (**plates**) *n* A **plate** is a round or oval flat dish used to hold food. طشتری

platform (**platforms**) *n* A **platform** is a flat raised structure or area on which someone or something can stand. چبوترہ، پلیٹ فارم

platinum *n* **Platinum** is a very valuable silvery-grey metal. پلیٹینم

play (**plays, playing, played**) *n* A **play** is a piece of writing performed in a theatre, on the radio, or on television. ڈراما ▷ *vi* When you **play**, you spend time using toys and taking part in games. کھیلنا ▷ *vt* If you **play** an instrument, you make music with it. بجانا

player (**players**) *n* A **player** in a sport or game is a person who takes part. کھلاڑی ▷ *n* You can use **player** to refer to a musician. سازندہ

playful *adj* A **playful** gesture is friendly and cheerful. خوش دلانہ

playground (**playgrounds**) *n* A **playground** is a piece of land where children can play. کھیل کا میدان

playgroup (**playgroups**) *n* A **playgroup** is an informal kind of school for very young children where they learn by playing. پلے گروپ

playing card (**playing cards**) *n* **Playing cards** are thin pieces of card with numbers and pictures on them, which are used to play games. تاش

playing field (**playing fields**) *n* A **playing field** is a large area of grass where people play sports. گھاس والا کھیل کا میدان

PlayStation® (**PlayStations**) *n* A **PlayStation** is a type of games console. کھیل کا اسٹیشن

playtime *n* In a school for young children, **playtime** is the period of time between lessons when they can play outside. کھیل کا گھنٹہ (اسکول میں)

play truant *v* If children **play truant**, they stay away from school without permission. گریزپا، اسکول سے بھاگنے کا کھیل

playwright (**playwrights**) *n* A **playwright** is a person who writes plays. ڈرامہ مصنف

pleasant (**pleasanter, pleasantest**) *adj* Something that is **pleasant** is enjoyable or attractive. پر کشش

please! *excl* You say **please!** when you are politely asking or inviting someone to do something. برائے کرم!

pleased *adj* If you are **pleased**, you are happy about something or satisfied with it. خوش، مطمئن

pleasure *n* If something gives you **pleasure**, you get a feeling of happiness, satisfaction, or enjoyment from it. خوشی

plenty *n* If there is **plenty** of something, there is a lot of it. افراط، بہتات

pliers *npl* **Pliers** are a tool with two handles at one end and two hard, flat, metal parts at the other. **Pliers** are used to hold or pull out things such as nails. پلایرز

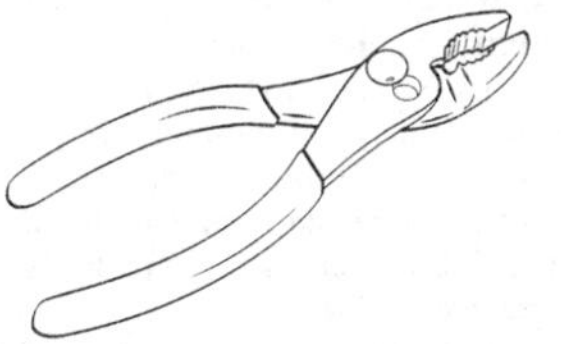

plot (**plots, plotting, plotted**) *n* A **plot** is a small piece of land, especially one that is intended for a purpose such as building houses or growing vegetables. قطعہ زمین ▷ *n* A **plot** is a secret plan to do something that is illegal or wrong. سازش

plough (**ploughs, ploughing, ploughed**) *n* A *plough* is a large farming tool with sharp blades, which is attached to a tractor or an animal and used to turn over the soil before planting. ہل ▷ *vt* When a farmer **ploughs** an area of land, they turn over the soil using a plough. ہل چلانا، کھیت جوتنا

plug (**plugs**) *n* A **plug** on a piece of electrical equipment is a small plastic object with two or three metal pins which fit into the holes of an electric socket. (بجلی) پلگ

plughole (**plugholes**) *n* A **plughole** is a small hole in a bath or sink which allows the water to flow away and into which you can put a plug. پلگ ان

plug in *v* If you **plug** a piece of electrical equipment **in**, you push its plug into an electric socket so that it can work. پلگ لگانا *I filled the kettle and plugged it in.*

plum (**plums**) *n* A **plum** is a small sweet fruit with a smooth red or yellow skin and a stone in the middle. آلو بخارا

plumber (**plumbers**) *n* A **plumber** is a person whose job is to connect and repair things such as water and drainage pipes, baths, and toilets. نل ساز

plumbing *n* The **plumbing** in a building consists of the water and drainage pipes, baths, and toilets in it. نل سازی

plump (**plumper, plumpest**) *adj* A **plump** person is rather fat. گول مٹول، چکنا

plunge (**plunges, plunging, plunged**) *vi* If something or someone **plunges** in a particular direction, especially into water, they fall, rush, or throw themselves in that direction. ڈبکی مارنا، غوطہ لگانا

plural (**plurals**) *n* The **plural** of a noun is the form of it that is used to refer to more than one person or thing. جمع

plus *prep* You use **plus** to show that one number or quantity is being added to another. جمع *Two plus two equals four.*

plywood *n* **Plywood** is wood that consists of thin layers of wood stuck together. پلائی وڈ (لکڑی کی پرت)

p.m. *abbr* **p.m.** is used after a number to show that you are referring to a particular time between noon and midnight. **p.m.** is an abbreviation for 'post meridiem'. دوپہر اور آدھی رات کے بیچ کا وقت (پاسٹ میریڈین)

pneumatic drill (**pneumatic drills**) *n* A **pneumatic drill** is operated by air under pressure and is very powerful. Pneumatic drills are often used for digging up roads. نیومیٹک ڈرل

pneumonia *n* **Pneumonia** is a serious disease which affects your lungs and makes breathing difficult. نمونیا

poached *adj* If fish, animals, or birds are **poached**, someone has caught them illegally on someone else's property. غیر قانونی طور پر جانوروں کو مارنا،چرانا ▷ *adj* **Poached** eggs, fish, or other food is cooked gently in boiling water, milk, or other liquid. کسی مائع میں ابالا ہوا

pocket (**pockets**) *n* A **pocket** is a small bag or pouch that forms part of a piece of clothing. جیب

pocket calculator (**pocket calculators**) *n* A **pocket calculator** is a very small electronic device that you use for making mathematical calculations. جیبی کیلکولیٹر

pocket money *n* **Pocket money** is a small amount of money given regularly to children by their parents. جیب خرچ

podcast (**podcasts**) *n* A **podcast** is an audio file that can be downloaded and listened to on a computer or iPod. پوڈکاسٹ

poem (**poems**) *n* A **poem** is a piece of writing in which the words are chosen for their beauty and sound and are carefully arranged, often in short lines. نظم

poet (**poets**) *n* A **poet** is a person who writes poems. شاعر

poetry *n* Poems, considered as a form of literature, are referred to as **poetry**. شاعری

point (**points, pointing, pointed**) *n* A **point** is an idea or a fact. نکتہ ▷ *n* A **point** is a mark that you win in a game or a sport. پوائنٹ ▷ *vi* If you **point** at something, you stick out your finger to show where it is. نشاندہی کرنا، اشارہ کرنا ▷ *n* The **point** of something is its thin, sharp end. Needles and knives have **points** . نوک

pointless *adj* Something that is **pointless** has no purpose. بے مطلب

point out *v* If you **point out** an object or place to someone, you direct their attention to it. نشاندہی کرنا *Now and then they would stop to point things out to each other.*

poison (**poisons, poisoning, poisoned**) *n* **Poison** is a substance that harms or kills people or animals if they swallow or absorb it. زہر ▷ *vt* To **poison** someone or something means to give poison to them or to add poison to them, causing them harm. زہر دینا

poisonous *adj* Something that is **poisonous** will kill you or harm you if you swallow or absorb it. زہریلا

poke (**pokes, poking, poked**) *vt* If you **poke** someone or something, you quickly push them with your finger or with a sharp object. گھسیڑنا (انگلیوں سے ڈھکیلنا)

poker *n* **Poker** is a card game that people usually play in order to win money. تاش کا ایک کھیل

Poland *n* **Poland** is a republic in central Europe, on the Baltic. پولینڈ

polar *adj* **Polar** refers to the area around the North and South Poles. قطبی

polar bear (**polar bears**) *n* A **polar bear** is a large white bear which is found near the North Pole. قطبی بھالو

Pole (**Poles**) *n* A **Pole** is a citizen of Poland, or a person of Polish origin. پولینڈ کا باشندہ

pole (**poles**) *n* A **pole** is a long, thin piece of wood or metal, used especially for supporting things. کھمبا، لمبی لکڑی

pole vault *n* **The pole vault** is an athletics event in which athletes jump over a high bar, using a long flexible pole to help lift themselves up. لمبی لکڑی کے سہارے جمپ لگانے کا کھیل

police *n* The **police** are the official organization that is responsible for making sure that people obey the law. پولیس

policeman (**policemen**) *n* A **policeman** is a man who is a member of the police force. پولیس والا

police officer (**police officers**) *n* A **police officer** is a member of the police force. پولیس افیسر

police station (**police stations**) *n* A **police station** is the local office of a police force in a particular area. تھانہ

policewoman (**policewomen**) *n* A **policewoman** is a woman who is a member of the police force. پولیس والی

polio *n* **Polio** is a serious infectious disease which can cause paralysis. پولیو

Polish *adj* **Polish** means belonging or relating to Poland, or to its people, language, or culture. پولینڈ کا باشندہ ▷ *n* **Polish** is the language spoken by people in Poland. پولینڈ کی زبان

polish (**polishes, polishing, polished**) *n* **Polish** is a substance that you put on the surface of an object in order to clean it, protect it, and make it shine. پالش ▷ *vt* If you **polish** something, you put polish on it or rub it with a cloth to make it shine. پالش کرنا

polite (**politer, politest**) *adj* A **polite** person has good manners and is not rude to other people. نرم خو

politely *adv* If you do something **politely**, you do it with good manners and without being rude to other people. نرمی سے

politeness *n* **Politeness** is good manners in front of other people. نرمی، اخلاق

political *adj* **Political** means relating to the way power is achieved and used in a country or society. سیاسی

politician (**politicians**) *n* A **politician** is a person whose job is in politics, especially a member of parliament. سیاست داں

p

politics *npl* **Politics** is the actions or activities concerned with achieving and using power in a country or organization. سیاست

poll (**polls**) *n* A **poll** is a survey in which people are asked their opinions about something. رائے شماری

pollen *n* **Pollen** is a powder produced by flowers in order to fertilize other flowers. زرگل

pollute (**pollutes, polluting, polluted**) *vt* To **pollute** water, air, or land means to make it dirty and dangerous to live in or to use, especially with poisonous chemicals or sewage. آلودہ کرنا

polluted *adj* If water, air, or land is **polluted**, it has been made dirty by poisonous substances. آلودہ

pollution *n* **Pollution** is poisonous substances that are polluting water, air, or land. آلودگی

polo-necked sweater (**polo-necked sweaters**) *n* A **polo-necked sweater** is a sweater with a high neck which folds over. گلے دار سویٹر

polo shirt (**polo shirts**) *n* A **polo shirt** is a soft short-sleeved piece of clothing with a collar, which you put on over your head. پولو قمیض (پولو کے کھیل کے لئے)

Polynesia *n* **Polynesia** is the division of islands in the Pacific which includes Samoa, Tonga, the Cook Islands, and Tuvalu. پولینیشیا

Polynesian (**Polynesians**) *adj* **Polynesian** means relating to Polynesia, its people, or any of their languages. پولینیشیائی ▷ *n* A **Polynesian** is a person who lives in Polynesia, or a person of Polynesian origin. پولینیشیائی ▷ *n* **Polynesian** is a branch of languages, which includes Māori, Hawaiian, and other languages of the South and central Pacific. پولینیشیائی زبان

polythene bag (**polythene bags**) *n* A **polythene bag** is a bag made of thin plastic, especially one used to store or protect food or household articles. پولیتھین (پلاسٹک) بیگ

pomegranate (**pomegranates**) *n* A **pomegranate** is a round fruit with a thick reddish skin. It contains lots of small seeds with juicy flesh around them. انار

pond (**ponds**) *n* A **pond** is a small, usually man-made, area of water. تالاب (انسان کا بنایا ہوا)

pony (**ponies**) *n* A **pony** is a type of small horse. گھوڑی (چھوٹے قد کی)

ponytail (**ponytails**) *n* If someone has their hair in a **ponytail**, it is tied up at the back so that it hangs down like a tail. چوٹی (دم کی طرح جھولتی ہوئی)

pony trekking *n* **Pony trekking** is the act of riding ponies cross-country, especially as a pastime. گھوڑی پر سوار ہو کر دیہاتوں کی سیر

poodle (**poodles**) *n* A **poodle** is a type of dog with thick curly hair. کتا (گھنے گھنگرالے بالوں والا)

pool (**pools**) *n* A **pool** of people, money, or things is a quantity or number of them that is available for use. وسائل ▷ *n* A **pool** is a small area of still water. تالاب

poor (**poorer, poorest**) *adj* Someone who is **poor** has very little money and few possessions. غریب

poorly *adj* If someone is **poorly**, they are ill. بیمار

popcorn *n* **Popcorn** is a snack which consists of grains of maize that have been heated until they have burst and become large and light. مکئی

pope (**popes**) *n* The **pope** is the head of the Roman Catholic Church. پوپ (رومن کیتھولک سربراہ)

poplar (**poplars**) *n* A **poplar** or a **poplar tree** is a type of tall thin tree. درخت حور

poppy (**poppies**) *n* A **poppy** is a plant with large, delicate, red flowers. گل لالہ

popular *adj* Someone or something that is **popular** is liked by a lot of people. مقبول

popularity *n* The **popularity** of someone or something is the degree to which they

are liked by other people. مقبولیت
population (**populations**) *n* The **population** of a place is the people who live there, or the number of people living there. آبادی
pop-up (**pop-ups**) *n* On a computer screen, a **pop-up** is a small window that appears on the screen when you perform particular operations. A **pop-up** may contain items such as a menu or advertisement. پوپ اپ
porch (**porches**) *n* A **porch** is a sheltered area at the entrance to a building. It has a roof and sometimes walls. ڈیوڑھی
porridge *n* **Porridge** is a thick sticky food made from oats cooked in water or milk and eaten hot, especially for breakfast. دلیہ
port (**ports**) *n* **Port** is a type of strong, sweet red wine. سرخ شراب ▷ *n* A **port** is a town or a harbour area with docks and warehouses, where ships load or unload goods or passengers. بندرگاہ
portable *adj* A **portable** machine or device is designed to be easily carried or moved. قابلِ انتقال
porter (**porters**) *n* A **porter** is a person whose job is to be in charge of the entrance of a building such as a hotel. حمال
portfolio (**portfolios**) *n* A **portfolio** is a set of pictures or photographs of someone's work, which they show to potential employers. پورٹفولیو
portion (**portions**) *n* A **portion of** something is a part of it. حصہ، جزو
portrait (**portraits**) *n* A **portrait** is a painting, drawing, or photograph of a person. خاکہ
Portugal *n* **Portugal** is a republic in south-west Europe, on the Atlantic. پرتگال
Portuguese (**Portuguese**) *adj* **Portuguese** means belonging or relating to Portugal, or its people, language, or culture. پرتگالی ▷ *n* The **Portuguese** are the people of Portugal. پرتگالی ▷ *n* **Portuguese** is the language spoken in Portugal, Brazil, Angola, and Mozambique. پرتگالی زبان
position (**positions**) *n* The **position** of someone or something is the place where they are. حالت
positive *adj* If you are **positive**, you are hopeful and confident, and think of the good aspects of a situation rather than the bad ones. مثبت
possess (**possesses, possessing, possessed**) *vt* If you **possess** something, you have it or own it. قابض ہونا، گرفت میں لینا
possession *n* If you are in **possession** of something, you have it, because you have obtained it or because it belongs to you. (*formal*) قبضہ، ملکیت
possibility (**possibilities**) *n* If you say there is a **possibility** that something is the case or that something will happen, you mean that it might be the case or it might happen. امکان
possible *adj* If it is **possible** to do something, it can be done. ممکن
possibly *adv* You use **possibly** to indicate that you are not sure whether something is true or will happen. ممکنہ طور پر
post (**posts, posting, posted**) *n* A **post** is a strong upright pole fixed into the ground. کھمبا ▷ *n* A **post** is a job or official position in a company or organization. نشست، عہدہ ▷ *n* The **post** is a system for collecting and delivering letters and parcels. ڈاک ▷ *vt* If you *post* a letter, you put a stamp on it and send it to someone. سپرد ڈاک کرنا، ڈاک سے بھیجنا
postage *n* **Postage** is the money that you pay for sending letters and parcels by post. ڈاک خرچ
postal order (**postal orders**) *n* A **postal order** is a piece of paper representing a sum of money which you can buy at a post office and send to someone as a way of sending them money by post. پوسٹل آرڈر
postbox (**postboxes**) *n* A **postbox** is a metal box in a public place, where you

put letters and packets to be collected. They are then sorted and delivered. پوسٹ باکس

postcard (**postcards**) *n* A **postcard** is a piece of card, often with a picture on one side, which you can write on and post to someone without using an envelope. پوسٹ کارڈ

postcode (**postcodes**) *n* Your **postcode** is a short sequence of numbers and letters at the end of your address. پن کوڈ

poster (**posters**) *n* A **poster** is a large notice, advertisement, or picture that you stick on a wall. پوسٹر

postgraduate (**postgraduates**) *n* A **postgraduate** is a student with a first degree from a university who is studying or doing research at a more advanced level. پوسٹ گریجویٹ

postman (**postmen**) *n* A **postman** is a man whose job is to collect and deliver letters and parcels that are sent by post. ڈاکیہ

postmark (**postmarks**) *n* A **postmark** is a mark which is printed on letters and packages at a post office. It shows the time and place at which something was posted. ڈاک کا نشان

post office (**post offices**) *n* A **post office** is a building where you can buy stamps, post letters, and parcels, and use other services provided by the national postal service. ڈاک خانہ

postpone (**postpones, postponing, postponed**) *vt* If you **postpone** an event, you arrange for it to take place at a later time than was originally planned. ملتوی کرنا

postwoman (**postwomen**) *n* A **postwoman** is a woman whose job is to collect and deliver letters, etc. خاتون ڈاکیہ

pot (**pots**) *n* A **pot** is a deep round container for cooking food. ہانڈی، پتیلا

potato (**potatoes**) *n* **Potatoes** are vegetables with brown or red skins and white insides. آلو

potato peeler (**potato peelers**) *n* A **potato peeler** is a special tool used for removing the skin from potatoes. آلو چھیلنے والا آلہ

potential *adj* You use **potential** to say that someone or something is capable of developing into the particular kind of person or thing. قوی ▷ *n* If something has **potential**, it is capable of being useful or successful in the future. صلاحیت

pothole (**potholes**) *n* A **pothole** is a large hole in the surface of a road, caused by traffic and bad weather. سڑک کا کھڈہ

pot plant (**pot plants**) *n* A **pot plant** is a plant which is grown in a container, especially indoors. برتن میں بڑا ہونے والا پودا

pottery *n* **Pottery** is objects made from clay. برتن سازی

potty (**potties**) *n* A **potty** is a deep bowl which a small child uses as a toilet. بچے کا قدمچہ (ہگنے کا کموڈ)

pound (**pounds**) *n* The **pound** is the unit of money which is used in Britain. It is represented by the symbol £. Some other countries, for example, Egypt, also have a unit of money called a **pound.** پاؤنڈ (کرنسی)

pound sterling (**pounds sterling**) *n* **Pound sterling** is the official name for the standard monetary unit of Britain. پاؤنڈ اسٹرلنگ (کرنسی)

pour (**pours, pouring, poured**) *vt* If you **pour** a liquid, you make it flow steadily out of a container by holding the container at an angle. انڈیلنا

poverty *n* **Poverty** is the state of being very poor. غربت

powder (**powders**) *n* **Powder** consists of many tiny particles of a solid substance. سفوف

power *n* If someone has **power**, they have control over people. اختیار ▷ *n* The **power** of something is its strength. قوت

power cut (**power cuts**) *n* A **power cut** is a period of time when the electricity supply to a particular building or area is stopped, sometimes deliberately. بجلی تخفیف

powerful *adj* A **powerful** person or organization is able to control or influence people and events. طاقتور، مقتدر

practical *adj* **Practical** means involving real situations, rather than ideas and theories. عملی

practically *adv* **Practically** means almost. عملی طور پر

practice (**practices**) *n* You can refer to something that people do regularly as a **practice**. عادت

practise (**practises, practising, practised**) *vt* If you **practise** something, you keep doing it regularly in order to do it better. عادی ہونا

praise (**praises, praising, praised**) *vt* If you **praise** someone or something, you express approval for their achievements or qualities. تعریف کرنا، ستائش کرنا

pram (**prams**) *n* A **pram** is like a baby's cot on wheels, which you can push along when you want to take the baby somewhere. بچہ گاڑی

prank (**pranks**) *n* A **prank** is a childish trick. (*old-fashioned*) شوخی، طفلانہ چالاکی

prawn (**prawns**) *n* A **prawn** is a small edible shellfish, similar to a shrimp. جھینگا

pray (**prays, praying, prayed**) *v* When people **pray**, they speak to God in order to give thanks or to ask for help. دعا مانگنا، نماز پڑھنا

prayer (**prayers**) *n* **Prayer** is the activity of speaking to God. دعا

precaution (**precautions**) *n* A **precaution** is an action that is intended to prevent something dangerous or unpleasant from happening. حفظ ماتقدم

preceding *adj* You refer to the period of time or the thing immediately before the one that you are talking about as the **preceding** one. گزشتہ، پہلے کی کوئی مثال

precinct (**precincts**) *n* A shopping **precinct** is an area in the centre of a town in which cars are not allowed. احاطہ، گردونواح

precious *adj* If you say that something such as a resource is **precious**, you mean that it is valuable and should not be wasted or used badly. قیمتی

precise *adj* You use **precise** to emphasize that you are referring to an exact thing, rather than something vague. ٹھیک ٹھیک

precisely *adv* **Precisely** means accurately and exactly. ٹھیک طور پر

predecessor (**predecessors**) *n* Your **predecessor** is the person who had your job before you. اپنے سے پہلے والا

predict (**predicts, predicting, predicted**) *vt* If you **predict** an event, you say that it will happen. پیش گوئی کرنا

predictable *adj* Something that is **predictable** is obvious in advance and will happen. قابل پیشگوئی

prefect (**prefects**) *n* In some schools, especially in Britain, a **prefect** is an older pupil who does special duties and helps the teachers to control the younger pupils. منکل

prefer (**prefers, preferring, preferred**) *vt* If you **prefer** someone or something, you like that person or thing better than another. ترجیح دینا

preferably *adv* You use **preferably** to show that something is more desirable or suitable. ترجیحاً

preference (**preferences**) *n* If you have a **preference** for something, you would

p

like to have or do that thing rather than something else. حوالہ

pregnancy *n* **Pregnancy** is the condition of being pregnant or the period of time during which a female is pregnant. حمل

pregnant *adj* If a woman or female animal is **pregnant**, she has a baby or babies developing in her body. حاملہ

prehistoric *adj* **Prehistoric** people and things existed at a time before information was written down. قبل تاریخ

prejudice (**prejudices**) *n* **Prejudice** is an unreasonable dislike of someone or something, or an unreasonable preference for one group over another. تعصب

prejudiced *adj* If someone is **prejudiced** against a particular group, they have an unreasonable dislike of them. متعصب

premature *adj* Something that is **premature** happens too early or earlier than expected. قبل از وقت

premiere (**premieres**) *n* The **premiere** of a new play or film is the first public performance of it. اول عوامی نمائش

premises *npl* The **premises** of a business or an institution are all the buildings and land that it occupies. احاطے

premonition (**premonitions**) *n* If you have a **premonition**, you have a feeling that something is going to happen, often something unpleasant. اندیشہ

preoccupied *adj* If you are **preoccupied**, you are thinking a lot about something or someone, and so you hardly notice other things. مسلط ہونا

prepaid *adj* **Prepaid** items are paid for in advance, before the time when you would normally pay for them. پیشگی ادا کردہ

preparation *n* **Preparation** is the process of getting something ready for use or for a particular purpose. تیاری

prepare (**prepares, preparing, prepared**) *vt* If you **prepare** something, you make it ready for something that is going to happen. تیاری کرنا

prepared *adj* If you are **prepared** to do something, you are willing to do it. تیار

prescribe (**prescribes, prescribing, prescribed**) *vt* If a doctor **prescribes** treatment, he or she states what medicine or treatment a patient should have. تجویز کرنا (دوا وغیرہ)

prescription (**prescriptions**) *n* A **prescription** is a medicine which a doctor has told you to take, or the form on which the doctor has written the details of that medicine. تجویز کردہ (نسخہ)

presence *n* Someone's **presence** in a place is the fact that they are there. موجودگی

present (**presents, presenting, presented**) *adj* If someone is **present** somewhere, they are there حاضر ہونا ▷ *n* A **present** is something that you give to someone for them to keep. موجود ہونا ▷ *n* The **present** is the period of time that is taking place now. موجودہ وقت، حال میں ▷ *vt* If you **present** someone with a prize or with information, you give it to them. تحفہ پیش کرنا

presentation (**presentations**) *n* A **presentation** is the act of formally giving something such as a prize or document. پیش

presenter (**presenters**) *n* A radio or television **presenter** is a person who introduces the items in a particular programme. پیش کرنے والا

presently *adv* If you say that something is **presently** happening, you mean that it is happening now. فی الحال

preservative (**preservatives**) *n* A **preservative** is a chemical that is added to substances to prevent them from decaying. محفوظ کار

president (**presidents**) *n* The **president** of a country that has no king or queen is the person who is the head of state of that country. صدر

press(**presses, pressing, pressed**) *n* The **press** refers to newspapers and the journalists who write them. پریس (اخباری دنیا) ▷ *vt* If you **press** something somewhere, you push it firmly against something else. دبانا (جسمانی طور پر)

press conference(**press conferences**) *n* A **press conference** is a meeting held by a famous or important person in which they answer journalists' questions. پریس کانفرنس

press-up(**press-ups**) *n* **Press-ups** are exercises that you do by lying with your face towards the floor and pushing with your hands to raise your body until your arms are straight. ڈنڈ

pressure(**pressures, pressuring, pressured**) *n* **Pressure** is the force produced when you press hard on something. دباؤ (جسمانی) ▷ *vt* If you **pressure** someone to do something, you try forcefully to persuade them to do it. دباؤ ڈالنا (نفسیاتی طور پر)

prestige *n* If a person, a country, or an organization has **prestige**, they are admired and respected because they are important or successful. ساکھ، عزت

prestigious *adj* A **prestigious** institution or activity is respected and admired by people. باوقار

presumably *adv* If you say that something is **presumably** the case, you mean that you think it is true, although you are not certain. مفروضہ کے طور پر

presume(**presumes, presuming, presumed**) *vt* If you **presume** that something is the case, you think that it is true, although you are not certain. فرض کرنا

pretend(**pretends, pretending, pretended**) *vt* If you **pretend** that something is true, you try to make people believe that it is true, although it is not. تسلیم کروانا

pretext(**pretexts**) *n* A **pretext** is a reason which you pretend has caused you to do something. بہانا، حیلہ

prettily *adv* If something is done or carried out **prettily** it is done or carried out in an attractive or pleasant manner. خوبصورتی سے، نفیس طور پر

pretty(**prettier, prettiest**) *adj* If you describe someone, especially a girl, as **pretty**, you mean that they look nice and are attractive in a delicate way. خوبصورت ▷ *adv* You can use **pretty** before an adjective or adverb to mean 'quite' or 'rather'. بالکل، بلکہ، بجائے

prevent(**prevents, preventing, prevented**) *vt* If you **prevent** something, you stop it happening or being done. روکنا

prevention *n* **Prevention** is the act of stopping something happening or being done. روک تھام

previous *adj* A **previous** event or thing is one that occurred before the one you are talking about. گزشتہ

previously *adv* **Previously** means at some time before the period that you are talking about. گزشتہ طور پر

prey *n* A creature's **prey** are the creatures that it hunts and eats in order to live. شکار

price(**prices**) *n* The **price** of something is the amount of money that you must pay to buy it. قیمت

price list(**price lists**) *n* A **price list** is a list of the prices of a good or service. قیمت فہرست

prick(**pricks, pricking, pricked**) *vt* If you **prick** something, you make small holes in it with a sharp object such as a pin. چبھو کر سوراخ کرنا

pride *n* **Pride** is a feeling of satisfaction which you have because you or people close to you have done something good or possess something good. فخر، اطمینان

primarily *adv* You use **primarily** to say what is mainly true in a particular situation. ابتدائی طور پر

primary *adj* You use **primary** to describe something that is extremely important or most important for someone or something. (*formal*) ابتدائی

primary school (**primary schools**) *n* A **primary school** is a school for children between the ages of 5 and 11. پرائمری اسکول

prime minister (**prime ministers**) *n* The leader of the government in some countries is called the **prime minister**. وزیرِ اعظم

primitive *adj* **Primitive** means belonging to a society in which people live in a very simple way, usually without industries or a writing system. پرانے زمانے کا

primrose (**primroses**) *n* A **primrose** is a wild plant with pale yellow flowers. پیلے پھولوں والا جنگلی پودا

prince (**princes**) *n* A **prince** is a male member of a royal family, especially the son of the king or queen of a country. شہزادہ

princess (**princesses**) *n* A **princess** is a female member of a royal family, usually the daughter of a king or queen or the wife of a prince. شہزادی

principal (**principals**) *adj* **Principal** means first in order of importance. خاص ▷ *n* The **principal** of a school or college is the person in charge of it. پرنسپل

principle (**principles**) *n* A **principle** is a belief that you have about the way you should behave. اصول

print (**prints, printing, printed**) *n* **Print** is all the letters and numbers in a printed document. چھپائی، طباعت ▷ *v* If you **print** something, you use a machine to put words or pictures on paper. پرنٹ کرنا، چھاپنا ▷ *v* If you **print** when you are writing, you do not join the letters together. جلی حروف میں لکھنا

printer (**printers**) *n* A **printer** is a person or firm whose job is printing books, leaflets, or similar material. چھاپنے والا ▷ *n* A **printer** is a machine that can be connected to a computer in order to make copies on paper of information held by the computer. پرنٹر

printout (**printouts**) *n* A **printout** is a piece of paper on which information from a computer has been printed. پرنٹ آوٹ

priority (**priorities**) *n* If something is a **priority**, it is the most important thing you have to achieve or deal with before everything else. ترجیح

prison (**prisons**) *n* A **prison** is a building where criminals are kept. جیل

prisoner (**prisoners**) *n* A **prisoner** is a person who is kept in a prison as a punishment or because they have been captured by an enemy. قیدی

prison officer (**prison officers**) *n* A **prison officer** is someone who works as a guard at a prison. جیل افسر

privacy *n* **Privacy** is the fact of being alone so that you can do things without being seen or disturbed. تخلیہ

private *adj* **Private** industries and services are owned and controlled by an individual person or group, rather than by the state. ذاتی

private property *n* **Private property** is land or belongings owned by a person or group and kept for their exclusive use. ذاتی جائداد

privatize (**privatizes, privatizing, privatized**) *vt* If an organization that is owned by the state **is privatized**, the government sells it to one or more private companies. نجی کاری کرنا

privilege (**privileges**) *n* A **privilege** is a special right or advantage that only one person or group has. اختیار خاص

prize (**prizes**) *n* A **prize** is something valuable, such as money or a trophy, that is given to the winner of a game or competition. اِنعام

prize-giving (**prize-givings**) *n* A **prize-giving** is a ceremony where prizes are awarded to people who have produced a very high standard of work. اِنعام دینا

prizewinner (**prizewinners**) *n* A

prizewinner is a person, animal, or thing that wins a prize. انعام جیتنے والا

probability (**probabilities**) *n* The **probability** of something happening is how likely it is to happen, sometimes expressed as a fraction or a percentage. امکان

probable *adj* Something that is **probable** is likely to be true or likely to happen. متوقع

probably *adv* If you say that something is **probably** true, you think that it is likely to be true, although you are not sure. امکانی طور پر

problem (**problems**) *n* A **problem** is an unsatisfactory situation that causes difficulties for people. الجھن، دشواری

proceedings *npl* Legal **proceedings** are legal action taken against someone. (*formal*) قانونی کاروائیاں

proceeds *npl* The **proceeds** of an event or activity are the money that has been obtained from it. کمائی، پیداوار

process (**processes**) *n* A **process** is a series of actions or events which have a particular result. سلسلۂ عمل

procession (**processions**) *n* A **procession** is a group of people who are walking, riding, or driving in a line as part of a public event. تقریب

produce (**produces, producing, produced**) *vt* To **produce** something means to cause it to happen. پیدا کرنا

producer (**producers**) *n* A **producer** is a person whose job is to produce plays, films, programmes, or CDs. پروڈیوسر (فلم وغیرہ)

product (**products**) *n* A **product** is something that is produced and sold in large quantities. مصنوع

production *n* **Production** is the process of manufacturing or growing something in large quantities, or the amount of goods manufactured or grown. پروڈکشن

productivity *n* **Productivity** is the rate at which goods are produced. پیداوار

profession (**professions**) *n* A **profession** is a type of job that requires advanced education or training. پیشہ

professional (**professionals**) *adj* **Professional** means relating to a person's work, especially work that requires special training. پیشہ وارانہ *His professional career started in a city law firm* ▷ *n* A **professional** is a person who belongs to or engages in one of the professions. پیشہ ور

professionally *adv* If someone is **professionally** trained or qualified it means they have received special training that relates to their job. پیشہ وارانہ طور پر

professor (**professors**) *n* A **professor** in a British university is the most senior teacher in a department. پروفیسر

profit (**profits**) *n* A **profit** is an amount of money that you gain when you are paid more for something than it cost you. نفع

profitable *adj* A **profitable** activity or organization makes a profit. نفع بخش

program (**programs, programming, programmed**) *n* A **program** is a set of instructions that a computer follows in order to perform a particular task. پروگرام ▷ *vt* When you **program** a computer, you give it a set of instructions to make it able to perform a particular task. پروگرام دینا

programme (**programmes**) *n* A **programme** of actions or events is a series of actions or events that are planned to be done. پروگرام

programmer (**programmers**) *n* A computer **programmer** is a person whose job involves writing programs for computers. پروگرامر

programming *n* **Programming** is the process of giving a set of instructions to a computer to make it able to perform a particular task. پروگرام سازی

progress *n* **Progress** is the process of gradually improving or getting nearer to achieving or completing something. پیش رفت

P

prohibit (**prohibits, prohibiting, prohibited**) *vt* If someone **prohibits** something, they forbid it or make it illegal. (*formal*) ممانعت کرنا

prohibited *adj* If something is **prohibited**, law or someone in authority forbids it or makes it illegal. ممنوعہ

project (**projects**) *n* A **project** is a carefully planned task that requires a lot of time and effort. منصوبہ بند کام

projector (**projectors**) *n* A **projector** is a machine that projects films or slides onto a screen or wall. پروجیکٹر

promenade (**promenades**) *n* In a seaside town, the **promenade** is the road by the sea where people go for a walk. سمندر کنارے سڑک، سیر گاہ

promise (**promises, promising, promised**) *n* A **promise** is a statement which you make to a person in which you say that you will definitely do something or give them something. وعدہ ▷ *vt* If you **promise** that you will do something, you say to someone that you will definitely do it. وعدہ کرنا

promising *adj* Someone or something that is **promising** seems likely to be very good or successful. کامیاب، برتر

promote (**promotes, promoting, promoted**) *vt* If people **promote** something, they help to make it happen, increase, or become more popular. ترقی، فروغ دینا

promotion (**promotions**) *n* A **promotion** is a means of making something happen, increase or become more popular. ترقی، فروغ

prompt *adj* A **prompt** action is done without any delay. فوری

promptly *adv* If you do something **promptly**, you do it immediately. فوری طور پر

pronoun (**pronouns**) *n* A **pronoun** is a word which is used instead of a noun group to refer to someone or something. 'He', 'she', 'them', and 'something' are pronouns. ضمیر

pronounce (**pronounces, pronouncing, pronounced**) *vt* To **pronounce** a word means to say it. تلفظ کرنا

pronunciation (**pronunciations**) *n* The **pronunciation** of words is the way they are pronounced. تلفظ

proof (**proofs**) *n* **Proof** is a fact or a piece of evidence which shows that something is true or exists. ثبوت ▷ *n* In publishing, the **proofs** of a book, magazine, or article are a first copy of it that is printed so that mistakes can be corrected before more copies are printed and published. پروف (طباعت سے پہلے پروف پڑھنا)

propaganda *n* **Propaganda** is information, often inaccurate information, which an organization publishes or broadcasts in order to influence people. پروپگنڈا (کسی کی شبیہ بنانا یا بگاڑنا)

proper *adj* You use **proper** to describe things that you consider to be real or satisfactory. ٹھیک، حق

properly *adv* If something is done **properly**, it is done in a correct and satisfactory way. ٹھیک طور پر

property *n* Someone's **property** consists of all the things that belong to them, or something that belongs to them. (*formal*) جائداد

proportion (**proportions**) *n* A **proportion** of an amount or group is a part of it. (*formal*) حصہ یا جزو

proportional *adj* If one amount is **proportional** to another, the two amounts increase and decrease at the same rate so there is always the same relationship between them. (*formal*) جزوی

proposal (**proposals**) *n* A **proposal** is a suggestion or plan, often a formal or written one. تجویز

propose (**proposes, proposing, proposed**) *vt* If you **propose** a plan or idea, you suggest it. تجویز پیش کرنا

prosecute (**prosecutes, prosecuting, prosecuted**) *v* If the authorities

prosecute someone, they charge them with a crime and put them on trial. مقدمہ چلانا

prospect (**prospects**) *n* A **prospect** is a possibility or a possible event. اِمکان، اِمکانی واقعہ

prospectus (**prospectuses**) *n* A **prospectus** is a document produced by a college, school, or company which gives details about it. نصاب

prosperity *n* **Prosperity** is a condition in which a person or community is being financially successful. خوشحالی

protect (**protects, protecting, protected**) *vt* To **protect** someone or something means to prevent them from being harmed or damaged. حفاظت کرنا

protection *n* If something gives **protection** against something unpleasant, it prevents people or things from being harmed or damaged by it. حفاظت

protein (**proteins**) *n* **Protein** is a substance which the body needs and which is found in meat, eggs, and milk. پروٹین (غذائی جزو)

protest (**protests, protesting, protested**) *n* A **protest** is the act of saying or showing publicly that you do not approve of something. اِحتجاج ▷ *v* To **protest** means to say or show publicly that you do not agree with something. احتجاج کرنا

proud (**prouder, proudest**) *adj* If you feel **proud**, you feel pleasure and satisfaction at something that you own, have done, or are connected with. فاخر

prove (**proves, proving, proved, proven**) *v* If something **proves** to be true or to have a particular quality, it becomes clear after a period of time that it is true or has that quality. ثابت ہونا، کرنا

proverb (**proverbs**) *n* A **proverb** is a short sentence that people often quote, which gives advice or tells you something about life. For example, 'A bird in the hand is worth two in the bush.' کہاوت، تمثیل

provide (**provides, providing, provided**) *vt* If you **provide** something that someone needs or wants, you give it to them or make it available to them. مہیا کرنا

provided *conj* If something will happen **provided** that another thing happens, the first thing will happen only if the second thing also happens. بشرطیکہ *He can go running, provided that he wears the right kind of shoes.*

provide for *v* If you **provide for** someone, you support them financially and make sure that they have the things that they need. ضروریات پوری کرنا *She won't let him provide for her.*

provisional *adj* You use **provisional** to describe something that has been arranged or appointed for the present, but may be changed soon. عبوری، عارضی

proximity *n* **Proximity** to a place or person is the fact of being near to them. (*formal*) قرابت

prune (**prunes**) *n* A **prune** is a dried plum. سوکھا آلو بخارا

pry (**pries, prying, pried**) *vi* If you say that someone is **prying**, you disapprove of them because they are trying to find out about someone else's private affairs. ٹوہ میں لگے رہنا

pseudonym (**pseudonyms**) *n* A **pseudonym** is a name which someone, usually a writer, uses instead of his or her real name. تخلص، قلمی نام

psychiatric *adj* **Psychiatric** means relating to psychiatry. طب نفسی سے متعلق

psychiatrist (**psychiatrists**) *n* A **psychiatrist** is a doctor who treats people suffering from mental illness. طبیب نفسی

psychological *adj* **Psychological** means concerned with a person's mind and thoughts. نفسیاتی

psychologist (**psychologists**) *n* A

psychologist is a person who studies the human mind and tries to explain why people behave in the way that they do. ماہرِ نفسیات

psychology *n* **Psychology** is the scientific study of the human mind and the reasons for people's behaviour. علم نفسیات

psychotherapy *n* **Psychotherapy** is the use of psychological methods to treat people who are mentally ill. نفسیاتی طریق علاج

PTO *abbr* **PTO** is a written abbreviation for 'please turn over'. You write it at the bottom of a page to indicate that there is more writing on the other side. برائے مہربانی صفحہ پلٹیے

public *adj* **Public** means relating to all the people in a country or community. عوامی ▷ *n* You can refer to people in general as **the public**. عوام

publication (**publications**) *n* The **publication** of a book or magazine is the act of printing it and making it available. اشاعت

public holiday (**public holidays**) *n* A **public holiday** is a holiday observed over the whole country. سرکاری چھٹی

publicity *n* **Publicity** is advertising, information, or actions intended to attract the public's attention to someone or something. تشہیر

public opinion *n* **Public opinion** is the opinion or attitude of the public regarding a particular matter. عوامی رائے، رائے عامہ

public relations *npl* **Public relations** are the state of the relationship between an organization and the public. تعلقات عامہ

public school (**public schools**) *n* In Britain, a **public school** is a private school that provides secondary education which parents have to pay for. عوامی اسکول

public transport *n* **Public transport** is a system of buses, trains, etc, running on fixed routes, on which the public may travel. عوامی نقل و حمل (ٹرانسپورٹ)

publish (**publishes, publishing, published**) *vt* When a company **publishes** a book or magazine, it prints copies of it, which are sent to shops and sold. شائع کرنا

publisher (**publishers**) *n* A **publisher** is a person or company that publishes books, newspapers, or magazines. ناشر

pudding (**puddings**) *n* A **pudding** is a cooked sweet food made with flour, fat, and eggs, and usually served hot. پڈنگ (مکئی کی کھیر)

puddle (**puddles**) *n* A **puddle** is a small shallow pool of rain or other liquid on the ground. پانی بھرے گڈھے

Puerto Rico *n* **Puerto Rico** is an autonomous commonwealth in the Caribbean. پیورٹو ریکو

puff pastry *n* **Puff pastry** is a type of pastry which is very light and consists of a lot of thin layers. پفدار پیسٹری

pull (**pulls, pulling, pulled**) *vt* When you **pull** something, you hold it and move it towards you. کھینچنا

pull down *v* To **pull down** a building or statue means to deliberately destroy it. گرا دینا، منہدم کرنا *They pulled the offices down, leaving a large open space.*

pull out *v* When a vehicle or driver **pulls out**, the vehicle moves out into the road or nearer the centre of the road. نکل جانا *She pulled out into the street.*

pullover (**pullovers**) *n* A **pullover** is a woollen piece of clothing that covers the upper part of your body and your arms. اونی قمیض

pull up *v* When a vehicle or driver **pulls up**, the vehicle slows down and stops. دھیمی ہوکر رک جانا *The car pulled up and the driver jumped out.*

pulse (**pulses** *n* Your **pulse** is the regular beating of blood through your body, which you can feel, for example, at your wrist or neck. دھڑکن

pulses *npl* Some large dried seeds which

can be cooked and eaten are called **pulses**, for example the seeds of peas, beans, and lentils. دالیں

pump (**pumps, pumping, pumped**) *n* A **pump** is a machine that is used to force a liquid or gas to flow in strong regular movements in a particular direction. پمپ (آلہ) ▷ *vt* To **pump** a liquid or gas in a certain direction means to force it to flow in that direction, using a pump. پمپ کرنا (ہوا سے کسی چیز کو دھکہ دینا)

pumpkin (**pumpkins**) *n* A **pumpkin** is a large, round, orange-coloured vegetable with a thick skin. کدو، لوکی

pump up *v* If you **pump up** something such as a tyre, you fill it with air, using a pump. ہوا بھرنا *Pump all the tyres up.*

punch (**punches, punching, punched**) *n* A **punch** is a blow with the fist. مکہ، پنچ ▷ *n* **Punch** is a drink usually made from wine or spirits mixed with sugar, fruit, and spices. شراب اور شکر کا جام ▷ *vt* If you **punch** someone or something, you hit them hard with your fist. مکہ مارنا

punctual *adj* Someone who is **punctual** arrives somewhere or does something at the right time and is not late. عادی

punctuation *n* **Punctuation** is the system of signs such as full stops, commas, and question marks that you use in writing to divide words into sentences and clauses. رموز اوقاف

puncture (**punctures**) *n* A **puncture** is a small hole in a car or bicycle tyre that has been made by a sharp object. سوراخ

punish (**punishes, punishing, punished**) *vt* To **punish** someone means to make them suffer in some way because they have done something wrong. سزا دینا

punishment *n* **Punishment** is the act of punishing someone or being punished. سزا

punk *n* **Punk** or **punk rock** is rock music that is played in a fast, loud, and aggressive way. Punk rock was particularly popular in the late 1970s. روک موسیقی

pupil (**pupils**) *n* The **pupils** of a school are the children who go to it. شاگرد ▷ *n* The **pupils** of your eyes are the small, round, black holes in the centre of them. آنکھ کی پتلی

puppet (**puppets**) *n* A **puppet** is a doll that you can move, either by pulling strings which are attached to it, or by putting your hand inside its body and moving your fingers. گڑیا

puppy (**puppies**) *n* A **puppy** is a young dog. پلہ

purchase (**purchases, purchasing, purchased**) *vt* When you **purchase** something, you buy it. (*formal*) خریدنا

pure (**purer, purest**) *adj* **Pure** means not mixed with anything else. خالص

purple *adj* Something that is **purple** is reddish-blue in colour. بینگنی

purpose (**purposes**) *n* The **purpose** of something is the reason for which it is made or done. مقصد

purr (**purrs, purring, purred**) *vi* When a cat **purrs**, it makes a low vibrating sound with its throat. بلی کی آواز، خرخراہٹ

purse (**purses**) *n* A **purse** is a very small bag that people, especially women, keep their money in. پرس (چرمی بیگ)

pursue (**pursues, pursuing, pursued**) *vt* If you **pursue** a particular aim or result, you make efforts to achieve it or to progress in it. (*formal*) اپنانا، تعاقب کرنا

pursuit *n* Your **pursuit** of something that you want consists of your attempts at achieving it. تعاقب

pus *n* **Pus** is a thick yellowish liquid that forms in wounds when they are infected. پس، مواد

push (**pushes, pushing, pushed**) *v* When you **push** something, you press it in order to move it away from you. دھکہ دینا

pushchair (**pushchairs**) *n* A **pushchair** is a small chair on wheels, in which a small

p

child can sit and be wheeled around. بچے دار کرسی

push-up (**push-ups**) *n* **Push-ups** are exercises to strengthen your arms and chest muscles. They are done by lying with your face towards the floor and pushing with your hands to raise your body until your arms are straight. (*US*) ڈنڈ

put (**puts, putting**) *vt* When you **put** something somewhere, you move it there. رکھنا

put aside *v* If you **put** something **aside**, you keep it to be dealt with or used at a later time. مختص کرنا *I put money aside each month because I'm saving for a holiday.*

put away *v* If you **put** something **away**, you put it into the place where it is normally kept when it is not being used. اپنی جگہ رکھنا *Put your maths books away, it's time for your history lesson.*

put back *v* To **put** something **back** means to delay it or postpone it. پیچھے کرنا *The trip has been put back to April.*

put forward *v* If you **put forward** a plan, proposal, or name, you suggest that it should be considered for a particular purpose or job. پیش کرنا *I asked my boss to put my name forward for the job in head office.*

put in *v* If you **put in** an amount of time or effort doing something, you spend that time or effort doing it. صرف کرنا *We put in three hours' work every evening.*

put off *v* If you **put** something **off**, you delay doing it. ملتوی کرنا *She put off telling him until the last moment.*

put up *v* If people **put up** a wall, building, tent, or other structure, they construct it. قائم کرنا *They put up their tents and settled down for the night.*

puzzle (**puzzles**) *n* A **puzzle** is a question, game, or toy which you have to think about carefully in order to answer it correctly or put it together properly. الجھن، پہیلیاں

puzzled *adj* Someone who is **puzzled** is confused because they do not understand something. حیران

puzzling *adj* If something is **puzzling**, it is confusing or difficult to understand. حیران کن

pyjamas *npl* A pair of **pyjamas** consists of loose trousers and a loose jacket that are worn in bed. لباس شب خوابی

pylon (**pylons**) *n* **Pylons** are very tall metal structures which hold electric cables high above the ground so that electricity can be transmitted over long distances. لوہے کا منارہ

pyramid (**pyramids**) *n* A **pyramid** is a three-dimensional shape with a flat base and flat triangular sides which slope upwards to a point. ہرم، تکونی مقبرے

q

Qatar *n* **Qatar** is a state in east Arabia, in the Persian Gulf. قطر

quail (**quails, quail**) *n* A **quail** is a small bird which is often shot and eaten. بٹیر

quaint (**quainter, quaintest**) *adj* Something that is **quaint** is attractive because it is unusual and rather old-fashioned. عجیب، جاذب

qualification (**qualifications**) *n* Your **qualifications** are the examinations that you have passed. تعلیمی لیاقت

qualified *adj* If you give someone or something **qualified** support or approval, you give support or approval that is not total and suggests that you have some doubts. تعلیم یافتہ

qualify (**qualifies, qualifying, qualified**) *v* When someone **qualifies**, they pass the examinations that they need to pass in order to work in a particular profession. معیار پر پورا اترنا

quality (**qualities**) *n* The **quality** of something is how good or bad it is. خوبی، کوالٹی

quantify (**quantifies, quantifying, quantified**) *v* If you try to **quantify** something, you try to calculate how much of it there is. مقدار کا اندازہ لگانا

quantity (**quantities**) *n* A **quantity** is an amount that you can measure or count. مقدار

quarantine *n* If a person or animal is in **quarantine**, they are kept separate from other people or animals in case they have an infectious disease. الگ تھلگ رکھنا

quarrel (**quarrels, quarrelling, quarrelled**) *n* A **quarrel** is an angry argument between two or more friends or family members. جھگڑا ▷ *vi* When two or more people **quarrel**, they have an angry argument. جھگڑا کرنا

quarry (**quarries**) *n* A **quarry** is an area that is dug out from a piece of land or mountainside in order to extract stone, slate, or minerals. پتھر کی کان

quarter (**quarters**) *n* A **quarter** is one of four equal parts of something. چوتھائی

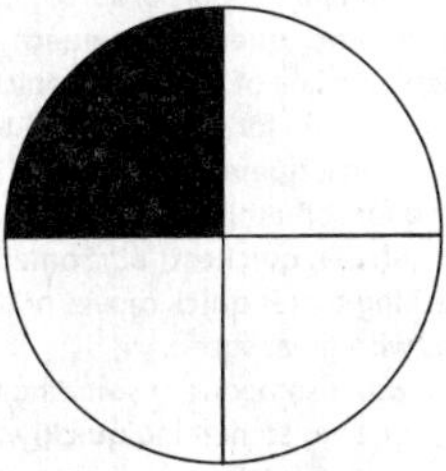

quarter final (**quarter finals**) *n* A **quarter final** is one of the four matches in a competition which decides which four players or teams will compete in the semi-final. کوارٹر فائنل

quartet (**quartets**) *n* A **quartet** is a group of four people who play musical instruments or sing together. چار لوگوں کا گروپ جو ساز بجاتے یا گاتے ہیں

quay (**quays**) *n* A **quay** is a long platform beside the sea or a river where boats can be tied. گھاٹ

queen (**queens**) *n* A **queen** is a woman who rules a country as its monarch. ملکہ

query (**queries, querying, queried**) *n* A **query** is a question about a particular point. سوال ▷ *vt* If you **query** something, you check it by asking about it because you are not sure if it is correct. سوال پوچھنا

question (**questions, questioning, questioned**) *n* A **question** is something which you say or write in order to ask about a particular matter. سوال ▷ *vt* If you **question** someone, you ask them questions about something. سوال کرنا

question mark (**question marks**) *n* A **question mark** is the punctuation mark (?) which is used in writing at the end of a question. سوالیہ نشان

questionnaire (**questionnaires**) *n* A **questionnaire** is a written list of questions which are answered by a number of people in order to provide information for a report or survey. سوالنامہ

queue (**queues, queuing, queued**) *n* A **queue** is a line of people or vehicles that are waiting for something. قطار ▷ *vi* When people **queue**, they stand in a line waiting for something. قطار میں لگنا، کھڑے ہونا

quick (**quicker, quickest**) *adj* Someone or something that is **quick** moves or does things with great speed. تیز

quickly *adv* If someone or something moves or does something **quickly** they move or do something with great speed. تیزی سے

quiet(**quieter, quietest**) *adj* Something or someone that is **quiet** makes only a small amount of noise. خاموش

quietly *adv* If someone or something does something **quietly** they do it with only a small amount of noise. خاموشی سے

quilt (**quilts**) *n* A **quilt** is a bed-cover filled with warm soft material, which is often decorated with lines of stitching. گدا

quit (**quits, quitting, quit**) *vt* If you **quit** your job, you choose to leave it. (*informal*) چھوڑ دینا

quite *adv* **Quite** means a bit but not a lot. تھوڑا

quiz (**quizzes**) *n* A **quiz** is a game or competition in which someone tests your knowledge by asking you questions. مقابلہ سوال جواب

quota (**quotas**) *n* A **quota** is the limited number or quantity which is officially allowed. کوٹا (مختص مقدار)

quotation (**quotations**) *n* A **quotation** is a sentence or phrase taken from a book, poem, or play. اقتباس (کسی اور کا جملہ یا تحریر مستعار لینا)

quotation marks *npl* **Quotation marks** are punctuation marks used in writing to show where speech or a quotation begins and ends. They are usually written or printed as (' ') and (" "). الٹے کوما، علامات اقتباس

quote (**quotes, quoting, quoted**) *n* A **quote** from a book, poem, or play is a sentence or phrase from it. قول ▷ *vt* If you **quote** something, you repeat what someone has written or said. If you **quote** someone as saying something, you repeat what they have written or said. کسی کے قول کا حوالہ دینا

r

rabbit (**rabbits**) *n* A **rabbit** is a small furry animal with long ears which is often kept as a pet. خرگوش

rabies *n* **Rabies** is a serious infectious disease which humans can get from the bite of an animal such as a dog which has the disease. جانور کے کاٹنے سے آلودگی

race (**races, racing, raced**) *n* you is a **all** in east Arabia, in the Persian Gulf. دوڑ مقابلہ ⊳ *n* A **race** is one of the major groups which human beings can be divided into according to their physical features, such as their skin colour. نسل ⊳ *v* If you **race**, you take part in a race. دوڑ میں مقابلہ کرنا

racecourse (**racecourses**) *n* A **racecourse** is a track on which horses race. گھڑدوڑ کا میدان

racehorse (**racehorses**) *n* A **racehorse** is a horse that is trained to run in races. ریس کا گھوڑا

racer (**racers**) *n* A **racer** is a person or animal that takes part in races. ریس کا جانور یا انسان

racetrack (**racetracks**) *n* A **racetrack** is a piece of ground that is used for races between runners, horses, dogs, cars, or motorcycles. ریس کا ٹریک (راستہ)

racial *adj* **Racial** describes things relating to people's race. نسلی

racing car (**racing cars**) *n* A **racing car** is a car that has been specially designed for motor racing. ریس کی کار

racing driver (**racing drivers**) *n* A **racing driver** is a person who takes part in motor racing. ریس ڈرائور

racism *n* **Racism** is the belief that people of some races are inferior to others. نسل پرستی

racist (**racists**) *adj* If you describe people, things, or behaviour as **racist**, you mean that they are influenced by the belief that some people are inferior because they belong to a particular race. نسلی برتری کا عقیدہ رکھنے والا ⊳ *n* A **racist**, or a person with **racist** views, believes that people of some races are inferior to others. نسلی پرست

rack (**racks**) *n* A **rack** is a piece of equipment used for holding things or for hanging things on. ریک (سامان رکھنے کا فریم)

racket (**rackets**) *n* A **racket**is a loud unpleasant noise. شور شرابہ

racoon (**racoons**) *n* A **racoon** is a small animal that has dark-coloured fur with white stripes on its face and on its long tail. Racoons live in forests in North and Central America and the West Indies. چھوٹا جنگلی فردار جانور

racquet (**racquets**) *n* A **racquet** is an oval-shaped bat with strings across it. Racquets are used in tennis, squash, and badminton. ٹینس ریکیٹ

radar *n* **Radar**is a way of discovering the position or speed of objects such as aircraft or ships by using radio signals. رڈار

radiation *n* **Radiation** is very small particles of a radioactive substance. Large amounts of radiation can cause illness and death. تابکاری

radiator (**radiators**) *n* A **radiator** is a hollow metal device which is connected to a central heating system and used to heat a room. ریڈیئٹر (کار انجن کا حصہ)

radio *n* **Radio** is the broadcasting of programmes for the public to listen to. ریڈیو

radioactive *adj* Something that is **radioactive** contains a substance that produces energy in the form of powerful rays which are harmful in large doses. تابکار

radio-controlled *adj* A **radio-controlled** device works by receiving radio signals which operate it. ریڈیو سگنل سے کنٹرول کی ہوئی

radio station (**radio stations**) *n* A **radio station** is an installation consisting of one or more transmitters or receivers, etc, used for radiocommunications. ریڈیو اسٹیشن

radish (**radishes**) *n* **Radishes** are small red or white vegetables that are the roots of a plant. They are eaten raw in salads. مولی

raffle (**raffles**) *n* A **raffle** is a competition in which you buy numbered tickets. Afterwards some numbers are chosen and if your ticket has one of these numbers on it, you win a prize. مقابلہ جس میں نمبر پڑے ٹکٹ خریدے جاتے ہیں

raft (**rafts**) *n* A **raft** is a floating platform made from large pieces of wood tied together. بے دیوار ناو

rag (**rags**) *n* A **rag** is a piece of old cloth which you can use to clean or wipe things. دھجی

rage (**rages**) *n* **Rage** is strong, uncontrollable anger. غصہ

raid (**raids, raiding, raided**) *n* A **raid** is a sudden surprise attack. اچانک حملہ ▷ *vt* When soldiers **raid** a place, they make a sudden armed attack against it, with the aim of causing damage rather than occupying any of the enemy's land. اچانک حملہ کرنا

rail (**rails**) *n* A **rail** is a horizontal bar which is fixed to something and used as a fence or a support, or to hang things on. باڑ، جنگلا

railcard (**railcards**) *n* A **railcard** is an identity card that allows people to buy train tickets cheaply. ریل کارڈ

railings *npl* A fence made from metal bars is called a **railing** or **railings**. باڑیں، جنگلے

railway (**railways**) *n* A **railway** is a route between two places along which trains travel on steel rails. ریلوے

railway station (**railway stations**) *n* A **railway station** is a building by a railway line where trains stop so that people can get on or off. ریلوے اسٹیشن

rain (**rains, raining, rained**) *n* **Rain** is water that falls from the clouds in small drops. بارش ▷ *vi* When **rain** falls, you can say that it is raining. بارش ہونا

rainbow (**rainbows**) *n* A **rainbow** is the arch of different colours that you sometimes see in the sky when it is raining. دھنک

raincoat (**raincoats**) *n* A **raincoat** is a waterproof coat. برساتی

rainforest (**rainforests**) *n* A **rainforest** is a thick forest of tall trees found in tropical areas where there is a lot of rain. لمبے درختوں کا گھنا جنگل

rainy (**rainier, rainiest**) *adj* If it is **rainy**, it is raining a lot. بارش بھرا

raise (**raises, raising, raised**) *vt* If you **raise** something, you move it to a higher position. اٹھانا

raisin (**raisins**) *n* **Raisins** are dried grapes. کشمش

rake (**rakes**) *n* A **rake** is a garden tool consisting of a row of metal teeth attached to a long handle. مالی کا اوزار

rally (**rallies**) *n* A **rally** is a large public meeting held in support of something such as a political party. ریلی

ram (**rams, ramming, rammed**) *n* A **ram** is an adult male sheep. نر ▷ *vt* If one vehicle **rams** another, it crashes into it with a lot of force. ٹکر ہونا

Ramadan *n* **Ramadan** is the ninth month of the Muslim year, when Muslims do not eat between the rising and setting of the sun. During Ramadan, Muslims celebrate the fact that it was in this month that God first revealed the words of the Quran to Mohammed. رمضان

rambler (**ramblers**) *n* A **rambler** is a person whose hobby is going on long walks in the countryside, often as part of an organized group. دیہاتوں کی سیر کے لیے منظم گروپ کا رکن

ramp (**ramps**) *n* A **ramp** is a sloping surface between two places that are at different levels. ڈھلان

random *adj* A **random** sample or method is one in which all the people or things involved have an equal chance of being chosen. اتفاقیہ

range (**ranges, ranging, ranged**) *n* The **range** of something is the maximum area within which it can reach things or detect things. دائرہ ▷ *vi* If things **range** between two points or **range** from one point to another, they vary within these points on a scale of measurement or quality. وسعت کی حدود ہونا

rank (**ranks, ranking, ranked**) *n* Someone's **rank** is their position in an organization, or in society. عہدہ ▷ *n* A **rank** of people or things is a row of them. درجہ ▷ *v* When someone or something is **ranked** a particular position, they are at that position on a scale. کسی حالت پر ہونا

ransom (**ransoms**) *n* A **ransom** is money that is demanded as payment for the return of someone who has been kidnapped. زر فدیہ

rape (**rapes, raping, raped**) *n* **Rape** is the crime of forcing someone to have sex. زنا بالجبر ▷ *n* **Rape** is a plant with yellow flowers which is grown as a crop. Its seeds are crushed to make cooking oil. سرسوں کی نسل کا پودا ▷ *vt* If someone is **raped**, they are forced to have sex, usually by violence or threats of violence. زنا بالجبر کرنا

rapids *npl* **Rapids** are a section of a river where the water moves very fast. ندی کے تیز دھارے

rapist (**rapists**) *n* A **rapist** is a man who has raped someone. زانی

rare (**rarer, rarest**) *adj* If something is **rare**, it is not common, and is therefore interesting, valuable, or unusual. نایاب ▷ *adj* Meat that is **rare** is cooked very lightly so that the inside is still red. ہلکا پکایا ہوا

rarely *adv* **Rarely** means not very often. شاذ و نادر طور پر

rash (**rashes**) *n* A **rash** is an area of red spots on your skin which appear when you are ill or have an allergy. سرخ باد

raspberry (**raspberries**) *n* A **raspberry** is a small, soft, red fruit that grows on bushes. رس بھری

rat (**rats**) *n* A **rat** is an animal which has a long tail and looks like a large mouse. چوہا

rate (**rates, rating, rated**) *n* The **rate** at which something happens is the speed or frequency with which it happens. شرح ▷ *vt* If you **rate** someone or something as good or bad, you consider them to be good or bad. درجہ بندی کرنا

rate of exchange (**rates of exchange**) *n* The **rate of exchange** of a country's unit of currency is the amount of another currency that you get in exchange for it. شرح مبادلہ

rather *adv* You use **rather** to mean 'a little bit'. تھوڑا، تھوڑی

ratio (**ratios**) *n* The **ratio** of something is the relationship between two things expressed in numbers or amounts, to show how much greater one is than the other. نسبت

rational *adj* **Rational** decisions and thoughts are based on reason rather than on emotion. عاقلانہ

rattle (**rattles**) *n* A **rattle** is a rapid

r

succession of short sharp sounds. گڑگڑاہٹ، شور

rattlesnake (**rattlesnakes**) *n* A **rattlesnake** is a poisonous American snake which can make a rattling noise with its tail. زہریلا امریکی سانپ

rave (**raves, raving, raved**) *n* A **rave** or a **rave** review is a very enthusiastic review. پرجوش جائزہ ▷ *v* If someone **raves**, they talk in an excited and uncontrolled way. جوش و جنون میں بات کرنا

raven (**ravens**) *n* A **raven** is a large bird with shiny black feathers and a deep harsh call. کوا

ravenous *adj* If you are **ravenous**, you are extremely hungry. انتہائی بھوکا

ravine (**ravines**) *n* A **ravine** is a very deep, narrow valley with steep sides. نہر

raw (**rawer, rawest**) *adj* A **raw** substance is in its natural state before being processed. خام

razor (**razors**) *n* A **razor** is a tool that people use for shaving. استرہ

razor blade (**razor blades**) *n* A **razor blade** is a small flat piece of metal with a very sharp edge which is put into a razor and used for shaving. ریزر بلیڈ

reach (**reaches, reaching, reached**) *vt* When you **reach** a place, you arrive there. رسائی پانا، پہنچنا ▷ *vi* If you **reach** somewhere, you move your arm and hand to take or touch something. پہنچنا

react (**reacts, reacting, reacted**) *vi* When you **react** to something that has happened to you, you behave in a particular way because of it. رد عمل کرنا

reaction (**reactions**) *n* Your **reaction** to something that has happened or something that you have experienced is what you feel, say, or do because of it. رد عمل

reactor (**reactors**) *n* A **reactor** is a device which produces nuclear energy. ری ایکٹر (جوہری توانائی پیدا کرنے والا)

read (**reads, reading**) *v* When you **read** something such as a book or article, you look at and understand the words that are written there. پڑھنا

reader (**readers**) *n* The **readers** of a book, newspaper, or magazine are the people who read it. قاری

readily *adv* If you do something **readily**, you do it willingly. آمادگی کے ساتھ

reading *n* **Reading** is the activity of reading books. خواندگی

read out *v* If you **read** something **out**, you say the words aloud, especially in a loud, clear voice. بول کر پڑھنا *We read plays out in class.*

ready (**readier, readiest**) *adj* If someone or something is **ready**, they have reached the required stage for something or they are properly prepared for action or use. آمادہ، تیار

ready-cooked *adj* If food that you buy is **ready-cooked**, you only have to heat it before eating it because it has already been cooked. پکا پکایا

real *adj* Something that is **real** is true and is not imagined. حقیقی ▷ *adj* If something is **real**, it is not a copy. اصلی

realistic *adj* If you are **realistic** about a situation, you recognize and accept its true nature and try to deal with it practically. حقیقت پسند

reality *n* You use **reality** to refer to real things or the real nature of things rather than imagined, invented, or theoretical ideas. حقیقت

reality TV *n* **Reality TV** is a type of television which aims to show how ordinary people behave in everyday life, or in situations, often created by the programme makers, which are intended to represent everyday life. ریئلیٹی ٹی وی (حقیقت دکھانے والا)

realize (**realizes, realizing, realized**) *n* If you **realize** that something is true, you become aware of that fact or understand it. حقیقت معلوم ہوجانا

really *adv* You say **really** to show how much you mean something. (*spoken*) واقعی، در حقیقت ▷ *adv* You say **really** to show that what you are saying is true. واقعی، حقیقتاً

rear *adj* **Rear** means situated in the back part of something or refers to the back part of something. پچھلا ▷ *n* The **rear** of something is the back part of it. عقبی

rear-view mirror(**rear-view mirrors**) *n* Inside a car, the **rear-view mirror** is the mirror that enables you to see the traffic behind when you are driving. پیچھے کا منظر دکھانے والا آئینہ

reason(**reasons**) *n* The **reason** for something is a fact or situation which explains why it happens. وجہ

reasonable *adj* If you think that someone is fair and sensible you can say they are **reasonable**. معقول

reasonably *adv* If someone behaves or acts **reasonably** they behave or act fairly and sensibly. معقول طور پر

reassure(**reassures, reassuring, reassured**) *vt* If you **reassure** someone, you say or do things to make them stop worrying about something. یقین دلانا

reassuring *adj* If you find someone's words or actions **reassuring**, they make you feel less worried. یقین دہانی

rebate(**rebates**) *n* A **rebate** is an amount of money which is paid to you when you have paid more tax, rent, or rates than you needed to. چھوٹ، رخصت

rebellious *adj* A **rebellious** person behaves in an unacceptable way and does not do what they are told. باغی

rebuild(**rebuilds, rebuilding, rebuilt**) *vt* When people **rebuild** something such as a building, they build it again after it has been damaged or destroyed. پھر سے بنانا

receipt(**receipts**) *n* A **receipt** is a piece of paper that you get from someone as confirmation that they have received money or goods from you. رسید

receive(**receives, receiving, received**) *vt* When you **receive** something, you get it after someone gives it to you or sends it to you. حاصل کرنا

receiver(**receivers**) *n* A telephone **receiver** is the part that you hold near to your ear and speak into. ٹیلیفون رسیور ▷ *n* A **receiver** is someone who is officially appointed to manage the affairs of a business, usually when it is facing financial failure. وصول کنندہ

recent *adj* A **recent** event or period of time happened only a short while ago. حالیہ

recently *adv* If you have done something **recently** or if something happened **recently**, it happened only a short time ago. حالیہ طور پر

reception(**receptions**) *n* In a hotel, office, or hospital, the **reception** is the place where people are received and their reservations, appointments, and inquiries are dealt with. استقبالیہ

receptionist(**receptionists**) *n* In a hotel, office, or hospital, the **receptionist** is the person whose job is to answer the telephone, arrange reservations, or appointments, and deal with people when they first arrive. ریسپشنسٹ

recession(**recessions**) *n* A **recession** is a period when the economy of a country is not very successful. کساد بازاری

recharge(**recharges, recharging, recharged**) *vt* If you **recharge** a battery, you put an electrical charge back into the battery by connecting it to a machine that draws power from another source of electricity such as the mains. بیٹری چارج کرنا

recipe(**recipes**) *n* A **recipe** is a list of ingredients and a set of instructions that tell you how to cook something. پکوان

recipient(**recipients**) *n* The **recipient** of something is the person who receives it. (*formal*) وصول کنندہ

reckon(**reckons, reckoning, reckoned**) *vt* If you **reckon** that something is true, you think that it is true. (*informal*) اندازہ لگانا سمجھنا

reclining *adj* A **reclining** seat has a back that you can lower so that it is more comfortable to sit in. نیم دراز حالت میں

recognizable *adj* Something that is **recognizable** is easy to recognize or identify. قابل شناخت

recognize (**recognizes, recognizing, recognized**) *vt* If you **recognize** someone or something, you know who or what they are, because you have seen or heard them before or because they have been described to you. شناخت کر لینا، پہچان لینا

recommend (**recommends, recommending, recommended**) *vt* If someone **recommends** something or someone to you, they suggest that you would find them good or useful. سفارش کرنا

recommendation (**recommendations**) *n* The **recommendations** of a person or a committee are their suggestions or advice on what is the best thing to do. سفارش

reconsider (**reconsiders, reconsidering, reconsidered**) *v* If you **reconsider** a decision or method, you think about it and try to decide whether it should be changed. دوبارہ غور کرنا

record (**records, recording, recorded**) *n* If you keep a **record** of something, you keep a written account or photographs of it so that it can be looked at later. ریکارڈ ▷ *vt* If you **record** a piece of information or an event, you write it down or photograph it so that in the future people can look at it. ریکارڈ کرنا ▷ *n* A **record** is the best result ever. ریکارڈ ▷ *vt* If you **record** something like a TV programme, you make a copy of it so that you can watch it later. ریکارڈ کرنا، نقل کرنا، محفوظ کرنا

recorded delivery *n* If you send a letter or parcel **recorded delivery**, you send it using a Post Office service which gives you an official record of the fact that it has been posted and delivered. درج کردہ حوالگی

recorder (**recorders**) *n* A **recorder** is a hollow musical instrument that you play by blowing down one end and covering a series of holes with your fingers. ریکارڈر ▷ *n* A **recorder** is a machine or instrument that keeps a record of something, for example, in an experiment or on a vehicle. ریکارڈ کنندہ

recording (**recordings**) *n* A **recording** of something such as moving pictures and sounds is a computer file or a disk on which they are stored. ریکارڈ کرنا

recover (**recovers, recovering, recovered**) *vi* When you **recover** from an illness or an injury, you become well again. شفایاب ہونا

recovery (**recoveries**) *n* If a sick person makes a **recovery**, he or she becomes well again. شفایابی

recruitment *n* The **recruitment** of workers, soldiers, or members is the act or process of selecting them for an organization or army and persuading them to join. بھرتی

rectangle (**rectangles**) *n* A **rectangle** is a shape with four sides whose angles are all right angles. Each side of a rectangle is the same length as the one opposite to it. مستطیل

rectangular *adj* Something that is **rectangular** is shaped like a rectangle. مستطیل نما

rectify (**rectifies, rectifying, rectified**) *vt* If you **rectify** something that is wrong, you change it so that it becomes correct or satisfactory. اصلاح کرنا

recurring *adj* Something that is **recurring** happens more than once. اعادی

recycle (**recycles, recycling, recycled**) *vt* If you **recycle** things that have already been used, such as bottles or sheets of paper, you process them so that they can be used again. بازاحیاء کرنا

recycling *n* **Recycling** is the means by which things that have already been used, such as bottles or sheets of paper, are processed so that they can be used again. بازاحیاء

red (**redder, reddest**) *adj* Something that is **red** is the colour of blood or tomatoes. سرخ

Red Cross *n* The **Red Cross** is an international organization that helps people who are suffering, for example, as a result of war, floods, or disease. ریڈکراس

redcurrant (**redcurrants**) *n* **Redcurrants** are very small, bright red berries that grow in bunches on a bush and can be eaten as a fruit or cooked to make a sauce for meat. بہت چھوٹی چمکدار سرخ بیری

redecorate (**redecorates, redecorating, redecorated**) *v* If you **redecorate** a room or a building, you put new paint or wallpaper on it. پھر سے سجانا

red-haired *adj* A **red-haired** person is a person whose hair is between red and brown in colour. سرخ بالوں والا

redhead (**redheads**) *n* A **redhead** is person, especially a woman, whose hair is a colour that is between red and brown. بھورے سرخ بالوں والی خاتون

red meat (**red meats**) *n* **Red meat** is meat such as beef or lamb, which is dark brown in colour after it has been cooked. سرخ گوشت

redo (**redoes, redoing, redid, redone**) *vt* If you **redo** a piece of work, you do it again in order to improve it or change it. پھر سے کرنا

Red Sea *n* The **Red Sea** is a long narrow sea between Arabia and north-east Africa. بحر احمر

reduce (**reduces, reducing, reduced**) *vt* If you **reduce** something, you make it smaller. گھٹانا

reduction (**reductions**) *n* When there is a **reduction** in something, it is made smaller. تخفیف

redundancy (**redundancies**) *n* If there are **redundancies** within an organization, some of its employees are dismissed because their jobs are no longer necessary or because the organization can no longer afford to pay them. چھٹنی

redundant *adj* If you are made **redundant**, you lose your job because it is no longer necessary or because your employer cannot afford to keep paying you. نکالا ہوا

red wine (**red wines**) *n* **Red wine** is wine that gets its red colour from the skins of the grapes. سرخ شراب

reed (**reeds**) *n* **Reeds** are tall plants that grow in shallow water or wet ground. سرکنڈا

reel (**reels**) *n* A **reel** is a cylinder-shaped object around which you wrap something such as thread or cinema film. ریل (دھاگے وغیرہ کی)

refer (**refers, referring, referred**) *vi* If you **refer** to a particular subject or person, you mention them. حوالہ دینا

referee (**referees**) *n* The **referee** is the official who controls a sports match. ریفری (میچ کا)

reference (**references**) *n* **Reference** to someone or something is the act of talking about them or mentioning them. A **reference** is a particular example of this. حوالہ

reference number (**reference numbers**) *n* A **reference number** is a number that tells you where you can obtain the information you want. حوالہ نمبر

refill (**refills, refilling, refilled**) *vt* If you **refill** something, you fill it again after it has been emptied. پھر سے بھرنا

refinery (**refineries**) *n* A **refinery** is a factory which refines a substance such as oil or sugar. ریفائنری

r

reflect (**reflects, reflecting, reflected**) *vt* If something **reflects** an attitude or situation, it shows that the attitude or situation exists. منعکس ہونا

reflection (**reflections**) *n* A **reflection** is an image that you can see in a mirror or in water. انعکاس

reflex (**reflexes**) *n* A **reflex** or a **reflex action** is a normal uncontrollable reaction of your body to something that you feel, see, or experience. غیر ارادی ردِ عمل

refresher course (**refresher courses**) *n* A **refresher course** is a training course in which people improve their knowledge or skills and learn about new developments that are related to the job that they do. ریفریشر کورس

refreshing *adj* A **refreshing** bath or drink makes you feel energetic or cool again after you have been tired or hot. تازہ کار

refreshments *npl* **Refreshments** are drinks and small amounts of food that are provided, for example, during a meeting or journey. چائے ناشتہ وغیرہ

refrigerator (**refrigerators**) *n* A **refrigerator** is a large container which is kept cool inside, usually by electricity, so that the food and drink in it stays fresh. ریفریجریٹر

refuel (**refuels, refuelling, refuelled**) *v* When an aircraft or other vehicle **refuels**, it is filled with more fuel so that it can continue its journey. پھر سے ایندھن بھرنا

refuge *n* If you take **refuge** somewhere, you try to protect yourself from physical harm by going there. پناہ

refugee (**refugees**) *n* **Refugees** are people who have been forced to leave their country because there is a war there or because of their political or religious beliefs. پناہ گزین

refund (**refunds, refunding, refunded**) *n* A **refund** is a sum of money which is returned to you, for example because you have returned goods to a shop. رقم واپسی ▷ *vt* If someone **refunds** your money, they return it to you. رقم واپس کرنا

refusal (**refusals**) *n* A **refusal** is the fact of firmly saying or showing that you will not do, allow, or accept something. انکار

refuse (**refuses, refusing, refused**) *n* **Refuse** consists of the rubbish and unwanted things in a house, shop, or factory that are regularly thrown away. کوڑا کرکٹ ▷ *v* If you **refuse** to do something, you deliberately do not do it, or say firmly that you will not do it. انکار کرنا

regain (**regains, regaining, regained**) *vt* If you **regain** something that you have lost, you get it back again. بحال ہونا یا کرنا

regard (**regards, regarding, regarded**) *n* If you have a high **regard** for someone, you have a lot of respect for them. وابستگی ▷ *vt* If you **regard** someone or something in a particular way, you think of them in that way, or have that opinion of them. سمجھنا

regarding *prep* You can use **regarding** to say what people are talking or writing about. متعلق *They refused to give any information regarding the accident.*

regiment (**regiments**) *n* A **regiment** is a large group of soldiers commanded by a colonel. رجمنٹ

region (**regions**) *n* A **region** is an area of a country or of the world. علاقہ

regional *adj* **Regional** is used to describe things which relate to a particular area of a country or of the world. علاقائی

register (**registers, registering, registered**) *n* A **register** is an official list or record. رجسٹر ▷ *vi* If you **register** for something, you put your name on an official list. اندراج کرنا

registered *adj* A **registered** letter or parcel is sent by a special postal service, for which you pay extra money for insurance in case it gets lost. درج شدہ

registration *n* The **registration** of something is the recording of it in an official list. اندراج

registry office (**registry offices**) *n* A **registry office** is a place where births, marriages, and deaths are officially recorded, and where people can get married without a religious ceremony. رجسٹری آفس

regret (**regrets, regretting, regretted**) *n* **Regret** is a feeling of sadness or disappointment. رنج ▷ *vt* If you **regret** something that you have done, you wish that you had not done it. معذرت طلب کرنا

regular *adj* **Regular** things happen at equal intervals, or involve things happening at equal intervals. مستقل

regularly *adv* If you do something **regularly** or something happens **regularly**, you do it or it happens at equal intervals. مستقلا

regulation *n* **Regulation** is the controlling of an activity or process, usually by means of rules. ضابط

rehearsal (**rehearsals**) *n* A **rehearsal** of a play, dance, or piece of music is the time when those taking part practise it. مشق

rehearse (**rehearses, rehearsing, rehearsed**) *v* When people **rehearse** a play, dance, or piece of music, they practise it. مشق کرنا

reimburse (**reimburses, reimbursing, reimbursed**) *vt* If you **reimburse** someone for something, you pay them back the money that they have spent or lost because of it. (*formal*) بازادائیگی کرنا

reindeer (**reindeer**) *n* A **reindeer** is a type of deer that lives in northern areas of Europe, Asia, and America. بارہ سنگا

reins *npl* **Reins** are the long leather straps attached to a horse's head which are used to make it go faster or stop. لگام

reject (**rejects, rejecting, rejected**) *vt* If you **reject** something such as a proposal or request, you do not accept it or agree to it. رد کرنا

relapse (**relapses**) *n* If someone has a **relapse** or if there is a **relapse** then that person starts to behave in a particular way again or a situation returns to how it was before. پہلے کی صورتحال پر واپس آنا

related *adj* If two or more things are **related**, there is a connection between them. وابستہ

relation (**relations**) *n* **Relations** between people, groups, or countries are contacts between them and the way they behave towards each other. رشتہ

relationship (**relationships**) *n* The **relationship** between two people or groups is the way they feel and behave towards each other. رشتہ داری

relative (**relatives**) *n* Your **relatives** are the members of your family. رشتہ دار

relatively *adv* **Relatively** means to a certain degree, especially when compared with other things of the same kind. نسبتا

relax (**relaxes, relaxing, relaxed**) *v* If you **relax**, or if something **relaxes** you, you feel calmer and less worried or tense. پر سکون ہونا

relaxation *n* **Relaxation** is a way of spending time in which you rest and feel comfortable. سکون

relaxed *adj* If you are **relaxed**, you are calm and not worried or tense. پر سکون

relaxing *adj* Something that is **relaxing** is pleasant and helps you to relax. سکون بخش

relay (**relays**) *n* A **relay** or a **relay race** is a race between two or more teams in which each member of the team runs or swims one section of the race. ریلے

release (**releases, releasing, released**) *n* When someone is released, you refer to their **release**. رہائی ▷ *vt* If a person or animal **is released** from somewhere where they have been locked up or looked after, they are set free or allowed to go. آزاد کرنا، ہونا

relegate (**relegates, relegating, relegated**) *vt* If a team that competes in a league **is relegated**, it is moved to

r

a lower division because it finished at or near the bottom of its division at the end of a season. نچلے درجہ میں بھیج دینا

relevant *adj* If something is **relevant** to a situation or person, it is important or significant in that situation or to that person. متعلقہ

reliable *adj* **Reliable** people or things can be trusted to work well or to behave in the way that you want them to. بھروسہ مند

relief *n* If you feel a sense of **relief**, you feel glad because something unpleasant has not happened or is no longer happening. راحت

relieve (**relieves, relieving, relieved**) *vt* If something **relieves** an unpleasant feeling or situation, it makes it less unpleasant or causes it to disappear completely. راحت رسانی

relieved *adj* If you are **relieved**, you feel glad because something unpleasant has not happened or is no longer happening. راحت زدہ

religion *n* **Religion** is belief in a god or gods. مذہب

religious *adj* **Religious** means connected with religion or with one particular religion. مذہبی

reluctant *adj* If you are **reluctant** to do something, you do not really want to do it. مزاحم

reluctantly *n* If you do something **reluctantly** you do not really want to do it. مزاحمت کے ساتھ

rely on *v* If you **rely on** someone or something, you need them and depend on them in order to live or work properly. انحصار ہونا | *The country relies heavily on tourism.*

remain (**remains, remaining, remained**) *v* To **remain** in a particular state means to stay in that state and not change. رہنا

remaining *adj* The **remaining** things or people out of a group are the things or people that still exist, are still present, or have not yet been dealt with. باقی بچا ہوا

remains *npl* The **remains** of something are the parts of it that are left after most of it has been taken away or destroyed. باقیات

remake (**remakes**) *n* A **remake** is a film that has the same story, and often the same title, as a film that was made earlier. پھر سے بنا ہوا

remark (**remarks**) *n* If you make a **remark** about something, you say something about it. پھبتی، تبصرہ

remarkable *adj* Someone or something that is **remarkable** is very impressive or unusual. غیر معمولی

remarkably *adv* **Remarkably** means impressively or unusually. غیر معمولی طور پر

remarry (**remarries, remarrying, remarried**) *vi* If someone **remarries**, they marry again after they have obtained a divorce from their previous husband or wife, or after their previous husband or wife has died. پھر سے شادی کرنا

remedy (**remedies**) *n* A **remedy** is a successful way of dealing with a problem. علاج، تدارک

remember (**remembers, remembering, remembered**) *v* If you **remember** people or events from the past, you still have an idea of them in your mind and you are able to think about them. یاد رکھنا، کرنا

remind (**reminds, reminding, reminded**) *vt* If someone **reminds** you of a fact or event that you already know about, they say something which makes you think about it. یاد دلانا

reminder (**reminders**) *n* If one thing is a **reminder** of another, the first thing makes you think about the second. (*written*) یاد دہانی

remorse *n* **Remorse** is a strong feeling of guilt and regret about something wrong that you have done. احساس جرم، پشیمانی

remote (**remoter, remotest**) *adj* **Remote**

areas are far away from places where most people live. دور کا

remote control *n* **Remote control** is a system of controlling a machine or vehicle from a distance by using radio or electronic signals. ریموٹ کنٹرول

remotely *adv* You use **remotely** to emphasize a negative statement. دور دراز کا

removable *adj* A **removable** part of something is a part that can easily be moved from its place or position. قابل بدل

removal *n* The **removal** of something is the act of removing it. اخراج

removal van (**removal vans**) *n* A **removal van** is a large vehicle that is used to transport furniture or equipment from one building to another. فرنیچر لانے لے جانے والی وین

remove (**removes, removing, removed**) *vt* If you **remove** something from a place, you take it away. (*written*) ہٹانا، نکالنا

rendezvous (**rendezvous**) *n* A **rendezvous** is a meeting, often a secret one, that you have arranged with someone for a particular time and place. خفیہ میٹنگ

renew (**renews, renewing, renewed**) *vt* If you **renew** an activity or a relationship, you begin it again. نیا بنانا

renewable *adj* **Renewable** resources are ones such as wind, water, and sunlight, which are constantly replacing themselves and therefore do not become used up. قابل تجدید

renovate (**renovates, renovating, renovated**) *vt* If someone **renovates** an old building or machine, they repair it and get it back into good condition. درست حالت میں واپس لانا

renowned *adj* A person or place that is **renowned** for something, usually something good, is well known because of it. شہرت یافتہ

rent (**rents, renting, rented**) *n* **Rent** is the amount of money that you pay regularly to use a house, flat, or piece of land. کرایہ ▷ *vt* If you **rent** something, you regularly pay its owner in order to have it and use it yourself. کرایہ پر لینا

rental (**rentals**) *n* The **rental** of something such as a car or television is the fact of paying an amount of money in order to have and use it. استعمال کے بدلے دی گئی رقم

reorganize (**reorganizes, reorganizing, reorganized**) *vt* To **reorganize** something means to change the way in which it is organized or done. ترتیب نو دینا

rep (**reps**) *n* A **rep** is a person who travels round selling their company's products or services to other companies. نمائندہ

repair (**repairs, repairing, repaired**) *n* A **repair** is something that you do to mend something that has been damaged. مرمت ▷ *vt* If you **repair** something that has been damaged or is not working properly, you mend it. مرمت کرنا

repair kit (**repair kits**) *n* A **repair kit** is a group of items that you keep together, usually in the same container, in case you need to repair something. مرمت کٹ (اوزاروں کا تھیلہ)

repay (**repays, repaying, repaid**) *vt* If you **repay** a debt, you pay back the money you owe to somebody. ادا کرنا (قرض وغیرہ کی رقم)

repayment (**repayments**) *n* A **repayment** is an amount of money paid at regular intervals in order to repay a debt. مستقل وقفوں پر ادائگی

repeat (**repeats, repeating, repeated**) *n* If there is a **repeat** of an event, usually an undesirable event, it happens again. اعادہ ▷ *vt* If you **repeat** something, you say or write it again. دوہرانا

repeatedly *adv* If you do something **repeatedly**, you do it many times. اعادی طور پر

repellent *adj* If you think that something is horrible and disgusting, you can say it is **repellent**. (*formal*) ہولناک

repercussions *npl* If an action or event

r

has **repercussions**, it causes unpleasant things to happen some time after the original action or event. (*formal*) ردِّ اعمال، نتائج

repetitive *adj* **Repetitive** actions are repeated many times and are therefore boring. اعادی

replace (**replaces, replacing, replaced**) *vt* To **replace** a person or thing means to put another person or thing in their place. بدلنا

replacement *n* If you refer to the **replacement** of one thing by another, you mean that the second thing takes the place of the first. بدل

replay (**replays, replaying, replayed**) *n* A **replay** is a showing again of a sequence of action, esp of part of a sporting contest immediately after it happens. ریپلے ▷ *vt* If a match between two sports teams **is replayed**, the two teams play it again, because neither team won the first time, or because the match was stopped because of bad weather. بار بار دکھانا

replica (**replicas**) *n* A **replica** of something such as a statue, machine, or weapon is an accurate copy of it. عکس

reply (**replies, replying, replied**) *n* A **reply** is something that you say or write when you answer someone or answer a letter or advertisement. جواب ▷ *vi* When you **reply** to something that someone has said or written to you, you say or write an answer to them. جواب دینا

report (**reports, reporting, reported**) *n* A **report** is a news article or broadcast which gives information about something that has just happened. رپورٹ ▷ *vt* If you **report** something that has happened, you tell people about it. رپورٹ کرنا ▷ *n* A **report** is an official written account of how well or how badly a pupil has done during the term or year that has just finished. احوال

reporter (**reporters**) *n* A **reporter** is someone who writes news articles or broadcasts news reports. نامہ نگار

represent (**represents, representing, represented**) *vt* If someone **represents** you, they act on your behalf. نمائندگی کرنا

representative *adj* A **representative** group acts on behalf of a larger group. نمائندہ

reproduction (**reproductions**) *n* A **reproduction** is a copy of something such as an antique or a painting. تخلیق نو

reptile (**reptiles**) *n* **Reptiles** are a group of animals which have scales on their skin and lay eggs. Snakes and crocodiles are reptiles. حشرات

republic (**republics**) *n* A **republic** is a country that has a president or whose system of government is based on the idea that every citizen has equal status. جمہوریہ

repulsive *adj* **Repulsive** means horrible and disgusting. ناپسندیدہ

reputable *adj* A **reputable** company or person is reliable and trustworthy. قابل اعتماد

reputation (**reputations**) *n* To have a **reputation** for something means to be known or remembered for it. ساکھ

request (**requests, requesting, requested**) *n* If you make a **request**, you politely ask for something or ask someone to do something. (*formal*) درخواست ▷ *vt* If you **request** something, you ask for it politely or formally. (*formal*) درخواست کرنا

require (**requires, requiring, required**) *vt* To **require** something means to need it. (*formal*) مطلوب ہونا

requirement (**requirements**) *n* A **requirement** is a quality or qualification that you must have in order to be allowed to do something or to be suitable for something. مطالبہ

rescue (**rescues, rescuing, rescued**) *n* A **rescue** is an attempt to save someone from a dangerous or unpleasant situation. بچاؤ ▷ *vt* If you **rescue** someone, you get them out of a dangerous or unpleasant situation. بچانا

research *n* **Research** is work that involves studying something and trying to discover facts about it. تحقیق

resemblance (**resemblances**) *n* If there is a **resemblance** between two people or things, they are similar to each other. یکسانیت

resemble (**resembles, resembling, resembled**) *vt* If one thing or person **resembles** another, they are similar to that thing or person. یکساں دکھائی دینا

resent (**resents, resenting, resented**) *vt* If you **resent** someone or something, you feel bitter and angry about them. ناپسند کرنا

resentful *adj* If you are **resentful**, you feel resentment. ناپسندیدہ

reservation (**reservations**) *n* If you have **reservations** about something, you are not sure that it is entirely good or right. ریزرویشن

reserve (**reserves, reserving, reserved**) *n* A **reserve** is a supply of something that is available for use when needed. ریزرو ▷ *n* A nature **reserve** is an area of land where animals, birds, and plants are officially protected. محفوظ ▷ *vt* If something **is reserved** for a particular person or purpose, it is kept specially for that person or purpose. محفوظ کرنا

reserved *adj* Someone who is **reserved** keeps their feelings hidden. محفوظ کردہ

reservoir (**reservoirs**) *n* A **reservoir** is a lake used for storing water before it is supplied to people. پانی جمع کرنے کے لئے جھیل یا تالاب

resident (**residents**) *n* The **residents** of a house or area are the people who live there. مکین

residential *adj* A **residential** area contains houses rather than offices or factories. رہائشی

resign (**resigns, resigning, resigned**) *vi* If you **resign** from a job or position, you formally announce that you are leaving it. استعفی دینا

resin (**resins**) *n* **Resin** is a sticky substance produced by some trees. گوند

resist (**resists, resisting, resisted**) *vt* If you **resist** a change, you refuse to accept it and try to prevent it. بند ہونا

resistance *n* **Resistance** to a change or a new idea is a refusal to accept it. مزاحمت

resit (**resits, resitting, resat**) *v* If someone **resits** a test or examination, they take it again, usually because they failed the first time. دوبارہ بیٹھنا (امتحان وغیرہ میں)

resolution (**resolutions**) *n* A **resolution** is a formal decision taken at a meeting by means of a vote. قرارداد

resort (**resorts**) *n* A holiday **resort** is a place where people can spend their holidays. تفریحی مقام

resort to *v* If you **resort to** a course of action that you do not really approve of, you adopt it because you cannot see any other way of achieving what you want. طریق کار اختیار کرنا *Some schools have resorted to recruiting teachers from overseas.*

resource (**resources**) *n* The **resources** of a country, organization, or person are the materials, money, and other things they have and can use. وسیلہ، ماخذ

respect (**respects, respecting, respected**) *n* If you have **respect** for someone, you have a good opinion of them. عزت ▷ *vt* If you **respect** someone, you have a good opinion of their character or ideas. عزت کرنا

respectable *adj* Someone or something that is **respectable** is approved of by society and considered to be morally correct. قابلِ احترام

respectively *adv* **Respectively** means in the same order as the items you have just mentioned. ترتیب کے طور پر

respond (**responds, responding, responded**) *vi* When you **respond** to something that is done or said, you react by doing or saying something. جواب دینا

response (**responses**) *n* Your **response** to an event or to something that is said is your reply or reaction to it. ردِ عمل

r

responsibility (**responsibilities**) *n* If you have **responsibility** for something or someone, it is your job or duty to deal with them. ذمہ داری

responsible *adj* If you are **responsible** for something bad that has happened, it is your fault. ذمہ دار، جوابدہ

rest (**rests, resting, rested**) *n* The **rest** is the parts of something that are left. باقی بچا ہوا ▷ *v* If you **rest** or if you **rest** your body, you sit or lie down and do not do anything active for a while. آرام کرنا

restaurant (**restaurants**) *n* A **restaurant** is a place where you can buy and eat a meal. ریستوراں

restful *adj* Something that is **restful** helps you to feel calm and relaxed. آرام دہ

restless *adj* If you are **restless**, you are bored or dissatisfied, and want to do something else. بے قرار

restore (**restores, restoring, restored**) *vt* To **restore** something means to cause it to exist again. بحال کرنا

restrict (**restricts, restricting, restricted**) *vt* If you **restrict** something, you put a limit on it to stop it becoming too large. پابندی لگانا

restructure (**restructures, restructuring, restructured**) *vt* To **restructure** an organization or system means to change the way it is organized, usually in order to make it work more effectively. تشکیل نو کرنا

result (**results, resulting, resulted**) *n* A **result** is something that happens or exists because of something else that has happened. نتیجہ ▷ *vi* If something **results in** a particular situation or event, it causes that situation or event to happen. نتیجہ نکالنا

resume (**resumes, resuming, resumed**) *v* If you **resume** an activity, it begins again. (*formal*) دوبارہ شامل ہونا

retail (**retails, retailing, retailed**) *n* **Retail** is the activity of selling goods direct to the public. خردہ ▷ *vi* If an item in a shop **retails** at or for a particular price, it is for sale at that price. خردہ قیمت ہونا

retailer (**retailers**) *n* A **retailer** is a person or business that sells goods to the public. خردہ فروش

retail price (**retail prices**) *n* The **retail price** of something is the price it is on sale for in a shop. خردہ قیمت

retire (**retires, retiring, retired**) *vi* When older people **retire**, they leave their job and stop working. سبکدوش ہوجانا

retired *adj* A **retired** person is an older person who has left his or her job and has usually stopped working completely. سبکدوش

retirement *n* **Retirement** is the time when a worker retires. سبکدوشی

retrace (**retraces, retracing, retraced**) *vt* If you **retrace** your steps, you return to where you started from, using the same route. الٹے قدموں لوٹنا

return (**returns, returning, returned**) *n* Your **return** is when you arrive back at a place where you were before. واپسی ▷ *n* The **return** on an investment is the amount of money you gain from it. منافع ▷ *vt* If you **return** something to someone, you give it back to them. واپس کرنا ▷ *vi* When you **return** to a place, you go back to it after you have been away. واپس ہونا ▷ *n* A **return** or a **return ticket** is a ticket that allows you to travel to a place and then back again. واپسی ٹکٹ

reunion (**reunions**) *n* A **reunion** is a party or occasion when people who have not seen each other for a long time meet again. پھر سے مل جانا

reuse (**reuses, reusing, reused**) *vt* When you **reuse** something, you use it again instead of throwing it away. دوبارہ استعمال کرنا

reveal (**reveals, revealing, revealed**) *vt* To **reveal** something means to make people aware of it. فاش کرنا

revenge *n* **Revenge** involves hurting someone who has hurt you. انتقام لینا

revenue *n* **Revenue** is money that a company, organization, or government receives from people. محصول

reverse (**reverses, reversing, reversed**) *n* If your car is in **reverse**, you have changed gear so that you can drive it backwards. الٹا ▷ *vt* To **reverse** a process, decision, or policy means to change it to its opposite. الٹ دینا

review (**reviews**) *n* A **review** of a situation or system is its formal examination by people in authority. This is usually done in order to see whether it can be improved or corrected. جائزہ

revise (**revises, revising, revised**) *vt* If you **revise** something, you alter it in order to make it better or more accurate. نظرثانی کرنا

revision (**revisions**) *n* To make a **revision** of something that is written or something that has been decided means to make changes to it in order to improve it, make it more modern, or make it more suitable for a particular purpose. نظرثانی

revive (**revives, reviving, revived**) *v* When something such as a feeling or a practice **revives or is revived**, it becomes active or successful again. فعال کرنا

revolting *adj* **Revolting** means horrible and disgusting. باغیانہ

revolution (**revolutions**) *n* A **revolution** is a successful attempt by a large group of people to change their country's political system, using force. انقلاب

revolutionary *adj* **Revolutionary** activities, organizations, or people have the aim of causing a political revolution. انقلابی

revolver (**revolvers**) *n* A **revolver** is a kind of hand gun. ریوالور

reward (**rewards**) *n* A **reward** is something that you are given because you have behaved well, worked hard, or provided a service to the community. صلہ

rewarding *adj* Something that is **rewarding** gives you satisfaction or brings you benefits. صلہ بخش

rewind (**rewinds, rewinding, rewound**) *v* When a recording on a tape, computer file, or disk **rewinds** or when you **rewind** it, the recording goes backwards so that you can play it again. لپیٹ لینا

rheumatism *n* **Rheumatism** is an illness that makes your joints or muscles stiff and painful. Older people, especially, suffer from rheumatism. جوڑوں کی جکڑن

rhubarb *n* **Rhubarb** is a plant with large leaves and long red stems. سرخ تنے والا درخت

rhythm (**rhythms**) *n* A **rhythm** is a regular series of sounds, movements, or actions. لب ولہجہ

rib (**ribs**) *n* Your **ribs** are the curved bones that go from your backbone around your chest. پسلی

ribbon (**ribbons**) *n* A **ribbon** is a long, narrow piece of cloth used as a fastening or decoration, for example on a birthday present. ربن

rice *n* **Rice** consists of white or brown grains taken from a cereal plant. چاول

rich (**richer, richest**) *adj* A **rich** person has a lot of money or valuable possessions. امیر

ride (**rides, riding, rode, ridden**) *n* you is a **all** in east Arabia, in the Persian Gulf. سواری ▷ *v* If you **ride** a horse, you sit on it and control its movements. سوار ہونا

rider (**riders**) *n* A **rider** is someone who rides a horse, bicycle, or motorcycle. سوار

ridiculous *adj* If you say that something or someone is **ridiculous**, you mean that they are very foolish. پشیمان

riding *n* **Riding** is the activity or sport of riding horses. گھڑسواری

rifle (**rifles**) *n* A **rifle** is a gun with a long barrel. رائفل

rig (**rigs**) *n* A **rig** is a large structure that is used for extracting oil or gas from the ground or the sea bed. تیل یا گیس نکالنے کے لئے استعمال کیا جانے والا ڈھانچہ

r

right *adj* If something is **right**, it is correct and there have been no mistakes. درست، صحیح ▷ *adj* The **right** side is the side that is towards the east when you look north. دایاں، داہنا ▷ *adv* If someone is **right** about something, they are correct. درست ▷ *n* **Right** is used to talk about actions that are good and acceptable. صحیح

right angle (**right angles**) *n* A right angle is an angle of ninety degrees. زاویہ قائمہ

right-hand *adj* If something is on the **right-hand** side of something, it is positioned on the right of it. دایاں ہاتھ

right-hand drive *n* In a motor vehicle, **right-hand drive** is a driving system in which the steering wheel is on the right side. Cars with **right-hand drive** are designed to be driven in countries where people drive on the left side of the road. داہنی طرف گاڑی چلانا

right-handed *adj* Someone who is **right-handed** uses their right hand rather than their left hand for activities such as writing and sports, and for picking things up. داہنا ہاتھ استعمال کرنے والا

rightly *adv* If you do something **rightly** you do it in accordance with the facts or correctly. صحیح طور پر

right of way (**rights of way**) *n* A **right of way** is a public path across private land. راستے کی داہنی سمت

right-wing *adj* A **right-wing** person or group has conservative or capitalist views. دایاں بازو، قدامت پرست طبقہ

rim (**rims**) *n* The **rim** of a container or a circular object is the edge which goes all the way round the top or round the outside. گول شیشے پر دھات کی کناری (رم)

ring (**rings, ringing, rang, rung**) *n* A **ring** is a round piece of metal that you wear on a finger. گھنٹی ▷ *vt* When you **ring** someone, you telephone them. فون کرنا ▷ *v* When a bell **rings**, or when you **ring** it, it makes a clear, loud sound. گھنٹی بجانا

ring back *v* If you **ring** someone **back**, you phone them, either because they phoned you earlier and you were out or because you did not finish an earlier conversation. واپسی فون کرنا *Tell her I'll ring back in a few minutes.*

ring binder (**ring binders**) *n* A **ring binder** is a file with hard covers, which you can insert pages into. The pages are held in by metal rings on a bar attached to the inside of the file. دھات کے رنگ والی فائل

ring road (**ring roads**) *n* A **ring road** is a road that goes round the edge of a town so that traffic does not have to go through the town centre. رنگ روڈ

ringtone (**ringtones**) *n* A **ringtone** is a musical tune played by a mobile phone when a call is received. رنگ ٹون

ring up *v* When you **ring** someone **up** you telephone them. فون کرنا *He rang up and invited us over for dinner.*

rink (**rinks**) *n* A **rink** is a large area where people go to skate. اسکیٹ کرنے کا علاقہ

rinse (**rinses, rinsing, rinsed**) *n* When you give something a **rinse**, you wash it in clean water in order to remove dirt or soap from it. رگڑ کر دھونے کا عمل ▷ *vt* When you **rinse** something, you wash it in clean water in order to remove dirt or soap from it. رگڑ کر دھونا

riot (**riots, rioting, rioted**) *n* When there is a **riot**, a crowd of people behave violently in a public place, for example they fight, throw stones, or damage buildings and vehicles. فساد ▷ *vi* If people **riot**, they behave violently in a public place. فساد کرنا

rip (**rips, ripping, ripped**) *v* If you **rip** something, you tear it forcefully with your hands or with a tool such as a knife. If something **rips**, it is torn forcefully. چیرنا

ripe (**riper, ripest**) *adj* **Ripe** fruit or grain is fully grown and ready to be harvested or eaten. پکا ہوا

rip off (**rip-offs**) *v* If someone **rips** you **off**, they cheat you by charging too much for goods or services. (*informal*) فریب کھانا *People are buying these products and getting ripped off.* ▷ *n* If you say that something that you bought was a **rip-off**, you mean that you were charged too much money or that it was of very poor quality. (*informal*) فریب دہی

rip up *v* If you **rip** something **up**, you tear it into small pieces. ٹکڑے کرنا *He ripped up the letter.*

rise (**rises, rising, rose, risen**) *n* If there is a **rise** in an amount, the amount increases. اضافہ ▷ *vi* If something **rises** or **rises up**, it moves upwards. اوپر اٹھنا

risk (**risks, risking, risked**) *n* If there is a **risk** of something unpleasant, there is a possibility that it will happen. جوکھم ▷ *vt* If you **risk** something unpleasant, you do something knowing that the unpleasant thing might happen as a result. جوکھم اٹھانا

risky (**riskier, riskiest**) *adj* If an activity or action is **risky**, it is dangerous or could fail. جوکھم بھری

ritual (**rituals**) *adj* **Ritual** activities happen as part of a ritual or tradition. رسمی ▷ *n* A **ritual** is a religious service or other ceremony which involves a series of actions performed in a fixed order. رسم

rival (**rivals**) *adj* **Rival** groups are groups of people that compete against each other. حریف (گروپ) ▷ *n* Your **rival** is a person, business, or organization who you are competing or fighting against in the same area or for the same things. حریف (شخص)

rivalry (**rivalries**) *n* **Rivalry** is competition or conflict between people or groups. مقابلہ آرائی

river (**rivers**) *n* A **river** is a large amount of fresh water flowing continuously in a long line across land, such as the Amazon or the Nile. ندی

road (**roads**) *n* A **road** is a long piece of hard ground built between two places so that people can drive or ride easily from one to the other. سڑک

roadblock (**roadblocks**) *n* When the police or the army put a **roadblock** across a road, they stop all the traffic going through, for example because they are looking for a criminal. سڑک جام

road map (**road maps**) *n* A **road map** is a map which shows the roads in a particular area in detail. روڈ میپ (نقشہ)

road rage *n* **Road rage** is an angry or violent reaction by a driver towards another road user. ڈرائیور کا پر تشدد ردِ عمل

road sign (**road signs**) *n* A road sign is a sign near a road giving information or instructions to drivers. ٹریفک نشان

road tax *n* **Road tax** is a tax paid every year by the owners of every motor vehicle which is being used on the roads. روڈ ٹیکس

roadworks *npl* **Roadworks** are repairs or other work being done on a road. سڑک مرمت وغیرہ

roast *adj* **Roast** meat has been roasted. بھنا ہوا

rob (**robs, robbing, robbed**) *vt* If a person or place **is robbed**, money or property is stolen from them, often using force. لوٹنا

robber (**robbers**) *n* A **robber** is someone who steals money or property from a bank, a shop, or a vehicle, often by using force or threats. لٹیرا

robbery (**robberies**) *n* **Robbery** is the crime of stealing money or property, often using force. لوٹ پاٹ

robin (**robins**) *n* A **robin** is a small brown bird with a red breast. سرخ چھاتی والی چڑیا

robot (**robots**) *n* A**robot** is a machine which moves and performs certain tasks automatically. روبوٹ

rock (**rocks, rocking, rocked**) *n* **Rock** is the hard material that is in the ground and in mountains. چٹان ▷ *v* If something **rocks**, it moves from side to side. شانہ بشانہ چلنا، ساتھ ساتھ چلنا، بغل میں چلنا ▷ *n* A **rock** is a piece of this material. کنکر، ڈھیلا

r

rock climbing *n* **Rock climbing** is the activity of climbing cliffs or large rocks, as a hobby or sport. پہاڑ پر چڑھائی

rocket (**rockets**) *n* A **rocket** is a space vehicle shaped like a long tube. راکیٹ

rocking chair (**rocking chairs**) *n* A **rocking chair** is a chair that is built on two curved pieces of wood so that you can rock yourself backwards and forwards when you are sitting in it. جھولنے والی کرسی

rocking horse (**rocking horses**) *n* A **rocking horse** is a toy horse which a child can sit on and which can be made to rock backwards and forwards. جھولنے والا کھلونا گھوڑا

rod (**rods**) *n* A **rod** is a long thin bar made of metal or wood. سلاخ

rodent (**rodents**) *n* **Rodents** are small mammals, for example rats and squirrels, with sharp front teeth. حشرات (چوہا وغیرہ)

role (**roles**) *n* The **role** of someone or something in a situation is their function or position in it. فرض، کردار

roll (**rolls, rolling, rolled**) *n* A **roll** of paper, plastic, cloth, or wire is a long piece of it that has been wrapped many times around itself or around a tube. لپیٹا ہوا ▷ *v* If something **rolls** or if you **roll** it, it moves along a surface, turning over many times. لپیٹنا، لڑھکانا

roll call (**roll call**) *n* If you take a **roll call**, you check which of the members of a group are present by reading their names out. حاضری

roller (**rollers**) *n* A **roller** is a cylinder that turns round in a machine or device. رولر (بیلن)

rollercoaster (**rollercoasters**) *n* A **rollercoaster** is a small railway at a fair that goes up and down steep slopes fast and that people ride on for pleasure or excitement. میلے کی ریل گاڑی (اوپر نیچے جانے والی)

rollerskates *npl* **Rollerskates** are shoes with four small wheels on the bottom. پہیے دار جوتے

rollerskating *n* **Rollerskating** is the activity of moving over a flat surface wearing rollerskates. رولر اسکیٹ (چار پہیوالے اسکیٹ جوتے)

rolling pin (**rolling pins**) *n* A rolling pin is a cylinder that you roll backwards and forwards over uncooked pastry in order to make the pastry flat. آگے پیچھے ہونے والا سلنڈر

Roman *adj* **Roman** means related to or connected with ancient Rome and its empire. رومی

romance (**romances**) *n* A **romance** is a relationship between two people who are in love with each other but who are not married to each other. رومان

Romanesque *adj* **Romanesque** architecture is in the style that was common in western Europe around the eleventh century. It is characterized by rounded arches and thick pillars. رومن طرز تعمیر

Romania *n* **Romania** is a republic in south-east Europe. رومانیہ

Romanian (**Romanians**) *adj* **Romanian** means belonging or relating to Romania, or to its people, language, or culture. رومانیائی ▷ *n* A **Romanian** is a person who comes from Romania. رومانیائی ▷ *n* **Romanian** is the language spoken in Romania. رومانیائی

romantic *adj* Someone who is **romantic** or does **romantic** things says and does things that make their partner feel special and loved. رومانی

roof (**roofs**) *n* The **roof** of a building or car is the covering on top of it. چھت

room (**rooms**) *n* A **room** is a part of a building that has its own walls. کمرہ ▷ *n* If there is **room** somewhere, there is a enough empty space. گنجائش، خالی جگہ

roommate (**roommates**) *n* Your **roommate** is the person you share an apartment or house with. ساتھی (کمرے کا)

room service *n* **Room service** is a service in a hotel by which meals or drinks are provided for guests in their rooms. روم سروس

root (**roots**) *n* The **roots** of a plant are the parts that grow underground. جڑ

rope (**ropes**) *n* A **rope** is a very thick cord, made by twisting together several thinner cords. رسی

rope in *v* If you say that you were **roped in** to do a particular task, you mean that someone persuaded you to help them do that task. (*informal*) سمجھا دیا گیا، منا لیا گیا *Visitors were roped in to help pick tomatoes.*

rose (**roses**) *n* A **rose** is a flower which has a pleasant smell and grows on a bush with thorns. گلاب

rosemary *n* **Rosemary** is a herb used in cooking. It comes from an evergreen plant with small narrow leaves. ایک سدا بہار خوشبودار پودا

rosé (**rosés**) *n* **Rosé** is wine which is pink in colour. گلابی شراب

rot (**rots, rotting, rotted**) *v* When food, wood, or other substances **rot**, or when something **rots** them, they decay and fall apart. سڑنا، سڑانا

rotten *adj* If food, wood, or another substance is **rotten**, it has decayed and can no longer be used. سڑا ہوا

rough (**rougher, roughest**) *adj* If something is **rough**, it is not smooth or even. کھردرا ▷ *adj* If you are **rough**, you are not being careful or gentle. غیر محتاط ہونا، سختی سے کرنا

roughly *adv* If you do something **roughly** you do it with too much force. اجڈ طریقے سے

roulette *n* **Roulette** is a gambling game in which a ball is dropped onto a revolving wheel with numbered holes in it. The players bet on which hole the ball will end up in. رولیٹ

round (**rounder, roundest, rounds**) *adj* Something **round** is in the shape of a ball or a circle. گول، دائرہ نما ▷ *n* A **round** of events is a series of similar events, especially one which comes after or before a similar series. دور، مرحلہ ▷ *n* A **round** is a circular shape. دائرہ ▷ *prep* **Round** a place or object means on all sides of it. اطراف *They were sitting round the kitchen table.*

roundabout (**roundabouts**) *n* A **roundabout** is a circle at a place where several roads meet. گول چکر

round trip (**round trips**) *n* If you make a **round trip**, you travel to a place and then back again. سفر پر جانا اور واپس لوٹنا

round up *v* If people or animals are rounded up, someone gathers them together. جمع کرنا *He had sought work as a cowboy, rounding up cattle.*

route (**routes**) *n* A **route** is a way from one place to another. روٹ

routine (**routines**) *n* A **routine** is the usual series of things that you do at a particular time in a particular order. معمول

row (**rows, rowing, rowed**) *n* A **row** is a line of things or people. قطار ▷ *n* A **row** is a serious disagreement or noisy argument. نزاع ▷ *v* When you **row**, or when you **row** a boat, you make it move through the water by using oars. کھینا (ناؤ) ▷ *vi* If two people **row**, they have a noisy argument. بحث و مباحثہ کرنا

rowing *n* **Rowing** is a sport in which people or teams race against each other in boats with oars. ناؤدوڑ

rowing boat (**rowing boats**) *n* A **rowing boat** is a small boat that you move through the water by using oars. چپو والی ناؤ

royal *adj* **Royal** means related to or belonging to a king, queen, or emperor, or to a member of their family. شاہی، شاہانہ

r

rub (**rubs, rubbing, rubbed**) *vt* If you **rub** something, you move your hand or a cloth backwards and forwards over it while pressing firmly. رگڑنا

rubber (**rubbers**) *n* **Rubber** is a strong material that stretches. **Rubber** is used to make things like tyres and boots for wet weather. ربڑ ▷ *n* A **rubber** is a small piece of rubber used to remove pencil mistakes. ربڑ (پنسل کے نشانات مٹانے والا)

rubber band (**rubber bands**) *n* A **rubber band** is a thin circle of very elastic rubber. You put it around things such as papers in order to keep them together. ربڑ بینڈ (ربڑ کا چھلہ)

rubber gloves *npl* **Rubber gloves** are gloves made of rubber that you wear to protect your hands, for example when you are washing up or gardening. ربڑ دستانے

rubbish *adj* If you think that someone is not very good at something, you can say that they are **rubbish** at it. (informal) بکواس ▷ *n* **Rubbish** consists of unwanted things or waste material such as old food. ردی، کوڑا کرکٹ

rubbish dump (**rubbish dumps**) *n* A **rubbish dump** is a place where rubbish is left, for example on open ground outside a town. کوڑا گاہ

rucksack (**rucksacks**) *n* A **rucksack** is a bag, often on a frame, used for carrying things on your back. پیٹھ پر لٹکانے والا بستر بند

rude (**ruder, rudest**) *adj* If someone is **rude**, they behave in a way that is not polite. غیر مہذب

rug (**rugs**) *n* A **rug** is a piece of thick material that you put on the floor and use like a carpet. قالین

rugby *n* **Rugby** is a game played by two teams, who try to get an oval ball past a line at their opponents' end of the pitch. رگبی (بیضوی گیند سے کھیلا جانے والا)

ruin (**ruins, ruining, ruined**) *n* **Ruin** is the state of no longer having any money. برباد ▷ *vt* To **ruin** something means to severely harm, damage, or spoil it. برباد کرنا

rule (**rules, ruling, ruled**) *n* **Rules** are instructions that tell you what you must do or must not do. اصول، قواعد ▷ *v* Someone who **rules** a country controls it. حکومت کرنا

rule out *v* If you **rule out** an idea or course of action, you reject it because it is impossible or unsuitable. مسترد کرنا *The Prime Minister is believed to have ruled out cuts in child benefit or pensions.*

ruler (**rulers**) *n* A **ruler** is also a person who rules a country. حکمراں ▷ *n* A **ruler** is a long, flat piece of wood or plastic with straight edges. You use a **ruler** for measuring things or drawing straight lines. پیمائش کا آلہ، رولر

rum (**rums**) *n* **Rum** is an alcoholic drink made from sugar cane juice. رم (گنے کی شراب)

rumour (**rumours**) *n* A **rumour** is a piece of information that may or may not be true, but that people are talking about. افواہ

run (**runs, running, ran, run**) *n* A **run** is a journey you make by running. دوڑ ▷ *vi* You say that something long, such as a road, **runs** in a particular direction when you are describing its course or position. دوڑنا ▷ *vi* When you **run**, you move very quickly on your legs. دوڑنا

run away *v* If you **run away** from a place, you secretly leave it. بھاگ جانا *I ran away from home when I was sixteen.*

runner (**runners**) *n* A **runner** is a person who runs, especially for sport or pleasure. دوڑنے والا (کھلاڑی)

runner bean (**runner beans**) *n* **Runner beans** are long green beans that are eaten as a vegetable. لمبی ہری پھلیاں (دانیدار)

runner-up (**runners-up**) *n* A **runner-up** is someone who finishes in second place in a race or competition. دوسرے نمبر پر آنے والا

running *n* **Running** is the activity of moving fast on foot, especially as a sport. دوڑنا

run out *v* If you **run out** of something, you have no more of it left. ذخیرہ ختم ہو جانا *By now the plane was running out of fuel.*
run over *v* If a vehicle **runs over** someone or something, it knocks them down. اوپر سے گزر جانا *He ran over an elderly man.*
runway (**runways**) *n* At an airport, the **runway** is the long strip of ground with a hard surface which an aeroplane takes off from or lands on. رن وے (جہاز دوڑانے کا راستہ)
rural *adj* **Rural** means relating to country areas as opposed to large towns. دیہاتی
rush (**rushes, rushing, rushed**) *n* A **rush** is a situation in which you need to go somewhere or do something very quickly. جلدی میں ▷ *vi* If you **rush** somewhere, you go there quickly. جلدی جانا
rush hour (**rush hours**) *n* The **rush hour** is one of the periods of the day when most people are travelling to or from work. مصروف اوقات
rusk (**rusks**) *n* **Rusks** are hard, dry biscuits that are given to babies and young children. بچوں کے سخت بسکٹ
Russia *n* **Russia** is the largest country in the world, covering north Eurasia. **Russia** borders on the Pacific and Arctic Oceans, and the Baltic, Black, and Caspian Seas. روس
Russian (**Russians**) *adj* **Russian** means belonging or relating to Russia, or to its people, language, or culture. روسی ▷ *n* A **Russian** is a person who comes from Russia. روسی ▷ *n* **Russian** is the language spoken in Russia, and other countries such as Belarus, Kazakhstan, and Kyrgyzstan. روسی (زبان)
rust *n* **Rust** is a brown substance that forms on iron or steel when it comes into contact with water. زنگ
rusty (**rustier, rustiest**) *adj* A **rusty** metal object has a lot of rust on it. زنگ آلود
ruthless *adj* Someone who is **ruthless** is very harsh or determined, and will do anything that is necessary to achieve their aim. جابرانہ
rye *n* **Rye** is a cereal grown in cold countries. Its grains can be used to make flour, bread, or other foods. رائی

r

S

sabotage(**sabotages, sabotaging, sabotaged**) *n* **Sabotage** is the deliberate destruction, disruption, or damage of equipment, a public service, etc, as by enemy agents, dissatisfied employees, etc. توڑ پھوڑ ▷ *vt* If a machine, railway line, or bridge **is sabotaged**, it is deliberately damaged or destroyed, for example in a war or as a protest. توڑ پھوڑ کرنا

sachet(**sachets**) *n* A **sachet** is a small closed plastic or paper bag, containing a small quantity of something. سیشے کی (چھوٹی تھیلی)

sack(**sacks, sacking, sacked**) *n* A **sack** is a large bag made of rough woven material. بوری ▷ *n* If your employers give you the **sack**, they tell you that you can no longer work for them. برطرفی ▷ *vt* If your employers **sack** you, they tell you that you can no longer work for them because you have done something that they did not like or because your work was not good enough. برطرف کرنا

sacred *adj* Something that is **sacred** is believed to be holy. مقدس

sacrifice(**sacrifices**) *n* To offer an animal as a **sacrifice**, means to kill it in a special religious ceremony. قربانی

sad(**sadder, saddes**) *adj* If you are **sad**, you feel unhappy. ناخوش، اداس

saddle(**saddles**) *n* A **saddle** is a leather seat that you put on the back of an animal so that you can ride the animal. زین، کاٹھی

saddlebag(**saddlebags**) *n* A **saddlebag** is a bag fastened to the saddle of a bicycle or motorcycle, or the saddle of a horse. موٹر سائکل کی سیٹ یا گھوڑے کی زین بندھا تھیلا

sadly *adv* If you feel or do something sadly, you feel or do it unhappily. دکھی دل کے ساتھ

safari(**safaris**) *n* A **safari** is an expedition for hunting or observing wild animals, especially in East Africa. شکار یا جنگلی جانور دیکھنے کے لئے سفر

safe(**safer, safest, safes**) *adj* Something that is **safe** does not cause physical harm or danger. محفوظ ▷ *n* A **safe** is a strong metal cupboard with special locks, in which you keep money, jewellery, or other valuable things. تجوری

safety *n* **Safety** is the state of being safe from harm or danger. حفاظت

safety belt(**safety belts**) *n* A **safety belt** is a strap that you fasten across your body for safety when travelling in a car or aeroplane. حفاظتی پیٹی

safety pin(**safety pins**) *n* A **safety pin** is a bent metal pin used for fastening things together. The point of the pin has a cover so that when the pin is closed it cannot hurt anyone. محفوظ پن

saffron *n* **Saffron** is a yellowish-orange powder obtained from a flower and used to give flavour and colouring to some foods. زعفران

Sagittarius *n* **Sagittarius** is one of the twelve signs of the zodiac. Its symbol is a creature that is half horse, half man, shooting an arrow. People who are born approximately between the 22nd of November and the 21st of December come under this sign. برج قوس

Sahara *n* The **Sahara** is a desert in North Africa, extending from the Atlantic to the Red Sea and from the Mediterranean to

central Mali, Niger, Chad, and the Sudan. صحرا ریگستان
sail (**sails, sailing, sailed**) *n* **Sails** are large pieces of material attached to the mast of a boat. پال، مستول، بادبان ▷ *v* If you **sail** a boat, or if a boat **sails**, it moves across water using its sails. کشتی چلانا
sailing (**sailings**) *n* A **sailing** is a voyage made by a ship carrying passengers. جہاز کا سفر
sailing boat (**sailing boats**) *n* A **sailing boat** is a boat with sails. بادبانی کشتی
sailor (**sailors**) *n* A **sailor** is a person who works on a ship as a member of its crew. جہازی، ملاح
saint (**saints**) *n* A **saint** is someone who has died and been officially recognized and honoured by the Christian church because his or her life was a perfect example of the way Christians should live. راہب
salad (**salads**) *n* A **salad** is a mixture of uncooked vegetables, eaten as part of a meal. سلاد
salad dressing (**salad dressings**) *n* **Salad dressing** is a mixture of oil, vinegar, herbs, and other flavourings, which you pour over a salad. سرکہ، جڑی بوٹیوں اور تیل کا مرکب
salami (**salamis**) *n* **Salami** is a type of strong-flavoured sausage. It is usually thinly sliced and eaten cold. تیز ذائقہ ساسیج
salary (**salaries**) *n* Your **salary** is the money that you are paid each month by your employer. تنخواہ
sale *n* The **sale** of goods is the selling of them for money. فروخت
sales assistant (**sales assistants**) *n* A **sales assistant** is a person who works in a shop selling things to customers. سیلس اسسٹینٹ
salesman (**salesmen**) *n* A **salesman** is a man whose job is selling things to people. سیلس مین
salesperson (**salespeople, salespersons**) *n* A **salesperson** is a person whose job is selling things to people. سیلس پرسن (مرد یا خاتون)
sales rep (**sales reps**) *n* A **sales rep** is an employee of a company who travels around a particular area selling the company's goods to shops, etc. سیلس نمائندہ
saleswoman (**saleswomen**) *n* A **saleswoman** is a woman who sells things, either in a shop or directly to customers on behalf of a company. سیلس ویمن
saliva *n* **Saliva** is the watery liquid that forms in your mouth. رال
salmon (**salmon**) *n* A **salmon** is a large edible silver-coloured fish with pink flesh. سالمن مچھلی
saloon (**saloons**) *n* A **saloon** or a **saloon car** is a car with seats for four or more people, a fixed roof, and a boot that is separated from the rear seats. کار (چار سے زیادہ سیٹوں والی)
salt *n* **Salt** is a substance in the form of white powder or crystals, used to improve the flavour of food or to preserve it. Salt occurs naturally in sea water. نمک
saltwater *adj* **Saltwater** fish live in water which is salty. **Saltwater** lakes contain salty water. نمکین پانی (کی مچھلی)
salty (**saltier, saltiest**) *adj* **Salty** things contain salt or taste of salt. نمکین
salute (**salutes, saluting, saluted**) *v* If you **salute** someone, you greet them or show your respect with a formal sign. Soldiers usually salute officers by raising their right hand so that their fingers touch their forehead. سلامی دینا
same *adj* If two things are the **same**, they are like one another. اس جیسا، یکساں
sample (**samples**) *n* A **sample** of a substance or product is a small quantity of it, showing you what it is like. نمونہ
sand *n* **Sand** is a powder that consists of extremely small pieces of stone. ریت
sandal (**sandals**) *n* **Sandals** are light shoes that have straps instead of a solid part over the top of your foot. سینڈل (جوتے)

S

sandcastle (**sandcastles**) *n* A **sandcastle** is a pile of sand made to look like a castle, usually by a child on a beach. ریت کا محل

sand dune (**sand dunes**) *n* A **sand dune** is a hill of sand near the sea or in a sand desert. ریت کا ٹیلہ

sandpaper *n* **Sandpaper** is strong paper that has a coating of sand on it. It is used for rubbing wood or metal surfaces to make them smoother. ریگمال (سینڈ پیپر)

sandpit (**sandpits**) *n* A **sandpit** is a shallow hole or box in the ground with sand in it where small children can play. ریت میں گڑھا

sandstone *n* **Sandstone** is a type of rock which contains a lot of sand. بلوا پتھر

sandwich (**sandwiches**) *n* A **sandwich** consists of two slices of bread with a layer of food between them. سینڈوچ (دو پرتی)

sanitary towel (**sanitary towels**) *n* A **sanitary towel** is a pad of thick soft material which women wear to absorb the blood during menstruation. ایام حیض میں استعمال کی گدی

San Marino *n* **San Marino** is a republic in south central Europe in the Apennines, forming an enclave in Italy. سین میرینو

sapphire (**sapphires**) *n* A **sapphire** is a precious stone which is blue in colour. نیلم

sarcastic *n* Someone who is **sarcastic** says the opposite of what they really mean in order to mock or insult someone. طنزیہ

sardine (**sardines**) *n* **Sardines** are a kind of small sea fish, often eaten as food. سارڈین، رایو مچھلی

satchel (**satchels**) *n* A **satchel** is a bag with a long strap that schoolchildren use for carrying books. لمبے پٹوں والا اسکول بیگ

satellite (**satellites**) *n* A **satellite** is an object which has been sent into space in order to collect information or to be part of a communications system. سیٹلائٹ، مصنوعی سیارہ

satellite dish (**satellite dishes**) *n* A **satellite dish** is a piece of equipment which receives satellite television signals. سیٹلائٹ ڈش (ٹی وی سگنل پکڑنے والی)

satisfaction *n* **Satisfaction** is the pleasure you feel when you do something you wanted or needed to do. اطمینان

satisfactory *adj* If something is **satisfactory**, it is acceptable to you or fulfils a particular need or purpose. اطمینان بخش

satisfied *adj* If you are **satisfied** with something, you are pleased because you have got what you wanted. مطمئن

satnav *n* **Satnav** is a system that uses information from satellites to find the best way of getting to a place. It is often found in cars. **Satnav** is an abbreviation for 'satellite navigation'. سیٹیلائٹ نیویگیشن

Saturday (**Saturdays**) *n* **Saturday** is the day after Friday and before Sunday. سنیچر

sauce (**sauces**) *n* A **sauce** is a thick liquid which is served with other food. ساس (چٹنی)

saucepan (**saucepans**) *n* A **saucepan** is a deep metal cooking pot, usually with a long handle and a lid. ساس پین (دستہ والا برتن)

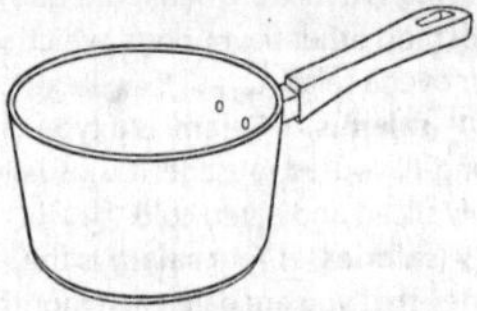

saucer (**saucers**) *n* A **saucer** is a small curved plate on which you stand a cup. طشتری

Saudi (**Saudis**) *adj* **Saudi** or **Saudi Arabian** means belonging or relating to Saudi Arabia or to its people, language, or culture. سعودی ▷ *n* The **Saudis** or **Saudi Arabians** are the people who come from Saudi Arabia. سعودی (لوگ)

Saudi Arabia *n* **Saudi Arabia** is a kingdom in south-west Asia, occupying most of the Arabian peninsula between

the Persian Gulf and the Red Sea. سعودی عرب
Saudi Arabian (Saudi Arabians) *adj* **Saudi** or **Saudi Arabian** means belonging or relating to Saudi Arabia or to its people, language, or culture. سعودی عرب کا ▷ *n* The **Saudi Arabians** or **Saudis** are the people who come from Saudi Arabia. سعودی اعرابی (لوگ)
sauna (saunas) *n* A **sauna** is a hot steam bath. سوانا (غسل)
sausage (sausages) *n* A **sausage** consists of minced meat, mixed with other ingredients, inside a long thin skin. ساسیج
save (saves, saving, saved) *vt* If you **save** someone or something, you help them to escape from danger. بچانا ▷ *vt* If you **save** something, you keep it because you will need it later. محفوظ کرنا
save up *v* If you **save up**, you gradually collect money by spending less than you get, usually in order to buy something that you want. پس انداز کرنا (بچانا)
savings *npl* Your **savings** are the money that you have saved, especially in a bank or a building society. بچت
savoury *adj* **Savoury** food has a salty or spicy flavour rather than a sweet one. مسالیدار کھانے
saw (saws) *n* A **saw** is a tool for cutting wood, which has a blade with sharp teeth along one edge. آری
sawdust *n* **Sawdust** is the very fine fragments of wood which are produced when you saw wood. برادہ
saxophone (saxophones) *n* A **saxophone** is a musical wind instrument in the shape of a curved metal tube with keys and a curved mouthpiece. سیکسوفون باجہ
say (says, saying, said) *vt* When you **say** something, you talk. کہنا
saying (sayings) *n* A **saying** is a traditional sentence that people often say and that gives advice or information about life. کہاوت
scaffolding *n* **Scaffolding** is a temporary framework of poles and boards that is used by workmen to stand on while they are working on the outside structure of a building. مچان بندی
scale (scales) *n* A **scale** is a set of levels or numbers which are used in a particular system of measuring things or comparing things. پیمانہ ▷ *n* The **scales** of a fish or reptile are the small, flat pieces of hard skin that cover its body. کھپرا
scales *npl* **Scales** are a piece of equipment for weighing things or people. پیمانہ
scallop (scallops) *n* **Scallops** are large shellfish with two flat fan-shaped shells. Scallops can be eaten. صدفی مچھلی
scam (scams) *n* A **scam** is an illegal trick, usually with the purpose of getting money from people or avoiding paying tax. (*informal*) گھوٹالا
scampi *npl* **Scampi** are large prawns, often served fried in breadcrumbs. بڑے جھینگے
scan (scans, scanning, scanned) *n* A **scan** is a medical test in which a machine sends a beam of X-rays over a part of your body in order to check whether your organs are healthy. مشین سے طبی جانچ ▷ *vt* When you **scan** an area, a group of things, or a piece of writing, you look at it carefully, usually because you are looking for something in particular. جائزہ لینا
scandal (scandals) *n* A **scandal** is a situation, event, or someone's behaviour that shocks a lot of people because they think it is immoral. فضیحت
Scandinavia *n* **Scandinavia** is the peninsula of north Europe occupied by Norway and Sweden. اسکینڈینیویا
Scandinavian *adj* **Scandinavian** means belonging or relating to a group of northern European countries that includes Denmark, Norway, and Sweden, or to the people, languages, or culture of those countries. اسکینڈینیویائی

S

scanner (**scanners**) *n* A **scanner** is a machine which is used to examine, identify, or record things, for example by moving a beam of light, sound, or X-rays over them. اسکین کرنے والی مشین

scar (**scars**) *n* A **scar** is a mark on the skin which is left after a wound has healed. زخم یا کٹے کا نشان

scarce (**scarcer, scarcest**) *adj* If something is **scarce**, there is not enough of it. کمیاب

scarcely *adv* You use **scarcely** to emphasize that something is only just true or only just the case. مشکل سے

scare (**scares, scaring, scared**) *n* If someone or something gives you a **scare**, they frighten you. ڈر ▷ *vt* If something **scares** you, it frightens or worries you. ڈرانا

scarecrow (**scarecrows**) *n* A **scarecrow** is an object in the shape of a person, which is put in a field where crops are growing in order to frighten birds away. پتلا، ڈراوا

scared *adj* If you are **scared** of someone or something, you are frightened of them. دہشت زدہ

scarf (**scarfs, scarves**) *n* A **scarf** is a piece of cloth that you wear round your neck or head, usually to keep yourself warm. رومال، سرپوش

scarlet *adj* Something that is **scarlet** is bright red. گہرا سرخ

scary (**scarier, scariest**) *adj* Something that is **scary** is rather frightening. ڈراونا - ڈروني

scene (**scenes**) *n* A **scene** in a play, film, or book is part of it in which a series of events happen in the same place. منظر

scenery *n* The **scenery** in a country area is the land, water, or plants that you can see around you. نظارہ

scent (**scents**) *n* The **scent** of something is the pleasant smell that it has. خوشبو

sceptical *adj* If you are **sceptical** about something, you have doubts about it. مشکوک

schedule (**schedules**) *n* A **schedule** is a plan that gives a list of events or tasks and the times at which each one should happen or be done. جدول

scheme (**schemes**) *n* A **scheme** is a plan or arrangement, especially one produced by a government or other organization. منصوبہ

schizophrenic *adj* Someone who is **schizophrenic** is suffering from schizophrenia. پراگندہ ذہنی، شقاق دماغی کا عارضہ

scholarship (**scholarships**) *n* If you get a **scholarship** to a school or university, your studies are paid for by the school or university, or by some other organization. وظیفہ

school (**schools**) *n* A **school** is a place where children are educated. You usually refer to this place as **school** when you are talking about the time that children spend there. اسکول

schoolbag (**schoolbags**) *n* A **schoolbag** is a bag that children use to carry books and other things to and from school. اسکول بیگ

schoolbook (**schoolbooks**) *n* **Schoolbooks** are books giving information about a particular subject, which children use at school. اسکول کتاب

schoolboy (**schoolboys**) *n* A **schoolboy** is a boy who goes to school. اسکول طالب علم

schoolchildren *npl* **Schoolchildren** are children who go to school. اسکول بچے

schoolgirl (**schoolgirls**) *n* A **schoolgirl** is a girl who goes to school. اسکول طالبہ

schoolteacher (**schoolteachers**) *n* A **schoolteacher** is a teacher in a school. اسکول ٹیچر (استاد)

school uniform (**school uniforms**) *n* A **school uniform** is a special set of clothes which some children wear at school. اسکول یونیفارم

science *n* **Science** is the study of the nature and behaviour of natural things and the knowledge that we obtain about them. سائنس

science fiction *n* **Science fiction** consists of stories and films about events that take place in the future or in other parts of the universe. سائنسی افسانہ

scientific *adj* **Scientific** is used to describe things that relate to science or to a particular science. سائنسی

scientist (**scientists**) *n* A **scientist** is someone who has studied science and whose job is to teach or do research in science. سائنس داں

sci-fi *n* **Sci-fi** consists of stories in books, magazines, and films about events that take place in the future or in other parts of the universe. **Sci-fi** is short for 'science fiction'. (*informal*) سائی۔ فائی (سائنسی تصور)

scissors *npl* **Scissors** are a small tool with two sharp blades which are screwed together. You use scissors for cutting things such as paper and cloth. قینچی

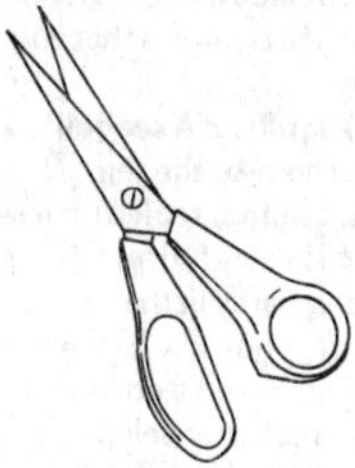

scoff (**scoffs, scoffing, scoffed**) *vi* If you **scoff**, you speak in a ridiculing way about something. تضحیک کرنا

scold (**scolds, scolding, scolded**) *vt* If you **scold** someone, you speak angrily to them because they have done something wrong. (*informal*) ڈانٹنا

scooter (**scooters**) *n* A **scooter** is a small lightweight motorcycle. اسکوٹر

score (**scores, scoring, scored**) *n* The **score** in a game is the number of points that each team or player has. حاصل نمبر (کھیل وغیرہ میں) ▷ *n* The **score** of a piece of music is the written version of it. تحریری موسیقی ▷ *v* If you **score** in a game, you get a goal, run, or point. اسکور

Scorpio *n* **Scorpio** is one of the twelve signs of the zodiac. Its symbol is a scorpion. People who are born approximately between the 23rd of October and the 21st of November come under this sign. برج بچھو

scorpion (**scorpions**) *n* A **scorpion** is a small creature which looks like a large insect. Scorpions have a long curved tail, and some of them are poisonous. بچھو

Scot (**Scots**) *n* A **Scot** is a person of Scottish origin. اسکاٹش، اسکاچستانی

Scotland *n* **Scotland** is a country that is part of the United Kingdom, occupying the north of Great Britain. اسکاٹ لینڈ

Scots *adj* **Scots** means belonging or relating to Scotland, its people, language, or culture. اسکاٹ لینڈ کا

Scotsman (**Scotsmen**) *n* A **Scotsman** is a man of Scottish origin. اسکاٹش نسل کا

Scotswoman (**Scotswomen**) *n* A **Scotswoman** is a woman of Scottish origin. اسکاٹش نسل کی خاتون

Scottish *adj* **Scottish** means belonging or relating to Scotland, its people, language, or culture. اسکاٹ فٹبال

scout (**scouts**) *n* A **scout** is someone who is sent to an area of countryside to find out the position of an enemy army. مخبر، جاسوس

scrambled eggs *npl* **Scrambled eggs** are eggs that have been broken, mixed together, and then heated and stirred in a pan. پھینٹ کر تلے ہوئے انڈوں کی ڈش

scrap (**scraps, scrapping, scrapped**) *n* A **scrap** of something is a very small piece or amount of it. ردی (چھوٹے ٹکڑے) ▷ *n* You can refer to a fight or an argument as a **scrap**. جھگڑا ▷ *vt* If you **scrap** something, you get rid of it or cancel it. ردی میں ڈال دینا

S

scrapbook (**scrapbooks**) *n* A **scrapbook** is a book with empty pages on which you can stick things such as pictures or newspaper articles in order to keep them. اسکریپ بک(سادہ اوراق والی کتاب)

scrap paper *n* **Scrap paper** is loose pieces of paper used for writing notes on. کھلے صفحات

scratch (**scratches, scratching, scratched**) *n* **Scratches** on someone or something are small cuts. خراش ▷ *v* If you **scratch** part of your body, you rub your nails against your skin. کھجانا، کھجلی کرنا ▷ *vt* If a sharp thing **scratches** someone or something, it makes small cuts on their skin or on its surface. کھرچنا

scream (**screams, screaming, screamed**) *n* A **scream** is a sharp piercing cry or sound, esp one denoting fear or pain. چیخ ▷ *vi* When someone **screams**, they make a very loud, high-pitched cry, for example because they are in pain or are very frightened. چیخنا

screen (**screens, screening, screened**) *n* A **screen** is the flat vertical surface on which pictures or words are shown on a television, on a computer, or in a cinema. اسکرین ▷ *vt* When a film or a television programme **is screened**, it is shown in the cinema or broadcast on television. پردے پر دکھانا

screensaver (**screensavers**) *n* A **screensaver** is a moving picture which appears on a computer screen when the computer is not being used. کمپیوٹر استعمال نہ ہونے پر اس کی اسکرین پر موجود متحرک تصویر

screw (**screws**) *n* A **screw** is a small metal device for fixing things together. It has a wide top, a pointed end, and a groove along its length. پیچ

screwdriver (**screwdrivers**) *n* A **screwdriver** is a tool for fixing screws into place. پیچ کس

scribble (**scribbles, scribbling, scribbled**) *v* If you **scribble** or **scribble** something, you write it quickly and untidily. شکستہ تحریر

scrub (**scrubs, scrubbing, scrubbed**) *vt* If you **scrub** something, you rub it hard in order to clean it, using a stiff brush and water. مٹانا

scuba diving *n* **Scuba diving** is the activity of swimming underwater using special breathing equipment. The equipment consists of cylinders of air which you carry on your back and which are connected to your mouth by rubber tubes. سانس لینے والے آلہ جات کے ساتھ زیر آب تیرنا

sculptor (**sculptors**) *n* A **sculptor** is someone who creates sculptures. مجسمہ ساز، بت تراش

sculpture (**sculptures**) *n* A **sculpture** is a work of art that is produced by carving or shaping materials such as stone or clay. مجسمہ ساز، بت تراش

sea *n* The **sea** is the salty water that covers much of the earth's surface. مجسمہ سازی، بت تراشی

seafood *n* **Seafood** refers to shellfish and other sea creatures that you can eat. سمندری غذائیں

seagull (**seagulls**) *n* A **seagull** is a type of bird that lives near the sea. سیگل

seal (**seals, sealing, sealed**) *n* A **seal** is an animal which eats fish and lives partly on land and partly in the sea. سیل (ایک جانور جو سمندر اور خشکی دونوں میں زندگی گزارتی ہے) ▷ *n* A **seal** is an official stamp on a document. مہر ▷ *vt* When you **seal** an envelope, you close it by folding part of it and sticking it down. مہربند کرنا، چپکا کر بند کر دینا

sea level *n* If you are at **sea level**, you are at the same level as the surface of the sea. سطح سمندر

seam (**seams**) *n* A **seam** is a line of stitches joining two pieces of cloth together. سلوٹ، سیون

seaman (**seamen**) *n* A **seaman** is a sailor. جہازی

search (**searches, searching, searched**) *n* A **search** is an attempt to find something by looking for it carefully. تلاش ▷ *v* If you **search for** something or someone, you look carefully for them. If you **search** a place, you look carefully for something there. تلاش کرنا

search engine (**search engines**) *n* A **search engine** is a computer program that searches for documents on the Internet. کمپیوٹر پروگرام برائے تلاش

search party (**search parties**) *n* A **search party** is an organized group of people who are searching for someone who is missing. سرچ (تلاش) پارٹی

seashore (**seashores**) *n* The **seashore** is the part of a coast where the land slopes down into the sea. ساحل

seasick *adj* If someone is **seasick** when they are travelling in a boat, they vomit or feel sick because of the way the boat is moving. سمندری آب وہوا کے سبب طبیعت کی خرابی، متلی قے وغیرہ ہونا

seaside *n* You can refer to an area that is close to the sea, especially where people go for their holidays, as the **seaside**. سمندر کے قریب

season (**seasons**) *n* The **seasons** are the periods into which a year is divided and which each have their own typical weather conditions. موسم

seasonal *adj* **Seasonal** means happening during one particular time of the year. موسمی

seasoning *n* **Seasoning** is salt, pepper, or spices that are added to food to improve its flavour. کھانے میں ذائقے کیلئے نمک مرچ یا مسالے ملانا

season ticket (**season tickets**) *n* A **season ticket** is a ticket for a series of events, such as football matches, or a number of journeys, that you usually buy at a reduced rate. سیزن ٹکٹ (خاص مواقع کے لئے)

seat (**seats**) *n* A **seat** is an object that you can sit on, for example a chair. نشست ▷ *n* When someone is elected to parliament, you can say that they or their party have won a **seat**. انتخابی نشست

seatbelt (**seatbelts**) *n* A **seatbelt** is a strap that you fasten across your body for safety when travelling in a car or aeroplane. سیٹ بیلٹ (کار یا ہوائی جہاز میں)

sea water *n* **Sea water** is salt water from the sea. سمندر کا پانی

seaweed (**seaweeds**) *n* **Seaweed** is a plant that grows in the sea. آبی پودا

second (**seconds**) *adj* The **second** thing in a number of things is the one that you count as number two. دوسرا ▷ *n* A **second** is an amount of time. There are sixty seconds in one minute. سیکنڈ

secondary school (**secondary schools**) *n* A **secondary school** is a school for pupils between the ages of 11 or 12 and 17 or 18. سیکنڈری اسکول (اسکول کے بعد کالج سے پہلے)

second class *n* **Second class** is accommodations on a train or ship which are cheaper and less comfortable than the first class accommodations. دوسرا درجہ ▷ *adj* **Second-class** things are regarded as less valuable or less important than others of the same kind. دوسرے درجہ کا

secondhand *adj* **Secondhand** things are not new and have been owned by someone else. سیکنڈ ہینڈ (اترن)

secondly *adv* You say **secondly** when you want to make a second point or give a second reason for something. دوم

second-rate *adj* If you describe something as **second-rate**, you mean that it is of poor quality. غیر معیاری

secret (**secrets**) *adj* If something is **secret**, it is known about by only a small number of people, and is not told or shown to anyone else. خفیہ، رازدارانہ ▷ *n* A **secret** is a fact that is known by only a small number of people, and is not told to anyone else. راز

secretary (**secretaries**) *n* A **secretary** is a person who is employed to do office work, such as typing letters or answering phone calls. سیکریٹری (دفتر میں)

secretly *adv* If you do something **secretly**,

S

it is known about by only a small number of people. خفیہ طور پر

secret service (**secret services**) *n* A country's **secret service** is a government department whose job is to find out enemy secrets and to prevent its own government's secrets from being discovered. خفیہ ادارہ

sect (**sects**) *n* A **sect** is a group of people that has separated from a larger group and has a particular set of religious or political beliefs. مکتبہ فکر

section (**sections**) *n* A **section** of something is one of the parts that it is divided into. حصہ

sector (**sectors**) *n* A **sector** of something, especially a country's economy, is a particular part of it. شعبہ

secure *adj* If something such as a job or institution is **secure**, it is safe and reliable, and unlikely to be lost or fail. محفوظ

security *n* **Security** refers to all the precautions that are taken to protect a place. حفاظت

security guard (**security guards**) *n* A **security guard** is someone whose job is to protect a building or to collect and deliver large amounts of money. سیکیورٹی گارڈ (محافظ)

sedative (**sedatives**) *n* A **sedative** is a drug that calms you or makes you sleep. سکون آور (دوا)

see (**sees, seeing, saw, seen**) *v* If you **see** something, you are looking at it or you notice it. دیکھنا ▷ *vt* If you **see** someone, you meet them. ملاقات کرنا

seed (**seeds**) *n* A **seed** is one of the small hard parts of a plant from which a new plant grows. بیج

seek (**seeks, seeking, sought**) *vt* If you **seek** something, you try to find it or obtain it. (*formal*) جستجو کرنا

seem (**seems, seeming, seemed**) *v* You use **seem** to say that someone or something gives the impression of having a particular quality, or that something gives the impression of happening in the way you describe. محسوس ہونا

seesaw (**seesaws**) *n* A **seesaw** is a long board which is balanced on a fixed part in the middle. To play on it, a child sits on each end, and when one end goes up, the other goes down. سی سا (اوپر نیچے کرنے والا تختہ)

see-through *adj* **See-through** clothes are made of thin cloth, so that you can see a person's body or underwear through them. آر پار دکھانے والا

seize (**seizes, seizing, seized**) *vt* If you **seize** something, you take hold of it quickly and firmly. ضبط کرنا

seizure (**seizures**) *n* If someone has a **seizure**, they have a heart attack or an epileptic fit. دورہ (مرض کا)

seldom *adv* If something **seldom** happens, it does not happen often. کبھی نہیں، اکثر نہیں

select (**selects, selecting, selected**) *vt* If you **select** something, you choose it from a number of things of the same kind. چننا

selection *n* **Selection** is the act of selecting one or more people or things from a group. انتخاب

self-assured *adj* Someone who is **self-assured** shows confidence in what they say and do because they are sure of their own abilities. پر یقین

self-catering *n* If you go on a **self-catering** holiday or you stay in **self-catering** accommodation, you stay in a place where you have to make your own meals. اپنا کھانا خود تیار کرنا

self-centred *adj* Someone who is **self-centred** is only concerned with their own wants and needs and never thinks about other people. خود غرض

self-conscious *adj* Someone who is **self-conscious** is easily embarrassed

and nervous about the way they look or appear. خودپسند
self-contained *adj* You can describe someone as **self-contained** when they do not need help or resources from other people. خوددار
self-control *n* Your **self-control** is your ability to control your feelings and appear calm. خود پر قابو
self-defence *n* **Self-defence** is the use of force to protect yourself against someone who is attacking you. دفاع، مدافعت
self-discipline *n* **Self-discipline** is the ability to control yourself and to make yourself work hard or behave in a particular way without needing anyone else to tell you what to do. خودانضباطی
self-employed *adj* If you are **self-employed**, you organize your own work and taxes and are paid by people for a service you provide, rather than being paid a regular salary by a person or a firm. خود کاروزگار کرنے والا
selfish *adj* If you say that someone is **selfish**, you disapprove of them because they care only about themselves, and not about other people. خود غرض
self-service *adj* A **self-service** shop, restaurant, or garage is one where you get things for yourself rather than being served by another person. خود اپنی پسند کی چیزیں لے لینا
sell (**sells, selling, sold**) *vt* If you **sell** something that you own, you let someone have it in return for money. فروخت کرنا
sell-by date (**sell-by dates**) *n* The **sell-by date** on a food container is the date by which the food should be sold or eaten before it starts to decay. کندہ تاریخ تک بیچ دینا چاہئے
selling price (**selling prices**) *n* The **selling price** of something is the price for which it is sold. قیمت فروخت
sell off *v* If you **sell** something **off**, you sell it because you need the money. اپنی ضرورت کے لئے بیچنا *The company is selling off some sites and concentrating on cutting debts.*
Sellotape® *n* **Sellotape** is a clear sticky tape that you use to stick paper or card together or onto a wall. سیلوٹیپ (ٹریڈ مارک)
sell out *v* If a shop **sells out** of something, it sells all its stocks of it. سارا ذخیرہ فروخت کرنا *The supermarket sold out of flour in a single day.*
semester (**semesters**) *n* In colleges and universities in the United States and some other countries, a **semester** is one of two periods into which the year is divided. چھماہی
semicircle (**semicircles**) *n* A **semicircle** is one half of a circle, or something having the shape of half a circle. دائرے کا نصف
semi-colon (**semi-colons**) *n* A **semi-colon** is the punctuation mark ; which is used to indicate a pause intermediate in value or length between that of a comma and that of a full stop. وقف ناقص
semi-detached house (**semi-detached houses**) *n* A **semi-detached house** is a house that is joined to another house on one side by a shared wall. ایک طرف سے دوسرے مکان سے متصل ہو
semifinal (**semifinals**) *n* A **semi-final** is one of the two matches or races in a competition that are held to decide who will compete in the final. فائنل سے پہلے
semi-skimmed milk *n* **Semi-skimmed milk** or **semi-skimmed** is milk from which some of the cream has been removed. کچھ کریم نکالا ہوا دودھ
send (**sends, sending, sent**) *vt* When you **send** someone something, you arrange for them to receive it, for example by post. بھیجنا
send back *v* When you **send** something **back**, you arrange for it to be taken and delivered to the person who sent it to you, for example by post. واپس بھیجنا *The camera was damaged, so I sent it back to the manufacturer.*

S

sender (**senders**) *n* **The sender** of a letter, package, or radio message is the person who sent it. بھیجنے والا

send off *v* If you **send off** a letter or parcel, you send it somewhere by post. بھیجنا (ڈاک سے)

send out *v* If you **send out** things such as leaflets or bills, you send them to a large number of people at the same time. بھیجنا (بڑی تعداد یا مقدار میں)

Senegal *n* **Senegal** is a republic in West Africa, on the Atlantic. سینیگل جمہوریہ

Senegalese (**Senegalese**) *adj* **Senegalese** means belonging or relating to Senegal, or to its people or culture. سینیگل ▷ *v* A **Senegalese** is a Senegalese citizen, or a person of Senegalese origin. سینیگل

senior *adj* The **senior** people in an organization have the highest and most important jobs in it. عمر، عہدے یا مرتبہ میں بڑا

senior citizen (**senior citizens**) *n* A **senior citizen** is a person who is old enough to receive an old-age pension. عمر رسیدہ شہری، بزرگ

sensational *adj* A **sensational** event or situation is so remarkable that it causes great excitement and interest. سنسنی خیز

sense (**senses**) *n* Your **senses** are the physical abilities of sight, smell, hearing, touch, and taste. حس

senseless *adj* A **senseless** action seems to have no meaning or purpose. ناقص العقل

sense of humour *n* Someone's **sense of humour** is the fact that they find certain things amusing. ظرافت

sensible *adj* A **sensible** person is able to make good decisions and judgements based on reason. حساس

sensitive *adj* If you are **sensitive** to other people's problems and feelings, you understand and are aware of them. حساس

sensuous *adj* **Sensuous** things give pleasure to the mind or body through the senses. حسی

sentence (**sentences, sentencing, sentenced**) *n* A **sentence** is a group of words which, when they are written down, begin with a capital letter and end with a full stop, question mark, or exclamation mark. Most sentences contain a subject and a verb. جملہ ▷ *n* In a law court, a **sentence** is the punishment that a person receives after they have been found guilty of a crime. سزا ▷ *vt* When a judge **sentences** someone, he or she states in court what their punishment will be. سزا سنانا

sentimental *adj* A **sentimental** person or thing feels or makes you feel emotions such as tenderness, affection, or sadness, sometimes in a way that is exaggerated or foolish. جذباتی

separate (**separates, separating, separated**) *adj* If one thing is **separate** from another, the two things are apart and are not connected. الگ ▷ *v* If you **separate** people or things that are together, or if they **separate**, they move apart. الگ کرنا، جدا کرنا

separately *adv* If people or things are dealt with **separately** or do something **separately**, they are dealt with or do something at different times or places, rather than together. جداگانہ طور پر

separation (**separations**) *v* The **separation** of two or more things or groups is the fact that they are separate or become separate, and are not linked. جدائی

September (**Septembers**) *n* **September** is the ninth month of the year in the Western calendar. ستمبر

septic tank (**septic tanks**) *n* A **septic tank** is an underground tank where faeces, urine, and other waste matter is made harmless using bacteria. سیپٹک ٹینک، (زیر زمین حوض جس میں پاخانے اور دیگر قابل ضیاع مادے جمع ہوتے ہیں)

sequel (**sequels**) *n* The **sequel** to a book

or film is another book or film which continues the story. سلسلہ

sequence (**sequences**) *n* A **sequence** of things is a number of them that come one after another in a particular order. ترتیب

Serbia *n* **Serbia** is a republic in south-east Europe. سربیا

Serbian (**Serbians**) *adj* **Serbian** means of, relating to, or characteristic of Serbia, its people, or their language (formerly regarded as a dialect of Serbo-Croat). سربیائی ▷ *n* A **Serbian** is a native or inhabitant of Serbia. سربیائی ▷ *n* **Serbian** is the language spoken in Serbia. سربیائی

sergeant (**sergeants**) *n* A **sergeant** is a non-commissioned officer of middle rank in the army, marines, or air force. سارجنٹ

serial (**serials**) *n* A **serial** is a story which is broadcast or published in a number of parts over a period of time. سیریل (سلسلہ وار کہانی)

series (**series**) *n* A **series** of things or events is a number of them that come one after the other. سلسلہ (واقعات یا واردات کا ایک کے بعد ایک رونما ہونا)

serious *adj* **Serious** problems or situations are very bad and cause people to be worried or afraid. سنگین

seriously *adv* **Seriously** means that something is done in a serious manner or to a serious degree. سنجیدگی سے

servant (**servants**) *n* A **servant** is someone who is employed to work in another person's house, for example to cook or clean. نوکر، ملازم

serve (**serves, serving, served**) *n* A **serve** is when you hit a ball or a shuttlecock in a game of tennis or badminton in order to start the game. سرو (گیند یا شٹل کاک کو مار کر دوسری طرف پھینکنا) ▷ *vt* If you **serve** your country, an organization, or a person, you do useful work for them. خدمت کرنا

server (**servers**) *n* A **server** is part of a computer network which does a particular task, for example storing or processing information, for all or part of the network. سرور (کمپیوٹر نیٹ ورک میں مرکزی کمپیوٹر) ▷ *n* In tennis and badminton, the **server** is the player whose turn it is to hit the ball or shuttlecock to start play. گیند کو سرو کرنے والا

service (**services, servicing, serviced**) *n* A **service** is an organization or system that provides something for the public. خدمت ▷ *vt* If you have a vehicle or machine **serviced**, you arrange for someone to examine, adjust, and clean it so that it will keep working efficiently and safely. سروس کرنا

service area (**service areas**) *n* A **service area** is a place beside a motorway where you can buy petrol and other things, or have a meal. راستے پر پیٹرول اور دیگر چیزیں خریدنے کا مقام

service charge (**service charges**) *n* A **service charge** is an amount that is added to your bill in a restaurant to pay for the work of the person who comes and serves you. خدمات کا معاوضہ

serviceman (**servicemen**) *n* A **serviceman** is a man who is in the army, navy, or air force. فوجی

service station (**service stations**) *n* A **service station** is a place that sells things such as petrol, oil, and spare parts. Service stations often sell food, drink, and other goods. سروس اسٹیشن

servicewoman (**servicewomen**) *n* A **servicewoman** is a woman who is in the army, navy, or air force. خاتون فوجی

serviette (**serviettes**) *n* A **serviette** is a square of cloth or paper that you use to protect your clothes or to wipe your mouth when you are eating. رومال

session (**sessions**) *n* A **session** is a meeting or series of meetings of a court, parliament, or other official group. اجلاس

set (**sets, setting**) *n* A **set** of things is a number of things that belong together. سیٹ (ایک گروپ کی چیزیں) ▷ *vt* If you **set**

S

something somewhere, you put it there. رکھنا، متعین کرنا

setback (**setbacks**) *n* A **setback** is an event that delays your progress or reverses some of the progress that you have made. دھچکہ، ترقی میں رکاوٹ

set off *v* When you **set off**, you start a journey. روانہ ہونا *He set off for the station.*

set out *v* When you **set out**, you start a journey. روانہ کرنا *I set out for the cottage.*

settee (**settees**) *n* A **settee** is a long comfortable seat with a back and arms, for two or three people. صوفہ

settle (**settles, settling, settled**) *vt* If two people **settle** an argument or problem, or if someone or something **settles** it, they solve it by making a decision about who is right or about what to do. تصفیہ کرنا

settle down *v* When someone **settles down**, they start living a quiet life in one place, especially when they get married or buy a house. تصفیہ ہوجانا *One day I'll settle down and have a family.*

seven *num* **Seven** is the number 7. سات

seventeen *num* **Seventeen** is the number 17. سترہ

seventeenth *adj* The **seventeenth** item in a series is the one that you count as number seventeen. سترہواں

seventh (**sevenths**) *adj* The **seventh** item in a series is the one that you count as number seven. ساتواں ▷ *n* A **seventh** is one of seven equal parts of something. ساتواں (حصہ)

seventy *num* **Seventy** is the number 70. ستر

several *det* **Several** is used to talk about a number of people or things that is not large but is greater than two. کئی *Several hundred students gathered on campus.* ▷ *pron* **Several** means a small number of people or things that is greater than two. متعدد *You may have to try several before you find the right treatment.* ▷ *adj* You use **several** for talking about a number of people or things that is not large but is greater than two. متعدد، کئی

sew (**sews, sewing, sewed, sewn**) *v* When you **sew** something such as clothes, you make them or repair them by joining pieces of cloth together by passing thread through them with a needle. سینا، سلائی کرنا

sewer (**sewers**) *n* A **sewer** is a large underground channel that carries waste matter and rainwater away. زیرزمین گٹر، سیم

sewing *n* **Sewing** is the activity of making or mending clothes or other things using a needle and thread. سلائی

sewing machine (**sewing machines**) *n* A **sewing machine** is a machine that you use for sewing. سلائی مشین

sew up *v* If you **sew up** pieces of cloth or tears in cloth or skin, you join them together using a needle and thread. سی دینا *Next day, Miss Stone decided to sew up the rip.*

sex (**sexes**) *n* The **sexes** are the two groups, male and female, into which people and animals are divided. جنس

sexism *n* **Sexism** is the belief that the members of one sex, usually women, are less intelligent or less capable than those of the other sex and need not be treated equally. جنسیت

sexist *adj* If you describe people or their behaviour as **sexist**, you mean that they are influenced by the belief that the members of one sex, usually women, are less intelligent or less capable than those of the other sex and need not be treated equally. ایک جنس کو کم عقل سمجھنے کا نظریہ

shabby (**shabbier, shabbiest**) *adj* **Shabby** things or places look old and in bad condition. پھٹے پرانے کپڑوں میں

shade *n* **Shade** is a cool area of darkness where the sun does not reach. سایا

shadow (**shadows**) *n* A **shadow** is a dark shape on a surface that is made when something stands between a light and the surface. پرچھائی

shake (**shakes, shaking, shook, shaken**) *vt* If you **shake** something, you hold it and move it quickly up and down. ہلانا ⊳ *v* If someone or something **shakes**, they move quickly backwards and forwards or up and down. کانپنا، تھر تھرانا

shaken *adj* If you are **shaken**, you are upset and unable to think calmly. پریشان حال، خوفزدہ

shaky (**shakier, shakiest**) *adj* If your body or your voice is **shaky**, you cannot control it properly and it trembles, for example because you are ill or nervous. لرزتی ہوئی

shall *v* You use **shall**, usually with 'I' and 'we', when you are talking about something that will happen in the future. گا/گی *I shall know more tomorrow.*

shallow (**shallower, shallowest**) *adj* A **shallow** hole, container, or layer of water measures only a short distance from the top to the bottom. کم گہرا

shambles *npl* If a place, event, or situation is a **shambles**, everything is in disorder. بے ترتیب

shame *n* **Shame** is an uncomfortable feeling that you have when you know that you have done something wrong or embarrassing, or when someone close to you has. شرم، غیرت

shampoo (**shampoos**) *n* **Shampoo** is a liquid that you use for washing your hair. شیمپو (بال دھونے کے لئے)

shape (**shapes**) *n* The **shape** of an object, a person, or an area is the form or pattern of its outline. شکل

share (**shares, sharing, shared**) *n* If you have or do your **share** of something, you have or do the amount that is reasonable or fair. حصہ ⊳ *vt* If you **share** something with another person, you both have it, use it, do it, or experience it. حصہ لگانا، ساجھی کرنا

shareholder (**shareholders**) *n* A **shareholder** is a person who owns shares in a company. شیر ہولڈر (حصص دار)

share out *v* If you **share** something **out**, you give each person in a group an equal or fair part of it. حصہ دینا *The funding will be shared out between universities, hospitals, and research bodies.*

shark (**sharks**) *n* **Sharks** are very large fish with sharp teeth. شارک (بڑی مچھلی)

sharp (**sharper, sharpest**) *adj* A **sharp** point or edge is very thin and can cut through things quickly. تیز دھار ⊳ *adj* A **sharp** feeling is sudden and is very big or strong. تیز

shave (**shaves, shaving, shaved**) *v* When a man **shaves**, he removes the hair from his face using a razor or shaver so that his face is smooth. چہرے کے بال صاف کرنا (شیو)

shaver (**shavers**) *n* A **shaver** is an electric device used for shaving hair from the face and body. شیو کرنے کا برقی آلہ

shaving cream (**shaving creams**) *n* **Shaving cream** is a soft soapy substance which men put on their face before they shave. شیونگ کریم

shaving foam (**shaving foams**) *n* **Shaving foam** is a soft soapy substance which men put on their face before they shave. شیونگ فوم (جھاگ)

shawl (**shawls**) *n* A **shawl** is a large piece of woollen cloth worn over a woman's shoulders or head, or wrapped around a baby to keep it warm. شال

she *pron* You use **she** to talk about a woman, a girl, or a female animal. وہ (خاتون)

shed (**sheds**) *n* A **shed** is a small building used for storing things such as garden tools. سائبان

sheep (**sheep**) *n* A **sheep** is a farm animal with a thick woolly coat. بھیڑ

sheepdog (**sheepdogs**) *n* A **sheepdog** is a breed of dog. Some sheepdogs are used for controlling sheep. بھیڑوں کی رکھوالی کرنے والا کتا

sheepskin (**sheepskins**) *n* **Sheepskin** is the skin of a sheep with the wool still

S

attached to it, used especially for making coats and rugs. بھیڑ کی کھال

sheer (**sheerer, sheerest**) *adj* You can use **sheer** to emphasize that a state or situation is complete and does not involve anything else. مکمل، شدید

sheet (**sheets**) *n* A **sheet** is a large piece of cloth that you sleep on or cover yourself with in bed. چادر ▷ *n* A **sheet** is a piece of paper, glass, plastic, or metal. صفحات

shelf (**shelves**) *n* A **shelf** is a flat piece of wood, metal, or glass which is attached to a wall or to the sides of a cupboard. دراز، الماری

shell (**shells**) *n* The **shell** of an egg or nut is its hard part. خول ▷ *n* The **shell** of an animal such as a snail is the hard part that covers its back and protects it. خول (گھونگھے وغیرہ کا)

shellfish (**shellfish**) *n* A **shellfish** is a small creature with a shell that lives in the sea. سیپی

shell suit (**shell suits**) *n* A **shell suit** is a casual suit which is made of thin nylon. پتلی نائلون کا سوٹ

shelter (**shelters**) *n* A **shelter** is a small building or covered place which is made to protect people from bad weather or danger. پناہ گاہ

shepherd (**shepherds**) *n* A **shepherd** is a person whose job is to look after sheep. چرواہا، گڈریا

sherry (**sherries**) *n* **Sherry** is a type of strong wine that is made in south-western Spain. شیری (ایک تیز شراب)

shield (**shields**) *n* A **shield** is a large piece of metal or leather which soldiers used to carry to protect their bodies while they were fighting. ڈھال

shift (**shifts, shifting, shifted**) *n* If someone's opinion, a situation, or a policy changes slightly, the change is called a **shift**. بدلاؤ، تبدیلی ▷ *v* If you **shift** something, or if it **shifts**, it moves slightly. بدلنا، بدلاؤ لانا

shifty *adj* Someone who looks **shifty** gives the impression of being dishonest. (*informal*) فریبی

shin (**shins**) *n* Your **shin** is the front part of your leg between your knee and ankle. پنڈلی کا سامنے والا حصہ

shine (**shines, shining, shined, shone**) *vi* When the sun or a light **shines**, it gives out bright light. چمکنا

shiny (**shinier, shiniest**) *adj* **Shiny** things are bright and reflect light. چمکدار

ship (**ships**) *n* A **ship** is a large boat which carries passengers or cargo. جہاز (بحری)

shipbuilding *n* **Shipbuilding** is the industry of building ships. جہاز کا کارخانہ

shipment (**shipments**) *n* A **shipment** is an amount of a particular kind of cargo that is sent to another country on a ship, train, aeroplane, or other vehicle. جہاز سے بھیجا جانے والا سامان

shipwreck (**shipwrecks**) *n* When there is a **shipwreck**, a ship is destroyed in an accident at sea. جہاز کا ملبہ

shipwrecked *adj* If someone is **shipwrecked**, their ship is destroyed in an accident at sea but they survive and manage to reach land. جہاز کی تباہی میں بچ جانے والا فرد

shipyard (**shipyards**) *n* A **shipyard** is a place where ships are built and repaired. جہاز کا کارخانہ اور مرمت گاہ

shirt (**shirts**) *n* A **shirt** is a piece of clothing worn on the upper part of your body with a collar, sleeves, and buttons down the front. قمیض

shiver (**shivers, shivering, shivered**) *vi* When you **shiver**, your body shakes slightly because you are cold or frightened. کانپنا

shock (**shocks, shocking, shocked**) *n* If you have a **shock**, you suddenly have an unpleasant or surprising experience. صدمہ ▷ *vt* If something **shocks** you, it makes you feel very upset. صدمہ دینا

shocking *adj* You can say that something

is **shocking** if you think that it is very bad. (*informal*) صدماتی

shoe (**shoes**) *n* **Shoes** are objects worn on your feet. Shoes cover most of your foot but not your ankle. جوتا

shoelace (**shoelaces**) *n* **Shoelaces** are long, narrow pieces of material like pieces of string that you use to fasten your shoes. جوتے کا تسمہ

shoe polish (**shoe polishes**) *n* **Shoe polish** is a substance that you put on your shoes in order to clean them, protect them, and make them shine. جوتا پالش

shoe shop (**shoe shops**) *n* A **shoe shop** is a shop that sells shoes. جوتے کی دوکان

shoot (**shoots, shooting, shot**) *vt* To **shoot** a person or animal means to kill or injure them by firing a gun at them. گولی مارنا

shooting (**shootings**) *n* A **shooting** is an occasion when someone is killed or injured by being shot with a gun. فائرنگ

shop (**shops**) *n* A **shop** is a building or part of a building where things are sold. دکان

shop assistant (**shop assistants**) *n* A **shop assistant** is a person who works in a shop selling things to customers. دکان کا ملازم

shopkeeper (**shopkeepers**) *n* A **shopkeeper** is a person who owns a small shop. دکاندار

shoplifting *n* **Shoplifting** is stealing from a shop by hiding things in a bag or in your clothes. دکان سے چوری

shopping *n* When you do the **shopping**, you go to shops and buy things. خریداری

shopping bag (**shopping bags**) *n* A **shopping bag** is a strong container with one or two handles, used to carry things in when you go shopping. خریداری بیگ

shopping centre (**shopping centres**) *n* A **shopping centre** is an area in a town where a lot of shops have been built close together. دوکانوں کا مجموعہ

shopping trolley (**shopping trolleys**) *n* A **shopping trolley** is a large metal basket on wheels which is provided by shops such as supermarkets for customers to use while they are in the shop. شاپنگ ٹرالی

shop window (**shop windows**) *n* A **shop window** is a large piece of glass along the front of a shop, behind which some of the goods that the shop sells are displayed. شیشیدار دکان

shore (**shores**) *n* The **shores** or the **shore** of a sea, lake, or wide river is the land along the edge of it. Someone who is **on shore** is on the land rather than on a ship. کنارا

short (**shorter, shortest**) *adj* If something is **short**, it does not last very long. مختصر
▷ *adj* A **short** thing is small in length, distance, or height. چھوٹا قد

shortage (**shortages**) *n* If there is a **shortage** of something, there is not enough of it. قلت

shortcoming (**shortcomings**) *n* The **shortcomings** of a person or thing are their faults or weaknesses. خامی، کمزوری

shortcrust pastry *n* **Shortcrust pastry** is a basic type of pastry that is made with half the quantity of fat to flour, and has a crisp but crumbly texture. خستہ تہ والی پیسٹری

shortcut (**shortcuts**) *n* A **shortcut** is a quicker way of getting somewhere than the usual route. نزدیک کا راستہ

shortfall (**shortfalls**) *n* If there is a **shortfall** in something, there is not enough of it. کمی، قلت

shorthand *n* **Shorthand** is a quick way of writing which uses signs to represent words or syllables. شارٹ ہینڈ

shortlist (**shortlists**) *n* A **shortlist** is a list of people or things which have been chosen from a larger group, for example for a job or a prize. The successful person or thing is then chosen from the small group. مجموعہ میں سے مختصر فہرست

S

shortly *adv* If something happens **shortly** after or before something else, it happens a short amount of time after or before it. مختصراً

shorts *npl* **Shorts** are trousers with short legs. گھٹنے(چھوٹے پائینچے کا پاجاما)

short-sighted *adj* If you are **short-sighted**, you cannot see things properly when they are far away, because there is something wrong with your eyes. جسکی قریب کی نظر خراب ہو

short-sleeved *adj* A **short-sleeved** shirt, dress, or other item of clothing has sleeves that cover the top part of your arms. چھوٹی آستین والی

short story (**short stories**) *n* A **short story** is a written story about imaginary events that is only a few pages long. مختصر افسانہ

shot (**shots**) *n* If you fire a **shot**, you fire a gun once. فائر

shotgun (**shotguns**) *n* A **shotgun** is a gun which fires a lot of small metal balls at one time. چھرےدار بندوق

should *v* You use **should** when you are saying what is the right thing to do. چاہیئے *He should tell us what happened.*

shoulder (**shoulders**) *n* Your **shoulders** are the parts of your body between your neck and the tops of your arms. کندھا

shoulder blade (**shoulder blades**) *n* Your **shoulder blades** are the two large, flat, triangular bones that you have in the upper part of your back, below your shoulders. کندھے کی تکونی ہڈی

shout (**shouts, shouting, shouted**) *n* A **shout** is the noise made when someone speaks very loudly. چیخ پکار ▷ *v* If you **shout**, you say something very loudly, usually because you want people a long distance away to hear you or because you are angry. چیخنا چلانا

shovel (**shovels**) *n* A **shovel** is a tool like a spade, used for lifting and moving earth, coal, or snow. بیلچہ

show (**shows, showing, showed, shown**) *n* A **show** of a feeling is an attempt by someone to make it clear that they have that feeling. اظہار ▷ *vt* If information or a fact **shows** that a situation exists, it proves it. اظہار کرنا ▷ *v* If you **show** someone something, you let them see it. دکھانا ▷ *vt* If you **show** someone how to do something, you teach them how to do it. کرکے دکھانا، کرکے بتانا، مظاہرہ کرنا

show business *n* **Show business** is the entertainment industry. شو بزنس

shower (**showers**) *n* A **shower** is a thing that you stand under, that covers you with water so you can wash yourself. اشاور (غسل کیلئے) ▷ *n* A **shower** is a short period of rain. پھوار پڑنا

shower cap (**shower caps**) *n* A **shower cap** is a waterproof cap that you wear in the shower to keep your hair dry. نہاتے وقت سرپوش (بالوں کو سوکھا رکھتا ہے)

shower gel (**shower gels**) *n* **Shower gel** is liquid soap you use in the shower. سیال صابن

showerproof *adj* If a garment etc is **showerproof**, it is resistant to or partly impervious to rain. بارش سے محفوظ

showing (**showings**) *n* A **showing** is a presentation, exhibition, or display. نمائش

show jumping *n* **Show jumping** is a sport in which horses are ridden in competitions to demonstrate their skill in jumping over fences and walls. گھوڑا کدانا

show off (**show-offs**) *n* If you say that someone **is showing off**, you are criticizing them for trying to impress people by showing in a very obvious way what they can do or what they own. دکھاوا کرنا *All right, there's no need to show off.* ▷ *n* If you say that someone is a **show-off**, you are criticizing them for trying to impress people by showing in a very obvious way what they can do or what they own. (*informal*) دکھاوا

show up *v* If a person you are expecting

to meet does not **show up**, they do not arrive at the place where you expect to meet them. دکھائی دینا *We waited until five o'clock, but he did not show up.*

shriek (**shrieks, shrieking, shrieked**) *vi* When someone **shrieks**, they make a short, very loud cry, for example, because they are suddenly surprised, are in pain, or are laughing. چیخ مارنا

shrimp (**shrimps, shrimp**) *n* **Shrimps** are small shellfish with long tails and many legs. جھینگا

shrine (**shrines**) *n* A **shrine** is a holy place associated with a sacred person or object. مقدس مقام

shrink (**shrinks, shrinking, shrank, shrunk**) *v* If something **shrinks** or you **shrink** it, it becomes smaller. سکڑنا

shrub (**shrubs**) *n* **Shrubs** are low plants like small trees with several stems instead of a trunk. جھاڑی

shrug (**shrugs, shrugging, shrugged**) *vi* If you **shrug**, you raise your shoulders to show that you are not interested in something or that you do not know or care about something. کندھے اچکانا

shrunken *adj* Someone or something that is **shrunken** has become smaller than they used to be. سکڑا، سمٹا ہوا

shudder (**shudders, shuddering, shuddered**) *vi* If you **shudder**, you shake with fear, horror, or disgust, or because you are cold. خوف سے کانپنا

shuffle (**shuffles, shuffling, shuffled**) *vi* If you **shuffle** somewhere, you walk there without lifting your feet properly off the ground. گھسٹنا

shut (**shuts, shutting, shut**) *v* If you **shut** something such as a door or if it **shuts**, it moves so that it fills a hole or a space. بند کرنا

shut down *v* If a factory or business **is shut down**, it is closed permanently. بند ہو جانا *Smaller contractors were forced to shut down.*

shutters *npl* **Shutters** are wooden or metal covers fitted on the outside of a window. They can be opened to let in the light, or closed to keep out the sun or the cold. شٹر (دروازہ)

shuttle (**shuttles**) *n* A **shuttle** is a spacecraft that is designed to travel into space and back to earth several times. خلائی گاڑی

shuttlecock (**shuttlecocks**) *n* A **shuttlecock** is the small object that you hit over the net in a game of badminton. شٹل کاک، بیڈمنٹن چڑیا

shut up *v* If you **shut up**, you stop talking. If you say **'shut up'** to someone, you are rudely telling them to stop talking. منہ بند کرنا *He wished she would shut up.*

shy (**shyer, shyest**) *adj* A **shy** person is nervous and uncomfortable in the company of other people. شرمیلا

Siberia *n* **Siberia** is a vast region of Russia and north Kazakhstan. سائبیریا

siblings *npl* Your **siblings** are your brothers and sisters. (*formal*) ایک ہی ماں باپ کی اولاد

sick (**sicker, sickest**) *adj* If you are **sick**, you are ill. **Sick** usually means physically ill, but it can sometimes be used to mean mentally ill. بیمار

sickening *adj* You describe something as **sickening** when it gives you feelings of horror or disgust, or makes you feel sick in your stomach. بیمار کرنے والا، جی خراب کرنے والا

sick leave *n* **Sick leave** is the time that a person spends away from work because of illness or injury. بیماری کی چھٹی

sickness *n* **Sickness** is the state of being ill or unhealthy. بیماری

sick note (**sick notes**) *n* A **sick note** is an official note signed by a doctor which states that someone is ill and needs to stay off work for a particular period of time. بیمار ہونے کی ڈاکٹری سند

sick pay *n* When you are ill and unable to work, **sick pay** is the money that you get from your employer instead of your normal wages. بیماری کے ایام کی تنخواہ

S

side (**sides**) *n* The **side** of something is a place to the left or right of it. پہلو، بغل ▷ *n* The **side** of something is also its edge. پہلو، بغل ▷ *n* The different **sides** in a game are the groups of people who are playing against each other. پہلو

sideboard (**sideboards**) *n* A **sideboard** is a long cupboard which is about the same height as a table. Sideboards are usually kept in dining rooms to put plates and glasses in. کپ بورڈ

side effect (**side effects**) *n* The **side effects** of a drug are the effects, usually bad ones, that the drug has on you in addition to its function of curing illness or pain. ضمنی اثرات

sidelight (**sidelights**) *n* The **sidelights** on a vehicle are the small lights at the front that help other drivers to notice the vehicle and to judge its width. گاڑی کی سامنے کی چھوٹی لائٹ

side street (**side streets**) *n* A **side street** is a quiet, often narrow street which leads off a busier street. سڑک سے نکلنے والی گلی

sideways *adv* **Sideways** means from or towards the side of something or someone. بغلی راستہ

sieve (**sieves**) *n* A **sieve** is a tool consisting of a metal or plastic ring with a fine wire net attached. It is used for separating liquids from solids or larger pieces of something from smaller pieces. چھلنی

sigh (**sighs, sighing, sighed**) *n* When you let out a **sigh**, you let out a deep breath. سانس ▷ *vi* When you **sigh**, you let out a deep breath, as a way of expressing feelings such as disappointment, tiredness, or pleasure. راحت کی سانس لینا

sight (**sights**) *n* Your **sight** is your ability to see. بینائی

sightseeing *n* **Sightseeing** is the activity of visiting the interesting places that tourists usually visit. سیاحتی مقامات کی سیر

sign (**signs, signing, signed**) *n* A **sign** is a mark or a shape that has a special meaning. علامت، نشان ▷ *v* When you **sign** a document, you write your name on it. دستخط کرنا ▷ *n* You can make a **sign** to somebody by moving something. اشارہ کرنا

signal (**signals, signalling, signalled**) *n* A **signal** is a sound or action which is intended to send a particular message. سگنل ▷ *v* If you **signal** something, or if you **signal** to someone, you make a gesture or sound in order to give someone a particular message. سگنل دینا

signature (**signatures**) *n* Your **signature** is your name, written in your own characteristic way. دستخط

significance *n* The **significance** of something is its importance. اہم، کافی زیادہ

significant *adj* A **significant** amount of something is large enough to be important or noticeable. اہم، کافی زیادہ

sign language (**sign languages**) *n* **Sign language** is movements of your hands and arms used to communicate. There are several official systems of sign language, used, for example, by deaf people. اشاراتی زبان

sign on *v* In the UK, when an unemployed person **signs on**, they officially inform the authorities that they are unemployed, so that they can receive money from the government in order to live. حاضری دینا *He has signed on at the job centre.*

signpost (**signposts**) *n* A **signpost** is a sign where roads meet that tells you which direction to go in to reach a particular place or different places. نشان راہ

Sikh (**Sikhs**) *n* A **Sikh** is a member of an Indian religion which separated from Hinduism in the sixteenth century and which teaches that there is only one God. سکھ ▷ *adj* **Sikh** means of or relating to Sikhs or their religious beliefs and customs. سکھ

silence (**silences**) *n* If there is **silence**, it is completely quiet. خاموشی

silencer (**silencers**) *n* A **silencer** is a device that is fitted onto a gun to make it very quiet when it is fired. سائلنسر

silent *adj* If something is **silent**, it is quiet, with no sound at all. خاموش، پرسکون ▷ *adj* If you are **silent**, you are not talking. خاموش

silicon chip (**silicon chips**) *n* A **silicon chip** is a very small piece of silicon inside a computer. It has electronic circuits on it and can hold large quantities of information or perform mathematical or logical operations. سلیکون چپ (چھوٹا برقی سرکٹ)

silk (**silks**) *n* **Silk** is a very smooth, fine cloth made from a substance produced by a kind of moth. ریشم

silly (**sillier, silliest**) *adj* Someone who is being **silly** is behaving in a foolish or childish way. بیوقوف

silver *n* **Silver** is a valuable greyish-white metal used for making jewellery and ornaments. چاندی

similar *adj* If one thing is **similar to** another, or if a number of things are **similar**, they have features that are the same. یکساں

similarity (**similarities**) *n* If there is a **similarity** between two or more things, they share some features that are the same. یکسانیت

simmer (**simmers, simmering, simmered**) *v* When you **simmer** food, you cook it gently at just below boiling point. دھیمی آنچ پر پکا

simple (**simpler, simplest**) *adj* If something is **simple**, it is not complicated, and is therefore easy to understand or do. سادہ

simplify (**simplifies, simplifying, simplified**) *vt* If you **simplify** something, you make it easier to understand. آسان بنا

simply *adv* **Simply** means in a simple and uncomplicated manner. سادہ طور پر

simultaneous *adj* Things which are **simultaneous** happen or exist at the same time. یک وقتی

simultaneously *adv* If things happen or exist **simultaneously** they happen or exist at the same time. یک وقتی طور پر

since *adv* You use **since** when you are talking about something that started in the past, and that has not stopped from then until now. سے ▷ *conj* You use **since** when you are talking about something that started in the past, and that has not stopped from then until now. جب سے *I've lived here since I was six years old.* ▷ *prep* You use **since** when you are talking about something that started in the past, and that has not stopped from then until now. تب سے اب تک *I've not seen her since my birthday.*

sincere *adj* If you say that someone is **sincere**, you approve of them because they really mean the things they say. مخلص

sincerely *adv* If you say or feel something **sincerely**, you really mean it or feel it. مخلصانہ طور پر

sing (**sings, singing, sang, sung**) *v* If you **sing**, you make musical sounds with your voice, usually producing words that fit a tune. گا

singer (**singers**) *n* A **singer** is a person who sings, especially as a job. گانے والا

singing *n* **Singing** is the activity of making musical sounds with your voice. گا

single (**singles**) *adj* You use **single** to emphasize that you are referring to one thing, and no more than one thing. واحد

single parent (**single parents**) *n* A **single parent** is someone who is bringing up a child or children on their own, because the other parent is not living with them. والدین میں صرف ایک

singles *npl* **Singles** is a game of tennis or badminton in which one player plays another. The plural **singles** can be used to refer to one or more of these matches. ایک ایک مقابل والا کھیل

single ticket (**single tickets**) *n* A **single ticket** is a ticket for a journey from one

S

place to another but not back again. ایک طرف کا ٹکٹ

singular *n* **The singular** of a noun is the form of it that is used to refer to one person or thing. واحد (جمع کی ضد)

sinister *adj* Someone or something that is **sinister** seems evil or harmful. شیطانی

sink (**sinks, sinking, sank, sunk**) *n* A **sink** is a basin with taps that supply water. بیسن ▷ *v* If a boat **sinks**, or if something **sinks** it, it disappears below the surface of a mass of water. ڈوبنا

sinus (**sinuses**) *n* Your **sinuses** are the spaces in the bone behind your nose. ناک کا اندرون

sir (**sirs**) *n* People sometimes say **sir** as a polite way of addressing a man whose name they do not know or a man of superior rank. 'Dear Sir' is used at the beginning of official letters addressed to men. جناب

siren (**sirens**) *n* A **siren** is a warning device which makes a long, loud, wailing noise. Most fire engines, ambulances, and police cars have sirens. سائرن (بھونپو)

sister (**sisters**) *n* Your **sister** is a girl or woman who has the same parents as you. بہن

sister-in-law (**sisters-in-law**) *n* Your **sister-in-law** is the sister of your husband or wife, or the woman who is married to your brother. سالی، نند

sit (**sits, sitting, sat**) *vi* If you **are sitting** somewhere, for example in a chair, your weight is supported by your buttocks rather than your feet. بیٹھنا

sitcom (**sitcoms**) *n* A **sitcom** is an amusing television drama series about a set of characters. **Sitcom** is an abbreviation for 'situation comedy'. ٹی وی کا مزاحیہ سلسلہ

sit down *v* When you **sit down** somewhere, you lower your body until you are sitting on something. بیٹھنا (بیٹھنے کا عمل)

site (**sites**) *n* A **site** is a piece of ground that is used for a particular purpose or where a particular thing happens or is situated. مقام

sitting room (**sitting rooms**) *n* A **sitting room** is a room in a house where people sit and relax. بیٹھک

situated *adj* If something is **situated** somewhere, it is in a particular place or position. واقع

situation (**situations**) *n* You use **situation** to refer generally to what is happening at a particular place and time, or to refer to what is happening to you. حالت، صورتحال

six *num* **Six** is the number 6. چھ

sixteen *num* **Sixteen** is the number 16. سولہ

sixteenth *adj* The **sixteenth** item in a series is the one that you count as number sixteen. سولواں

sixth *adj* The **sixth** item in a series is the one that you count as number six. چھٹا

sixty *num* **Sixty** is the number 60. ساٹھ

size (**sizes**) *n* The **size** of something is how big or small it is. سائز (قد)

skate (**skates, skating, skated**) *vi* If you **skate**, you move about wearing ice-skates or roller-skates. اسکیٹ یا گراری دار اسکیٹ پہن کر پھسلنا

skateboard (**skateboards**) *n* A **skateboard** is a narrow board with wheels at each end, which people stand on and ride for pleasure. پہیے دار پٹری، اسکیٹ بورڈ

skateboarding *n* **Skateboarding** is the activity of riding on a skateboard. اسکیٹ بورڈ تگ، چوٹی پر پہونچانے والی

skates *npl* **Skates** are boots with a thin metal blade underneath that people wear to move quickly on ice. پہیے یا پھسلنے والے بوٹ

skating *n* **Skating** is the act or process of moving about wearing ice-skates or roller-skates. اسکیٹ پہن کر پھسلنا

skating rink (**skating rinks**) *n* A **skating rink** is a large area covered with ice where people go to ice-skate, or a large area of concrete where people go to roller-skate. برف کا میدان (اسکیٹنگ کے لیے)

skeleton (**skeletons**) *n* Your **skeleton** is the framework of bones in your body. ہڈیوں کا ڈھانچہ

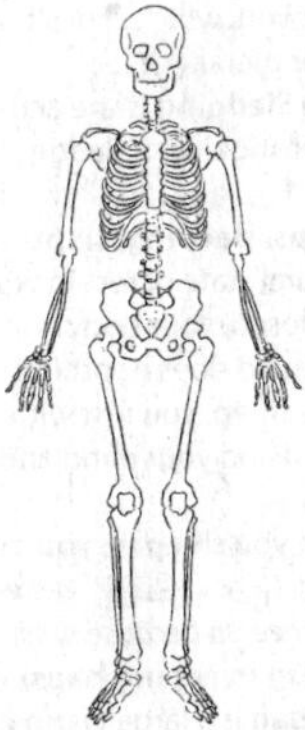

sketch (**sketches, sketching, sketched**) *n* A **sketch** is a drawing that is done quickly without a lot of details. خاکہ ▷ *v* If you **sketch** something, you make a quick rough drawing of it. خاکہ کھینچنا

skewer (**skewers**) *n* A **skewer** is a long metal pin which is used to hold pieces of food together during cooking. سیخ، سلاخ

ski (**skis, skiing, skied**) *n* **Skis** are long, flat, narrow pieces of wood, metal, or plastic that are fastened to boots so that you can move easily over snow. اسکی (پیر کی نیچے باندھ کر پھسلنے کے پٹے) ▷ *vi* When people **ski**, they move over snow on skis. پیروں میں پٹے باندھ کر برف پر پھسلنا

skid (**skids, skidding, skidded**) *vi* If a vehicle **skids**, it slides sideways or forwards while moving, for example when you are trying to stop it suddenly on a wet road. جھٹک جانا

skier (**skiers**) *n* A **skier** is a person who moves over snow on skis. اسکی کرنے والا (پھسلنے والا)

skiing *n* **Skiing** is the act or process of moving over snow on skis. برف پر پھسلنے کا عمل

skilful *adj* Someone who is **skilful** at something does it very well. ماہر

ski lift (**ski lifts**) *n* A **ski lift** is a machine for taking people to the top of a slope so that they can ski down it. It consists of a series of seats hanging down from a moving wire. ڈھلوان کی چوٹی پر پہنچانے والی لفٹ

skill (**skills**) *n* A **skill** is a type of activity or work which requires special training or knowledge. مہارت

skilled *adj* Someone who is **skilled** has the knowledge and ability to do something well. ماہر فن

skimmed milk *n* **Skimmed milk** is milk from which the cream has been removed. کریم نکالا ہوا دودھ

skimpy (**skimpier, skimpiest**) *adj* **Skimpy** means too small in size or quantity. چھوٹا، تھوڑا

skin (**skins**) *n* Your **skin** covers your whole body. جلد، چمڑی ▷ *n* The **skin** of a fruit or vegetable covers the outside of it. چھلکا

skinhead (**skinheads**) *n* A **skinhead** is a young person whose hair is shaved or cut very short. Skinheads are usually regarded as violent and aggressive. گنجا یا چھوٹے بالوں والا نوجوان

skinny (**skinnier, skinniest**) *adj* If you say that someone is **skinny**, you mean that they are very thin in a way you find unattractive. (*informal*) دبلا

skin-tight *adj* **Skin-tight** clothes fit very tightly so that they show the shape of your body. تنگ (کپڑا)

skip (**skips, skipping, skipped**) *vi* If you **skip** along, you move along jumping from one foot to the other. کودنا، اچھلنا ▷ *vt* If you **skip** something, you decide not to do it. چھوڑ دینا

skirt (**skirts**) *n* A **skirt** is a piece of clothing worn by women and girls. It fastens at the waist and hangs down around the legs. اِسکرٹ (لہنگا)

skirting board (**skirting boards**) *n* **Skirting board** or **skirting** is a narrow length of wood which goes along the bottom of a wall in a room and makes a border between the walls and the floor. لکڑی کی پٹی (دیوار اور فرش کی سرحد پر)

skive (**skives, skiving, skived**) *v* If you **skive**, you avoid working, especially by staying away from the place where you should be working. (*informal*) غائب رہ کر کام سے بچنا

skull (**skulls**) *n* Your **skull** is the bony part of your head which holds your brain. کھوپڑی

sky (**skies**) *n* The **sky** is the space around the earth which you can see when you stand outside and look upwards. آسمان

skyscraper (**skyscrapers**) *n* A **skyscraper** is a very tall building in a city. اونچی عمارت

slack (**slacker, slackest**) *adj* Something that is **slack** is loose and not tightly stretched. ڈھیلا

slag off *v* To **slag** someone **off** means to criticize them in an unpleasant way. (*informal*) ناگوار تنقید کیڑے نکالنا *All bands slag off their record companies. It's just the way it is.*

slam (**slams, slamming, slammed**) *v* If you **slam** a door or window, or if it **slams**, it shuts noisily and with great force. زوردار آواز کے ساتھ بند کرنا

slang *n* **Slang** is words, expressions, and meanings that are informal and are used by people who know each other very well or who have the same interests. بے تکلفانہ زبان

slap (**slaps, slapping, slapped**) *vt* If you **slap** someone, you hit them with the palm of your hand. تھپڑ مارنا

slate *n* **Slate** is a dark grey rock that can be easily split into thin layers. سلیٹ

slave (**slaves, slaving, slaved**) *n* A **slave** is a person who is owned by another person and has to work for that person without pay. غلام ▷ *vi* If you say that a person **is slaving over** something or **is slaving for** something, you mean that they are working very hard. سخت محنت کرنا

sledge (**sledges**) *n* A **sledge** is an object used for travelling over snow. It consists of a framework which slides on two strips of wood or metal. برف گاڑی

sledging *n* **Sledging** is the activity of riding over snow on a sledge. سلیج پر بیٹھ کر برف پر پھسلنا

sleep (**sleeps, sleeping, slept**) *n* **Sleep** is the natural state of rest in which your eyes are closed, your body is inactive, and your mind does not think. نیند ▷ *vi* When you **sleep**, you rest with your eyes closed and your mind and body inactive. سونا

sleep in *v* If you **sleep in**, you sleep longer than usual. معمول سے زیادہ دیر سونا *Yesterday, few players turned up because most slept in.*

sleeping bag (**sleeping bags**) *n* A **sleeping bag** is a large warm bag for sleeping in, especially when you are camping. سلیپنگ بیگ

sleeping car (**sleeping cars**) *n* A **sleeping car** is a railway carriage containing beds for passengers to sleep in at night. ریل کا سونے کی سیٹوں والا ڈبہ

sleeping pill (**sleeping pills**) *n* A **sleeping pill** is a pill that you can take to help you sleep. خواب آور دوا

sleepwalk (**sleepwalks, sleepwalking, sleepwalked**) *vi* If someone **sleepwalks**, they walk around while they are asleep. نیند میں چلنا

sleepy (**sleepier, sleepiest**) *adj* If you feel **sleepy**, you feel tired and ready to go to sleep. نیند محسوس کرنا

sleet (**sleets, sleeting, sleeted**) *n* **Sleet** is rain that is partly frozen. ژالہ باری ▷ *v* When partly melted snow or hail, or partly frozen rain, falls from the clouds, you can say that it is **sleeting**. اولے گرنا

sleeve (**sleeves**) *n* The **sleeves** of a coat,

shirt, or other item of clothing are the parts that cover your arms. آستین

sleeveless *adj* A **sleeveless** dress, top, or other item of clothing has no sleeves. بغیر آستین

slender *adj* A **slender** person is thin and graceful in an attractive way. (*written*) چست، تراشیدہ بدن

slice (**slices, slicing, sliced**) *n* A **slice** of bread, meat, fruit, or other food is a thin piece that has been cut from a larger piece. پارچہ، سلائس ▷ *vt* If you **slice** food, you cut it into thin pieces. ٹکڑے کرنا

slide (**slides, sliding, slid**) *n* A **slide** in a playground is a structure that has a steep slope for children to slide down. پھسلنے کا ڈھانچہ ▷ *v* When something **slides** somewhere, or when you **slide** it somewhere, it moves there smoothly over or against something else. اوپر سے نیچے کی طرف پھسلنا

slight (**slighter, slightest**) *adj* Something that is **slight** is very small in degree or quantity. ہلکا، تھوڑا سا

slightly *adv* **Slightly** means to some degree but not much. ہلکے طور پر

slim (**slimmer, slimmest**) *adj* A **slim** person has a thin nicely shaped body. تراشیدہ جسم

sling (**slings**) *n* A **sling** is an object made of ropes, straps, or cloth that is used for carrying things. لٹکانے کا تھیلا، جھولا

slip (**slips, slipping, slipped**) *n* A **slip** is a small or unimportant mistake. معمولی غلطی ▷ *n* A **slip** of paper is a small piece of paper. کاغذ کی پرچی ▷ *n* A **slip** is a thin piece of clothing that a woman wears under her dress or skirt. استر ▷ *vi* If you **slip**, you accidentally slide and lose your balance. پھسل جانا

slipped disc (**slipped discs**) *n* If you have a **slipped disc**, you have a bad back because one of the discs in your spine has moved out of its proper position. ریڑھ کا مہرہ کھسک جانا

slipper (**slippers**) *n* **Slippers** are loose soft shoes that you wear in the house. چپل

slippery *adj* Something that is **slippery** is smooth, wet, or greasy, making it difficult to walk on or to hold. پھسلن بھرا

slip road (**slip roads**) *n* A **slip road** is a road which cars use to drive on and off a motorway. بغلی راستہ

slip up (**slip-ups**) *v* If you **slip up**, you make a small or unimportant mistake. معمولی غلطی یا سہو کرنا *We slipped up a few times.* ▷ *n* A **slip-up** is a small or unimportant mistake. (*informal*) معمولی غلطی

slope (**slopes**) *n* A **slope** is a surface that is at an angle, so that one end is higher than the other. ڈھلان

sloppy (**sloppier, sloppiest**) *adj* Work that is **sloppy** is messy and careless. لاپرواہی اور تتر بتر انداز میں کام

slot (**slots**) *n* A **slot** is a narrow opening in a machine or container, for example a hole that you put coins in to make a machine work. گالا، شگاف

slot machine (**slot machines**) *n* A **slot machine** is a machine from which you can get food or cigarettes or on which you can gamble. You make it work by putting coins into a slot. شگاف مشین (شگاف میں رقم ڈال کر سامان لے لینا)

Slovak (**Slovaks**) *adj* **Slovak** means of, relating to, or characteristic of Slovakia, its people, or their language. سلوواک ▷ *n* **Slovak** is the official language of Slovakia, belonging to the West Slavonic branch of the Indo-European family. Slovak is closely related to Czech, they are mutually intelligible. سلوواکی ▷ *n* A **Slovak** is a native or inhabitant of Slovakia. سلوواکی

Slovakia *n* **Slovakia** is a country in central Europe. سلوواکیا

Slovenia *n* **Slovenia** is a republic in south central Europe. سلووینیا

Slovenian (**Slovenians**) *adj* **Slovenian** means belonging or relating to Slovenia, or to its people, language, or culture.

S

سلووینیائی ▷ *n* A **Slovenian** is a person of Slovenian origin. سلووینیائی ▷ n **Slovenian** is the language spoken in Slovenia. سلووینیائی

slow (**slower, slowest**) *adj* Something that is **slow** moves, happens, or is done without much speed. سست

slow down *v* If something **slows down,** or if you **slow** it **down**, it starts to move or happen more slowly. دھیا ہونا، کرنا *The car slowed down.*

slowly *adv* If something happens or is done **slowly**, it happens or is done without much speed. دھیرے دھیرے، آہستگی سے

slug (**slugs**) *n* A **slug** is a small slow-moving creature, with a long slippery body, like a snail without a shell. گھونگھا

slum (**slums**) *n* A **slum** is an area of a city where living conditions are very bad. جھونپڑپٹی

slush *n* **Slush** is snow that has begun to melt and is therefore very wet and dirty. برف کی کیچڑ

sly *adj* A **sly** look, expression, or remark shows that you know something that other people do not know. معنی خیز

smack (**smacks, smacking, smacked**) *vt* If you **smack** someone, you hit them with your hand. چپت لگانا

small (**smaller, smallest**) *adj* If something is **small**, it is not large in size or amount. چھوٹا

small ads *npl* The **small ads** in a newspaper are short advertisements in which you can advertise something such as an object for sale or a room to let. چھوٹے اِشتہار

smart (**smarter, smartest**) *adj* **Smart** people and things are pleasantly neat and clean in appearance. خوبرو

smart phone (**smart phones**) *n* A **smart phone** is a type of cellphone that can perform many of the operations that a computer does, such as accessing the Internet. کثیرالمقصد فون

smash (**smashes, smashing, smashed**) *v* If something **smashes**, or if you **smash** it, it breaks into many pieces, for example when it is hit or dropped. ٹکڑے کر ڈالنا

smashing *adj* If you describe something or someone as **smashing**, you mean that you like them very much. (*informal*) شاندار

smear (**smears**) *n* A **smear** or a **smear test** is a medical test in which a few cells are taken from a woman's cervix and examined to see if any cancer cells are present. بچہ دانی کے سرطان کا پتہ لگانے کے لیے طبی جانچ

smell (**smells, smelling, smelled, smelt**) *n* The **smell** of something is a quality it has which you become aware of through your nose. بو ▷ *vt* If you **smell** something, you become aware of it through your nose. سونگھنا، بو محسوس کرنا ▷ *vi* If something **smells** of a particular thing, it has a particular quality which you become aware of through your nose. بو آنا، بو محسوس ہونا

smelly (**smellier, smelliest**) *adj* Something that is **smelly** has an unpleasant smell. بدبودار

smile (**smiles, smiling, smiled**) *n* A **smile** is the expression that you have on your face when you smile. مسکراہٹ ▷ *vi* When you **smile**, the corners of your mouth curve up and you sometimes show your teeth. People smile when they are pleased or amused, or when they are being friendly. مسکرانا

smiley (**smileys**) *n* A **smiley** is a symbol used in e-mail to show how someone is feeling. :-) is a smiley showing happiness. (*informal*) مسکراہٹ کا علامتی نشان

smoke (**smokes, smoking, smoked**) *n* **Smoke** consists of gas and small bits of solid material that are sent into the air when something burns. دھواں ▷ *vi* If something **is smoking**, smoke is coming from it. دھواں اٹھنا

smoke alarm (**smoke alarms**) *n* A **smoke alarm** or a **smoke detector** is a device fixed to the ceiling of a room which makes a loud noise if there is smoke in the air, to warn people. آگ یا دھوئیں سے خبردار کرنے والا الارم

smoked *adj* **Smoked** glass has been made darker by being treated with smoke. دھوئیں سے کالا کیا ہوا

smoker (**smoker**) *n* A **smoker** is a person who habitually smokes tobacco. تمباکو نوش

smoking *n* **Smoking** is the act or habit of smoking cigarettes, cigars, or a pipe. تمباکو نوشی

smooth (**smoother, smoothest**) *adj* A **smooth** surface has no roughness or holes. ہموار، چکنا

SMS *n* **SMS** is a way of sending short written messages from one mobile phone to another. **SMS** is an abbreviation for 'short message system'. ایس ایم ایس (تحریری پیغام موبائل پر)

smudge (**smudges**) *n* A **smudge** is a dirty, blurred mark. گندا دھندلا نشان

smug *adj* If you say that someone is **smug**, you are criticizing the fact they seem very pleased with how good, clever, or fortunate they are. اپنے منہ میاں مٹھو بننے کی کیفیت

smuggle (**smuggles, smuggling, smuggled**) *vt* If someone **smuggles** things or people into a place or out of it, they take them there illegally or secretly. غیر قانونی طور پر ملک میں لانا

smuggler (**smugglers**) *n* **Smugglers** are people who take goods into or out of a country illegally. اسمگلر

smuggling *n* **Smuggling** is the act of taking things or people into a place or out of it, illegally or secretly. اسمگلنگ

snack (**snacks**) *n* A **snack** is a small, quick meal, or something eaten between meals. ہلکا ناشتہ

snack bar (**snack bars**) *n* A **snack bar** is a place where you can buy drinks and simple meals such as sandwiches. ناشتہ، نمکین کی دوکان

snail (**snails**) *n* A **snail** is a small animal that has a spiral shell. It moves slowly, leaving behind a trail of slime. گھونگا

snake (**snakes**) *n* A **snake** is a long, thin reptile with no legs. سانپ

snap (**snaps, snapping, snapped**) *v* If something **snaps** or if you **snap** it, it breaks suddenly, usually with a sharp cracking noise. توڑ لینا

snapshot (**snapshots**) *n* A **snapshot** is a photograph that is taken quickly and casually. اچانک لیا ہوا فوٹو

snarl (**snarls, snarling, snarled**) *vi* When an animal **snarls**, it makes a fierce, rough sound in its throat while showing its teeth. غرانا

snatch (**snatches, snatching, snatched**) *v* If you **snatch** something, or if you **snatch at** it, you take it or pull it away quickly. چھینا

sneeze (**sneezes, sneezing, sneezed**) *vi* When you **sneeze**, you suddenly take in your breath and then blow it down your nose noisily without being able to stop yourself, for example because you have a cold. چھینکنا

sniff (**sniffs, sniffing, sniffed**) *v* When you **sniff**, you breathe in air through your nose hard enough to make a sound, for example when you are trying not to cry, or in order to show disapproval. سسکی لینا

snigger (**sniggers, sniggering, sniggered**) *vi* If someone **sniggers**, they laugh quietly in a disrespectful way, for example at something rude or unkind. ہتک آمیز طور پر دھیرے سے ہنسنا

snob (**snobs**) *n* If you call someone a **snob**, you disapprove of them because they admire upper-class people and dislike lower-class people. اِنسانوں میں فرق کرنے والا

snooker *n* **Snooker** is a game involving balls on a large table. The players use long sticks called cues to hit a white ball, and score points by knocking coloured balls into the pockets at the sides of the table. اسنوکر (بڑی میز پر لکڑی کی گیندوں والا کھیل)

snooze (**snoozes, snoozing, snoozed**) *n*

A **snooze** is a short, light sleep, especially during the day. (*informal*) قیلولہ ▷ *vi* If you **snooze**, you sleep lightly for a short period of time. (*informal*) قیلولہ کرنا

snore (**snores, snoring, snored**) *vi* When someone who is asleep **snores**, they make a loud noise each time they breathe. خراٹے لینا

snorkel (**snorkels**) *n* A **snorkel** is a tube through which a person swimming just under the surface of the sea can breathe. ایک ٹیوب جس کے سہارے سانس لیکر زیر آب تیرا جا سکتا ہے

snow (**snows, snowing, snowed**) *n* **Snow** is the soft white bits of frozen water that fall from the sky in cold weather. برف ▷ *vi* When it **snows**, snow falls from the sky. برفباری ہونا

snowball (**snowballs**) *n* A **snowball** is a ball of snow. برف کے گولے

snowflake (**snowflakes**) *n* A **snowflake** is one of the soft, white bits of frozen water that fall as snow. جما ہوا پانی (برفباری)

snowman (**snowmen**) *n* A **snowman** is a large shape which is made out of snow, especially by children, and is supposed to look like a person. برف سے بنا آدمی

snowplough (**snowploughs**) *n* A **snowplough** is a vehicle which is used to push snow off roads or railway lines. برف ہٹانے والی گاڑی

snowstorm (**snowstorms**) *n* A **snowstorm** is a very heavy fall of snow, usually when there is also a strong wind blowing at the same time. بھاری برفباری

so *adv* You use **so** to talk about something without repeating the same words. ایسا ▷ *conj* You use **so** and **so that** to talk about the reason for doing something. تاکہ *They went outside so that nobody would hear them.* ▷ *adv* You can use **so** in front of adjectives and adverbs to make them stronger. کافی

soak (**soaks, soaking, soaked**) *v* When you **soak** something, or when you leave it to **soak**, you put it into a liquid and leave it there. ڈبونا

soaked *adj* If someone or something gets **soaked** or **soaked through,** water or some other liquid makes them extremely wet. جذب کردہ، بھیگا ہوا

soap (**soaps**) *n* **Soap** is a substance that you use with water for washing yourself or sometimes for washing clothes. صابن

soap dish (**soap dishes**) *n* A **soap dish** is a shallow container with a wide uncovered top, used in a bathroom for holding soap. صابندانی

soap opera (**soap operas**) *n* A **soap opera** is a television drama serial about the daily lives of a group of people. روزمرہ کی زندگی پر ڈرامہ

soap powder (**soap powders**) *n* **Soap powder** is a powder made from soap and other substances that you use for washing your clothes, especially in a machine. سفوف صابن

sob (**sobs, sobbing, sobbed**) *vi* When someone **sobs**, they cry in a noisy way, breathing in short breaths. سسکنا

sober *adj* When you are **sober**, you are not drunk. ہوش میں

sociable *adj* **Sociable** people enjoy meeting and talking to other people. سماجی، ملنسار

social *adj* **Social** means relating to society. سماج سے متعلق

socialism *n* **Socialism** is a set of left-wing political principles whose general aim is to create a system in which everyone has an equal opportunity to benefit from a country's wealth. Under socialism, the country's main industries are usually owned by the state. سماجواد

socialist (**socialists**) *adj* **Socialist** means based on socialism or relating to socialism. سماجوادی ▷ *n* A **socialist** is a person who believes in socialism or who is a member of a socialist party. سماجواد میں اعتماد رکھنے والا

social security *n* **Social security** is money that is paid by the government to people who are unemployed, poor, or ill. معاشرتی تحفظ

social services *npl* **Social services** are services provided by the local authority to help people who have serious family problems or financial problems. سماجی خدمات

social worker (**social workers**) *n* A **social worker** is a person whose job is to do social work. سماجی کارکن

society (**societies**) *n* **Society** consists of all the people in a country or region, considered as a group. سماج، معاشرہ

sociology *n* **Sociology** is the study of society or of the way society is organized. سماجیات

sock (**socks**) *n* **Socks** are pieces of clothing which cover your foot and ankle and are worn inside shoes. موزہ

socket (**sockets**) *n* A **socket** is a device on a piece of electrical equipment into which you can put a plug or bulb. جس میں کوئی برقی آلہ لگایا جائے

sofa (**sofas**) *n* A **sofa** is a long, comfortable seat with a back and arms, which two or three people can sit on. صوفہ

sofa bed (**sofa beds**) *n* A **sofa bed** is a type of sofa whose seat folds out so that it can also be used as a bed. صوفہ جسے کھول کر پلنگ بنا لیا جائے

soft (**softer, softest**) *adj* Something that is **soft** is nice to touch, and not rough or hard. ملائم، نرم ▷ *adj* A **soft** sound or light is very gentle. نرم، ہلکی

soft drink (**soft drinks**) *n* A **soft drink** is a cold, non-alcoholic drink such as lemonade. ہلکے مشروب (الکحل کے بغیر)

software *n* Computer programs are referred to as **software**. کمپیوٹر پروگرام

soggy (**soggier, soggiest**) *adj* Something that is **soggy** is unpleasantly wet. ناگوار حد تک بھیگا ہوا

soil *n* **Soil** is the substance on the surface of the earth in which plants grow. مٹی

solar *adj* **Solar** is used to describe things relating to the sun. آفتابی

solar power *n* **Solar power** is heat radiation from the sun converted into electrical power. آفتابی قوت

solar system (**solar systems**) *n* The **solar system** is the sun and all the planets that go round it. نظام شمسی

soldier (**soldiers**) *n* A **soldier** is a person who works in an army. سپاہی

sold out *adj* If a performance, sports event, or other entertainment is **sold out**, all the tickets for it have been sold. سبھی ٹکٹ بک جانا

solicitor (**solicitors**) *n* In Britain, a **solicitor** is a lawyer who gives legal advice, prepares legal documents and cases, and represents clients in the lower courts of law. وکیل

solid *adj* Something that is **solid** stays the same shape whether it is in a container or not. ٹھوس ▷ *adj* Something that is **solid** is not hollow. سخت، ٹھوس

solo (**solos**) *n* A **solo** is a piece of music or a dance performed by one person. اکیلا

soloist (**soloists**) *n* A **soloist** is a person who performs a solo, usually a piece of music. اکیلا کارکردگی انجام دینے والا

soluble *adj* A substance that is **soluble** will dissolve in a liquid. تحلیل پذیر

solution (**solutions**) *n* A **solution** to a

S

problem is a way of dealing with it so that the difficulty is removed. حل

solve (**solves, solving, solved**) *vt* If you **solve** a problem or a question, you find a solution or an answer to it. حل کرنا

solvent (**solvents**) *n* A **solvent** is a liquid that can dissolve other substances. محلل

Somali (**Somalis**) *adj* **Somali** means of, relating to, or characteristic of Somalia, the Somalis, or their language. صومالی ▷ *n* A **Somali** is a member of a tall dark-skinned people inhabiting Somalia. صومالیائی ▷ *n* **Somali** is the language spoken by the Somali people. صومالیائی

Somalia *n* **Somalia** is a republic in north-east Africa, on the Indian Ocean and the Gulf of Aden. صومالیہ

some *det* You use **some** to talk about an amount of something. کچھ، تھوڑا *Can I have some orange juice, please?* ▷ *pron* **Some** means a quantity of something or a number of people or things. کچھ (چیز)

somebody *pron* You use **somebody** to talk about a person without saying who you mean. کوئی شخص

somehow *adv* You use **somehow** when you cannot say how somebody did something, or how somebody will do something. کسی بھی طرح

someone *pron* You use **someone** to talk about a person without saying who you mean. کوئی *I need someone to help me.*

someplace *adv* You use **someplace** to talk about a place without saying where you mean. کسی جگہ

something *pron* You use **something** to talk about a thing without saying what it is. کوئی چیز/ کچھ چیز

sometime *adv* You use **sometime** to talk about a time in the future or the past that is not known. کبھی کبھی

sometimes *adv* You use **sometimes** to talk about things that do not take place all the time. کبھی بھی (آنے والے وقت میں)

somewhere *adv* You use **somewhere** to talk about a place without saying where you mean. کسی جگہ

son (**sons**) *n* A person's **son** is their male child. بیٹا

song (**songs**) *n* A **song** is a piece of music with words and music sung together. گیت

son-in-law (**sons-in-law**) *n* A person's **son-in-law** is the husband of their daughter. داماد

soon *adv* If something is going to happen **soon**, it will happen after a short time. جلد

soot *n* **Soot** is black powder which rises in the smoke from a fire and collects on the inside of chimneys. کالک

sophisticated *adj* A **sophisticated** person is comfortable in social situations and knows about culture, fashion, and other matters that are considered socially important. شائستہ

soppy (**soppier, soppiest**) *adj* If you describe someone or something as **soppy**, you mean that they are foolishly sentimental. جذباتی

soprano (**sopranos**) *n* A **soprano** is a woman, girl, or boy with a high singing voice. بہترین گلوکار، گلوکارہ

sorbet (**sorbets**) *n* **Sorbet** is a frozen dessert made with fruit juice, sugar, and water. شربت

sorcerer (**sorcerers**) *n* In fairy stories, a **sorcerer** is a person who performs magic by using the power of evil spirits. ساحر، ساحرہ

sore (**sorer, sorest, sores**) *adj* If part of your body is **sore**, it causes you pain and discomfort. خراش، چھالا ▷ *n* A **sore** is a painful spot on your body where the skin is infected. چھالا

sorry *excl* You say '**Sorry!**' as a way of apologizing to someone for something that you have done which has upset them or caused them difficulties, or when you bump into them accidentally. معذرت! ▷ *adj* If you are **sorry** about something, you feel sad about it. معذرت

خواہی، افسوس ہونا ▷ *adj* If you feel **sorry** for someone, you feel sad for them. دکھ محسوس کرنا، غمزدہ ہونا

sort (**sorts**) *n* A particular **sort** of something is one of its different kinds or types. قسم

sort out *v* If you **sort out** a group of things, you organize or tidy them. چھانٹنا *We try to sort out the truth from the lies.*

SOS *n* An **SOS** is a signal which indicates to other people that you are in danger and need help quickly. خطرہ سے آگاہی اور مدد کا سگنل

so-so *adv* **So-so** means in an average or indifferent manner. (*informal*) بس یوں ہی

soul (**souls**) *n* A person's **soul** is the spiritual part of them which some people believe continues existing after their body is dead. روح

sound (**sounder, soundest, sounds**) *adj* If something is **sound**, it is in good condition or healthy. مضبوط، بے عیب ▷ *n* A **sound** is something that you hear. آواز

soundtrack (**soundtracks**) *n* The **soundtrack** of a film is its sound, speech, and especially the music. فلم کی صرف آواز

soup (**soups**) *n* **Soup** is liquid food made by cooking meat, fish, or vegetables in water. شوربہ

sour *adj* Something that is **sour** has a sharp taste like the taste of a lemon. کھٹا

south *adj* The **south** edge, corner, or part of a place or country is the part which is towards the south. جنوب ▷ *adv* If you go **south**, you travel towards the south. جنوبی ▷ *n* **The south** is the direction on your right when you are looking towards the place where the sun rises. جنوبی سمت

South Africa *n* **South Africa** is a republic occupying the southernmost part of the African continent. جنوبی افریقہ

South African (**South Africans**) *adj* **South African** means of or relating to the Republic of South Africa, its inhabitants, or any of their languages. جنوبی افریقی ▷ *n* A **South African** is a native or inhabitant of the Republic of South Africa. جنوبی افریقی

South America *n* **South America** is the fourth largest of the continents, bordering on the Caribbean in the north, the Pacific in the west, and the Atlantic in the east and joined to Central America by the Isthmus of Panama. جنوبی امریکہ

South American (**South Americans**) *adj* **South American** means of or relating to the continent of South America or its inhabitants. جنوبی امریکہ ▷ *n* A **South American** is a native or inhabitant of South America. جنوبی امریکی

southbound *adj* **Southbound** roads or vehicles lead or are travelling towards the south. جنوب طرفی

southeast *n* The **southeast** is the direction which is halfway between south and east. جنوب مشرق

southern *adj* **Southern** means in or from the south of a region or country. جنوبی

South Korea *n* **South Korea** is a republic in north-east Asia. جنوبی کوریا

South Pole *n* **The South Pole** is the place on the surface of the earth which is farthest towards the south. قطبِ جنوبی

southwest *n* The **southwest** is the direction which is halfway between south and west. جنوب مشرق

souvenir (**souvenirs**) *n* A **souvenir** is something which you buy or keep to remind you of a holiday, place, or event. سوونیر(چھٹی، واقعات کی یاد دلانیوالا)

soya *n* **Soya** flour, butter, or other food is made from soya beans. سویا

soy sauce *n* **Soy sauce** is a dark brown liquid made from soya beans and used as a flavouring, especially in Chinese cooking. سویا سوس

spa (**spas**) *n* A **spa** is a place where water with minerals in it bubbles out of the ground. معدنیات سے بھرپور چشمہ

space (**spaces**) *n* You use **space** to talk

S

about an area that is empty. خالی جگہ ▷ *n* **Space** is the area past the Earth, where the stars and planets are. خلاء

spacecraft (**spacecraft**) *n* A **spacecraft** is a rocket or other vehicle that can travel in space. خلائی راکٹ / گاڑی

spade (**spades**) *n* A **spade** is a tool used for digging, with a flat metal blade and a long handle. پھاوڑا

spaghetti *n* **Spaghetti** is a type of pasta which looks like long pieces of string. چوڑی سوئیاں

Spain *n* **Spain** is a kingdom of south-west Europe, occupying the Iberian peninsula between the Mediterranean and the Atlantic. اسپین

spam (**spams**) *n* **Spam** is unwanted e-mail that is sent to a large number of people, usually as advertising. فضول ای میل

Spaniard (**Spaniards**) *n* A **Spaniard** is a Spanish citizen, or a person of Spanish origin. اسپینی باشندہ

spaniel (**spaniels**) *n* A **spaniel** is a type of dog with long ears that hang down. لمبے لٹکے کانوں والا کتا

Spanish *adj* **Spanish** means belonging or relating to Spain, or to its people, language, or culture. اسپینی ▷ *n* **Spanish** is the main language spoken in Spain, and in many countries in South and Central America. اسپینی (زبان)

spank (**spanks, spanking, spanked**) *vt* If someone **spanks** a child, they punish them by hitting them on the bottom several times. سرین پر مارنا

spanner (**spanners**) *n* A **spanner** is a metal tool used for tightening a nut. پانہ

spare (**spares, sparing, spared**) *adj* You use **spare** to describe something that is the same as things that you are already using, but that you do not need yet and are keeping ready in case another one is needed. فاضل ▷ *vi* If you have something such as time, money, or space to **spare**, you have some extra time, money, or space that you have not used or which you do not need. فاضل ہونا (وقت، رقم وغیرہ)

spare part (**spare parts**) *n* **Spare parts** are parts that you can buy separately to replace old or broken parts in a piece of equipment. فاضل پرزے

spare room (**spare rooms**) *n* A **spare room** is a bedroom which is kept especially for visitors to sleep in. فاضل کمرہ

spare time *n* Your **spare time** is the time during which you do not have to work and you can do whatever you like. فاضل وقت

spare tyre (**spare tyres**) *n* A **spare tyre** is a wheel with a tyre on it that you keep in your car in case you get a flat tyre and need to replace one of your wheels. فالتو ٹائر

spare wheel (**spare wheels**) *n* A **spare wheel** is a wheel with a tyre on it that you keep in your car in case you get a flat tyre and need to replace one of your wheels. فاضل پہیا

spark (**sparks**) *n* A **spark** is a tiny bright piece of burning material that flies up from something that is burning. چنگاری

sparkling water (**sparkling waters**) *n* **Sparkling water** is slightly fizzy water. شفاف پانی

spark plug (**spark plugs**) *n* A **spark plug** is a device in the engine of a motor vehicle, which produces electric sparks to make the petrol burn. اسپارک پلگ (چنگاری پیدا کرنے والا)

sparrow (**sparrows**) *n* A **sparrow** is a small brown bird that is common in Britain. چڑیا (گوریا)

spasm (**spasms**) *n* A **spasm** is a sudden tightening of your muscles, which you cannot control. عضلات کی جکڑن

spatula (**spatulas**) *n* A **spatula** is an object like a knife with a wide, flat blade. Spatulas are used in cooking. کفچہ (باورچی خانے کا اوزار)

speak (**speaks, speaking, spoke, spoken**) *v* When you **speak**, you use your voice in order to say something. بولنا

speaker (**speakers**) *n* A **speaker** at a meeting, conference, or other gathering is a person who is making a speech or giving a talk. مقرر

speak up *v* If you ask someone to **speak up**, you are asking them to speak more loudly. زور سے بولنا *I'm quite deaf – you'll have to speak up.*

special *adj* Someone or something that is **special** is different from normal, often in a way that makes them better or more important than other people or things. خاص

specialist (**specialists**) *n* A **specialist** is a person who has a particular skill or knows a lot about a particular subject. ماہر فن

speciality (**specialities**) *n* Someone's **speciality** is the kind of work they do best or the subject they know most about. مہارت

specialize (**specializes, specializing, specialized**) *vi* If you **specialize in** an area of study or a type of work, you know a lot about it and spend a lot of your time and attention on it. کسی بھی فن میں خاص مہارت حاصل کرنا

specially *adv* If something has been done **specially** for a particular person or purpose, it has been done only for that person or purpose. خاص طور سے

special offer (**special offers**) *n* A **special offer** is a product, service, or programme that is offered at reduced prices or rates. خاص پیشکش

species (**species**) *n* A **species** is a class of plants or animals whose members have the same characteristics and are able to breed with each other. پودوں اور جانداروں کی نسلیں

specific *adj* You use **specific** to emphasize that you are talking about a particular thing or subject. مخصوص

specifically *adv* You use **specifically** to emphasize that a subject is being considered separately from other subjects. مخصوص طور پر

specify (**specifies, specifying, specified**) *vt* If you **specify** something, you state it precisely. مخصوص کرنا

spectacles *npl* **Spectacles** are two lenses in a frame that some people wear in front of their eyes in order to help them see better. (*formal*) دونوں لینس فریم میں (عینک)

spectacular *adj* adj قابل دید

spectator (**spectators**) *n* A **spectator** is someone who watches something, especially a sporting event. ناظر

speculate (**speculates, speculating, speculated**) *v* If you **speculate** about something, you guess about its nature or identity, or about what might happen. اندازہ لگانا (مستقبل کا)

speech *n* **Speech** is the ability to speak or the act of speaking. تقریر، گویائی

speechless *adj* If you are **speechless**, you are temporarily unable to speak, usually because something has shocked you. منہ سے آواز نہ نکلنا

speed (**speeds**) *n* The **speed** of something is the rate at which it moves, happens, or is done. رفتار

speedboat (**speedboats**) *n* A **speedboat** is a boat that can go very fast because it has a powerful engine. تیز رفتار کشتی

speeding *n* **Speeding** means the act or process of moving or travelling quickly. تیز رفتار

speed limit (**speed limits**) *n* The **speed limit** on a road is the maximum speed at which you are legally allowed to drive. رفتار کی حد

speedometer (**speedometers**) *n* A **speedometer** is the instrument in a vehicle which shows how fast the vehicle is moving. رفتار پیما

speed up *v* When something **speeds up**, it moves, happens, or is done more quickly. رفتار بڑھانا *Try to speed up your breathing and stretch your legs.*

spell (**spells, spelling, spelled, spelt**) *n* A **spell** of a particular type of weather or a particular activity is a short period of time during which this type of weather or activity occurs. مدت ▷ *n* A **spell** is a situation in which events are controlled by a magical power. سحر ▷ *vt* When you **spell** a word, you write or speak each letter in the word in the correct order. ہجے کرنا

spellchecker (**spellcheckers**) *n* A **spellchecker** is a special program on a computer which you can use to check for spelling mistakes. ہجے چیک کرنے والا کمپیوٹر پروگرام

spelling (**spellings**) *n* The **spelling** of a word is the correct sequence of letters in it. ہجے

spend (**spends, spending, spent**) *vt* When you **spend** money, you buy things with it. خرچ کرنا ▷ *vt* To **spend** time or energy is to use it doing something. گزارنا

sperm (**sperms, sperm**) *n* A **sperm** is a cell produced in the sex organs of a male animal which can enter a female animal's egg and fertilize it. نطفی خلیہ

spice (**spices**) *n* A **spice** is a part of a plant, or a powder made from that part, which you put in food to give it flavour. مسالہ

spicy (**spicier, spiciest**) *adj* **Spicy** food is strongly flavoured with spices. مسالیدار

spider (**spiders**) *n* A **spider** is a small creature with eight legs. مکڑی

spill (**spills, spilling, spilled, spilt**) *v* If a liquid **spills** or if you **spill** it, it accidentally flows over the edge of a container. چھلک جانا

spinach *n* **Spinach** is a vegetable with large green leaves. پالک

spinal cord (**spinal cords**) *n* Your **spinal cord** is a thick cord of nerves inside your spine which connects your brain to nerves in all parts of your body. اعصابی رسی (ریڑھ کی ہڈی سے گزرنے والی)

spin drier (**spin driers**) *n* A **spin drier** is a machine that partly dries clothes that you have washed by turning them round and round very fast to remove the water. کپڑے سکھانے والی (مشین)

spine (**spines**) *n* Your **spine** is the row of bones down your back. ریڑھ کی ہڈی کا منکا

spinster (**spinsters**) *n* A **spinster** is a woman who has never been married; used especially when talking about an old or middle-aged woman. (*old-fashioned*) ادھیڑ یا بوڑھی عمر کی کنواری،

spire (**spires**) *n* The **spire** of a church is a tall cone-shaped structure on top of a tower. تکون مینار (چرچ کی)

spirit *n* Your **spirit** is the part of you that is not physical and that is connected with your deepest thoughts and feelings. روح، جذبہ

spirits *npl* You can refer to your **spirits** when saying how happy or unhappy you are. For example, if your spirits are high, you are happy. حوصلے، جینے کی امنگ

spiritual *adj* **Spiritual** means relating to people's deepest thoughts and beliefs, rather than to their bodies and physical surroundings. روحانی

spit (**spits, spitting, spat**) *n* **Spit** is the watery liquid produced in your mouth. تھوک ▷ *v* If someone **spits**, they force an amount of spit out of their mouth. If you **spit** liquid or food somewhere, you force a small amount of it out of your mouth. تھوکنا

spite *n* If you do something cruel out of **spite**, you do it because you want to hurt or upset someone. انتقام، چوٹ پہنچانے کی نیت سے ▷ *vt* If you do something cruel to **spite** someone, you do it in order to hurt or upset them. انتقام لینا، چوٹ پہنچانا

spiteful *adj* Someone who is **spiteful** does cruel things to hurt people they dislike. منتقم، ظالم

splash (**splashes, splashing, splashed**) *vi* If you **splash** about or **splash** around in water, you hit or disturb the water in a noisy way, causing some of it to fly up into the air. پانی کے چھینٹے اڑانا

splendid *adj* If you say that something is **splendid**, you mean that it is very good. شاندار

splint (**splints**) *n* A **splint** is a long piece of wood or metal that is fastened to a broken arm, leg, or back to keep it still. کھپچی (ہڈی کو سیدھا رکھنے کے لئے)

splinter (**splinters**) *n* A **splinter** is a very thin sharp piece of wood or glass which has broken off from a larger piece. کرچی

split (**splits, splitting**) *v* If something **splits**, or if you **split** it, it is divided into two or more parts. پھٹنا، ٹکڑے ہونا

split up *v* If two people **split up**, they end their relationship or marriage. جدائی ہونا *I split up with my boyfriend.*

spoil (**spoils, spoiling, spoiled, spoilt**) *vt* If you **spoil** something, you damage it or stop it from working as it should. برباد کرنا، روکنا، ختم کرنا ▷ *vt* If you **spoil** children, you give them everything they want or ask for. بگاڑنا

spoilsport (**spoilsports**) *n* If you say that someone is a **spoilsport**, you mean that they are behaving in a way that ruins other people's pleasure or enjoyment. (*informal*) دوسروں کو برباد کرنے والا

spoilt *adj* A **spoilt** child is a child who has been given everything he wants which has a bad effect on his character. بگڑا ہوا

spoke (**spokes**) *n* The **spokes** of a wheel are the bars that join the outer ring to the centre. پہیے کی مرکزی پلیٹ سے جڑی سلاخیں

spokesman (**spokesmen**) *n* A **spokesman** is a male spokesperson. ترجمان مرد

spokesperson (**spokespersons, spokespeople**) *n* A **spokesperson** is a person who speaks as the representative of a group or organization. ترجمان شخص

spokeswoman (**spokeswomen**) *n* A **spokeswoman** is a female spokesperson. ترجمان خاتون

sponge (**sponges**) *n* A **sponge** is a piece of sponge that you use for washing yourself or for cleaning things. اسفنج ▷ *n* A **sponge** is a light cake or pudding made from flour, eggs, sugar, and sometimes fat. کیک یا پڈنگ

sponge bag (**sponge bags**) *n* A **sponge bag** is a small bag in which you keep things such as soap and a toothbrush when you are travelling. چھوٹا سفری بیگ (صابن ٹوتھ برش رکھنے کو)

sponsor (**sponsors, sponsoring, sponsored**) *n* A **sponsor** is a person or organization that sponsors something or someone. کفیل ▷ *vt* If an organization **sponsors** something such as an event, it pays some or all of the expenses connected with it, often in order to get publicity for itself. کفالت کرنا

sponsorship *n* **Sponsorship** is financial support given by a sponsor. کفالت

spontaneous *adj* **Spontaneous** acts are not planned or arranged, but are done because someone suddenly wants to do them. فی البدیہہ، فوری، اچانک

spooky (**spookier, spookiest**) *adj* If something is **spooky**, it has a frightening and unnatural atmosphere. (*informal*) بھوتیا

spoon (**spoons**) *n* A **spoon** is a tool used for eating, stirring, and serving food. It is shaped like a small shallow bowl with a long handle. چمچ

spoonful (**spoonfuls**) *n* You can refer to an amount of food resting on a spoon as a **spoonful** of food. چمچ بھر

sport (**sports**) *n* **Sports** are games and other competitive activities which need physical effort and skill. کھیل

sportsman (**sportsmen**) *n* A **sportsman** is a man who takes part in sports. کھلاڑی

sportswear *n* **Sportswear** is the special clothing worn for playing sports or for informal leisure activities. کھلاڑیوں کے لباس

sportswoman (**sportswomen**) *n* A **sportswoman** is a woman who takes part in sports. خاتون کھلاڑی

S

sporty (**sportier, sportiest**) *adj* A **sporty** person enjoys playing sport. کھیلوں سے وابستہ

spot (**spots, spotting, spotted**) *n* **Spots** are small, round, coloured areas on a surface. دھبہ ▷ *n* You can refer to a particular place as a **spot**. مقام ▷ *vt* If you **spot** something or someone, you notice them. نظر میں لانا

spotless *adj* Something that is **spotless** is completely clean. بے داغ

spotlight (**spotlights**) *n* A **spotlight** is a powerful light, used for example in a theatre, which can be directed so that it lights up a small area. اسپوٹ لائٹ (ایک مقام پر تیز روشنی ڈالنے والی)

spotty (**spottier, spottiest**) *adj* Someone who is **spotty** has spots on their face. چہرے پر داغ دھبہ والا

spouse (**spouses**) *n* Someone's **spouse** is the person they are married to. زوج

sprain (**sprains, spraining, sprained**) *n* A **sprain** is the injury caused by spraining a joint. جوڑ کا کھنچاؤ ▷ *vt* If you your ankle or wrist, you accidentally damage it by twisting it, for example, when you fall. جوڑ کے کھنچاؤ کا شکار ہونا

spray (**sprays, spraying, sprayed**) *n* **Spray** consists of a lot of small drops of water which are being splashed or forced into the air. چھڑکاؤ ▷ *v* If you **spray** drops of a liquid or small pieces of something somewhere, or if they **spray** somewhere, they cover a place or shower someone. چھڑکاؤ کرنا

spread (**spreads, spreading, spread**) *n* A **spread** is a soft food which you put on bread. بریڈ پر لگانے والی چیز ▷ *vt* If you **spread** something somewhere, you open it out. پھیلانا ▷ *vt* If you **spread** something on a surface, you put it all over the surface. پھیلانا ▷ *vi* If something **spreads**, it reaches a larger area. پھیلنا

spread out *v* If people, animals, or vehicles **spread out**, they move apart from each other. بکھر جانا، پھیل جانا *They spread out to search the area.*

spreadsheet (**spreadsheets**) *n* A **spreadsheet** is a computer program that is used for displaying and dealing with numbers. Spreadsheets are used mainly for financial planning. اعداد سے متعلق کمپیوٹر پروگرام

spring (**springs**) *n* **Spring** is the season between winter and summer when the weather becomes warmer and plants start to grow again. موسم بہار ▷ *n* A **spring** is a long piece of metal that goes round and round, It goes back to the same shape after you pull it. اسپرنگ

spring-cleaning *n* **Spring-cleaning** is the process of thoroughly cleaning a place, especially your home. You can also say that you give a place a **spring-cleaning**. کسی مقام خاص طور سے گھر کی مکمل صفائی

spring onion (**spring onions**) *n* **Spring onions** are small onions with long green leaves. They are often eaten raw in salads. کچی پیاز کا پودا

springtime *n* **Springtime** is the period of time during which spring lasts. موسم بہار کا اثر

sprinkler (**sprinklers**) *n* A **sprinkler** is a device used to spray water. Sprinklers are used to water plants or grass, or to put out fires in buildings. پانی چھڑکنے والا

sprint (**sprints, sprinting, sprinted**) *n* A **sprint** is a short fast race. کم دوری کی تیز دوڑ ▷ *vi* If you **sprint**, you run or ride as fast as you can over a short distance. تیز دوڑنا یا سواری کرنا (کم دوری تک)

sprinter (**sprinters**) *n* A **sprinter** is a person who takes part in short, fast races. کم دوری تیز دوڑوں میں حصہ لینے والا

sprouts *npl* **Sprouts** are vegetables that look like tiny cabbages. انکرائی ہوئی سبزیاں

spy (**spies, spying, spied**) *n* A **spy** is a person whose job is to find out secret information about another country or organization. جاسوس ▷ *vi* Someone who **spies** for a country or organization tries to find out secret information for them about other countries or organizations. جاسوسی کرنا کا شکار ہونا

spying *n* **Spying** is the act or process of finding out secret information for a country or organization about other countries or organizations. جاسوسی

squabble (**squabbles, squabbling, squabbled**) *vi* When people **squabble**, they quarrel about something that is not really important. بے سبب جھگڑنا

squander (**squanders, squandering, squandered**) *vt* If you **squander** money, resources, or opportunities, you waste them. ضائع کرنا

square (**squares**) *adj* If something is **square**, it has a shape similar to a square. مربع شکل ▷ *n* A **square** is a shape with four sides of the same length and four corners that are all right angles. مربع

squash (**squashes, squashing, squashed**) *n* **Squash** is a game in which two players hit a small rubber ball against the walls of a court using rackets. کھیل (دو کھلاڑی ربر کی گیند کو دیوار پر مارتے ہیں) ▷ *vt* If someone or something is **squashed**, they are pressed or crushed with such force that they become injured or lose their shape. ٹکرا جانا، کچلا جانا

squeak (**squeaks, squeaking, squeaked**) *vi* If something or someone **squeaks**, they make a short, high-pitched sound. کوکنا

squeeze (**squeezes, squeezing, squeezed**) *vt* If you **squeeze** something, you press it firmly, usually with your hands. بھینچنا، نچوڑنا

squeeze in *v* If you **squeeze** a person or thing **in** somewhere or if they **squeeze in** there, they manage to get through or into a small space. تنگ جگہ کی وجہ سے بھینچے جانا *They went down in the lift, squeezing in with half a dozen guests.*

squid (**squids, squid**) *n* A **squid** is a sea creature with a long soft body and many tentacles. آکٹوپس

squint (**squints, squinting, squinted**) *vi* If you **squint** at something, you look at it with your eyes partly closed. نیم وا آنکھوں سے دیکھنا

squirrel (**squirrels**) *n* A **squirrel** is a small furry wild animal with a long bushy tail. گلہری

Sri Lanka *n* **Sri Lanka** is a republic in South Asia, occupying the island of Ceylon. سری لنکا

stab (**stabs, stabbing, stabbed**) *vt* If someone **stabs** another person, they push a knife into their body. چاقو مارنا، پیوست کرنا، گھونپنا

stability *n* **Stability** is the quality of being stable. استقلال، استحکام

stable (**stabler, stablest, stables**) *adj* If something is **stable**, it is not likely to change or come to an end suddenly. مستقل ▷ *n* A **stable** or **stables** is a building in which horses are kept. اصطبل

stack (**stacks**) *n* A **stack** of things is a neat pile of them. ڈھیر

stadium (**stadiums, stadia**) *n* A **stadium** is a large sports ground with rows of seats all round it. اسٹیڈیم (کرسیوں کی قطاروں کے ساتھ کھیل کا میدان)

staff (**staffs**) *npl* The **staff** of an organization are the people who work for it. عملہ ▷ *n* A **staff** is a stout rod or stick. ڈنڈا

staffroom (**staffrooms**) *n* The **staffroom** is a room that an organization provides for the use of the people who work for it. عملہ کا کمرہ

stage (**stages**) *n* A **stage** of an activity, process, or period is one part of it. اسٹیج

stagger (**staggers, staggering, staggered**) *vi* If you **stagger**, you walk very unsteadily, for example because you are ill or drunk. لڑکھڑانا

stag night (**stag nights**) *n* A **stag night** is a party for a man who is getting married very soon, to which only men are invited. (جلد شادی کرنے والے کے لئے دی گئی پارٹی)

stain (**stains, staining, stained**) *n* A **stain**

is a mark on something that is difficult to remove. داغ ▷ *vt* If a liquid **stains** something, the thing becomes coloured or marked by the liquid. داغ لگنا

stained glass *n* **Stained glass** consists of pieces of glass of different colours used to make decorative windows or other objects. مختلف رنگوں کے کانچ کے ٹکڑے

stainless steel *n* **Stainless steel** is a metal which does not rust, made from steel and chromium. اسٹیل جس میں زنگ نہیں لگتا

stain remover (**stain removers**) *n* **Stain remover** is a substance that you use for removing an unwanted stain from a surface. داغ ہٹانے والا

staircase (**staircases**) *n* A **staircase** is a set of stairs inside a house. سیڑھیوں کے سیٹ

stairs *npl* **Stairs** are a set of steps inside a building which go from one floor to another. سیڑھیاں

stale (**staler, stalest**) *adj* **Stale** food or air is no longer fresh. باسی

stalemate (**stalemates**) *n* **Stalemate** is a situation in which neither side in an argument or contest can make progress. جمود

stall (**stalls**) *n* A **stall** is a large table on which you put goods that you want to sell, or information that you want to give people. اسٹال (بڑی میز۔ کتاب یا فوڈ اسٹال)

stamina *n* **Stamina** is the physical or mental energy needed to do a tiring activity for a long time. دم خم

stammer (**stammers, stammering, stammered**) *v* If you **stammer**, you speak with difficulty, hesitating and repeating words or sounds. ہکلانا

stamp (**stamps, stamping, stamped**) *n* A **stamp** or a **postage stamp** is a small piece of paper which you stick on an envelope or parcel, to show that you have paid the cost of posting it. مہر ▷ *vt* If you **stamp** a mark or word on an object, you press the mark or word onto the object, using a stamp. مہر لگانا

stand (**stands, standing, stood**) *vi* When you **are standing**, you are on your feet. کھڑے ہونا ▷ *n* A **stand** at a sports ground is where people sit or stand to watch. چبوترہ

standard (**standards**) *adj* **Standard** means usual and normal. معیاری ▷ *n* A **standard** is a level of quality or achievement, especially a level that is thought to be acceptable. معیار

standard of living (**standards of living**) *n* Your **standard of living** is the level of comfort and wealth which you have. جینے کا معیار

stand for *v* If letters **stand for** particular words, they are an abbreviation for those words. ۔۔۔ کا مفہوم ہونا *CCTV stands for Closed Circuit Television.*

standing order (**standing orders**) *n* A **standing order** is an instruction to your bank to pay a fixed amount of money to someone at regular times. جاری ہدایت

stand out *v* If something **stands out**, it can be clearly noticed or is clearly better or more important than other similar things. موجودگی نظر میں آنا *The dark shape of the castle stands out clearly on the skyline.*

standpoint (**standpoints**) *n* If you look at an event, situation, or idea from a particular **standpoint**, you look at it in a particular way. نکتۂ نگاہ

stand up *v* When you are **standing up**, your body is upright, your legs are straight, and your weight is supported by your feet. کھڑے ہونا *Shop assistants have to stand up all day.*

staple (**staples, stapling, stapled**) *n* **Staples** are small pieces of bent wire that are used mainly for holding sheets of paper together firmly. You put the staples into the paper using a device called a stapler. پن ▷ *n* A **staple** is a food, product, or activity that is basic and important in people's everyday lives. بنیادی، اہم ▷ *vt* If you **staple** something, you fasten it to something else or fix it in place using staples. تھی کرنا

stapler (**staplers**) *n* A **stapler** is a device used for putting staples into sheets of paper. تھی کرنے والا آلہ

star (**stars, starring, starred**) *n* A **star** is a large ball of burning gas in space. Stars look like small points of light in the sky. ستارہ، تارے ▷ *n* A **star** is somebody who is famous for doing something, for example acting or singing. اسٹار، مقبول شخص ▷ *v* If an actor or actress **stars** in a play or film, he or she has one of the most important parts in it. You can also say that a play or film stars a famous actor or actress. فلموں میں اہم رول ادا کرنا ▷ *n* A **star** is a shape that has four, five, or more points sticking out of it in a pattern. ستارہ

starch (**starches**) *n* **Starch** is a carbohydrate found in foods such as bread, potatoes, and rice. کلف (کاربوہائڈریٹ)

stare (**stares, staring, stared**) *vi* If you **stare** at someone or something, you look at them for a long time. گھورنا

stark (**starker, starkest**) *adj* **Stark** choices or statements are harsh and unpleasant. سخت

start (**starts, starting, started**) *n* If you make a **start** on doing something, you begin to do it. شروعات ▷ *vt* If you **start** to do something, you begin to do it. شروع کرنا ▷ *v* When something **starts**, it begins. آغاز ہونا، شروع ہونا

starter (**starters**) *n* A **starter** is a small quantity of food served as the first course of a meal. کھانے میں پہلے پیش کی جانے والی چیز

startle (**startles, startling, startled**) *vt* If something sudden and unexpected **startles** you, it surprises you and frightens you slightly. بیقرار کرنا

start off *v* If you **start off** by doing something, you do it as the first part of an activity. شروعات کرنا *I started off by setting out the facts.*

starve (**starves, starving, starved**) *vi* If people **starve**, they suffer greatly and may die from lack of food. بھوکوں مرنا

state (**states, stating, stated**) *n* You can refer to countries as **states**, particularly when you are discussing politics. ریاست ▷ *vt* If you **state** something, you say or write it in a formal or definite way. بیان کرنا

stately home (**stately homes**) *n* A **stately home** is a very large old house, especially one that people can pay to visit. شاہی محل

statement (**statements**) *n* A **statement** is something that you say or write which gives information in a formal or definite way. بیان

station (**stations**) *n* A **station** is a building by a railway line where a train stops. اسٹیشن

stationer (**stationers**) *n* A **stationer** or a **stationer's** is a shop that sells paper, envelopes, and other materials or equipment used for writing. لکھنے سے متعلق سامان کی دوکان

stationery *n* **Stationery** is paper, envelopes, and writing equipment. لکھنے سے متعلق سازوسامان

S

statistics *npl* **Statistics** are facts obtained from analyzing information that is expressed in numbers. حسابیات

statue (**statues**) *n* A **statue** is a large sculpture of a person or an animal, made of stone, bronze, or some other hard material. بت، مجسمہ

status quo *n* The **status quo** is the situation that exists at a particular time. موجودہ حالت کا قائم رہنا

stay (**stays, staying, stayed**) *n* The time you spend in a place is your **stay** there. قیام ▷ *vi* If you **stay** in a place, you do not move away from it. ٹھہرنا، برقرار رہنا ▷ *vi* If you **stay** somewhere, you live there for a short time. قیام کرنا، ٹھہرنا

stay in *v* If you **stay in**, you remain at home during the evening and do not go out. گھر کے اندر ٹھہرنا *We decided to stay in and have dinner at home.*

stay up *v* If you **stay up**, you remain out of bed at a later time than normal. دیر تک جاگنا *I used to stay up late with my mum and watch movies.*

steady (**steadier, steadiest**) *adj* Something that is **steady** continues or develops gradually without any interruptions and is unlikely to change suddenly. مضبوط

steak (**steaks**) *n* **Steak** is beef without much fat on it. بغیر چربی والا بڑے کا گوشت

steal (**steals, stealing, stole, stolen**) *v* If you **steal** something from someone, you take it away from them without their permission and without intending to return it. چرانا

steam *n* **Steam** is the hot mist that forms when water boils. **Steam** vehicles and machines are powered by steam. بھاپ

steel *n* **Steel** is a very strong metal made mainly from iron. فولاد

steep (**steeper, steepest**) *adj* A **steep** slope rises at a very sharp angle and is difficult to go up. ڈھلوان

steeple (**steeples**) *n* A **steeple** is a tall pointed structure on top of the tower of a church. چرچ کی مینار کی چوٹی پر نوکدار ڈھانچہ

steering *n* The **steering** in a car or other vehicle is the mechanical parts of it which make it possible to steer. اسٹیرنگ

steering wheel (**steering wheels**) *n* The **steering wheel** in a vehicle is the wheel which the driver holds to steer the vehicle. اسٹیرنگ

step (**steps**) *n* If you take a **step**, you lift your foot and put it down in a different place. قدم ▷ *n* A **step** is a flat surface that you put your feet on to walk up or down to somewhere. سیڑھی

stepbrother (**stepbrothers**) *n* Someone's **stepbrother** is the son of their stepfather or stepmother. سوتیلا بھائی

stepdaughter (**stepdaughters**) *n* Someone's **stepdaughter** is a daughter that was born to their husband or wife during a previous relationship. سوتیلی بیٹی

stepfather (**stepfathers**) *n* Your **stepfather** is the man who has married your mother after the death of your father or divorce of your parents. سوتیلا باپ

stepladder (**stepladders**) *n* A **stepladder** is a portable ladder that is made of two sloping parts that are hinged together at the top so that it will stand up on its own. پہیے دار سیڑھی

stepmother (**stepmothers**) *n* Your **stepmother** is the woman who has married your father after the death of your mother or the divorce of your parents. سوتیلی ماں

stepsister (**stepsisters**) *n* Someone's **stepsister** is the daughter of their stepfather or stepmother. سوتیلی بہن

stepson (**stepsons**) *n* Someone's **stepson** is a son born to their husband or wife during a previous relationship. سوتیلا بیٹا

stereo (**stereos**) *n* A **stereo** is a record player with two speakers. دو اسپیکر کے ساتھ ریکورڈ پلیئر

stereotype (**stereotypes**) *n* A **stereotype** is a fixed general image or set of characteristics representing a particular type of person or thing, but which may not be true in reality. جھوٹی شبیہ

sterile *adj* Something that is **sterile** is completely clean and free of germs. جراثیم سے پاک

sterilize (**sterilizes, sterilizing, sterilized**) *vt* If you **sterilize** a thing or place, you make it completely clean and free from germs. جراثیم سے پاک کرنا

sterling *n* **Sterling** is the money system of Great Britain. اسٹرلنگ (برطانوی کرنسی)

steroid (**steroids**) *n* A **steroid** is a type of chemical substance which occurs naturally in the body, and can also be made artificially. کیمیاوی مادہ (بدن میں پیدا ہویا مصنوعی طور پر بنایا جائے)

stew (**stews**) *n* A **stew** is a meal made by cooking meat and vegetables in liquid at a low temperature. شوربہ

steward (**stewards**) *n* A **steward** is a man whose job is to look after passengers on a ship, plane, or train. جہاز، ہوائی جہاز، ٹرین کے مسافروں کا خیال رکھنے والا

stick (**sticks, sticking, stuck**) *n* A **stick** is a long, thin piece of wood. تیلیاں، ٹہنی ▷ *vt* If you **stick** one thing to another, you join them together using glue. چپکنا، چپکانا

sticker (**stickers**) *n* A **sticker** is a small piece of paper or plastic with writing or a picture on it, that you can stick onto a surface. پٹی پر تحریر جس کے پیچھے گوند لگا ہو

stick insect (**stick insects**) *n* A **stick insect** is an insect with a long thin body and legs. چپکو کیڑا

stick out *v* If something **sticks out**, or if you **stick it out**, it extends beyond something else. باہر کی طرف نکلنا *A newspaper was sticking out of his back pocket.*

sticky (**stickier, stickiest**) *adj* A **sticky** substance can stick to other things. **Sticky** things are covered with a sticky substance. چپکنے والا

stiff (**stiffer, stiffest**) *adj* Something that is **stiff** is firm and does not bend easily. سخت، بے لچک

stifling *adj* **Stifling** heat is so hot that it makes you feel uncomfortable. شدید

still (**stiller, stillest**) *adj* If you are **still**, you are not moving. بلا حرکت، جامد ▷ *adv* If a situation **still** exists, it has continued and exists now. اب بھی

sting (**stings, stinging, stung**) *n* The **sting** of an insect is the part that stings you. ڈنک ▷ *v* If an insect or plant **stings** you, it pricks your skin, usually with poison, so that you feel a sharp pain. ڈنک مارنا

stingy (**stingier, stingiest**) *adj* If you describe someone as **stingy**, you are criticizing them for being unwilling to spend money. (*informal*) کنجوس

stink (**stinks, stinking, stank, stunk**) *n* A **stink** is a strong foul smell or stench. سڑاندھ ▷ *vt* To **stink** means to smell extremely unpleasant. سڑنا

stir (**stirs, stirring, stirred**) *vt* When you **stir** a liquid, you mix it inside a container using something such as a spoon. تحریک پیدا کرنا، ہلانا

stitch (**stitches, stitching, stitched**) *n* **Stitches** are the pieces of thread that have been sewn in a piece of cloth. ٹانکا ▷ *vt* If you **stitch** cloth, you use a needle and thread to join two pieces together or to make a decoration. ٹانکے لگانا، سلائی کرنا،چپکانا

stock (**stocks, stocking, stocked**) *n* **Stocks** are shares in the ownership of a company. A company's **stock** consists of all the shares that people have bought in it. کمپنی کے حصص ▷ *vt* A shop that **stocks** particular goods keeps a supply of them to sell. مال کی دوکان

stockbroker (**stockbrokers**) *n* A **stockbroker** is someone whose profession is buying and selling stocks and shares for clients. دلال

stock cube (**stock cubes**) *n* A **stock cube** is a solid cube made from dried meat or vegetable juices and other flavourings. Stock cubes are used to add flavour to dishes such as stews and soups. خشک گوشت یا سبزیوں سے بنائے گئے مکعب

stock exchange (**stock exchanges**) *n* A **stock exchange** is a place where people buy and sell stocks and shares. اسٹوک ایکسچینج (حصص بازار)

stock market (**stock markets**) *n* **The stock market** consists of the activity of buying stocks and shares, and the people and institutions that organize it. بازار حصص

stock up *v* If you **stock up** with something or **stock up** on it, you buy a lot of it, in case you cannot get it later. جمع خوری کرنا *People are stocking up on fuel.*

stomach (**stomachs**) *n* Your **stomach** is the organ inside your body where food is digested. پیٹ

stomachache (**stomachaches**) *n* If you have a **stomachache**, you have a pain in your stomach. پیٹ درد

stone (**stones**) *n* **Stone** is a hard solid material that is found in the ground. It is often used for building. پتھر ▷ *n* A **stone** is a small piece of rock that is found on the ground. کنکر

stool (**stools**) *n* A **stool** is a seat with legs but no support for your back or arms. اسٹول (بغیر ہتھے اور پیٹھ کی کرسی)

stop (**stops, stopping, stopped**) *n* If something that is moving comes to a **stop**, it slows down and no longer moves. رکاوٹ ▷ *v* If you **stop** doing something, you do not do it any more. روکنا

stopover (**stopovers**) *n* A **stopover** is a short stay in a place in between parts of a journey. پڑاؤ

stopwatch (**stopwatches**) *n* A **stopwatch** is a watch with buttons which you press at the beginning and end of an event, so that you can measure exactly how long it takes. وقت کے مقررہ وقفے کی پیمائش والی گھڑی

storage *n* **Storage** is the process of keeping something in a particular place until it is needed. ذخیرہ

store (**stores, storing, stored**) *n* A **store** is a shop. **Store** is used mainly to refer to a large shop selling a variety of goods, but in American English, a **store** can be any shop. دوکان (زیادہ مال رکھنے والی) ▷ *vt* When you **store** things, you put them in a container or other place and leave them there until they are needed. ذخیرہ کرنا

storm (**storms**) *n* A **storm** is very bad weather, with heavy rain, strong winds, and often thunder and lightning. طوفان

stormy (**stormier, stormiest**) *adj* If there is **stormy** weather, there is a strong wind and heavy rain. طوفانی

story (**stories**) *n* A **story** is a description of imaginary people and events, which is written or told in order to entertain. داستان

stove (**stoves**) *n* A **stove** is a piece of equipment for heating a room or cooking. اسٹوو

straight (**straighter, straightest**) *adj* A **straight** line or edge continues in the same direction and does not bend or curve. سیدھی، راست

straighteners *npl* **Straighteners** are a heated device that you use to make your hair straight. سیدھا کرنے والا آلہ (بال وغیرہ)

straightforward *adj* If something is **straightforward**, it is not complicated to do or understand. سادہ، سلجھی ہوئی

straight on *adv* You use **straight on** to indicate that the way from one place to another is forward. براہ راست

strain (**strains, straining, strained**) *n* If **strain** is put on a person or organization, they have to do more than they are really able to do. دباؤ، تناؤ ▷ *vt* To **strain** something means to make it do more than it is really able to do. دباؤ ڈالنا، تناؤ ڈالنا

strained *adj* If someone's appearance, voice, or behaviour is **strained**, they seem worried and nervous. تناؤزدہ، دباؤزدہ

stranded *adj* If you are **stranded**, you are prevented from leaving a place, for example because of bad weather. پھنسے ہوئے

strange (**stranger, strangest**) *adj* **Strange** means unusual or unexpected. عجیب

stranger (**strangers**) *n* A **stranger** is someone you have not met before or do not know at all. If two people are **strangers**, they have never met or do not know each other at all. اجنبی

strangle (**strangles, strangling, strangled**) *vt* To **strangle** someone means to kill them by tightly squeezing their throat. گلا گھونٹنا

strap (**straps**) *n* A **strap** is a narrow piece of leather, cloth, or other material. Straps are used to carry things or hold them in place. پٹہ

strategic *adj* **Strategic** means relating to the most important, general aspects of something such as a military operation or political policy. مبنی بر حکمت عملی

strategy (**strategies**) *n* A **strategy** is a

general plan or set of plans intended to achieve something, especially over a long period. حکمت عملی

straw (**straws**) *n* **Straw** is the dry, yellow stems of crops. تنکا ▷ *n* A **straw** is a thin tube that you use to suck a drink into your mouth. اسٹرا، نلکی

strawberry (**strawberries**) *n* A **strawberry** is a small red fruit with tiny seeds in its skin. اسٹرابیری

stray (**strays**) *n* A **stray** is a domestic animal, fowl, etc, that has wandered away from its place of keeping and is lost. آوارہ

stream (**streams**) *n* A **stream** is a small narrow river. دھارا، چھوٹا دریا

street (**streets**) *n* A **street** is a road in a town or village, usually with houses along it. گلی، گلیارا

streetlamp (**streetlamps**) *n* A **streetlamp** is a tall post with a light at the top, which stands by the side of the road to light it up, usually in a town. سڑک کنارے کی روشنی

street map (**street maps**) *n* A **street map** is a map of a town or city, showing the positions and names of all the streets. شہر کا نقشہ (سب سڑکیں گلیاں دکھائی ہوں)

streetwise *adj* Someone who is **streetwise** knows how to deal with difficult or dangerous situations in big cities.(*informal*) جاندیدہ

strength *n* Your **strength** is the physical energy that you have, which gives you the ability to do things such as lift heavy objects. طاقت

strengthen (**strengthens, strengthening, strengthened**) *vt* To **strengthen** something means to make it stronger. طاقتور بنانا

stress (**stresses, stressing, stressed**) *n* If you lay **stress** on a point, you emphasize it because you think it is important. زور ▷ *vt* If you **stress** a point in a discussion, you put extra emphasis on it because you think it is important. زور دینا نلکی

stressed *adj* If you feel **stressed**, you feel tension and anxiety because of difficulties in your life. تناؤزدہ

stressful *adj* A **stressful** situation or experience causes someone to feel stress. تناؤ بھرا

stretch (**stretches, stretching, stretched**) *vi* Something that **stretches** over an area covers all of it. پھیلنا ▷ *vi* When you **stretch**, you hold out part of your body as far as you can. پھیلانا

stretcher (**stretchers**) *n* A **stretcher** is a long piece of canvas with a pole along each side, which is used to carry an injured person. اسٹریچر

stretchy (**stretchier, stretchiest**) *adj* **Stretchy** material is slightly elastic and stretches easily. پھیلنے کی سکت والا

strict (**stricter, strictest**) *adj* A **strict** rule or order is very precise or severe and must be obeyed absolutely. سخت

strictly *adv* If something is done **strictly** it is done severely and must be obeyed absolutely. شدید طور پر

strike (**strikes, striking, struck, stricken**) *n* When there is a **strike**, workers stop doing their work for a period of time, usually in order to try to get better pay or conditions for themselves. ہڑتال ▷ *vt* If you **strike** someone or something, you deliberately hit them. ضرب لگانا، مارنا ▷ *vt* When workers **strike**, they stop working for a period of time, usually to try to get better pay or conditions. کام بند کر دینا ▷ *v* To **strike** someone or something means to attack them or to affect them, quickly and violently. حملہ ور ہونا

striker (**strikers**) *n* A **striker** is a person who is on strike. ہڑتالی

striking *adj* Something that is **striking** is very noticeable or unusual. آنکھوں میں چبھنے والا یا غیر معمولی

string (**strings**) *n* **String** is thin rope that is made of twisted threads. رسی ▷ *n* The **strings** on an instrument are the thin

S

pieces of wire that are stretched across it and that make sounds when the instrument is played. تار

strip (**strips, stripping, stripped**) *n* A **strip** of something is a long narrow piece of it. ٹکڑا، پٹی ▷ *v* If you **strip**, or if someone **strips** you, your clothes are removed from your body. کپڑے اتار دینا

stripe (**stripes**) *n* A **stripe** is a long line which is a different colour from the areas next to it. دھاری، پٹی

striped *adj* Something that is **striped** has stripes on it. دھاریدار، پٹیدار

stripy *adj* Something that is **stripy** has stripes on it. (*informal* دھاریدار، پٹیدار

stroke (**strokes, stroking, stroked**) *n* If someone has a **stroke**, a blood vessel in their brain bursts or gets blocked, which may kill them or cause one side of their body to be paralysed. نس پھٹنا یا خون رک جانا ▷ *vt* If you **stroke** someone or something, you move your hand slowly and gently over them. ہاتھ اوپر پھیرنا دینا

stroll (**strolls**) *n* A **stroll** is a leisurely walk. چہل قدمی

strong (**stronger, strongest**) *adj* Someone who is **strong** is healthy with good muscles. طاقتور ▷ *adj* **Strong** things are not easy to break. مضبوط

strongly *adv* If something is built **strongly**, it means it is not easily broken. مضبوطی سے

structure (**structures**) *n* The **structure** of something is the way in which it is made, built, or organized. ڈھانچہ

struggle (**struggles, struggling, struggled**) *n* A **struggle** is an attempt to obtain something or to defeat someone who is denying you something. جدوجہد ▷ *v* If you **struggle** or **struggle** to do something difficult, you try hard to do it. جدوجہد کرنا

stub (**stubs**) *n* The **stub** of a cigarette or a pencil is the short piece which remains when the rest has been used. بٹ، ٹوٹا

stubborn *adj* A **stubborn** person is determined to do what they want and refuses to change their mind. ضدی

stub out *v* When someone **stubs out** a cigarette, they put it out by pressing it against something hard. مسل دینا *A sign told visitors to stub out their cigarettes.*

stuck *adj* If something is **stuck** in a place, it cannot move. پھنسا ہوا ▷ *adj* If you get **stuck**, you can't go on doing something because it is too difficult. رکا ہوا

stuck-up *adj* If you say that someone is **stuck-up**, you mean that are very proud and unfriendly because they think they are very important. (*informal*) لاتعلق

stud (**studs**) *n* **Studs** are small pieces of metal which are attached to a surface for decoration. دھات پارے

student (**students**) *n* A **student** is a person who is studying at a university, college, or school. طالب علم

student discount (**student discounts**) *n* A **student discount** is a reduction in the usual price of something that students are allowed to pay. طلباء کے لئے قیمت میں کمی

studio (**studios**) *n* A **studio** is a room where a designer, painter, or photographer works. اسٹوڈیو (فیلم یا فنکار کا)

studio flat (**studio flats**) *n* A **studio flat** is a small flat with one room for living and sleeping in, a kitchen, and a bathroom. You can also talk about a **studio**. چھوٹے فلیٹ میں اسٹوڈیو

study (**studies, studying, studied**) *v* If you **study**, you spend time learning about a particular subject or subjects. مطالعہ کرنا

stuff *n* You can use **stuff** to refer to things in a general way, without mentioning the things themselves by name. (*informal*) کوئی بھی چیز

stuffy (**stuffier, stuffiest**) *adj* If you describe a person or institution as **stuffy**, you are criticizing them for being formal and old-fashioned. مصنوعی، بناوٹی

stumble (**stumbles, stumbling, stumbled**) *vi* If you **stumble**, you nearly fall while walking or running. لڑکھڑانا

stunned *adj* **Stunned** means shocked or astonished. حیرت زدہ

stunning *adj* A **stunning** person or thing is extremely beautiful or impressive. حیرت میں ڈالنے والا

stunt (**stunts**) *n* A **stunt** is something interesting that someone does to get attention or publicity. کرتب بازی

stuntman (**stuntmen**) *n* A **stuntman** is a man whose job is to do dangerous things, either for publicity, or in a film instead of an actor so that the actor does not risk being injured. کرتب باز

stupid (**stupider, stupidest**) *adj* If you say that someone or something is **stupid**, you mean that they show a lack of good judgement or intelligence and they are not at all sensible. بیوقوف

stutter (**stutters, stuttering, stuttered**) *vi* If someone **stutters**, they have difficulty speaking because they find it hard to say the first sound of a word. صاف نہ بول پانا

style (**styles**) *n* The **style** of something is the general way it is done or presented. اسٹائل

stylist (**stylists**) *n* A **stylist** is a person whose job is to cut and arrange people's hair. اسٹائل والا

subject (**subjects**) *n* The **subject** of a conversation, letter, or book is the person or thing that is being discussed or written about. موضوع

submarine (**submarines**) *n* A **submarine** is a ship that can travel below the surface of the sea. آبدوز

subscription (**subscriptions**) *n* A **subscription** is an amount of money that you pay regularly to receive a service or magazine, or to belong to or support an organization. چندہ، عطیہ

subsidiary (**subsidiaries**) *n* A **subsidiary** is a company which is part of a larger and more important company. ذیلی

subsidize (**subsidizes, subsidizing, subsidized**) *vt* If an authority **subsidizes** something, they pay part of the cost of it. امداد دینا

subsidy (**subsidies**) *n* A **subsidy** is money paid by an authority in order to help an industry or business, or to pay for a public service. امداد

substance (**substances**) *n* A **substance** is a solid, powder, liquid, or gas. مادہ

substitute (**substitutes, substituting, substituted**) *n* A **substitute** is something or someone that you use instead of something or someone else. بدل ▷ *v* If you **substitute** one thing for another, you use it instead of the other thing. بدل کرنا

subtitled *adj* If a foreign film is **subtitled**, a printed translation of the words is shown at the bottom of the picture. ذیلی عنوانات والے

subtitles *npl* **Subtitles** are a printed translation of the words of a foreign film that are shown at the bottom of the picture. ذیلی عنوانات

subtle (**subtler, subtlest**) *adj* Something **subtle** is not immediately obvious or noticeable. باریک ترین، تیز ترین

subtract (**subtracts, subtracting, subtracted**) *vt* If you **subtract** one number from another, you take the first number away from the second. نفی کرنا

suburb (**suburbs**) *n* The **suburbs** of a city are the areas on the edge of it where people live. قصبہ

suburban *adj* **Suburban** means relating to a suburb. قصباتی

subway (**subways**) *n* A **subway** is a passage for pedestrians underneath a busy road. زیر زمین فٹپاتھ

succeed (**succeeds, succeeding, succeeded**) *vi* To **succeed** means to achieve the result that you wanted or to

S

perform in a satisfactory way. کامیاب ہونا

success *n* **Success** is the achievement of something you have wanted to achieve. کامیابی

successful *adj* Someone or something that is **successful** achieves a desired result or performs in a satisfactory way. کامیاب

successfully *adv* If something happens or is carried out successfully, it achieves a desired result or performs in a satisfactory way. کامیابی سے

successive *adj* **Successive** means happening or existing one after another without a break. متواتر

successor (**successor**) *n* Someone's **successor** is the person who takes their job after they have left. وارث

such *det* You use **such** to refer back to the thing or person that you have just mentioned, or a thing or person like the one that you have just mentioned. ایسا *We regard such methods as entirely unacceptable.* ▷ *det* You use **such** in front of an adjective followed by a noun to make the adjective stronger. بہت، کافی *They're such good friends.* ▷ *det* **Such** means like this or like that. جیسا، کے جیسا *How could you do such a thing?* ▷ *det* You use **such a** or **such an** in front of an adjective followed by a noun to make the adjective stronger. اتنا، بہت زیادہ *It's such an ugly building.*

suck (**sucks, sucking, sucked**) *v* If you **suck** something, you hold it in your mouth and pull at it with the muscles in your cheeks and tongue, for example in order to get liquid out of it. چوسنا

Sudan *n* **Sudan** is a republic in north-east Africa, on the Red Sea. سوڈان

Sudanese (**Sudanese**) *adj* **Sudanese** means belonging or relating to Sudan, or to its people or culture. سوڈانی ▷ *npl* The **Sudanese** are the people of Sudan. سوڈانی

sudden *adj* Something that is **sudden** happens quickly and unexpectedly. اچانک

suddenly *adv* If something happens **suddenly**, it happens quickly and unexpectedly. اچانک طور پر

sue (**sues, suing, sued**) *v* If you **sue** someone, you start a legal case against them to claim money from them because they have harmed you in some way. مقدمہ دائر کرنا

suede *n* **Suede** is thin soft leather with a slightly rough surface. نرم کھردرا چمڑا

suffer (**suffers, suffering, suffered**) *v* If you **suffer** pain or an illness, or if you **suffer from** a pain or illness, you are badly affected by it. بھگتنا، مبتلا ہونا

suffocate (**suffocates, suffocating, suffocated**) *vi* If someone **suffocates**, they die because there is no air for them to breathe. If someone suffocates, they die because there is no air for them to breathe. دم گھٹنا

sugar *n* **Sugar** is a sweet substance, often in the form of white or brown crystals, used to sweeten food and drink. شکر

sugar-free *adj* **Sugar-free** drinks do not contain any sugar. بغیر شکر

suggest (**suggests, suggesting, suggested**) *vt* If you **suggest** something, you put forward a plan or idea for someone to consider. مشورہ دینا

suggestion (**suggestions**) *n* If you make a **suggestion**, you put forward an idea or plan for someone to think about. مشورہ دینا

suicide (**suicides**) *n* People who commit **suicide** deliberately kill themselves. خودکشی کرنا

suicide bomber (**suicide bombers**) *n* A **suicide bomber** is a terrorist who carries out a bomb attack, knowing that he or she will be killed in the explosion. خودکش بمبار

suit (**suits, suiting, suited**) *n* A **suit** is a matching jacket and trousers, or a matching jacket and skirt. سوٹ (کوٹ پینٹ جیکٹ) ▷ *vt* If a piece of clothing or a particular style or colour **suits** you, it makes you look attractive. راس آنا، اچھا

suitable *adj* Someone or something that is **suitable** for a particular purpose or occasion is right or acceptable for it. موزوں

suitcase (**suitcases**) *n* A **suitcase** is a case for carrying clothes when you are travelling. سوٹکیس

suite (**suites**) *n* A **suite** is a set of rooms in a hotel or other building. سوئٹ (ہوٹل روم)

sulk (**sulks, sulking, sulked**) *vi* If you **sulk**, you are silent and bad-tempered for a while because you are annoyed about something. اچانک بھڑک جانا

sulky *adj* Someone who is **sulky** is sulking or is unwilling to enjoy themselves. نالاں

sultana (**sultanas**) *n* **Sultanas** are dried white grapes. کشمش

sum (**sums**) *n* A **sum** of money is an amount of money. رقم، مقدار ▷ *n* In maths, a **sum** is a problem you work out using numbers. جوڑ، مثبت

summarize (**summarizes, summarizing, summarized**) *v* If you **summarize** something, you give a brief description of its main points. تلخیص کرنا

summary (**summaries**) *n* A **summary** is a short account of something giving the main points but not the details. تلخیص

summer (**summers**) *n* **Summer** is the season between spring and autumn. In summer the weather is usually warm or hot. موسم گرما

summer holidays *npl* Your **summer holidays** are a period of time in the summer during which you relax and enjoy yourself away from home. گرمی کی چھٹیاں

summertime *n* **Summertime** is the period of time during which summer lasts. موسم گرما

summit (**summits**) *n* A **summit** is a meeting between the leaders of two or more countries to discuss important matters. دو ممالک کی بیٹھک

sum up *v* If you **sum up** or **sum** something **up**, you briefly describe the main features of something. مختصراً بیان کرنا *Well, to sum up, what is the message that you are trying to communicate?*

sun *n* The **sun** is the ball of fire in the sky that the Earth goes round, and that gives us heat and light. سورج

sunbathe (**sunbathes, sunbathing, sunbathed**) *vi* When people **sunbathe**, they sit or lie in a place where the sun shines on them, in order to get a suntan. دھوپ کھانا

sunbed (**sunbeds**) *n* A **sunbed** is a piece of equipment with ultraviolet lights. You lie on it to make your skin browner. آفتابی لیمپ کے نیچے لیٹنے کا بستر

sunblock (**sunblocks**) *n* **Sunblock** is a cream which you put on your skin to protect it completely from the sun. دھوپ سے جلد کو بچانے کے لئے کریم

sunburn (**sunburns**) *n* If someone has **sunburn**, their skin is red and sore because they have spent too much time in the sun. دھوپ سے جل جانا

sunburnt *adj* Someone who is **sunburnt** has sore bright pink skin because they have spent too much time in hot sunshine. دھوپ سے جلا ہوا

suncream (**suncreams**) *n* **Suncream** is a cream that protects your skin from the sun's rays, especially in hot weather. دھوپ کی کریم

Sunday (**Sundays**) *n* **Sunday** is the day after Saturday and before Monday. اِتوار

sunflower (**sunflowers**) *n* A **sunflower** is a tall plant with large yellow flowers. سورج مکھی

sunglasses *npl* **Sunglasses** are spectacles with dark lenses to protect your eyes from bright sunlight. دھوپ کا چشمہ

sunlight *n* **Sunlight** is the light that comes from the sun. دھوپ

sunny (**sunnier, sunniest**) *adj* When it is **sunny**, the sun is shining brightly. دھوپ دار

sunrise *n* **Sunrise** is the time in the

morning when the sun first appears. طلوع آفتاب

sunroof (**sunroofs**) *n* A **sunroof** is a panel in the roof of a car that opens to let sunshine and air enter the car. چھت سی دھوپ آنے کے لئیشگاف

sunscreen (**sunscreens**) *n* A **sunscreen** is a cream that protects your skin from the sun's rays in hot weather. دھوپ سے بچنے کے لئے کریم

sunset *n* **Sunset** is the time in the evening when the sun disappears. غروبِ آفتاب

sunshine *n* **Sunshine** is the light and heat that comes from the sun. سورج کی دھوپ اور گرمی

sunstroke *n* **Sunstroke** is an illness caused by spending too much time in hot sunshine. لولگنا

suntan (**suntans**) *n* If you have a **suntan**, the sun has turned your skin a brown colour. دھوپ سے جلد کا تانبئی ہوجانا

suntan lotion (**suntan lotions**) *n* **Suntan lotion** protects your skin from the sun. دھوپ سے جلد کو کالا ہونے سے بچانے کا لوشن

suntan oil (**suntan oils**) *n* **Suntan oil** protects your skin from the sun. جلد کو بچانے والا تیل

super *adj* **Super** means very nice or good. (*informal, old-fashioned*) بہترین

superb *adj* If something is **superb**, it is very good indeed. عظیم

superficial *adj* If you describe someone as **superficial**, you disapprove of them because they do not think deeply, and have little understanding of anything serious or important. سطحی

superior (**superiors**) *adj* You use **superior** to describe someone or something that is better than other similar people or things. برتر ▷ *n* Your **superior** in an organization that you work for is a person who has a higher rank than you. اعلیٰ

supermarket (**supermarkets**) *n* A **supermarket** is a large shop which sells all kinds of food and some household goods. سبھی سامان کی دوکان

supernatural *adj* **Supernatural** creatures, forces, and events are believed by some people to exist or happen, although they are impossible according to scientific laws. غیر قدرتی، ساحرانہ

superstitious *adj* People who are **superstitious** believe in things that are not real or possible, for example magic. وہمی

supervise (**supervises, supervising, supervised**) *vt* If you **supervise** an activity or a person, you make sure that the activity is done correctly or that the person is behaving correctly. اصلاح کرنا

supervisor (**supervisors**) *n* A **supervisor** is a person who supervises activities or people, especially workers or students. نگراں

supper (**suppers**) *n* Some people refer to the main meal eaten in the early part of the evening as **supper**. شام کا کھانا

supplement (**supplements**) *n* A **supplement** is something which is added to another thing in order to improve it. تکملہ

supplier (**suppliers**) *n* A **supplier** is a person or company that provides you with goods or equipment. سپلائی کرنیوالا

supplies *npl* You can use **supplies** to refer to food, equipment, and other essential things that people need, especially when these are provided in large quantities. فراہم کردہ اشیاء

supply (**supplies, supplying, supplied**) *n* A **supply** of something is an amount of it which is available for use. If something is in short **supply**, there is very little of it available. فراہمی ▷ *vt* If you **supply** someone with something, you provide them with it. فراہم کرنا

supply teacher (**supply teachers**) *n* A **supply teacher** is a teacher whose job is to take the place of other teachers at different schools when they are unable to be there. دوسروں کے مقام پر آکر پڑھانے والا

support (**supports, supporting, supported**) *n* If you give someone your **support**, you agree with them, and perhaps try to help them because you want them to succeed. حمایت ▷ *vt* If you **support** someone or their ideas or aims, you agree with them, and perhaps help them because you want them to succeed. حمایت کرنا

supporter (**supporters**) *n* **Supporters** are people who support someone or something, for example a political leader or a sports team. حامی

suppose (**supposes, supposing, supposed**) *vt* You use **suppose** or **supposing** when you are considering a possible situation or action and trying to think what effects it would have. فرض کرنا

supposedly *adv* **Supposedly** means that the following word or description is misleading and is not definitely known to be true. مفروضہ کے طور پر

supposing *conj* You say **supposing** to ask someone to pretend that something is true or to imagine that something will happen. فرض کر لینا *Supposing he sees us?*

surcharge (**surcharges**) *n* A **surcharge** is an extra payment of money in addition to the usual payment for something. It is added for a specific reason, for example by a company because costs have risen or by a government as a tax. فاضل ادائگی

sure (**surer, surest**) *adj* If you are **sure** that something is true, you are certain that it is true. If you are not **sure** about something, you do not know for certain what the true situation is. یقینی

surely *adv* You use **surely** to emphasize that you think something should be true, and you would be surprised if it was not true. یقیناً

surf (**surfs, surfing, surfed**) *n* **Surf** is the mass of white foam formed by waves as they fall on the shore. سمندری جھاگ ▷ *vt* If you **surf**, you ride on big waves on a special board. لہروں پر تیرنا

surface (**surfaces**) *n* The **surface** of something is the top part of it or the outside of it. سطح

surfboard (**surfboards**) *n* A **surfboard** is a long narrow board that is used for surfing. بورڈ جس پر کھڑے ہوکر سمندری لہروں پر تیرتے ہیں

surfer (**surfers**) *n* A **surfer** rides on big waves on a special board. لہروں پر تیرنے والا

surfing *n* **Surfing** is the sport of riding on the top of a wave while standing or lying on a special board. لہروں پر تیراکی

surge (**surges**) *n* A **surge** is a sudden large increase in something that has previously been steady, or has only increased or developed slowly. بڑھوتری

surgeon (**surgeons**) *n* A **surgeon** is a doctor who performs surgery. سرجن (جراح)

surgery (**surgeries**) *n* **Surgery** is medical treatment which involves cutting open a person's body in order to repair or remove a diseased or damaged part. جراحی ▷ *n* A **surgery** is the room or house where a doctor or dentist works. جراحی کا کمرہ

surname (**surnames**) *n* Your **surname** is the name that you share with other members of your family. خاندانی نام

surplus (**surpluses**) *adj* **Surplus** is used to describe something that is extra or that is more than is needed. فاضل، اضافی ▷ *n* If there is a **surplus** of something, there is more than is needed. ضرورت سے زیادہ ▷ *n* If there is a **surplus** of something, there is more than is needed. ضرورت سے زیادہ

surprise (**surprises**) *n* A **surprise** is an unexpected event, fact, or piece of news. حیرت

surprised *adj* If you are **surprised** at something, you have a feeling of surprise, because it is unexpected or unusual. حیرت زدہ

surprising *adj* Something that is

surprising is unexpected or unusual and makes you feel surprised. تحیر آمیز
surprisingly *adv* **Surprisingly** means unexpectedly or unusually. حیرت انگیز طور پر
surrender (**surrenders, surrendering, surrendered**) *vi* If you **surrender**, you stop fighting or resisting someone and agree that you have been beaten. حوالے کر دینا
surrogate mother (**surrogate mothers**) *n* A **surrogate mother** is a woman who has agreed to give birth to a baby on behalf of another woman. کوکھ کرایہ پر دینے والی
surround (**surrounds, surrounding, surrounded**) *vt* If something or someone **is surrounded** by something, that thing is situated all around them. گھیرنے والا
surroundings *npl* The place where someone or something is can be referred to as their **surroundings**. اطراف
survey (**surveys**) *n* If you carry out a **survey**, you try to find out detailed information about a lot of different people or things, usually by asking people a series of questions. مشاہدہ، سروے
surveyor (**surveyors**) *n* A **surveyor** is a person whose job is to survey land. مشاہد
survival *n* **Survival** is the fact of continuing to live or exist in spite of great danger or difficulty. باقی رہنے کی حالت
survive (**survives, surviving, survived**) *v* If someone **survives** in a dangerous situation, they do not die. باقی رہنا
survivor (**survivors**) *n* A **survivor** of a disaster, accident, or illness is someone who continues to live afterwards in spite of coming close to death. باقی رہنے والا
suspect (**suspects, suspecting, suspected**) *n* A **suspect** is a person who the police think may be guilty of a crime. مشکوک ▷ *vt* If you say that you **suspect** that something is true, you mean that you believe it is probably true, but you want to make it sound less strong or direct. شک کرنا
suspend (**suspends, suspending, suspended**) *vt* If you **suspend** something, you delay or stop it for a while. معطل کرنا
suspense *n* **Suspense** is a state of excitement or anxiety about something that is going to happen very soon. شش و پنج
suspension *n* The **suspension** of something is the act of delaying or stopping it for a while. التوا
suspension bridge (**suspension bridges**) *n* A **suspension bridge** is a type of bridge that is supported from above by cables. لوہے کی رسیوں سے سہارا دیا ہوا پل
suspicious *adj* If you are **suspicious** of someone or something, you do not trust them. مشکوک
swallow (**swallows, swallowing, swallowed**) *n* When you take a **swallow**, you cause something to go from your mouth down into your stomach. نگلنے کا عمل ▷ *vt* If you **swallow** something, you cause it to go from your mouth down into your stomach. نگلنا ▷ *vi* When you **swallow**, you cause something to go from your mouth down into your stomach. نگل جانا
swamp (**swamps**) *n* A **swamp** is an area of wet land with wild plants growing in it. بیہڑ، کچھار
swan (**swans**) *n* A **swan** is a large white bird with a long neck that lives on rivers and lakes. ہنس
swap (**swaps, swapping, swapped**) *v* If you **swap** something with someone, you give it to them and receive a different thing in exchange. بدلے میں کچھ دینا
swat (**swats, swatting, swatted**) *vt* If you **swat** an insect, you hit it with a quick, swinging movement. جھپٹنا
sway (**sways, swaying, swayed**) *vi* When people or things **sway**, they lean or swing slowly from one side to the other. جھولنا

Swaziland *n* **Swaziland** is a kingdom in southern Africa. سوازیلینڈ

swear (**swears, swearing, swore, sworn**) *vi* If someone **swears**, they use language that is considered to be rude or offensive. قسم اٹھانا، دھمکانا

swearword (**swearwords**) *n* A **swearword** is a word which is considered to be rude or offensive. Swearwords are usually used when people are angry. سخت الفاظ

sweat (**sweats, sweating, sweated**) *n* **Sweat** is the salty colourless liquid which comes through your skin when you are hot, ill, or afraid. پسینہ ▷ *vi* When you **sweat**, sweat comes through your skin. پسینہ آنا

sweater (**sweaters**) *n* A **sweater** is a warm knitted piece of clothing which covers the upper part of your body and your arms. سویٹر

sweatshirt (**sweatshirts**) *n* A **sweatshirt** is a loose warm piece of casual clothing, usually made of thick cotton, which covers the upper part of your body and your arms. گرم کپڑے کی قمیض

sweaty (**sweatier, sweatiest**) *adj* If your clothing or body is **sweaty**, it is soaked or covered with sweat. پسینے سے بھیگا ہوا

Swede (**Swedes**) *n* A **Swede** is a person who comes from Sweden. سویڈن کا

swede (**swedes**) *n* A **swede** is a round yellow root vegetable with a brown or purple skin. بینگن

Sweden *n* **Sweden** is a kingdom in north-west Europe, occupying the eastern part of the Scandinavian Peninsula, on the Gulf of Bothnia and the Baltic. سویڈن

Swedish *adj* **Swedish** means belonging or relating to Sweden, or to its people, language, or culture. سویڈش ▷ *n* **Swedish** is the language spoken in Sweden. سویڈش

sweep (**sweeps, sweeping, swept**) *vt* If you **sweep** an area of ground, you push dirt or rubbish off it with a broom. پونچھنا

sweet (**sweeter, sweetest, sweets**) *adj* **Sweet** food or drink contains a lot of sugar. میٹھا ▷ *adj* If you describe something as **sweet**, you mean that it gives you great pleasure and satisfaction. شیریں ▷ *n* A **sweet** is something sweet, such as fruit or a pudding, that you eat at the end of a meal. مٹھائی

sweetcorn *n* **Sweetcorn** consists of the yellow seeds of the maize plant, which are eaten as a vegetable. سویٹن

sweetener (**sweeteners**) *n* A **sweetener** is an artificial substance that can be used instead of sugar. میٹھا کرنے والا

sweets *npl* **Sweets** are small sweet things such as toffees, chocolates, and mints. مٹھائیاں

sweltering *adj* If the weather is **sweltering**, it is very hot. شدید گرم

swerve (**swerves, swerving, swerved**) *v* If a vehicle or other moving thing **swerves**, it suddenly changes direction, often in order to avoid hitting something. جھٹکے سے سمت بدل لینا

swim (**swims, swimming, swam, swum**) *vi* When you **swim**, you move through water by making movements with your arms and legs. تیرنا

swimmer (**swimmers**) *n* A **swimmer** is a person who swims, especially for sport or pleasure, or a person who is swimming. تیراک

swimming *n* **Swimming** is the activity of swimming, especially as a sport or for pleasure. تیراکی

swimming costume (**swimming costumes**) *n* A **swimming costume** is a piece of clothing that is worn for swimming, especially by women and girls. تیراکی لباس

swimming pool (**swimming pools**) *n* A **swimming pool** is a place that has been built for people to swim in. It consists of a large hole that has been tiled and filled with water. تیراکی تالاب

S

swimming trunks *npl* **Swimming trunks** are the shorts that a man wears when he goes swimming. (تیراکی لباس (مردوں کے لیے
swimsuit (**swimsuits**) *n* A **swimsuit** is a piece of clothing that is worn for swimming, especially by women and girls. تیراکی سوٹ
swing (**swings, swinging, swung**) *n* A **swing** is the act or manner of swinging or the distance covered while swinging. جھولا ▷ *v* If something **swings** or if you **swing** it, it moves repeatedly backwards and forwards or from side to side from a fixed point. جھولنا
Swiss *adj* **Swiss** means belonging or relating to Switzerland, or to its people or culture. سوس ▷ *npl* The **Swiss** are the people of Switzerland. سوس
switch (**switches, switching, switched**) *n* A **switch** is a small control for an electrical device which you use to turn the device on or off. سوچ، بٹن ▷ *vi* If you **switch** to something different, for example to a different system, task, or subject of conversation, you change to it from what you were doing or saying before. طرح بدلنا
switchboard (**switchboards**) *n* A **switchboard** is a place in a large office or business where all the telephone calls are connected. سوئچ بورڈ
switch off *v* If you **switch off** an electrical device, you stop it working by operating a switch. بٹن بند کرنا *The driver switched off the headlights.*
switch on *v* If you **switch on** an electrical device, you make it start working by operating a switch. بٹن چالو کرنا *We switched on the radio.*
Switzerland *n* **Switzerland** is a federal republic in west central Europe. سوئزرلینڈ
swollen *adj* If a part of your body is **swollen**, it is larger and rounder than normal, usually as a result of injury or illness. متورم
sword (**swords**) *n* A **sword** is a weapon with a handle and a long blade. تلوار
swordfish (**swordfish**) *n* A **swordfish** is a large sea fish with a very long upper jaw. تلوار کی نوک جیسے منہ والی مچھلی
swot (**swots, swotting, swotted**) *vi* If you **swot**, you study very hard, especially when you are preparing for an examination. سخت مطالعہ کرنا
syllable (**syllables**) *n* A **syllable** is a part of a word that contains a single vowel sound and that is pronounced as a unit. For example, 'book' has one syllable, and 'reading' has two syllables. لفظ جس میں واحد حرفِ صوت کی آواز ہو
syllabus (**syllabuses**) *n* You can refer to the subjects that are studied in a particular course as the **syllabus**. نصاب
symbol (**symbols**) *n* A **symbol** of something such as an idea is a shape or design that is used to represent it. علامت
symmetrical *adj* If something is **symmetrical**, it has two halves which are exactly the same, except that one half is the mirror image of the other. بالکل یکساں
sympathetic *adj* If you are **sympathetic** to someone who has had a misfortune, you are kind to them and show that you understand how they are feeling. ہمدرد
sympathize (**sympathizes, sympathizing, sympathized**) *vi* If you **sympathize** with someone who has had a misfortune, you show that you are sorry for them. ہمدردی کرنا
sympathy (**sympathies**) *n* If you have **sympathy** for someone who has had a misfortune, you are sorry for them, and show this in the way you behave towards them. ہمدردی
symphony (**symphonies**) *n* A **symphony** is a piece of music written to be played by an orchestra, usually in four parts. آرکیسٹرا کی موسیقی
symptom (**symptoms**) *n* A **symptom** of

an illness is something wrong with your body that is a sign of the illness. علامت

synagogue (**synagogues**) *n* A **synagogue** is a building where Jewish people worship. یہودیوں کی عبادت گاہ

Syria *n* **Syria** is a republic in West Asia, on the Mediterranean. ملک شام

Syrian (**Syrians**) *adj* **Syrian** means belonging or relating to Syria, or to its people or culture. شامی ▷ *n* A **Syrian** is a Syrian citizen, or a person of Syrian origin. شامی باشندہ

syringe (**syringes**) *n* A **syringe** is a small tube with a fine hollow needle, used for injecting drugs or for taking blood from someone's body. سیرنج

syrup (**syrups**) *n* **Syrup** is a sweet liquid made by cooking sugar with water or fruit juice. شربت

system (**systems**) *n* A **system** is a way of working, organizing, or doing something which follows a fixed plan or set of rules. نظام

systematic *adj* Something that is done in a **systematic** way is done according to a fixed plan, in a thorough and efficient way. منظم

systems analyst (**systems analysts**) *n* A **systems analyst** is someone whose job is to decide what computer equipment and software a company needs, and to provide it. نظام تجزیہ کار

t

table (**tables**) *n* A **table** is a piece of furniture with a flat top that you put things on or sit at. میز ▷ *n* A **table** is a set of facts or figures arranged in columns and rows. جدول

tablecloth (**tablecloths**) *n* A **tablecloth** is a large piece of material used to cover a table, especially during a meal. میز پوش

tablespoon (**tablespoons**) *n* A **tablespoon** is a fairly large spoon used for serving food and in cookery. بڑا چمچ

tablet (**tablets**) *n* A **tablet** is a small, solid, round mass of medicine which you swallow. ٹیبلیٹ

table tennis *n* **Table tennis** is a game played inside by two or four people. The players stand at each end of a table which has a low net across the middle and hit a small light ball over the net, using small bats. ٹیبل ٹینس

table wine (**table wines**) *n* **Table wine** is fairly cheap wine that is drunk with meals. سستی شراب (کھانے کے ساتھ پی جانے والی)

taboo (**taboos**) *adj* If a subject or activity is **taboo**, it is a social custom to avoid doing that activity or talking about that subject, because people find it embarrassing or offensive. حرام، ممنوعہ ▷ *n* If there is a **taboo** on a subject or activity, it is a social custom to avoid doing that activity or talking about that subject, because people find it embarrassing or offensive. ممانعت

tackle (**tackles, tackling, tackled**) *n* A **tackle** is when you try to take the ball away from someone in a game such as football. (گیری کرنا) لے چلنا ⊳ *vt* If you **tackle** a difficult task, you start dealing with it in a determined way. سنبھالنا

tact *n* (**Tact**) is the ability to avoid upsetting or offending people by being careful not to say or do things that would hurt their feelings. سلیقہ

tactful *adj* If you describe someone as **tactful**, you approve of them because they are careful not to say or do anything that would offend or upset other people. سلیقہ مند

tactics *npl* **Tactics** are the methods that you choose in order to achieve what you want. چالبازی

tactless *adj* If you describe someone as tactless, you think what they say or do is likely to offend other people. بے سلیقہ

tadpole (**tadpoles**) *n* **Tadpoles** are small water creatures which grow into frogs or toads. مینڈک کا بچہ

tag (**tags**) *n* A **tag** is a small piece of card or cloth which is attached to an object and has information about that object on it. اطلاع (قیمت، نام، پتہ) کی پرچی

Tahiti *n* **Tahiti** is an island in the South Pacific, in the Windward group of the Society Islands. تاہیتی

tail (**tails**) *n* The **tail** of an animal is the part extending beyond the end of its body. دم

tailor (**tailors**) *n* A **tailor** is a person who makes clothes, especially for men. درزی

Taiwan *n* **Taiwan** is an island in south-east Asia between the East China Sea and the South China Sea, off the south-east coast of the People's Republic of China. تائیوان

wanese (**Taiwanese**) *adj* **Taiwanese** eans of or relating to Taiwan or its inhabitants. تائیوانی ⊳ *n* A **Taiwanese** is a native or inhabitant of Taiwan. تائیوانی

Tajikistan *n* **Tajikistan** is a republic in central Asia. تاجکستان

take (**takes, taking, took, taken**) *vt* If you **take** a vehicle, you ride in it from one place to another. پکڑنا، سوار ہونا ⊳ *vt* If you **take** something, you move it or carry it. لینا ⊳ *vt* If you **take** something that does not belong to you, you steal it. لینا

take after *v* If you **take after** a member of your family, you look or behave like them. اس جیسا ہونا، انداز اختیار کرنا *He takes after his dad.*

take apart *v* If you **take** something **apart**, you separate it into its different parts. الگ کرنا *When the clock stopped, he took it apart.*

take away (**takeaways**) *v* If you **take** something **away** from someone, you remove it from them. لے جانا، لے لینا *If you don't like it, we'll take it away for free.* ⊳ *n* A **takeaway** is a shop or restaurant which sells hot food to be eaten elsewhere. A meal that you buy there is also called a **takeaway**. دکان یا ریستوراں (گرم کھانا کہیں اور لے جا کر کھانے کے لئے)

take back *v* If you **take** something **back**, you return it. لوٹانا، واپس لینا *I once took back a pair of shoes that fell apart after a week.*

take off (**takeoffs**) *v* When an aircraft **takes off**, it leaves the ground and starts flying. پرواز شروع کرنا *We took off at 11 o'clock.* ⊳ *n* **Takeoff** is the beginning of a flight, when an aircraft leaves the ground. پرواز کی شروعات

take over (**takeovers**) *v* To **take over** something such as a company or country means to gain control of it. اختیار میں لے لینا *The company has been taken over by a multinational corporation.* ⊳ *n* A **takeover** is the act of gaining control of a company by buying a majority of its shares. اختیار میں لینا

takings *npl* The **takings** of a business such as a shop or cinema consist of the amount of money it gets from selling its goods or tickets during a certain period. مال یا ٹکٹ بیچنے سے حاصل رقم

talcum powder *n* **Talcum powder** is fine powder with a pleasant smell which people put on their bodies after they have had a bath or a shower. ٹیلکم پاؤڈر

tale (**tales**) *n* A **tale** is a story, especially one involving adventure or magic. کہانی

talent (**talents**) *n* **Talent** is the natural ability to do something well. صلاحیت، ذہانت

talented *adj* Someone who is **talented** has a natural ability to do something well. ذہین، با صلاحیت

talk (**talks, talking, talked**) *n* **Talk** is the things you say to someone when you talk. بات ▷ *vi* When you **talk**, you use spoken language to express your thoughts, ideas, or feelings. بات کرنا

talkative *adj* Someone who is **talkative** talks a lot. باتونی

talk to *v* If you **talk to** someone, you have a conversation with them. بات چیت کرنا
I talked to him yesterday.

tall (**taller, tallest**) *adj* Someone or something that is **tall** is above average height. لمبا

tame (**tamer, tamest**) *adj* A **tame** animal or bird is not afraid of humans. پالتو، سدھایا ہوا

tampon (**tampons**) *n* A **tampon** is a firm piece of cotton wool that a woman puts inside her vagina when she is menstruating, in order to absorb the blood. جسم کی صفائی کا تولیہ

tan (**tans**) *n* If you have a **tan**, your skin has become darker than usual because you have been in the sun. دھوپ سے جلد کا سانولا ہوجانا

tandem (**tandems**) *n* A **tandem** is a bicycle designed for two riders. دوگدی والی سائیکل

tangerine (**tangerines**) *n* A **tangerine** is a small sweet orange. سنترہ، سنگترہ

tank (**tanks**) *n* A **tank** is a large container for holding liquid or gas. ٹنکی ▷ *n* A **tank** is a military vehicle covered with armour and equipped with guns or rockets. (ٹینک (توپ بردار

tanker (**tankers**) *n* A **tanker** is a ship or lorry used for transporting large quantities of gas or liquid, especially oil. تیل بردار ٹرک یا جہاز

tanned *adj* If someone is **tanned**, his or her skin is darker because of the time he or she has spent in the sun. سانولا

tantrum (**tantrums**) *n* If a child has a **tantrum**, it suddenly loses its temper in a noisy and uncontrolled way. جھلاہٹ، بدمزاجی کا غلبہ

Tanzania *n* (**Tanzania**) is a republic in East Africa, on the Indian Ocean. تنزانیہ

Tanzanian (**Tanzanians**) *adj* **Tanzanian** means of or relating to Tanzania or its inhabitants. تنزانیائی ▷ *n* A **Tanzanian** is a native or inhabitant of Tanzania. تنزانیائی

tap (**taps**) *n* A **tap** is a device that controls the flow of a liquid or gas from a pipe or container. نل

tap-dancing *n* **Tap-dancing** is a style of dancing in which the dancers wear special shoes with pieces of metal on the heels and toes. The shoes make loud sharp sounds as the dancers move their feet. دھات کے تلیدار جوتے پہن کر رقص کرنا

tape (**tapes, taping, taped**) *n* **Tape** is a narrow plastic strip covered with a magnetic substance. It is used to record sounds, pictures, and computer information. (ٹیپ (پلاسٹک کی پٹی پر چپندہ مادہ ▷ *vt* If you **tape** music, sounds, or television pictures, you record them using a tape recorder or a video recorder. ٹیپ کرنا(آواز ٹیپ کرنا)

tape measure (**tape measures**) *n* A **tape measure** is a strip of metal, plastic, or cloth with marks on it, used for measuring, especially for clothes and DIY. پیمائش کا فیتہ

t

tape recorder (**tape recorders**) *n* A **tape recorder** is a machine used for recording and playing music, speech, or other sounds. ٹیپ ریکارڈر
target (**targets**) *n* A **target** is something that someone is trying to hit with a weapon or other object. ہدف
tariff (**tariffs**) *n* A **tariff** is a tax on goods coming into a country. درآمد پر ٹیکس
tarmac *n* **Tarmac** is a material used for making road surfaces, consisting of crushed stones mixed with tar. **Tarmac** is a trademark. کولتار اور بجری
tarpaulin *n* **Tarpaulin** is a fabric made of canvas or similar material coated with tar, wax, paint, or some other waterproof substance. ترپال
tarragon *n* **Tarragon** is a European herb with narrow leaves which are used to add flavour to food. کندرو جیسا ایک پودا
tart (**tarts**) *n* A **tart** is a shallow pastry case with a filling of sweet food or fruit. ترش، کھٹا، تلخ
tartan *adj* **Tartan** cloth, which traditionally comes from Scotland, has different coloured stripes crossing each other. چارخانے دار رنگین اونی کپڑا
task (**tasks**) *n* A **task** is an activity or piece of work which you have to do. کام، مصروفیت
Tasmania *n* **Tasmania** is an island in the South Pacific, south of mainland Australia. تسمانیہ
taste (**tastes, tasting, tasted**) *n* Your sense of **taste** is your ability to recognize the flavour of things with your tongue. ذائقہ ▷ *vi* If food or drink **tastes** of something, it has that particular flavour. ذائقہ دینا، ذائقہ محسوس ہونا
tasteful *adj* If you describe something as **tasteful**, you mean that it is attractive and elegant. ذائقہ دار
tasteless *adj* If you describe something as **tasteless**, you mean that it is vulgar and unattractive. بے ذائقہ
tasty (**tastier, tastiest**) *adj* If you say that food, especially savoury food, is **tasty**, you mean that it has a pleasant and fairly strong flavour which makes it good to eat. لذیذ
tattoo (**tattoos**) *n* A **tattoo** is a design on someone's skin, made by pricking little holes and filling them with coloured dye. گودنا
Taurus *n* **Taurus** is one of the twelve signs of the zodiac. Its symbol is a bull. People who are born approximately between the 20th of April and the 20th of May come under this sign. برج ثور
tax (**taxes**) *n* **Tax** is an amount of money that you have to pay to the government so that it can pay for public services. ٹیکس محصول
taxi (**taxis**) *n* A **taxi** is a car driven by a person whose job is to take people where they want to go in return for money. ٹیکسی (کرایہ کی کار)
taxi driver (**taxi drivers**) *n* A **taxi driver** is a person whose job is to take people in a car to the place they want to go to in return for money. ٹیکسی ڈرائیور
taxpayer (**taxpayers**) *n* **Taxpayers** are people who pay a percentage of their income to the government as tax. ٹیکس ادا کرنے والا
tax return (**tax returns**) *n* A **tax return** is an official form that you fill in with details about your income and personal situation, so that the tax you owe can be calculated. ٹیکس ریٹرن
TB *n* **TB** is a very serious infectious disease that affects someone's lungs and other parts of their body. **TB** is an abbreviation for 'tuberculosis'. ٹی بی، تپ دق
tea (**teas**) *n* **Tea** is a drink. You make it by pouring hot water on to the dry leaves of a plant called the tea bush. چائے ▷ *n* **Tea** is a meal that you eat in the afternoon or the early evening. ہلکے ناشتے کے ساتھ چائے
tea bag (**tea bags**) *n* **Tea bags** are small

paper bags with tea leaves in them. You put them into hot water to make tea. ٹی بیگ

teach (**teaches, teaching, taught**) *vt* If you **teach** someone something, you give them instructions so that they know about it or know how to do it. پڑھانا

teacher (**teachers**) *n* A **teacher** is a person who teaches, usually as a job at a school or similar institution. استاد

teaching *n* **Teaching** is the work that a teacher does in helping students to learn. پڑھائی، پڑھانے کا عمل

teacup (**teacups**) *n* A **teacup** is a cup that you use for drinking tea. چائے کی پیالی

team (**teams**) *n* A **team** is a group of people who play together against another group in a sport or game. گروہ، دستہ، ٹیم

teapot (**teapots**) *n* A **teapot** is a container with a lid, a handle, and a spout, used for making and serving tea. چائے دانی

tear (**tears, tearing, tore, torn**) *n* **Tears** are the liquid that comes out of your eyes when you cry. آنسو ▷ *n* A **tear** in something is a hole that has been made in it. شگاف ▷ *vt* If you **tear** something, you pull it into pieces or make a hole in it. پھاڑنا

tear gas *n* **Tear gas** is a gas that causes your eyes to sting and fill with tears so that you cannot see. It is sometimes used by the police or army to control crowds. آنسو گیس

tear up *v* If you **tear up** a piece of paper, you tear it into a lot of small pieces. ٹکڑے ٹکڑے کرنا *Don't you dare tear up her ticket.*

tease (**teases, teasing, teased**) *vt* To **tease** someone means to laugh at them or make jokes about them in order to embarrass, annoy, or upset them. ستانا، ہنسی اڑانا

teaspoon (**teaspoons**) *n* A **teaspoon** is a small spoon that you use to put sugar into tea or coffee. چائے کا چمچ

teatime (**teatimes**) *n* **Teatime** is the period of the day when people have their tea. It can be eaten in the late afternoon or in the early part of the evening. چائے کا وقت

tea towel (**tea towels**) *n* A **tea towel** is a cloth used to dry dishes after they have been washed. پلیٹیں خشک کرنے کا کپڑا

technical *adj* **Technical** means involving the sorts of machines, processes, and materials used in industry, transport, and communications. تکنیکی

technician (**technicians**) *n* A **technician** is someone whose job involves skilled practical work with scientific equipment, for example in a laboratory. تکنیشین

technique (**techniques**) *n* A **technique** is a particular method of doing an activity, usually a method that involves practical skills. تکنیک

techno *n* **Techno** is a form of modern electronic music with a very fast beat. تیز بیٹ والا برقی میوزک

technological *adj* **Technological** means relating to or associated with technology. تکنیکی

technology (**technologies**) *n* **Technology** refers to things which are the result of scientific knowledge being used for practical purposes. ٹکنالوجی

teddy bear (**teddy bears**) *n* A **teddy bear** or a **teddy** is a soft toy that looks like a bear. بھالو کی شکل کا ملائم کھلونا

tee (**tees**) *n* In golf, a **tee** is a small piece of wood or plastic which is used to support the ball before it is hit at the start of each hole. (گولف کے کھیل میں گیند کا سہارا) ٹی

teenager (**teenagers**) *n* A **teenager** is someone between 13 and 19 years of age. نوخیز، نوعمر، نوجوان

teens *npl* If you are in your **teens**, you are between 13 and 19 years old. تیرہ سے انیس سال کے درمیان

tee-shirt (**tee-shirts**) *n* A **tee-shirt** is a cotton shirt with short sleeves and no collar or buttons. آدھی آستین کی سوتی قمیض

t

teethe (**teethes, teething, teethed**) *vi* When babies **are teething**, their teeth are starting to appear through their gums. بچے کے (دانت نکالنا، دانت نکلنا)

teetotal *adj* Someone who is **teetotal** does not drink alcohol. بہت چائے پینے والا

telecommunications *npl* **Telecommunications** is the technology of sending signals and messages over long distances using electronic equipment, for example by radio and telephone. برقی آلات سے دور تک رابطہ کرنا

telegram (**telegrams**) *n* A **telegram** is a message that is sent by electricity or radio and then printed and delivered to someone's home or office. تار، ٹیلیگرام

telephone (**telephones**) *n* The **telephone** is an electrical system used to talk to someone in another place by dialling a number on a piece of equipment and speaking into it. ٹیلیفون

telephone directory (**telephone directories**) *n* The **telephone directory** is a book that contains an alphabetical list of the names, addresses, and telephone numbers of the people in a particular area. ٹیلیفون ڈائریکٹری

telesales *n* **Telesales** is a method of selling in which someone employed by a company telephones people to try to persuade them to buy the company's products or services. فون پر خریدی کے لئے آمادہ کرنا

telescope (**telescopes**) *n* A **telescope** is an instrument shaped like a tube. It has lenses inside it that make distant things seem larger and nearer when you look through it. دوربین

television (**televisions**) *n* A **television** or a **television set** is a piece of electrical equipment consisting of a box with a screen on which you can watch programmes with pictures and sounds. ٹیلیویژن

tell (**tells, telling, told**) *vt* If you **tell** someone something, you let them know about it. بتانا، کہنا ▷ *vt* If you **tell** someone to do something, you say that they must do it. کہنا ▷ *vt* If you can **tell** something, you know it. بتانا

teller (**tellers**) *n* A **teller** is someone who works in a bank and who customers pay money to or get money from. بینک میں رقم لینے دینے والا

tell off *v* If you **tell** someone **off**, you speak to them angrily or seriously because they have done something wrong. باتیں سنانا *I'm always getting told off for being late.*

telly (**tellies**) *n* A **telly** is a piece of equipment consisting of a box with a glass screen on it on which you can watch programmes with pictures and sounds. (*informal*) بائسکوپ

temp (**temps**) *n* A **temp** is a person who is employed by an agency that sends them to work in different offices for short periods of time, for example to replace someone who is ill or on holiday. عارضی ملازم

temper (**tempers**) *n* If you say that someone has a **temper**, you mean that they become angry very easily. مزاج

temperature (**temperatures**) *n* The **temperature** of something is how hot or cold it is. حرارت

temple (**temples**) *n* A **temple** is a building used for the worship of a god or gods, especially in the Buddhist and Hindu religions. مندر

temporary *adj* Something that is **temporary** lasts for only a limited time. عارضی

tempt (**tempts, tempting, tempted**) *v* Something that **tempts** you attracts you and makes you want it, even though it may be wrong or harmful. للچانا، اکسانا، ترغیب دینا

temptation (**temptations**) *n* **Temptation** is the state you are in when you want to do or have something, although you know it might be wrong or harmful. لالچ، تحریص، ترغیب

tempting *adj* If something is **tempting**, it makes you want to do it or have it. للچانے والا

ten *num* **Ten** is the number 10. دس

tenant (tenants) *n* A **tenant** is someone who pays rent for the place they live in, or for land or buildings that they use. کرایہ دار

tend (tends, tending, tended) *vi* If something **tends** to happen, it usually happens or it happens often. رجحان ہونا، رجحان پایا جانا

tendency (tendencies) *n* A **tendency** is a worrying or unpleasant habit or action that keeps occurring. رجحان

tender (tenderer, tenderest) *adj* Someone or something that is **tender** is kind and gentle. نرم

tendon (tendons) *n* A **tendon** is a strong cord of tissue in your body joining a muscle to a bone. عضلہ

tennis *n* **Tennis** is a game played by two or four players on a rectangular court with a net across the middle. The players use rackets to hit a ball over the net. ٹینس

tennis court (tennis courts) *n* A **tennis court** is an area in which you play the game of tennis. ٹینس کا میدان

tennis player (tennis players) *n* A **tennis player** is a person who plays tennis, either as a job or for fun. ٹینس کا کھلاڑی

tennis racket (tennis rackets) *n* A **tennis racket** is the racket that you use when you play tennis. (ٹینس ریکیٹ (بلا

tenor (tenors) *n* A **tenor** is a male singer with a fairly high voice. بلند آواز گلوکار

tenpin bowling *n* **Tenpin bowling** is a game in which you try to knock down ten objects shaped like bottles by rolling a heavy ball towards them. It is usually played in a place called a bowling alley. بھاری گیند سے دس بوتلیں گرانے کا عمل

tense (tenser, tensest, tenses) *adj* If you are **tense**, you are worried and nervous, and cannot relax. تناؤزدہ ▷ *n* The **tense** of a verb group is its form, which usually shows whether you are referring to past, present, or future time. زمانہ

tension (tensions) *n* **Tension** is a feeling of fear or nervousness produced before a difficult, dangerous, or important event. تناؤزدہ

tent (tents) *n* A **tent** is a shelter made of canvas or nylon and held up by poles and ropes, used mainly by people who are camping. خیمہ، تنبو

tenth (tenths) *adj* The **tenth** item in a series is the one that you count as number ten. دسواں ▷ *n* A **tenth** is one of ten equal parts of something. دسواں حصہ

term (terms) *n* A **term** is a word or expression with a specific meaning. اصطلاح ▷ *n* A **term** is one of the periods of time that a school, college, or university year is divided into. میعاد

terminal terminals *adj* A **terminal** illness or disease cannot be cured and eventually causes death. جان لیوا سرطان ▷ *n* A **terminal** is a place where vehicles, passengers, or goods begin or end a journey. ٹرمنل

terminally *adv* If someone is **terminally** ill, it means that they will die of an illness or disease that cannot be cured. ہلاکت خیزی کے طور پر

terrace (terraces) *n* A **terrace** is a row of similar houses joined together by their side walls. ٹیریس

terraced *adj* A **terraced** slope or side of a hill has flat areas like steps cut into it, where crops or other plants can be grown. (زینہ دار (پہاڑی ڈھلان

terrible *adj* **Terrible** means extremely bad. خوفناک، انتہائی خراب

terribly *adv* **Terribly** means in an extremely bad manner. شدید طور پر

terrier (terriers) *n* A **terrier** is a small breed of dog. There are many different types of terrier. چھوٹی نسل کا کتا

terrific *adj* If you describe something or

t

someone as **terrific**, you are very pleased with them or very impressed by them. (*informal*) شاندار

terrified *adj* If you are **terrified**, you are extremely frightened. خوفزدہ

terrify (**terrifies, terrifying, terrified**) *vt* If something **terrifies** you, it makes you feel extremely frightened. ڈرانا

territory (**territories**) *n* **Territory** is land which is controlled by a particular country or ruler. علاقہ

terrorism *n* **Terrorism** is the use of violence in order to achieve political aims or to force a government to do something. دہشت گردی

terrorist (**terrorists**) *n* A **terrorist** is a person who uses violence in order to achieve political aims. دہشت گرد

terrorist attack (**terrorist attacks**) *n* A **terrorist attack** is a violent incident, usually involving murder and bombing, carried out by people who are trying to achieve political aims. دہشت گردانہ حملہ

test (**tests, testing, tested**) *n* A **test** is an action or experiment to find out how well something works. ٹیسٹ، جانچ ▷ *vt* If you **test** something, you try it to see what it is like, or how it works. جانچنا ▷ *n* A **test** is something you do to show how much you know or what you can do. ٹیسٹ، امتحان

testicle (**testicles**) *n* A man's **testicles** are the two sex glands that produce sperm. خصیہ، فوطہ

test tube (**test tubes**) *n* A **test tube** is a small tube-shaped container made from glass. Test tubes are used in laboratories. جانچ نلی

tetanus *n* **Tetanus** is a serious painful disease caused by bacteria getting into wounds. It makes your muscles, especially your jaw muscles, go stiff. ٹیٹنس، جبڑے بھنچ جانا

text (**texts, texting, texted**) *n* **Text** is any written material. متن ▷ *vt* If you **text** someone, you send them a text message on a mobile phone. (متنی پیغام بھیجنا) موبائل پر

textbook (**textbooks**) *n* A **textbook** is a book about a particular subject that is intended for students. نصابی کتاب

textile (**textiles**) *n* **Textiles** are types of woven cloth. تانے بانے کا کپڑا، بنا ہوا کپڑا

text message (**text messages**) *n* A **text message** is a message that you send using a mobile phone. (متنی پیغام بھیجنا) موبائل پر

Thai (**Thais**) *adj* **Thai** means belonging or relating to Thailand, or to its people, language, or culture. (تھائی) ملک ▷ *n* A **Thai** is a person who comes from Thailand. (تھائی) باشندہ ▷ *n* **Thai** is the language spoken in Thailand. (تھائی) زبان

Thailand *n* **Thailand** is a kingdom in south-east Asia, on the Andaman Sea and the Gulf of Thailand. تھائی لینڈ

than *prep* You use **than** when you are talking about the difference between two people or things. ایک کے مقابلے میں دوسرا *Children learn faster than adults.*

thank (**thanks, thanking, thanked**) *vt* When you **thank** someone for something, you express your gratitude to them for it. شکریہ ادا کرنا

thanks! *excl* You can say '**thanks!**' to show that you are grateful to someone for something they have done. شکریہ!

that *det* You use **that** to talk about something that you have mentioned before. (وہ) جو، جو کہ *For that reason the claims procedure is as simple and helpful as possible.* ▷ *conj* You use **that** to join two different things you are saying. کہ *I felt sad that he was leaving.* ▷ *pron* You use **that** to talk about something that you have mentioned before. وہ *They said you wanted to talk to me. Why was that?* ▷ *det* You use **that** to talk about somebody or something a distance away from you. وہ *Look at that car over there. Who's that beautiful girl?* ▷ *pron* You use **that** to talk about somebody or something a distance away from you. وہ

Who's that? ▷ *pron* You use **that** to show which person or thing you are talking about. جس کے، وہ *There's the girl that I told you about.*

thatched *adj* A **thatched** house has a roof made of straw or reeds. چھپر والا، کھپریل والا

the *det* You use **the** before a noun when it is clear which person or thing you are talking about. (دی) آرٹیکل *It's always hard to think about the future.* ▷ *det* You use **the** before a noun to talk about things of that type in general. کسی اسم سے قبل استعمال ہونے والا حرف تخصیص *The computer has developed very quickly in recent years.*

theatre (**theatres**) *n* A **theatre** is a building with a stage on which plays and other entertainments are performed. تھیٹر

theft (**thefts**) *n* **Theft** is the criminal act of stealing. چوری

their *det* You use **their** to say that something belongs to a group of people, animals, or things. ان کا

theirs *pron* You use **theirs** to say that something belongs to a group of people, animals, or things. ان کی

them *pron* You use **them** to talk about more than one person, animal, or thing. ان کو

theme (**themes**) *n* A **theme** in a piece of writing, a discussion, or a work of art is an important idea or subject in it. مرکزی خیال، موضوع

theme park (**theme parks**) *n* A **theme park** is a large outdoor area where people pay to go to enjoy themselves. All the different activities in a theme park are usually based on a particular idea or theme. کسی خاص خیال سے جڑی حرکات کا پارک

themselves *pron* You use **themselves** to talk about people, animals, or things that you have just talked about. وہ لوگ خود

then *adv* **Then** means at that time. کے مقابلے ▷ *conj* You also use **then** to say that one thing happens after another. (*informal*) پھر

theology *n* **Theology** is the study of religion. دینیات

theory (**theories**) *n* A **theory** is a formal idea or set of ideas intended to explain something. کلیہ، اصول

therapy *n* **Therapy** is the treatment of mental or physical illness without the use of drugs or operations. علاج، طریق علاج

there *adv* **There** also means to a place, or at a place. وہاں ▷ *pron* You use **there** to say that something is in a place or is happening, or to make someone notice it. وہاں

therefore *adv* You use **therefore** when you are talking about the result of something. اس لیے

thermometer (**thermometers**) *n* A **thermometer** is an instrument for measuring the temperature of a room or of a person's body. تھرمامیٹر

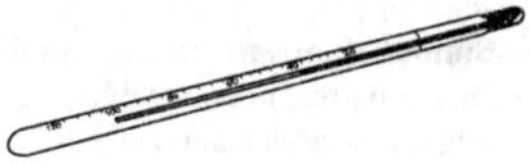

Thermos® (**Thermoses**) *n* A **Thermos** or **Thermos flask** is a container which is used to keep hot drinks hot or cold drinks cold. It has two thin shiny glass walls with no air between them. تھرمس

thermostat (**thermostats**) *n* A **thermostat** is a device that switches a system or motor on or off according to the temperature. Thermostats are used, for example, in central heating systems and fridges. حرارت کو محسوس کرکے نظام یا موٹر کو چالو یا بند کرنے والا آلہ

these *det* You use **these** to talk about someone or something that you have already mentioned. یہ *These people need more support.* ▷ *pron* You use **these** to talk about people or things that are near you. (یہ) جمع *I like these, on this table.* ▷ *det* You use **these** to talk about people or things that are near you. (یہ) جمع *These* *bags are very heavy.* ▷ *det* You use **these** to introduce people or things that you are going to talk about. ے (یہ) *If you're looking for a builder, these phone numbers will be useful.*

they *pron* You use **they** when you are talking about more than one person, animal, or thing. وہ، لوگ *They are all in the same class.*

thick (**thicker, thickest**) *adj* If something is **thick**, it is deep or wide between one side and the other. موٹا ▷ *adj* If a liquid is **thick**, it flows slowly. گاڑھا

thickness (**thicknesses**) *n* The **thickness** of something is the distance between its two opposite surfaces. موٹائی

thief (**thieves**) *n* A **thief** is a person who steals something from another person. چور

thigh (**thighs**) *n* Your **thighs** are the top parts of your legs, between your knees and your hips. ہانگ

thin (**thinner, thinnest**) *adj* If something is **thin**, it is narrow between one side and the other. پتلا ▷ *adj* If a person or animal is **thin**, they are not fat and they do not weigh much. دبلا

thing (**things**) *n* You use **thing** as a substitute for another word when you are unable to be more precise, or you do not need or want to be more precise. چیز

think (**thinks, thinking, thought**) *v* If you **think** something, you believe that it is true. سوچنا ▷ *vi* When you **think**, you use your mind. سوچنا، غور کرنا

third (**thirds**) *adj* The **third** item in a series is the one that you count as number three. تیسرا ▷ *n* A **third** is one of three equal parts of something. تیسرا حصہ

thirdly *adv* You use **thirdly** when you are about to mention the third thing in a series of items. (تیسرے شمار پر)

third-party insurance *n* **Third-party insurance** is insurance that covers you if you injure someone or damage someone's property. فریق ثالث والا بیمہ

thirst (**thirsts**) *n* **Thirst** is the feeling that you need to drink something. پیاس

thirsty (**thirstier, thirstiest**) *adj* If you are **thirsty**, you feel a need to drink something. پیاسا

thirteen *num* **Thirteen** is the number 13. تیرہ

thirteenth *adj* The **thirteenth** item in a series is the one that you count as number thirteen. تیرہواں

thirty *num* **Thirty** is the number 30. تیس

this *det* You use **this** to talk about someone or something that you have already mentioned. یہ *How can we resolve this problem?* ▷ *pron* You use **this** to talk about somebody or something near you. یہ *'Would you like a different one?'—'No, this is great.'* ▷ *det* You use **this** followed by a noun, or followed by an adjective and a noun, to talk about somebody or something that is near you. یہ *I like this room much better than the other one.* ▷ *pron* You use **this** to introduce someone or something that you are going to talk about. یہ *This is what I will do. I will call her and explain.*

thistle (**thistles**) *n* A **thistle** is a wild plant which has leaves with sharp points and purple flowers. گوکھرو

thorn (**thorns**) *n* **Thorns** are the sharp points on some plants and trees such as roses and holly. کانٹا

thorough *adj* A **thorough** action is done very carefully and methodically. مکمل، ایک سرے سے دوسرے سرے تک

thoroughly *adv* If somebody does something **thoroughly**, they do it with great care. اچھی طرح سے، بخوبی

those *det* You use **those** to talk about people or things that have already been mentioned. وہ، لوگ *I don't know any of those people you mentioned.* ▷ *pron* You use **those** to talk about people or things a distance away from you. وہ *Those are nice shoes.* ▷ *det* You use **those** to talk about people or things a distance away from you. „ *What are those buildings?*

though *adv* You use **though** when talking about an idea that is not what you would expect. اگرچہ، باوجودیکہ ▷ *conj* You use **though** to add information that changes what you have already said. حالانکہ *They went to the same school, though they never met there.* ▷ *conj* You use **though** to start talking about an idea that is not what you would expect. اگرچہ، باوجودیکہ *He plays in adult tennis games even though he is only 15.*

thought (**thoughts**) *n* A **thought** is an idea or opinion. خیال

thoughtful *adj* If you are **thoughtful**, you are quiet and serious because you are thinking about something. متفکر

thoughtless *adj* If you describe someone as **thoughtless**, you are critical of them because they forget or ignore other people's wants, needs, or feelings. کم سوجھ بوجھ والے

thousand *num* A **thousand** or one **thousand** is the number 1,000. ہزار

thousandth (**thousandths**) *adj* The **thousandth** item in a series is the one you count as number one thousand. ہزارواں ▷ *n* A **thousandth** is one of a thousand equal parts of something. ہزارواں حصہ

thread (**threads**) *n* **Thread** or a **thread** is a long very thin piece of a material such as cotton, nylon, or silk, especially one that is used in sewing. دھاگا

threat (**threats**) *n* A **threat** to someone or something is a danger that something unpleasant might happen to them. دھمکی

threaten (**threatens, threatening, threatened**) *vt* If someone **threatens** to do something unpleasant to you, or if they **threaten** you, they say or imply that they will do something unpleasant to you, especially if you do not do what they want. دھمکی دینا

threatening *adj* You can describe someone's behaviour as **threatening** when you think that they are trying to harm you. دھمکی آمیز

three *num* **Three** is the number 3. تین

three-dimensional *adj* A **three-dimensional** object is solid rather than flat, because it can be measured in three dimensions, usually the height, length, and width. تین ابعاد والا

thrifty (**thriftier, thriftiest**) *adj* If you say that someone is **thrifty**, you are praising them for saving money, not buying unnecessary things, and not wasting things. کفایت

thrill (**thrills**) *n* If something gives you a **thrill**, it gives you a sudden feeling of great excitement, pleasure, or fear. سنسنی

thrilled *adj* If you are **thrilled** about something, you are pleased and excited about it. ہیجان انگیز، سنسنی پیدا کرنے والا

thriller (**thrillers**) *n* A **thriller** is a book, film, or play that tells an exciting story about something such as criminal activities or spying. (جذبات انگیز (کتاب، فلم، ڈراما

thrilling *adj* Something that is **thrilling** is very exciting and enjoyable. جذباتی

throat (**throats**) *n* Your **throat** is the back part of your mouth that you use to swallow and to breathe. حلق ▷ *n* Your **throat** is the front part of your neck. گلا

throb (**throbs, throbbing, throbbed**) *vi* If part of your body **throbs**, you feel a series of strong and usually painful beats there. دھڑکنا

throne (**thrones**) *n* A **throne** is an ornate chair used by a king, queen, or emperor on important occasions. تخت شاہی

through *prep* **Through** means going all the way from one side of something to the other side. اول تا آخر *We walked through the forest.*

throughout *prep* If something happens **throughout** a period of time, it happens for all of that period. کسی چیز کے ہر حصے میں، ہر جگہ *It rained heavily throughout the game.*

t

throw (**throws, throwing, threw, thrown**) *vt* If you **throw** an object that you are holding, you move your hand quickly and let go of the object, so that it moves through the air. پھینکا

throw away *v* If you **throw away** or **throw out** something you do not want, you get rid of it. پھینک دینا *I never throw anything away.*

throw out *v* When you **throw out** something that you do not want, you get rid of it. نکالنا، باہر پھینک دینا

throw up *v* To **throw up** means to vomit. (*informal*) قے کرنا *She threw up after reading reports of the trial.*

thrush (**thrushes**) *n* A **thrush** is a small brown bird with small marks on its chest. ترشہ

thug (**thugs**) *n* If you refer to someone as a **thug**, you think they are violent or a criminal. ٹھگ

thumb (**thumbs**) *n* Your **thumb** is the short, thick digit on the side of your hand next to your first finger. انگوٹھا

thumbtack (**thumbtacks**) *n* A **thumbtack** is a short pin with a broad flat top which is used for fastening papers or pictures to a board, wall, or other surface. US بڑے ماتھے کی پن

thump (**thumps, thumping, thumped**) *v* If you **thump** something, you hit it hard, usually with your fist. زور سے ہاتھ (مکہ) مارنا

thunder *n* **Thunder** is the loud noise that you hear from the sky after a flash of lightning, especially during a storm. گرج، گھن گرج

thunderstorm (**thunderstorms**) *n* A **thunderstorm** is a storm in which there is thunder, lightning, and heavy rain. گرجدار طوفان

thundery *adj* When the weather is **thundery**, there is a lot of thunder, or there are heavy clouds which make you think that there will be thunder soon. گرجدار طوفانی

Thursday (**Thursdays**) *n* **Thursday** is the day after Wednesday and before Friday. جمعرات

thyme *n* **Thyme** is a type of herb. صعتر (بوٹی)

Tibet *n* **Tibet** is an autonomous region of south-west China. تبت

Tibetan (**Tibetans**) *adj* **Tibetan** means of, relating to, or characteristic of Tibet, its people, or their language. تبتی ▷ *n* A **Tibetan** is a native or inhabitant of Tibet. تبتی ▷ *n* **Tibetan** is a language spoken by people who live in Tibet. تبتی

tick (**ticks, ticking, ticked**) *n* A **tick** is a written mark like a *v* with the right side extended. You use it to show that something is correct or has been dealt with. صحیح کا نشان ▷ *vt* If you **tick** something that is written on a piece of paper, you put a tick next to it. ٹک کرنا

ticket (**tickets**) *n* A **ticket** is an official piece of paper or card which shows that you have paid for a journey or have paid to enter a place of entertainment. ٹکٹ

ticket machine (**ticket machines**) *n* A **ticket machine** is a machine, for example in a railway station, from which you can get tickets by putting in money and pressing a button. ٹکٹ مشین

ticket office (**ticket offices**) *n* A **ticket office** is a place, for example at a theatre, cinema, or railway station, where tickets are sold. ٹکٹ دفتر

tickle (**tickles, tickling, tickled**) *vt* When you **tickle** someone, you move your fingers lightly over their body, often in order to make them laugh. گدگدانا

ticklish *adj* A **ticklish** problem, situation, or task is difficult and needs to be dealt with carefully. نازک

tick off *v* If you **tick off** an item on a list, you put a tick by it to show that it has been dealt with. ٹک کا نشان لگانا *He ticked off my name on a piece of paper.*

tide (**tides**) *n* The **tide** is the regular

change in the level of the sea on the shore. اتار چڑھاؤ، جوار بھاٹا

tidy (**tidier, tidiest, tidies, tidying, tidied**) *adj* Something that is **tidy** is neat and arranged in an orderly way. صاف ستھرا ▷ *vt* When you **tidy** a place, you make it neat by putting things in their proper places. صاف کرنا

tidy up *v* When you **tidy up** or **tidy** a place **up**, you put things back in their proper places so that everything is neat. سنوارنا *She spent an hour tidying up the shop.*

tie (**ties, tying, tied**) *n* A tie is a long, narrow piece of cloth that you tie a knot in and wear around your neck with a shirt. ٹائی ▷ *vt* If you **tie** something, you fasten it with string or a rope. باندھنا

tie up *v* When you **tie** something **up**, you fasten string or rope round it so that it is firm or secure. باندھنا *He tied up the bag and took it outside.*

tiger (**tigers**) *n* A **tiger** is a large fierce animal belonging to the cat family. Tigers are orange with black stripes. شیر

tight (**tighter, tightest**) *adj* If clothes are **tight**, they are so small that they fit very close to your body. تنگ ▷ *adj* Something that is **tight** is fastened so that it is not easy to move it. سخت

tighten (**tightens, tightening, tightened**) *v* If you **tighten** your grip on something, or if your grip on something **tightens**, you hold it more firmly or securely. تنگ کرنا، کسنا

tights *npl* **Tights** are a piece of clothing made of thin material such as nylon that covers your hips and each of your legs and feet separately. تنگ لچکدار کپڑے

tile (**tiles**) *n* **Tiles** are flat square pieces of baked clay, carpet, cork, or other substance, which are fixed as a covering onto a floor, wall, or roof. کھپریل

tiled *adj* A **tiled** surface is covered with tiles. کھپریل والا

till (**tills**) *conj* If something happens **till** something else happens, the first thing happens before the other thing and stops when the other thing happens. (*informal*) یہاں تک کہ *They slept till the alarm woke them.* ▷ *n* In a shop, a **till** is a cash register where money is kept, and where customers pay for what they have bought. ادائگی کیش کاؤنٹر ▷ *prep* If something happens **till** a time, it happens before that time and stops at that time. (*informal*) تک *She lived there till last year.* ▷ *prep* If something does not happen **till** a time, it does not happen before that time and only starts happening at that time. (*informal*) تک *The shop doesn't open till half past nine.*

timber *n* **Timber** is wood used for building houses and making furniture. لکڑی

time *n* **Time** is how long something takes to happen. We measure **time** in minutes, hours, days, weeks, months, and years. وقت ▷ *n* The **time** is a moment in the day that you describe in hours and minutes. وقت

time bomb (**time bombs**) *n* A **time bomb** is a bomb with a mechanism that causes it to explode at a particular time. ٹائم بم

time off *n* If you have **time off**, you do not go to work or school, for example, because you are ill or it is a day when you do not usually work. چھٹی کا دن

timer (**timers**) *n* A **timer** is a device that measures time, especially one that is part of a machine and causes it to start or stop working at specific times. ٹائمر (وقت پیما آلہ جو مشین شروع کر دیتا ہے)

timetable (**timetables**) *n* A **timetable** is a plan of the times when particular events are to take place. ٹائم ٹیبل

time zone (**time zones**) *n* A **time zone** is one of the areas into which the world is divided where the time is calculated as being a particular number of hours behind or ahead of GMT. منطقہ وقت (وقت کی تقسیم جی ایم ٹی کے اعتبار سے)

tin (**tins**) *n* **Tin** is a kind of soft, pale grey metal. ٹن ▷ *n* A **tin** is a metal container for food. ٹن، ڈبا

tinfoil *n* **Tinfoil** consists of shiny metal in the form of a thin sheet which is used for wrapping food. جھلی نما پتلی دھات کا اندرونی ڈھکن

tinned *adj* **Tinned** food has been preserved by being sealed in a tin. ڈبہ بند

tin opener (**tin openers**) *n* A **tin opener** is a tool that is used for opening tins of food. ڈبہ کھولنے والا

tinsel *n* **Tinsel** consists of small strips of shiny paper attached to long pieces of thread. People use tinsel as a decoration. سستی دھات کے چمکدار ورق، گوٹا وغیرہ

tinted *adj* If something is **tinted**, it has a small amount of a particular colour or dye in it. ہلکا رنگا ہوا

tiny (**tinier, tiniest**) *adj* Someone or something that is **tiny** is extremely small. چھوٹا سا

tip (**tips, tipping, tipped**) *n* The **tip** of something long and narrow is the end of it. نوک ▷ *n* If you give someone such as a waiter a **tip**, you give them some money for their services. بخشش ▷ *n* A **tip** is a useful piece of advice. صلاح ▷ *v* If an object or part of your body **tips**, or if you **tip** it, it moves into a sloping position with one end or side higher than the other. ایک طرف سے اونچا ہونا، جھکنا، جھکانا ▷ *vt* If you **tip** someone such as a waiter, you give them some money for their services. بخشش دینا

tipsy *adj* If someone is **tipsy**, they are slightly drunk. مدہوش، نشہ میں چور

tired *adj* If you are **tired**, you feel that you want to rest or sleep. تھکا ہوا

tiring *adj* If you describe something as **tiring**, you mean that it makes you tired so that you want to rest or sleep. تھکادینے والا

tissue (**tissues**) *n* In animals and plants, **tissue** consists of cells that are similar in appearance and function. نسیج

title (**titles**) *n* The **title** of a book, play, film, or piece of music is its name. عنوان

to *prep* You use **to** when you are talking about the position or direction of something. کو *She went to the window and looked out.* ▷ *prep* You use **to** before the infinitive the simple form of a verb. کا *It was time to leave.*

toad (**toads**) *n* A **toad** is an animal like a frog, but with a drier skin. مینڈک کی ایک قسم

toadstool (**toadstools**) *n* A **toadstool** is a fungus that you cannot eat because it is poisonous. سانپ کی چھتری، کگرمتا

toast (**toasts**) *n* **Toast** is slices of bread heated until they are brown and crisp. توش، ٹوسٹ ▷ *n* When you drink a **toast** to someone, you wish them success or good health, and then drink some alcoholic drink. نیک خواہش کے لئے پی جانے والی شراب

toaster (**toasters**) *n* A **toaster** is a piece of electric equipment used to toast bread. ٹوسٹ سینکنے والا

tobacco (**tobaccos**) *n* **Tobacco** is the dried leaves of a plant which people smoke in pipes, cigars, and cigarettes. تمباکو

tobacconist (**tobbaconists**) *n* A **tobacconist** or a **tobacconist's** is a shop that sells cigarettes, tobacco, etc. تمباکو کے سامان بیچنے والا

toboggan (**toboggans**) *n* A **toboggan** is a light wooden board with a curved front, used for travelling down hills on snow or ice. دستی برف گاڑی

tobogganing *n* **Tobogganing** is the activity of travelling down a slope on snow or ice using a toboggan. دستی برف گاڑی چلانا

today *adv* You use **today** to refer to the day on which you are speaking or writing. آج

toddler (**toddlers**) *n* A **toddler** is a young child who has only just learnt to walk. گھٹنوں پر چلنے والا

toe (**toes**) *n* Your **toes** are the five

movable parts at the end of each foot. پیر کا پنجہ

toffee (**toffees**) *n* A **toffee** is a sweet made by boiling sugar and butter together with water. ٹافی

together *adv* If people do something **together**, they do it with each other. ساتھ ساتھ

Togo *n* **Togo** is a republic in West Africa, on the Gulf of Guinea. (ٹوگو) جمہوریہ

toilet (**toilets**) *n* A **toilet** is a large bowl connected to the drains which you use when you want to get rid of urine or faeces from your body. بیت الخلاء

toilet bag (**toilet bags**) *n* A **toilet bag** is a small bag in which you keep things such as soap, a flannel, and a toothbrush when you are travelling. صابن ٹوتھ برش رکھنے کا بیگ

toilet paper *n* **Toilet paper** is paper that you use to clean yourself after getting rid of urine or faeces from your body. رفع حاجت کے بعد پونچھنے کا کاغذ

toiletries *npl* **Toiletries** are products such as soap and toothpaste that you use when cleaning or taking care of your body. صابن ٹوتھ برش وغیرہ

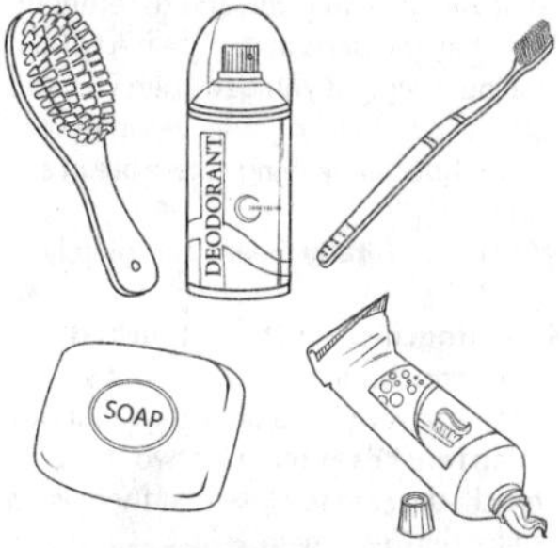

toilet roll (**toilet rolls**) *n* A **toilet roll** is a long narrow strip of toilet paper that is wound around a small cardboard tube. ٹائلٹ پیپر رول

token (**tokens**) *n* A **token** is a piece of paper, plastic, or metal which can be used instead of money. نِشانی، ثبوت

tolerant *adj* If you are **tolerant**, you let other people say and do what they like, even if you do not agree with it or approve of it. بردبار، متحمّل مزاج

toll (**tolls**) *n* A **toll** is a sum of money that you have to pay in order to use a particular bridge or road. چنگی

tomato (**tomatoes**) *n* A **tomato** is a small, soft, red fruit that is used in cooking as a vegetable or eaten raw in salads. ٹماٹر

tomato sauce *n* **Tomato sauce** is a thick sauce made with tomatoes and often served with pasta. ٹماٹر کی چٹنی

tomb (**tombs**) *n* A **tomb** is a stone structure containing the body of a dead person. مقبرہ

tomboy (**tomboys**) *n* If you say that a girl is a **tomboy**, you mean that she likes playing rough or noisy games, or doing things that were traditionally considered to be things that boys enjoy. شور و غل مچانے والی شوخ لڑکی

t

tomorrow *adv* You use **tomorrow** to refer to the day after today. آنے والا کل

ton (**tons**) *n* A non-metric **ton** is a unit of weight equal to 2,240 pounds in Britain and 2,000 pounds in the United States. (ٹن) (وزن)

tongue (**tongues**) *n* Your **tongue** is the soft movable part inside your mouth that you use for tasting, licking, and speaking. زبان

tonic (**tonics**) *n* **Tonic** or **tonic water** is a colourless, fizzy drink that has a slightly bitter flavour. (ٹانک) مقوی دوا

tonight *adv* **Tonight** is used to refer to the evening of today or the night that follows today. اِس رات کو، آج رات کو

tonsillitis *n* **Tonsillitis** is a painful swelling of your tonsils caused by an infection. حلق کی گلٹیوں کا ورم

tonsils *npl* Your **tonsils** are the two small soft lumps in your throat at the back of your mouth. گلوئے

too *adv* **Too** means also. بھی ▷ *adv* You also use **too** to mean more than you want or need. کافی

tool (**tools**) *n* A **tool** is any instrument or simple piece of equipment, for example, a hammer or a knife, that you hold in your hands and use to do a particular kind of work. آلہ

tooth (**teeth**) *n* Your **teeth** are the hard, white things in your mouth that you use to bite and chew food. دانت ▷ *n* The **teeth** of a comb, a saw, or a zip are the parts that are in a row along its edge. دندانے

toothache *n* **Toothache** is pain in one of your teeth. دانت درد

toothbrush (**toothbrushes**) *n* A **toothbrush** is a small brush used for cleaning your teeth. ٹوتھ برش

toothpaste (**toothpastes**) *n* **Toothpaste** is a thick substance which you use to clean your teeth. ٹوتھ پیسٹ

toothpick (**toothpicks**) *n* A **toothpick** is a small stick which you use to remove food from between your teeth. خلال

top (**tops**) *n* The **top** thing is the highest one. چوٹی، سرفہرست ▷ *n* The **top** of something is the highest part of it. چوٹی ▷ *n* The **top** of something is the part that fits over the end of it. اوپری سرا، اوپر

topic (**topics**) *n* A **topic** is a particular subject that you write about or discuss. مضمون

topical *adj* **Topical** means relating to events that are happening at the time when you are speaking or writing. مسائل حاضرہ سے متعلق

top-secret *adj* **Top-secret** information or activity is intended to be kept completely secret. انتہائی رازدارانہ

top-up card (**top-up cards**) *n* A **top-up card** is a card bought by a mobile-phone user entitling him or her to a stipulated amount of credit for future calls. کارڈ کوری چارج کرنا

torch (**torches**) *n* A **torch** is a small, battery-powered electric light which you carry in your hand. ٹارچ

tornado (**tornadoes, tornados**) *n* A **tornado** is a violent storm with strong circular winds. سخت آندھی طوفان

tortoise (**tortoises**) *n* A **tortoise** is a slow-moving animal with a shell into which it can pull its head and legs for protection. کچھوا

torture (**tortures, torturing, tortured**) *n* If someone is subjected to **torture**, another person deliberately causes them great pain, in order to punish them or make them reveal information. سخت اذیت ▷ *vt* If someone **is tortured**, another person deliberately causes them great pain over a period of time, in order to punish them or to make them reveal information. سخت اذیت دینا

toss (**tosses, tossing, tossed**) *vt* If you **toss** something somewhere, you throw it there lightly and carelessly. اچھالنا

total (**totals**) *adj* The **total** number or cost of something is the number or cost that you get when you add together or count all the parts in it. کل ▷ *n* A **total** is the number that you get when you add several numbers together or when you count how many things there are in a group. کل جمع

totally *adv* **Totally** means completely. کلی طور پر

touch (**touches, touching, touched**) *vt* If you **touch** something, you put your fingers or your hand on it. چھونا ▷ *v* If one thing **touches** another, or two things **touch**, they are so close that there is no space between them. چھونا، پہنچنا

touchdown (**touchdowns**) *n* **Touchdown** is the landing of an aircraft or spacecraft. ہوائی یا خلائی جہاز کا زمین کو چھونا

touched *adj* If you are **touched**, you

are affected or moved to sympathy or emotion. متاثرہ

touching *adj* If something is **touching**, it causes feelings of sadness or sympathy. دِل کو چھو لینے والا

touchline *n* In sports such as rugby and football, the **touchline** is one of the two lines which mark the side of the playing area. رگبی فٹبال میں تقسیمی خط

touch pad (**touch pads**) *n* A **touch pad** is a flat pad on some computers that you slide your finger over in order to move the cursor. ماؤس رکھنے والا پیڈ

touchy (**touchier, touchiest**) *adj* **Touchy** people are easily upset or irritated. حساس

tough (**tougher, toughest**) *adj* A **tough** person has a strong character and can tolerate difficulty or hardship. سخت جان

toupee (**toupees**) *n* A **toupee** is a piece of artificial hair worn by a man to cover a patch on his head where he has lost his hair. نقلی بالوں کا گچھا

tour (**tours, touring, toured**) *n* A **tour** is an organized trip that people such as musicians, politicians, or theatre companies go on to several different places, stopping to meet people or perform. سیر، ٹور ▷ *v* When people such as musicians, politicians, or theatre companies **tour**, they go on a tour, for example in order to perform or to meet people. سیر کرنا

tour guide (**tour guides**) *n* A **tour guide** is someone who helps tourists who are on holiday or shows them round a place. ٹور گائڈ

tourism *n* **Tourism** is the business of providing services for people on holiday. سیاحت

tourist (**tourists**) *n* A **tourist** is a person who is visiting a place for pleasure, especially when they are on holiday. سیاح

tourist office (**tourist offices**) *n* A **tourist office** is a place where tourists can go to get information, to make bookings, etc. ٹورسٹ دفتر

tournament (**tournaments**) *n* A **tournament** is a sports competition in which players who win a match continue to play further matches until just one person or team is left. ٹورنامنٹ (کھیل مقابلہ)

towards *prep* **Towards** means in the direction of something. طرف، جانب *He moved towards the door.*

tow away *v* If one vehicle **tows away** another, it removes it by pulling it along behind it. کھینچ کر ہٹا دینا *They threatened to tow away my car.*

towel (**towels**) *n* A **towel** is a piece of thick, soft cloth that you use to dry yourself with. تولیہ

tower (**towers**) *n* A **tower** is a tall narrow structure that is often part of a castle. مینار

town (**towns**) *n* A **town** is a place with many streets and buildings where people live and work. شہر

town centre (**town centres**) *n* The **town centre** is the main part of a town, where the shops are. مرکزِ شہر

town hall (**town halls**) *n* The **town hall** in a town is a large building owned and used by the town council, often as its headquarters. ٹاؤن ہال

town planning *n* **Town planning** is the planning and design of all the new buildings, roads, and parks in a place in order to make them attractive and convenient for the people who live there. شہر کی منصوبہ بندی

toxic *adj* A **toxic** substance is poisonous. زہریلا

toy (**toys**) *n* A **toy** is an object that children play with, for example, a doll or a model car. کھلونا

trace (**traces**) *n* A **trace** of something is a very small amount of it. آثار

tracing paper *n* **Tracing paper** is transparent paper which you put over a picture so that you can draw over its lines in order to produce a copy of it. ٹریسنگ پیپر

t

track (**tracks**) *n* A **track** is a narrow road or path. راستہ، پٹری
track down *v* If you **track down** someone or something, you find them after a long and difficult search. سراغ لگانا، سراغ پانا *It took two years to track him down.*
tracksuit (**tracksuits**) *n* A **tracksuit** is a loose, warm suit consisting of trousers and a top, worn mainly when exercising. ٹریک سوٹ (ورزشی سوٹ)
tractor (**tractors**) *n* A **tractor** is a farm vehicle that is used for pulling farm machinery. ٹریکٹر
trade (**trades**) *n* **Trade** is the activity of buying, selling, or exchanging goods or services between people, firms, or countries. تجارت
trademark (**trademarks**) *n* A **trademark** is a name or symbol that a company uses on its products and that cannot legally be used by another company. ٹریڈمارک
trade union (**trade unions**) *n* A **trade union** is an organization formed by workers in order to represent their rights and interests to their employers. ٹریڈیونین
trade unionist (**trade unionists**) *n* A **trade unionist** is an active member of a trade union. ٹریڈیونین والا
tradition (**traditions**) *n* A **tradition** is a custom or belief that has existed for a long time. روایت
traditional *adj* **Traditional** customs, beliefs, or methods are ones that have existed for a long time without changing. روایتی
traffic *n* **Traffic** refers to all the vehicles that are moving along the roads in an area. ٹریفک (نقل و حمل)
traffic jam (**traffic jams**) *n* A **traffic jam** is a long line of vehicles that cannot move because there is too much traffic, or because the road is blocked. ٹریفک جام
traffic lights *npl* **Traffic lights** are the coloured lights at road junctions which control the flow of traffic. ٹریفک کی بتی
traffic warden (**traffic wardens**) *n* A **traffic warden** is a person whose job is to make sure that cars are not parked illegally. ٹریفک وارڈن (کارپارک نگراں)
tragedy (**tragedies**) *n* A **tragedy** is an extremely sad event or situation. المیہ
tragic *adj* Something that is **tragic** is extremely sad, usually because it involves suffering. المناک
trailer (**trailers**) *n* A **trailer** is a vehicle without an engine which is pulled by a car or lorry. گاڑی سے منسلک باربرداری کا چھکڑا
train (**trains, training, trained**) *n* A **train** is a long vehicle that is pulled by an engine along a railway line. ٹرین، ریل گاڑی
▷ *vt* If you **train** to do something, you learn the skills that you need in order to do it. تربیت دینا
trained *adj* A person who is **trained** in a particular kind of work has learned the skills that you need in order to do it. تربیت یافتہ
trainee (**trainees**) *n* A **trainee** is a junior employee who is being taught how to do a job. زیر تربیت
trainer (**trainers**) *n* A **trainer** is someone who teaches you the skills you need to be able to do something. تربیت کار، تربیت دہندہ
trainers *npl* **Trainers** are shoes that people wear, especially for running and other sports. دوڑنے کیلئے بنے جوتے
training *n* **Training** is the process of learning the skills that you need for a particular job or activity. تربیت
training course (**training courses**) *n* A **training course** is a series of lessons or lectures teaching the skills that you need for a particular job or activity. تربیتی نصاب
tram (**trams**) *n* A **tram** is a public transport vehicle, usually powered by electricity, which travels along rails laid in the surface of a street. سڑک پر بچھی پٹری پر بجلی سے چلنے والی بس
tramp (**tramps**) *n* A **tramp** is a person with no home or job who travels around

and gets money by doing occasional work or by begging. بے گھر در شخص سفر میں مانگ کر یا کام کر کے گزارہ کرنے والا ▷ *n* A **tramp** is a difficult and long walk. دشوار اور طویل سفر

trampoline (trampolines) *n* A **trampoline** is a piece of equipment on which you jump up and down as a sport. It consists of a large piece of strong cloth held by springs in a frame. کودنے کے لیے اسپرنگ سے بندھا مضبوط کپڑا

tranquillizer (tranquillizers) *n* A **tranquillizer** is a drug that is used to make people or animals become sleepy or unconscious. بیہوش کرنے والا، پر سکون کرنے والا

transaction (transactions) *n* A **transaction** is a business deal. (*formal*) سودا، لین دین

transcript (transcripts) *n* A **transcript** of something that is spoken is a written copy of it. مکالموں کی تحریر

transfer (transfers) *n* The **transfer** of something or someone is the act of transferring them. تبادلہ

transform (transforms, transforming, transformed) *vt* To **transform** someone or something means to change them completely. کایا پلٹنا

transfusion (transfusions) *n* A blood **transfusion** is a process in which blood is injected into the body of a person who is badly injured or ill. اِنتقالِ خون

transistor (transistors) *n* A **transistor** is a small electronic component in something such as a television or radio, which is used to amplify or control electronic signals. ٹرانسسٹر (برقی پرزہ)

transit *n* **Transit** is the carrying of goods or people by vehicle from one place to another. نقل و حمل

transition (transitions) *n* **Transition** is the process in which something changes from one state to another. حالت کی تبدیلی

translate (translates, translating, translated) *vt* If something that someone has said or written **is translated**, it is said or written again in a different language. ترجمہ کرنا

translation (translations) *n* A **translation** is a piece of writing or speech that has been translated from a different language. ترجمہ

translator (translators) *n* A **translator** is a person whose job is translating writing or speech from one language to another. ترجمان

transparent *adj* If an object or substance is **transparent**, you can see through it. شفاف

transplant (transplants) *n* A **transplant** is a surgical operation in which a part of a person's body is replaced because it is diseased. اعضاء کی تبدیلی

transport (transports, transporting, transported) *n* **Transport** refers to any type of vehicle that you can travel in. سواری ▷ *vt* When goods or people **are transported** from one place to another, they are moved there. نقل و حمل کا انتظام کرنا

transvestite (transvestites) *n* A **transvestite** is a person, usually a man, who enjoys wearing clothes normally worn by people of the opposite sex. زنانہ کپڑے پہن کر خوش ہونے والا مرد

trap (traps) *n* A **trap** is a device which is placed somewhere or a hole which is dug somewhere in order to catch animals or birds. جال

traumatic *adj* A **traumatic** experience is very shocking or upsetting, and may cause psychological damage. صدماتی

travel (travels, travelling, travelled) *n* **Travel** is the act of travelling. سفر ▷ *vi* If you **travel**, you go from one place to another, often to a place that is far away. سفر کرنا

travel agency (travel agencies) *n* A **travel agency** is a business which makes arrangements for people's holidays and journeys. (ٹریول ایجنسی) سفر کا انتظام کرنے والی کمپنی

travel agent (travel agents) *n* A **travel**

agent is a person who arranges people's holidays and journeys. ٹریول ایجنٹ کی دکان

travel insurance *n* **Travel insurance** is an arrangement in which you pay money to a company, and they pay money to you if your property is stolen or damaged, or if you get a serious illness. سفری بیمہ

traveller (**travellers**) *n* A **traveller** is a person who is making a journey or who travels a lot. مسافر

traveller's cheque (**traveller's cheques**) *n* **Traveller's cheques** are special cheques that you can exchange for local currency when you are abroad. مسافر چیک

travelling *n* **Travelling** is the process of going from one place to another, often one that is far away. سفر

tray (**trays**) *n* A **tray** is a flat piece of wood, plastic, or metal that has raised edges and that is used for carrying food or drinks. ٹرے، طشت

treacle *n* **Treacle** is a thick, sweet, sticky liquid that is obtained when sugar is processed. It is used in making cakes and puddings. شیرہ، راب

tread (**treads, treading, trod, trodden**) *vi* If you **tread on** something, you put your foot on it when you are walking or standing. قدم رکھنا

treasure *n* In children's stories, **treasure** is a collection of valuable old objects, such as gold coins and jewels. literary خزانہ

treasurer (**treasurers**) *n* The **treasurer** of a society or organization is the person in charge of its finances. خازن

treat (**treats, treating, treated**) *n* If you give someone a **treat**, you buy or arrange something special for them which they will enjoy. سلوک ▷ *vt* If you **treat** someone or something in a particular way, you behave towards them in that way. سلوک کرنا

treatment (**treatments**) *n* **Treatment** is medical attention given to a sick or injured person or animal. طبی علاج

treaty (**treaties**) *n* A **treaty** is a written agreement between countries. اقرارنامہ، معاہدہ

treble (**trebles, trebling, trebled**) *v* If something **trebles**, or if you **treble** it, it becomes three times greater in number or amount. تین گنا کرنا، تگنا کرنا

tree (**trees**) *n* A **tree** is a tall plant with a hard trunk, branches, and leaves. درخت

trek (**treks, trekking, trekked**) *n* A **trek** is a long and often difficult journey. مشکل پیدل سفر ▷ *vi* If you **trek** somewhere, you go on a journey across difficult country, usually on foot. بیل گاڑی یا پیدل سفر کرنا

tremble (**trembles, trembling, trembled**) *vi* If you **tremble**, you shake slightly, usually because you are frightened or cold. کپکپانا

tremendous *adj* You use **tremendous** to emphasize how strong a feeling or quality is, or how large an amount is. مہیب

trench (**trenches**) *n* A **trench** is a long narrow channel dug in the ground. خندق

trend (**trends**) *n* A **trend** is a change towards something different. رخ، رجحان

trendy (**trendier, trendiest**) *adj* If you say that something or someone is **trendy**, you mean that they are very fashionable and modern. (*informal*) روایت پرست، روایت پسند

trial (**trials**) *n* A **trial** is a formal meeting in a law court, at which a judge and jury listen to evidence and decide whether a person is guilty of a crime. آزمائش

trial period (**trial periods**) *n* If you are on a **trial period** for a job, you do the job for a short period of time to see if you are suitable for it. آزمائشی مدت، مدت آزمائش

triangle (**triangles**) *n* A **triangle** is a shape with three straight sides. مثلث ▷ *n* A **triangle** is an instrument made of metal in the shape of a triangle that you hit with a stick to make music. (ٹرینگل (ساز

tribe (**tribes**) *n* **Tribe** is sometimes used to refer to a group of people of the same race, language, and customs, especially in a developing country. قبیلہ

tribunal (**tribunals**) *n* A **tribunal** is a special court or committee that is appointed to deal with particular problems. خصوصی عدالت

trick (**tricks, tricking, tricked**) *n* A **trick** is an action that is intended to deceive someone. فریب، دھوکہ، چال ▷ *vt* If someone **tricks** you, they deceive you, often in order to make you do something. دھوکہ کرنا

tricky (**trickier, trickiest**) *adj* A **tricky** task or problem is difficult to deal with. پرپیچ، پر فریب

tricycle (**tricycles**) *n* A **tricycle** is a cycle with three wheels, two at the back and one at the front. Tricycles are usually ridden by children. تین پہیوں والی سائیکل

trifle (**trifles**) *n* **Trifles** are things that are not considered important. ادنیٰ بات

trim (**trims, trimming, trimmed**) *vt* If you **trim** something, for example, someone's hair, you cut off small amounts of it in order to make it look neater and tidier. تراشنا، کاٹ چھانٹ کرنا

Trinidad and Tobago *n* **Trinidad and Tobago** is an independent republic in the Caribbean. (ٹرنیداد اور ٹوبیگو (جمہوریہ

trip (**trips, tripping, tripped**) *n* A **trip** is a journey that you make to a place and back again. سفر (آنے جانے کا) ▷ *vi* If you **trip** when you are walking, you knock your foot against something and fall or nearly fall. سفر کرنا

triple *adj* **Triple** means consisting of three things or parts. تگنا

triplets *npl* **Triplets** are three children born at the same time to the same mother. جڑواں تین

triumph (**triumphs, triumphing, triumphed**) *n* A **triumph** is a great success or achievement. فتح ▷ *vi* If you triumph, you win a victory or succeed in overcoming something. جیتنا

trivial *adj* If you describe something as **trivial**, you think that it is unimportant and not serious. معمولی، غیر اہم

trolley (**trolleys**) *n* A **trolley** is a small cart on wheels that you use to carry things such as shopping or luggage. ٹرالی

trombone (**trombones**) *n* A **trombone** is a long brass musical instrument which you play by blowing into it and sliding part of it backwards and forwards. بڑا بگل

troops *npl* **Troops** are soldiers. فوجی

trophy (**trophies**) *n* A **trophy** is a prize such as a cup, given to the winner of a competition. ٹرافی

tropical *adj* **Tropical** means belonging to or typical of the tropics. سرطانی

trot (**trots, trotting, trotted**) *vi* If you **trot** somewhere, you move fairly fast at a speed between walking and running, taking small quick steps. تیز چلنا

trouble (**troubles**) *n* You can refer to problems or difficulties as **trouble**. زحمت، تکلیف

troublemaker (**troublemakers**) *n* A **troublemaker** is someone who causes trouble. تکلیف دہ

trough (**troughs**) *n* A **trough** is a long container from which farm animals drink or eat. ناند لگن

trousers *npl* **Trousers** are a piece of clothing that you wear over your body from the waist downwards, and that cover each leg separately. You can also say a pair of trousers. پتلون

trout (**trout, trouts**) *n* A **trout** is a kind of fish that lives in rivers and streams. تازہ پانی کی مچھلی

trowel (**trowels**) *n* A **trowel** is a small garden tool which you use for digging small holes or removing weeds. کرنی، رانبی

truce (**truces**) *n* A **truce** is an agreement between two people or groups to stop fighting or quarrelling for a short time. جنگ بندی کا معاہدہ

truck (**trucks**) *n* A **truck** is a large vehicle that is used to transport goods by road. US ٹرک

t

truck driver (**truck drivers**) *n* A **truck driver** is someone who drives a truck as their job. US ٹرک ڈرائیور

true (**truer, truest**) *adj* If a story is **true**, it really happened. درست، صحیح، سچ ▷ *adj* If something is **true**, it is right or correct. سچ

truly *adv* **Truly** means completely and genuinely. سچائی سے

trumpet (**trumpets**) *n* A **trumpet** is a brass wind instrument. بگل

trunk (**trunks**) *n* A **trunk** is the thick stem of a tree. The branches and roots grow from the **trunk**. تنا ▷ *n* An elephant's **trunk** is its long nose. Elephants use their **trunks** to suck up water and to lift things. سونڈ ▷ *n* A **trunk** is a large, strong box that you use to keep things in. ٹرنک، صندوق

trunks *npl* **Trunks** are shorts that a man wears when he goes swimming. تیراکی زیر جامہ (مردانہ)

trust (**trusts, trusting, trusted**) *n* Your **trust** in someone is your belief that they are honest and sincere and will not deliberately do anything to harm you. اعتماد، بھروسہ ▷ *vt* If you **trust** someone, you believe that they are honest and sincere and will not deliberately do anything to harm you. بھروسہ کرنا

trusting *adj* A **trusting** person believes that people are honest and sincere and do not intend to harm him or her. لوگوں پر بھروسہ کرنے والا

truth *n* The **truth** about something is all the facts about it, rather than things that are imagined or invented. سچ

truthful *adj* If a person or their comments are truthful, they are honest and do not tell any lies. صادق، سچا

try (**tries, trying, tried**) *n* If you have a **try** at doing something, you make an effort to do it. کوشش ▷ *vi* If you **try** to do something, you do it as well as you can. کوشش کرنا ▷ *vt* If you **try** something, you test it to see what it is like or how it works. آزمانا

try on *v* If you **try on** a piece of clothing, you put it on to see if it fits you or if it looks nice. پہن کر دیکھنا، موزوں بنانا *Try on clothing and shoes to make sure they fit.*

try out *v* If you **try** something **out**, you test it in order to find out how useful or effective it is. آزمانا *The company hopes to try out the system in September.*

T-shirt T-shirts *n* A **T-shirt** is a cotton shirt with short sleeves and no collar or buttons. ٹی ۔ شرٹ (آدھی آستین کی قمیض)

tsunami (**tsunamis**) *n* A **tsunami** is a very large wave, often caused by an earthquake, that flows onto the land and destroys things. سونامی (سمندر میں زلزلہ)

tube (**tubes**) *n* A **tube** is a long, round, hollow piece of metal, rubber, or plastic. نلی ▷ *n* A **tube** is a soft metal or plastic container that you press to make what is in it come out. ٹیوب

tuberculosis *n* **Tuberculosis**, or **TB**, is a serious infectious disease that affects the lungs. تپ دق

Tuesday (**Tuesdays**) *n* **Tuesday** is the day after Monday and before Wednesday. منگل

tug-of-war (**tugs-of-war**) *n* A **tug-of-war** is a sports event in which two teams test their strength by pulling against each other on opposite ends of a rope. رسہ کشی

tuition *n* If you are given **tuition** in a particular subject, you are taught about that subject, especially on your own or in a small group. ٹیوشن فیس

tuition fees *npl* **Tuition fees** are the money that you pay to be taught, especially in a college or university. ٹیوشن فیس

tulip (**tulips**) *n* **Tulips** are garden flowers that grow in the spring. لالہ

tumble dryer (**tumble dryers**) *n* A **tumble dryer** is an electric machine which dries washing by turning it over and over and blowing warm air onto it. الٹ پلٹ کرکے سکھانے کی مشین

tummy (**tummies**) *n* Your **tummy** is your stomach. پیٹ، شکم

tumour (**tumours**) *n* A **tumour** is a mass of diseased or abnormal cells that has grown in someone's body. رسولی

tuna (**tuna, tunas**) *n* A **tuna** or a **tuna fish** is a large fish that lives in warm seas. ٹیونا مچھلی

tune (**tunes** *n* A **tune** is a series of musical notes that is pleasant to listen to. دھن

Tunisia *n* **Tunisia** is a republic in North Africa, on the Mediterranean. ٹیونیشیا

Tunisian (**Tunisians**) *adj* **Tunisian** means belonging to or relating to Tunisia, or to its people or culture. ٹیونیشیائی ▷ *n* A **Tunisian** is a person who comes from Tunisia. ٹیونیشیائی

tunnel (**tunnels**) *n* A **tunnel** is a long passage which has been made under the ground, usually through a hill or under the sea. سرنگ

turbulence *n* **Turbulence** is a state of confusion and disorganized change. سرکشی، مفسدہ پردازی

Turk (**Turks**) *n* A **Turk** is a person who comes from Turkey. ترک

Turkey *n* **Turkey** is a Eurasian republic in western Asia and south-eastern Europe. ترکی

turkey (**turkeys**) *n* A **turkey** is a large bird that is kept on a farm for its meat. ترکی مرغ، ترکی

Turkish *adj* **Turkish** means belonging or relating to Turkey, or to its people, language, or culture. ترکی ▷ *n* **Turkish** is the main language spoken in Turkey. ترکی (زبان))

turn (**turns, turning, turned**) *n* A **turn** is a change of direction. گھماؤ ▷ *v* When you **turn**, you move in a different direction. واپس مڑنا ▷ *v* When something **turns**, it moves around in a circle. گھومنا ▷ *vi* If one thing **turns** into another thing, it becomes that thing. تبدیل ہونا

turn around *v* To **turn around** means to move in a different direction or to move into a different position. مختلف سمت یا حالت پر گھوم جانا *She turned around to see a woman standing there. I felt a tapping on my shoulder and I turned around.*

turn back *v* If you **turn back**, or if someone **turns** you **back** when you are going somewhere, you change direction and go towards where you started from. پیٹھ پھیر لینا *Police attempted to turn back protesters.*

turn down *v* If you **turn down** a person or their request or offer, you refuse their request or offer. مسترد کرنا *After careful consideration I turned the invitation down.*

turning (**turnings**) *n* If you take a particular **turning**, you go along a road which leads away from the side of another road. موڑ

turnip (**turnips**) *n* A **turnip** is a round vegetable with a green and white skin. شلجم

turn off *v* If you **turn off** the road or path you are going along, you start going along a different road or path which leads away from it. پہلے راستے سے ہٹ کر دوسرا راستہ پکڑنا *Turn off at the bridge.*

turn on *v* When you **turn on** a piece of equipment or a supply of something, you cause heat, sound, or water to be produced by adjusting the controls. چالو کرنا، شروع کرنا *She asked them why they hadn't turned the lights on.*

turn out *v* If something **turns out** a particular way, it happens in that way or has the result or degree of success indicated. (پھر جانا، بدل جانا (مثبت طور پر *I was positive things were going to turn out fine.*

turnover *n* The **turnover** of a company is the value of goods or services sold during a particular period of time. ٹرن اوور

turn up *v* If you say that someone or something **turns up**, you mean that they arrive, often unexpectedly, or after you have been waiting a long time. آموجود ہونا *We waited for the bus, but it never turned up.*

turquoise *adj* **Turquoise** is used to

describe things that are of a light greenish-blue colour. (ہرے نیلے رنگ کی) چیزیں

turtle (**turtles**) *n* A **turtle** is a large reptile with a thick shell which lives in the sea. بحری کچھوا

tutor (**tutors**) *n* A **tutor** is a teacher at a British university or college. خانگی معلم، اتالیق

tutorial (**tutorials**) *n* In a British university or college, a **tutorial** is a regular meeting between a tutor and one or several students for discussion of a subject that is being studied. تدریس

tuxedo (**tuxedos**) *n* A **tuxedo** is a black or white jacket worn by men for formal social events. ڈنر جیکیٹ

TV (**TVs**) *n* A **TV** is a piece of electrical equipment with a glass screen on which you can watch programmes with pictures and sounds. **TV** is an abbreviation for 'television'. ٹیلی ویژن

tweezers *npl* **Tweezers** are a small tool that you use for tasks such as picking up small objects or pulling out hairs. Tweezers consist of two strips of metal or plastic joined together at one end. موچنا، بال کھینچنے کے لیے

twelfth *adj* The **twelfth** item in a series is the one that you count as number twelve. بارہواں

twelve *num* **Twelve** is the number 12. بارہ

twentieth *adj* The **twentieth** item in a series is the one that you count as number twenty. بیسواں

twenty *num* **Twenty** is the number 20. بیس

twice *adv* If something happens **twice**, it happens two times. دو بار

twin (**twins**) *n* If two people are **twins**, they have the same mother and were born on the same day. جڑواں

twin beds *npl* (**Twin beds**) are two single beds in one bedroom. جڑواں پلنگ

twinned *adj* When a place or organization in one country is **twinned** with a place or organization in another country, a special relationship is formally established between them. (جڑواں (ادارے، دو ممالک میں

twist (**twists, twisting, twisted**) *vt* If you **twist** something, you turn it to make a spiral shape, for example by turning the two ends of it in opposite directions. بٹنا، بل دینا

twit (**twits**) *n* If you call someone a **twit**, you are insulting them and saying that they are silly or stupid. (*informal*) ...کا طعنہ دینا

two *num* **Two** is the number 2. دو

type types, typing, typed *n* A **type** of something is the kind of thing that it is. قسم ▷ *v* If you **type** something, you write it with a machine, for example a computer. ٹائپ کرنا

typewriter (**typewriters**) *n* A **typewriter** is a machine with keys which are pressed in order to print letters, numbers, or other characters onto paper. ٹائپ کرنا

typhoid *n* **Typhoid** or **typhoid fever** is a serious infectious disease that produces fever and diarrhoea and can cause death. It is spread by dirty water or food. میعادی بخار

typical *adj* You use **typical** to describe someone or something that shows the most usual characteristics of a particular type of person or thing, and is therefore a good example of that type. مثالی، اشارتی

typist (**typists**) *n* A **typist** is someone who works in an office typing letters and other documents. ٹائپسٹ

tyre (**tyres**) *n* A **tyre** is a thick ring of rubber filled with air and fitted round the wheel of a vehicle. (ٹائر (ہوا بھری ٹیوب کے ساتھ

U

UFO (**UFOs**) *abbr* A **UFO** is an object seen in the sky or landing on Earth which cannot be identified and which is often believed to be from another planet. **UFO** is an abbreviation for 'unidentified flying object'. اڑن طشتری

Uganda *n* **Uganda** is a republic in East Africa. یوگانڈا

Ugandan (**Ugandans**) *adj* **Ugandan** means belonging or relating to Uganda or to its people or culture. یوگانڈیائی ▷ *n* A **Ugandan** is a Ugandan citizen, or a person of Ugandan origin. یوگانڈیائی

ugh! *excl* **Ugh!** is used in writing to represent the sound that people make if they think something is unpleasant, horrible, or disgusting. اف!

ugly (**uglier, ugliest**) *adj* If you say that someone or something is **ugly**, you mean that they are unattractive and unpleasant to look at. بدشکل، بھدا

UHT milk *n* **UHT milk** is milk which has been treated at a very high temperature so that it can be kept for a long time if the container is not opened. **UHT** is an abbreviation for 'ultra-heat-treated'. انتہائی درجہ حرارت پر ابالا ہوا دودھ

UK *n* The **UK** is Great Britain and Northern Ireland. **UK** is an abbreviation for 'United Kingdom'. یونائیٹڈ کنگڈم (برطانیہ)

Ukraine *n* **Ukraine** is a republic in south-east Europe, on the Black Sea and the Sea of Azov. یوکرین

Ukrainian (**Ukrainians**) *adj* **Ukrainian** means of or relating to Ukraine, its people, or their language. یوکرینیائی ▷ *n* A **Ukrainian** is a Ukrainian citizen, or a person of Ukrainian origin. یوکرینیائی ▷ *n* **Ukrainian** is the official language of Ukraine. It is an East Slavonic language closely related to Russian. یوکرینیائی

ulcer (**ulcers**) *n* An **ulcer** is a sore area on or inside a part of your body which is very painful and may bleed. پیٹ کا ناسور

Ulster *n* **Ulster** is a province and former kingdom of Northern Ireland. شمالی آئرلینڈ کی ایک سابقہ ریاست

ultimate *adj* You use **ultimate** to describe the final result or the original cause of a long series of events. حتمی

ultimately *adv* **Ultimately** means finally, after a long series of events. حتمی طور پر

ultimatum (**ultimatums, ultimata**) *n* An **ultimatum** is a warning that unless someone acts in a particular way within a particular time limit, action will be taken against them. انتباہ

ultrasound *n* **Ultrasound** refers to sound waves which travel at such a high frequency that they cannot be heard by humans. الٹراساؤنڈ (کی تیزترین لہریں)

umbrella (**umbrellas**) *n* An **umbrella** is an object which you use to protect yourself from the rain. It consists of a long stick with a folding frame covered in cloth. چھاتا

umpire (**umpires**) *n* An **umpire** is a person whose job is to make sure that a sports match or contest is played fairly and that the rules are not broken. حکم، امپائر

UN *abbr* The **UN** is an organization which most countries belong to. Its role is to encourage international peace, co-operation, and friendship. **UN** is an abbreviation for 'United Nations'. یونائیٹڈ نیشنز (اقوام متحدہ)

unable *adj* If you are **unable** to do something, it is impossible for you to do it. بے سکت

unacceptable *adj* If you describe something as **unacceptable**, you strongly disapprove of it or object to it and feel that it should not be allowed to happen or continue. ناقابلِ قبول

unanimous *adj* When a group of people or their opinion is **unanimous**, they all agree about something. اتفاقِ رائے سے

unattended *adj* When people or things are left **unattended**, they are not being watched or looked after. متروک

unavoidable *adj* If something bad is **unavoidable**, it cannot be avoided or prevented. ناقابلِ دفع

unbearable *adj* If you describe something as **unbearable**, you mean that it is so unpleasant, painful, or upsetting that you feel unable to accept it or deal with it. ناقابلِ برداشت

unbeatable *adj* If you describe something as **unbeatable**, you mean that it is the best thing of its kind. ناقابلِ شکست

unbelievable *adj* If you say that something is **unbelievable**, you are emphasizing that it is very extreme, impressive, or shocking. ناقابلِ یقین

unbreakable *adj* **Unbreakable** objects cannot be broken, usually because they are made of a very strong material. ناقابلِ شکستگی

uncanny *adj* If something is **uncanny**, it is strange and difficult to explain. غیر ارضی، پر اسرار

uncertain *adj* If you are **uncertain** about something, you do not know what to do. متزلزل

uncertainty (**uncertainties**) *n* **Uncertainty** is a state of doubt about the future or about what is the right thing to do. غیر یقینی حالت

unchanged *adj* Something that is **unchanged** has stayed the same during a period of time. مستقل

uncivilized *adj* If you describe someone's behaviour as **uncivilized**, you find it unacceptable, for example because it is very cruel or very rude. غیر مہذب

uncle (**uncles**) *n* Your **uncle** is the brother of your mother or father, or the husband of your aunt. چچا، ماموں

unclear *adj* If something is **unclear**, it is not known or not certain. غیر واضح

uncomfortable *adj* If you are **uncomfortable**, you are not physically relaxed, and feel slight pain or discomfort. بے آرام

unconditional *adj* Something that is **unconditional** is done or given to someone freely, without anything being required in return. بے شرط

unconscious *adj* Someone who is **unconscious** is in a state similar to sleep, as a result of a shock, accident, or injury. بے ہوش

uncontrollable *adj* If something such as an emotion is **uncontrollable**, you can do nothing to prevent it or control it. بے قابو

unconventional *adj* If someone is **unconventional**, they do not behave in the same way as most other people in their society. غیر روایتی

undecided *adj* If you are **undecided** about something, you have not yet made a decision about it. بے فیصلہ

undeniable *adj* If something is **undeniable**, it is definitely true or definitely exists. ناقابلِ انکار

under *prep* If one thing is **under** another thing, it is lower down than it, or the second thing covers the first thing. تحت، نیچے *There was a dog under the table.* ❑ *He was standing under a large painting.*

underage *adj* Someone who is **underage** is not legally old enough to do something. کم عمر

underestimate (**underestimates, underestimating, underestimated**) *vt*

If you **underestimate** something, you do not realize how large it is or will be. کم قیمت سمجھنا

undergo (**undergoes, undergoing, underwent, undergone**) *vt* If you **undergo** something necessary or unpleasant, it happens to you. سے گزرنا

undergraduate (**undergraduates**) *n* An **undergraduate** is a student at a university or college who is studying for his or her first degree. نچلا طالب علم

underground *adv* Something that is **underground** is below the surface of the ground. زیرزمین ▷ *n* The **underground** in a city is the railway system in which electric trains travel below the ground in tunnels. زیرزمین (ریلوے)

underground station (**underground stations**) *n* An **underground station** is a station of an underground railway system. زیرزمین اسٹیشن

underline (**underlines, underlining, underlined**) *vt* If a person or event **underlines** something, they draw attention to it and emphasize its importance. توجہ دلانا

underneath *adv* If one thing is **underneath** another thing, the second thing covers the first thing. نیچے، کے نیچے ▷ *prep* If one thing is **underneath** another thing, the second thing covers the first thing. نیچے *The ring was underneath the sofa.*

underpaid *adj* People who are **underpaid** are not paid enough money for the job that they do. کم ادائگی پانے والے

underpants *npl* **Underpants** are a piece of underwear with two holes for your legs and elastic around the waist. **Underpants** refers only to men's underwear. زیر جامے

underpass (**underpasses**) *n* An **underpass** is a road or path that goes underneath a railway or another road. ریلوے کے نیچے سے گزرنے والا رستہ

underskirt (**underskirts**) *n* An **underskirt** is any skirt like garment worn under a skirt. پانچہ والا انڈرویر

understand (**understands, understanding, understood**) *vt* If you **understand** someone, or if you **understand** what they are saying, you know what they mean. سمجھنا

understandable *adj* If you describe someone's behaviour or feelings as **understandable**, you mean that they have reacted to a situation in a natural way or in the way you would expect. سمجھے لائق

understanding *adj* If you are **understanding** towards someone, you are kind and forgiving. سمجھ، فہم

undertaker (**undertakers**) *n* An **undertaker** is a person whose job is to deal with the bodies of people who have died and to arrange funerals. تجہیز و تکفین کرنے والا

underwater *adv* Something that exists or happens **underwater** exists or happens below the surface of the sea, a river, or a lake. زیرآب

underwear *n* **Underwear** is clothing which you wear next to your skin under your other clothes, such as a bra, a vest, and underpants. انڈرویر

undisputed *adj* If you describe something as **undisputed**, you mean that everyone accepts that it exists or is true. بے اختلاف، متفقہ

undo (**undoes, undoing, undid, undone**) *vt* If you **undo** something, you unfasten, loosen, or untie it. کھولنا، کئے ہوئے کو الٹنا

undoubtedly *adv* **Undoubtedly** means certainly, definitely or unquestionably. بلا شک

undress (**undresses, undressing, undressed**) *v* When you **undress**, you take off your clothes. If you **undress** someone, you take off their clothes. کپڑے اتارنا

U

unemployed *adj* Someone who is **unemployed** does not have a job. بے روزگار

unemployment *n* **Unemployment** is the fact that people who want jobs cannot get them. بیروزگاری

unexpected *adj* Something that is **unexpected** surprises you because you did not think it was likely to happen. غیر متوقع

unexpectedly *adv* **Unexpectedly** means surprisingly. غیر متوقع طور پر

unfair *adj* Something that is **unfair** is not right or not just. نامناسب

unfaithful *adj* If someone is **unfaithful** to their lover or to the person they are married to, they have a sexual relationship with someone else. بے وفا

unfamiliar *adj* If something is **unfamiliar** to you, or if you are **unfamiliar** with it, you know very little about it and have not seen or experienced it before. غیر معروف

unfashionable *adj* If something is **unfashionable**, it is not approved of or done by most people. قدیم، غیر رولتی

unfavourable *adj* **Unfavourable** conditions or circumstances cause problems and reduce the chance of success. ناسازگار

unfit *adj* If you are **unfit**, your body is not in good condition because you have not been taking regular exercise. غیر موزوں

unforgettable *adj* If something is **unforgettable**, it is so impressive that you are likely to remember it for a long time. ناقابل فراموش

unfortunately *adv* You can use **unfortunately** to express regret about what you are saying. بد قسمتی سے

unfriendly *adj* If you describe someone as **unfriendly**, you mean that they behave in an unkind or hostile way. غیر دوستانہ

ungrateful *adj* If you describe someone as **ungrateful**, you are criticizing them for not showing thanks or for being unkind to someone who has helped them or done them a favour. ناشکرا

unhappy (**unhappier, unhappiest**) *adj* If you are **unhappy**, you are sad and depressed. ناخوش

unhealthy (**unhealthier, unhealthiest**) *adj* Something that is **unhealthy** is likely to cause illness or poor health. غیر صحت مند

unhelpful *adj* If you say that someone or something is **unhelpful**, you mean that they do not help you or improve a situation, and may even make things worse. نامددگار

uni (**unis**) *n* A **uni** is an institution where students study for degrees and where academic research is done. **Uni** is short for 'university'. (*informal*) یونیورسٹی، تعلیم گاہ

unidentified *adj* If you describe someone or something as **unidentified**, you mean that nobody knows who or what they are. بے شناخت

uniform (**uniforms**) *n* A **uniform** is a special set of clothes which some people wear to work in, and which some children wear at school. وردی

unimportant *adj* If you describe something or someone as **unimportant**, you mean that they do not have much effect or value, and are therefore not worth considering. غیر اہم

uninhabited *adj* An **uninhabited** place is one where nobody lives. ویران

unintentional *adj* Something that is **unintentional** is not done deliberately, but happens by accident. بے ارادہ

union (**unions**) *n* A **union** is an organization that has been formed by workers in order to represent their rights and interests to their employers, for example in order to improve working conditions or wages. یونین

unique *adj* Something that is **unique** is the only one of its kind. یکتہ، انوکھی

unit (**units**) *n* If you consider something as a **unit**, you consider it as a single complete thing. اکائی

unite (**unites, uniting, united**) *v* If a group of people or things **unite**, they join together and act as a group. متحد کرنا

United Arab Emirates *npl* The **United Arab Emirates** are a group of seven emirates in south-west Asia, on the Persian Gulf, consisting of Abu Dhabi, Dubai, Sharjah, Ajman, Umm al Qaiwain, Ras el Khaimah, and Fujairah. متحدہ عرب امیرات

United Kingdom *n* The **United Kingdom** is the official name for the country consisting of Great Britain and Northern Ireland. برطانیہ

United Nations *n* The **United Nations** is a worldwide organization which most countries belong to. Its role is to encourage international peace, cooperation, and friendship. دولت مشترکہ

United States *n* **The United States of America** is the official name for the country in North America that consists of fifty states and the District of Columbia. It is bordered by Canada in the north and Mexico in the south. The form **United States** is also used. امریکہ

universe *n* The **universe** is the whole of space, and all the stars, planets, and other forms of matter and energy in it. کائنات، آفاق

university (**universities**) *n* A **university** is an institution where students study for degrees and where academic research is done. یونیورسٹی

unknown *adj* If something is **unknown** to you, you have no knowledge of it. نا معلوم

unleaded *n* Unleaded fuels contain a reduced amount of lead in order to reduce the pollution caused when they are burned. You can refer to such fuels as **unleaded**. سیسہ سے پاک یا کم سے کم

unleaded petrol *n* **Unleaded petrol** contains a smaller amount of lead than most fuels so that it produces fewer harmful substances when it is burned. بے سیسہ پیٹرول

unless *conj* **Unless** means if the thing you are talking about does not happen. یہاں تک کہ *He says he won't go to the party, unless I go too.*

unlike *prep* If one thing is **unlike** another thing, the two things are different. بر خلاف *You're so unlike your father!*

unlikely (**unlikelier, unlikeliest**) *adj* If you say that something is **unlikely** to happen or **unlikely** to be true, you believe that it will not happen or that it is not true, although you are not completely sure. نا آمادہ

unlisted *adj* If a person or their telephone number is **unlisted**, the number is not listed in the telephone book, and the telephone company will refuse to give it to people who ask for it. نا فہرست زد، غیر مندرج

unload (**unloads, unloading, unloaded**) *vt* If you **unload** goods from a vehicle, you remove the goods from the vehicle. بوجھ اتارنا

unlock (**unlocks, unlocking, unlocked**) *vt* If you **unlock** something such as a door, a room, or a container, you open it using a key. کھولنا

unlucky (**unluckier, unluckiest**) *adj* If you are **unlucky**, you have bad luck. بدنصیب

unmarried *adj* Someone who is **unmarried** is not married. غیر شادی شدہ

unnecessary *adj* If you describe something as **unnecessary**, you mean that it is not needed or does not have to be done. غیر ضروری

unofficial *adj* An **unofficial** action is not authorized, approved, or organized by a person in authority. غیر سرکاری

unpack (**unpacks, unpacking, unpacked**) *v* When you **unpack** a suitcase, box, or bag, you take the things out of it. بیگ خالی کرنا

unpaid *adj* If you do **unpaid** work, you do a job without receiving any money for it. بے معاوضہ

unpleasant *adj* If something is

unpleasant, it gives you bad feelings, for example by making you feel upset or uncomfortable. ناپسندیدہ

unplug (**unplugs, unplugging, unplugged**) *vt* If you **unplug** a piece of electrical equipment, you take its plug out of the socket. پلگ نکالنا

unpopular *adj* If something or someone is **unpopular**, most people do not like them. غیر مشہور

unprecedented *adj* If something is **unprecedented**, it has never happened before. پہلے نہ ہوا ہو

unpredictable *adj* If someone or something is **unpredictable**, you cannot tell what they are going to do or how they are going to behave. ناقابل پیش گوئی

unreal *adj* If you say that a situation is **unreal**, you mean that it is so strange that you find it difficult to believe it is happening. غیر اصل

unrealistic *adj* If you say that someone is being **unrealistic**, you mean that they do not recognize the truth about a situation, especially about the difficulties involved. سچائی کو تسلیم نہ کرنے والا

unreasonable *adj* If you say that someone is being **unreasonable**, you mean that they are behaving in a way that is not fair or sensible. غیر منطقی

unreliable *adj* If you describe a person, machine, or method as **unreliable**, you mean that you cannot trust them to do or provide what you want. بے بھروسہ

unroll (**unrolls, unrolling, unrolled**) *v* If you **unroll** something such as a sheet of paper or cloth, it opens up and becomes flat when it was previously rolled in a cylindrical shape. کھولنا

unsatisfactory *adj* If you describe something as **unsatisfactory**, you mean that it is not as good as it should be, and cannot be considered acceptable. غیر تسلی بخش

unscrew (**unscrews, unscrewing, unscrewed**) *v* If you **unscrew** something such as a lid, or if it **unscrews**, you keep turning it until you can remove it. پیچ کھولنا

unshaven *adj* If a man is **unshaven**, he has not shaved recently and there are short hairs on his face or chin. بے شیو

unskilled *adj* People who are **unskilled** do not have any special training for a job. غیر کاریگر

unstable *adj* You can describe something as **unstable** if it is likely to change suddenly, especially if this creates difficulty. غیر مستقل

unsteady *adj* If you are **unsteady**, you have difficulty doing something because you cannot completely control your body. کمزور

unsuccessful *adj* Something that is **unsuccessful** does not achieve what it was intended to achieve. ناکامیاب

unsuitable *adj* Someone or something that is **unsuitable** for a particular purpose or situation does not have the right qualities for it. غیر موزوں

unsure *adj* If you are **unsure** of yourself, you don't have much confidence. غیر مطمئن

untidy *adj* Something that is **untidy** is messy, and not neatly arranged. بے ترتیب

untie (**unties, untying, untied**) *vt* If you **untie** something that is tied to another thing, or if you **untie** two things that are tied together, you remove the string or rope that holds them. کھولنا, گرہ کھولنا

until *conj* **Until** a particular time means during the period before that time. ہونے تک *I waited until it got dark.* ▷ *prep* If something happens **until** a time, it happens before that time and then stops at that time. تک *Wait here until I come back.*

unusual *adj* If something is **unusual**, it does not happen very often or you do not see it or hear it very often. غیر عادی

unwell *adj* If you are **unwell**, you are ill. غیر صحت مند

unwind (**unwinds, unwinding,**

unwound) *vi* When you **unwind** after working hard, you relax. آرام کرنا

unwise *adj* Something that is **unwise** is foolish. بے عقل

unwrap (**unwraps, unwrapping, unwrapped**) *vt* When you **unwrap** something, you take off the paper or covering that is around it. پیکنگ کھولنا

unzip (**unzips, unzipping, unzipped**) *vt* To **unzip** an item of clothing or a bag means to unfasten its zip. زپ (چین) کھولنا

up *adv* When something moves **up**, it moves from a lower place to a higher place. اوپر

upbringing *n* Your **upbringing** is the way your parents treat you and0 the things that they teach you when you are growing up. پرورش

update (**updates, updating, updated**) *vt* If you **update** something, you make it more modern, usually by adding newer parts to it. جدید کرنا

uphill *adv* If something or someone is **uphill** or is moving **uphill**, they are near the top of a hill or are going up a slope. چوٹی کی طرف، پر

upon *prep* **Upon** means the same as **on**. پر، کے اوپر

upper *adj* You use **upper** to describe something that is above something else. اوپر والا

upright *adv* If you are sitting or standing **upright**, you have your back straight and are not bending or lying down. سیدھا، کمر سیدھی

upset (**upsets, upsetting, upset**) *adj* If you are **upset**, you are unhappy or disappointed because something unpleasant has happened. پراگندہ ⊳ *vt* If something **upsets** you, it makes you feel worried or unhappy. پراگندہ کرنا، ہونا

upside down *adv* If you hang **upside down**, your head is below your feet. الٹا ⊳ *adj* If something is **upside down**, the part that is usually at the bottom is at the top. الٹا

upstairs *adv* If you go **upstairs** in a building, you go up a staircase towards a higher floor. سیڑھیوں پر

uptight *adj* If someone is **uptight**, they are very tense, because they are worried or annoyed about something. (*informal*) تناؤ میں

up-to-date *adj* If something is **up-to-date**, it is the newest thing of its kind. جدید ترین

upwards *adv* If someone moves or looks **upwards**, they move or look up towards a higher place. اوپر کی طرف

uranium *n* **Uranium** is a radioactive metal that is used to produce nuclear energy and weapons. یورینیم (ایک تابکار دھات)

urgency ***Urgency*** *is the quality of being urgent or pressing.* mean that it is good nough. ہنگامی حالت

urgent *adj* If something is **urgent**, it needs to be dealt with as soon as possible. فوری توجہ کی حامل

urine *n* **Urine** is the liquid that you get rid of from your body when you go to the toilet. پیشاب

URL (**URLs**) *n* A **URL** is an address that shows where a particular page can be found on the World Wide Web. **URL** is an abbreviation for 'Uniform Resource Locator'. یونیفورم ریسورس لوکیٹر (ویب کا خبر)

Uruguay *n* **Uruguay** is a republic in South America, on the Atlantic. یوروگوے کا

Uruguayan (**Uruguayans**) *adj* **Uruguayan** means of or relating to Uruguay or its inhabitants. یوروگوے کا باشندہ ⊳ *n* A **Uruguayan** is a native or inhabitant of Uruguay. اروگوائی

US *n* The **US** is an abbreviation for 'the United States'. ریاستہائے متحدہ (امریکہ)

us *pron* You use **us** to talk about yourself and the person or people with you. ہم *He has invited us to a party.*

USA *n* The **USA** is an abbreviation for 'the United States of America'. ریاستہائے متحدہ امریکہ

use (**uses, using, used**) *n* Your **use** of

u

something is the action or fact of your using it. استعمال ▷ *vt* If you **use** something, you do something with it. استعمال کرنا

used *adj* A **used** handkerchief, glass, or other object is dirty or spoiled because it has been used. استعمال شدہ ▷ *v* You use **used to** to talk about something that was true in the past but is not true now. عادی ہونا

useful *adj* If something is **useful**, you can use it to do something or to help you. فائدے مند

useless *adj* If something is **useless**, you cannot use it. بیفائدہ

user (**users**) *n* The **users** of a product, machine, service, or place are the people who use it. صارف

user-friendly *adj* If you describe something such as a machine or system as **user-friendly**, you mean that it is well designed and easy to use. صارف دوست

use up *v* If you **use up** a supply of something, you finish it so that none of it is left. استعمال کرکے ختم کر ڈالنا *Did you use up the milk?*

usual *adj* **Usual** is used to describe what happens or what is done most often in a particular situation. معمول کا

usually *adv* If something **usually** happens, it is the thing that most often happens in a particular situation. عام طور سے

utility room (**utility rooms**) *n* A **utility room** is a room in a house which is usually connected to the kitchen and which contains things such as a washing machine, sink, and cleaning equipment. باورچی خانے سے متصل کمرہ

U-turn (**U-turns**) *n* If you make a **U-turn** when you are driving or cycling, you turn in a half circle in one movement, so that you are then going in the opposite direction. الٹا گھوم جانے کی حالت

Uzbekistan *n* **Uzbekistan** is a republic in central Asia. ازبکستان

V

vacancy (**vacancies**) *n* A **vacancy** is a job or position which has not been filled. خالی نشست

vacant *adj* If something is **vacant**, it is not being used by anyone. خالی

vacate (**vacates, vacating, vacated**) *vt* If you **vacate** a place or a job, you leave it and make it available for other people. خالی کرنا

vaccinate (**vaccinates, vaccinating, vaccinated**) *vt* If a person or animal **is vaccinated**, they are given, usually by injection, a substance containing a harmless form of a disease, to prevent them from getting that disease. ٹیکہ لگانا

vaccination (**vaccinations**) *n* **Vaccination** is the process of giving a person or animal, usually by injection, a substance containing a harmless form of a disease, to prevent them from getting that disease. ٹیکہ، نشتر

vacuum (**vacuums, vacuuming, vacuumed**) *v* If you **vacuum** something, you clean it using a vacuum cleaner. برقی مشین سے صفائی کرنا

vacuum cleaner (**vacuum cleaners**) *n* A **vacuum cleaner** or a **vacuum** is an electric machine which sucks up dust and dirt from carpets. برقی مشین (ویکیوم کلینر)

vague (**vaguer, vaguest**) *adj* If something is **vague**, it is not clear, distinct, or definite. مبہم، غیر واضح

vain (**vainer, vainest**) *adj* A **vain** attempt or action is one that fails to achieve what was intended. لاحاصل

Valentine's Day *n* On **Valentine's Day**, the 14th of February, people send a greetings card to someone that they are in love with or are attracted to, usually without signing their name. یوم ویلنٹائن

valid *adj* A **valid** reason or argument is logical and reasonable, and therefore worth taking seriously. قانونی، معقول

valley (**valleys**) *n* A **valley** is a low area of land between hills, often with a river flowing through it. وادی

valuable *adj* Something that is **valuable** is very useful. قیمتی

valuables *npl* **Valuables** are things that you own that are worth a lot of money, especially small objects such as jewellery. قیمتی سامان

value *n* The **value** of something such as a quality or a method is its importance or usefulness. قدر و قیمت

vampire (**vampires**) *n* In horror stories, **vampires** are creatures who come out of their graves at night and suck the blood of living people. ویمپائر، خوں خوار درندہ

van (**vans**) *n* A **van** is a medium-sized road vehicle that is used for carrying goods. وین (موٹر گاڑی)

vandal (**vandals**) *n* A **vandal** is someone who deliberately damages things, especially public property. غارتگر

vandalism *n* **Vandalism** is the deliberate damaging of things, especially public property. غارتگری

vandalize (**vandalizes, vandalizing, vandalized**) *v* If something **is vandalized** by someone, they deliberately damage it. غارت کرنا، توڑ پھوڑ کرنا

vanilla *n* **Vanilla** is a flavouring used in ice cream and other sweet food. ونیلا (ذائقہ)

vanish (**vanishes, vanishing, vanished**) *vi* If someone or something **vanishes**, they disappear suddenly or cease to exist altogether. دفعتاً غائب ہوجانا

variable *adj* Something that is **variable** is likely to change at any time. تغیر پذیر

varied *adj* Something that is **varied** consists of things of different types, sizes, or qualities. مختلف قسموں کا

variety (**varieties**) *n* If something has **variety**, it consists of things which are different from each other. قسم

various *adj* If you say that there are **various** things, you mean there are several different things of the type mentioned. مختلف، متعدد

varnish (**varnishes, varnishing, varnished**) *n* **Varnish** is an oily liquid which is painted onto wood to give it a hard, clear, shiny surface. وارنش ▷ *vt* If you **varnish** something, you paint it with varnish. وارنش کرنا

vary (**varies, varying, varied**) *vi* If things **vary**, they are different in size, amount, or degree. مختلف ہونا، متعدد ہونا

vase (**vases**) *n* A **vase** is a jar used for holding cut flowers or as an ornament. گلدان

VAT *abbr* **VAT** is a tax that is added to the price of goods or services. **VAT** is an abbreviation for 'value added tax'. ایک چیز پر کئی بار ٹیکس

Vatican *n* **The Vatican** is the city state in Rome ruled by the pope which is the centre of the Roman Catholic Church. رومن کیتھولک چرچ کا مرکز

veal *n* **Veal** is meat from a calf. بچھڑے کا گوشت

vegan (**vegans**) *n* A **vegan** is someone who never eats meat or any animal products such as milk, butter, or cheese. گوشت سے پرہیز کرنے والا

vegetable (**vegetables**) *n* **Vegetables** are edible plants such as cabbages, potatoes, and onions. سبزی ترکاری

vegetarian (**vegetarians**) *adj* Someone

who is **vegetarian** never eats meat or fish. سبزی خور ▷ *n* A **vegetarian** is someone who does not eat meat or fish. گوشت خور کی ضد

vegetation *n* **Vegetation** is plants, trees, and flowers. نباتات

vehicle (**vehicles**) *n* A **vehicle** is a machine with an engine, for example a car, that carries people or things from place to place. موٹر گاڑی

veil (**veils**) *n* A **veil** is a piece of thin soft cloth that women sometimes wear over their heads and which can also cover their face. گھونگھٹ

vein (**veins**) *n* Your **veins** are the tubes in your body through which your blood flows towards your heart. رگ، ورید

Velcro® *n* **Velcro** is a material consisting of two strips of nylon fabric which you press together to close things such as pockets and bags. نائلون کی دو پٹیاں جو کر بند ہو جانے والی

velvet *n* **Velvet** is a soft fabric with a thick layer of short cut threads on one side. مخمل

vending machine (**vending machines**) *n* A **vending machine** is a machine from which you can get things such as cigarettes, chocolate, or coffee by putting in money and pressing a button. وینڈنگ مشین

vendor (**vendors**) *n* A **vendor** is someone who sells things such as newspapers or hamburgers from a small stall or cart. خوانچہ والا

Venetian blind (**Venetian blinds**) *n* A **Venetian blind** is a window blind made of thin horizontal strips which can be adjusted to let in more or less light. بینائی میں مددگار پتلی پٹیاں

Venezuela *n* **Venezuela** is a republic in South America, on the Caribbean. وینیزویلا

Venezuelan (**Venezuelans**) *adj* **Venezuelan** means of or relating to Venezuela or its inhabitants. وینیزویلین ▷ *n* A **Venezuelan** is a native or inhabitant of Venezuela. وینیزویلین

venison *n* **Venison** is the meat of a deer. ہرن کا گوشت

venom *n* **Venom** is a feeling of great bitterness or anger towards someone. زہر، گہری تلخی

ventilation *n* **Ventilation** is the act or process of allowing fresh air to get into a room or building. روشندان

venue (**venues**) *n* The **venue** for an event or activity is the place where it will happen. جائے وقوع

verb (**verbs**) *n* A **verb** is a word such as 'sing' or 'feel' which is used to say what someone or something does or what happens to them, or to give information about them. فعل

verdict (**verdicts**) *n* In a law court, a **verdict** is the decision that is given by the jury or judge at the end of a trial. جیوری کا فیصلہ

versatile *adj* If you say that a person is **versatile**, you approve of them because they have many different skills. ہمہ گیر

version (**versions**) *n* A **version** of something is a form of it in which some details are different from earlier or later forms. ترجمہ

versus *prep* **Versus** is used for showing that two teams or people are on different sides in a game. بمقابلہ

vertical *adj* Something that is **vertical** stands or points straight upwards. عمودی

vertigo *n* If you get **vertigo** when you look down from a high place, you feel unsteady and sick. چکر

very *adv* **Very** is used before a word to make it stronger. بہت

vest (**vests**) *n* A **vest** is a piece of underwear which is worn to keep the top part of your body warm. بنیان

vet (**vets**) *n* A **vet** is someone who is qualified to treat sick or injured animals. جانوروں کا ڈاکٹر، سلوتری

veteran (**veterans**) *adj* A **veteran** campaigner, actor, or other person is someone who has been involved in their particular activity for a long time. بڑا تجربہ کار ▷ *n* A **veteran** is someone who has served in the armed forces of their country, especially during a war. جنگ میں شامل رہا فوجی

veto (**vetoes**) *n* If someone in authority puts a **veto** on something, they forbid it, or stop it being put into action. حق استرداد

via *prep* If you go somewhere **via** a place, you go through that place on the way. براہ

vice (**vices**) *n* A **vice** is a habit which is regarded as a weakness in someone's character, but not usually as a serious fault. گناہ

vice versa *adv* **Vice versa** is used to indicate that the reverse of what you have said is also true. For example, 'Women may bring their husbands with them, and vice versa' means that men may also bring their wives with them. -- کی پلٹ بھی صحیح

vicinity *n* If something is in the **vicinity** of a place, it is in the nearby area. قرب وجوار

vicious *adj* A **vicious** person is violent and cruel. زہریلا

victim (**victims**) *n* A **victim** is someone who has been hurt or killed by someone or something. شکار

victory (**victories**) *n* A **victory** is a success in a war or a competition. فتح

video (**videos**) *n* A **video** is a film or television programme recorded on magnetic tape. ویڈیو

video camera (**video cameras**) *n* A **video camera** is a camera that you use to record something that is happening so that you can watch it later. ویڈیو کیمرا

videophone (**videophones**) *n* A **videophone** is a telephone which has a camera and screen so that people who are using the phone can see and hear each other. ویڈیو فون

Vietnam *n* **Vietnam** is a republic in south-east Asia. ویتنام

Vietnamese (**Vietnamese**) *adj* **Vietnamese** means of, relating to, or characteristic of Vietnam, its people, or their language. ویتنامی ▷ *n* A **Vietnamese** is a native or inhabitant of Vietnam. ویتنامی ▷ *n* **Vietnamese** is the language spoken in Vietnam. ویتنامی

view (**views**) *n* Your **views** on something are the opinions or beliefs that you have about it. نظارہ، منظر

viewer (**viewers**) *n* **Viewers** are people who watch television. ناظر

viewpoint (**viewpoints**) *n* Someone's **viewpoint** is the way they think about things in general or about a particular thing. نقطہ نگاہ

vile (**viler, vilest**) *adj* If you say that someone or something is **vile**, you mean that they are extremely unpleasant. شرمناک

villa (**villas**) *n* A **villa** is a fairly large house, especially one that is used for holidays in Mediterranean countries. کوٹھی

village (**villages**) *n* A **village** consists of a group of houses, together with other buildings such as a school, in a country area. گاؤں

villain (**villains**) *n* A **villain** is someone who deliberately harms other people or breaks the law in order to get what he or she wants. بدمعاش، ولن

vinaigrette (**vinaigrettes**) *n* **Vinaigrette** is a dressing made by mixing oil, vinegar, salt, pepper, and herbs, which is put on salad. سلاد کا غلاف

vine (**vines**) *n* A **vine** is a climbing or trailing plant, especially one which produces grapes. انگور کی بیل

vinegar *n* **Vinegar** is a sharp-tasting liquid, usually made from sour wine or malt, which is used to make things such as salad dressing. سرکہ

vineyard (**vineyards**) *n* A **vineyard** is an area of land where grapevines are grown in order to produce wine. انگور کا باغ، چمن

viola (**violas**) *n* A **viola** is a musical

instrument which looks like a violin but is slightly larger. بڑی وائلن

violence *n* **Violence** is behaviour which is intended to hurt or kill people. تشدد

violent *adj* If someone is **violent**, or if they do something which is **violent**, they use physical force or weapons to hurt other people. متشدد

violin (**violins**) *n* A **violin** is a musical instrument with four strings stretched over a shaped hollow box. You hold a violin under your chin and play it with a bow. ولایتی سارنگی

violinist (**violinists**) *n* A **violinist** is someone who plays the violin. وائلن نواز

virgin (**virgins**) *n* A **virgin** is someone who has never had sex. کنواری

Virgo *n* **Virgo** is one of the twelve signs of the zodiac. Its symbol is a young woman. People who are born approximately between the 23rd of August and the 22nd of September come under this sign. برج عورت، سنبلہ

virtual *adj* You can use **virtual** to indicate that something is so nearly true that for most purposes it can be regarded as being true. واقعاتی

virtual reality *n* **Virtual reality** is an environment which is produced by a computer and seems very like reality to the person experiencing it. واقعاتی حقیقت

virus (**viruses**) *n* A **virus** is a kind of germ that can cause disease. وائرس

visa (**visas**) *n* A **visa** is an official document or a stamp put in your passport which allows you to enter or leave a particular country. ویزا

visibility *n* **Visibility** is how far or how clearly you can see in particular weather conditions. بینائی

visible *adj* If an object is **visible**, it can be seen. مرئی، قابل دید

visit (**visits, visiting, visited**) *n* If you pay someone a **visit**, you go to see them and spend time with them. ملاقات ▷ *vt* If you **visit** someone, you go to see them and spend time with them. ملاقات کرنا

visiting hours *npl* In an institution such as a hospital or prison, **visiting hours** are the times during which people from outside the institution are officially allowed to visit people who are staying at the institution. ملاقاتی اوقات

visitor (**visitors**) *n* A **visitor** is someone who is visiting a person or place. ملاقاتی

visitor centre (**visitor centres**) *n* A **visitor centre** at a place of interest is a building or group of buildings that provides information, often with video displays and exhibitions. ملاقاتی مرکز

visual *adj* **Visual** means relating to sight, or to things that you can see. مرئی، دیدنی

visualize (**visualizes, visualizing, visualized**) *vt* If you **visualize** something, you imagine what it is like by forming a mental picture of it. سوچ کے ذریعہ دیکھنا

vital *adj* If something is **vital**, it is necessary or very important. حیاتی

vitamin (**vitamins**) *n* **Vitamins** are organic substances in food which you need in order to remain healthy. وٹامن

vivid *adj* **Vivid** memories and descriptions are very clear and detailed. صاف، واضح

vocabulary (**vocabularies**) *n* Your **vocabulary** is the total number of words you know in a particular language. فہرست الفاظ، فرہنگ

vocational *adj* **Vocational** training and skills are the training and skills needed for a particular job or profession. پیشہ ورانہ

vodka (**vodkas**) *n* **Vodka** is a strong, clear, alcoholic drink. ووڈکا (بے رنگ بے بو روسی شراب)

voice (**voices**) *n* When someone speaks or sings, you hear their **voice**. آواز

voicemail *n* **Voicemail** is an electronic system which can store telephone messages, so that someone can listen to them later. وائس میل (ریکورڈ آواز)

void (**voids**) *adj* Something that is **void** is officially considered to have no value or authority. خالی، مسترد ▷ *n* If you describe a situation or a feeling as a **void**, you mean that it seems empty because there is nothing interesting or worthwhile about it. خلا

volcano (**volcanoes**) *n* A **volcano** is a mountain from which hot melted rock, gas, steam, and ash sometimes burst. آتش فشاں پہاڑ

volleyball *n* **Volleyball** is a sport in which two teams use their hands to hit a large ball over a high net. والی بال

volt (**volts**) *n* A **volt** is a unit used to measure the force of an electric current. برق کی اکائی

voltage (**voltages**) *n* The **voltage** of an electrical current is its force measured in volts. وولٹیج (کل قوت برق)

volume (**volumes**) *n* The **volume** of something is the amount of it that there is. حجم، جسامت

voluntarily *adv* If something is done **voluntarily**, it is done because you choose to do it and not because you have to do it. رضاکارانہ طور پر

voluntary *adj* **Voluntary** is used to describe actions and activities that you do because you choose them, rather than because you have to do them. رضاکارانہ

volunteer (**volunteers, volunteering, volunteered**) *n* A **volunteer** is someone who does work without being paid for it, especially for an organization such as a charity. رضاکار ▷ *v* If you **volunteer** to do something, you offer to do it without being forced to do it. رضاکار کے طور پر پیش کرنا (خود کو)

vomit (**vomits, vomiting, vomited**) *vi* If you **vomit**, food and drink comes back up from your stomach and out through your mouth. قے کرنا

vote (**votes, voting, voted**) *n* A **vote** is a choice made by a particular person or group in a meeting or an election. رائے دھندگی، ووٹ ▷ *v* When you **vote**, you indicate your choice officially at a meeting or in an election, for example, by raising your hand or writing on a piece of paper. ووٹ دینا

voucher (**vouchers**) *n* A **voucher** is a piece of paper that can be used instead of money to pay for something. رقم ادائگی کا رقعہ

vowel (**vowels**) *n* A **vowel** is a sound such as the ones represented in writing by the letters 'a', 'e', 'i', 'o', and 'u', which you pronounce with your mouth open, allowing the air to flow through it. حرفِ علت

vulgar *adj* If you describe something as **vulgar**, you think it is in bad taste or of poor artistic quality. بازاری، سستا

vulnerable (**adj**) *n* If someone or something is **vulnerable** to something, they have some weakness or disadvantage which makes them more likely to be harmed or affected by that thing. غیر محفوظ، ہدف بننے والا

vulture (**vultures**) *n* A **vulture** is a large bird which lives in hot countries and eats the flesh of dead animals. گدھ، کرگس

W

wafer (**wafers**) *n* A **wafer** is a thin crisp biscuit, often eaten with ice cream. نمکین

waffle (**waffles, waffling, waffled**) *n* If someone talks or writes a lot without saying anything clear or important, you can call what they say or write **waffle**. (*informal*) بے معنی ▷ *vi* If you say that someone **waffles**, you are critical of them because they talk or write a lot without actually making any clear or important points. (*informal*) بے معنی لکھنا

wage (**wages**) *n* Someone's **wages** are the amount of money that is regularly paid to them for the work that they do. مزدوری

waist (**waists**) *n* Your **waist** is the middle part of your body, above your hips. کمر

waistcoat (**waistcoats**) *n* A **waistcoat** is a sleeveless piece of clothing with buttons, usually worn over a shirt. واسکٹ

wait (**waits, waiting, waited**) *vi* If you say that something can **wait**, you mean that it is not important, so you will do it later. کسی کے لیے انتظار کرنا

waiter (**waiters**) *n* A **waiter** is a man who serves food and drink in a restaurant. ویٹر (ریسٹورینٹ یا ہوٹل میں)

waiting list (**waiting lists**) *n* A **waiting list** is a list of people who have asked for something which they cannot receive immediately, for example medical treatment or housing, and so who must wait until it is available. فہرست منتظرین

waiting room (**waiting rooms**) *n* A **waiting room** is a room in a place such as a railway station or a clinic, where people can sit down while they wait. انتظار خانہ

waitress (**waitresses**) *n* A **waitress** is a woman who serves food and drink in a restaurant. خاتون ویٹر

wait up *v* If you **wait up**, you deliberately do not go to bed, especially because you are expecting someone to return home late at night. سونے سے رک کر انتظار کرنا *I hope he doesn't expect you to wait up for him.*

waive (**waives, waiving, waived**) *vt* If you **waive** your right to something, for example legal representation, or if someone else **waives** it, you no longer have the right to receive it. منسوخ کرنا، ترک کر دینا

wake up *v* When you **wake up**, you become conscious again after being asleep. جاگنا *It's lovely to wake up every morning and see a blue sky.*

Wales *n* **Wales** is a principality that is part of the United Kingdom, in the west of Great Britain. ویلز

walk (**walks, walking, walked**) *n* A **walk** is a journey that you make by walking. چہل قدمی ▷ *vi* When you **walk**, you move along by putting one foot in front of the other. چلنا، ٹہلنا

walkie-talkie (**walkie-talkies**) *n* A **walkie-talkie** is a small portable radio which you can talk into and hear messages through so that you can communicate with someone far away. وائرلیس (بے تار ریڈیو جس پر بات کی جاسکتی ہے)

walking *n* **Walking** is the activity of going for walks in the country. چلنے کا عمل

walking stick (**walking sticks**) *n* A **walking stick** is a long wooden stick which a person can lean on while walking. چلنے کی چھڑی

walkway (**walkways**) *n* A **walkway**

is a path or passage for pedestrians, especially one which is raised above the ground. پیدل راستہ

wall (**walls**) *n* A **wall** is one of the vertical sides of a building or room. دیوار

wallet (**wallets**) *n* A **wallet** is a small flat folded case where you can keep banknotes and credit cards. بٹوا

wallpaper (**wallpapers**) *n* **Wallpaper** is thick coloured or patterned paper that is used to decorate the walls of rooms. رنگین ڈیزائن والا کاغذ

walnut (**walnuts**) *n* **Walnuts** are light brown edible nuts which have a wrinkled shape and a very hard round shell. اخروٹ

walrus (**walruses**) *n* A **walrus** is a large, fat animal which lives in the sea. It has two long teeth called tusks that point downwards. سمندری گھوڑا نما مچھلی

waltz (**waltzes, waltzing, waltzed**) *n* A **waltz** is a piece of music with a rhythm of three beats in each bar, which people can dance to. والز ناچ، رقص ▷ *vi* If you **waltz** with someone, you dance a waltz with them. والز رقص کرنا

wander (**wanders, wandering, wandered**) *vi* If you **wander** in a place, you walk around there in a casual way, often without intending to go in any particular direction. گھومنا

want (**wants, wanting, wanted**) *vt* If you **want** something, you would like to have it. چاہنا

war (**wars**) *n* A **war** is a period of fighting between countries. جنگ

ward (**wards**) *n* A **ward** is a room in a hospital which has beds for many people, often people who need similar treatment. کمرہ، وارڈ ▷ *n* A **ward** is a district which forms part of a political constituency or local council. محلہ

warden (**wardens**) *n* A **warden** is an official who is responsible for a particular place or thing, and for making sure that certain laws are obeyed. نگراں

wardrobe (**wardrobes**) *n* A **wardrobe** is a tall cupboard in which you hang your clothes. کپڑوں کی آلماری

warehouse (**warehouses**) *n* A **warehouse** is a large building where raw materials or manufactured goods are stored before they are taken to a shop. گودام

warm (**warmer, warmest**) *adj* Something that is **warm** has some heat but not enough to be hot. گرم

warm up *v* If you **warm** something **up**, or if it **warms up**, it gets hotter. گرم کرنا *Have you warmed the milk up, Mum?*

warn (**warns, warning, warned**) *v* If you **warn** someone about a possible danger or problem, you tell them about it so that they are aware of it. خبردار کرنا، آگاہ کرنا

warning (**warnings**) *n* A **warning** is something which is said or written to tell people of a possible danger, problem, or other unpleasant thing that might happen. آگاہی

warranty (**warranties**) *n* A **warranty** is a written guarantee which enables you to get a product repaired or replaced free of charge within a certain period of time. وارنٹی (ضمانت)

wart (**warts**) *n* A **wart** is a small lump which grows on your skin and which is usually caused by a virus. گومڑا (وائرس کی وجہ سے جلد پر ابھار)

wash (**washes, washing, washed**) *vt* If you **wash** something, you clean it using water and usually a substance such as soap or detergent. دھونا

washbasin (**washbasins**) *n* A **washbasin** is a large bowl for washing your hands and face. It is usually fixed to a wall, with taps for hot and cold water. واش بیسن (منہ ہاتھ دھونے کو)

washing *n* **Washing** is clothes, sheets, and other things that need to be washed, are being washed, or have just been washed. دھلائی

W

washing line (**washing lines**) *n* A **washing line** is a strong cord which you can hang wet clothes on while they dry. الگنی
washing machine (**washing machines**) *n* A **washing machine** is a machine that you use to wash clothes in. واشنگ مشین
washing powder (**washing powders**) *n* **Washing powder** is a powder that you use with water to wash clothes. واشنگ پاوڈر
washing-up *n* To do the **washing-up** means to wash the pans, plates, cups, and cutlery which have been used in cooking and eating a meal. برتن دھلائی
washing-up liquid (**washing-up liquids**) *n* **Washing-up liquid** is a thick soapy liquid which you add to hot water to clean dirty dishes. دھلنے والا سیال مادہ
wash up *v* If you **wash up**, you wash the pans, plates, cups, and cutlery which have been used in cooking and eating a meal. دھو ڈالنا *I made breakfast and then washed up the plates.*
wasp (**wasps**) *n* A **wasp** is a small insect with a painful sting. It has yellow and black stripes across its body. بھڑ، بر
waste (**wastes, wasting, wasted**) *n* If you waste something such as time, money, or energy, you use too much of it doing something that is not important or necessary, or is unlikely to succeed. You can say that doing this is a **waste** of time, money, or energy. اصراف، بربادی ▷ *vt* If you **waste** something such as time, money, or energy, you use too much of it doing something that is not important or necessary, or is unlikely to succeed. ضائع کرنا
wastepaper basket (**wastepaper baskets**) *n* A **wastepaper basket** is a container for rubbish, especially paper, which is usually placed on the floor in the corner of a room or next to a desk. ردی کی ٹوکری
watch (**watches, watching, watched**) *n* A **watch** is a small clock that you wear on your wrist. دستی گھڑی ▷ *v* If you **watch** something, you look at it for a period of time. نگرانی کرنا، دیکھنا
watch out *v* If you tell someone to **watch out**, you are warning them to be careful, because something unpleasant might happen to them or they might get into difficulties. خبردار کرنا *You have to watch out – there are dangers everywhere.*
watch strap (**watch straps**) *n* A **watch strap** is a strap of leather, cloth, etc, attached to a watch for fastening it round the wrist. گھڑی کا پٹہ
water (**waters, watering, watered**) *n* **Water** is a clear thin liquid that has no colour or taste when it is pure. It falls from clouds as rain. پانی ▷ *vt* If you **water** plants, you pour water over them in order to help them to grow. پانی دینا، آب پاشی کرنا
watercolour (**watercolours**) *n* **Watercolours** are coloured paints, used for painting pictures, which you apply with a wet brush or dissolve in water first. آبی رنگ
watercress *n* **Watercress** is a small plant with white flowers which grows in streams and pools. Its leaves taste hot and are eaten raw in salads. آبی سلاد
waterfall (**waterfalls**) *n* A **waterfall** is a place where water flows over the edge of a steep cliff or rocks and falls into a pool below, such as Niagara Falls and Victoria Falls. جھرنا
watering can (**watering cans**) *n* A **watering can** is a container with a long spout which is used to water plants. ہزارہ (ٹونٹی میں سیکڑوں سوراخ)
watermelon (**watermelons**) *n* A **watermelon** is a large, round fruit with green skin, pink flesh, and black seeds. تربوز
waterproof *adj* Something that is **waterproof** does not let water pass through it. پانی سے محفوظ

water-skiing *n* **Water-skiing** is the act of standing on skis in the water while being pulled along by a boat. پانی پر اسکی کی مدد سے تیرنا
wave (**waves, waving, waved**) *n* If you give a **wave**, you move your hand from side to side in the air, usually to say hello or goodbye to someone. ہاتھ ہلانا (ہلو یا الوداع کہنے کے لئے) ▷ *v* If you **wave** your hand, you move it from side to side, usually to say hello or goodbye. ہاتھ ہلانا، الوداع کہنا ▷ *n* **Waves** on the surface of the sea are the parts that move up and down. لہر
wavelength (**wavelengths**) *n* A **wavelength** is the distance between the same point on two waves of energy such as light or sound that are next to each other. دو لہروں کے بیچ کی دوری
wavy (**wavier, waviest**) *adj* **Wavy** hair is not straight or curly, but curves slightly. ہلکا گھنگرالا
wax *n* **Wax** is a solid, slightly shiny substance made of fat or oil which is used to make candles and polish. موم
way (**ways**) *n* A **way** of doing something is how you do it. طریقہ ▷ *n* The **way** to a place is how you get there. راستہ
way in (**ways in**) *n* The **way in** is the point where you enter a place, for example, a door or gate. داخلہ کا راستہ
way out (**ways out**) *n* The **way out** is the point where you leave a place, for example, a door or gate. نکاسی کا راستہ
we *pron* You use **we** to talk about yourself and one or more other people as a group. ہم *We said we would always be friends.*
weak (**weaker, weakest**) *adj* If someone is **weak**, they do not have very much strength or energy. کمزور
weakness (**weaknesses**) *n* **Weakness** is the state or quality of having little strength or energy. کمزوری
wealth *n* **Wealth** is a large amount of money or property owned by someone, or the possession of it. دولت
wealthy (**wealthier, wealthiest**) *adj* Someone who is **wealthy** has a large amount of money, property, or valuable possessions. دولتمند
weapon (**weapons**) *n* A **weapon** is an object such as a gun, knife, or missile. ہتھیار
wear (**wears, wearing, wore, worn**) *vt* When you **wear** clothes, shoes, or jewellery, you have them on your body. پہننا
weasel (**weasels**) *n* A **weasel** is a small wild animal with a long thin body, a tail, short legs, and reddish-brown fur. ایک قسم کا نیولا
weather *n* The **weather** is the condition of the atmosphere in an area at a particular time, for example, if it is raining, hot, or windy. موسم
weather forecast (**weather forecasts**) *n* A **weather forecast** is a statement saying what the weather will be like the next day or for the next few days. موسمی پیشن گوئی
web (**webs**) *n* A **web** is the thin net made by a spider from a string that comes out of its body. جال
Web *n* The **Web** is made up of a very large number of websites all joined together. You can use it anywhere in the world to search for information. **Web** is short for World Wide Web. ویب
Web 2.0 *n* **Web 2.0** is the Internet viewed as a medium in which interactive experience, in the form of blogs, wikis, forums, etc, plays a more important role than simply accessing information. انٹرنیٹ ویب
web address (**web addresses**) *n* A **web address** is a website's location on the Internet. ویب پتہ
web browser (**web browsers**) *n* A **web browser** is a piece of computer software that you use to search for information on the Internet, especially on the World Wide Web. تلاش کے لئے سافٹ ویر
webcam (**webcams**) *n* A **webcam** is a video camera that takes pictures which

can be viewed on a website. The pictures are often of something that is happening while you watch. ویب کیمرا

webmaster (**webmasters**) *n* A **webmaster** is someone who is in charge of a website, especially someone who does that as their job. ویب انچارج پیشہ ور

website (**websites**) *n* A **website** is a set of data and information about a particular subject which is available on the Internet. ویب سائٹ

webzine (**webzines**) *n* A **webzine** is a website which contains the kind of articles, pictures, and advertisements that you would find in a magazine. ویب میگزین

wedding (**weddings**) *n* A **wedding** is a marriage ceremony and the celebration that often takes place afterwards. شادی

wedding anniversary (**wedding anniversaries**) *n* Your **wedding anniversary** is a date that you remember or celebrate because you got married on that date in a previous year. شادی کی سالگرہ

wedding dress (**wedding dresses**) *n* A **wedding dress** is a special dress that a woman wears at her wedding. لباس عروسی

wedding ring (**wedding rings**) *n* A **wedding ring** is a ring that you wear to show that you are married. شادی کی انگوٹھی

Wednesday (**Wednesdays**) *n* **Wednesday** is the day after Tuesday and before Thursday. بدھ

weed (**weeds**) *n* A **weed** is a wild plant growing where it is not wanted, for example in a garden. کھرپتوار

weedkiller (**weedkillers**) *n* **Weedkiller** is a substance you put on your garden to kill weeds. کھرپتوار کش

week (**weeks**) *n* A **week** is a period of seven days, which is often considered to start on Monday and end on Sunday. ہفتہ

weekday (**weekdays**) *n* A **weekday** is any day of the week except Saturday and Sunday. سنیچر اتوار کے علاوہ کوئی بھی دن

weekend (**weekends**) *n* A **weekend** is Saturday and Sunday. ہفتے کا آخر (سنیچر اتوار)

weep (**weeps, weeping, wept**) *v* If someone **weeps**, they cry. (*literary*) رونا

weigh (**weighs, weighing, weighed**) *vt* If someone or something **weighs** a particular amount, that is how heavy they are. وزن کرنا

weight (**weights**) *n* The **weight** of a person or thing is how heavy they are, measured in units such as kilos or pounds. وزن کرنا

weightlifter (**weightlifters**) *n* A **weightlifter** is a person who does weightlifting. وزن اٹھانے والا (کھلاڑی)

weightlifting *n* **Weightlifting** is a sport in which the competitor who can lift the heaviest weight wins. وزن اٹھانے کا کھیل

weird (**weirder, weirdest**) *adj* **Weird** means strange and peculiar. (*informal*) عجوبہ، مافوق الفطرت

welcome! (**welcomes, welcoming, welcomed**) *excl* You say **'Welcome!'** when you are greeting someone who has just arrived somewhere. خوش آمدید ▷ *n* If you give someone a **welcome**, you greet them in a friendly way when they arrive. خوشآمدید ▷ *vt* If you **welcome** someone, you greet them in a friendly way when they arrive somewhere. خیر مقدم کرنا

well (**better, best, wells**) *adj* If you are **well**, you are healthy and not ill. اچھا، صحتمند ▷ *adv* If you do something **well**, you do it in a good way. اچھا ▷ *n* A **well** is a deep hole in the ground from which people take water, oil, or gas. کنواں

well-behaved *adj* If you describe someone, especially a child, as **well-behaved**, you mean that they behave in a way that adults generally like and think is correct. مہذب

well done! *excl* You say **'Well done!'** to indicate that you are pleased that someone has done something good. بہت خوب!

wellingtons *npl* **Wellingtons** are long rubber boots which you wear to keep your feet dry. لمبے ربر بوٹ

well-known *adj* Something or someone that is **well-known** is famous or familiar. جانا پہچانا

well-off *adj* Someone who is **well-off** is rich enough to be able to do and buy most of the things that they want. (*informal*) کھاتا پیتا

well-paid *adj* If you say that a person or their job is **well-paid**, you mean that they receive a lot of money for the work that they do. اچھی تنخواہ والا

Welsh *adj* **Welsh** means belonging or relating to Wales, or to its people, language, or culture. ویلز (ریاست) کا ▷ *n* **Welsh** is a language of Wales. ویلز کی زبان

west *adj* The **west** part of a place, country, or region is the part which is towards the west. مغربی ▷ *adv* If you go **west**, you travel towards the west. مغرب ▷ *n* The **west** is the direction in which you look to see the sun set. مغربی سمت

westbound *adj* **Westbound** roads or vehicles lead to or are travelling towards the west. غربی

western (**westerns**) *adj* **Western** means in or from the west of a region or country. مغربی ▷ *n* A **western** is a film or book about the life of cowboys. مغربی

West Indian (**West Indians**) *adj* **West Indian** means belonging or relating to the West Indies, or to its people or culture. ویسٹ انڈیز کا ▷ *n* A **West Indian** is a person who comes from the West Indies. ویسٹ انڈیز کا باشندہ

West Indies *npl* The **West Indies** is an archipelago off Central America, extending over 2400 km (1500 miles) in an arc from the peninsula of Florida to Venezuela, separating the Caribbean Sea from the Atlantic Ocean. ویسٹ انڈیز

wet (**wetter, wettest**) *adj* If something is **wet**, it is covered in water or another liquid. بھیگا، گیلا

wetsuit (**wetsuits**) *n* A **wetsuit** is a close-fitting rubber suit which an underwater swimmer wears in order to keep their body warm. زیرآب تیراکی کیلئے ربر سوٹ

whale (**whales**) *n* A **whale** is a very large sea mammal. وھیل

what *det* You use **what** with a noun, when you ask for information. کیا *What time is it?* ▷ *pron* You use **what** in questions when you ask for information. کیا *What do you want?*

whatever *conj* You use **whatever** to talk about anything or everything of a type. جو کچھ *We can do whatever you want.*

wheat *n* **Wheat** is a cereal crop grown for its grain, which is ground into flour to make bread. گیہوں

wheat intolerance *n* If you have a **wheat intolerance**, you become ill if you eat food containing wheat. گیہوں ہضم نہ ہونا

wheel (**wheels**) *n* A **wheel** is a circular object which turns round on a rod attached to its centre. Wheels are fixed underneath vehicles so that they can move along. پہیہ

wheelbarrow (**wheelbarrows**) *n* A **wheelbarrow** is a small open cart with one wheel and handles that is used for carrying things, for example in the garden. یک پہیہ گاڑی

wheelchair (**wheelchairs**) *n* A **wheelchair** is a chair with wheels that sick or disabled people use in order to move about. پہیہ دار کرسی

when *adv* You use **when** to ask what time something happened or will happen. کب ▷ *conj* You use **when** to talk about the time at which something happens. جب *I asked him when he'd be back.*

whenever *conj* You use **whenever** to talk about any time or every time that something happens. جب کبھی *Whenever I talked to him, he seemed quite nice.*

where *adv* You use **where** to ask questions about the place something is in. کہاں ▷ *conj* You use **where** to talk about the place in which something is situated or happens. جہاں *People were wondering where the noise was coming from.*

whether *conj* You use **whether** when you are talking about a choice between two or more things. آیا، خواہ، چاہے، ہو یا نہ ہو *They now have two weeks to decide whether or not to buy the house.*

which *det* You use **which** when you want help to choose between things. کون *Which shoes should I put on?* ▷ *pron* You use **which** to ask questions when there are two or more possible answers. کون سی *Which is your room?*

whichever *det* **Whichever** means any person or thing. جو کوئی *Whichever way we do this, it isn't going to work.*

while *conj* If one thing happens **while** another thing is happening, the two things are happening at the same time. جبکہ، دوران *She goes to work while her children are at school.* ▷ *n* A **while** is a period of time. لمحہ

whip (**whips**) *n* A **whip** is a long thin piece of leather or rope fastened to a handle. It is used for hitting animals or people. کوڑا، دُرّا

whipped cream *n* **Whipped cream** is cream that has been stirred very fast until it is thick or stiff. خوب پھینٹی ہوئی کریم

whisk (**whisks**) *n* A **whisk** is a kitchen tool used for whisking eggs or cream. چھوٹی بلونی

whiskers *npl* The **whiskers** of an animal such as a cat or a mouse are the long stiff hairs that grow near its mouth. بلی کی مونچھ کے بال

whisky (**whiskies**) *n* **Whisky** is a strong alcoholic drink made, especially in Scotland, from grain such as barley or rye. الکحل والا مشروب

whisper (**whispers, whispering, whispered**) *v* When you **whisper**, you say something very quietly, using your breath rather than your throat, so that only one person can hear you. دھیمی آواز سے کچھ کہنا

whistle (**whistles, whistling, whistled**) *n* A **whistle** is a small metal tube which you blow in order to produce a loud sound and attract someone's attention. سیٹی ▷ *v* When you **whistle**, you make sounds by forcing your breath out between your lips or teeth. سیٹی بجانا

white (**whiter, whitest**) *adj* Something that is **white** is the colour of snow or milk. سفید

whiteboard (**whiteboards**) *n* A **whiteboard** is a shiny white board on which people draw or write using special pens. Whiteboards are often used for teaching or giving talks. سفید تختہ (پین سے لکھنے کے لئے)

whitewash (**whitewashes, whitewashing, whitewashed**) *v* **Whitewash** is a mixture of lime or chalk and water used for painting walls white. چونے سے پتائی کرنا

whiting (**whitings, whiting**) *n* A **whiting** is a black and silver fish that lives in the sea. کالی سفید مچھلی

who *pron* You use **who** in questions when you ask about someone's name. کون *Who won the quiz?*

whoever *conj* You use **whoever** to talk about somebody when you do not know who they are. جو بھی *Whoever wins the prize is going to be famous for life.*

whole *adj* The **whole** of something is all of it. کل، سالم، مکمل، پورا ▷ *n* A **whole** is a single thing which contains several different parts. مکمل

wholefoods *npl* **Wholefoods** are foods which have not been processed much and which have not had artificial ingredients added. مصنوعی چیزوں سے پاک ثابت کھانے

wholemeal *adj* **Wholemeal** flour is made from the complete grain of the wheat plant, including the outer part. **Wholemeal** bread or pasta is made from wholemeal flour. بغیر چھنے آٹے کا کھانا

wholesale *adj* **Wholesale** goods are bought cheaply in large quantities and then sold again to shops. تھوک فروشی ▷ *n* **Wholesale** is the activity of buying and selling goods in large quantities and therefore at cheaper prices, usually to shopkeepers who then sell them to the public. بڑے پیمانے کی فروخت

whom *pron* **Whom** is used in formal or written English instead of 'who' when somebody does something to somebody. (*formal*) جن کا، جن کے *The book is about her husband, whom she married ten years ago.*

whose *det* You use **whose** to ask who something belongs to. کس کی *Whose bag is this?* ▷ *pron* You use **whose** to explain who something belongs to. جس کی *He shouted at the driver whose car was blocking the street.*

why *adv* You use **why** when you are asking about the reason for something. کیوں

wicked *adj* You use **wicked** to describe someone or something that is very bad in a way that is deliberately harmful to people. بدمعاش

wide (**wider, widest**) *adj* Something that is **wide** is a large distance from one side to the other. وسیع، کشادہ، چوڑا ▷ *adv* If you open something **wide**, you open it fully. چوڑا

widespread *adj* Something that is **widespread** exists or happens over a large area or to a very great extent. سب جگہ پھیلی ہوئی

widow (**widows**) *n* A **widow** is a woman whose husband has died. بیوہ

widower (**widowers**) *n* A **widower** is a man whose wife has died. رنڈوا

width (**widths**) *n* The **width** of something is the distance that it measures from one side to the other. چوڑائی

wife (**wives**) *n* A man's **wife** is the woman he is married to. بیوی

Wi-Fi *n* **Wi-Fi** is a system for using the Internet from laptop computers with wireless connections. **Wi-Fi** is an abbreviation of 'wireless fidelity'. وائی فائی (بے تار موڈم سے کمپیوٹر پر انٹرنیٹ استعمال کرنا)

wig (**wigs**) *n* A **wig** is a mass of false hair which is worn on your head. نقلی بال

wild (**wilder, wildest**) *adj* **Wild** animals and plants live or grow in natural surroundings and are not looked after by people. جنگلی

wildlife *n* You can use **wildlife** to refer to animals and other living things that live in the wild. جنگل کی زندگی

will (**wills**) *n* **Will** is the determination to do something. عزم، خواہش ▷ *n* A **will** is a legal document stating what you want to happen to your money when you die. وصیت ▷ *v* You use **will** to talk about things that are going to happen in the future. کرے گا (مستقبل)

willing *adj* If someone is **willing** to do something, they do not mind doing it or have no objection to doing it. آمادہ

willingly *adv* If someone does something **willingly**, they have no objection to doing it. ارادی طور پر، بالارادہ، عمداً

willow (**willows**) *n* A **willow** is a tree with long narrow leaves and branches that hang down. بید

willpower *n* **Willpower** is a very strong determination to do something. عزم و حوصلہ

wilt (**wilts, wilting, wilted**) *vi* If a plant **wilts**, it gradually bends downwards and becomes weak, because it needs more water or is dying. مرجھانا، کمہلانا

W

win (**wins, winning, won**) *v* If you **win** something such as a competition, battle, or argument, you defeat those people you are competing or fighting against, or you do better than everyone else involved. جیتنا

wind (**winds, winding, winded, wound**) *n* **Wind** is air that moves. ہوا ▷ *vt* If you are **winded** by something, you have difficulty breathing for a short time. ہوا بھرنا ▷ *vi* If a road or river **winds**, it twists and turns. مڑنا ▷ *vt* When you **wind** something long around something, you wrap it around several times. لپیٹنا

windmill (**windmills**) *n* A **windmill** is a tall building with sails which turn as the wind blows. Windmills are used to grind grain or pump water. بادی چکی

window (**windows**) *n* A **window** is a space in the wall of a building or in the side of a vehicle, which has glass in it so that light can pass through and people can see in or out. کھڑکی

window pane (**window panes**) *n* A **window pane** is a piece of glass in the window of a building. کھڑکی کا فریم

window seat (**window seats**) *n* A **window seat** is a seat which is fixed to the wall underneath a window in a room. کھڑکی کے ساتھ والی نشست

windowsill (**windowsills**) *n* A **windowsill** is a shelf along the bottom of a window, either inside or outside a building. کھڑکی کے تلے سے جڑی آلماری (اندر یا باہر)

windscreen (**windscreens**) *n* The **windscreen** of a car or other vehicle is the glass window at the front through which the driver looks. کار کا سامنے کا شیشہ

windscreen wiper (**windscreen wipers**) *n* A **windscreen wiper** is a device that wipes rain from a vehicle's windscreen. سامنے کا شیشہ صاف کرنے والے (وائپر)

windsurfing *n* **Windsurfing** is a sport in which you move along the surface of the sea or a lake on a long narrow board with a sail on it. ایک پٹے پر کھڑے ہوکر سمندر یا جھیل پر تیرنا

windy (**windier, windiest**) *adj* If it is **windy**, the wind is blowing a lot. ہوادار

wine (**wines**) *n* **Wine** is an alcoholic drink, usually made from grapes. شراب

wineglass (**wineglasses**) *n* A **wineglass** is a glass drinking vessel, typically having a small bowl on a stem, with a flared foot. بلوری جام

wine list (**wine lists**) *n* A restaurant's **wine list** is a list of all the wines that it has available. ریسٹورینٹ کی شراب کی فہرست

wing (**wings**) *n* The **wings** of a bird or insect are the parts of its body that it uses for flying. بازو، ڈینے

wing mirror (**wing mirrors**) *n* The **wing mirrors** on a car are the mirrors on each side of the car on the outside. بازو کے شیشے

wink (**winks, winking, winked**) *vi* When you **wink** at someone, you look towards them and close one eye very briefly, usually as a signal that something is a joke or a secret. آنکھ مارنا

winner (**winners**) *n* The **winner** of a prize, race, or competition is the person, animal, or thing that wins it. فاتح

winning *adj* You can use **winning** to describe a person or thing that wins something such as a competition, game, or election. فتح

winter (**winters**) *n* **Winter** is the season between autumn and spring. In winter the weather is usually cold. سردی کا موسم

winter sports *npl* **Winter sports** are sports that take place on ice or snow, for example skating and skiing. موسم سرما کے کھیل

wipe (**wipes, wiping, wiped**) *vt* If you **wipe** something, you rub its surface to remove dirt or liquid from it. پونچھنا

wipe up *v* If you **wipe up** dirt or liquid from something, you remove it using a cloth. پونچھ ڈالنا *Wipe up spills immediately.*

wire (**wires**) *n* A **wire** is a long thin piece of metal that is used to fasten things or to carry electric current. تار

wisdom *n* **Wisdom** is the ability to use your experience and knowledge to make sensible decisions and judgments. ذہانت، عقل

wisdom tooth (**wisdom teeth**) *n* Your **wisdom teeth** are the four large teeth at the back of your mouth which usually grow much later than your other teeth. عقل داڑھ

wise (**wiser, wisest**) *adj* A **wise** person is able to use their experience and knowledge to make sensible decisions and judgments. عاقل، فہیم

wish (**wishes, wishing, wished**) *n* A **wish** is a desire for something. خواہش ▷ *vi* If you **wish** to do something, you want to do it. خواہش کرنا

wit *n* **Wit** is the ability to use words or ideas in an amusing and clever way. ظرافت

witch (**witches**) *n* A **witch** is a woman who is believed to have magic powers, especially evil ones. ساحرہ

with *prep* If one person is **with** another, they are together in one place. ساتھ *He's watching a film with his friends.* ▷ *prep* You use **with** to say that someone has something. کے ساتھ *My daughter is the girl with brown hair.*

withdraw (**withdraws, withdrawing, withdrew, withdrawn**) *vt* If you **withdraw** something from a place, you remove it or take it away. (*formal*) نکالنا

withdrawal (**withdrawals**) *n* The **withdrawal** of something is the act or process of removing it or ending it. (*formal*) نکاسی

within *prep* If something is **within** a place, area, or object, it is inside it or surrounded by it. (*formal*) بغیر *He went without me.*

without *prep* If you do something **without** someone, they are not in the same place as you are, or they are not doing the same thing as you. بغیر

witness (**witnesses**) *n* A **witness** to an event such as an accident or crime is a person who saw it. گواہ

witty (**wittier, wittiest**) *adj* Someone or something that is **witty** is amusing in a clever way. ظریف

wolf (**wolves**) *n* A **wolf** is a wild animal that looks like a large dog. بھیڑیا

woman (**women**) *n* A **woman** is an adult female human being. عورت

wonder (**wonders, wondering, wondered**) *vt* If you **wonder** about something, you think about it and try to guess or understand more about it. حیرت کرنا

wonderful *adj* If you describe something or someone as **wonderful**, you think they are extremely good. حیرت انگیز

wood (**woods**) *n* **Wood** is the hard material that trees are made of. لکڑی ▷ *n* A **wood** is a large area of trees growing near each other. جنگل

wooden *adj* A **wooden** object is made of wood. لکڑی کا

woodwind *adj* **Woodwind** instruments are musical instruments such as flutes, clarinets, and recorders that you play by blowing into them. ہوائی ساز (بانسری وغیرہ)

woodwork *n* You can refer to the doors and other wooden parts of a house as the **woodwork**. لکڑی کا سامان (دروازہ وغیرہ)

wool *n* **Wool** is the hair that grows on sheep and on some other animals. اون

woollen *adj* **Woollen** clothes are made from wool. اونی

woollens *npl* **Woollens** are clothes, especially sweaters, that are made of wool. اونی کپڑے

word (**words**) *n* **Words** are things that you say or write. لفظ

work (**works, working, worked**) *n* People who have **work** have a job. کام ▷ *vi* When you **work**, you do something that uses a lot of your time or effort. کام کرنا ▷ *vi* If a machine **works**, it does its job. کام کرنا

worker (**workers**) *n* **Workers** are people who are employed in industry or business and who are not managers. کام کرنے والا، مزدور

W

work experience *n* **Work experience** is a period of time that a young person, especially a student, spends working in a company as a form of training. کام کا تجربہ

workforce (**workforces**) *n* The **workforce** is the total number of people in a country or region who are physically able to do a job and are available for work. کام کرنے لائق لوگوں کی تعداد

working-class *adj* If you are **working-class**, you are a member of the group of people in a society who do not own much property, who have low social status, and who do jobs which involve using physical skills rather than intellectual skills. کام کرنے لائق لوگوں کا طبقہ

workman (**workmen**) *n* A **workman** is a man who works with his hands, for example a builder or plumber. کاریگر، دستکار

work of art (**works of art**) *n* A **work of art** is a painting or piece of sculpture of high quality. آرٹ کا کام (شاہکار)

work out *v* If you **work out** a solution to a problem or mystery, you find the solution by thinking or talking about it. نتیجے پر پہنچنا، حل تلاش کرنا *They are planning to meet later today to work out a solution.*

work permit (**work permits**) *n* A **work permit** is an official document that someone needs in order to work in a particular foreign country. کام کا اجازت نامہ

workplace (**workplaces**) *n* Your **workplace** is the place where you work. مہیا کرائی گئی جگہ

workshop (**workshops**) *n* A **workshop** is a room or building containing tools or machinery for making or repairing things. کاریگر خانہ

workspace *n* A person's **workspace** is the area, especially in an office, that is allocated for them to work in. کام کے لئے مہیا کرائی گئی جگہ

workstation (**workstations**) *n* A **workstation** is a computer. کمپیوٹر

world *n* The **world** is the planet that we live on. دنیا

World Cup *n* The **World Cup** is an international competition held between national teams in various sports, most notably association football. عالمی کپ

worm (**worms**) *n* A **worm** is a small thin animal without bones or legs which lives in the soil. کیڑا

worn *adj* **Worn** things are damaged or thin because they are old and have been used a lot. پھٹی پرانی، گئی گزری

worried *adj* When you are **worried**, you are unhappy because you keep thinking about problems that you have or about unpleasant things that might happen in the future. فکر مند

worry (**worries, worrying, worried**) *vi* If you **worry**, you keep thinking about a problem or about something unpleasant that might happen. فکر کرنا

worrying *adj* If something is **worrying**, it causes people to worry. باعث فکر

worse *adj* **Worse** is the comparative of **bad** and **badly**. It means more bad. خراب ▷ *adv* **Worse** is the comparative of **badly**.It means more badly. خراب‌تر

worsen (**worsens, worsening, worsened**) *v* If a situation **worsens**, it becomes more difficult, unpleasant, or unacceptable. خراب کرنا

worship (**worships, worshipping, worshipped**) *v* If you **worship** a god, you show your respect to the god, for example by saying prayers. عبادت کرنا

worst *adj* **Worst** is the superlative of **bad**. It means most bad. سب سے برا

worth *n* Someone's **worth** is their value, usefulness, or importance. قیمت، ساکھ

worthless *adj* Something that is **worthless** is of no real use or value. بے قیمت، بے وقعت

would *v* You use **would** to say that someone agreed to do something. کرے گا *They said they would come to my party.*

wound (**wounds, wounding, wounded**) *n* A **wound** is a part of your body that you have hurt with something like a knife or a gun. زخم، ضرب ▷ *vi* If somebody or something **wounds** you, they hurt you. زخمی کرنا

wrap (**wraps, wrapping, wrapped**) *vt* When you **wrap** something, you fold paper or cloth tightly round it to cover it completely, for example in order to protect it or so that you can give it to someone as a present. لپیٹنا

wrapping paper (**wrapping papers**) *n* **Wrapping paper** is special paper which is used for wrapping presents. لپیٹنے کا کاغذ

wrap up *v* If you **wrap** something **up**, you fold paper or cloth tightly round it to cover it. لپیٹنا (کاغذ یا کپڑے وغیرہ میں)

wreck (**wrecks, wrecking, wrecked**) *n* A **wreck** is something such as ship, car, plane, or building which has been destroyed, usually in an accident. ملبہ ▷ *vi* To **wreck** something means to completely destroy or ruin it. ملبہ کر دینا، توڑ پھوڑ ڈالنا

wreckage *n* wreckage توڑ پھوڑ کر بنا ہوا ملبہ

wren (**wrens**) *n* A **wren** is a very small brown bird. رن چڑیا

wrench (**wrenches, wrenching, wrenched**) *n* If you say that leaving someone or something is a **wrench**, you feel very sad about it. جدائی، فراق کا صدمہ ▷ *vt* If you **wrench** something, usually something that is in a fixed position, you pull or twist it violently. چھین کر جدا کر دینا (کسی چیز کو)

wrestler (**wrestlers**) *n* A **wrestler** is someone who wrestles as a sport. پہلوان

wrestling *n* **Wrestling** is a sport in which two people wrestle and try to throw each other to the ground. پہلوانی

wrinkle (**wrinkles**) *n* Wrinkles are lines which form on someone's face as they grow old. جھری

wrinkled *adj* Someone who has **wrinkled** skin has a lot of wrinkles. جھریدار

wrist (**wrists**) *n* Your **wrist** is the part of your body between your hand and arm which bends when you move your hand. کلائی

write (**writes, writing, wrote, written**) *v* When you **write** something on a surface, you use something such as a pen or pencil to produce words, letters, or numbers on it. لکھنا

write down *v* When you **write** something **down**, you record it on a piece of paper using a pen or pencil. قلم سے کاغذ پر لکھنا *I wrote down exactly what I thought.*

writer (**writers**) *n* A **writer** is a person whose job is writing books, stories, or articles. مصنف

writing *n* **Writing** is something that has been written or printed. تحریر، تصنیف

writing paper (**writing papers**) *n* **Writing paper** is paper for writing letters on. It is usually of good, smooth quality. لکھنے کا کاغذ

wrong *adj* If there is something **wrong**, there is something that is not as it should be. غلط ▷ *adj* If you say that an answer is **wrong**, you mean that it is not right. غلط، صحیح نہ ہونا ▷ *adj* If you say that something someone does is **wrong**, you mean that it is bad. غلط، خراب

wrong number (**wrong numbers**) *n* A **wrong number** is a telephone number dialled in error. غلطی سے لگ جانے والا ٹیلیفون نمبر

W

x

Xmas (**Xmases**) *n* **Xmas** is used in written English to represent the word Christmas. informal. کرسمس

X-ray (**X-rays, X-raying, X-rayed**) *n An* **X-ray** is a type of radiation that can pass through most solid materials. **X-rays** are used by doctors to examine the bones or organs inside your body, and at airports to see inside people's luggage. ایکسرے (شعاعوں کو جسم سے گزارنا) ▷ *vt* If someone or something **is X-rayed**, an X-ray picture is taken of them. ایکسرے کرنا

xylophone (**xylophones**) *n* A **xylophone** is a musical instrument which consists of a row of wooden bars of different lengths. You play the xylophone by hitting the bars with special hammers. چوبی باجہ

y

yacht (**yachts**) *n* A **yacht** is a large boat with sails or a motor, used for racing or for pleasure trips. بحری مقابلے یا سیر کی کشتی

yard (**yards**) *n* A **yard** is a unit of length equal to 36 inches or approximately 91.4 centimetres. گز ▷ *n* A **yard** is a flat area of concrete or stone that is next to a building and often has a wall around it. احاطہ

yawn (**yawns, yawning, yawned**) *vi* If you **yawn**, you open your mouth very wide and breathe in more air than usual, often when you are tired or when you are not interested in something. جمائی لینا

year (**years**) *n* A **year** is a period of twelve months, beginning on the first of January and ending on the thirty-first of December. سال

yearly *adj A* **yearly** event happens once a year or every year. سالانہ ▷ *adv* If something happens **yearly**, it happens once a year or every year. سالانہ طور پر

yeast (**yeasts**) *n* **Yeast** is a kind of fungus which is used to make bread rise, and in making alcoholic drinks such as beer. خمیر

yell (**yells, yelling, yelled**) *v* If you **yell**, you shout loudly, usually because you are excited, angry, or in pain. زور سے چلانا

yellow *adj* Something that is **yellow** is the colour of lemons, butter, or the middle part of an egg. پیلا، زرد

Yellow Pages® *n* **Yellow Pages** is a

book that contains advertisements and telephone numbers for businesses and organizations in a particular area, grouped according to the type of business they do. یلو پیجز

Yemen *n* **Yemen** is a republic in south-west Arabia, on the Red Sea and the Gulf of Aden. یمن

yes! *excl* You say '**yes!**' to give a positive response to a question. ہاں!

yesterday (**allies**) *adv* You use **yesterday** to refer to the day before today. گزشتہ کل

yet *adv* You use **yet** when you expect something to happen, but it hasn't happened. پھر بھی

yew (**yews**) *n* A **yew** or a **yew tree** is an evergreen tree. It has sharp leaves which are broad and flat, and red berries. سدا بہار درخت

yield (**yields, yielding, yielded**) *vi* If you **yield** to someone or something, you stop resisting them. مان جانا، تسلیم کرنا

yoga *n* **Yoga** is a type of exercise in which you move your body into various positions in order to become more fit or flexible, to improve your breathing, and to relax your mind. یوگا

yoghurt (**yoghurts**) *n* **Yoghurt** is a slightly sour thick liquid made by adding bacteria to milk. دہی، رائب

yolk (**yolks**) *n* The **yolk** of an egg is the yellow part in the middle. زردی

you (**allies**) *pron* **You** means the person or people that someone is talking or writing to. تم، آپ

young (**younger, youngest**) *adj* A **young** person, animal, or plant has not lived for very long. نوجوان

younger *adj* A **younger** person or animal has lived for a shorter time than another. چھوٹا (عمر میں)

youngest *adj* The **youngest** person or animal of a group has lived for the shortest time of all of them. سب سے چھوٹا (عمر میں)

your *det* You use **your** to show that something belongs to the people that you are talking to. تمہارا، آپ کا

yours *pron* **Yours** refers to something belonging to the people that you are talking to. آپ کا

yourself *pron* **Yourself** means you alone. آپ خود

yourselves *pron* A speaker or writer uses **yourselves** to refer to the people that they are talking or writing to. **Yourselves** is used when the object of a verb or preposition refers to the same people as the subject of the verb. آپ خود

youth *n* Someone's **youth** is the period of their life when they are a child, before they are a fully mature adult. جوانی

youth club (**youth clubs**) *n* A **youth club** is a club where young people can go to meet each other and take part in various leisure activities. Youth clubs are often run by a church or local authority. نوجوانوں کا کلب (یوتھ کلب)

youth hostel (**youth hostels**) *n* A **youth hostel** is a place where people can stay cheaply when they are travelling. نوجوانوں کا ہاسٹل

X

Z

Zambia *n* **Zambia** is a republic in southern Africa. زامبیا (جمہوریہ)

Zambian (**Zambians**) *adj* **Zambian** means of or relating to Zambia or its inhabitants. زامبیائی ▷ *n* A **Zambian** is a native or inhabitant of Zambia. زامبیا کا باشندہ

zebra (**zebras, zebra**) *n* A **zebra** is an African wild horse which has black and white stripes. گوگھر

zebra crossing (**zebra crossings**) *n* In Britain, a **zebra crossing** is a place on the road that is marked with black and white stripes, where vehicles are supposed to stop so that people can walk across. پیدل چلنے والوں کے لئے سڑک پار کرنے کے لئے پٹی دار راستہ

zero (**zeros, zeroes**) *n* **Zero** is freezing point on the Centigrade scale. It is often written as 0 � C. صفر

zest *n* **Zest** is a feeling of pleasure and enthusiasm. مزا، چٹخارہ ▷ *n* The **zest** of a lemon, orange, or lime is the outer skin when it is used to give flavour to something such as a cake or drink. چھلکا

Zimbabwe *n* **Zimbabwe** is a country in south-east Africa. زمبابوے

Zimbabwean (**Zimbabweans**) *adj* **Zimbabwean** means of or relating to Zimbabwe or its inhabitants. زمبابوے کا ▷ *n* A **Zimbabwean** is a native or inhabitant of Zimbabwe. زمبابوے کا باشندہ

Zimmer® frame (**Zimmer frames**) *n* A **Zimmer frame** or a **Zimmer** is a frame that old or ill people sometimes use to help them walk. چلنے کے لئے استعمال ہونے والا فریم

zinc *n* **Zinc** is a bluish-white metal which is used to make other metals such as brass, or to cover other metals such as iron to stop them rusting. جستہ

zip (**zips, zipping, zipped**) *n* A **zip** is a device used to open and close parts of clothes and bags. It consists of two rows of metal or plastic teeth which separate or fasten together as you pull a small tag along them. زپ، چین ▷ *vt* When you **zip** something, you fasten it using a zip. زپ، چین بند کرنا

zit (**zits**) *n* **Zits** are spots on someone's skin, especially a young person's. جلد کے دھبے

zodiac *n* The **zodiac** is a diagram used by astrologers to represent the positions of the planets and stars. It is divided into twelve sections, each with a special name and symbol. بروج (ستاروں کے ۱۲ مجسموں کی خیالی تصاویر)

zone (**zones**) *n* A **zone** is an area that has particular features or characteristics. پٹی، حلقہ

zoo (**zoos**) *n* A **zoo** is a park where live animals are kept so that people can look at them. چڑیا گھر

zoology *n* **Zoology** is the scientific study of animals. حیوانیات

zoom lens (**zoom lenses**) *n* A **zoom lens** is a lens that you can attach to a camera, which allows you to make the details larger or smaller while always keeping the picture clear. چیزوں کو بڑا چھوٹا کرکے دooo کھانے والا عدسہ

INDEX

اِشاریہ

یقینی definite, sure
یقینی بنانا ensure
یمن Yemen
یوروپ Europe
یوروپیائی European
یوروپین European
یوروپی چڑیا grouse
یوروپی یونین European Union
یوروگوے کا Uruguay
یوروگوے کا باشندہ Uruguayan
یورینیم (ایک تابکار دھات) uranium
یوم ویلنٹائن Valentine's Day
یوم پیدائش birthday
یونان Greece
یونانی Greek
یونانی زبان Greek
یونائیٹڈ نیشنز (بالواسطہ یہودی ادارہ) UN
یونائیٹڈ کنگڈم (برطانیہ) UK
یونین union
یونیفورم ریسورس لوکیٹر (ویب کا پتہ) URL
یونیورسٹی university
یونیورسٹی، تعلیم گاہ uni
یوکرین Ukraine
یوکرینیائی Ukrainian
یوکرینیائی Ukrainian
یوگا yoga
یوگانڈا Uganda
یوگانڈیائی Ugandan
یک بہ یک abruptly
یکتا، انوکھی unique
یکسانی، اکتا دینے والا monotonous
یکسانیت resemblance, similarity
یکساں identical, similar
یکساں دکھائی دینا resemble
یکسوئی concentration
یکسو ہونا concentrate
یک وقتی simultaneous
یک وقتی طور پر simultaneously
یک پہیہ گاڑی wheelbarrow
یہ these, this
یہاں here
یہاں تک کہ till, unless
یہ (بے جان کے لئے) it
یہ (جمع) these
یہود کا Jewish
یہودی Jew
یہودیوں کی عبادت گاہ synagogue
۔۔ سے آنا come from
۔۔ سے گزرنا undergo
۔۔ پر کوشش کرنا، موزوں بنانا try on
۔۔ کا طعنہ دینا twit
۔۔ کا مفہوم ہونا stand for
۔۔ کی وجہ سے، ۔۔ کی بناء پر owing to
۔۔ کی پلٹ بھی صحیح vice versa
۔۔ ہونے تک until
۔۔۔ سے قبل earlier
۔۔۔ کے قابل ہونا fit in
۔۔۔ کے لئے پکارنا call for
بنکوں کی عام تعطیل (۳۰ جون) bank holiday

ہرجانہ compensation
ہرجانہ دینا compensate
ہرجگہ everywhere
ہرم، تکونی مقبرے pyramid
ہرن deer
ہرن کا گوشت venison
ہرکوئی everybody
ہرگھنٹے hourly
ہرے نیلے رنگ کی (چیزیں) turquoise
ہزار thousand
ہزارواں thousandth
ہزارواں حصہ thousandth
ہزارہ millennium
ہزارہ (ٹونٹی میں سیکڑوں سوراخ) watering can
ہسپتال hospital
ہضم ہونا digest
ہفتہ week
ہل plough
ہلانا shake
ہل چلانا، کھیت جوتنا plough
ہلکا mild
ہلکا، تھوڑا سا slight
ہلکا ارغوانی mauve
ہلکا رنگا ہوا tinted
ہلکا ناشتہ snack
ہلکا پکایا ہوا rare
ہلکا گرم lukewarm
ہلکا گھنگرالا wavy
ہلکا ر ہلکی light
ہلکا ر ہلکی ہونا light
ہلکی نیند سونا doze off
ہلکے طور پر slightly
ہلکے مشروب (الکحل کے بغیر) soft drink
ہلکے ناشتے کے ساتھ چائے tea
ہلکے پیلے رنگ کا fair
ہم us, we
ہمارا our
ہم آہنگ بنانا adjust
ہم آہنگی adjustment
ہم آہنگی communion
ہمت courage
ہمت، جرآت nerve
ہمت افزا encouraging
ہمت افزائی encouragement
ہمت افزائی کرنا encourage
ہمت توڑنا discourage
ہمت ور courageous
ہمت کرنا dare
ہمتی daring
ہم خود ourselves
ہمدرد sympathetic
ہمدردی sympathy
ہمدردی کرنا sympathize
ہمزاد clone
ہمزاد بنانا clone
ہم زمانہ contemporary
ہم سبھی ourselves
ہموار even, flat
ہموار، چکنا smooth
ہمہ گیر versatile
ہمیشہ always
ہمیشہ کے لیے forever
ہندسی، ڈیجیٹل digital
ہندوستان India
ہندوستانی Indian
ہندو (غیر مسلم) Hindu
ہندو مذہب Hinduism
ہندو (کثیر العقیدہ) Hindu
ہنس goose, swan
ہنسلی کی ہڈی collarbone
ہنسنا laugh
ہنسی laugh, laughter
ہنگامی حالت urgency
ہنگامی صورت حال emergency
ہنگامی نکاسی emergency exit
ہنگری Hungary
ہنگریائی Hungarian
ہنگری کا باشندہ Hungarian
ہوا air, wind
ہوابند airtight
ہوا بھرا تھیلا airbag
ہوا بھرنا pump up
ہوا بھری ر بھرا ہوا inflatable
ہوا بہنا wind
ہوادار windy
ہوا میں تیرنا، جھولنا float
ہوا میں پکڑنا catch
ہوائی اڈہ airport
ہوائی جہاز plane
ہوائی سفر کا بیمار airsick
ہوائی فضا airspace
ہوائی چپل flip-flops
ہوائی ڈاک airmail
ہواپاشی aerobics
ہوا کا جھونکا draught
ہوشمند conscious
ہوش میں sober
ہوش میں آنا come round
ہوش و شعور consciousness
ہوشیاری سے carefully
ہولناک repellent
ہومیوپیتھک homeopathic
ہومیوپیتھی homeopathy
ہونا be, become, get, happen, should
ہونٹ lip
ہونٹ تر، خشک یا پھٹے ہونٹوں کا لوشن lip salve
ہونٹوں کی سرخی، لپسٹک lipstick
ہونڈوراس Honduras
ہٹنا off
ہٹانا، نکالنا remove
ہچکچانا hesitate
ہچکیاں hiccups
ہڈیوں کا ڈھانچہ skeleton
ہڈی bone
ہڈی ٹوٹ جانا fracture
ہڑتال strike
ہڑتالی striker
ہک hook
ہکدار زیور brooch
ہکلانا stammer
ہیتی Haiti
ہیجان انگیز، سنسنی پیدا کرنے والا thrilled
ہیرا diamond
ہینڈل، دستہ handle
یا or
یا تو ۔ ۔ ۔ یا either ... or
یادداشت memo, memory
یاد دلانا remind
یاد دلانے والا بیپ beeper
یاد دہانی reminder
یاد رکھنا، کرنا remember
یاد کرنا memorize
یادگار memorial
یادگار، نشانی memento
یادگار (عمارت) monument
یتیم orphan
یرغمال hostage
یرقان jaundice
یقیناً definitely, surely
یقین دلانا assure, reassure
یقین دہانی reassuring
یقین سے certainly

گونگا dumb
گوٹی pebble
گوکھر، زیبرا zebra
گوکھرو thistle
گیانا جمہوریہ Guyana
گیراج، کار مرمت کرنے کی جگہ garage
گدھ، کرگس vulture
گرا دینا، منہدم کرنا pull down
گروہ، دستہ، ٹیم team
گرہ، گانٹھ knot
گلہری squirrel
گنی جمہوریہ Guinea
گٹار guitar
گٹھیا arthritis
گپ شپ gossip
گپ شپ کرنا gossip
گچھا bunch
گڈمڈ muddle
گڑگڑاہٹ، شور rattle
گڑیا doll, puppet
گھاس grass
گھاس کا انبار haystack
گھاس کا میدان lawn
گھانا Ghana
گھانائی Ghanaian
گھاٹ quay
گھاٹا deficit
گھاٹ کی کشتی ferry
گھر home, house
گھر، رہائش apartment
گھرانہ household
گھر کا بنا home-made
گھر کا پتہ home address
گھر کی یاد سے پریشان homesick
گھر کے اندر inside
گھر کے اندر ٹھہرنا stay in
گھر کے طور پر home
گھریلو domestic
گھریلو کام housework
گھس پیٹھیا intruder
گھسیٹنا drag
گھسیڑنا (انگلیوں سے دھکیلنا) poke
گھماؤ turn
گھنا dense
گھناپن density
گھنٹہ hour
گھنٹی bell
گھنٹی بجانا ring
گھنٹے بھر کا hourly
گھنٹے کے اعتبار سے hourly
گھنڈی، ہینڈل، ہتھہ knob
گھنے گھنگرالے poorly
گھورا dump
گھورنا stare
گھورنا، ٹکٹکی لگا کر دیکھنا gaze
گھومنا turn, wander
گھونسلہ nest
گھونگا snail
گھونگھا slug
گھونگھٹ veil
گھوٹالا scam
گھوڑا horse
گھوڑا کدانا show jumping
گھوڑی mare
گھوڑی (چھوٹے قد کی) pony
گھٹانا decrease, reduce
گھٹنا diminish, knee
گھٹنوں پر چلنے والا toddler
گھٹنوں کے بل زمین پر جھکنا kneel down
گھٹنے (چھوٹے پائینچے کا پاجاما) shorts
گھٹیا lousy
گھڑ دوڑ horse racing
گھڑ دوڑ کا میدان racecourse
گھڑسواری horse riding
گھڑی clock
گھڑیال alligator
گھڑی کا پٹہ watch strap
گھڑی کی الٹی سمت anticlockwise
گھڑی کی سوئیوں کی سمت میں clockwise
گھیرنے والا surround
گھیرے ہوئے around
گہرا dark, deep
گہرا سرخ scarlet
گہرائی depth
گہرائی سے deeply
گہری ز گہرے intimate
گیارہ eleven
گیارہواں eleventh
گیبن Gabon
گیت song
گیت کے بول lyrics
گیس gas
گیلی لکڑی کا کندہ، لٹھ log
گیم، کھیل game
گیمبیا Gambia
گیند ball
گیندا marigold
گیند کو سرو کرنے والا server
گیہوں wheat
گیہوں ہضم نہ ہونا wheat intolerance
ہوائی ساز (بانسری وغیرہ) woodwind
ہاتھ hand
ہاتھ اوپر پھیرنا stroke
ہاتھ سے دینا hand
ہاتھوں اور ناخنوں کی صفائی manicure
ہاتھوں اور ناخنوں کی صفائی کرنا manicure
ہاتھ کا بنا ہوا handmade
ہاتھ ہلانا، الوداع کہنا wave
ہاتھ ہلانا (ہلو یا الوداع کہنے کے لئے) wave
ہاتھی elephant
ہاتھی دانت ivory
ہار جانا lose
ہارن horn
ہارڈبورڈ hardboard
ہاضمہ digestion
ہال hall
ہالینڈ Holland
ہانڈی، پتیلا pot
ہاں! yes!
ہتک آمیز offensive
ہتک آمیز طور پر دھیرے سے ہنسنا snigger
ہتھوڑا hammer
ہتھہ، دستہ lever
ہتھکڑی handcuffs
ہتھیار weapon
ہتھیار ڈالنا، جھک جانا give in
ہتھیانا grab
ہتھیلی palm
ہجرت migration
ہجے spelling
ہجے چیک کرنے والا کمپیوٹر پروگرام spellchecker
ہجے کرنا spell
ہدایات instructions
ہدایت briefing, directions
ہدایت دینا instruct
ہدایت کار director
ہدایتی کتاب manual
ہدف target
ہر either
ہرا green
ہراسانی harassment
ہرانا defeat
ہر ایک each, everyone

because کیوں کہ
mud کیچڑ
muddy کیچڑ زدہ
mudguard کیچڑ محافظ (مڈ گارڈ)
bug, pest, worm کیڑا
insect کیڑا، حشرہ
pesticide کیڑے مار دوا
crab کیکڑا
sponge کیک یا پڈنگ
onto کے اوپر
of کے بارے میں
although کے باوجود
with کے ساتھ
along کے ساتھ، پر
against کے سہارے
capable کے قابل
then کے مقابلے
carrot گاجر
cheek گال
slot گالا، شگاف
cheekbone گال کی ہڈیاں
sing, singing گانا
cyst گانٹھ
singer گانے والا
village گاؤں
cow گائے
thick گاڑھا
cart گاڑی
trailer گاڑی سے منسلک باربرداری کا چھکڑا
drive گاڑی چلانا
sidelight گاڑی کی سامنے کی چھوٹی لائٹ
shall گا، گی
cushion گدا
quilt گدا
tickle گدگدانا
donkey گدھا
knock down گرادینا
graph گراف
gram گرام
drop, fall گراوٹ
گرائی اور اٹھائی جانے والی چھت کی کی
گاڑی convertible
thunder گرج، گھن گرج
church گرجا
thunderstorm گرجدار طوفان
thundery گرجدار طوفانی
cyclone, hurricane گردابی طوفان
conjugation گردان (تصریف) فعل کا صیغہ

neck گردن
kidney گردہ
arrest, capture گرفتار کرنا
arrest, detention گرفتاری
catch up گرفت میں لینا
grasp گرفت میں لینا، ہڑپ لینا
hot, warm گرم
cosy گرم اور آرام دہ
heat, warm up گرم کرنا
heat up گرم کرنا (ٹھنڈے کھانے کو)
sweatshirt گرم کپڑے کی قمیض
heat گرمی
summer holidays گرمی کی چھٹیاں
drop, fall گرنا
gang, group گروہ
mortgage گروی رکھنا
fall down گر پڑنا
pickpocket گرہ کٹ، جیب کترہ
play truant گریزپا، اسکول سے بھاگنے کا کھیل
Greenland گرین لینڈ
yard گز
spend گزارنا
live on گزارہ کرنا
gone گزرا ہوا
cost of living گزر بسر کی لاگت
go by, go through, pass گزرنا
previous گزشتہ
preceding گزشتہ، پہلے کی کوئی مثال
previously گزشتہ طور پر
yesterday گزشتہ کل
cheeky گستاخ
patrol گشت
march گشت کرنا
patrol car گشتی کار
negotiate گفت و شنید کرنا
negotiations گفت و شنید، معاملہ داری
conversation گفتگو
throat گلا
rose گلاب
pink گلابی
rosé گلابی شراب
glass گلاس
strangle گلا گھونٹنا
vase گلدان
chrysanthemum, daisy گل داؤدی
bouquet گلدستہ
mumps, tonsils گلسوئے
florist گلفروش

carnation گلنار
muffler گلوبند، مفلر
glucose گلوکوز
poppy گل لالہ
lane گلی
street گلی، گلیارا
corridor گلیارا
necklace گلے کا ہار
misleading گمراہ کن
missing گم شدہ
plant pot گملا
anonymous گمنام
vice گناہ
count گنتی کرنا
count on گنتے جانا
bald گنجا
room گنجائش، خالی جگہ
hold گنجائش ہونا
skinhead گنجا یا چھوٹے بالوں والا نوجوان
dirty گندا
smudge گندا دھندلا نشان
dirt گندگی
dough گندھا آٹا
Guatemala گوائٹے مالا جمہوریہ
witness گواہ
lap گود
warehouse گودام
adopt گود لینا
tattoo گودنا
pier گودی
gorilla گوریلا
meat گوشت
mutton گوشت (بکری بھیڑ کا)
vegetarian گوشت خور کی ضد
vegan گوشت سے پرہیز کرنے والا
fillet گوشت سے ہڈی نکالنا
joint گوشت کا بڑا ٹکڑا
round گول، دائرہ نما
broad bean گول دانے
plump گول مٹول، چکنا
roundabout گول چکر
beret گول ہیٹ
pellet گولی (آٹے وغیرہ کی)
pill گولی (دوا)
shoot گولی مارنا
wart گومڑا (وائرس کی وجہ سے جلد پر ابھار)
resin گوند
glue گوند، سریش

کسی مقام خاص طور سے گھر کی مکمل صفائی spring-cleaning
کسی مقام پر رکھنا placement
کسی کے لئے انتظار کرنا wait
کشمش sultana
کفالت sponsorship
کفالت کرنا sponsor
کنارا shore
کھلاڑی player
کٹنے کا زخم cut
کٹوتی cutback
کپ بورڈ sideboard
کپتان captain
کپڑا cloth
کپڑا، لباس garment
کپڑوں کی الماری wardrobe
کپڑے clothes
کپڑے اتار دینا strip
کپڑے اتارنا undress
کپڑے دھونے کا عمل laundry
کپڑے سکھانے والی (مشین) spin drier
کپکپانا tremble
کچلنا crush
کچھ any, few
کچھ، تھوڑا some
کچھ بھی نہیں nothing
کچھوا tortoise
کچھ (چیز) some
کچھ کریم نکالا ہوا دودھ semi-skimmed milk
کچی پیاز کا پودا spring onion
کڑھائی pan
کڑھی curry
کڑھی سفوف curry powder
کگرمتا mushroom
کھاتہ account
کھاتہ نمبر account number
کھاد fertilizer, manure
کھانا eat, meal
کھانا، خوراک food
کھانا زہریلا ہونا food poisoning
کھانسنا cough
کھانسی bronchitis, cough
کھانسی کا آمیزہ cough mixture
کھانے میں پہلے پیش کی جانے والی چیز starter
کھانے کا سوڈا bicarbonate of soda
کھانے کا وقت mealtime
کھانے کے لئے پاک (یہودیت کے مطابق) kosher
کھجانا، کھجلی کرنا scratch
کھجلی itch
کھردرا rough
کھرپتوار weed
کھرپتوار کش weedkiller
کھرچنا scratch
کھلا bare
کھلانا، پلانا feed
کھلنا open
کھلنے کے اوقات opening hours
کھلکھلانا giggle
کھلی open
کھلے صفحات scrap paper
کھلے میں out-of-doors
کھمبا pillar
کھمبا، لمبی لکڑی pole
کھودنا dig
کھولنا open, unlock, unroll
کھولنا، کئے ہوئے کو الٹنا undo
کھولنا، گرہ کھولنا untie
کھولنے اور بند کرنے والی چھت کی گاڑی convertible
کھونا lose
کھوپڑی skull
کھوکھلا hollow
کھویا ہوا lost
کھسکنا shuffle
کھلاڑی sportsman
کھلاڑیوں کے لباس sportswear
کھلونا toy
کھڑکی window
کھڑکی کا فریم window pane
کھڑکی کے تلے سے جڑی الماری (اندر یا باہر) windowsill
کھڑکی کے ساتھ والی نشست window seat
کھٹا sour
کھپرا scale
کھپریل tile
کھپریل والا tiled
کھچی (ہڈی کو سیدھا رکھنے کے لئے) splint
کھڈا dent
کھڈا کرنا dent
کھریا chalk
کھڑے ہونا stand, stand up
کھیت field
کھیتی باڑی farming
کھیرا cucumber
کھیل sport
کھیل، گیم game
کھیل (دو کھلاڑی ربر کی گیند کو دیوار پر مارتے ہیں) squash
کھیلنا play
کھیلوں سے وابستہ sporty
کھیل کا میدان playground
کھینا (ناؤ) row
کھینچنا draw, pull
کھینچ کر ہٹا دینا tow away
کہ that
کہانی tale
کہاوت saying
کہاوت، تمثیل proverb
کہاں where
کہرا fog
کہرا، دھند mist
کہر آلود misty
کہر آلود foggy
کہرے میں دیکھنے میں مدد کرنے والی تیز لائٹ fog light
کہنا say, tell
کہنا، مجبور کرنا make
کہنی elbow
کہیں اور elsewhere
کہیں بھی anywhere
کہیں نہیں nowhere
کیا what
کیا ہوا done
کیتلی kettle
کیریبیائی Caribbean
کیسے، کس طرح how
کیفین caffeine
کیفے ٹیریا۔ قہوہ خانہ cafeteria
کیل، میخ nail
کیلا banana
کیلئے for
کیمیا chemistry
کیمیاوی مادہ (بدن میں پیدا ہویا مصنوعی طور پر بنایا جائے) steroid
کیمیرون Cameroon
کینٹین canteen
کینیا Kenya
کینیائی Kenyan
کینیڈا Canada
کینیڈین Canadian
کیوبا Cuba
کیوبائی Cuban
کیوں why

کشمش currant, raisin
کشمیرا cashmere
کشیدہ کاری embroidery
کشیدہ کاری کرنا embroider
کفایت enough
کفایت شعاری سے خرچ کرنا economize
کفایتی economical
کفایتی درجہ economy class
کفچہ (باورچی خانے کا اوزار) spatula
کفیل sponsor
کل total
کل، سالم، مکمل، پورا whole
کلائی wrist
کل جمع total
کلف (کاربوہائڈریٹ) starch
کل وقتی full-time
کلومیٹر فی گھنٹہ km/h
کلہاڑی axe
کلی طور پر totally
کلیہ، اصول theory
کم less
کم، تھوڑا less
کم ادائگی پانے والے underpaid
کم از کم at least, minimum
کمان bow
کمانا earn
کمائی earnings
کمائی، پیداوار proceeds
کمبل blanket
کمبوڈیائی Cambodian
کمبوڈیا Cambodia
کمبوڈیائی Cambodian
کمتر inferior
کمتر (رقم وغیرہ) least
کم دوری تیز دوڑوں میں حصہ لینے والا sprinter
کم دوری کی تیز دوڑ sprint
کمر waist
کم روغنی low-fat
کمرہ room
کمرہ، وارڈ ward
کمرۂ طعام dining room
کمزور frail, pale, unsteady, weak
کمزوری weakness
کم سوجھ بوجھ والے thoughtless
کم صلاحیت incompetent
کم عمر underage
کم قیمت سمجھنا underestimate
کمنٹری کرنے والا تبصرہ کرنے والا commentator
کمینہ mean
کم پانی والا تالاب (بچوں کے لئے) paddling pool
کمپنی کے حصص stock
کمپیوٹر پروگرام برائے تلاش search engine
کمپیوٹر workstation
کمپیوٹر استعمال نہ ہونے پر اس کی اسکرین پر موجود متحرک تصویر screensaver
کمپیوٹر پروگرام software
کمپیوٹر کا حفاظتی نظام firewall
کم گہرا shallow
کمی lack
کمی، قلت shortfall
کمیاب scarce
کمیشن commission
کمی محسوس کرنا miss
کمی کرنا cut down
کنارا edge
کنجوس miser, stingy
کندھا shoulder
کندھے اچکانا shrug
کندھے کی تکونی ہڈی shoulder blade
کندہ تاریخ تک بیچ دینا چاہئے sell-by date
کنستر canister
کنوارہ bachelor
کنواری Miss, virgin
کنواں well
کنڈلی horoscope
کنکر gravel, stone
کنکر، سنگریزہ grit
کنکر، ڈھیلا rock
کنگارو kangaroo
کنگھا comb
کنگھی کرنا comb
کو to
کوا crow
کودنا، اچھلنا skip
کوریا Korea
کوریائی Korean
کوسوو Kosovo
کوسٹاریکا Costa Rica
کوشش attempt, effort
کوشش کرنا attempt, try
کوشش try
کوفتے meatball
کولتار اور بجری tarmac
کولمبیا Colombia
کولمبیائی Colombian
کولہے کی ہڈیاں pelvis
کوما، دماغی موت coma
کون which, who
کونسل ہاؤس council house
کون سی which
کونہ corner
کونے سلی چادر fitted sheet
کوئل cuckoo
کوئلہ coal
کوئی someone
کوئی شخص somebody
کوئی چیز (کچھ چیز) something
کوئلے کی کان colliery
کوئی any
کوئی، کوئی ایک a, an
کوئی ایک either
کوئی بھی anyone
کوئی بھی نہیں neither
کوئی بھی چیز stuff
کوئی شخص anybody
کوئی نہیں nobody, none, no one
کوئی چیز anything
کوا raven
کوٹ coat
کوٹھی villa
کوچ، فوجی انداز میں روانگی march
کوڑا، درّا whip
کوڑا دان litter bin
کوڑا کرکٹ litter, refuse
کوڑے دان bin, dustbin
کوڑے کا برتن dustpan
کوکنا squeak
کوکھ کرایہ پر دینے والی surrogate mother
کوہپیما mountaineer
کوہپیمائی mountaineering
کوہپیمائی کا لباس cagoule
کویت Kuwait
کویتی Kuwaiti
کئی several
کتابچہ leaflet
کرایہ rent
کرایہ پر لینا rent
کس کی whose
کسی جگہ someplace, somewhere

کارتوس **cartridge**
کارخانہ **factory, plant**
کارروائی **action**
کارروائی کرنا **act**
کارواں **caravan**
کارٹون فلم **cartoon**
کار (چار سے زیادہ سیٹوں والی) **saloon**
کارڈ، موٹا سخت کاغذ **card**
کار ڈھونے والی ناو **car ferry**
کار کا سامنے کا شیشہ **windscreen**
کارکردگی **performance**
کار کی چابیاں **car keys**
کاری ضرب لگانا **bash**
کاریگر، دستکار **workman**
کاریگر خانہ **workshop**
کاغذ **paper**
کاغذ کی پرچی **slip**
کاغذی، پلاسٹک بیگ **carrier bag**
کاغذی نوٹ **banknote**
کاغذی کارروائی **paperwork**
کافی **so, too**
کافی، بہت زیادہ **lot**
کافی، حسب ضرورت **enough**
کافی، قہوہ **coffee**
کافی کی میز **coffee table**
کافی کے دانے **coffee bean**
کالا **black**
کالج **college**
کالک **soot**
کالی سفید مچھلی **whiting**
کالی مرچ **pepper**
کالی مرچ کی چکی **peppermill**
کالی کافی **black coffee**
کام **work**
کام بند کر دینا **strike**
کام طور پر، بلا شرکت غیرے **exclusively**
کاملیت **perfection**
کام کا اجازت نامہ **work permit**
کام کا تجربہ **work experience**
کام کرنا **work**
کام کرنے لائق لوگوں کا طبقہ **working-class**
کام کرنے لائق لوگوں کی تعداد **workforce**
کام کرنے والا، مزدور **worker**
کام کے لئے مہیا کرائی گئی جگہ **workspace**
کامیاب **pass, successful**
کامیاب، برتر **promising**
کامیاب ہونا **succeed**
کامیابی **achievement, success**
کامیابی سے **successfully**
کان **ear**
کان، کھان **mine**
کان درد **earache**
کانسہ **bronze**
کانٹا **fork, thorn**
کانٹے دار تار **barbed wire**
کانپنا **shiver**
کانپنا، تھرتھرانا **shake**
کانکن **miner**
کانکنی **mining**
کان کی بالی / بالا **earring**
کان کی جھلی **eardrum**
کانگو **Congo**
کائنات، آفاق **universe**
کائی **moss**
کاٹ لینا **cut**
کاٹنا **bite, cross out, cut, mow**
کاٹ پھینکنا **cut off**
کاکروچ **cockroach**
کاگ **cork**
کاہو، سلاد **lettuce**
کا ہونا، کی ملکیت ہونا **one's**
کایا پلٹنا **transform**
کب **when**
کباب **beefburger, cutlet, kebab**
کبوتر **pigeon**
کبھی **ever**
کبھی بھی (آنے والے وقت میں) **sometimes**
کبھی نہیں **never**
کبھی نہیں، اکثر نہیں **seldom**
کبھی کبھی **sometime**
کتا **dog**
کتاب **book**
کتابچہ **booklet, handbook**
کتاب کا خانہ **bookcase, bookshelf**
کتاب کی دکان **bookshop**
کتبہ **gravestone**
کتنے، کتنا **how**
کتیا **bitch**
کثیرالمقصد فون **smart phone**
کثیر الوقوع **frequent**
کثیر بافتی تصلب **multiple sclerosis**
کثیر ملکی **multinational**
کدو، لوکی **pumpkin**
کدوکش کرنا **grate**
کراب کرنا **worsen**
کراٹے (خالی ہاتھ) **karate**
کراہ **groan**
کراہنا **moan**
کرایہ **fare, hire**
کرایہ دار **tenant**
کرایہ پر لینا **hire**
کرتب باز **stuntman**
کرتب بازی **stunt**
کردار **character**
کردار ادا کرنا **act**
کرسی **chair**
کرشمہ **miracle**
کرغزستان **Kyrgyzstan**
کرنا **do, make**
کرنی، رانبی **trowel**
کروشیا **Croatia, crochet**
کروشیائی **Croatian**
کروشیائی زبان **Croatian**
کروندا **cranberry**
کروڑپتی **millionaire**
کرہ، سیارہ **planet**
کرچی **splinter**
کرکٹ **cricket**
کرکے دکھانا، کرکے بتانا، مظاہرہ کرنا **show**
کرہ ارض **globe**
کریانہ دوکان **grocer**
کریم نکلا ہوا دودھ **skimmed milk**
کریڈٹ کارڈ **credit card**
کریہہ **hideous**
کرے گا (مستقبل) **will**
کساد بازاری **recession**
کسنا (ٹائٹ کرنا) **do up**
کسوٹی، معیار **criterion**
کسی بھی طرح **somehow**
کسی ریستراں کی سب سے سستی شراب **house wine**
کسی طرح **anyhow, anyway**
کسی فرقے یا قوم کی روایتی داستانیں، لباس اور عادتیں **folklore**
کسی نے بھی نہیں **neither**
کسی وقت **anytime**
کسی کھاتے سے نکالی رقم کا اندراج **debit**
کسی کے قول کا حوالہ دینا **quote**
کشادہ ذہن **broad-minded**
کشتی چلانا **sail**
کشش **attraction, charm**

چھلہ، کی رنگ keyring
چھلہ کار curler
چھ ماہی semester
چھننی، چھلنی colander
چھونا touch
چھوٹ، رخصت rebate
چھوٹا inferior, small
چھوٹا، تھوڑا skimpy
چھوٹا، چھوٹی little
چھوٹا، کمتر، کم low
چھوٹا بھورا جانور hedgehog
چھوٹا تولیہ، دست پاک napkin
چھوٹا سا tiny
چھوٹا سفری بیگ (صابن ٹوتھ برش رکھنے کو) sponge bag
چھوٹا (عمر میں) younger
چھوٹا قد short
چھوٹا ٹکڑا grain
چھوٹا پودا bush
چھوٹ جانا، چلے جانا go off
چھوٹ دینا discount
چھوٹی آستین والی short-sleeved
چھوٹی بلونی whisk
چھوٹی ناؤ dinghy
چھوٹے اشتہار small ads
چھوٹے فلیٹ میں اسٹوڈیو studio flat
چھچھوندر mole
چھوڑا ہوا سامان left luggage
چھوڑ دینا quit, skip
چھوڑ دینا، ترک کر دینا give up
چھوڑنا abandon, leave, opt out
چھوکرا brat
چھلکا peel, zest
چھلکا اتارنا peel
چھٹک جانا skid
چھپکلی lizard
چھڑکاؤ spray
چھڑکاؤ کرنا spray
چھٹا sixth
چھٹنی redundancy
چھٹی leave
چھٹکارا escape
چھٹکنا drift
چھٹی holiday
چھٹی کا دن time off
چھپانا hide
چھپانا، پردہ پوشی کرنا hide
چھپائی، طباعت print

چھپنا hide
چھپر والا، کھپریل والا thatched
چھپی ہوئی hidden
چھڑی club
چھیدنا pierce
چھیننا snatch
چھین کر جدا کر دینا (کسی چیز کو) wrench
چھینکنا sneeze
چہرہ face
چہرہ صاف کرنے کا تولیہ face cloth
چہرے سے متعلق facial
چہرے پر داغ دھبہ والا spotty
چہرے کے بال صاف کرنا (شیو) shave
چہل قدمی stroll, walk
چیتا، تیندوا leopard
چیخ cry, scream
چیخ مارنا shriek
چیخنا scream
چیخنا چلانا shout
چیخ پکار shout
چیرنا rip
چیز object, thing
چیزوں کو بڑا چھوٹا کر کے دکھانے والا عدسہ zoom lens
چین China
چینی Chinese
چینی زبان Chinese
چینی مٹی ceramic, china
چیونٹی ant
چیرس، مرحبا! cheers!
چیچنیا Chechnya
چیچک chickenpox
چیک باشندہ Czech
چیک جمہوریہ Czech Republic
چیک زبان Czech
چیکوسلواکیا سے متعلق Czech
ڈانٹنا scold
ڈاؤن لوڈ کرنا download
ڈاکٹر doctor
ڈاک کا نشان postmark
ڈاکیہ postman
ڈبونا dip, soak
ڈبہ بند tinned
ڈبکی مارنا، غوطہ لگانا plunge
ڈبہ container
ڈبہ، ٹن can
ڈبے carriage
ڈر fright, horror, scare

ڈرامائی dramatic
ڈرانا scare, terrify
ڈراونا frightening, horrible
ڈراونا خواب یا تجربہ nightmare
ڈراونی فلم horror film
ڈراونا - ڈرونی scary
ڈرا ہوا afraid, frightened
ڈرنا fear
ڈرنا، ڈرانا frighten
ڈنمارک Denmark
ڈنڈا staff
ڈنک sting
ڈنک مارنا sting
ڈوبنا drown, sink
ڈوری بنسی fishing tackle
ڈومنیکن جمہوریہ Dominican Republic
ڈونٹ doughnut
ڈوئی ladle
ڈپلوما diploma
ڈکار burp
ڈکار لینا burp
ڈگری یافتہ، گریجویٹ graduate
ڈھال shield
ڈھانچہ apparatus, structure
ڈھلان ramp, slope
ڈھلوان steep
ڈھلوان کی چوٹی پر پہنچانے والی لفٹ ski lift
ڈھول drum
ڈھولچی drummer
ڈھکنا cover
ڈھکن lid
ڈھیر heap, pile, stack
ڈھیر، ڈلا mass
ڈھیر، ڈھیلا lump
ڈھیلا loose, slack
ڈھیلا لباس baggy
ڈھیلا ڈھالا loose
ڈھے جانا collapse
ڈنمارکی Dane
ڈینگ مارنا boast
ڈیوڑھی porch
ژالہ باری sleet
کا of, to
کا، کی، کے of
کالی مکھی dragonfly
کاجو cashew
کار car
کارآموز apprentice

پیچھے کی سمت backside
پیچھے کی طرف backwards
پیچیدگی complication
پیچیدہ complex
پیکنگ کھولنا unwrap
پیک کرنا pack
چابی، کنجی key
چادر sheet
چادر تکیے غلاف bed linen
چادریں غلاف bedclothes
چار four
چاقو، چھری knife
چاقو مارنا، پیوست کرنا، گھونپنا stab
چالاک clever
چالاکی سے کام نکالنا manipulate
چالبازی tactics
چالو، چلتی حالت میں on
چالو کرنا، شروع کرنا turn on
چالو کھاتہ current account
چالیس forty
چاند moon
چاندی silver
چاول rice
چائے tea
چائے دانی teapot
چائے کا وقت teatime
چائے کا چمچ teaspoon
چائے کی پیالی teacup
چاٹنا lick
چاڈ Chad
چاہت obsession
چاہنا want
چبانا chew
چبوترہ stand
چبھو کر سوراخ کرنا prick
چتلا کوا magpie
چربی fat
چرند پرند (حیوانات) fauna
چرواہا، گڈریا shepherd
چرچ کی مینار کی چوٹی پر نوکدار ڈھانچہ steeple
چست، تراشیدہ بدن slender
چشمہ glasses
چقندر beetroot
چلانا conduct, operate
چلتا پھرتا گھر mobile home
چلنا، ٹہلنا walk
چلنے کا عمل walking
چلنے کی چھڑی walking stick
چلین Chilean
چلے جانا go away
چمنی chimney
چمپینزی chimpanzee
چمچ بھر spoonful
چمچ spoon
چمڑا leather
چمکدار bright, fluorescent, shiny
چمکنا shine
چمکیلا، بھڑکیلا bright
چمگادڑ bat
چناؤ election
چنا ہوا chosen
چند، تھوڑا few
چندہ، عطیہ subscription
چننا choose, elect, select
چنگی toll
چوبی باجہ xylophone
چوتڑ، سرین bottom
چوتھا fourth
چوتھائی quarter
چودہ fourteen
چودہواں fourteenth
چور thief
چوراہا crossroads
چوری theft
چوزہ chick
چوسنا suck
چومنا kiss
چونا lime
چونا پتھر limestone
چونچ beak
چونے سے پتائی کرنا whitewash
چوٹی top
چوٹی، سرفہرست top
چوٹی (دم کی طرح جھولتی ہوئی) ponytail
چوٹی کی طرف، پر uphill
چوپڑ draughts
چوپہیہ گاڑی (سب پہیوں کو انجن سے راست توانائی ملتی ہے) four-wheel drive
چوڑا wide
چوڑائی width
چوڑی سویاں spaghetti
چوڑی سڑک motorway
چوکور diamond
چوکھا frame
چوہا mouse, rat
چوہا گھر mouse mat
چیونگم gum
چرانا steal
چبوترہ، پلیٹ فارم platform
چراغ، بلب lamp
چراغ کا کھمبا lamppost
چلی Chile
چنگاری spark
چپکنے والا sticky
چپکو کیڑا stick insect
چڑیا (گوریا) sparrow
چڑیا گھر zoo
چھدا ہوا pierced
چٹان rock
چٹائی mat
چٹنی ketchup
چٹکی بھرنا pinch
چپت لگانا smack
چپو oar
چپل slipper
چپٹا اسکرین (کمپیوٹر، ٹی وی) flat-screen
چپکانا glue, paste
چپکنا، چپکانا stick
چچا، ماموں uncle
چچازاد بھائی یا بہن cousin
چچی، خالہ، پھوپی aunt, auntie
چڑھائی climbing
چڑھتی بیل honeysuckle
چڑھنا climb
چڑھنا، بڑھنا mount up
چڑھنے والا climber
چڑیا bird
چکوترہ grapefruit
چکور pheasant
چکر vertigo
چکی mill
چھ six
چھاتا umbrella
چھاتی کے بل تیرنا breaststroke
چھالہ sore
چھاننا filter
چھانٹنا sort out
چھاپنے والا printer
چھت ceiling, roof
چھت سی دھوپ آنے کے لیےشگاف sunroof
چھرےدار بندوق shotgun
چھلنی sieve
چھلکا bran, skin
چھلک جانا spill

پھول flower
پھول آنا، بہار آنا flower
پھول گوبھی cauliflower
پھونک مارنا blow
پھوہار drizzle
پھر بھی yet
پھر جانا، بدل جانا (مثبت طور پر) turn out
پھر سے بنانا rebuild
پھر سے سجانا redecorate
پھر سے شادی کرنا remarry
پھر سے مل جانا reunion
پھسل جانا slip
پھسلن بھرا slippery
پھسلنے کا ڈھانچہ slide
پھٹنا burst
پھٹا، ٹکڑے ہوا split
پھٹی پرانی، گھسی گزری worn
پھپھوندی mould
پھپھوندی لگی ہوئی mouldy
پھڑپھڑانا flap
پھیلانا spread, stretch
پھیلنا spread, stretch
پھیلنے کی سکت والا stretchy
پھینٹ کرتے ہوئے انڈوں کی ڈش scrambled eggs
پھینک دینا throw away
پھینکنا throw
پھیپھڑا lung
پہاڑ، کوہ mountain
پہاڑ پر چڑھائی rock climbing
پہاڑی hill
پہاڑی سلسلہ mountainous
پہاڑی علاقے میں چلنا hill-walking
پہلا نام first name
پہلو aspect, side
پہلو، بغل side
پہلوان wrestler
پہلوانی wrestling
پہلوانی مقابلہ (ہر ایک کو ۵ بار موقع) pentathlon
پہلی بار first
پہلے before, first
پہلے، بعد والا later
پہلے، جلدی early
پہلے سے already
پہلے سے ہی beforehand
پہلے نہ ہوا ہو unprecedented
پہلے کی شام eve
پہننا wear
پہنچنا approach, get, reach
پہچاننا pick out
پہیلی crossword
پہیہ wheel
پہیہ دار کرسی wheelchair
پہیہ دار سیڑھی stepladder
پہیہ دار پٹری، اسکیٹ بورڈ skateboard
پہیے دار کرسی pushchair
پہیے کی مرکزی پلیٹ سے جڑی سلاخیں spoke
پہیے یا پھسلنے والے بوٹ skates
پیادہ فوج infantry
پیار love
پیارا affectionate, cute, lovely
پیار کرنا، محبت کرنا خیال رکھنا love
پیاری darling
پیاز onion
پیاس thirst
پیاسا thirsty
پیالی cup
پیتل brass
پیتل کا ساز cornet
پیداوار breed
پیداواریت productivity
پیدائش birth
پیدائشی born
پیدا کرنا breed, produce
پیدل paddle
پیدل راستہ walkway
پیدل چلانا paddle
پیدل سفر hiking
پیر feet, foot, Monday
پیراگوائی Paraguayan
پیراگوئے Paraguay
پیرو Peru
پیروویائی Peruvian
پیروں سے متعلق بیماری کا ڈاکٹر chiropodist
پیروں میں پٹے باندھ کر برف پر پھسلنا ski
پیر کا پنجہ toe
پیر یا جوتے کا نشان footprint
پیسنا grind
پیسٹ کرنا (کمپیوٹر) paste
پیشاب urine
پیشانی forehead
پیش بینی کرنا foresee
پیشرفت progress
پیشقدمی، پہلا قدم initiative
پیشین گوئی کرنا predict
پیش کرنا offer, put forward
پیش کرنے والا presenter
پیشکش offer
پیشگی advance
پیشگی ادا کردہ prepaid
پیشہ career, occupation, profession
پیشہ ور professional
پیشہ ورانہ professional, vocational
پیشہ ورانہ طور پر professionally
پیشہ ور سازندہ گلوکار busker
پیشی presentation
پیغام message
پیغامبر messenger
پیلا، زرد yellow
پیلے پھول والا پودا buttercup
پیمانہ metric, scale, scales
پیمائش کا آلہ، رولر ruler
پیمائش کا فیتہ tape measure
پیمائش کرنا، تخمینہ لگانا measure
پیمائشیں measurements
پینا drink
پین جس کے نب میں روشنائی نمدے سے آتی ہے felt-tip
پیچ screw
پیچ کس screwdriver
پینے کا پانی drinking water
پیورٹو ریکو Puerto Rico
پیوست کردہ canned
پیوند patch
پیوند لگا ہوا patched
پیٹ abdomen, stomach
پیٹ، شکم tummy
پیٹ، پیڑو belly
پیٹ درد stomachache
پیٹ کا ناسور ulcer
پیٹھ back
پیٹھ درد backache, back pain
پیٹھ پھیر لینا turn back
پیٹھ کے بل تیرنا backstroke
پیپر منٹ peppermint
پیچ کھولنا unscrew
پیچھا چھڑانا ditch
پیچھا کرنا go after
پیچھے after, back, behind, past
پیچھے رہ جانا lag behind
پیچھے چھوڑ کر گزر جانا go past
پیچھے کرنا put back

پرچھائی shadow
پرچہ pamphlet
پرکشش attractive, charming
پرکشش، جکڑنے والی gripping
پرکشش pleasant
پر کی آواز، خرخراہٹ purr
پر (ہوا) on, over
پر ہونا، اس جگہ پر ہونا belong
پری fairy
پریشان desperate
پریشان حال، خوفزدہ shaken
پریشان کن alarming
پریشانی despair
پریشانی میں desperately
پریقین certain
پریقین confident, self-assured
پس، مواد pus
پس انداز کرنا (بچانا) save up
پستان دار جانور (پستان سے دودھ پلانے والے) mammal
پستان سے دودھ پلانا breast-feed
پستان پوش bra
پسلی rib
پس منظر background
پسند choice, favourite
پسند کرنا like
پسندیدہ favourite
پسو flea
پس ورق paperback
پسینہ perspiration, sweat
پسینہ آنا sweat
پسینہ مخالف antiperspirant
پسینے سے بھیگا ہوا sweaty
پشت back, behind
پشت میں ایک فاضل دروازے والی کار hatchback
پشتہ، بند embankment
پشم، بال fur
پشیمان ridiculous
پل bridge
پل، لمحہ moment
پلاسٹر، زخم پر لگانے والی پٹی plaster
پلنگ couch
پلنگ پوش bedspread
پلنگڑی، کھٹولا cot
پلک eyelid
پلک جھپکنا blink
پلکوں کے بال eyelash
پلگ نکالنا unplug
پناما Panama
پناہ asylum, refuge
پناہ گاہ shelter
پناہ گزین refugee
پناہ گزیں asylum seeker
پنجرہ cage
پنجہ claw, clutch, paw
پندرہ fifteen
پندرہ دن fortnight
پندرہواں fifteenth
پنساری grocer
پنڈلی calf
پنکھ feather
پنکھے کی بیلٹ (کار میں) fan belt
پنیر cheese
پوائنٹ point
پوتا، نواسا grandson
پوتی granddaughter
پوتے پوتیاں grandchild
پودا plant
پودوں اور جانداروں کی نسلیں species
پودینہ mint
پورا کرنا (وعدہ، خواب۔۔۔) fulfil
پوری طرح، مکمل طور پر fully
پوشاک costume
پولس والا cop
پولینڈ Poland
پولینڈ کا باشندہ Pole
پولینیشیا Polynesia
پولینیشیائی Polynesian
پونچھنا sweep, wipe
پونچھ ڈالنا wipe up
پوپ (رومن کیتھولک سربراہ) pope
پوچھ تاچھ enquiry
پوچھ تاچھ دفتر inquiries office
پوچھنا ask
پوچھنا، دریافت کرنا inquire
پوچھ گچھ inquiry
پوکھر bog
پتلا، ڈراوا scarecrow
پر مزاح، ہنسانے والا funny
پت gail bladder
پستان breast
پلہ puppy
پن staple
پنڈلی کا سامنے والا حصہ shin
پچھلا rear
پھر سے بنا ہوا remake
پھر سے بھرنا refill
پھینک دینا fling
پٹہ lease, strap
پٹہ پر دینا، لینا lease
پٹی، علاقہ zone
پٹھا، عضلہ muscle
پٹھولادے مسافر backpacker
پٹہ، پالتو جانور کے گردن میں لگی پٹی نما شئے collar
پٹی belt, brace
پٹی باندھنا bandage
پٹی پر تحریر جس کے پیچھے گوند لگا ہو sticker
پچاس fifty
پچی کاری mosaic
پڑاؤ stopover
پڑوس neighbourhood
پڑوسی neighbour
پڑھانا teach
پڑھائی، پڑھانے کا عمل teaching
پڑھنا read
پڑھنے لائق، صاف دید legible
پکارنا call
پکارنا، نام دینا call
پکانا cook
پکانے کا فن cookery
پکا پکایا ready-cooked
پکا ہوا ripe
پکوان recipe
پکڑنا catch, grip, hold
پکڑنا، سوار ہونا take
پکڑے رکھنا hold on
پگھلانا melt
پگھلنا melt
پھاوڑا spade
پھاٹک gate
پھاڑنا tear
پھبتی، تبصرہ remark
پھر then
پھر بھی، باوجود اس کے however
پھل fruit
پھلوں کا باغ orchard
پھلوں کا سلاد fruit salad
پھل کا رس (جوس) fruit juice
پھلی یا پھلی کے دانے bean
پھنسا ہوا stuck
پھنسی abscess
پھنسے ہوئے stranded
پھوار پڑنا shower

ٹکرانا collide, crash
ٹکر مارنا crash
ٹکر ہونا ram
ٹکسال mint
ٹکر crash
ٹکڑا bit, chop, piece
ٹکڑا، پٹی strip
ٹکڑے ٹکڑے کرنا tear up
ٹکڑے کاٹنا cut up
ٹکڑے کرنا chop, rip up, slice
ٹکڑے کر ڈالنا smash
ٹھسا ٹھس بھرا jammed
ٹھنسا ہوا crammed
ٹھنڈا cold, cool
ٹھنڈا کرنا chill
ٹھنڈی chilly
ٹھنڈی دانے cold sore
ٹھوس solid
ٹھوس، پختہ concrete
ٹھونسنا cram
ٹھوڑی chin
ٹھگ thug
ٹھہرنا، برقرار رہنا stay
ٹھہرنا۔ ٹھہرانا camp
ٹھیک، حق proper
ٹھیک طور پر exactly, precisely, properly
ٹھیک ٹھیک exact, precise
ٹھیک کرنا fix
ٹھیکہ contract
ٹھیک ہونا fine
ٹھیک ہے! OK!
ٹھیکے دار contractor
ٹی بی، تپ دق TB
ٹیسٹ، امتحان test
ٹیلا cliff
ٹیوب tube
ٹیونیشیائی Tunisian
ٹیونیشیا Tunisia
ٹی وی کا مزاحیہ سلسلہ sitcom
ٹیکہ، نشتر vaccination
ٹیکہ لگانا vaccinate
پابندی ban
پابندی لگانا ban, restrict
پارچہ chip
پارچہ، سلائس slice
پارک، ٹہلنے یا ورزش کرنے اور کھیلنے کی جگہ park
پارہ، سیماب mercury

پاس pass
پاستہ pasta
پاس کرنا، کامیاب ہونا pass
پال، مستول، بادبان sail
پالتو pet
پالتو، سدھایا ہوا tame
پالدار کشتی sailing boat
پالنا bring up, carrycot, cradle
پالنا، پرورش کرنا foster
پالک spinach
پانا find
پانا، حاصل ہونا get
پانسہ dice
پانچ five
پانچواں fifth
پانہ spanner
پانی water
پانی بھر جانا flood
پانی بھرے گڑھے puddle
پانی دینا، آب پاشی کرنا water
پانی سے محفوظ waterproof
پانی پر اسکی کی مدد سے تیرنا water-skiing
پانی پہ حرکت کرنا paddle
پانی چھڑکنے والا sprinkler
پانی کے چھینٹے اڑانا splash
پائنچہ والا انڈرویر underskirt
پائنچہ leg
پاپیادہ pedestrian
پاپیادہ علاقہ (گاڑیاں ممنوع) pedestrian precinct
پاپیادہ چوراہا pedestrian crossing
پاکستان Pakistan
پاکستانی Pakistani
پاگل lunatic, mad, nutter
پاگل، دیوانہ insane
پاگل آدمی madman
پاگلپن madness
پتلا thin
پتلون pants, trousers
پتلی iris
پتلی سپاٹ پیندے کی مال بردار کشتی barge
پتلی نائلون کا سوٹ shell suit
پتنگ kite
پتھر کی کان quarry
پتہ، پتی leaf
پتھر stone
پتھر ہو جانا (خوف یا غم سے) petrified
پتہ address

پختہ، بالغ mature
پختہ کار طالب علم mature student
پر، کے اوپر upon
پراسرار mysterious
پرامن peaceful
پرامید hopeful
پرانا، پرانی old
پرانی out of date
پرانی وضع کا old-fashioned
پرانے زمانے کا primitive
پراگندہ upset
پراگندہ ذہنی، شقاق دماغی کا عارضہ schizophrenic
پراگندہ کرنا، ہونا upset
پرایا، غیر مانوس impersonal
پرت layer
پرتعیش luxurious
پرتگال Portugal
پرتگالی Portuguese
پرتگالی زبان Portuguese
پرجوش، جوشیلا enthusiastic
پرجوش جائزہ rave
پردادا great-grandfather
پردہ curtain
پردیسی alien
پردے پر دکھانا screen
پرزہ component
پرستش کرنا adore
پرسکون calm, relaxed
پرسکون ہونا calm down, relax
پرعزم ambitious
پرنانی great-grandmother
پرندہ بینی birdwatching
پرنٹ کرنا، چھاپنا print
پرواز flight
پرواز خادم flight attendant
پرواز شروع کرنا take off
پرواز کی شروعات take off
پروانہ، پتنگا moth
پرورش upbringing
پرورش کرنا، دیکھ بھال کرنا look after
پروف (طباعت سے پہلے پروف پڑھنا) proof
پروگرام program, programme
پروگرام دینا program
پروگرامر programmer
پروگرام سازی programming
پرپیچ، پرفریب tricky
پرچم، جھنڈا flag

وائلن نواز violinist
وائرس virus
وائس میل (ریکورڈ آواز) voicemail
واپس بھیجنا send back
واپس لانا bring back
واپس لوٹانا pay back
واپس مڑنا move back, turn
واپس پانا get back
واپس کرنا return
واپس ہونا back out, return
واپسی return
واپسی ٹکٹ day return
واپسی کرنا come back
وبائی epidemic
وبائی حالت outbreak
وتری diagonal
وثیقہ dead
وجود میں ہونا exist
وجہ cause, reason
وجہ سے due to
وحشی bully
وحشیانہ barbaric
وراثت heritage, inheritance
وردی uniform
ورزش، کثرت exercise
ورم ام دماغ meningitis
ورم نرخرہ laryngitis
ورنہ، نہیں تو otherwise
وزارت ministry
وزن اٹھانے والا (کھلاڑی) weightlifter
وزن اٹھانے کا کھیل weightlifting
وزن کرنا weigh, weight
وزیر minister
وزیر اعظم prime minister
وسائل pool
وسط افریقی جمہوریہ
Central African Republic
وسطی امریکہ Central America
وسعت، حد extent
وسیع broad, extensive
وسیع، کشادہ، چوڑا wide
وسیع پیمانے پر extensively
وسیلہ، ماخذ resource
وصول کنندہ receiver, recipient
وصیت will
وصیت will
وضاحت کرنا account for, clarify
وضاحت یا بیان outline

وضع gesture
وضع کرنا devise
وظیفہ scholarship
وعدہ promise
وعدہ کرنا promise
وغیرہ etc
وفادار faithful
وفادارانہ طور پر faithfully
وفاداری loyalty
وقار dignity
وقت time
وقت طلب demanding
وقت عشائیہ dinner time
وقت پر on time
وقت کے مقررہ وقفے کی پیمائش والی گھڑی
stopwatch
وقت گزاری pastime
وقتی momentary, occasional
وقتی طور پر occasionally
وقعات سے پر eventful
وقف dedicated, dedication
وقف لازم full stop
وقف ناقص semi-colon
وقفہ interval
وقفہ، مدت period
ولائتی سارنگی violin
ولولہ enthusiasm
ونیلا (ذائقہ) vanilla
وولٹیج (کل قوت برق) voltage
ووٹ دینا vote
ووڈکا (بیرنگ بے بو روسی شراب) vodka
وٹامن vitamin
وکیل solicitor
وکیل (قانون داں) lawyer
وھیل whale
وہ that, those
وہاں there
وہ (خاتون) she
وہ (خاتون) خود herself
وہ لوگ they, those
وہ لوگ خود themselves
وہ (مذکر) he
وہ (مرد) خود himself
وہمی superstitious
ویب Web
ویب انچارج پیشہ ور webmaster
ویب سائٹ website
ویب میگزین webzine

ویب پتہ web address
ویب کیمرا webcam
ویران uninhabited
ویران جزیرہ desert island
ویزا visa
ویسٹ انڈیز West Indies
ویلز (ریاست) کا Welsh
ویمپائر، خون خوار درندہ vampire
وینڈنگ مشین vending machine
وینیزویلا Venezuela
وینیزویلن Venezuelan
وین (موٹر گاڑی) van
ویتنام Vietnam
ویتنامی Vietnamese
ویڈیو video
ویڈیو فون videophone
ویڈیو کیمرا video camera
یسٹونیائی زبان Estonian
صحافت journalism
ٹالنا avoid
ٹانکہ stitch
ٹانکے لگانا، سلائی کرنا stitch
ٹانگ leg
ٹخنہ ankle
ٹرن اوور turnover
ٹرنک، صندوق trunk
ٹرینیداد اور ٹوبیگو (جمہوریہ) Trinidad and
Tobago
ٹرک truck
ٹرینگل (ساز) triangle
ٹریک سوٹ (ورزشی سوٹ) tracksuit
ٹرے، طشت tray
ٹماٹر tomato
ٹماٹر کی چٹنی tomato sauce
ٹن، ڈبا tin
ٹن (وزن) ton
ٹنکی tank
ٹوگو (جمہوریہ) Togo
ٹوٹنا break, break up
ٹوٹ کر گرنا fall out
ٹوٹی ہوئی broken
ٹوپی cap
ٹوکری basket
ٹوہ میں لگے رہنا pry
ٹٹولنا grope
ٹڈا، جھینگر grasshopper
ٹکر collision, ram
ٹکرا جانا، کچلا جانا squash

نو nine
نوادرات antique
نوادرات کی دوکان antique shop
نواں ninth
نواں حصہ ninth
نوجوان young
نوجوان مرغا cockerel
نوجوانی adolescence
نوجواں adolescent
نوخیز، نوعمر، نوجوان teenager
نوزائیدہ newborn
نوعمر گھوڑا foal
نومبر November
نووارد newcomer
نوے ninety
نوک point, tip
نوکر، ملازم servant
نوکر شاہی bureaucracy
نجکاری کرنا privatize
نشاندہی کرنا point out
نشانی، ثبوت token
نصاب prospectus, syllabus
نصابی کتاب textbook
نظام system
نظام تجزیہ کار systems analyst
نظام شمسی solar system
نکاراگوا Nicaragua
نکاراگوائی Nicaraguan
نکاسی withdrawal
نکاسی کا رستہ way out
نکالا ہوا redundant
نکالنا withdraw
نکل جانا pull out
نگاہ look
نگراں supervisor, warden
نگل جانا swallow
نگلنا swallow
نگلنے کا عمل swallow
نٹ acrobat
نپٹنا deal with
نچلا حصہ، پیندا bottom
نچلی منزل downstairs
نکاراگوا کا شہری Nicaraguan
نکاسی exit
نکاسی پائپ drainpipe
نکاسی کرنا drain
نکال دینا eliminate
نکالنا expel
نکالنا، باہر پھینک دینا throw out
نکتہ point
نکتہ نگاہ standpoint
نکتہ چینی criticism
نکتہ چینی کرنا criticize
نکتہ چیں، نقاد critic
نکسیر پھوٹنا nosebleed
نکل جانا get out
نگران اطفال childminder
نگرانی oversight
نگرانی کرنا، دیکھنا watch
نگراں caretaker
نگہداشت care
نگہداشت طفل childcare
نگہداشت یونٹ انتہائی intensive care unit
نگینہ، جواہر jewel
نہاتے وقت سرپوش (بالوں کو سوکھا رکھتا ہے)
shower cap
نہانا bathe
نہایت مضحکہ خیز hilarious
نہایت وفادار devoted
نہ تو، نہ ہی neither ... nor
نہر canal
نہ ہی nor
نہیں no, not
نیا new
نیا بنانا renew
نیا سال New Year
نیا، نئی new
نیاپن makeover
نیدرلینڈز (یورپی ملک) Netherlands
نیزہ javelin
نیل lilac
نیل، لیلیک پودا lilac
نیلا blue
نیلامی auction
نیلم sapphire
نیلے رنگ کی navy
نیم خوابیدہ drowsy
نیم دراز حالت میں reclining
نیم وا آنکھوں سے دیکھنا squint
نیند sleep
نیند محسوس کرنا sleepy
نیند میں چلنا sleepwalk
نیوزی لینڈ (ملک) New Zealand
نیومیٹک ڈرل pneumatic drill
نیون گیس neon
نیپال Nepal
نیچائی پر low
نیچے below, beneath, down,
underneath
نیچے، کے نیچے underneath
نیچے آنا come down
نیچے جانا go down
نیچے، پست ہونا low
نیچے کرنا، نیچے اتارنا lower
نیچے کو below
نیک good-natured
نیک شخص gentleman
وابستگی association
وابستہ concerned
وابستہ ہونا، متعلق ہونا، کا ہونا belong
وابستگی regard
وابستہ related
واجب اخراجات overheads
واحد single
واحد (جمع کی ضد) singular
وادی valley
وارث heir
وارث (خاتون) heiress
وارث ہونا inherit
وارد ہونا dash
وارنش varnish
وارنش کرنا varnish
وارنٹی (ضمانت) warranty
وارث successor
واسکٹ waistcoat
واش بیسن (منہ ہاتھ دھونے کو) washbasin
واشنگ مشین washing machine
واشنگ پاؤڈر washing powder
واضح apparent, blatant, clear
واضح طور پر apparently
واقع situated
واقعاتی virtual
واقعاتی حقیقت virtual reality
واقعتاً actually, eventually
واقعہ affair, event, incident,
occurrence
واقعہ، سلسلے کا جزو episode
واقعی literally
واقعی، حقیقتاً indeed, really
واقعی، درحقیقت really
والدین parent
والز رقص کرنا waltz
والز ناچ، رقص waltz
والی بال volleyball

نتیجہ نکالنا result
نتیجہ نکالنا conclude
نتیجے پر پہنچنا، حل تلاش کرنا work out
نتیجے کے طور پر consequently
نحیف faint
نخلستان oasis
ندی river
ندی پار ناؤ کا سفر crossing
نرم tender
نرم، ہلکی soft
نرم خو humble, polite
نرم لحاف duvet
نرم کھردرا چمڑا suede
نرم ہوا breeze
نرمی، اخلاق politeness
نرمی سے gently, politely
نرگس daffodil
نزاع row
نزدیک early
نزدیک close, close by
نزدیک والا nearby
نزدیک کا راستہ shortcut
نزلہ زکام میں مبتلا ہونا cold
نسبت ratio
نسبتاً relatively
نسبتاً تھوڑے fewer
نسل generation, race
نسل انسانی mankind
نسل پرستی racism
نسلی ethnic, racial
نسلی برتری کا عقیدہ رکھنے والا racist
نسلی پرست racist
نسوانی feminine
نس پھٹنا یا خون رک جانا stroke
نسیج tissue
نشان mark
نشان، علامت icon
نشاندہی کرنا، اشارہ کرنا point
نشان راہ signpost
نشان لگانا mark
نشان منزل landmark
نشان کتاب bookmark
نشر کرنا broadcast
نشریہ broadcast
نشست berth
نشوونما پانا develop
نشوونما ہونا grow
نشست seat

نشست، عہدہ post
نشہ باز addicted, drunk
نشہ میں دھت drunk
نشہ کا خمار hangover
نشے میں گاڑی چلانا drink-driving
نصاب course, curriculum
نصف، آدھا half
نصف النہار midday
نصف شب midnight
نصف ۔ نصف fifty-fifty
نصف ۔ نصف حاصل کرنا fifty-fifty
نطفی خلیہ sperm
نظارہ scenery
نظارہ، منظر view
نظام مدافعت immune system
نظرانداز کرنا neglect
نظرانداز کرنا ignore
نظر آنا look
نظرثانی revision
نظرثانی کرنا revise
نظر میں لانا spot
نظر کرنا look at
نظریہ ideology, outlook
نظم poem
نظم وضبط کی تربیت discipline
نظم کرنا organize
نعرہ تحسین cheer
نعرہ مارنا cheer
نعمت خانہ larder
نفرت hatred
نفرت انگیز disgusting
نفرت کرنا despise, hate
نفسیاتی psychological
نفسیاتی طریق علاج psychotherapy
نفع profit
نفع، ماحصل gain
نفع بخش lucrative, profitable
نفی negative
نفیس nice
نفی کرنا subtract
نقاب، مکھوٹہ mask
نقاشی painting
نقب زن burglar
نقب زن الارم burglar alarm
نقب زنی burglary
نقب لگانا burgle
نقدی cash
نقدی تقسیم کار مشین cash dispenser

نقش inscription
نقش نگاری کرنا engrave
نقشہ map
نقص defect, flaw
نقصان damage, disadvantage, loss
نقصاندہ harmful
نقصان پہنچانا، مضروب کرنا harm
نقصان کرنا damage
نقطہ dot
نقطہ نگاہ viewpoint
نقل copy, imitation
نقل، مجسمہ dummy
نقل اتارنا mimic
نقل تیار کرنا (عکسی) photocopy
نقل وحرکت movement
نقل وحمل transit
نقل وحمل کا انتظام کرنا transport
نقل کرنا copy, imitate, mock
نقلی mock
نقلی بال wig
نقلی بالوں کا گچھا toupee
نقلی دانت dentures
نل tap
نل ساز plumber
نل سازی plumbing
نم damp, humid, moist
نمائش showing
نمائش، میلا fair
نمائندہ representative
نمائش demo, display, exhibition
نمائش کرنا display
نمائندگی کرنا represent
نمائندہ rep
نم آور moisturizer
نمایاں طور پر fairly
نمدا felt
نمدہ gasket
نمونہ model, pattern, sample
نمٹنا cope, handle
نمک salt
نمکین salty, wafer
نمکین پانی (کی مچھلی) saltwater
نمی moisture
نن (راہبہ) nun
ننگا naked
ننگے پیر barefoot
ننگے پیروں barefoot

مہمان خانہ، ہوٹل guesthouse
مہمان نوازی hospitality
مہم جو adventurous
مہم جوئی adventure
مہم جوئی کرنا mount
مہندس، انجینئر engineer
مہنگا expensive
مہوگنی لکڑی mahogany
مہم operation
مہیا کرنا provide
مہیب tremendous
میانمار (کل کا برما) Myanmar
میدانی علاقہ plain
میرا mine, my
میز table
میزبان host
میزبانی compere
میز پوش tablecloth
میسر available
میعاد term
میل mile
میلا گاہ، نمائش گاہ fairground
مینار tower
میناکاری enamel
مینو، طعام نامہ menu
مینڈک کا بچہ tadpole
میٹھا afters, sweet
میٹھا پویہ چلنا چلانا canter
میٹھا کرنے والا sweetener
میڈاگاسکر Madagascar
مینڈک frog
میکسیکو Mexico
میکسیکن Mexican
میں I, in
میں خود myself
میں سے، ایک سرے سے دوسرے سرے تک thorough
مقصد motive
ناامید hopeless
ناانصافی injustice
ناآمادہ unlikely
نااہل قرار دینا disqualify
نابالغ minor
نابینا blind
ناتجربہ کار inexperienced
ناخن nail
ناخن پالش nail polish
ناخواندہ illiterate

ناخوش unhappy
ناخوش، اداس sad
نادیدہ invisible
نادیدہ برف کی پرت black ice
ناراض angry
ناراض کرنا annoy
نارنجی بھورا ginger
نارنجی مچھلی goldfish
نارنگی (پھل) orange
نارنگی کا مربہ marmalade
نارویجین Norwegian
ناروے Norway
ناریل coconut
نازبو oregano
نازک delicate, ticklish
ناسازگار unfavourable
ناشاد، بے مہر grim
ناشائستگی سے grossly
ناشائستہ gross
ناشتہ breakfast
ناشتہ، نمکین کی دوکان snack bar
ناشر publisher
ناشپاتی pear
ناشکرا ungrateful
ناظرین، سامعین audience
ناظر spectator, viewer
ناف belly button, navel
نافرمان disobedient
نافرمانی کرنا disobey
نافہرست زد، غیر مندرج unlisted
ناقابل عمل impractical
ناقابل انکار undeniable
ناقابل برداشت unbearable
ناقابل دفع unavoidable
ناقابل شکستگی unbreakable
ناقابل شکست unbeatable
ناقابل فراموش unforgettable
ناقابل قبول unacceptable
ناقابل پیش گوئی unpredictable
ناقابل یقین unbelievable
ناقص العقل senseless
نال horseshoe
نالاں sulky
نالی drain
نام name
نامددگار unhelpful
نامزد کرنا nominate
نامزدگی nomination

نامعلوم unknown
ناممکن impossible
نامناسب unfair
نام و پتہ کی کتاب address book
نامکمل incomplete
نامہ نگار correspondent, reporter
ناند، لگن trough
ناؤ boat, canoe
ناؤ دوڑ canoeing, rowing
ناول novel
ناول نگار novelist
ناؤ (ڈوبنے والوں کو بچانے کے لئے) lifeboat
ناؤ یا جہاز پر چھٹی cruise
نائی barber
نائجر Niger
نائجیریائی Nigeria, Nigerian
نائلون، پلاسٹک دھاگہ nylon
نائلون کی دو پٹیاں جڑ کر بند ہو جانے والی Velcro®
نائی کی دوکان hairdresser
ناپختہ immature
ناپسند کرنا dislike
ناپسند کرنا resent
ناپسندیدہ obnoxious, repulsive, resentful, unpleasant
ناک nose
ناکارہ broken down, invalid
ناکارہ ہونا break down
ناکافی inadequate, insufficient
ناکام ہونا fail
ناکامی break down, failure, flop
ناکامیاب unsuccessful
ناک بہنا catarrh
ناک والا، نکو nosy
ناک کا اندرون sinus
ناگزیر indispensable, inevitable
ناگوار awful, dreadful, nasty
ناگوار انداز میں awfully
ناگوار تنقید کیڑے نکالنا slag off
ناگوار حد تک بھیگا ہوا soggy
نایاب extinct, rare
ناقص faulty
نباتات flora, vegetation
نتھی کرنا staple
نتھنا nostril
نتھی کرنے والا آلہ stapler
نتیجہ conclusion, consequence, outcome, result
نتیجہ میں accordingly

منکسر مزاج modest
منگل Tuesday
منگنی کی انگوٹھی engagement ring
منگولیا Mongolia
منگولیائی Mongolian
منگیتر (خاتون) fiancée
منگیتر (مرد) fiancé
منہ mouth
منہ بند کرنا shut up
منہ بولا بچہ foster child
منہ تک بھرنا fill up
منہدم کرنا demolish
منہ سے آواز نہ نکلنا speechless
منہ پھٹ blunt
منہ پھٹ، کھری کھری سنانے والا outspoken
مواد content
موازنہ comparison
مواصلت communication
موت death
موت کی سزا capital punishment
موتی pearl
موتیابند cataract
موجد inventor
موجودگی presence
موجودگی نظر میں آنا stand out
موجودہ حالت کا قائم رہنا status quo
موجودہ معاملات current affairs
موجودہ وقت، حال میں present
موجود ہونا be, present
مور peacock
موروثی hereditary
موریشس Mauritius
موریطانیہ جمہوریہ Mauritania
موزمبیق Mozambique
موزوں appropriate, suitable
موزہ sock
موسلادھار downpour
موسم season, weather
موسم بہار blossom, spring
موسم بہار کا اخیر springtime
موسم سرما کے کھیل winter sports
موسم گرما summer, summertime
موسمی seasonal
موسمی پیشن گوئی weather forecast
موسیقار composer, musician
موسیقارانہ musical
موسیقی blues, music
موسیقی دار musical
موسیقی کے سازوسامان
musical instrument
موضوع subject
موضوع بحث issue
موقع chance, occasion,
opportunity
مول بھاؤ bargain
مول بھاؤ کرنا haggle
مولڈویائی Moldovan
مولی horseradish
موم wax
موم بتی candle
موم بتی دان candlestick
مومیائی ہوئی لاش mummy
مونچھ moustache
مونگا coral
مونگ پھلی peanut
مورخ historian
موٹا chubby, fat, obese, thick
موٹائی thickness
موٹاپا overweight
موٹر گاڑی vehicle
موچنا، بال کھینچنے کے لئے tweezers
موڑ bend, turning
موڑنا bend
موکل client
مویشی cattle
معادی بخار typhoid
مئی May
مثالی، اشارتی typical
مزاج mood, temper
مقدار quantity
مقدار کا اندازہ لگانا quantify
ملا جلا سلاد mixed salad
ملان match
ملانا meet, mix
ملنا meet
ملنا scrub
مٹھائی sweet
مٹھائیاں sweets
مٹی soil
مٹانا delete, erase
متحدہ عرب امیرات
United Arab Emirates
مٹر peas
مٹھی fist
مٹی clay, earth
مٹی کا تیل kerosene
مچان بندی scaffolding
مچھر mosquito
مچھلی fish
مچھلی مارنا fish
مچھیرا، ماہیگیر fisherman
مڑنا wind
مکالموں کی تحریر transcript
مکالمہ dialogue
مکان plane
مکان مالک landlord
مکان مالکن landlady
مکتبہ فکر sect
مکعب cube
مکعبی cubic
مکمل complete, prefect
مکمل، کامل perfect
مکمل طور پر completely
مکمل طور پر، پوری طرح سے entirely
مکمل چاند full moon
مکمل whole
مکمل، شدید sheer
مکئی کے پھولے cornflakes
مکئی corn, maize, popcorn
مکئی کا آٹا cornflour
مکڑی spider
مکڑی کا جالا cobweb
مکھن butter
مکھوٹا لگائے ہوئے masked
مکھی fly
مکہ Mecca
مکہ، پنچ punch
مکہ مارنا punch
مکین resident
مکے باز boxer
مکے بازی boxing
مگ mug
مگرمچھ crocodile
مہاجر immigrant
مہارت skill, speciality
مہاسہ acne, pimple
مہذب well-behaved
مہر seal, stamp
مہربان، رحم دل kind
مہربند کرنا، چپکا کر بند کر دینا seal
مہر لگانا stamp
مہلک fatal
مہم campaign, expedition
مہمان guest

مغرور arrogant, bigheaded
مغرب west
مغربی west, western
مغربی سمت west
مغز brain
مغزیات nut
مغزیات سے الرجی nut allergy
مفت free
مفروضہ کے طور پر presumably, supposedly
مفصل detailed
مقابل adversary, competitor, contestant, front
مقابل کے میدان پر میچ away match
مقابلہ competition, contest
مقابلہ، میچ match
مقابلہ آرا competitive
مقابلہ سوال جواب quiz
مقابلہ کرنا compete
مقابلے میں برابری پر رہنا draw
مقابل opposite
مقابلہ آرائی rivalry
مقام site, spot
مقام انتظار (روانگی سے پہلے) departure lounge
مقام تعمیر building site
مقام دوا فروشی chemist
مقام زر مبادلہ bureau de change
مقام اتصال (جنکشن) junction
مقامی local
مقامی بیہوشی آور local anaesthetic
مقبرہ tomb
مقبوضات belongings
مقبول popular
مقبول، جانا پہچانا familiar
مقبولیت popularity
مقدار amount
مقدر fortune
مقدس holy
مقدس مقامات کو سفر pilgrimage
مقدس چبوترہ altar
مقدمہ چلانا prosecute
مقدس sacred
مقدس مقام shrine
مقدمہ دائر کرنا sue
مقرر کرنا appoint
مقررہ وقت deadline
مقرر speaker
مقصد cause, objective, purpose
مقصد ہونا mean
مقناطیس magnet
مقناطیسی magnetic
مقیم inmate
ملازم employee
ملازمت employment, job
ملازمت کا مرکز job centre
ملازم رکھنا employ
ملاقات meeting, visit
ملاقات کرنا meet up, see, visit
ملاقاتی visitor
ملاقاتی اوقات visiting hours
ملاقاتی مرکز visitor centre
ملال grief
ملامت کرنا condemn
ملانا combine
ملاوی جمہوریہ Malawi
ملائم، نرم soft
ملا کر، کل ملا کر altogether
ملبوس dressed
ملبہ wreck
ملبہ کر دینا، توڑ پھوڑ ڈالنا wreck
ملتا جلتا matching
ملتوی کرنا call off, postpone, put off
ملزم accused
ملسط ہونا preoccupied
ملوث نہ ہونا keep out
ملوث کرنا involve
ملکہ queen
ملک country
ملک، قوم nation
ملک بدر کرنا deport
ملک شام Syria
ملکی، قومی national
ملکی پیدائشی native
ملکیت میں ہونا own
ملگجے shabby
ملی جلی mixed
ملیریا malaria
ملیشیا Malaysia
ملیشیائی Malaysian
ملین laxative
مماثل ہونا match
ممانعت کرنا prohibit
ممانعت taboo
ممتحن examiner, invigilator
ممنوع forbidden
ممنوعہ banned, prohibited
ممکن possible
ممکنہ طور پر possibly
مناسب ہونا، موزوں ہونا fit
مناسب fit
منافع return
منتخب pick
منتظم manager
منتظمہ manageress
منتقل کرنا، حرکت دینا move
منتقل ہونا، گھر بدلنا move
منتقم، ظالم spiteful
منتہا peak
منجانب on behalf of
منجمد کرنا freeze
منحصر ہونا depend
مندر temple
مندمل ہونا heal
مندوب، ڈیلیگیٹ delegate
مندوب بنانا، اختیار دینا delegate
منزل destination, floor
منسلک attached
منسوخ abolition
منسوخ کرنا abolish
منسوخ کرنا، ترک کر دینا waive
منسوخی cancellation
منصفانہ fair
منصف مزاجی fairness
منصوبہ plan, scheme
منصوبہ بند کام project
منصوبہ بندی planning
منصوبہ بندی کرنا plan
منطقۂ وقت (وقت کی تقسیم جی ایم ٹی کے اعتبار سے) time zone
منطقی logical
منظر scene
منظور کرنا approve
منظوری approval
منظم systematic
منع کرنا forbid
منعکس ہونا reflect
منفی negative
منفی کرنا deduct
منقطع کرنا disconnect
منڈی marketplace
منکا bead
منکرانہ طور پر no
منکر خدا atheist

مسرور delighted
مسرور کن delightful
مسطح level
مسلح armed
مسل دینا stub out
مسلسل continually
مسلم Moslem
مسلمان، اسلام کا پیرو Muslim
مسلمان یا ان کے مذہب سے متعلق Muslim
مسودہ draft
مسودہ (غیر مطبوعہ) manuscript
مسور lentils
مسکارہ mascara
مسکرانا grin, smile
مسکراہٹ grin, smile
مسکراہٹ کا علامتی نشان smiley
مسیح Christ
مسیحی Christian
مشاہدہ گاہ observatory
مشاہد observer, surveyor
مشاہدہ، سروے survey
مشترک collective
مشترکہ joint
مشترکہ کھاتہ joint account
مشتعل excited
مشتمل ہونا consist of
مشرق east
مشرق وسطی Middle East
مشرق کو east
مشرق کی طرف eastbound
مشرقی east, eastern
مشروب drink
مشروط conditional
مشرقی ایشیا Orient
مشغول engaged
مشق exercise, rehearsal
مشق کرنا rehearse
مشمول included
مشمولات contents
مشورہ دینا advise, suggest, suggestion
مشورہ کرنا consult
مشکل difficult, hurdle
مشکل سے hardly
مشکل صورت حال dilemma
مشکوک doubtful, sceptical, suspect, suspicious
مشکل سے scarcely
مشکل پیدل سفر trek
مشہور famous
مشین appliance
مشین سے طبی جانچ scan
مصر Egypt
مصروف busy
مصروف اوقات rush hour
مصروف ترین اوقات peak hours
مصروفیت engagement
مصری Egyptian
مصری شہری Egyptian
مصری چنا chickpea
مصنف author, writer
مصنوع product
مصنوعی artificial
مصنوعی، بناوٹی stuffy
مصیبت nuisance
مضاف additive
مضافات countryside
مضبوط firm, steady, strong
مضبوط، بے عیب sound
مضبوطی سے strongly
مضطرب neurotic
مضمون article, essay, topic
مضمون حساب maths
مطابقت پذیر compatible
مطالبہ demand
مطالبہ کرنا demand
مطالعہ کرنا study
مطالبہ requirement
مطب clinic
مطلب ہونا mean
مطلع کرنا inform, notify
مطلقہ divorced
مطلوب ہونا require
مطمئن content, satisfied
مظاہرہ demonstration
مظاہرہ کرنا demonstrate, perform
معاشرتی تحفظ social security
معاشیات economic, economics
معاف کر دینا forgive
معافی pardon
معافی مانگنا apologize
معافی چاہتا ہوں! pardon
معالج دندان dentist
معاملہ case, matter
معانقہ hug
معانقہ کرنا، گلے لگانا hug
معاون assistant
معائنہ check
معائنہ کرنا check
معائنہ کار، انسپکٹر inspector
معائنہ کرنا inspect
معاہدہ deal
معاہدہ کرنا observe
معتدل normal
معدن mineral
معدنی mineral
معدنیات سے بھرپور چشمہ spa
معذرت apology
معذرت! sorry
معذرت خواہی، افسوس ہونا sorry
معذرت طلب کرنا regret
معذرت کرنا excuse
معذور disabled
معذوری disability
معطل کرنا suspend
معقول reasonable
معقول طور پر reasonably
معلومات information
معلومات دفتر information office
معلوماتی informative
معلوم کرنا enquire
معلوم ہونا، پتہ لگنا notice
معلم instructor
معمار bricklayer
معمول routine
معمول سے زیادہ دیر سونا sleep in
معمول کا usual
معمول کے طور پر normally
معمولی ordinary
معمولی، تھوڑی سی minute
معمولی، غیر اہم trivial
معمولی دشواری hitch
معمولی غلطی slip, slip up
معمولی غلطی یا سہو کرنا slip up
معنی، مطلب meaning
معنی، مفہوم mean
معنی خیز sly
معیار standard
معیار زندگی lifestyle
معیار پر پورا اترنا qualify
معیاری standard
معیشت economy
مغربی western
مغربی لوک کہانیوں کا کردار cowboy

محفوظ کار preservative
محفوظ کردہ reserved
محفوظ کرنا reserve, save
محل castle, palace
محلل solvent
محلہ ward
محنت labour
محنت طلب challenging
مخالف contrast
مخالف، مقابل opponent
مخالفت کرنا oppose
مخالف opposed, opposing, opposite
مخالفت opposition
مخبر grass
مخبر، جاسوس scout
مختصر brief, minor, short
مختصر افسانہ short story
مختصراً briefly, shortly
مختصراً بیان کرنا sum up
مختصر تصویر miniature
مختصر عنوان caption
مختص کرنا put aside
مختلف different
مختلف الاوقاتی کام کے گھنٹے flexitime
مختلف، متعدد various
مختلف رنگوں کے کانچ کے ٹکڑے stained glass
مختلف سمت یا حالت پر گھوم جانا turn around
مختلف قسموں کا varied
مختلف ہونا، متعدد ہونا vary
مخروط cone
مخصوص particular, specific
مخصوص طور پر specifically
مخصوص غذا کھانا diet
مخصوص کرنا specify
مخفف abbreviation
مخلوط نسل کا (کتا) mongrel
مخلص sincere
مخلصانہ طور پر sincerely
مخمل velvet
مداری conjurer, juggler
مدبر، سلیقہ مند ingenious
مدت duration
مدد help
مدد کرنا help
مددگار helpful
مدعا علیہ، حامی defender
مدعی defendant
مدغم ہونا merge
مدور circular
مدت spell
مدھم dim
مدھم، ہلکا dull
مدہوش، نشہ میں چور tipsy
مدیر editor
مذاق کرنا joke
مذاقیہ jolly
مذاکرات کار negotiator
مذکر male
مذہب religion
مذہبی religious
مراعات incentive
مراقبہ meditation
مراقش Morocco
مراقشی Moroccan
مربع square
مربع شکل square
مرتبان jar
مرجھانا، کمہلانا wilt
مرحوم late
مرد male
مردانہ masculine
مردم شماری census
مردوں کا gents
مردہ dead
مردہ گھر morgue
مرض الزائمر Alzheimer's disease
مرطوب humid
مرغ chicken
مرغا cock
مرغزار، سبزہ زار meadow
مرغ کا گوشت chicken
مرغی hen
مرمت repair
مرمت کرنا repair
مرنا die, pass out
مرئی، دیدنی visual
مرئی، قابل دید visible
مرچ chilli
مرچ، مرچی pepper
مرکب mixture
مرکز توجہ focus
مرکز centre, core
مرکز شہر city centre, town centre
مرکز خط mainland
مرکزی central
مرکزی حرارت central heating
مرکزی خیال، موضوع theme
مرہم lotion, ointment
مرہم پٹی bandage
مریض patient
مزاح humour
مزاحم reluctant
مزاحمت resistance
مزاحمت کے ساتھ reluctantly
مزاح کا تصویری سلسلہ comic strip
مزاحیہ comedy, comic, humorous
مزاحیہ کتاب comic book
مزدور labourer
مزدوری labour, wage
مزید more
مزید، آگے کی further
مزید، زیادہ more
مزید نہ ہونا anymore
مسابقت دینا challenge
مسافر commuter, traveller
مسالہ flavouring, spice
مسالیدار spicy
مسالیدار کھانے savoury
مساوات equation
مساوی equal
مساوی کرنا equalize
مسائل حاضرہ سے متعلق topical
مسائی catching
مستثنیٰ exception
مستحق ہونا deserve
مسترد کرنا dismiss, overrule, rule out, turn down
مستری mechanic
مستطیل rectangle
مستطیل نما rectangular
مستقبل future
مستقل constant, permanent
مستقلاً constantly, permanently, regularly
مستقل regular, stable, unchanged
مستند authentic
مستول mast
مسجد mosque
مسخرہ clown, comedian

مالٹیز Maltese
مالک master
مالک ہونا، ماہر ہونا master
مال کی دوکان stock
مالی gardener, monetary
مالی، رقوماتی financial
مالیاتی سال fiscal year
مالی سال financial year
مالی کا اوزار rake
مان جانا، تسلیم کرنا yield
مانسون monsoon
مانع حمل contraceptive
مانگنا beg
ماؤس (کمپیوٹر کا) mouse
مایوس راداس beg
مائل کرنا canvass
ماپ، پیمانہ gauge
ماپنا، ناپنا gauge
ماچس کی تیلی match
ماڈل، شخصی نمونہ model
ماں mother, mum
ماہ month
ماہانہ monthly
ماہر expert
ماہر آثار قدیمہ archaeologist
ماہر معاشیات economist
ماہر امراض نسواں gynaecologist
ماہر ہونا good
ماہر skilful
ماہر فن skilled, specialist
ماہر لسانیات linguist
ماہر نفسیات psychologist
ماہی خانہ aquarium
ماہی فروش fishmonger
ماہیگیری fishing
ماہیگیری ناؤ fishing boat
مایوس disappointed
مایوس کرنا disappoint, let down
مایوس کن bleak, disappointing, dismal
مایوسی disappointment
مباحثہ discussion
مباحثہ کرنا discuss
مبارکباد congratulations
مبارکباد دینا congratulate
مبالغہ exaggeration
مبالغہ کرنا exaggerate

مبتدی beginner
مبتلا ہونا catch
مبنی based
مبنی بر حکمت عملی strategic
مبہم dubious
مبہم، غیر واضح vague
مبینہ alleged
متاثر impressed
متاثر کرنا impress
متاثرہ touched
متاخر delayed
متبادل alternative
متبادل طور پر alternatively
متبنیٰ adopted
متجسس curious, inquisitive
متحرک dynamic, mobile, moving
متذبذب bewildered, confused
متذبذب ہونا confuse
مترجم interpreter
متروک neglected, obsolete
متروکہ unattended
متزلزل uncertain
متزوج خاتون کا شادی سے پہلے کا نام maiden name
متشدد violent
متصادم ہونا clash
متصل adjacent
متعدد several
متعدد، کئی several
متعدد numerous
متعدد بار پوچھے گئے سوالات FAQ
متعدی contagious
متعصب prejudiced
متعلق فعل adverb
متعلقہ concerning
متعلق ہونا، کا ہونا، وابستہ ہونا belong to
متعلم learner
متعلق regarding
متعلقہ relevant
متفرق miscellaneous
متفق نہ ہونا disagree
متفق ہونا agree
متفکر thoughtful
متلی nausea
متن text
متنازعہ controversial
متواتر successive

متوازن balanced
متوازی parallel
متوحش کرنا bully
متورم swollen
متوسط درجے کا medium-sized
متوقع probable
متحد کرنا unite
مثال example, instance
مثال کے طور پر ideally
مثالی ideal, model
مثانہ bladder
مثانے کی سوزش cystitis
مثبت positive
مثلاً .i.e
مثلاً .e.g
مثلث triangle
مجرم criminal
مجرمانہ criminal
مجرموں کے گروہ کا سرغنہ godfather
مجرم گروہ کا رکن gangster
مجسمہ ساز، بت تراش sculptor, sculpture
مجسمہ سازی، بت تراشی sea
مجلس، کونسل council
مجموعہ collection, complex, pack
مجموعہ میں سے مختصر فہرست shortlist
مجموعی طور پر overall
مجنونانہ madly
مجھے me
محاسبہ کرنا audit
محافظ bodyguard
محاورے کی کتاب phrasebook
محبت کرنا، پیار کرنا love
محبوب boyfriend
محبوبہ girlfriend
محب وطن patriotic
محتاط careful, cautious
محترمہ، مادام madam
محتسب auditor
محدب عدسہ lens
محراب arch
محسوس کرنا feel
محسوس ہونا seem
محصول revenue
محفل موسیقی concert
محفوظ reserve, safe, secure
محفوظ وسائل back up
محفوظ پن safety pin

لبنانی Lebanese
لب ولہجہ rhythm
لحیم شحیم gigantic
لذیذ delicious, tasty
لرزتی ہوئی shaky
لسانی قواعد grammatical
لطف joy
لطف اندوز ہو enjoy
لطف کا نقطۂ عروج ecstasy
لطیف enjoyable
لطیفہ joke
لغت dictionary
لفافہ envelope
لفظ word
لفظ جس میں واحد حرف صوت کی آواز ہو syllable
لقمہ bite
لقوہ زدہ paralysed
للچانا، اکسانا، ترغیب دینا tempt
للچانے والا tempting
لمبا tall
لمبا راستہ detour
لمبائی length
لمبا کرنا، بڑھانا long
لمبی دوڑ (۲۰ تا ۲۶ میل) یونانی میراتھن marathon
لمبی لکڑی کے سہارے pole vault
لمبی مدت long
لمبے بال والا کتہ collie
لمبے ربر بوٹ wellingtons
لمبے عرصے کا longer
لمبے لٹکے کانوں والا کتا spaniel
لمبے پٹوں والا اسکول بیگ satchel
لمحاتی طور پر momentarily
لمحہ while
لندن London
لنگر anchor
لنگڑا lame
لنگڑا کر چلنا limp
لوری (بچہ کو سلانے کے لئے گایا جانے والا
گیت) lullaby
لو لگنا sunstroke
لومڑی fox
لونگ clove
لوٹانا give back
لوٹانا، واپس لینا take back
لوٹنا rob
لوٹ پاٹ robbery
لوگ people
لوہا، فولاد iron

لوہے کا منارہ pylon
لوہے کی رسیوں سے سہارا دیا ہوا
پل suspension bridge
لئے for
لباس شب خوابی nightdress, pyjamas
لباس عروسی wedding dress
لتھوانیا Lithuania
لتھوانیائی Lithuanian
لسانی linguistic
لکھنا write
لکھنے سے متعلق سازو سامان stationery
لکھنے سے متعلق سامان کی دوکان stationer
لکھنے کا کاغذ writing paper
لٹویا کا شہری Latvian
لٹویا کی زبان Latvian
لٹویا (ایک ملک) Latvia
لٹویائی Latvia
لٹکانا hang
لٹکانے کا تھیلا، جھولا sling
لٹکنا hang
لٹیرا robber
لپٹ flame
لپیٹا ہوا roll
لپیٹ لینا rewind
لپیٹنا wind, wrap
لپیٹنا، لڑھکانا roll
لپیٹنا (کاغذ یا کپڑے وغیرہ میں) wrap up
لپیٹنے کا کاغذ wrapping paper
لچکدار flexible
لچیلا elastic
لڑائی battle
لڑائی fight
لڑائی، جنگ fighting
لڑنا fight
لڑکا boy, chap, lad
لڑکھڑانا stagger, stumble
لڑکی girl
لکا چھپی hide-and-seek
لکڑی timber, wood
لکڑی کا wooden
لکڑی کا سامان (دروازہ وغیرہ) woodwork
لکڑی کی پٹی (دیوار اور فرش کی سرحد پر)
skirting board
لگاتار continuous
لگام reins
لگانا، نصب کرنا fix
لگزمبرگ (ایک ملک کا نام) Luxembourg
لہجہ dialect

لہر Wave, wave
لہروں پر تیراکی surfing
لہروں پر تیرنا surf
لہروں پر تیرنے والا surfer
لہسن garlic
لہسن، جھائیاں freckles
لیبیا Libya
لیبیائی Libyan
لیس، زری چمکدار پٹی lace
لیشٹنسٹائن Liechtenstein
لیموں lemon
لیموں کا مشروب lemonade
لینا take
لیٹنا lie
لیکن but
لیگ league
لے جانا carry, collect
لے جانا، لے لینا take away
ماتم mourning
ماتھے کی زلف fringe
ماحول environment
ماحول دوست ecofriendly
ماحولیات ecology
ماحولیاتی ecological, environmental
مادر وطن homeland
مادری maternal
مادری زبان mother tongue
مادری زبان بولنے والا native speaker
مادّہ substance
مادہ material
مادہ، میٹیریل material
مارفین morphine
مارنا beat
مارنا، قتل کرنا kill
مارنا، ٹھوکر لگانا hit
مارچ March
مارچوبہ، ناگ دون asparagus
مارکسی نظریہ Marxism
ماضی past
ماضی میں جانا go back
ماضی کا past
مال goods
مال بردار جہاز cargo
مالدووا Moldova
مالک owner
مالٹا Malta
مالٹائی Maltese
مالٹائی زبان Maltese

قتل کرنا **murder**
قحط **famine**
قحط سالی **drought**
قد **height**
قدامت پرست **conservative**
قدرتی **organic**
قدرتی وسائل **natural resources**
قدرتی گیس **natural gas**
قدر و قیمت **value**
قدم **step**
قدم رکھنا **tread**
قدموں کی آواز **footstep**
قدیم **ancient**
قدیم، غیر رواجی **unfashionable**
قرابت **proximity**
قرارداد **resolution**
قرارنامہ **agreement**
قرآن **Koran**
قربانی **sacrifice**
قرب و جوار **vicinity**
قرض **debt, loan**
قرضدار ہونا **owe**
قرض دینا **loan**
قرون وسطیٰ کا **mediaeval**
قریبی، نزدیکی **near**
قریب **near**
قریب ترین رشتہ دار **next of kin**
قریب دکھنے والا حصہ (تصویر میں) **foreground**
قریب سے **closely**
قریب قریب **approximate**
قریب کی نظر والا **near-sighted**
قریب ہونا **close**
قریبی **nearby**
قریبی طور پر **near**
قزاقستان **Kazakhstan**
قسط **instalment**
قسم **form, kind, type**
قسم اٹھانا، دھمکانا **swear**
قصائی کی دکان **butcher**
قصباتی **suburban**
قصبہ **suburb**
قصور **fault**
قصوروار **guilty**
قصاب **butcher**
قطار **queue, row**
قطار میں لگنا، کھڑے ہونا **queue**
قطب جنوبی **South Pole**
قطب شمالی **North Pole**
قطبی **polar**
قطبی بھالو **polar bear**
قطر **diameter, Qatar**
قطعہ زمین **plot**
قلاش **broke**
قلت تغذیہ **malnutrition**
قلعہ **fort**
قلم **pen**
قلم سے کاغذ پر لکھنا **write down**
قلمی دوست **penfriend**
قلیل **minimal**
قمار بازی **gambling**
قمیض **shirt**
قنوطیت پسند **pessimist, pessimistic**
قواعد لسان **grammar**
قوت **power**
قوسین **brackets**
قول **quote**
قوم پرست **nationalist**
قوم پرستی **nationalism**
قومیانا **nationalize**
قومی پارک **national park**
قومی گیت **national anthem**
قونصل **consul**
قوی **potential**
قوی کرنا **boost**
قسم **sort, variety**
قسمت **luck**
قسمت سے **luckily**
قسمت والا **lucky**
قلت **shortage**
قہوہ دانی **coffeepot**
قیام **camping, stay**
قیام کرنا، ٹھہرنا **stay**
قید خانہ **jail**
قید کرنا **jail**
قیدی **prisoner**
قیراط **carat**
قیف **funnel**
قیلولہ **snooze**
قیلولہ، جھپکی **nap**
قیلولہ کرنا **snooze**
قیمت **charge**
قیمت، ساکھ **worth**
قیمت فہرست **price list**
قیمت فروخت **selling price**
قیمت ہونا **cost**
قیمتی **precious, price, valuable**
قیمتی، مہنگی **dear**
قیمتی سامان **valuables**
قیمہ **mince**
قینچی **scissors**
قے کرنا **throw up, vomit**
لات **kick**
لاتعلق **stuck-up**
لات مارنا **kick**
لاحاصل **vain**
لاروا **caterpillar**
لاروا (کیڑے کا) **grub**
لازم، واجب **due**
لازمہ **accessory**
لازمی **compulsory, essential**
لازمی طور پر **have to**
لاش **corpse**
لاطینی **Latin**
لاطینی امریکہ **Latin America**
لاطینی امریکی **Latin American**
لالچ، تحریص، ترغیب **temptation**
لالچی **greedy**
لانا **bring**
لانا، حاصل کرنا **get**
لاوا **lava**
لاؤس **Laos**
لائبریری **library**
لائبریرین **librarian**
لائبیریا **Liberia**
لائبیریائی **Liberian**
لائسنس **licence**
لائق **able**
لاپرواہی اور تتر بتر انداز میں کام **sloppy**
لاپرواہ **careless**
لاکھ کا روغن، وارنش **lacquer**
لاگت **cost**
لبادہ **apron**
لبادے (پینٹ اور جیکٹ ایک ہی کپڑے میں تراشے ہوئے) **overalls**
لباس **clothing, dress**
لباس تبدیل کرنا **change**
لباس غسل **bathing suit**
لباس و سامان **gear**
لباس پہننا **dress**
لباس (کسی خاص مقصد کے لئے) **outfit**
لبریز **full**
لیس زیب تن کرنا **dress up**
لبنان **Lebanon**

فلم (سنیما)	film
فلو	flu
فلوپی ڈسک	floppy disk
فلپائنی	Filipino
فلپائنی باشندہ	Filipino
فلپرس (تیراکی پنجے)	flippers
فلیش (کیمرا میں)	flash
فلیٹ (گھر)	flat
فن تعمیر	architecture
فنون لطیفہ	art
فنکار	artist
فنی	artistic
فوارہ	fountain
فوج	army, military
فوجی	serviceman
فورمولا	formula
فورمیٹ (ترتیب)	format
فورمیٹ کرنا (کمپیوٹر کو)	format
فوری	immediate, instant, prompt
فوری توجہ کی حامل	urgent
فوری طور پر	immediately, promptly
فولاد	steel
فولڈر، کاغذ رکھنے کی فاءل	folder
فون رکھ دینا	hang up
فون کرنا، کال کرنا	call
فوڈ پروسیسر (برقی آلہ)	food processor
فلموں میں اہم رول ادا کرنا	star
فلم کی صرف آواز	soundtrack
فلٹر (چھننے والا)	filter
فن لینڈ	Finland
فنی	Finnish
فنی باشندے	Finn
فنی زبان	Finnish
فٹ، مناسب	fit
فکر مند	worried
فکر کرنا	worry
فٹبال	football
فٹبالر	footballer
فٹبال میچ	football match
فٹ بال میچ کیدوران چوٹ لگنے پر کھیل میں خلل پڑنے پر دیا جانے والا اضافی وقت	injury time
فٹبال کھلاڑی	football player
فٹنگ روم (درزی کے یاں)	fitting room
فٹ پاتھ	footpath
فٹ کی ہوئی قالین	fitted carpet
فکر مند ہونا	fret
فکس کیا ہوا	fixed
فہرست الفاظ، فرہنگ	vocabulary
فہرست (کل چیزوں کی)	inventory
فہرست	list
فہرست بنانا	list
فہرست منتظرین	waiting list
فہم	comprehension
فہیم	wise
فی	per
فی البدیہہ، فوری، اچانک	spontaneous
فی الحال	currently, lately, presently
فی الفور	instantly
فیتہ	lace
فیریٹ (چوہا خرگوش مار بلی نما جاور)	ferret
فیس	charge
فیس، حق خدمت	fee
فیشن	fashion
فیشن پرست	cool
فیشنیبل، فیشن پرست	fashionable
فیشیل (چہرے کا مساج)	facial
فی صد	per cent, percentage
فیصلہ	decision
فیصلہ کرنا	decide
فیصلہ کرنا، انصاف کرنا	judge
فیصلہ کن	decisive
فلیش مارنا	flash
فیوز بکس	fuse box
فیچر (نمایاں حصہ)	feature
فیڈبیک، تعامل	feedback
فیکس (تحریری ترسیل)	fax
فیکس کرنا	fax
قابل استطاعت	affordable
قابل اعتبار	credible
قابل بازاحیاء	biodegradable
قابل تبدیل	changeable
قابل تجدید	renewable
قابل رحم	miserable
قابل رسائی	accessible
قابل شناخت	recognizable
قابل ضیاع	disposable
قابل عمل	feasible
قابل قبول	acceptable, convincing
قابل مشورہ	advisable
قابل موازنہ	comparable
قابل انتظام	manageable
قابل حرکت چیز سے مارنے کا عمل	hit
قابلیت	ability
قابلیت کے ساتھ	efficiently
قابو	control
قابو پانا	overcome
قابو پانا، پیچھے چھوڑ دینا	get over
قابو کرنا	control
قابض ہونا، گرفت میں لینا	possess
قابل ادائیگی	payable
قابل اعتماد	reputable
قابل احترام	respectable
قابل انتقال	portable
قابل بدل	removable
قابل توجہ	noticeable
قابل دید	spectacular
قابل رحم	pathetic
قابل قدر	outstanding
قابل پیشگوئی	predictable
قاتل	killer, murderer
قاری	reader
قافلہ	convoy
قالین	carpet, rug
قاموس	encyclopaedia
قانون	code, law
قانون سازی	legislation
قانون پڑھانے والا ادارہ	law school
قانونی	legal
قانونی، معقول	valid
قانونی مسودہ	bill
قانونی کاروائیاں	proceedings
قائل کرنا	convince
قائل کرنا، منوا لینا	persuade
قائل کرنے والا	persuasive
قائم مقام	acting
قائم کرنا	put up
قبر	grave
قبرستان	cemetery, graveyard
قبرص	Cyprus
قبرص سے متعلق	Cypriot
قبض زدہ	constipated
قبضہ	hinge, occupation
قبضہ، ملکیت	possession
قبضہ کرنا	occupy
قبل	before
قبل، پہلے	ago, before
قبل از وقت	premature
قبل از ولادت	antenatal
قبل مسیح	BC
قبل تاریخ	prehistoric
قبول کرنا	accept
قبیلہ	tribe
قتل	murder
قتل عام	massacre

غیر محتاط ہونا، سختی سے کرنا rough
غیر محفوظ insecure
غیر محفوظ، ہدف بننے والا vulnerable
غیر مختتم endless
غیر مخلص insincere
غیر مستقل unstable
غیر مشہور unpopular
غیر مطمئن unsure
غیر مطمئن dissatisfied
غیر معروف unfamiliar
غیر معمولی extraordinary, remarkable
غیر معمولی طور پر remarkably
غیر معیاری second-rate
غیر ملکی foreigner
غیر ملکی، بیرونی exotic
غیر منطقی unreasonable
غیر موجودگی absence, disappearance
غیر موزوں unfit, unsuitable
غیر مہذب rude
غیر مہذب uncivilized
غیر نمکین پانی کی مچھلی freshwater fish
غیر وابستہ irrelevant
غیر واضح illegible, unclear
غیر کاریگر unskilled
غیر یقینی fragile
غیر یقینی حالت uncertainty
فاتح winner
فاختہ dove
فاخر proud
فارسی Persian
فارم (کھیت مع گھر) farm
فارم ہاؤس (فارم کا گھر) farmhouse
فاش، صریح (غلطی) glaring
فاش غلطی blunder
فاش کرنا disclose, reveal
فاصلہ distance
فاضل extra
فاضل، اضافی surplus
فاضل spare
فاضل ادئگی surcharge
فاضل سامان excess baggage
فاضل وقت spare time
فاضل پرزے spare part
فاضل پہیا spare wheel
فاضل کمرہ spare room
فاضل ہونا (وقت، رقم وغیرہ) spare
فالتو ٹائر spare tyre
فاؤنٹین پین fountain pen
فائبر شیشہ fibreglass
فائنل سے پہلے semifinal
فائنل (فیصلہ کن) final
فائدہ advantage, benefit
فائدہ اٹھانا benefit
فائدہ مند useful
فائر shot
فائرنگ shooting
فائل file
فائل میں رکھنا file
فایر الارم fire alarm
فایر برگیڈ fire brigade
فایر مین fireman
فتح triumph, victory, winning
فجائیہ نشان exclamation mark
فجی (جمہوریہ ۸۴۴ جزائر) Fiji
فخر، اطمینان pride
فراخ دل generous
فراخ دلی generosity
فرار ہونا flee, get away
فرانس France
فرانسیسی French
فرانسیسی خاتون Frenchwoman
فرانسیسی زبان French
فرانسیسی (شخص) Frenchman
فراہم کردہ اشیاء supplies
فراہم کرنا supply
فراہمی supply
فرد individual
فرسٹ ایڈ (ابتدائی طبی علاج) first aid
فرسٹ ایڈ کٹ first-aid kit
فرسٹ کلاس first-class
فرش floor, ground
فرشتہ angel
فرشپوش lino
فرش کی طرف downstairs
فرشی منزل ground floor
فرض، کردار role
فرض کرلینا supposing
فرض کرنا assume, presume, suppose
فرضی، نقلی fake
فرق difference
فرقہ community
فرماں بردار obedient
فرماں برداری کرنا obey
فرم (تجارتی ادارہ) firm
فرنیچر، کرسی میز وغیرہ furniture
فروخت sale
فروخت کرنا sell
فروری February
فروغ دینا develop
فروگزاشت / غلطی سے oversight
فرج fridge
فریب، دھوکہ fraud
فریب، دھوکہ، چال trick
فریب دہی rip off
فریب کھانا rip off
فریبی shifty
فریضہ duty
فریفتہ obsessed
فریق ثالث والا بیمہ third-party insurance
فرنچ بینس (پھلی کے دانے) French beans
فرنچ ہورن (موسیقی ساز) French horn
فریکوینسی (ہونے کی شرح) frequency
فری کک (فٹبال میں) free kick
فساد riot
فساد کرنا riot
فشار خون blood pressure
فصل crop, harvest
فصل اگانا harvest
فضا atmosphere
فضائیہ air force
فضول absurd, junk
فضول ای میل spam
فضول بکھراہٹ clutter
فضول خرچ extravagant
فضولیات پر توجہ دینے والا fussy
فضیحت scandal
فطرت، قدرت nature
فطرت پسند naturalist
فطری طور پر naturally
فعال active
فعل verb
فعل کی حالت (جانا، کھانا وغیرہ) infinitive
فعال کرنا revive
فقرہ phrase
فلالین flannel
فلان (کیک) flan
فلسطین Palestine
فلسطینی Palestinian
فلسفہ philosophy
فلم اسٹار (اداکار) film star

علامت symbol, symptom
علامت، نشان sign
علامت تخفیف حروف apostrophe
علم ارضیات geology
علم افلاک astronomy
علم الاساطیر mythology
علم آثار قدیمہ archaeology
علم نجوم astrology
عمارات وغیرہ پر لکھی تحریر graffiti
عمارت ساز builder
عمارت سازی building
عمان Oman
عمدہ ترین، خصوصی fancy
عمر age
عمر، عہدے یا مرتبہ میں بڑا senior
عمر رسیدہ elderly
عمر رسیدہ، بالغ نظر grown-up
عمر رسیدہ شہری، بزرگ senior citizen
عمر کا aged
عمر کی قید age limit
عمل act
عمل تکثیف condensation
عملہ staff
عملہ کا کمرہ staffroom
عملی practical
عملی طور پر practically
عمودی vertical
عموماً mainly
عمومی common
عمومی بنانا generalize
عمومی شعور common sense
عمومی معلومات general knowledge
عنبر amber
عنصر element
عنصر، جزو ingredient
عنوان title
عوام public
عوامی public
عوامی رائے، رائے عامہ public opinion
عوامی مالیاتی fiscal
عوامی موسیقی folk music
عوامی نقل و حمل (ٹرانسپورٹ)
public transport
عورت woman
عبادت کرنا worship
عشائے ربانی کی رسم Mass
علاج، تدارک remedy

علاج، طریق علاج therapy
علاقائی regional
علاقہ region, territory
علم، معلومات knowledge
علم نفسیات psychology
عکس illustration, replica
عہدہ post, rank
عیار cunning
عیسائی Christian
عیسائیت Christianity
عیسائی خانقاہ monastery
عیسیٰ مسیح (پیغمبر خدا) Jesus
عیش و عشرت luxury
غار cave
غارت کرنا، توڑ پھوڑ کرنا vandalize
غارتگر vandal
غارتگری vandalism
غازہ blusher
غافل ignorant
غائب رہ کر کام سے بچنا skive
غائب دماغ absent-minded
غائب ہونا disappear
غائب ہونا، چلا جانا out
غبارہ balloon
غدود gland
غذا diet
غذائیت بخش nutritious
غربت poverty
غربی westbound
غروب آفتاب sunset
غرانا growl
غرانا snarl
غریب poor
غسل خانہ bathroom
غصہ anger, rage
غصہ سے گھورنا glare
غصہ میں پاگل mad
غضبناک، طیش میں furious
غفلت ignorance, neglect
غلام slave
غلط false, wrong
غلط، خراب wrong
غلط، صحیح نہ ہونا wrong
غلط راہ پر ڈالنا mislay
غلط سمجھنا misunderstand
غلط فہمی misunderstanding,
mistaken

غلط فہمی سے mistakenly
غلط فیصلہ کرنا misjudge
غلطی error, mistake
غلطی سے accident
غلطی سے لگ جانے والا ٹیلیفون نمبر
wrong number
غلطی کرنا mistake
غلیظ filthy
غلیظ، گندا foul
غوطہ خور diver
غوطہ خوری diving
غوطہ لگانا dive
غذائی عنصر nutrient
غپ شپ chat
غپ شپ کا کمرہ chatroom
غپ شپ کرنا chat
غیر اخلاقی immoral
غیر ارضی، پر اسرار uncanny
غیر اصل unreal
غیر ارادی ردِّ عمل reflex
غیر اہم unimportant
غیر برقی acoustic
غیر تسلی بخش unsatisfactory
غیر تمباکو نوش non-smoker
غیر تمباکو نوشی non-smoking
غیر جانب دار neutral
غیر جانبدار impartial
غیر حاضر absent
غیر دوستانہ unfriendly
غیر ذمہ دار irresponsible
غیر رسمی informal
غیر رواجی unconventional
غیر سرکاری unofficial
غیر شادی شدہ unmarried
غیر صحت مند unhealthy, unwell
غیر صحیح inaccurate, incorrect
غیر ضروری unnecessary
غیر عادی unusual
غیر فوجی civilian
غیر قانونی illegal
غیر قانونی طور پر ملک میں لانا smuggle
غیر قدرتی، ساحرانہ supernatural
غیر متحمل intolerant
غیر متصل گھر detached house
غیر متوقع آفت catastrophe
غیر متوقع unexpected
غیر متوقع طور پر unexpectedly

ضرب لگانا، مارنا strike
ضرب لگنا hurt
ضرورت necessity, need
ضرورت سے زیادہ surplus
ضرورت ہونا need
ضروری necessary
ضروریات پوری کرنا provide for
ضروری طور پر necessarily
ضروری ہونا must
ضلع district
ضمانت guarantee
ضمانت دینا، لینا guarantee
ضمانتی رقم deposit
ضم ہونا mix up
ضمیر conscience, pronoun
ضمنی اثرات side effect
طاقت strength
طاقت، زور force
طاقتور strong
طاقتور، مقتدر powerful
طاقتور بنانا strengthen
طاق (عدد) odd
طالب علم student
طالب لسان بعوض گھریلو کام کاج au pair
طباعت کی غلطی misprint
طبعیات physics
طب نفسی سے متعلق psychiatric
طبی medical
طبیب نفسی psychiatrist
طبی سند medical certificate
طراوت دار، گھنا lush
طرح بدلنا switch
طرف، جانب towards
طرفداری favour
طریق کار اختیار کرنا resort to
طریقہ way
طریقہ، طریق method
طشتری plate, saucer
طشتری، تھالی dish
طلاق divorce
طلباء کے لئے قیمت میں کمی student discount
طلب کرنا ask for
طلوع dawn
طلوع آفتاب sunrise
طنز irony
طنزیہ ironic, sarcastic

طور، طریقہ manner
طوطا parrot
طوفان storm
طوفانی stormy
طول البلد longitude
طویل، لمبا long
طویل چہل قدمی hike
طبی علاج treatment
طیارہ aircraft
طیش آمیز infuriating
ظالم cruel
ظاہر ہونا appear
ظرافت sense of humour, wit
ظریف witty
ظہور appearance
عادات و خصلت character
عادت habit, practice
عادی addict, punctual
عادی ہونا adjust, practise, used
عارضی temporary
عارضی ملازم temp
عاقل intelligent
عاقلانہ rational
عالم گیریت globalization
عالمی، آفاقی global
عالمی حدت global warming
عالمی کپ World Cup
عالم، جانکار knowledgeable
عالیشان classical
عام general
عام انتخابات general election
عام بیہوشی آور general anaesthetic
عام شہری civilian
عام طور سے usually
عام طور پر generally
عامل executive
عبقری genius
عبوری، عارضی provisional
عجائب گھر museum
عجوبہ، مافوق الفطرت weird
عجیب eccentric, funny, peculiar, strange
عجیب، جاذب quaint
عدالت court
عدد figure, number
عدل justice
عدم اتفاق disagreement

عدم اشتہا anorexia
عدم اشتہا کا مریض anorexic
عذر excuse
عذر عدم موجودگی alibi
عراق Iraq
عراقی Iraqi
عرب Arab
عربی Arab, Arabic
عربی زبان Arabic
عرشہ deck
عرشہ پر رکھی کرسی deckchair
عرض البلد latitude
عرضی petition
عرف alias
عرفیت nickname
عزت honour, respect
عزت کرنا respect
عزم ambition
عزم، خواہش will
عزم و حوصلہ willpower
عزیز dear
عشائیہ dinner
عشائیہ تقریب dinner party
عشق کا شکار ہونا، دام میں پھنسنا fall for
عصب nerve
عضلات کی جکڑن spasm
عضلاتی muscular
عضلہ tendon
عضو organ
عطائی سامان کی دوکان charity shop
عطا کرنا contribute
عطیہ charity, contribution
عطیہ دینا donate
عطیہ کنندہ donor
عظیم enormous, grand, superb
عظیم، بہت بڑا/بڑی great
عظیم، کافی بڑا، عظیم الشان great
عظیم الجثہ ہاتھی (ناپید) mammoth
عظیم (ساکھ یا رتبہ میں) giant
عفریت monster
عقب میں back
عقبی rear
عقل داڑھ wisdom tooth
عقیدہ belief
عقیدہ رکھنا believe
علاقہ area
علاقہ قطب شمالی Arctic

شوروغل مچانے والی شوخ لڑکی tomboy
شور کرنے والا noisy
شوری، جیوری jury
شوق hobby
شوقین amateur
شوہر husband
شے item
شکار prey, victim
شگاف leak, tear
شگاف مشین (شگاف میں رقم ڈال کر سامان لے لینا)
slot machine
شگاف پڑنا crack
شیئر ہولڈر (حصص دار) shareholder
شٹر (دروازہ) shutters
شٹل کاک، بیڈ منٹن چڑیا shuttlecock
شک doubt
شکار کا عمل hunting
شکار کرنا hunt
شکاری hunter
شکاری پرندہ bird of prey
شکایت complaint, grouse
شکایت کرنا complain
شکرگزار grateful
شکریہ! thanks!
شکریہ ادا کرنا thank
شکست defeat
شکست خوردہ frustrated
شکست خوردہ، ہارا ہوا loser
شکست دینا، ہرانا beat
شکستہ تحریر scribble
شکل shape
شکر sugar
شک کرنا doubt, suspect
شگاف crack, gap
شگاف دار cracked
شہادت کی انگلی index finger
شہد honey
شہد کی مکھی bee
شہر city, town
شہرت fame
شہرت یافتہ renowned
شہر کا نقشہ (سب سڑکیں گلیاں دکھائی ہوں)
street map
شہر کی منصوبہ بندی town planning
شہری citizen
شہریت citizenship, nationality
شہزادہ prince
شہزادی princess
شہنشاہ emperor
شہید martyr
شیر lion, tiger
شیر دنداں dandelion
شیرنی lioness
شیر کا بچہ cub
شیرہ، راب treacle
شیری (ایک تیز شراب) sherry
شیریں sweet
شیشہ، بلور glass
شیشیدار دکان shop window
شیطان Devil
شیطانی evil, sinister
شیف، باورچی chef
شیمپو (بال دھونے کی لئی) shampoo
شیونگ فوم (جھاگ) shaving foam
شیونگ کریم shaving cream
شیو کرنے کا برقی آلہ shaver
صابن soap
صابندانی soap dish
صادق، سچا truthful
صارف consumer
صارف user
صارف دوست user-friendly
صاف clean, clear
صاف، واضح obvious, vivid
صاف ستھرا neat, tidy
صاف طور پر clearly, frankly,
obviously
صاف نہ بول پانا stutter
صاف کرنا clear, tidy
صافی، پونچھا cloth
صبح a.m., morning
صبح کی کسل مندی morning sickness
صبر patience
صحرا ریگستان Sahara
صحافی journalist
صحت health
صحت بخش healthy
صحت مند healthy
صحیح correct, correction, right
صحیح طور پر correctly, rightly
صحیح ٹھہرانا، توجیہ کرنا justify
صحیح کا نشان tick
صحیح کرنا correct
صدر president
صدر دفتر head office
صدر مرکز headquarters
صدماتی shocking, traumatic
صدمہ shock
صدمہ دینا shock
صدی centenary, century
صرف only
صرف، محض mere
صرف، واحد only
صرف ایک والدین single parent
صرف کرنا put in
صعتر (بوٹی) thyme
صفائی والی chambermaid,
cleaning lady
صفائی کار cleaner
صفائی کرنا cleaning, clear up
صفائی سے neatly
صفائی والا dustman
صفائی کرنا clean
صفحات sheet
صفحہ page
صفر nil, nought, zero
صلاح tip
صلاحکار consultant
صلاحیت capacity, potential
صلاحیت، ذہانت talent
صلہ reward
صلہ بخش rewarding
صلیب cross
صلیب مع مسیح crucifix
صنعت کار manufacturer
صنعتی industrial
صنف gender
صنوبر کا درخت fir tree
صوابدید discretion
صوفہ settee, sofa
صوفہ جسے کھول کر پلنگ بنایا جائے sofa bed
صومالی Somali
صومالیائی Somali
صومالیہ Somalia
ضابطہ regulation
ضائع کرنا squander, waste
ضائعگی، بربادی waste
ضبط کرنا confiscate, seize
ضد جسم antibody
ضدی obstinate, stubborn
ضدی، بار بار ہونے والی persistent
ضرب multiplication
ضرب، زخم، ضرر injury
ضرب دینا multiply

سینیگال جمہوریہ Senegal

سینیگالی Senegalese

سیاح tourist

سیال liquid

سیال صابن shower gel

سیٹ (ایک گروپ کی چیزیں) set

سیٹلائٹ، مصنوعی سیارہ satellite

سیٹلائٹ ڈش (ٹی وی سگنل پکڑنے والی) satellite dish

سیٹی whistle

سیٹی بجانا whistle

سیٹیلائٹ نیویگیشن satnav

سیپ scallop

سیپی oyster, shellfish

سیڑھی ladder, step

سیڑھیاں stairs

سیڑھیوں پر upstairs

سیڑھیوں کے سیٹ staircase

سیکریٹری (دفتر میں) secretary

سیکسوفون باجہ saxophone

سیکنڈ second

سیکھنا، علم حاصل کرنا learn

سیکیورٹی گارڈ (محافظ) security guard

سیگل seagull

سے from, since

شاخ branch

شادی wedding

شادی، نکاح marriage

شادی شدہ married

شادی کرنا marry

شادی کی انگوٹھی wedding ring

شادی کی سالگرہ wedding anniversary

شاذونادر طور پر rarely

شارٹ ہینڈ shorthand

شارک (بڑی مچھلی) shark

شاعر poet

شاعری poetry

شال shawl

شام dusk, evening

شامل کرنا include

شامل کرنا، ملانا add

شامل ہونا join

شام کا کھانا supper

شامی Syrian

شامی باشندہ Syrian

شامی کباب، ٹکیہ pie

شان glory, majesty

شاندار fantastic, glorious, graceful, magnificent, smashing, splendid, terrific

شانہ بشانہ چلنا، ساتھ ساتھ چلنا، بغل میں چلنا rock

شاور (غسل کیلئے) shower

شائستہ decent, sophisticated

شائع کرنا publish

شائق keen

شائق، شوقین fan

شاپنگ ٹرالی shopping trolley

شاگرد pupil

شاہ بلوط oak

شاہ بلوط کا پھل acorn

شاہراہ main road

شاہکار masterpiece

شاہی، شاہانہ royal

شاہی محل stately home

شاید maybe, perhaps

شاید ہی، نہیں کے برابر hardly

شبینہ اسکول night school

شبینہ تفریح گاہیں nightlife

شبیہ image

شترمرغ ostrich

شتری خاکستری رنگ beige

شخص bloke, guy, person

شخصیت personality

شدید drastic, fierce, intense, intensive, stifling

شدید طور پر heavily, strictly, terribly

شدید گرم sweltering

شراب wine

شراب اور شکر کا جام punch

شراب خانہ bar

شراب کی بھٹی distillery

شرارت mischief

شرارتی mischievous

شربت sorbet, syrup

شرح rate

شرح سود interest rate

شرح مبادلہ rate of exchange

شرم، غیرت shame

شرمانا blush

شرمسار embarrassed

شرمناک embarrassing, vile

شرمندہ ashamed

شرمیلا shy

شروعات beginning, kick off, start

شروعات میں outset

شروعات کرنا start off

شروع کرنا begin, kick off, start

شریان artery

شریف gentle

شریک جرم accomplice

شستہ elegant

شش وپنج suspense

شطرنج chess

شعاعی پٹی beam

شعبہ department, sector

شفا cure

شفاف clear

شفایاب ہونا cure, recover

شفایابی recovery

شفتالو nectarine

شفاف transparent

شفاف پانی sparkling water

شفیق caring

شق clause

شل numb

شلغم turnip

شمار کرنا، گنتی کرنا count

شمارہ edition

شمال north

شمالاً north

شمال طرفی northbound

شمال مشرق northeast

شمال مغرب northwest

شمالی northern

شمالی افریقہ North Africa

شمالی افریقی North African

شمالی امریکہ North America

شمالی امریکی North American

شمالی آئرلینڈ Northern Ireland

شمالی سمت north

شمالی کوریا North Korea

شمشان crematorium

شناخت identification, identity

شناخت کر لینا، پہچان لینا recognize

شناخت کرنا identify

شناخت کی چوری identity theft

شناسا known

شوبزنس show business

شوخ، شرارتی naughty

شوخی، طفلانہ چالاکی prank

شور noise

شوراء، جیوری jury

شوربہ broth, gravy, soup, stew

شورشرابہ racket

سوراخ کرنا drill
سورج sun
سورج مکھی sunflower
سورج کی دھوپ اور گرمی sunshine
سور کا گوشت bacon
سوزش زدہ inflamed
سوزش دل heartburn
سوزش inflammation
سوسن، للی lily
سوسن کا پودا lily of the valley
سولہ sixteen
سولواں sixteenth
سونا sleep
سونف aniseed
سونپنا deliver
سونڈ trunk
سونگھنا، بو محسوس کرنا smell
سونے سے رک کر انتظار کرنا wait up
سونے کا وقت bedtime
سووینیر (چھوٹی، واقعات کی یاد دلانیوالا) souvenir
سوئٹ (ہوٹل روم) suite
سوئزرلینڈ Switzerland
سوئچ بورڈ switchboard
سوئی needle
سوئی لگانا inject
سوئیٹر sweater
سوس Swiss
سوچ، بٹن switch
سوٹ (کوٹ پینٹ جیکیٹ) suit
سوٹکیس suitcase
سوچنا think
سوچنا، غور کرنا think
سوچ کے ذریعہ دیکھنا visualize
سوڈان Sudan
سوڈانی Sudanese
سوکھا آلو بخارا prune
سوکھی گھاس hay
سویا soya
سویا سوس soy sauce
سویڈش Swedish
سویڈن Sweden, sweetcorn
سویڈن کا Swede
سویڈش Swedish
سیاحوں کا موسم high season
ستمبر September
سرکہ vinegar
سرکہ، جڑی بوٹیوں اور تیل کا مرکب salad dressing
سنکی لینا sniff
سفارش recommendation
سفارش کرنا recommend
سلائی sewing
سلائی مشین sewing machine
سلسلہ range, sequel
سلسلہ (واقعات یا واردات کا ایک کے بعد ایک رونما ہونا) series
سلوواک Slovak
سلوواکی Slovak
سلوواکیا Slovakia
سلووینیا Slovenia
سلووینیائی Slovenian
سلوٹ، سیون seam
سلوٹدار creased
سلیکون چپ (چھوٹا برقی سرکٹ) silicon chip
سوئی noodles
سپاہی soldier
سکڑا، سمٹا ہوا shrunken
سکڑنا shrink
سکھ Sikh
سگنل signal
سگنل دینا signal
سیاست politics
سیاسی political
سٹہ bet
سٹہ لگانا bet
سپردگی delivery
سپلائی کرنیوالا supplier
سچ true, truth
سچائی کو تسلیم نہ کرنے والا unrealistic
سڑاندھ stink
سڑا ہوا rotten
سڑنا decay, stink
سڑنا، سڑانا rot
سڑک road
سڑک جام roadblock
سڑک سے نکلنے والی گلی side street
سڑک مرمت وغیرہ roadworks
سڑک کا کنارا hard shoulder
سڑک کا کھڈہ pothole
سڑک کنارے کی روشنی streetlamp
سکنا may, might
سکنا، کرنے کے قابل ہونا can
سکون relaxation
سکون آور (دوا) sedative
سکون بخش relaxing
سکہ coin
سہل، مفید handy
سہولت بخش convenient
سہولیات facilities
سہ پہر afternoon
سیاحت tourism
سیاحتی مقامات کی سیر sightseeing
سیاست داں politician
سیاق وسباق context
سیب apple
سیب کی شراب cider
سیخ grill
سیخ، سلاخ skewer
سیخ پر پکانا grill
سیخ-سلاخ bar
سیدھا، کمر سیدھی upright
سیدھا کرنے والا آلہ (بال وغیرہ) straighteners
سیدھی، راست straight
سی دینا sew up
سیرنج syringe
سیریل (سلسلہ وار کہانی) serial
سیر کرنا tour
سی سا (اوپر نیچے کرنے والا تختہ) seesaw
سیسہ lead
سیسہ سے پاک lead-free
سیسہ سے پاک یا کم سے کم unleaded
سیشے (چھوٹی تھیلی) sachet
سیلاب flood
سیلاب آنا flood
سیل (ایک جانور جو سمندر اور خشکی دونوں میں زندگی گزارتی ہے) seal
سیلز اسسٹنٹ sales assistant
سیلزمین salesman
سیلز نمائندہ sales rep
سیلز ویمن saleswoman
سیلز پرسن (مرد یا خاتون) salesperson
سیلوٹیپ (ٹریڈ مارک) •Sellotape
سینا، سلائی کرنا sew
سین میرینو San Marino
سینڈل (جوتے) sandal
سینڈوچ (دو روٹی) sandwich
سینکا ہوا baked
سینکنا bake
سینگ horn
سینہ chest

سزا punishment, sentence
سزا، جرمانہ penalty
سزا دینا penalize, punish
سزا سنانا sentence
سزا سنایا جانا convict
سزائے موت execution
سزائے موت دینا execute
سست lazy, slow
سست، کام چور idle
سستا inexpensive
سستا ریستراں diner
سستی cheap
سستے چھوٹ جانا get off
سسر father-in-law
سسرالی رشتے دار mother-in-law
سسکنا sob
سطح surface
سطح (ناپنے کا نشان) level
سطح سمندر sea level
سطحی superficial
سعودی Saudi
سعودی اعرابی (لوگ) Saudi Arabian
سعودی عرب Saudi Arabia
سعودی عرب کا Saudi Arabian
سعودی (لوگ) Saudi
سفارت خانہ consulate, embassy
سفارتی diplomatic
سفر journey, outing, travel, travelling
سفر (آنے جانے کا) trip
سفر کرنا commute, travel, trip
سفری بیمہ travel insurance
سفری منصوبہ (جگہوں اور روٹ کی وضاحت کے ساتھ) itinerary
سفوف powder
سفوف صابن soap powder
سفاک brutal
سفید white
سفید تختہ (پین سے لکھنے کے لئے) whiteboard
سفیر ambassador, diplomat
سلاخ rod
سلاد coleslaw, salad
سلاد کا غلاف vinaigrette
سلام دعا کرنا greet
سلامی دینا salute
سلجھانا، مشکل حل کرنا handle

سلسلہ عمل process
سلسلے وار consecutive
سلطنت empire
سلوٹ crease
سلوٹ، تہ fold
سلوک treat
سلوک کرنا behave, treat
سلیقہ tact
سلیقہ مند tactful
سلیٹ slate
سلیپنگ بیگ sleeping bag
سماج، معاشرہ society
سماج سے متعلق social
سماجواد socialism
سماجواد میں اعتماد رکھنے والا socialist
سماجوادی socialist
سماجی، ملنسار sociable
سماجیات sociology
سماجی خدمات social services
سماجی کارکن social worker
سماعت hearing
سماعتی آلہ hearing aid
سمانا accommodate
سمت direction
سمت نما compass
سمجھ، فہم understanding
سمجھا دیا گیا، منا لیا گیا rope in
سمجھنا consider, regard, understand
سمجھنے لائق understandable
سمجھوتا compromise
سمجھوتا کرنا compromise
سمندر ocean
سمندر کا پانی sea water
سمندر کی سطح سے یا کسی سطح سے بلندی altitude
سمندر کے قریب seaside
سمندری، بحری Oceania
سمندری جھاگ surf
سمندری غذائیں seafood
سمندری مچھلی haddock
سمندری گھوڑا نما مچھلی walrus
سن ایاس menopause
سنبھالنا tackle
سنترہ orange
سنترہ، سنگترہ tangerine
سنترے کا رس orange juice
سنجیدگی سے seriously

سند certificate
سند نکاح marriage certificate
سند پیدائش birth certificate
سند یافتگی، گریجوئیشن graduation
سنسنی thrill
سنسنی خیز sensational
سنمورہ anchovy
سننا hear, listen
سنوارنا tidy up
سنوارنے والا conditioner
سنگ مرمر marble
سنگ مثانہ gallstone
سنگین serious
سنہری golden
سنہری ملمع gold-plated
سنیچر Saturday
سو hundred
سوس Swiss
سوار rider
سوار ہونا ride
سواری passenger, ride, transport
سوازیلینڈ Swaziland
سوال query, question
سوالنامہ questionnaire
سوال پوچھنا query
سوال کرنا question
سوالیہ نشان question mark
سونا (غسل) sauna
سوانح حیات autobiography
سوانحی خاکہ curriculum vitae, CV
سوائے apart from, except
سوتی cotton
سوتی دھاگہ cotton
سوتیلا باپ stepfather
سوتیلا بھائی stepbrother
سوتیلا بیٹا stepson
سوتیلی بہن stepsister
سوتیلی بیٹی stepdaughter
سوتیلی ماں stepmother
سوتی کپڑا fabric
سوختہ شکر caramel
سود interest
سودا، لین دین transaction
سوداگر dealer
سور pig
سوراخ aperture, hole, puncture
سوراخ (جسم کے کسی حصہ میں) piercing

سالی، نند sister-in-law
سامان، اسباب luggage
سامان بستر bedding
سامان سفر baggage
سامع listener
سامنے front
سامنے، بالمقابل opposite
سامنے کا شیشہ صاف کرنے والے (واپر) windscreen wiper
سانس breath, sigh
سانس اندر لینا breathe in
سانس خارج کرنا breathe out
سانس لینا breathe
سانس لینے والے آلہ جات کے ساتھ زیر آب تیرا scuba diving
سانولا tanned
سانپ snake
سانپ کی چھتری، کگرمتا toadstool
سانچہ mould
سانڈ bull
سائبیریا Siberia
سائز (قد) size
سائنس science
سائنس داں scientist
سائنسی scientific
سائبان shed
سائرن (بھونپو) siren
سائلنسر silencer
سائنسی افسانہ science fiction
سائکل چلانا cycle
سائیکل bicycle
ساٹھ sixty
ساکھ reputation
ساکھ عزت prestige
سایا shade
سب، سارا entire
سبب بننا cause
سب جاننا know-all
سبزی ترکاری vegetable
سبزی خور vegetarian
سبزی (لمبی سفید مغز) marrow
سب سے برا worst
سب سے بڑا eldest
سب سے زیادہ most
سب سے چھوٹا (عمر میں) youngest
سبق lesson
سبکدوش retired
سبکدوش ہو جانا retire
سبکدوشی retirement
سب کچھ everything
سبھی all, every
سبھی، تمام all
سبھی سامان کی دوکان supermarket
سبھی ٹکٹ بک جانا sold out
ستارہ star
ستارہ، تارے star
ستانا، ہنسی اڑانا tease
ستائش کرنا appreciate
ستون column
ستر seventy
سترہ seventeen
سترہواں seventeenth
سجانا decorate
سجانے والا decorator
سحر spell
سخت hard, stark, strict, tight
سخت، بے لچک stiff
سخت، دشوار hard
سخت، ٹھوس solid
سخت، کھردرا harsh
سخت اذیت torture
سخت اذیت دینا torture
سخت الفاظ swearword
سخت آزمائش ordeal
سخت آندھی طوفان tornado
سخت جان tough
سخت محنت کرنا slave
سخت مطالعہ کرنا swot
سخت نفرت کرنا loathe
سختی سے hard
سختی سے کاٹنا hack
سدا بہار درخت yew
سدا بہار درخت اور جھاڑیوں کا مجموعہ holly
سدھار، اصلاح improvement
سدھارنا، مرمت کرنا mend
سدھارکرنا improve
سر head
سرا، اختتامی حصہ end
سراغ clue, cue
سراغ رساں detective
سر اور کاندھوں کا مجسمہ bust
سرائے inn
سربراہ، صدر، قائد head
سربیا Serbia
سربیائی Serbian
سرجن (جراح) surgeon
سرحد border, frontier
سرخ red
سرخباد rash
سرخ بھورا auburn
سرخ شراب port, red wine
سرخ گوشت red meat
سرخی headline, highlight
سرخی، تمتماہٹ flush
سرخی لگانا، واضح کرنا highlight
سردرد headache
سرد علاقوں کے درخت conifer
سرد مہری والا laid-back
سردی لگنا، ٹھنڈک محسوس کرنا cold
سردی کا موسم winter
سسرالی رشتے دار in-laws
سرسوں، رائی mustard
سرطان cancer
سرطانی tropical
سرعت acceleration
سرغنہ chief
سرمایہ capital, investment
سرمایہ داری capitalism
سرمایہ لگانا invest
سرمایہ کار investor
سرنامیہ acronym
سرنگ tunnel
سرور delight
سرور (کمپیوٹر نیٹ ورک میں مرکزی کمپیوٹر) server
سروس اسٹیشن service station
سروس کرنا service
سرو (گیند یا شٹل کاک کو مار کر دوسری طرف بھیجنا) serve
سرپوش headscarf
سرپوش hood
سرپٹ gallop
سرپٹ دوڑانا gallop
سرچ (تلاش) پارٹی search party
سرکاری چھٹی public holiday
سرکشی، مفسدہ پردازی turbulence
سرکنڈا reed
سرگراں dizzy
سرگرمی activity
سرگزشت account
سر ہلا کر رضامندی دینا nod
سری لنکا Sri Lanka
سرین bum, buttocks, hip
سرین پر مارنا spank

زاویہ قائمہ right angle
زاویہ نگاہ perspective
زائد extra
زائرین pilgrim
زبان language, tongue
زبانی، دہنی oral
زبانی امتحان oral
زبانی تبصرہ commentary
زبانی خبر دینا page
زحمت، تکلیف trouble
زحمت، دشواری inconvenience
زخم، ضرب wound
زخم خوردگی، ہلاکت casualty
زخمی hurt, injured
زخم یا کٹنے کا نشان scar
زخمی کرنا wound
زخمی کرنا، مضروب کرنا injure
زراعت agriculture
زراعتی agricultural
زرخیز fertile
زردی yolk
زرضمانت bail
زرفدیہ ransom
زرق برق، ٹھاٹھ دار gorgeous
زرمبادلہ کی شرح exchange rate
زرگل pollen
زرہ armour
زعفران saffron
زلزلہ earthquake
زمانہ tense
زمبابوے کا Zimbabwean
زمبابوے کا باشندہ Zimbabwean
زمرہ category
زمین earth, land
زمین بوس ہونا crouch down
زمین کا مالک landowner
زن، خاتون female
زنانہ، نسوانی female
زنجیر chain
زندہ alive
زندہ رہنا live
زنگ rust
زنگ آلودہ rusty
زوج spouse
زور stress
زوردار آواز کے ساتھ بند کرنا slam
زور دینا emphasize, stress
زور سے aloud, loudly

زور سے بولنا speak up
زور سے چلانا yell
زور سے ہاتھ (مکہ) مارنا thump
زور لگا کر پھینکنا pitch
زور ڈالنا force
زمبابوے Zimbabwe
زنا بالجبر کرنا rape
زنا بالجبر rape
زندگی life
زندہ live
زندہ دل lively
زپ، چین zip
زپ، چین بند کرنا zip
زپ (چین) کھولنا unzip
زچگی کی چھٹیاں maternity leave
زچہ ہسپتال maternity hospital
زہر poison
زہر، گہری تلخی venom
زہر دینا poison
زہریلا poisonous, toxic, vicious
زیادہ most, much
زیادہ تر most, mostly
زیادہ دور far
زیادہ سے زیادہ (بڑے سے بڑا) maximum
زیادہ سے زیادہ (ممکن حد تک) maximum
زیادہ معاوضہ بتانا overcharge
زیبائشی سامان cosmetics
زیبائشی سامان، میک اپ کا سامان make up
زیتون olive
زیتون کا تیل olive oil
زیتون کا درخت olive
زیر تربیت trainee
زیر جامے briefs, underpants
زیر غور considering
زیر آب underwater
زیر آب تیراکی کیلئے، ربر سوٹ wetsuit
زیر زمین (ریلوے) underground
زیر زمین فٹپاتھ subway
زیر زمین گٹر سسٹم sewer
زیرہ cumin
زیریں lower
زین، کاٹھی saddle
زینہ دار (پہاڑی ڈھلان) terraced
زیور jewel, ornament
زیورات، جواہرات jewellery
زیورات کی دوکان jeweller
زیر زمین underground
سابق former

سابق شوہر ex-husband
سابقہ بیوی ex-wife
سابقہ طور پر formerly
سات seven
ساتواں seventh
ساتواں (حصہ) seventh
ساتھ along, with
ساتھ آنا، مجتمع ہونا get together
ساتھ دینا accompany
ساتھ ساتھ together
ساتھ ہونا club together
ساتھی companion, mate
ساتھی (کمرے کا) roommate
ساجھی دار partner
ساحر، ساحرہ sorcerer
ساحل beach, coast
ساحل کا محافظ coastguard
ساحلی سیرگاہ کا لنگر marina
ساحرہ witch
ساحل seashore
سادگی austerity
سادہ plain, simple
سادہ، سلجھی ہوئی straightforward
سادہ طور پر simply
سادہ لوح naive
سادہ چیک blank cheque
سارا ذخیرہ فروخت کرنا sell out
سارجنٹ sergeant
سارس flamingo
سارس، بگلا crane
سارڈین، رایو مچھلی sardine
سازش conspiracy
ساز و سامان equipment
ساز و سامان سے لیس equipped
سازش plot
سازندہ player
ساس پین (دستہ والا برتن) saucepan
ساس (چٹنی) sauce
ساسیج sausage
ساق پوش (لچیلے کپڑے کے پائجامے) leggings
سال year
سالا، بہنوئی brother-in-law
سالانہ annual, annually, yearly
سالانہ اجلاس عام AGM
سالانہ طور پر yearly
سالمن مچھلی salmon
سالمہ molecule
سالگرہ anniversary

رقم، مقدار **sum**
رقم ادائگی کا رقعہ **voucher**
رقم واپس کرنا **refund**
رقم واپسی **refund**
رقومات **funds**
رقیق بنانا **dilute**
رقیق کردہ **dilute**
رمضان **Ramadan**
رموز اوقاف **punctuation**
رنج **misery, regret**
رنڈوا **widower**
رنگ **colour, colouring, dye, paint**
رنگ برش **paintbrush**
رنگساز **painter**
رنگ سے تصویر بنانا **paint**
رنگنا **dye**
رنگ کا اندھاپن **colour-blind**
رنگ کرنا، رنگنا **paint**
رنگین **colourful**
رنگین چشمہ **goggles**
رنگین ڈیزائن والا کاغذ **wallpaper**
رنگین کاغذ کے ٹکڑے **confetti**
رواج **custom**
روانگی **check out, departure**
روانہ کرنا **set out**
روانہ ہونا **depart, set off**
روانہ ہونا، روانگی **leave**
رواں زینہ **escalator**
روایت پرست، روایت پسند **trendy**
روایتی **conventional**
روایتی داستان **legend**
روایتی لباس **fancy dress**
روایتی نظم **nursery rhyme**
روایت **tradition**
روایتی **traditional**
روح **soul**
روح، جذبہ **spirit**
روحانی **spiritual**
روز، دن **day**
روزانہ **daily**
روز مرہ کی زندگی پر ڈرامہ **soap opera**
روزنامچہ **diary**
روزگار مرکز **job centre**
روزی **living**
روس **Russia**
روسی **dandruff, Russian**
روسی (زبان) **Russian**
روشنائی **ink**
روشندان **ventilation**
روشن ہونا **light**
روشنی **light, lighting**
روشنی کا بلب **light bulb**
روشنی کا مینار **lighthouse**
رومال **handkerchief, hankie, serviette**
رومال، سرپوش **scarf**
رومان **romance**
رومانی **romantic**
رومانیائی **Romanian**
رومانیہ **Romania**
رومن طرز تعمیر **Romanesque**
رومن کیتھولک چرچ کا مرکز **Vatican**
رومی **Roman**
رونا **cry, weep**
رونما کرنا **bring forward**
رونما ہونا **occur**
روئی **cotton wool**
روٹی **bread**
روٹی دان **bread bin**
روٹی کے پارچے **crumb**
روٹی کے چھوٹے ٹکڑے **breadcrumbs**
روک تھام **prevention**
روکنا **prevent, stop**
رئیسی غذا **main course**
ربن **ribbon**
رسنا **leak**
رشتہ **relation**
رشتہ دار **relative**
رشتہ داری **relationship**
رہائشی **residential**
رکاوٹ **band, barrier, block, blockage, break, curb, interruption, obstacle, pause, stop**
رکاوٹ، وقف **halt**
رکاوٹ ڈالنا **block**
رکاوٹ ڈالنا **interrupt, obstruct**
رکا ہوا **stuck**
رکن **member**
رکنا، ٹھہر جانا **stop**
رکنیت **membership**
رکھنا **contain, have, keep, place, put**
رکھنا، متعین کرنا **set**
رکھنا، پھیلانا **lay**
رگ، ورید **vein**
رگڑنا **rub**
رگڑ کر دھونا **rinse**
رگڑ کر دھونے کا عمل **rinse**
رہائش **accommodation**
رہائی **release**
رہن **mortgage**
رہنا **live, remain**
رہنما **leader**
رہنمائی کرنا **head, lead**
رہنما کتابچہ **guidebook**
رہنما گلوکار **lead singer**
ریاست **state**
ریاستہائے متحدہ امریکہ **USA**
ریاستہائے متحدہ (امریکہ) **US**
ریاضی **mathematics**
ریت **sand**
ریت میں گڑھا **sandpit**
ریتنا **file**
ریت کا محل **sandcastle**
ریت کا ٹیلہ **sand dune**
ریتی **file**
ریستوران **restaurant**
ریستوراں کی شراب کی فہرست **wine list**
ریسٹورینٹ یا ہوٹل میں **waiter**
ریس کا جانور یا انسان **racer**
ریس کا گھوڑا **racehorse**
ریشم **silk**
ریشہ **fibre**
ریل (دھاگے وغیرہ کی) **reel**
ریلنگ **banister**
ریلوے **railway**
ریلوے پھاٹک **level crossing**
ریلوے کے نیچے سے گزرنے والا رستہ **underpass**
ریل کا سونے کی سیٹوں والا ڈبہ **sleeping car**
رین چڑیا **wren**
رینگنا **crawl, creep**
ریڑھ کا مہرہ کھسک جانا **slipped disc**
ریڑھ کی ہڈی کا منکا **spine**
ریڑھ کی ہڈی **backbone**
ریکارڈ **record**
ریکارڈ کرنا، نقل کرنا، محفوظ کرنا **record**
ریگستان **desert**
ریگمال (سینڈ پیپر) **sandpaper**
زامبیا (جمہوریہ) **Zambia**
زامبیائی **Zambian**
زانی **rapist**
زاویہ **angle**

دہشت گردانہ حملہ terrorist attack
دہشت گردی terrorism
دہقان، کسان farmer
دیر late
دیر تک جاگنا stay up
دیرپا خم (بالوں کے) perm
دیرینہ chronic
دینا، حوالے کرنا pass
دینا، دو give
دینیات theology
دیوار wall
دیوالیہ bankrupt
دیوانا maniac
دیوانگی mania
دیوانی حقوق civil rights
دیوانی ملازم civil servant
دیومالائی داستان myth
دیکھ بھال کرنا، نگہداشت کرنا care
دیکھ ریکھ maintenance
دیکھنا look, see
دیکھنا (تحریر میں) look up
دیہاتی rural
دیہی علاقہ country
ذاتی personal, private
ذاتی جائداد private property
ذاتی سڑک driveway
ذاتی طور پر personally
ذاتی معاون (پرسنل اسسٹنٹ) personal assistant
ذاتی منتظم personal organizer
ذائقہ taste
ذائقہ، فلے ور flavour
ذائقہ دار tasteful
ذائقہ دینا، ذائقہ محسوس ہونا taste
ذخیرہ storage
ذخیرہ کرنا store
ذرائع ابلاغ media
ذرائع وسائل means
ذرہ، جوہر atom
ذریعہ by
ذمہ دار، جوابدہ responsible
ذمہ دار account
ذمہ داری responsibility
ذولسانی bilingual
ذکر کرنا mention
ذہانت، عقل wisdom
ذہنیت mentality
ذہین brilliant
ذہین brainy
ذہین، باصلاحیت talented
ذیابیطس diabetes
ذیابیطس سے متعلق diabetic
ذیابیطس کا مریض diabetic
ذیلی subsidiary
ذیلی عنوانات subtitles
ذیلی عنوانات والے subtitled
رابطہ contact
رابطہ کرنا contact
رات night
رات پالی night shift
راحت relief
راحت رسانی relieve
راحت زدہ relieved
راحت کی سانس لینا sigh
راز confidence, secret
رازدارانہ confidential
راس آنا، جچنا suit
راست آگ پر پکایا ہوا grilled
راستہ way
راستہ (پاتھ) path
راستے پر پیٹرول اور دیگر چیزیں خریدنے کا مقام service area
راغب کرنا attract
رال saliva
رانگ، جستہ pewter
رائی rye
رائے opinion
رائے دھندگی، ووٹ vote
رائے شماری opinion poll
راکھ دانی ashtray
راہب saint
راہداری passage
ربر rubber
ربر دستانے rubber gloves
ربر (پنسل کے نشانات مٹانے والا) rubber
ربط link
ربط کرنا، جوڑنا link
رجائیت optimism
رجائیت پسند optimist
رجائیت پسندی optimistic
رجحان attitude, tendency
رجحان ہونا، رجحان پایا جانا tend
رحم kindness, mercy, pity
رحدلانہ طور پر kindly
رحم کرنا pity
رخ، رجحان trend
رخ کرنا direct, face
رد عمل reaction
رد عمل کرنا react
رد عمل response
ردّ اعمال، نتائج repercussions
ردّ کرنا reject
ردی، کوڑا کرکٹ rubbish
ردی میں ڈال دینا scrap
ردی (چھوٹے ٹکڑے) scrap
ردی کی ٹوکری wastepaper basket
رد کرنا cancel
رس، جوس juice
رسالہ magazine
رسائی access
رسائی حاصل کرنا access
رسائی پانا، پہنچنا reach
رس بھری raspberry
رسم ritual
رسمی ritual
رسولی tumour
رسہ کشی tug-of-war
رسی rope
رسی string
رسید receipt
رشوت bribery
رشوت دینا bribe
رشک کرنا envy
رضامند agreed
رضامند okay
رضاکار volunteer
رضاکارانہ voluntary
رضاکارانہ طور پر voluntarily
رضاکار کے طور پر پیش کرنا (خود کو) volunteer
رطوبت humidity
رعایت concession
رعب میں لینا offend
رفتار pace, speed
رفتار بڑھانا accelerate
رفتار بڑھانا speed up
رفتار پیما mileometer, speedometer
رفتار کی حد speed limit
رفیق کار associate, colleague
رقاص dancer
رقص dance, dancing
رقص کرنا dance
رقم money, payment
رقم، مال finance
رقم، مال دینا finance

دوا فروش pharmacist
دوام eternity
دو اسپیکر کے ساتھ ریکارڈ پلیئر stereo
دوا کی دوکان pharmacy
دو ایک couple
دو بار twice
دوبارہ again
دوبارہ استعمال کرنا reuse
دوبارہ بیٹھنا (امتحان وغیرہ میں) resit
دوبارہ شامل ہونا resume
دوبارہ غور کرنا reconsider
دودھ milk
دودھ دوہنا milk
دور away, cycle, far
دور، مرحلہ round
دوران circulation, during
دوربین binoculars
دوربین telescope
دور کا distant, remote
دورہ لگانا go round
دورہ (مرض کا) seizure
دوزانو ہونا kneel
دوست friend, pal
دوستانہ friendly
دوستی friendship
دوسرا other, second
دوسرا، ایک اور another
دوسرا درجہ second class
دوسروں کو برباد کرنے والا spoilsport
دوسروں کے مقام پر آکر پڑھانے والا supply teacher
دوسرے درجہ کا second class
دوشیزہ، لڑکی lass
دو صامی صدفیہ mussel
دولت wealth
دولتمند wealthy
دولت مشترکہ United Nations
دولہا bridegroom
دو لہروں کے بیچ کی دوری wavelength
دوم secondly
دو ممالک کی بیٹھک summit
دونوں both
دونوں لینس فریم میں (عینک) spectacles
دونوں طرف either
دونوں میں سے کوئی نہیں neither
دوپہر noon
دوپہر کا کھانا (ظہرانہ) lunch
دو چیزوں کو ملانے والا، جوڑ joint

دوڑ مقابلہ race
دوڑ میں مقابلہ کرنا race
دوڑنا running
دوکان (زیادہ مال رکھنے والی) store
دوکانوں کا مجموعہ shopping centre
دو گدی والی سائکل tandem
دوگنا double
دوگنا ہوجانا double
دوہرانا repeat
دق کرنا nag
دل کو چھو لینے والا touching
دکھاوا show off
دکھاوا کرنا show off
دکھائی دینا show up
دکان shop
دکاندار shopkeeper
دکان سے چوری shoplifting
دکان کا ملازم shop assistant
دکھانا show
دکھ محسوس کرنا، غمزدہ ہونا sorry
دکھی دل کے ساتھ sadly
دھات metal
دھات پارے stud
دھاتی سیڑھی fire escape
دھاتی پیچ clasp
دھاتی کاغذ foil
دھار blade
دھارا، چھوٹا دریا stream
دھار دار edgy
دھاری، پٹی stripe
دھاریدار، پٹیدار striped, stripy
دھاوا بولنا، گرفت کرنا crack down on
دھاگا thread
دھبہ spot
دھبہ mark
دھجی rag
دھلائی washing
دھلائی مائع washing-up liquid
دھماکہ bang, blast, explosion
دھماکہ خیز اشیاء explosive
دھماکہ کرنا bang
دھماکے سے پھٹنا explode
دھمکانا intimidate
دھمکی threat
دھمکی آمیز threatening
دھمکی دینا threaten
دھن composition, melody, tune
دھندلانا fade

دھنک rainbow
دھنیا coriander
دھواں smoke
دھواں اٹھنا smoke
دھول dust
دھول بھرا dusty
دھول جھاڑنا dust
دھول مٹی صاف کرنا hoover
دھونا wash
دھوئیں سے کالا کیا ہوا smoked
دھوپ sunlight
دھوپ دار sunny
دھوپ سے بچنے کے لئے کریم sunscreen
دھوپ سے جلا ہوا sunburnt
دھوپ سے جل جانا sunburn
دھوپ سے جلد کا سانولا ہوجانا tan
دھوپ سے جلد کا تانبئی ہو جانا suntan
دھوپ سے جلد کو بچانے کے لئے کریم sunblock
دھوپ سے جلد کو کالا ہونے سے بچانے کا لوشن suntan lotion
دھوپ کا چشمہ sunglasses
دھوپ کھانا sunbathe
دھوپ کی کریم suncream
دھو ڈالنا wash up
دھوکہ bluff
دھوکہ، بہروپ illusion
دھوکہ باز cheat
دھوکہ دینا bluff, cheat, deceive
دھوکہ کرنا trick
دھچکہ، ترقی میں رکاوٹ setback
دھچکے دار bumpy
دھڑکن pulse
دھڑکنا throb
دھکہ blow
دھکہ دینا push
دھیان نہ دینا، چوک جانا miss
دھیرے دھیرے، آہستگی سے slowly
دھیرے دھیرے چلنا creep
دھیما ہونا، کرنا slow down
دھیمی آنچ پر پکانا simmer
دھیمی آواز سے کچھ کہنا whisper
دھیمی آواز سے کچھ کہنا widespread
دھیمی ہو کر رک جانا pull up
دہائی decade
دہشت زدہ scared
دہشت ناک horrendous
دہشت گرد terrorist

دانشور intellectual
دائرہ circle
دائرہ round
دائرہ range
دائرہ قطب شمالی Arctic Circle
دائرے کا نصف semicircle
دائمی eternal
داڑھی beard
داڑھی والا bearded
دایاں، داہنا right
دایاں بازو، قدامت پرست طبقہ right-wing
داہنی کی طرف right-hand
دایہ midwife
دبانا (جسمانی طور پر) press
دباؤ (جسمانی) pressure
دباؤ، تناؤ strain
دباؤ ڈالنا، تناؤ ڈالنا strain
دباؤ ڈالنا (نفسیاتی طور پر) pressure
دبلا skinny, thin
دراز chest of drawers, drawer, dresser
دراز، الماری shelf
درآمد import
درآمد کرنا import
دراڑ crack
دربان doorman
دربان، نگہبان janitor
درج شدہ registered
درجن dozen
درج کردہ حوالگی recorded delivery
درجہ class, rank
درجہ، ڈگری degree
درجہ بندی کرنا mark, rate
درخت tree
درخت حور poplar
درخواست appeal, application, request
درخواست دینا apply
درخواست فارم application form
درخواست کرنا appeal, request
درخواست گزار applicant
درد ache, pain
درد بھرا painful
درد کش painkiller
درد ہونا ache
درزی tailor
درست accurate, right
درست، صحیح right
درست، صحیح، سچ true
درست حالت میں واپس لانا renovate
درست طور پر accurately
درستگی accuracy
درست ہونا، مناسب ہونا ought
درمیان among, between, mid, middle
درمیان کا وقت meantime
درمیانہ طبقہ middle-class
درمیانی intermediate
دروازہ door, entrance
دروازے کا دستہ door handle
دروغ حلفی perjury
درہ pass
درہم برہم کرنا disrupt
دریافت کرنا discover
دریافت کرنا، معلوم کرنا find out
دس ten
دستانہ glove
دستانہ (ایک ہی خانہ) mitten
دستاویز document
دستاویزات documents
دستاویز بندی documentation
دستاویزی فلم documentary
دستخط signature
دستخط کرنا sign
دستور constitution
دستک knock
دست کار craftsman
دستک دینا knock
دستہ والا چاقو penknife
دستیابی availability
دستی تحریر autograph
دستی گھڑی watch
دس لاکھ million
دسمبر December
دسواں tenth
دسواں حصہ tenth
دشمن enemy
دشمن بنانا antagonize
دشوار اور طویل سفر tramp
دشوار گزار inconvenient
دشواری difficulty
دعا prayer
دعا مانگنا، نماز پڑھنا pray
دعوت invitation
دعوت دینا invite, party
دعوت مبارزت دینا challenge
دعوی claim
دعوی فارم claim form
دعوی کرنا claim
دفاع defence
دفاع، مدافعت self-defence
دفاع کرنا defend
دفتر office
دفتری، باضابطہ official
دفتری اوقات office hours
دفعتاً غائب ہو جانا vanish
دفعتہ، اچانک abrupt
دفع کرنا clear off
دفنانا bury
دل heart
دلال agent
دل بہلانا entertain
دل بہلانے والا entertainer
دلدل marsh
دلدلی کوئلہ peat
دل شکستہ heartbroken
دلفریب fascinating
دلو Aquarius
دلچسپ interesting
دلچسپ لگنا interest
دلچسپی interest
دل کا صدمہ، ہارٹ اٹیک heart attack
دل کو ٹھیس پہنچانا offend
دلہن bride
دلہن کی سہیلی bridesmaid
دلیل argument
دلیہ porridge
دم tail
دماغ mind
دماغی mental
دماغی صدمہ concussion
دماغی ہسپتال mental hospital
دم خم stamina
دمدار ستارہ comet
دم گھٹنا choke, suffocate
دمہ asthma
دن day
دندانی dental
دندانے tooth
ڈنڈ press-up, push-up
دن کا وقت daytime
دنیا world
دو two
دوا drug, medicine

خطاب address
خط استوا equator
خطبہ lecture
خطبہ دینا، تقریر کرنا lecture
خطرناک dangerous
خطرہ danger
خطرہ سے آگاہی اور مدد کا سگنل SOS
خطرے میں ڈالنا endanger
خط و کتابت correspondence
خطیب، مقرر، لیکچرر lecturer
خفیہ طور پر secretly
خفیہ میٹنگ rendezvous
خفیہ ادارہ secret service
خفیہ، رازدارانہ secret
خلا void
خلاء space
خلاباز astronaut
خلاف against
خلاف قاعدہ foul
خلاف معمول abnormal
خلائی راکٹ / گاڑی spacecraft
خلائی گاڑی shuttle
خلل ڈالنا disturb
خلیج bay
خلیجی ریاستیں Gulf States
خلیہ cell
خم curl
خم دار curly
خمدار لٹ lock
خمیدہ bent
خمیر baking powder, yeast
خندق moat, trench
خندق، کھائی ditch
خواب dream
خواب آور دوا sleeping pill
خواب دیکھنا dream
خواب گاہ bedroom
خوابیدہ asleep
خواتین کا ladies
خواندگی reading
خوانچہ والا vendor
خواہاں interested
خواہش desire
خواہش کرنا desire
خواہش wish
خواہش کرنا wish
خوبانی apricot
خوب تلنا deep-fry

خوب رو handsome
خوبرو smart
خوبصورت beautiful, pretty
خوبصورتی beauty
خوبصورتی سے beautifully
خوبصورتی سے، نفیس طور پر prettily
خوب پھینٹی ہوئی کریم whipped cream
خوبی، کوالٹی quality
خوبی بیان کرنا compliment
خوداعتمادی confidence
خودانضباطی self-discipline
خود اپنی پسند کی چیزیں لے لینا self-service
خود بخود automatically
خوددار self-contained
خود غرض self-centred, selfish
خود مختار independent
خود مختار نظام autonomy
خود مختاری autonomous
خود پر قابو self-control
خودپسند self-conscious
خود کار automatic
خود کا روزگار کرنے والا self-employed
خودکش بمبار suicide bomber
خودکشی کرنا suicide
خوراک dose
خوش glad, happy, merry
خوش، مطمئن pleased
خوشامد کرنا flatter
خوش آمدید welcome!
خوشآمدید welcome!
خوش باش cheerful
خوشبو aroma, perfume, scent
خوشبودار پھول کا پودا (سنبل) hyacinth
خوشبو سے علاج aromatherapy
خوشحالی prosperity
خوش دلانہ playful
خوش قسمت fortunate
خوش قسمتی سے fortunately
خوش مزاج easy-going
خوشی happiness, pleasure
خوف fear
خوفزدہ terrified
خوف سے کانپنا shudder
خوفناک appalling, gruesome, horrifying
خوفناک، انتہائی خراب terrible
خوف وہراس panic
خول case, shell

خول، ڈھکن cover
خول (گھونگھے وغیرہ کا) shell
خون blood
خون بہنا bleed
خون کی اقسام blood group
خون کی زہرآلودگی blood poisoning
خیر مقدم کرنا hail
خدمات کا معاوضہ service charge
خدمت کرنا serve
خلال toothpick
خچر mule
خیال idea, thought
خیال رکھنا care
خیال کرنا mind
خیال کرنا، تصور کرنا imagine
خیالی abstract, imaginary
خیرات dole
خیرمقدم کرنا welcome!
خیمہ، تنبو tent
داخل کرنا admit
داخلہ admission, admittance
داخلہ فیس entrance fee
داخل ہونا enter, get into, move in
داخل ہونا، پرچڑھنا onto
داخلہ کا راستہ way in
داد applause, eczema
دادا granddad, grandpa
دادا، دادی، نانا، نانی grandparents
دادا، نانا grandfather
داد دینا applaud
دادی grandma
دادی، نانی grandmother, granny
دارالسلطنت، دارالحکومت، راجدھانی capital
دارالصبیان crèche
دارچینی cinnamon
داستان story
داغ stain
داغ لگنا stain
داغ ہٹانے والا stain remover
دافع افسردگی antidepressant
دافع انجماد antifreeze
دافع عفونت antiseptic
دالیں pulses
داماد son-in-law
دانائی intelligence
دانت tooth
دانت درد toothache
دانت نکالنا، دانت نکلنا (بچے کے) teethe

حوصلہ، جینے کی امنگ spirits
حویلی، فلیٹوں والی عمارت mansion
حکم order
حس sense
حسابیات statistics
حساس touchy
حسی sensuous
حصہ دینا share out
حصہ لگانا، ساجھی کرنا share
حصہ section, share
حصہ، جزو portion
حصہ یا جزو proportion
حفاظت protection, safety, security
حفاظت کرنا protect
حفاظتی پیٹی safety belt
حمایت support
حمایت کرنا support
حکمت عملی strategy
حکم command
حکم، امپائر umpire
حکم دینا order
حکمراں ruler
حکم چلانے والا bossy
حکومت government
حکومت کرنا rule
حیاتی vital
حیاتیات biology
حیاتیاتی biological
حیاتیاتی کیمیا biochemistry
حیران puzzled
حیران کن puzzling
حیرت surprise
حیرت انگیز amazing, marvellous, wonderful
حیرت انگیز طور پر surprisingly
حیرت زدہ amazed, astonished, stunned, surprised
حیرت زدہ کرنا amaze, astonish
حیرت میں ڈالنے والا stunning
حیرت ناک incredible
حیرت کرنا wonder
حیوانیات zoology
ختم finished
خاتمہ ending
خاتون lady
خاتون خانہ housewife
خاتون خدمتگار، نوکرانی maid
خاتون فوجی servicewoman

خاتون ویٹر waitress
خاتون کھلاڑی sportswoman
خارج کرنا exclude
خارشی itchy
خازن treasurer
خاص chief, principal, special
خاص، اہم main
خاص طور سے especially, particularly
خاص لائن میں مہارت حاصل کرنا specialize
خاص پیشکش special offer
خاصیت characteristic
خاطر میں لانا bother
خالص pure
خالی blank, empty, vacant
خالی، مسترد void
خالی جگہ blank, space
خالی نشست vacancy
خالی وقت leisure
خالی کرنا empty, evacuate, vacate
خام crude, raw
خاموش quiet, silent
خاموش، پرسکون silent
خاموش تماشائی onlooker
خاموشی silence
خاموشی سے quietly
خامی drawback
خامی، کمزوری shortcoming
خاندان family
خاندانی نام surname
خانگی معلم، اتالیق tutor
خانہ compartment
خانہ بدوش gypsy
خانہ جنگی civil war
خانہ پری کرنا fill in
خانے دار checked
خائف apprehensive
خاکستری رنگ grey
خاکستری رنگین grey-haired
خاکہ chart, diagram, drawing, portrait, sketch
خاکہ کھینچنا sketch
خاکے، گرافکس graphics
خبر news
خبردار alert
خبردار کرنا alert, watch out
خبردار کرنا، آگاہ کرنا warn
خبر مرگ (شائع شدہ) obituary
خبر پڑھنے والا newsreader

ختم کرنا end, finish
ختم ہونا expire, over
خدا حافظ goodbye!
خدا حافظ! bye-bye!
خدا حافظ! bye!
خداداد صلاحیت والا gifted
خدمت service
خراب bad
خراب، بدمعاش bad
خراب تر worse
خراب ترین worse
خراب کرنا mess up
خراش bruise, scratch
خراش، چھالہ sore
خربوزہ melon
خردحیاتیہ organism
خردہ retail
خردہ فروش retailer
خردہ قیمت retail price
خردہ قیمت ہونا retail
خراٹے لینا snore
خرچ، صرفہ expenditure
خرچ کرنا spend
خرگوش hare, rabbit
خریدار buyer
خریدار، صارف customer
خریداری shopping
خریداری بیگ shopping bag
خریدنا buy, purchase
خزانچی cashier
خزانہ treasure
خزاں autumn
خستہ crisp, crispy
خستہ (بسکٹ) cracker
خستہ تہ والی پیسٹری shortcrust pastry
خسرہ measles
خش اسلوب fluent
خشک dry
خشک میوہ اور ناشتے کا دلیہ muesli
خشک کار dryer
خشک کردہ dried
خشک کرنا dry
خشک گوشت یا سبزیوں سے بنائے گئے مکعب stock cube
خصوصی عدالت tribunal
خصیہ، فوطہ testicle
خط letter, line
خطا mix up

جھلاہٹ، بدمزاجی کا غلبہ tantrum
جھنڈ flock
جھولا swing
جھولنا sway, swing
جھونپڑا cottage
جھونپڑپٹی slum
جھونپڑی hut
جھوٹا liar
جھوٹا الارم false alarm
جھوٹ بولنا lie
جھوٹی شبیہ stereotype
جھینگا lobster
جھریدار wrinkled
جھٹکے سے سمت بدل لینا swerve
جھپٹنا swat
جھکنا bend down, lean
جھکڑ gale, gust
جھگڑا conflict, quarrel, scrap
جھگڑا کرنا quarrel
جھیل lake
جھینگا prawn, shrimp
جھینگر cricket
جہاز craft
جہاز، ہوائی جہاز، ٹرین کے مسافروں کا خیال رکھنے والا steward
جہاز (بحری) ship
جہاز سے بھیجا جانے والا سامان shipment
جہاز کا سفر sailing
جہاز کا عملہ cabin crew
جہاز کا ملبہ shipwreck
جہاز کا کارخانہ shipbuilding
جہاز کی تباہی میں بچ جانے والا فرد shipwrecked
جہازی seaman
جہازی، کشتی راں sailor
جہازی بیڑہ fleet
جہاں where
جہاندیدہ streetwise
جہنم hell
جیب pocket
جیب خرچ pocket money
جی بہلانا، دل خوش کرنا amuse
جیتنا conquer, triumph, win
جیسا such
جیسا، کے جیسا such
جیل prison
جیل افسر prison officer
جیل تہ خانہ (قلعہ میں) dungeon
جینیاتی genetic
جینے کا معیار standard of living
جیوری کا فیصلہ verdict
حاجز insulation
حادثاتی accidental
حادثاتی طور پر accidentally, accident and emergency
حادثاتی ٹکراؤ bump
حادثہ بیمہ accident insurance
حاسد envious, jealous
حاشیہ margin
حاصل کرنا achieve, gain, obtain
حاصل نمبر (کھیل وغیرہ میں) score
حاصل کرنا receive
حاضر ہونا present
حاضری attendance
حاضری دینا attend
حاضری roll call
حاضری دینا sign on
حافظہ memory
حالات circumstances
حالات حاضرہ current
حالانکہ though
حالانکہ، اگرچہ although
حالت condition, position
حالت، صورتحال situation
حالت کی تبدیلی transition
حالیہ recent
حالیہ طور پر recently
حاملہ pregnant
حامی supporter
حامیٔ نسواں feminist
حتمی ultimate
حتمی طور پر ultimately
حتی الامکان جلد سے جلد asap
حجام hairdresser
حجر شہابی meteorite
حجم، جسامت volume
حد boundary, limit
حد سے زیادہ excessive
حرارت heating, temperature
حرام، ممنوعہ taboo
حرف letter
حرف صامت consonant
حرف علت vowel
حروف تہجی alphabet
حرکت move
حریف (شخص) rival
حریف (گروپ) rival
حساب calculation
حساب کتاب accountancy
حساب کتاب کرنا computing
حساب کرنا calculate
حسابی mathematical
حسب ضرورت customized
حسد، رشک envy
حساس sensible, sensitive
حسین مقام beauty spot
حشرات reptile
حشرات (چوہا وغیرہ) rodent
حصہ passage
حصہ، جزو part
حصہ لگانا، ساجھی کرنا part with
حصہ لینا participate
حفاظت خانہ پودگھر conservatory
حفاظت سے رکھنا keep
حفاظت کرنا guard
حفاظتی انجکشن jab
حفظان صحت hygiene
حفظ ماتقدم precaution
حق اشاعت copyright
حق استرداد veto
حقیقت fact, reality
حقیقت معلوم ہو جانا realize
حقیقت پسند realistic
حقیقی actual, real
حل solution
حلف oath
حلق throat
حلق کی گلٹیوں کا ورم tonsillitis
حل کرنا figure out, solve
حمال porter
حمام baths
حمایت backing
حمل pregnancy
حملہ attack, mugging
حملہ ور mugger
حملہ ور ہونا strike
حملہ کرنا attack, invade
حملہ کرنا، ڈھانپ لینا mug
حوالہ preference
حوالہ دینا refer
حوالہ نمبر reference number
حوالے کر دینا surrender
حوصلہ morale
حوصلہ شکستہ nervous

جزیرہ نما peninsula
جستجو کرنا seek
جست لگانا، کودنا jump
جستہ zinc
جسم body
جسمانی سزا corporal punishment
جسم بنانا bodybuilding
جسم میں سوئی چبھونے کے ذریعے مرض کے علاج کا
طریقہ ۔ acupuncture
جسم کی صفائی کا تولیہ tampon
جس کی خوشامد کی گئی ہو flattered
جس کے، وہ that
جشن bash, celebration
جشن منانا celebrate
جعل سازی forgery
جعل سازی کرنا forge
جغرافیہ geography
جفت عدد، برابر even
جلانا burn, light
جلاوطن exile
جلا ڈالنا burn down
جلا ہوا burn
جلد soon
جلد، چمڑی skin
جلد شادی کرنے والے کے لیے دی گئی پارٹی)
stag night
جلدی early, hurry
جلدی جانا rush
جلدی رنگ complexion
جلدی سے hastily
جلدی سے لکھنا jot down
جلدی میں rush
جلدی کرنا hurry
جلدی کرو hurry up
جلنا burn
جلنے سے محفوظ ovenproof
جل پری mermaid
جلی حروف میں لکھنا print
جمانے والا (فرج) freezer
جما ہوا frozen
جما ہوا پانی (برفباری) snowflake
جمائی لینا yawn
جمع plural, plus
جمع خوری کرنا stock up
جمعرات Thursday
جمع کرنا add up, collect, round up
جمع کرنے والا collector
جمعہ Friday

جملہ sentence
جمنا freeze
جمناسٹک ورزش gymnastics
جمود hold up, stalemate
جمیکا کا باشندہ Jamaican
جمہوری democratic
جمہوریت democracy
جمہوریہ republic
جمیکن Jamaican
جناب sir
جنت heaven, paradise
جنس زعفران، سوسنی جنس کا پھول crocus
جنوب south
جنوب طرف southbound
جنوب مشرق southeast, southwest
جنوبی south, southern
جنوبی افریقہ South Africa
جنوبی افریقی South African
جنوبی امریکہ South America,
South American
جنوبی امریکی South American
جنوبی سمت south
جنوبی کوریا South Korea
جنوری January
جنونی crazy, fanatic
جن کا، جن کے whom
جنگ war
جنگ بندی کا معاہدہ truce
جنگل forest, jungle, wood
جنگلا، باڑا fence
جنگلی wild
جنگ میں شامل رہا فوجی veteran
جنین foetus
جو barley
جو، جو کچھ whatever
جواب answer, reply
جواب دینا answer, reply, respond
جواری gambler
جوانی youth
جوا کھیلنا، اندھا جوکھم اٹھانا gamble
جوا گھر casino
جواہر، نگینہ gem
جو بھی whoever
جوتا shoe
جوتا پالش shoe polish
جوتے کا تسمہ shoelace
جوتے کی دوکان shoe shop
جو (جو کہ) that

جوس کی مشین blender
جوش وجنون میں بات کرنا rave
جولائی July
جون June
جوڑ connection
جوڑ مثبت sum
جوڑا couple, pair
جوڑنا add, attach
جوڑنا، ملانا join
جوڑوں کی جکڑن rheumatism
جوڑ کا کھنچاؤ sprain
جوڑ کے کھنچاؤ کا شکار ہونا sprain
جوکوئی whichever
جوکھم risk
جوکھم اٹھانا risk
جوکھم بھری risky
جوں، لیکھ lice
جوہری atomic, jeweller
جوہری بم atom bomb
جئی (جو جیسا) oats
جئی کا آٹا oatmeal
جسمانی physical
جس میں کوئی برقی آلہ لگایا جائے socket
جس کی whose
جسکی قریب کی نظر خراب ہو short-sighted
جلد کو بچانے والا تیل suntan oil
جلد کے دھبے zit
جنس sex
جنسیت sexism
جگر liver
جھری wrinkle
جڑ root
جڑا ہوا کچن (دیوار سے) fitted kitchen
جڑواں twin
جڑواں (ادارے، دو ممالک میں) twinned
جڑواں تین triplets
جڑواں پلنگ twin beds
جڑی بوٹیاں herbs
جڑی کی پتیاں chives
جگ jug
جگہ، مقام location, place
جگہ پر رکھنا away
جھانج مجیرے cymbals
جھاڑنا، صاف کرنا mop up
جھاڑو broom, mop
جھاڑی bush, hedge, shrub
جھجک inhibition
جھرنا cataract, waterfall

تیز دوڑنا یا سواری کرنا (کم دوری تک) sprint
تیز دھار sharp
تیز ذائقہ ساسج salami
تیز رفتار speeding
تیز رفتار کشتی speedboat
تیز سر درد migraine
تیز شور din
تیز لائٹ (کھیل کے میدان میں) floodlight
تیز نگاہ observant
تیز پتہ bay leaf
تیز چلنا trot
تیزی سے fast, quickly
تیس thirty, thrifty
تیسرا third
تیسرا حصہ third
تیسرے (شمار پر) thirdly
تیقن certainty
تیل oil
تیل ڈالنا، چکنا کرنا oil
تیل کا کنواں oil well
تیلیاں، ٹہنی stick
تین three
تین ابعاد والا three-dimensional
تیندوا، گلدار panther
تین گنا کرنا، تگنا کرنا treble
تیوری چڑھانا frown
تیوہار festival
تیکھا bitter
ثابت intact
ثابت قدم determined
ثابت قدم رہنا persevere
ثابت ہونا، کرنا prove
ثالثی arbitration
ثبوت evidence, proof
ثقافتی cultural
جابرانہ ruthless
جادو magic
جادوئی magic
جادوئی، ساحرانہ magical
جادوگر، ساحر magician
جاذب نظر good-looking
جارجیا جمہوریہ Georgia
جارجیا ریاست Georgia
جارجیائی Georgian
جارجیائی شخص Georgian
جارح aggressive
جاری رکھنا carry on, continue, go on
جاری رکھنا، برقرار رکھنا keep
جاری رہنا continue
جاری کرنا issue
جاری کرنا، بھیجنا launch
جاری ہدایت standing order
جاز (موسیقی) jazz
جاسوس mole, spy
جاسوسی espionage, spying
جاسوسی کرنا spy
جال grid, trap, web
جال (سڑکوں، نسوں وغیرہ کا) network
جالیدار کپڑا hammock
جام carafe, congestion
جامد passive
جامع comprehensive
جانا go
جانا پہچانا well-known
جانبدار bent, biased
جان بچانے والی life-saving
جاندار creature
جان لیوا سرطان terminal
جان محافظ (ڈوبنے والوں کو بچانے والا) lifeguard
جاننا know
جاننا، معلوم ہونا know
جانور animal
جانور اور پرندوں کا دو پیر پر کودنا hop
جانوروں کا ڈاکٹر، سلوتری vet
جانور کا آواز کرنا howl
جانچنا check-up, examine, test
جانچ نلی test tube
جانگھ thigh
جائداد property
جائزہ review
جائزہ لینا scan
جائفل nutmeg
جائے وقوعہ venue
جائے پیدائش birthplace
جائے پیدائش place of birth
جاپان Japan
جاپانی Japanese
جاپانی زبان Japanese
جاکر لانا fetch
جاگنا wake up
جاگنا، جگانا awake
جاگیر estate
جب when
جبری داخلہ break in
جب سے since
جبلت، وجدان instinct
جبڑا jaw
جب کبھی whenever
جبکہ، دوران while
جدائی، فراق کا صدمہ wrench
جدائی parting, separation
جدائی ہونا split up
جداگانہ طور پر separately
جدول schedule, table
جدوجہد struggle
جدوجہد کرنا struggle
جدید advanced, modern
جدید ترین up-to-date
جدید زبانیں modern languages
جدید سہولیات mod cons
جدید کاری modernize
جدید کرنا update
جذبات انگیز (کتاب، فلم، ڈراما) thriller
جذباتی emotional, sentimental, soppy, thrilling
جذب کردہ، بھیگا ہوا soaked
جذبہ emotion
جذبہ، احساس feeling
جراثیم ربا disinfectant
جراثیم سے پاک pasteurized, sterile
جراثیم سے پاک کرنا sterilize
جراحی (چیر پھاڑ) operation
مہیا کرائی گئی جگہ workplace
جراحی کا کمرہ surgery
جراحی کرنا operate
جراف giraffe
جرثومہ bacteria, germ
جرم crime, offence
جرمانہ fine
جرمن German
جرمن خسرہ German measles
جرمن زبان German
جرمنی Germany
جراحی surgery
جزائر فارو Faroe Islands
جز وقتی part-time
جز وقتی طور پر part-time
جزوی partial, proportional
جزوی طور پر partly
جزیرہ island

تقریباً تاریک gloomy
تقریر، گویائی speech
تقسیم division
تقسیم کار dispenser, distributor
تقسیم کاری assortment
تقسیم کر دینا give out
تقسیم کرنا distribute, divide
تلاش search
تلاش کرنا browse, hunt, look for, search
تلا ہوا fried
تلخیص summary
تلخیص کرنا summarize
تلخی کینہ بغض grudge
تلسی basil
تلفظ pronunciation
تلفظ کرنا pronounce
تلنا fry
تلنے کا مخصوص برتن frying pan
تلوار sword
تلوار کی نوک جیسے منہ والی مچھلی swordfish
تلے اوپر پلنگ bunk beds
تلے کا bottom
تم، آپ you
تمباکو tobacco
تمباکو نوش smoker
تمباکو نوشی smoking
تمتمانا flush
تمغہ medal
تمہارا، آپ کا your
تمیز سے پیش آنا behave
تنا trunk
تناؤ بھرا stressful
تناور درخت beech
تناؤ زدہ stressed
تناؤ زدہ tense, tension
تناؤ زدہ، دباؤ زدہ strained
تناؤ میں uptight
تنبیہ caution
تنخواہ pay, salary
تنزانیائی Tanzanian
تنزانیہ Tanzania
تنظیم organization
تنفس breathing
تنقید کرنا pick on
تنکا straw
تنگ مزاج irritable
تنگ narrow, tight
تنگ جگہ کی وجہ سے بھینچے جانا squeeze in
تنگ دست hard-up
تنگ راستہ alley
تنگ چکدار کپڑے tights
تنگ نظر narrow-minded
تنگ کرنا، کسنا tighten
تنگ (کپڑا) skin-tight
تنہا alone
تنہائی loneliness
توازن balance
توانا energetic
توانائی energy
توجہ دلانا underline
توجہ attention
توجہ مرکوز کرنا focus
توجہ ہٹانا distract
توسیع extension
توش، ٹوسٹ toast
توقع کرنا expect
تولیہ towel
توڑ لینا snap
توڑنا chip
توڑ پھوڑ sabotage
توڑ پھوڑ کر بنا ہوا ملبہ wreckage
توڑ پھوڑ کرنا sabotage
تبت Tibet
تبتی Tibetan
تجارت trade
تجوری safe
ترپال tarpaulin
ترچھی لائن forward slash
تل mole
تکون مینار (چرچ کی) spire
تگنا triple
تپ دق tuberculosis
تپ کاہی hay fever
تک till, until
تکفین گھر funeral parlour
تکلیف دہ troublemaker
تکملہ supplement
تکمیلی complementary
تکنیک know-how, technique
تکیہ pillow
تھانہ police station
تھائی (باشندہ) Thai
تھائی (زبان) Thai
تھائی لینڈ Thailand
تھائی (ملک) Thai
تھاپ (والے ساز) percussion
تھرموس flask
تھل تھل بدن flabby
تھوڑا quite
تھوڑا، تھوڑی rather
تھوک spit
تھوک فروشی wholesale
تھوکنا spit
تھوہر hawthorn
تھپڑ مارنا slap
تھکا دینے والا tiring
تھکا ہوا tired
تھکی ہوئی exhausted
تھیلا bag
تہ خانہ cellar
تہدار folding
تہذیب civilization, culture
تہنیت greeting
تہنیت نامہ greetings card
تہ کرنا fold
تہہ خانہ basement
تیار prepared
تیاری preparation
تیاری کرنا prepare
تیتر partridge
تیر arrow
تیراک swimmer
تیراک چیز float
تیراکی swimming
تیراکی تالاب swimming pool
تیراکی جیکٹ life jacket
تیراکی زیر جامے (مردانہ) trunks
تیراکی سوٹ swimsuit
تیراکی لباس swimming costume
تیراکی لباس (مردوں کے لئے) swimming trunks
تیرنا float, swim
تیر کا نشان arrow
تیرہ thirteen
تیرہواں thirteenth
تیز fast, quick, sharp
تیزاب acid
تیزابی بارش acid rain
تیز آواز crash
تیز آواز شور loud

تحریک motivation
تحریک پیدا کرنا، ہلانا stir
تحریک یافتہ motivated
تحفظ conservation
تحفہ gift
تحفہ پیش کرنا present
تحقیر contempt
تحقیق research
تحلیل پذیر soluble
تحلیل ہونا dissolve
تحمل مزاج، برداشت کرنے والا، صابر patient
تحویل custody
تحیر آمیز astonishing, surprising
تخت شاہی throne
تختہ block, board
تختہ سیاہ blackboard
تختہ مشق، بلی کا بکرا guinea pig
تختی index
تخریب destruction
تخفیف decrease, reduction
تخلص، قلمی نام pseudonym
تخلیق creation
تخلیق نو reproduction
تخلیق کرنا create
تخلیقی creative
تخلیہ privacy
تخمینہ estimate
تخمینہ لگانا estimate
تخیل imagination
تدریجی gradual
تدریس tutorial
تذبذب confusion
تراشنا carve
تراشنا، کاٹ چھانٹ کرنا trim
تراشہ (اخبار کا) cutting
تراشیدہ جسم slim
ترانہ anthem
تربوز watermelon
تربیت training
تربیتی نصاب training course
تربیت یافتہ trained
تربیت کار coach
تربیت کار، تربیت دہندہ trainer
تربیت دینا train
ترتیب sequence
ترتیب دینا arrange
ترتیب نو دینا reorganize
ترتیب کے طور پر respectively
ترجمان translator
ترجمان خاتون spokeswoman
ترجمان شخص spokesperson
ترجمان مرد spokesman
ترجمانی کرنا interpret
ترجمہ translation, version
ترجمہ کرنا translate
ترجیح priority
ترجیحاً preferably
ترجیح دینا prefer
تردید کرنا contradict
ترش lime
ترش، کھٹا، تلخ tart
ترشہ thrush
ترقی، فروغ promotion
ترقی، فروغ دینا promote
ترقی development
ترقی پذیر ملک developing country
ترمیم، تبدیلی modification
ترمیم کرنا modify
ترک Turk
ترک وطن کرنا emigrate
ترکی Turkey, Turkish
ترکی (زبان) Turkish
ترکی مرغ، ترکی turkey
تریاق antidote
تسلا basin
تسلسل سے continual
تسلیم کروانا pretend
تسمانیہ Tasmania
تسمہ braces
تشخیص diagnosis
تشدد violence
تشریح، وضاحت explanation
تشریح کرنا، وضاحت کرنا explain
تشویش concern
تشکیل نو کرنا restructure
تشہیر advertising, publicity
تصدیق confirmation
تصدیق کرنا confirm
تصفیہ کرنا settle
تصفیہ ہو جانا settle down
تصور، تخیل fiction
تصور کرنا، تمنا کرنا fancy
تصویر picture
تصویر بنانا draw
تصویر نما picturesque
تضاد contradiction
تضحیک کرنا scoff
تعارف کروانا introduce
تعاقب chase, pursuit
تعاقب کرنا chase, follow
تعاون cooperation
تعریف admiration, definition, introduction
تعریف، تحسین compliment
تعریف کرنا admire, define
تعریف کرنا، ستائش کرنا praise
تعریفی complimentary
تعصب prejudice
تعلقات عامہ public relations
تعلق ہونا get on
تعلیم education
تعلیم بالغاں adult education
تعلیمی academic, educational
تعلیم یافتہ qualified
تعلیمی سال academic year
تعلیمی لیاقت qualification
تعمیر construction
تعمیراتی ماہر architect
تعمیر کرنا construct
تعمیری constructive
تغذیہ nutrition
تغیر پذیر variable
تفتیش investigation
تفتیش قتل inquest
تفتیش کرنا interrogate
تفریح fun
تفریحاً عشق جتانا flirt
تفریحاً محبت flirt
تفریح گاہ amusement arcade
تفریحی entertaining, fun
تفریحی مقام resort
تفریحی میلا funfair
تفریق کرنا distinguish
تفصیل detail
تفویض assignment
تقابل کرنا compare
تقابلی طور پر comparatively
تقدیر destiny, fate
تقرری appointment
تقریب ceremony, party, procession
تقریباً almost
تقریباً approximately, nearly
تقریباً، لگ بھگ about

بیٹھنا sit
بیٹھنا (بیٹھنے کا عمل) sit down
بیٹھک bedsit, living room, sitting room
بیٹھک خانہ lounge
بیٹی daughter
بیچلر طالب علم undergraduate
بیچ میں among
بیکری bakery
بیکری والا baker
بیگ خالی کرنا unpack
بینگن aubergine
بیہوش کر دینا knock out
بیہوش ہونا faint
بیہوشی آور anaesthetic
بیہڑ moor, ravine
بیہڑ، کچھار swamp
بے اختلاف، متفقہ undisputed
بے ارادہ unintentional
بے آب dehydrated
بے آرام uncomfortable
بے ایمان crook, dishonest
بے بھروسہ unreliable
بے تار cordless
بے ترتیب untidy
بے ترتیب irregular, shambles
بے ترتیب، غیر منظم messy
بے ترتیب حالت mess
بے تکلفانہ زبان slang
بے ثباتی، ناپائداری instability
بے جوڑ الگ odd
بے حس و حرکت motionless
بےحس insensitive
بے داغ spotless
بے ذائقہ tasteless
بے روزگار unemployed
بے روزگاری unemployment
بے زار bored
بے زار کن boring
بے زاری boredom
بے سبب جھگڑنا squabble
بے سلیقہ tactless
بے سکت unable
بے سیسہ پیٹرول unleaded petrol
بے شرط unconditional
بے شناخت unidentified
بے شیو unshaven
بے صبر impatient
بے صبری impatience
بے صبری سے impatiently
بے صلاحیت inefficient
بے ضرر harmless
بے عقل unwise
بے عزتی insult
بے عزتی کرنا insult
بیفائدہ useless
بے فیصلہ undecided
بے قابو uncontrollable
بے قرار restless
بے قصور innocent
بیقیمت، بے وقعت worthless
بے لچک inflexible
بے مطلب pointless
بے معاوضہ unpaid
بے معنی waffle
بے معنی لکھنا waffle
بے منصوبہ کام کرنا mess about
بے وفا unfaithful
بے وقعت disgraceful
بیوقوف fool, silly, stupid
بے وقوفانہ daft
بے پھول پودا fern
بے ڈھنگا clumsy
بے گھر homeless
بے ہنگم inconsistent
بے ہوش unconscious
بے ہڈی گوشت fillet
تابوت coffin
تابکار radioactive
تابکاری radiation
تاثر impression
تاج crown
تاجر businessman
تاجرہ businesswoman
تاجکستان Tajikistan
تاخیر delay
تاخیر سے late
تاخیر کرنا delay
تار string, wire
تارکول charcoal
تاریخ date, history
تاریخ اختتام expiry date
تاریخ سالمیت best-before date
تاریخ کا وسطی دور Middle Ages
تازہ fresh
تازہ پانی کی مچھلی trout
تازہ کار refreshing
تازہ کرنا، ہونا freshen up
تاش card, playing card
تالا lock
تالاب pool
تالاب (انسان کا بنایا ہوا) pond
تالا بندی lock out
تالا لگانا lock
تالی بجانا clap
تانبہ copper
تائید کرنا back up
تائیوان Taiwan
تائیوانی Taiwanese
تاڑ (پیڑ) palm
تاکہ so
تاہم، پھر بھی nevertheless
تاہیتی Tahiti
تبادلہ transfer
تبادلہ، مبادلہ change
تباہ devastated
تباہ کن devastating, disastrous
تبدیل کرنا change
تبدیل ہونا turn
تبدیلی change
تبدیلی آب و ہوا climate change
تب سے اب تک since
تبصرہ comment
تبصرہ کرنا comment
تبنیت adoption
تتلی butterfly
تجارت business
تجارتی commercial
تجارتی وقفہ commercial break
تجربہ experience, experiment
تجربہ کار experienced
تجربہ گاہ، لیبارٹری laboratory
تجزیہ analysis
تجزیہ کرنا analyse
تجویز proposal
تجویز پیش کرنا propose
تجویز کردہ (نسخہ) prescription
تجویز کرنا (دوا وغیرہ) prescribe
تجہیز و تکفین funeral
تجہیز و تکفین کرنے والا undertaker
تحت، نیچے under
تحریر handwriting
تحریر، تصنیف writing
تحریری موسیقی score

coarse, drab بھدی
recruitment بھرتی
trust بھروسہ کرنا
fill بھرنا
reliable بھروسہ مند
roast بھنا ہوا
hum بھنبھناہٹ
beetle بھونرا
ghost بھوت
spooky بھوتیا
brown بھورا
brown rice بھورا چاول
brown bread بھوری روٹی
maze بھول بھلیاں
forget بھولنا
forgotten بھولی ہوئی
baked potato بھونا ہوا آلو
baking بھوننا، سینکنا
baffled بھونچکا
bark بھونکنا
appetite, hunger بھوک
hungry بھوکا
starve بھوکوں مرنا
wasp بھڑ، بر
glamorous بھڑکیلا
beggar بھکاری
suffer بھگتنا، مبتلا ہونا
drench بھگونا
also, either, even, too بھی
within بھیتر
send بھیجنا
send out بھیجنا (بڑی تعداد یا مقدار میں)
send off بھیجنا (ڈاک سے)
sender بھیجنے والا
buffalo بھینس
squeeze بھینچنا، نچوڑنا
crowd, ewe, sheep بھیڑ
crowded بھیڑ بھرا
busy بھیڑ بھرا، مصروف
sheepdog بھیڑوں کی رکھوالی کرنے والا کتا
wolf بھیڑیا
lamb بھیڑ کا بچہ
fleece بھیڑ کی اون
wet بھیگا، گیلی
brave بہادر
bravery بہادری
blossom بہار آنا
Bahamas بہاماس

pretext بہانا، حیلہ
current بہاو
much, very بہت
many بہت، متعدد
such بہت، کافی
buoy بہتا نشان
momentous بہت اہم
giant بہت بڑا، جسیم
hypermarket بہت بڑا سپر مارکیٹ
massive بہت بڑی
bone dry بہت خشک
excellent, well done! بہت خوب
better بہتر
best بہتر طور پر
best, super بہترین
great بہترین، بہت اچھا
best man بہترین شخص
soprano بہترین گلوکار، گلوکارہ
much بہت زیادہ
many بہت سارے
deaf بہرا
disguise بہروپ بھرنا
deafening بہرا کرنے والی آواز
break in بہ زور گھسنا
according to بہ مطابق، کے مطابق
sister بہن
blow, flow بہنا
daughter-in-law بہو
statement بیان
description بیان، حلیہ
describe, state بیان کرنا
lavatory, loo, toilet بیت الخلاء
seed بیج
Beijing بیجنگ
insomnia بے خوابی
willow بید
awake بیدار
berry بیر
barrel بیرل
jobless بیروزگار
abroad بیرون ملک
foreign, overseas بیرون ملک
external, outdoor بیرونی
outdoors, outside بیرونی طور پر
disgusted, fed up, moody بیزار
dull بیزار کن، پھیکا
bore بیزار ہونا
twenty بیس

crutch بیساکھی
baseball بیس بال
baseball cap بیس بال ٹوپی
twentieth بیسواں
sink بیسن
oblong, oval بیضوی
egg white بیضوی سفید
eggcup بیضہ دان
ovary بیضہ دانی
startle بیقرار کرنا
Belarus بیلا روس
Belarussian بیلا روسی
Belarussian بیلا روسی زبان
Belgian بیلجین
Belgium بیلجیم
balance sheet بیلنس شیٹ
shovel بیلچہ
trek بیل گاڑی یا پیدل سفر کرنا
ill, sick بیمار
sickening بیمار کرنے والا، جی خراب کرنے والا
infirmary بیمار گھر (ہسپتال)
sick note بیمار ہونے کی ڈاکٹری سند
disease, illness, sickness بیماری
sick leave بیماری کی چھٹی
sick pay بیماری کے ایام کی تنخواہ
insurance بیمہ
insurance certificate بیمہ سند
insured بیمہ شدہ
insurance policy بیمہ پالیسی
insure بیمہ کرنا، کرانا
international بین الاقوامی
sight بینائی
eyesight, visibility بینائی
Venetian blind بینائی میں مددگار پتلی پٹیاں
bank بینک
banker بینک کار
bank statement بینک کا گوشوارہ
بینک کو اخراجات کے عوض ادا کی جانے والی رقم
bank charges
swede بینگن
purple بینگنی
idiot بیوقوف
idiotic بیوقوفانہ
fool بیوقوف بنانا
widow بیوہ
wife بیوی
beat بیٹ
son بیٹا

بند جگہوں سے خوفزدہ claustrophobic
بندر monkey
بندرگاہ harbour, port
بندرگاہ، گودی dock
بند سرا dead end
بندوبست arrangement
بندوق gun
بند کرنا close, shut
بند کرنے کا وقت closing time
بند گوبھی cabbage
بندھن bond
بند ہو جانا shut down
بندی closure
بنسی fishing rod
بنسی باز angler
بنسی بازی angling
بننا knit
بننے کی سلائیاں knitting needle
بنگلا bungalow
بنگلہ دیش Bangladesh
بنگلہ دیشی Bangladeshi
بنیاد basis
بنیاد، دلیل پر مبنی ہونا ground
بنیادی basic
بنیادی، اہم staple
بنیادی حقائق basics
بنیادی سہولیات infrastructure
بنیادی طور پر basically
بنیادیں foundations
بنیان vest
بو smell
بو، بو odour
بواسیر piles
بواسیری مسے haemorrhoids
بو آنا، بو محسوس ہونا smell
بوتسوانا Botswana
بوتل bottle
بوتل کشا bottle-opener
بوجھ burden
بوجھ، گٹھر load
بوجھ اتارنا unload
بوجھ اٹھانا bear
بودھ Buddhist
بودھ مذہب Buddhism
بودھ مذہبی پیشوا monk
بورڈ جس پر کھڑے ہو کر سمندری لہروں پر تیرتے ہیں
surfboard
بوری sack

بوسنیا اور ہرزیگووینا Bosnia-Herzegovina
بوسنیائی Bosnian
بوسہ kiss
بوقت، بمقام at
بوقیدار elm
بولنا speak
بولنگ ایلی bowling alley
بول کر پڑھنا read out
بولی لگانا bid
بولیویائی Bolivian
بولیویا Bolivia
بونا dwarf, plant
بوند drip
بوندیں گرنا drip
بوڑھا، بوڑھی، عمر رسیدہ old
بجلی lightning
بجلی تخفیف power cut
بل invoice
بلا شک undoubtedly
بل بھیجنا invoice
بلور crystal
بلوری جام wineglass
بلی کی مونچھ کے بال whiskers
بچھو scorpion
بکھر جانا، پھیل جانا spread out
بگل trumpet
بگڑا ہوا spoilt
بیر beer
بٹ، ٹوٹا stub
بٹنا، بل دینا twist
بٹن بند کرنا switch off
بٹن چالو کرنا switch on
بٹوا wallet
بٹیر quail
بچانا rescue, save
بچاؤ rescue
بچاؤ! help
بچت savings
بچ نکلنا dodge, escape
بچپن childhood
بچکانہ childish
بچکانہ بات کرنا kid
بچھوا nettle
بچھڑا calf
بچھڑے کا گوشت veal
بچہ baby, child, kid
بچہ دانی کے سرطان کا پتہ لگانے کے لئے طبی جانچ
smear

بچہ نگرانی babysitting
بچہ نگراں babysitter
بچہ کا دودھ baby milk
بچہ کھلائی babysit
بچہ کی بوتل baby's bottle
بڑا elder
بڑا، جسیم large
بڑا تجربہ کار veteran
بڑا تمغہ medallion
بڑا جنگی جہاز battleship
بڑا جہاز jumbo jet
بڑا ٹکڑا chunk
بڑا پیالا bowl
بڑا چمچ tablespoon
بڑا چھلکے سمیت بھنا آلو jacket potato
بڑبڑانا mutter
بڑھوتری surge
بڑھئی carpenter
بڑھئی گیری carpentry
بڑھئی، جوڑنے والا joiner
بڑھیا کا کاتا candyfloss
بڑی big, major
بڑی، دیو ہیکل huge
بڑی، عظیم mammoth
بڑی، کثیر mega
بڑی آنت کا درد appendicitis
بڑی حد تک further
بڑی دوکان department store
بڑی مقدار میں سامان host
بڑی وائلن viola
بڑے جھینگے scampi
بڑے ماتھے کی پن thumbtack
بڑے پیمانے پر landslide, largely
بڑے پیمانے کی فروخت wholesale
بڑے کا گوشت beef
بکری goat
بکسوا buckle
بکواس rubbish
بکواس، بے معنی nonsense
بگاڑنا spoil
بگھی buggy
بھاری heavy
بھاری برفباری snowstorm
بھاری بکس chest
بھالو bear
بھائی brother
بھاپ steam
بھتیجہ، بھانجہ nephew, niece

برآمد export
برآمد کرنا export
براہ via
براہ راست direct, straight on
براہ راست نکاسی direct debit
برباد ruin
برباد کرنا destroy, ruin
برباد کرنا، روکنا، ختم کرنا spoil
برتاؤ behaviour
برتر superior
برتن دھلائی washing-up
برتن سازی pottery
برتن پونچھنے کا کپڑا dishcloth
برج اسد Leo
برج بچھو Scorpio
برج ثور Taurus
برج جدی Capricorn
برج جیمینی Gemini
برج حمل Aries
برج سرطان Cancer
برج عورت، سنبلہ Virgo
برج قوس Sagittarius
برج میزان Libra
برخلاف unlike
برداشت کرنا bear up
بردبار، متحمل مزاج tolerant
برساتی raincoat
برش brush
برش کرنا brush
برطانوی British
برطانیہ Britain, United Kingdom
برطانیہ عظمی Great Britain
برطرف کرنا sack
برطرف کرنا (کام نہ ہونے کے سبب) lay off
برطرفی sack
برعکس contrary
برف snow
برف آس snow
برفانی icy
برفانی تودہ avalanche, glacier, iceberg
برفانی طوفان blizzard
برفانی میدان (مصنوعی) ice rink
برفباری ہونا snow
برف سے بنا آدمی snowman
برف نما شکر icing sugar
برف پر پھسلنے کا عمل skiing

برف کا میدان (اسکیٹنگ کے لئے) skating rink
برف کی کیچڑ slush
برف کے گولے snowball
برف گاڑی sledge
برف ہٹانے والی گاڑی snowplough
برقرار رکھنا keep up, maintain
برقیات electronics
برق کی اکائی volt
برقی electric
برقی مشین سے صفائی کرنا vacuum
برقی مشین (ویکیوم کلینر) vacuum cleaner
برمی burgle
برمی زبان burgle
بروج (ستاروں کے ۱۲ جھرمٹوں کی خیالی تصاویر) zodiac
برچ birch
برکت bliss
برکت کی دعا دینا bless
برہمی irritating
برہنہ (تصویر وغیرہ) nude
برہنہ (شخص) nude
برہنہ کرنا bare
بریڈ پر لگانے والی چیز spread
برے طریقہ سے badly
بزدل coward
بزدلانہ cowardly
بس ابھی، ٹھیک just
بساطی کھیل board game
بستر bed
بستربند holdall
بسولہ chisel, plane
بسیار خوابی oversleep
بسیار فروش bestseller
بس یوں ہی so-so
بشرطیکہ provided
بشریات anthropology
بشمول including
بصورت دیگر otherwise
بصورت دیگر، دوسری صورت میں otherwise
بضد ہونا resist
بطخ duck
بطرف، منجانب from
بطور as
بطور سلاد استعمال ہونے والا پودا cress
بعد after, dimension
بعد ازاں afterwards

بعد میں after
بعد مسیح AD
بعید مشرق Far East
بغل armpit, beside
بغلی راستہ aisle, sideways, slip road
بغور سننا listen
بغیر excluding, without
بغیر آستین sleeveless
بغیر رکے non-stop
بغیر سوچے قدم اٹھانا panic
بغیر شکر sugar-free
بغیر چربی والا بڑے کا گوشت steak
بغیر چھنے آٹے کا کھانا wholemeal
بقایا arrears
بل bill
بلا badge, bat
بلا، حادثہ disaster
بلا حرکت، جامد still
بل ادائیگی کا کاؤنٹر check out
بلا رکاوٹ directly
بلبل زرد canary
بلبلہ bubble
بلبلہ کار bubble bath
بلبلے دار مشروب fizzy
بلب کا سایہ lampshade
بلغاریائی Bulgarian
بلغاریا Bulgaria
بلغاری زبان Bulgarian
بلقانی Balkan
بلند high
بلند درجہ classic
بلوا پتھر sandstone
بل کھانا bend over
بلی cat
بلی کا بچہ kitten
بم bomb
بم باری کرنا bomb, bombing
بمشکل barely
بمعیت inclusive
بمقابلہ versus
بنانا build, make
بنانے والا maker
بناؤ سنگار کرنا make up
بناوٹ make
بناوٹی fake
بنائی knitting
بند blocked, closed, off

باقاعدہ formal
باقیات leftovers
باقی left
باقیات remains
باقی بچا ہوا remaining, rest
باقی دھواں، بخارات exhaust fumes
باقی رہنا survive
باقی رہنے والا survivor
باقی رہنے کی حالت survival
باقی ہونا، بچا ہوا past
بال football, hair
بالائی cream
بالارادہ intentional
بالاپوش bib
بال تراشی، حجامت haircut
بال دار hairy
بالدار شہد کی مکھی bumblebee
بالدار دانے goose pimples
بالدار کوٹ fur coat
بالغ adult
بالغ ہونا grow up
بال لڑھکانا bowling
بالواسطہ indirect
بالوں کی جیل hair gel
بالٹی bucket, pail
بالکل absolutely
بالکل، بلکہ، بجائے pretty
بالکل نئی brand-new
بالکل ٹھیک all right
بالکل یکساں symmetrical
بالیدگی growth
بامروت considerate
بام مچھلی eel
بانجھ infertile
باندھ dam
باندھنا tie up
بانس bamboo
بانسری flute
بانٹنا، تقسیم کرنا deal
باوجود despite
باوجودیکہ instead of
باورچی cook
باورچی خانہ kitchen
باورچی خانے سے متصل کمرہ utility room
باوقار prestigious
بائسکل (دوپہیہ) cycle
بائیں left
باٹی dumpling
باپ father
باڑ، جنگلا rail
باڑا barn
باڑھ flooding
باڑیں، جنگلے railings
باہر out
باہر آنا come out
باہر جانا go out
باہر جانے والی outgoing
باہر نکالنا leave out
باہر کی طرف outside
باہر کی طرف جھکنا lean out
باہر کی طرف نکلنا stick out
باہری exterior, outside
باہمی mutual
بایاں بازو left-wing
بایاں ہاتھ left-hand
بھیڑ کی کھال sheepskin
بت، مجسمہ statue
بتانا tell
بتانا، کہنا tell
بتدریج gradually
بجانا play
بجائے instead
بجلی electricity
بجلی آلہ سے جڑا کیبل flex
بجلی مستری electrician
بجو badger
بجھانے والا extinguisher
بحال کرنا restore
بحال ہونا یا کرنا regain
بحث debate
بحث و مباحثہ کرنا row
بحث کرنا argue, debate
بحران crisis
بحرانی critical
بحر اوقیانوس Mediterranean
بحر شمالی North Sea
بحر قطب شمالی Arctic Ocean
بحر احمر Red Sea
بحر اوقیانوس کا Mediterranean
بحر ہند Indian Ocean
بحری maritime, naval
بحری جھیل lagoon
بحری قزاق pirate
بحری مقابلے یا سیر کی کشتی yacht
بحرین Bahrain
بحری کچھوا turtle
بحریہ navy
بحفاظت لے جانا escort
بحوالہ، بقول according to
بخار، حرارت fever
بخارات fumes
بخشش tip
بخشش دینا tip
بدبدانا lip-read
بدبودار smelly
بدتمیزی کرنا misbehave
بدحواس frantic
بدخواہ malicious
بددعا curse
بدشکل، بھدا ugly
بدعنوان corrupt
بدعنوانی corruption
بدقسمتی misfortune
بدقسمتی سے unfortunately
بدل alternative, replacement, substitute
بدلاؤ، تبدیلی shift
بدلنا alter, convert, replace
بدلنا، بدلاؤ لانا shift
بدل کرنا substitute
بدلے میں کچھ دینا swap
بدمزاج bad-tempered
بدمزاج، چڑچڑا grumpy
بدمعاش culprit, wicked
بدمعاش، ولن villain
بدنصیب unlucky
بدوضع، بے ڈول awkward
بدھ Buddha, Wednesday
بدہضمی indigestion
بذات خود itself
برابر equivalent
براہ برتاؤ کرنا ill-treat
برابر کرنا equal
برابری equality
برادہ sawdust
برازیل Brazil
برازیلی Brazilian
براعظم continent
براؤزر browser
برائے مہربانی صفحہ پلٹیے PTO
برائے کرم! please!

اچھا good, well
اچھا، صحت مند better
اچھا، اچھی، ٹھیک all right
اچھالنا toss
اچھا ہونا fine
اچھلنا bounce
اچھلنا، جست لگانا leap
اچھی طرح درج کریں NB
اچھی طرح سے، کلی thoroughly
اڑا دینا (دھماکے سے) blow up
اڑ جانا fly away
اڑنا fly
اڑن طشتری UFO
اژدہا dragon
اکا ace
اکادمی academy
اکتوبر October
اکثر often
اکثریت majority
اکواڈور جمہوریہ Ecuador
اکیلا lonely, solo
اکیلا / اکیلی only
اکیلا کارکردگی انجام دینے والا soloist
اگنا grow
اگر if
اگرچہ، باوجودیکہ though
اگست August
اگلا، اگلے next
اہلکار personnel
اہم important
اہم، ضروری important
اہم، کافی زیادہ significance, significant
اہم شخصیت celebrity
اہم ہونا matter
اہمیت importance
ایام حیض menstruation
ایام حیض میں استعمال کی گدی sanitary towel
ایام عسل honeymoon
ایتھوپیا Ethiopia
ایتھوپیائی Ethiopian
ایتھوپیائی باشندہ Ethiopian
ایجاد innovation
ایجاد، دریافت invention
ایجاد کرنا invent
ایذا دینا persecute
ایران Iran
ایرانی Iranian
ایریٹریا Eritrea
ایسا so
ایسا ہوٹل جس میں صبح کا ناشتہ اور شام کے کھانے کی قیمت کرایہ میں شامل ہو half board
ایس ایم ایس (تحریری پیغام موبائل پر) SMS
اسٹونیا Estonia
اسٹونیائی باشندہ Estonian
اسٹونیائی زبان Estonian
ایشیائی Asian
ایشیا Asia
ایشیائی Asian
ایماندار honest
ایمانداری سے honestly
ایمانداری honesty
انجائنا (سینے کا درد) angina
ایندھن fuel, paraffin
اینٹ brick
ایپل پائی apple pie
ایڑی heel
ایک one
ایک ایک مقابل والا کھیل singles
ایک بار once
ایک جنس کو کم عقل سمجھنے کا نظریہ sexist
ایک سدا بہار خوشبودار پودا rosemary
ایک طرف سے اونچا ہونا، جھکنا، جھکانا tip
ایک طرف سے دوسرے مکان سے متصل ہو semi-detached house
ایک طرف کا ٹکٹ single ticket
ایک طرف کرنا، کنارے کرنا aside
ایک قسم کا نیولا weasel
ایک نظر glance
ایک نظر ڈالنا glance
ایک ٹیوب جس کے سہارے سانس لیکر زیر آب تیرا جا سکتا ہے snorkel
ایک پٹے پر کھڑے ہو کر سمندر یا جھیل پر تیرنا windsurfing
ایک چیز پر کئی بار ٹیکس VAT
ایکڑ acre
ایک ہی ماں باپ کی اولاد siblings
بااصول consistent
باب chapter
بات talk
باتونی pester, talkative
بات چیت کرنا talk to
بات کرنا communicate, talk
باتیں سنانا tell off
باجہ harp
باخبر aware
بادام almond
بادام کا حلوہ marzipan
بادامی قرمزی رنگ maroon
بادشاہ king, monarch
بادشاہت kingdom, monarchy
بادل cloud
بادی چکی windmill
بارباڈوس Barbados
باربرداری freight
بارش rain
بارش بھرا rainy
بارش سے محفوظ showerproof
بارش ہونا rain
بار کرنا، لادنا load
بارہ twelve
بارہ سنگا reindeer
بارہ سنگھا antelope
بارہواں twelfth
باری باری alternate
باریک fine
باریک ترین، تیز ترین subtle
بارے میں about
باز eagle
بازاحیاء recycling
بازاحیاء کرنا recycle
بازادائیگی کرنا reimburse
بازار market
بازار حصص stock market
بازاری، سستا vulgar
بازو arm
بازو، ڈینے wing
بازوبند bracelet
بازو کے شیشے wing mirror
بازگشت echo
باس گیری کرنا، حکم چلانا boss around
باسی stale
باس۔ سرغنہ boss
باشندہ inhabitant
باصلاحیت capable, competent, efficient
باضابطگی formality
باضمیر conscientious
باعث فکر worrying
باغبانی gardening
باغیانہ revolting
باغی hostile, rebellious
باغیچہ garden

آدھے راستے میں halfway
آراستہ (سازو سامان فرنیچر سے) furnished
آرام دہ comfortable, restful
آرام کرسی armchair, easy chair
آرام کرنا rest, unwind
آرائشی تختی، کتبہ plaque
آرائشی سرجری cosmetic surgery
آرمینیا Armenia
آرمینیائی Armenian
آرمینیائی زبان Armenian
آرٹ کا کام (شاہکار) work of art
آرپار across
آرپار دکھانے والا see-through
آرکیسٹرا کی موسیقی symphony
آری saw
آزاد free
آزادانہ طور پر freelance
آزاد خیال liberal
آزاد (صحافی) freelance
آزاد کرنا free
آزاد کرنا، ہونا release
آزادی freedom
آزادی، حریت liberation
آزادی (خود مختاری) independence
آذربائجان Azerbaijan
آذربائجانی Azerbaijani
آزمانا try, try out
آزمائش trial
آزمائشی مدت، مدت آزمائش trial period
آسان easy
آسان بنانا simplify
آسانی سے easily
آسائشیں amenities
آستین sleeve
آسمان sky
آس پاس، قریب around
آسیب زدہ haunted
آغاز ہونا، شروع ہونا start
آغوش cuddle
آغوش میں لینا cuddle
آفتابی solar
آفتابی قوت solar power
آفتابی لیمپ کے نیچے لیٹنے کا بستر sunbed
آلو potato
آلوبخارا plum
آلودگی pollution
آلودگی، چھوت infection
آلودہ polluted
آلودہ، جان لیوا malignant
آلودہ، متعدی infectious
آلودہ کرنا pollute
آلو چپس crisps
آل کی پیاز leek
آلہ device, tool
آلہ، اوزار instrument
آلہ موسیقی instrument
آم mango
آمادگی کے ساتھ readily
آمادہ willing
آمادہ، تیار ready
آمد advent, arrival
آمدنی income
آمر dictator
آموجود ہونا turn up
آمیزہ mix, paste
آنا check in, come
آنت gut
آنتیں bowels
آنسو tear
آنسو گیس tear gas
آنکھ eye
آنکھ مارنا wink
آنکھوں میں چبھنے والا یا غیر معمولی striking
آنکھوں پر پٹی باندھنا blindfold
آنکھ کا ماہر optician
آنکھ کی پتلی pupil
آنگن courtyard
آنے دینا let in
آنے والا coming
آنے والا کل tomorrow
آنے والے following
آوارہ stray
آواز sound, voice
آئرلینڈ کا Irish
آئرلینڈ کی زبان Irish
آئس لینڈ جمہوریہ Iceland
آئس لینڈ کی زبان Icelandic
آئندہ future
آئرلینڈ کا آدمی Irishman
آئرلینڈ کی عورت Irishwoman
آئی شیڈو eye shadow
آئینہ mirror
آٹا flour
آٹھ eight
آٹھواں eighth
آٹھواں حصہ eighth
آپ بیتی biography
آپ خود yourself, yourselves
آپ کا yours
آڑا کٹا معما (تصویر کے ٹکڑے جوڑنا) jigsaw
آڑو، شفتالو peach
آکٹوپس squid
آگ blaze, bonfire
آگاہی warning
آگ بجھانے والا fire extinguisher
آگ زنی arson
آگ یا دھوئیں سے خبردار کرنے والا الارم smoke alarm
آگے ahead
آگے beyond, forward, next to
آگے بڑھنا advance, go ahead, move forward
آگے بھیجنا forward
آگے نکل جانا، جا لینا overtake
آگے کی طرف جھکنا lean forward
آگے ہونا، بڑھت حاصل کرنا lead
آگے ہونے والی next
آہستہ دوڑ jogging
آہستہ دوڑنا jog
آیا nanny
آیا، خواہ، چاہے، ہو یا نہ ہو whether
اٹاری attic
اٹھارہ eighteen
اٹھارہواں eighteenth
اٹھانا lift, pick up, raise
اٹھانا، لے جانا pick
اٹھنا get up
اپریل April
اپنا، ذاتی own
اپنانا، تعاقب کرنا pursue
اپنا کھانا خود تیار کرنا self-catering
اپنی جگہ رکھنا put away
اپنی ضرورت کے لئے بیچنا sell off
اپنے ساتھ سوار کر لینا lift
اپنے لئے oneself
اپنے منہ میاں مٹھو بننے کی کیفیت smug
اچانک sudden
اچانک بھڑک جانا sulk
اچانک حملہ raid
اچانک حملہ کرنا raid
اچانک طور پر suddenly
اچانک لیا ہوا فوٹو snapshot
اچانک مل جانا bump into
اچھا، صحتمند well

اوکے (ٹھیک ہے) **okay**

ایک قسم کی گھاس (مروا) **okay**

انیس **nineteen**

ابتدائی طور پر **primarily**

ابتدائی **initial, primary**

اتوار **Sunday**

اتحادی **ally**

اتفاق رائے **consensus**

اتفاق رائے سے **unanimous**

اجارہ داری **monopoly**

اجازت **permission**

اجتماعی خوابگاہ **dormitory**

اجلاس **session**

احاطہ، گرد و نواح **precinct**

احتجاج **protest**

احساس جرم، پشیمانی **remorse**

استعمال **use**

استعمال شدہ **used**

استعمال کر کے ختم کر ڈالنا **use up**

استقبالیہ **reception**

استقلال، استحکام **stability**

اس رات کو، آج رات کو **tonight**

اسقاط حمل **miscarriage**

اسلامی **Islamic**

اس لئے **therefore**

اسم **noun**

اسمگلر **smuggler**

اسنوکر (بڑی میز پر لکڑی کی گیندوں والا کھیل) **snooker**

اسٹال (بڑی میز، کتاب یا فوڈ اسٹال) **stall**

اسٹائل **style**

اسٹائل والا **stylist**

اسٹرابیری **strawberry**

اسٹرلنگ (برطانوی کرنسی) **sterling**

اسٹریچر **stretcher**

اسٹول (بغیر ہتھے اور پیٹھ کی کرسی) **stool**

اسٹوو **stove**

اسٹوڈیو (فلم یا فنکار کا) **studio**

اسٹاک ایکسچینج (حصص بازار) **stock exchange**

اسٹیج **stage**

اسٹیشن **station**

اسٹیل جس میں زنگ نہیں لگتا **stainless steel**

اسٹیڈیم (کرسیوں کی قطاروں کے ساتھ کھیل کا میدان) **stadium**

اسپارک پلگ (چنگاری پیدا کرنے والا) **spark plug**

اسپوٹ لائٹ (ایک مقام پر تیز روشنی ڈالنے والی) **spotlight**

اسپین **Spain**

اسپینی باشندہ **Spaniard**

اسکاٹش نسل کا **Scotsman**

اسکاٹ فٹبال **Scottish**

اسکرٹ (لہنگا) **skirt**

اسکریپ بک (سادہ اوراق والی کتاب) **scrapbook**

اسکول **school**

اسکول بیگ **schoolbag**

اسکولی بچے **schoolchildren**

اسکولی طالب علم **schoolboy**

اسکولی طالبہ **schoolgirl**

اسکول یونیفارم **school uniform**

اسکولی کتاب **schoolbook**

اسکوٹر **scooter**

اسکینڈینیویا **Scandinavia**

اسکینڈینیویائی **Scandinavian**

اسکین کرنے والی مشین **scanner**

اسکیٹ کرنے کا علاقہ **rink**

اسکی (پیر کی نیچے باندھ کر پھسلنے کے پٹے) **ski**

اسکی کرنے والا (پھسلنے والا) **skier**

اشاریہ **index**

اشاعت **publication**

اشتعال انگیز **outrageous**

اصرار کرنا **insist**

اضافہ **rise**

اضافہ کرنا **increase**

اضافی **more**

اطالوی **Italian**

اطلاع **notice**

اطلاعی تختہ **noticeboard**

اطمینان **satisfaction**

اطمینان بخش **satisfactory**

اقتباس (کسی اور کا جملہ یا تحریر مستعار لینا) **quotation**

التوا **suspension**

الزام **blame**

امداد **subsidy**

امداد دینا **subsidize**

امکان **possibility, probability**

امکان، امکانی واقعہ **prospect**

انتقال خون **transfusion**

انتقام، چوٹ پہنچانے کی نیت سے **spite**

انتقام لینا **revenge**

انتقام لینا، چوٹ پہنچانا **spite**

انتباہ **ultimatum**

انتہائی رازدارانہ **top-secret**

انتہائی بھوکا **ravenous**

انجماد **frost**

انحصار ہونا **rely on**

انحصار کرنا **lean on**

ان دنوں **nowadays**

انسانوں میں فرق کرنے والا **snob**

انعام **prize**

انعام جیتنے والا **prizewinner**

انعام دینا **prize-giving**

انقلاب **revolution**

انقلابی **revolutionary**

انٹرنیٹ ویب **Web 2.0**

انڈونیشیائی **Indonesian**

انکار **refusal**

انکار کرنا **refuse**

اکائی **unit**

اکٹھا کرنا **gather**

آبادی **population**

آباواجداد **ancestor**

آبدوز **submarine**

آبلہ **blister**

آب و ہوا **climate**

آبی رنگ **watercolour**

آبی سلاد **watercress**

آبی پودا **seaweed**

آبی چھپکلی **newt**

آتشبازی **fireworks**

آتش دان **fireplace**

آتشی اشیاء **flammable**

آتش فشاں پہاڑ **volcano**

آثار **trace**

آج **today**

آجر **employer**

آخر **finish**

آخرکار **eventually**

آخرکار **finally**

آخری **last**

آخری، اختتامی **last**

آخری (فائنل) **final**

آخری نتیجہ تک پہنچانا، پہنچانا **finalize**

آخرش **last**

آخر میں **lastly**

آخر ہونا، اخیر ہونا **last**

آخری **late**

آدمی **man**

آدمی کا ایک پیر پر کودنا **hop**

آدھا گھنٹہ **half-hour**

آدھی قیمت **half-price**

آدھی قیمت پر **half-price**

الگ تھلگ، تنہا isolated
الگ تھلگ رکھنا quarantine
الگنی clothes line, peg, washing line
الگ کرنا apart, take apart
الگ کرنا، جدا کرنا separate
الہام intuition
امتحان exam, examination
امتزاج combination
امتناع حمل contraception
امتیاز discrimination, distinction
امتیازی distinctive
امداد aid
امداد، گرانٹ grant
امربیل mistletoe
امریکہ America, United States
امریکی American
امریکی چوہا guinea pig
املا dictation
امن peace
امکان likely
امکانی طور پر probably
امید hope
امیدوار candidate
امید کرنا hope
امید کے ساتھ hopefully
امیر rich
اناج grain
اناج، سیریل cereal
اناج کا پودا cereal
انار pomegranate
اناڑی، ناتجربہ کار green
انتباہ alarm
انتخاب selection
انتخابی نشست seat
انتظار کرانا hang on
انتظار خانہ waiting room
انتظام کرنا arrange, manage
انتظامی administrative
انتظامیہ administration, management
انتہائی طور پر perfectly
انتہائی extreme
انتہائی درجہ حرارت پر ابالا ہوا دودھ UHT milk
انتہائی طور پر extremely
انتہاپسند extremist
انتہاپسندی extremism
انجام دینا carry out
انجانے طور پر inadvertently
انجمادی freezing, frosty
انجن engine
انجن کا ڈھکنا bonnet
انجیر fig
انجیل Bible
انحراف diversion, drift
اندازہ سمجھنا reckon
اندازہ guess
اندازہ لگانا (مستقبل کا) speculate
اندازہ کرنا guess
اندر in, inside, into
اندراج entry, registration
اندراج کرنا register
اندراج کرنا، درج کرنا note down
اندر آنا come in
اندر جانا go in, into
اندرون inside, interior
اندرون دروازہ indoor
اندرونی inner, internal
اندرونی طور پر indoors
اندھیرا blackout, dark, darkness
اندیشہ premonition
انسان human being
انسانی human
انسانیت نواز humanitarian
انسانی حقوق human rights
انسلاک attachment
انعام award
انعکاس reflection
اناناس pineapple
اناناس درخت pine
انیسواں nineteenth
انڈا egg
انڈرویر underwear
انڈونیشیا Indonesia
انڈیلنا pour
انڈے دینا lay
انڈے کی زردی egg yolk
ان کا their
انکار کرنا deny
انکرائی ہوئی سبزیاں sprouts
انکرائے دانے beansprouts
ان کو them
ان کی theirs
انگریز English, Englishman
انگریزی زبان English
انگریزی کا بڑا حروف capital
انگلی finger
انگلینڈ England
انگلیوں کے نشان fingerprint
انگلی کے ناخن fingernail
انگور grape
انگور کا باغ، چمن vineyard
انگور کی بیل vine
انگولا Angola
انگولائی Angolan
انگوٹھا thumb
انگیٹھی کا حاشیہ mantelpiece
انیمیا کا مریض anaemic
اودبلاؤ beaver
اودبلاؤ otter
اور and, else
اوسط average, medium
اول one
اولا hail
اولاً first
اولین طور پر firstly
اولے گرنا sleet
اون wool
اونٹ camel
اونچا high
اونچا اٹھانا hold up
اونچائی میں high
اونچا ہونا go up
اونچی ایڑی high heels
اونچی تنخواہ والا well-paid
اونچی جدید عمارت high-rise
اونچی عمارت skyscraper
اونچی کرسی highchair
اونچی کود long jump
اونچی کود، جست high jump
اونگھنا doze
اونی woollen
اونی قمیض pullover
اونی کپڑے woollens
اوون oven
اول تا آخر through
اوپر above, up
اوپر آنا come up
اوپر اٹھنا rise
اوپر سے دیکھنا rise
اوپر سے نیچے کی طرف پھسلنا slide
اوپر والا upper
اوپر کی طرف upwards
اوپری سرا، اوپر top

سکول سے آگے کی تعلیم (ہایر سیکنڈری)
further educatio
سکول ٹیچر (استاد) schoolteacher
سکولی میعاد کے درمیان قلیل چھٹی half-term
ں کو (مرد کو) him
ں کی (خاتون کی) hers
کیٹ بورڈنگ skateboarding
کیٹ پہن کر پھسلنا skating
کیٹ یا گراری دار اسکیٹ پہن کر پھسلنا skate
ں کے علاوہ besides
ال، دست diarrhoea
ں eighty
ں طرح besides
راتی زبان sign language
رہ hint
رہ کرنا hint, indicate, sign
یہ indicator
اک کرنا collaborate
کی communist
کیت communism
ال انگیز annoying, exciting,
nerve-racki
ور سیال aperitif
ad, advertisement
دینا advertise
خوردونوش groceries
بنانا، تیار کرنا (بڑے پیمانے پر)
manufact
، بربادی waste
ں stable
ح term
origin
ح کرنا rectify, supervise
طور پر originally
ں کے مطابق بنانا model
ں genuine, original, real
ں principle
ں، قواعد rule
ۃ increase
ۃ، توسیع increase
ی additional
ی تنخواہ bonus
ی طور پر increasingly
راب anxiety
ی زبان Italian
ں Italy
ت around, surroundings
ت کا جائزہ لینا look round

اطلاعاتی ٹیکنالوجی IT
اظہار expression, show
اظہار کرنا express, show
اعادہ repeat
اعادی recurring, repetitive
اعادی طور پر repeatedly
اعانت assistance
اعتدال پسند moderate
اعتدال پسندی moderation
اعتراض objection
اعتراف acknowledgement, confession
اعتراف کرنا admit, confess
اعتقاد رکھنا believe
اعتماد confidence
اعتماد، عقیدہ faith
اعتماد، بھروسہ trust
اعتماد توڑنا betray
اعداد سے متعلق کمپیوٹر پروگرام spreadsheet
اعشاریہ decimal
اعصابی رسی (ریڑھ کی ہڈی سے گزرنے والی)
spinal cord
اعضاء کی تبدیلی transplant
اعلان announcement
اعلان کرنا announce, declare
اعلیٰ superior
اعلیٰ تعلیم higher education
اعلیٰ درجہ کے classic
اغواکار hijacker
اغوا کرنا abduct, hijack, kidnap
اف! ugh!
ابال آنا boil over
افراتفری chaos, fuss
افراتفری والی chaotic
افرادی قوت manpower
افراط، بہتات plenty
افراط زر inflation
افریقہ Africa
افریقی African
افسر officer
افسردگی depression
افسردہ depressed
افسردہ کن depressing
افسوسناک حادثہ mishap
افغان Afghan
افغانستان Afghanistan
افغانستانی Afghan
افق horizon

افقی horizontal
افواہ rumour
اقامتی اسکول boarding school
اقامتی مدرسے کا طالب علم boarder
اقرار نامہ، معاہدہ treaty
اقل minimum
اقلیتی فرقہ minority
الارم گھڑی alarm clock
البانیائی Albanian
البانی Albanian
البانیہ Albania
البم album
الجزائری Algerian
الجھن، دشواری problem
الجھن، پہیلی puzzle
الجھن آمیز confusing
الجھے ہوئے، پیچیدہ complicated
الجیریا Algeria
الجیریائی Algerian
الرجی allergy
الرجی زا allergic
الرجی مخالف دوا antihistamine
الزام charge
الزام تراشی accusation
الزام دینا accuse, blame
الزام لگانا charge
الغوزہ clarinet
الفاظ نمایاں کرنے والی قلم highlighter
الف لیلوی داستان fairy tale
اللہ Allah
اللہ، رب، خالق کائنات God
الماری cabinet, cupboard
المناک tragic
المیہ tragedy
الوداع farewell!
الو owl
الٹا reverse, upside down
الٹا، معکوس، پیچھے کی طرف opposite
الٹا گھوم جانے کی حالت U-turn
الٹ جانا backfire, capsize
الٹ دینا reverse
الٹرا ساؤنڈ (کی تیز ترین لہریں) ultrasound
الٹی طرف backwards
الٹے قدموں لوٹنا retrace
الٹے کوما inverted commas
الٹے کوما، علامات اقتباس quotation marks
الکحل والا مشروب whisky
الگ apart, separate

اب now
ابا dad
ابالنا boil
اب بھی still
ابتدائی طور پر initially
ابتر ہونا deteriorate
ابر آلود cloudy
ابرو eyebrow
ابلا ہوا boiled
ابلتی ہوئی boiling
ابلنا، کافی گرم ہونا boil
ابو daddy
ابوظہبی Abu Dhabi
اتارنا، توڑنا pick
اتار چڑھاؤ، جوار بھاٹا tide
اتحاد alliance
اترنا descend
اتصال conjunction
اتفاق coincidence
اتفاق سے coincide
اتفاق ہونا coincide
اتفاقی طور پر casually
اتفاقیہ casual, random
اتنا، اتنا as ... as
اتنا، بہت زیادہ such
اثاثہ asset
اثر effect, influence
اثر، تاثر impact
اثر انداز ہونا affect
اثر دار effective
اثردار impressive
اثر دار طریقے سے effectively
اثر ڈالنا influence
اجازت دینا allow, let
اجداد ancestor
اجلاس، اجتماع assembly
اجنبی stranger
اجنبی، غیر معمولی، مناسب نہ ہونا، بے جوڑ odd
اجوائن celery
اجڈ طریقے سے roughly
ایسے as
احاطہ yard
احاطے premises
احتساب audit
احتجاج کرنا protest
احتیاط سے cautiously
احساس feel
احساس جرم guilt
احوال report
اخبار newspaper
اختراعی innovative
اختصاری، جامع concise
اختیار میں لینا take over
اختیار میں لے لینا take over
اختیار خاص privilege
اختیار option, power
اختیار دینا authorize
اختیاری optional
اخراج removal
اخراجات expenses
اخروٹ chestnut, walnut
اخلاق واطوار morals
اخلاق وعادات manners
اخلاقی ethical, moral
ادارہ institute, institution
ادا شدہ paid
اداکار actor
اداکارہ actress
اداکاری acting
ادا کرنا pay
ادا کرنا (قرض وغیرہ کی رقم) repay
ادب literature
ادرک ginger
ادغام merger
ادلا بدلی کرنا exchange
ادنی بات trifle
ادھار دینا lend
ادھار لینا borrow
ادھار کھاتے میں اندراج کرنا debit
ادھیڑ عمر middle-aged
ادھیڑ یا بوڑھی عمر کی کنواری، spinster
ارادتاً deliberate
ارادہ aim, intention
ارادہ رکھنا intend
ارادہ کرنا aim
ارادی طور پر deliberately
ارادی طور پر، بالارادہ، عمداً willingly
ارتقاء evolution
ارتکاب کرنا commit
اردن Jordan
اردنی Jordanian
اردگرد around
ارضی منظر landscape
اروگوائی Uruguayan
ازبکستان Uzbekistan
ازدواجی حیثیت marital status
اساس base
استاد teacher
استاد کا معاون classroom assistant
استثنائی exceptional
استحالیت metabolism
استحصال exploitation
استحصال کرنا exploit
استحصالی extortionate
استر slip
استرہ razor
استری iron
استری کرنا iron
استری کرنے کا عمل ironing
استشراقی oriental
استطاعت رکھنا afford
استعمال شدہ سامان کی دوکان flea market
استعمال کرنا use
استعفی دینا resign
استوائی گنی Equatorial Guinea
اس جیسا، یکساں same
اس جیسا ہونا، انداز اختیار کرنا take after
اس دوران meanwhile
اسرار (راز) mystery
اسرائیل Israel
اسرائیلی Israeli
اسرائیلی باشندہ Israeli
اسفنج sponge
اسلام (دین فطرت) Islam
اس (مرد) کی his
اسم صفت adjective
اسمگلنگ smuggling
اسناد اعتبار credentials
اسٹار، مقبول شخص star
اسٹرا، نلکی straw
اسٹیرنگ steering, steering wheel
اسپرنگ spring
اسپینی Spanish
اسپینی (زبان) Spanish
اس کا his, its
اس کا (خاتون کا) her
اسکاٹش، اسکاچتانی Scot
اسکاٹش نسل کی خاتون Scotswoman
اسکاٹ لینڈ Scotland
اسکاٹ لینڈ کا Scots
اسکرین screen
اس کو (خاتون کو) her
اسکور score
اسکول دن کے درمیان چھٹی کا وقفہ half-time

INDEX

اِشاریہ